Learning Mechanisms In Food Selection

Learning Mechanisms in Food Selection

Edited by

Lewis M. Barker
BAYLOR UNIVERSITY

Michael R. Best
SOUTHERN METHODIST UNIVERSITY

Michael Domjan
UNIVERSITY OF TEXAS AT AUSTIN

Baylor University Press

Printed in the United States of America

Library of Congress Cataloging in Publication Data

Barker, Lewis M. 1942-
    Learning mechanisms in food selection.
    632 pages, includes indexes and bibliography.
    1. Learning   2. Food selection   I. Best,
Michael R. 1947-   II. Domjan, Michael 1947-
III. Title
LC Catalogue No. 77-76779
ISBN 0-918954-19-3

PREFACE

In the fall of 1975 the co-editors of this volume met at Baylor University to discuss research of mutual interest. The idea of holding a symposium gradually developed from this discussion. Dr. Herbert H. Reynolds, Executive Vice President and Dean of Baylor University was approached concerning such a formal meeting, and he subsequently made available personnel, facilities, and funds sufficient to plan and conduct a major symposium, including the present publication of proceedings. On October 14, 1975, fourteen individuals were initially selected to discuss five topic areas within the general area of "learning about foods." More extensive coverage of critical areas was deemed advisable, and eventually twenty-two individuals from the United States and Canada gathered at Baylor University on March 3-5, 1976, to participate in a Symposium on Learning Mechanisms in Food Selection.

The present volume consists of edited versions of seventeen papers formally presented at the symposium. In numerous instances, the discussion which ensued following a paper presentation was incorporated into a revised manuscript which each participant eventually submitted for inclusion in this volume. Five additional manuscripts and the Appendix were solicited for balance and breadth, bringing the final volume to twenty-three chapters. Summer sabbaticals from each of our respective institutions allowed us to complete editorial treatment of all manuscripts by December, 1976.

Our appreciation is expressed to the many individuals at Baylor University whose support and expertise made possible the symposium and this volume. We especially are grateful to Dr. Herbert H. Reynolds, for his vision of excellence in academic pursuits and his confidence in our ability to share a part of that vision. We also wish to thank the contributors to the volume for their cooperation in meeting unreasonable deadlines and for their good humor and tolerance of our editorial suggestions. Finally, we are grateful to the staff of Baylor University Press for their diligence, patience, and expertise in translating our efforts into this handsome volume.

LMB   March 3, 1977
MRB
MD

CREDITS

We wish to express our appreciation to Mr. John C. Sittner for the still photographs taken at the Baylor Conference, and for his help in videotaping the proceedings. Mr. Bill Bright also contributed a photograph in the present collection.

We also wish to thank the following publishers for their kind permission to reprint the following figures, tables, and text:

Academic Press for Chapter 14, Figures 4 and 5; Chapter 18, Figures 1, 2, 3, 4, 5, and 6; Chapter 20, Figures 1, 2, and 3.

The *American Psychological Association* for Chapter 4, Figures 4 and 6; Chapter 5, Figure 3; Chapter 6, Figures 2, 3, 4, 9, 10, and 11; Chapter 7, Figures 3, 6, 7, 8, and 9; Chapter 8, Figure 2 and Tables 1 and 2; Chapter 11, Figures 1, 2, 3, 4, and 5; Chapter 12, Figure 2; Chapter 13, Figures 1 and 2; Chapter 14, Figure 1; Chapter 15, Figures 1 and 2; Chapter 16, Figure 1.

Bailliere, Tindall & Cassell Limited for Chapter 5, Table 1.

MacMillan Journals Limited for Chapter 5, Figures 5 and 6.

Pergamon Press for Chapter 7, Figure 2.

The *Psychonomic Society* for Chapter 5, Figure 2; Chapter 6, Figure 7; Chapter 7, Figures 4 and 5; Chapter 8, Figure 3; Chapter 14, Figure 2.

Springer-Verlag for Chapter 19, Figures 4 and 7.

The *University of Chicago Press* for Chapter 4, Figure 1.

TABLE OF CONTENTS

PART FOUR: FOOD AVERSION LEARNING

PART FOUR-A: LONG-DELAY LEARNING

... The two-presentation experiment: Evidence for learned safety ... The two-presentation experiment: Effects of the second presentation ... The effects of extensive preexposure on the delay of reinforcement gradient ... The two presentation experiment: Interactions

PART FOUR-B: NON-GUSTATORY ASPECTS OF FOOD AVERSION LEARNING

PART SIX: APPENDIX

Learning Mechanisms In Food Selection

Row 1: Bennett Galef, Jr., Michael Domjan, Marvin Nachman, James C. Smith, John Garcia.

Row 2: Carl Gustavson, Abram Amsel, E. Martin Suarez, James W. Kalat.

Row 3: Thomas J. Testa, Jerry Hogan, Richard L. Solomon, Hardy C. Wilcoxon, Patrick J. Capretta.

Row 4: Donna Zahorik, Phillip J. Best, Michael R. Best, Samuel Revusky, Elkan Gamzu, Norman S. Braveman, Paul Rozin, Lewis M. Barker.

P. Best

N. Braveman

P. Capretta

C. Gustavson

M. Best, L. Barker, M. Domjan

J. Galef

E. Gamzu

J. Garcia

J. Hogan

J. Kalat

M. Nachman

S. Revusky

P. Rozin

R. Solomon

T. Testa

H. Wilcoxon

D. Zahorik

INTRODUCTION

I

ON THE ORIGIN OF
FOOD AVERSION PARADIGMS

JOHN GARCIA AND WALTER G. HANKINS
University of California, Los Angeles

Charles Darwin, writing in *Descent of Man* (1896), reflected on the beauty of many butterflies and commented on the utility of their colorful patterns for sexual selection. He was puzzled because some larval caterpillars were also splendidly colored in patterns which were not closely correlated with those of the adult form of the insect. Furthermore, the behavior of the gaudy yet tender "sexless embryos" seemed maladaptive, for they habitually displayed themselves openly, catching the eye of every passing bird. He turned to Alfred R. Wallace, who had an "innate genius" for solving such difficulties, and he describes Wallace's answer in the following passage.

> "From such considerations Mr. Wallace thought it probable that conspicuously-coloured caterpillars were protected by having a nauseous taste; but as their skin is extremely tender, and as their intestines readily protrude from a wound, a slight peck from the beak of a bird would be as fatal to them as if they had been devoured. Hence, as Mr. Wallace remarks, 'distastefulness alone would be insufficient to protect a caterpillar unless some outward sign indicated to its would-be destroyer that its prey was a disgusting morsel.' Under these circumstances it would be highly advantageous to a caterpillar to be instantaneously and certainly recognized as unpalatable by all birds and other animals. Thus the most gaudy colours would be serviceable, and might have been gained by variation and the survival of the most easily-recognised individuals."

3

A. R. Wallace presented this bold hypothesis to the Entomological Society of London on December 3, 1866, and it stimulated research on predation of insect larvae by birds, lizards, frogs and other vertebrates. Twenty years later, E. B. Poulton (1887) summarized the data collected for the Zoological Society of London in a paper entitled, "The Experimental Proof of the Protective Value of Color and Markings in Insects in Reference to their Vertebrate Enemies."

We have listed a series of propositions on the behavioral mechanisms for selecting food and avoiding poison. Poulton's remarkable 83 pages bear directly upon a number of these "modern" notions in learning. We present the relevant passages following the first three propositions, because they describe the issues so graphically.

Proposition 1: Food aversion learning. Acceptable food becomes aversive when it is followed by illness.

"In addition to this, I am assured by a very keen observer, Rev. G. J. Burch, that recently hatched chickens certainly do peck at insects which they afterwards learn to avoid without trial, and he believes that the hen assists in their education by indicating that certain insects are not fit for food. His observations were chiefly made upon a common phytophagous Hymenopterous larva which is found upon gooseberry (doubtless *Nematus ribesii*). Another observation made by Mr. Burch bears upon the same question. He offered his chickens a quantity of chickweed, knowing that this plant was often given as food to Linnets. The chickens ate the plant readily enough, but they were all extremely unwell in consequence, and vomited freely. After this Mr. Burch again offered them chickweed, but they had profited by the experience and would not touch it."

Obviously, Poulton knew (a) that aversions were learned, (b) that illness was the reinforcing agent or unconditioned stimulus, and (c) that food stimuli were the critical cues or conditioned stimuli. Furthermore, he believed that positive changes in palatability were also possible if feeding was followed by nutrition, as stated in the following proposition.

Proposition 2: Food preference learning. Unattractive food becomes more acceptable if it is followed by general repletion of hunger.

"If once the vertebrate enemies were driven to eat any such

4

insect in spite of the unpleasant taste, they would almost certainly soon acquire a relish for what was previously disagreeable, and the insect would be in great danger of extermination, having in the meantime become conspicuous by gaining warning colours."

Poulton (1887) was not completely clear as to which food stimuli were the critical cues, but he believed that flavor played a primary role while visual cues played a secondary role in both reptiles and birds. This point is still under debate, however, so the following proposition is put forth as a hypothesis.

Proposition 3: Flavor mediation. Visual avoidances are mediated by aversive flavors.

"And this was seen in its treatment by the Lizard, for the larva was recognized at once as something which was expected to be palatable, and was at first seized with great vigour, and it was only when the larva was injured beyond hope of recovery that its enemy recognized the unpleasant attributes and relinquished it. I witnessed the whole process; it afforded the most instructive comparison with the reluctant and hesitating way in which a very hungry Lizard would approach a highly coloured larva which it knew to be distasteful. It was quite obvious that the Lizard fully expected a palatable insect, and was greatly surprised at the unwelcome result.

"All hairy caterpillars (experimented upon) were uniformly uneaten;" viz. *Arclia caja, Eriogaster lanestris, Porthesia auriflua,* and *Orgyia antiqua.* "None of these species were even examined." The writer believes that the hairs are not themselves disliked, but that they "serve as a caution to the birds that the larvae so clothed are uneatable." This suggestion is supported by the fact that the young and comparatively hairless larvae of *Spilosoma menthastri* were tasted by the Siskin, Redpoll, and by a West-African Finch (*Textor erythrorhyachus*), but these three birds evidently found the larvae disagreeable, and soon left them alone."

Poulton cites the research upon mimicry by Bates (1862) and Muller (1879); thus, he also knew that discrimination and generalization were manifested in the bird's avoidance of aversive-tasting insects.

"But if, as I shall endeavour to show, there is a superficial resemblance between the colours employed by very different insects, and frequently even a similarity of pattern, we see that a comparatively few unpleasant experiences would be sufficient to create a prejudice against any insect with colours and patterns at all resembling the nauseous forms which have already produced so indelible an impression upon the memory. And thus it is most probable that the conspicuous appearance which astonishes one sense becomes associated in the mind of the Vertebrate insect-eater with the well-remembered effect of other qualities upon other senses."

A. R. Wallace's hypothesis that visual stimuli provided by the insect become a conditioned signal for predatory animals through association with its noxious taste was formulated 24 years before I. P. Pavlov was elected Professor of Pharmacology at the Military Medical Academy of St. Petersburg. Several years later, Pavlov was to begin his studies there on "psychic" reflexes, employing visual and auditory stimuli to signal the taste of acid or meat powder in the mouth of dogs. Poulton's summary of two decades of comparative animal research upon the positive effects of satisfying foods and the negative effects of annoying tastes was presented eleven years before E. L. Thorndike's (1897) doctoral thesis on animal intelligence and the law of effect. Pavlov and Thorndike went on to investigate conditioned responses more rigorously, and ultimately their students operationally defined a series of methodological "laws" which were essentially disembodied from the rats, cats, dogs and pigeons who served as laboratory subjects. This pall of rigor had not yet fallen upon behavioral description when Darwin wrote the following passage in 1896. He unabashedly commits the sin of anthropomorphism and anticipates ethology as he embeds learning where it truly belongs, in the adaptive nature of birds, lizards, frogs, and other animals.

"When the birds rejected a caterpillar, they plainly shewed, by shaking their heads, and cleansing their beaks, that they were disgusted by the taste. Three conspicuous kinds of caterpillars and moths were also given to some lizards and frogs, by Mr. A. Butler, and were rejected, though other kinds were eagerly eaten. Thus the probability of Mr. Wallace's view is confirmed, namely, that certain caterpillars have been made conspicuous for their own good, so as to be easily recognised by their enemies, on nearly the same principle that poisons are sold in coloured bottles by druggists for the good of man."

Proposition 4: Flavor-thiamine learning. Flavors become preferred when they are followed by recuperation from thiamine deficiency.

This proposition, which is a more specific corollary of the proposition on food preference learning, was proclaimed in 1933 in another remarkable paper published in the proceedings of the Royal Society of London. Authored by Leslie J. Harris, Janet Clay, Florence J. Hargreaves and Alfred Ward and entitled "Appetite and Choice of Diet. The Ability of the Vitamin B Deficient Rat to Discriminate between Diets Containing and Lacking the Vitamin," this 29-page paper describes 18 experiments conducted during the period of 1928-1931. Young growing rats were maintained on carefully measured diets, and offered various flavors as signals for presence or absence of Vitamin B in various food cups. They "obtained good evidence that the behavior of the animal is due not so much to instinct as to *experience, i.e.,* of the beneficial effect produced by a particular foodstuff."

These authors repeatedly stressed learning, for they observed that "previous experience may at times lead the animal into error, causing it to choose the wrong diet, and deceiving it into associating its recovery not with the beneficial ingredient actually responsible but with some other feature of the diet acting upon its special senses." However, they believed that this learning occurred without awareness. This conclusion resembles the recent position taken by Seligman (1972) and Rozin and Kalat (1972). We quote a statement taken from Harris et al. as our fifth proposition.

Proposition 5: Non-cognitive processing. "The association between flavor and effect of food is often subconscious rather than fully reasoned and tends to pass into an automatic habit."

Aversions seem to rise independent of knowledge or information concerning relationship of the food to the illness. Ships' passengers acquire aversions for food eaten prior to sea sickness, even though they know that the true cause of their malaise was the motion of the ship, not the food. Animal studies indicate that aversions can be formed when the illness is induced while the rat is under general anesthesia (Roll & Smith, 1972) or the rat's cortex is electrically depressed by potassium chloride (Buresova & Bures, 1973, 1974), provided that the animal is allowed to complete his drinking bout while fully awake. Control rats indicate that the illness agent produces an aversive effect above and beyond that produced by the incapacitating agent.

7

Harris and his associates noted the prompt effect of Vitamin B (thiamine) upon the deficient rat. They concluded that the negative results they obtained with other dietary essentials, namely Vitamin A, Vitamin D and protein, were "because they failed to evoke the stimulus of sufficiently immediate and marked remedial effect." Thus, it remained for Julian Rzoska (1953, 1954) of University College, Khartoum, to indicate that long-delay learning was possible.

Proposition 6: Long-delay learning. Aversions can be established with long intervals separating the flavor and the illness.

Rzoska was interested in getting rats to accept poison, rather than beneficial foods, and his method was direct and simple. He fed lumps of paste made of bread and water to hungry rats by hand. The first bit of bread paste weighed one gram and usually contained the poison calculated to body weight; then he gave 0.25 g lumps of plain bread paste to the rats at 5-min intervals until they refused the bread. Without poisoning, the rats would accept and eat the bread paste for over 7 hr. When the first lump contained poison, he found that rats would later begin to hesitate and ultimately they would refuse the bread. The time of onset of these refusal symptoms was a function of the logarithm of the dose for any given poison. For low doses, the refusals came hours after ingesting the poisoned bread baits. Rzoska wrote, "The rats turned their heads away when the bait was brought near them, some pushed it aside with their forepaws or grasped it fiercely, droppped it, or buried it in the litter." Most of his experiments resembled long CS trace conditioning rather than long delayed US conditioning; nevertheless, he appears to have evidence for long-delay learning. Rzoska concluded (a) "Survivors of an initial poison bait showed a more or less definite refusal or shyness to further baits . . ." (b) "Base shyness develops quickly or slowly following the action of the poison; it may appear in a range of one-half hour to several days . . ." and (c) "The memory of a red squill bait may last as long as 374 days . . ."

More conclusive evidence for the proposition on long-delay learning came from research upon the effects of ionizing radiation beginning in the 1950's. Ionizing rays such as gamma radiation or high energy X-rays had a methodological advantage over ingested toxins as an unconditioned stimulus. These rays can be delivered in precise doses independent of the animal's consummatory behavior without immediate pain or excessive disturbance of the animal. It soon became evident that ionizing rays could produce food aversions even when animals were exposed to low doses several minutes after drinking saccharin water. This radiation treatment produced no immediate illness, though a mild effect may have occurred hours later (Garcia & Kimeldorf, 1960; Kimeldorf & Hunt, 1965). The early investigations were directed at the biological effects of radiation rather than its conditioning effects. Ultimately, it was demonstrated that transfusions of blood from irradiated donor rats (Hunt, Carroll, & Kimeldorf, 1965), or even injections of serum from irradiated donors given 5 min after saccharin drinking (Garcia, Ervin, & Koelling, 1967), would produce aversions in other rats. Apparently the aversive agent is a histamine-like by-product of exposure (Levy, Ervin, & Garcia, 1970; Levy, Carroll, Smith, & Hofer, 1974). Thus, aversive effects could be produced by delaying the radiation exposure (Smith & Roll, 1967; Revusky, 1968) or delaying the injection of an emetic drug (Garcia, Ervin, & Koelling, 1966). Since the effects of radiation exposure were delayed for an hour or more, rats would acquire an aversion even if they drank saccharin water after they were exposed (McLaurin, Farley, Scarborough, & Rawlings, 1964; Smith, Taylor, Morris, & Hendricks, 1965; Barker & Smith, 1974; see also Barker, Smith, & Suarez, this volume).

Proposition 7: Memorial mediation. Aversions do not depend on lingering physical traces of ingested substances.

Recently, Bitterman (1975, 1976) raised a strenuous objection to the notion that flavor aversions were established by long delayed illness reinforcement. In essence, he argues that when a rat consumes a large quantity of saccharin-flavored water and then becomes ill, some traces of saccharin may linger long enough to coincide with the delayed illness. He suggests that saccharin could flavor the saliva continuously bathing the taste receptors, citing the research of Bradley and Mistretta (1971), who obtained an aversion by injecting saccharin into the tail vein of rats prior to illness. Bitterman fails to note that these investigators used delayed illness, i.e., after the intravenous saccharin they applied radiation which produces delayed effects and, furthermore, the actual exposure was delayed up to 20 min. As an alternative explanation, Bitterman seems to be proposing conditioning with a long CS, i.e., a CS which begins hours before the US and endures until the US occurs. Conditioning with such a long CS would be a phenomenon no less remarkable than conditioning where a long delay intervenes between the CS and US. We would scarcely expect a light avoidance if we turned on a signal light and left it on several hours before we shocked an animal.

Bitterman also reminds us of another possibility. Although the rat does not vomit, it does retch, and retching could bring up traces of saccharin to restimulate the taste receptors during illness. This might be true of emetic agents, but low doses of X-rays produce aversions without producing retching or any other visible sign of illness. Furthermore, a trace of hydrochloric acid in the water, which is lost in the higher acid concentration of the stomach, or a trace of starch or sugar in food which is rapidly transformed by the digestive process, serves as well as saccharin (Garcia, Hankins, & Rusiniak, 1974). Also, saccharin preferences have been increased by delayed injections of thiamine which have beneficial effects upon the animal (Garcia, Ervin, Yorke, & Koelling, 1967; Zahorik & Maier, 1969). Viewed in its entirety, the evidence from the aversion literature leads most of us to accept the proposition that a memorial process bridges the CS-US gap in long-delay learning.

Proposition 8: Taste Primacy. Taste stimuli are favored as cues for illness.

Radiation aversion studies in the 1950's yielded another paradox. Although rats quickly learned an aversion for subtle taste cues paired with delayed radiation illness, it was much more difficult for them to learn a motor avoidance away from a distinctive compartment in which they suffered the radiation exposure (Garcia, Kimeldorf, & Hunt, 1957, 1961). While rats could be trained to avoid the radiation compartment on the basis of visual, tactual, and other cues, the conditioned avoidances seemed too weak to insure their survival if these nongustatory cues were the only signals for toxicosis (see Best, Best, & Henggeler, this volume). Since this issue is not yet completely resolved, perhaps we should consider the proposition of taste primacy an hypothesis for the moment.

Affirmative evidence for this hypothesis comes from research with an experimental arrangement called the cue-consequence paradigm. In the original cue-consequence experiment, thirsty rats were trained to obtain water in a drinkometer box which recorded each contact of the rat's tongue with the spout. Under this arrangement, "bright-noisy water" could be produced by switching a clicking relay controlling a light into the lick circuit and "tasty water" by simply adding saccharin or salt to the water. Both cues (CS) were contingent upon the rat's licking response. Groups of rats were punished for drinking bright-noisy and tasty water with two classes of consequences (US): foot-shock or illness induced by lithium chloride consumption or exposure to X-rays. The two cue conditions were juxtaposed against the two consequences in a simple fourfold experimental design and inhibition of licking was the response measure in all four cells.

The results were clear-cut. Rats punished with foot-shock quickly learned to inhibit drinking bright-noisy water, but continued to drink tasty water. Conversely, rats punished with illness quickly learned to avoid drinking tasty water but continued to drink bright-noisy water (Garcia & Koelling, 1966). The original experiment has been critically tested in a number of laboratories, where care was taken (a) to insure that both classes of cues were more comparably bound to the product consumed (Garcia, McGowan, Ervin, & Koelling, 1968), (b) to present the two cues independent of the rats' responses in the classical Pavlovian manner (Domjan & Wilson, 1972a, 1972b), and (c) to schedule the illness and shock so that they had a comparable effect upon the response measure (Green, Bouzas, & Rachlin, 1972). Under all variations, the same curious inequalities persisted; apparently rats could neither learn that the taste of food and drink was paired with the pain of shock nor that the auditory-visual signal was paired with illness before learning was complete in the bright noise-pain cell and the taste-illness cell. While studies with other species indicate that avoidances can be obtained by pairing nongustatory signals with illness (Green & Garcia, 1970; Braveman, 1974; Best, Best, & Mickley, 1973; Johnson, Beaton, & Hall, 1975), taste is the favored cue whenever a comparison is made. This is true for odors as well, for though Taukulis (1974) has demonstrated that odor aversions may be established with delayed illness, we (Hankins, Garcia, & Rusiniak, 1973; Hankins, Rusiniak, & Garcia, 1976) have shown that taste cues are much more effective than odor cues when paired with illness. Conversely, odor cues are more effective than taste cues when paired with foot shock.

Bitterman (1975, 1976) rejects the cue-consequence data on procedural grounds, deeming that proof of a CS-US association is *sine qua non* for each and every conditioning study. He writes ". . . there were no pseudoconditioning controls, yet illness might have produced aversion to saccharin, and shock might have produced aversions to the sound of a buzzer, quite independently of pairing." This procedural distinction is irrelevant since differential responding presents the same theoretical problem for traditional learning theory whether the effect is due to some priming action of illness as opposed to pain, or to a "legitimate" CS-US pairing with illness as opposed to pain. Unfortunately, this procedural objection is

11

simply incorrect as well, since a cursory review of the literature reveals that stable illness aversions, like stable shock avoidances, require associative procedures. As a matter of fact, in the very first radiation-induced saccharin aversion study (Garcia, Kimeldorf, & Koelling, 1955), where independent groups were subjected to associative and nonassociative stimulation in a balanced experimental design, radiation did not cause a saccharin aversion independent of pairing.

It may be more fruitful to turn from such ritualistic devotions to operationalism and to consider the behavioral phenomena before us. Rats acquire conditioned flavor aversions when the toxic US: (a) produces no visible discomfort or escape responses, (b) is delayed for hours, or (c) is administered under soporific drug states. Conditioned responses to auditory and visual signals are difficult to establish under similar conditions, leading us to believe that flavor or, more specifically, taste, is favored over all other stimuli as a cue for illness. The single exception to this rule so far has been found in birds.

Proposition 9: Visual primacy in birds. Birds may favor visual stimuli as signals for illness.

Historically, Wallace's hypothesis on visual avoidance of gaudy toxic caterpillars in 1886 and Poulton's review of aversions and avoidances were largely concerned with birds. The following passage from Riddle and Burns (1931) clearly indicates that emetic reflex in the pigeon can be conditioned to visual cues and perhaps other nongustatory cues.

> "In 1912 one of us administered a series of daily doses of yohimbine hydrochloride to several pairs of pigeons and doves which were kept in quite large cages. It was our custom to walk into a cage, catch the pair of birds, and then place the dry pellets of the drug into the upper throat with long, curve-tipped artery forceps. These pellets were readily swallowed but, unless restrained, many of the birds almost immediately regurgitated part or all of the contents of their crops. Several days after beginning this treatment it was observed that some of these birds began to vomit as soon as the person administering the drug entered their cage for this purpose—and *before* the bird was caught for dosage."

This paper goes on to describe subsequent studies which indicated that three to eight trials were needed to condition doves and pigeons with the same drug. Conditioned emesis was also obtained with injections of digitalis and ergot extracts by Lieb and Mulinos (1934), who reported:

"As long as the pigeon is conditioned, it will vomit only when the conditions of the experiment under which it was trained are duplicated, and at no other time. The birds become so sensitive to the routine previously described that the omission of any major part of it, such as the period of starvation, will usually render the other stimuli innocuous."

It seems that this classically conditioned emetic response in birds may be very "situation specific," in contrast to the food aversions of mammals, which appear flavor specific and generalize to many situations. Dramatic examples of this generalization capacity were obtained in coyotes and wolves by Gustavson and his associates (Gustavson, Garcia, Hankins, & Rusiniak, 1974; Gustavson, Kelly, Sweeney, & Garcia, 1976). One or two meals of chopped prey flesh paired with lithium chloride is sufficient to block attacks upon living prey in a choice arena. However, as we have noted above, avoidance of the situational cues associated with illness has been obtained with rats also, but the compartment avoidance response is not nearly as sensitive as the flavor-aversion response. From a practical, survival point of view, higher-order conditioning of visual cues (see **Proposition 5: Flavor mediation**.) seems more important than direct association between visual cues and illness in the absence of differential taste for most species.

The best evidence that birds may prefer visual cues over taste cues is provided by Wilcoxon, Dragoin, and Kral (1971), who compared the quail's and the rat's responses to blue sour water paired with illness. While the quail did show aversions to the sour taste, they demonstrated an even stronger avoidance of the blue visual cue, which appeared to overshadow the taste cue completely in some cases. The rats preferred the taste cue and showed no conditioning to the color cue.

Studies with predatory birds yielded results unlike those observed in the seed-eating quail. When black and/or bitter mice were paired with subsequent lithium illness in broad-winged hawks, stronger aversions were obtained to the bitter taste than to the visual cue. When the two cues were combined, the taste cue appeared to potentiate the visual cue, rather than to overshadow it. Specifically, when the poison mouse was both bitter and black, visual avoidances were observed after a single trial. When the poison mouse was black only, visual avoidances appeared after two or three illness trials and a general aversion developed for both black and white mice. When the mouse was bitter only, an aversion was obtained in one trial (Brett, Hankins, & Garcia, 1976).

Studies with the predatory blue jay by Brower and his associates (1969, 1975) yielded results similar to those observed in hawks. In this case, the poison prey was the Monarch butterfly, which naturally becomes toxic if in the larval stage it feeds on milkweeds containing bitter glycosides. Apparently, the blue jay can learn to avoid the Monarch butterfly on sight, but if driven by hunger it will seize the insects, releasing the toxic ones and consuming the nontoxic ones. The critical cue controlling consumption appears to be taste in the blue jay as well as the hawk. For the moment, the quail and perhaps its seed-eating relatives, are the only species which appear to prefer visual signals over taste in tests of food-aversion conditioning.

Proposition 10: Incentive modification. Taste aversions result from an automatic process in which the hedonic value of a peripheral stimulus is adjusted commensurate with its homeostatic utility.

This rather theoretical proposition did not originate with us, as we have previously pointed out (Garcia, Hankins, & Rusiniak, 1974). Essentially we proposed the following dichotomy: (a) Noise-shock conditioning represents an information acquisition process in which the animal learns that an external signal (noise) is related to a peripheral discomfort (shock) in an external time-space context; (b) Flavor-illness conditioning represents a motivational process in which the hedonic tone of a peripheral stimulus (flavor) is appropriately modified according to its usefulness in maintaining an internal homeostatic balance. Now, we simply wish to present some empirical data which indicates that the acquisition of signal information is relatively independent of hedonic adjustment.

Rats were tested with a strong saccharin solution (7.0 g/L) in one bottle and water in another bottle at the ends of a shuttlebox. The bottles were changed unsystematically from end to end for ten trials per day. Half of the animals were rendered anosmic by zinc sulfate treatment (Alberts & Galef, 1971). The first day served as a pretest without shock, but for nine days thereafter animals were always shocked for drinking saccharin. After these nine days the animals' preference for saccharin as opposed to water was tested in the home cage.

14

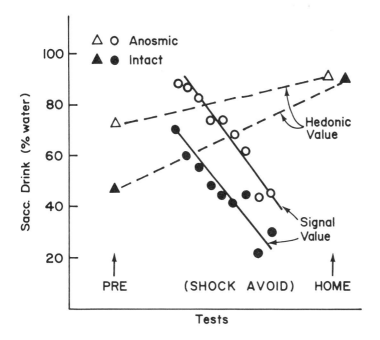

Figure 1
Saccharin preference of rats before (Pre), during (Shock Avoid),
and after (Home) shock avoidance training.

The results are illustrated in Figure 1. Note that for both groups
of animals the hedonic value of saccharin increased from pretest to
posttest in the home cage despite the fact that in the interim the
rats were learning to run away from saccharin because it signalled
shock in the shuttlebox. In one sense, this experiment can be considered a cue to consequence experiment where the same stimulus
(saccharin) serves to signal shock and also to quench the rats'
thirst. Since it signals shock in the shuttlebox, the animals learn to
run away from the saccharin spout, but since saccharin water also
proves useful to correct the homeostatic water deficit, the thirsty
animals come to hedonically regard saccharin water as equivalent
to tap water. Hedonic changes and signal acquisition work in opposite directions without apparent conflict.

Interpretation of the differential conditioning obtained under the
cue-consequence arrangement has returned us to the *nature-nurture*
issue and evolutionary thought. For example, Seligman and Hager
(1972) point out that evolutionary pressures have prepared animals
to quickly learn the contingencies found in the natural niche. The

crack of a twig under the footfall of the predator is apt to be followed by a painful bite. The taste of a toxic plant is apt to be followed by a malaise. Animals are not prepared to make the unnatural taste-pain and noise-illness associations arbitrarily arranged by the experimenter with electronic gear. Rozin and Kalat (1972) also proclaim *Nature,* arguing that all learning and memory mechanisms should be considered situation-specific adaptations. Mackintosh (1974), true to British empiricism, defends *Nurture,* pointing out that during ontogeny each individual gains experience with natural contingencies but not with unnatural ones. However, neuroanatomical evidence seems to indicate that the mammals are biologically prepared to make taste-illness and noise-pain associations (Garcia & Ervin, 1968). We have argued (Garcia & Hankins, 1975; Garcia, Hankins, & Coil, 1976) that, for important environmental contingencies, *Nature* and *Nurture* must act in concert, as beautifully described by the passages quoted in our introduction. The *tabula rasa* is inherited after all, and when that slate is written upon by stable environmental sequences during ontogeny, this nurtured message becomes functionally identical to a naturally coded genetic message. Given that genetic material is in a constant mutational flux, variant offspring opting for the plastic *tabula rasa* and others opting for the fixed genetic message could logically be expected to evolve. As the two classes compete for reproductive advantage, the vagaries of the natural niche pragmatically determine which variant will survive. It is our happy and exciting quest to search out just how nature and nurture interact to yield any given behavioral pattern for any given species at any point in time.

ACKNOWLEDGEMENT

Our research was supported by USPHS Grant 1-RO1-NS 11618 and USPHS Program Project Grant HD-05958.

REFERENCES

Alberts, J., & Galef, B. Acute anosmia in the rat: A behavioral test of a peripherally induced olfactory deficit. **Physiology and Behavior,** 1971, **6,** 619-621.

Barker, L. M., & Smith, J. C. A comparison of taste aversions induced by radiation and lithium chloride in CS-US and US-CS paradigms. **Journal of Comparative and Physiological Psychology,** 1974, **87,** 644-654.

Bates, H. W. Contributions to an insect fauna of the Amazon Valley, *Lepidoptera*: Heliconidae. **Transactions of the Linnaean Society, London,** 1862, **23,** 495-566.

Best, P., Best, M., & Mickley, G. Conditioned aversion to distinct environmental stimuli resulting from gastrointestinal distress. **Journal of Comparative and Physiological Psychology,** 1973, **85,** 250-257.

Bitterman, M. E. The comparative analysis of learning. **Science,** 1975, **188,** 699-709.

Bitterman, M. E. Flavor aversion studies. **Science,** 1976, **192,** 265-267.

Bradley, R. M., & Mistretta, C. Intravascular taste in rats as demonstrated by conditioned aversion to sodium saccharin. **Journal of Comparative and Physiological Psychology,** 1971, **75,** 186-189.

Braveman, N. S. Poison-based avoidance learning with flavored or colored water in guinea pigs. **Learning and Motivation,** 1974, **5,** 182-194.

Brett, L. P., Hankins, W. G., & Garcia, J. Prey-lithium aversions III: Buteo hawks. **Behavioral Biology,** 1976, **17,** 87-98.

Brower, L. P. Ecological chemistry. **Scientific American,** 1969, **220,** 22-29.

Brower, L. P., & Glazier, S. C. Localization of heart poisons in the monarch butterfly. **Science,** 1975, **188,** 19-25.

Buresova, O., & Bures, J. Cortical and subcortical components of the conditioned saccharin aversion. **Physiology and Behavior,** 1973, **11,** 435-439.

Buresova, O., & Bures, J. Functional decortication in the CS-US interval decrease efficiency of taste aversion learning. **Behavioral Biology,** 1974, **12,** 357-364.

Darwin, C. **The descent of man and selection in relation to sex.** London: Murray, 1871.

Domjan, M., & Wilson, N. E. Contribution of ingestive behaviors to taste-aversion learning in the rat. **Journal of Comparative and Physiological Psychology,** 1972, **80,** 403-412. (a)

Domjan, M., & Wilson, N. E. Specificity of cue to consequence in aversion learning in the rat. **Psychonomic Science,** 1972, **26,** 143-145. (b)

Garcia, J., & Ervin, F. R. Gustatory-visceral and telereceptor-cutaneous conditioning—adaptation in internal and external mileus. **Communications in Behavioral Biology,** 1968, **1,** 389-415.

Garcia, J., Ervin, F. R., & Koelling, R. A. Learning with prolonged delay of reinforcement. **Psychonomic Science,** 1966, **5,** 121-122.

Garcia, J., Ervin, F. R., & Koelling, R. A. Toxicity of serum from irradiated donors. **Nature,** 1967, **213,** 682-683.

Garcia, J., Ervin, F. R., Yorke, C., & Koelling, R. A. Conditioning with delayed vitamin injections. **Science,** 1967, **155,** 716-718.

17

Garcia, J., & Hankins, W. G. The evolution of bitter and the acquisition of toxiphobia. In D. A. Denton & J. P. Coghlan (Eds.), **Olfaction and taste** (Vol. 5). New York: Academic Press, 1975.

Garcia, J., Hankins, W. G., & Coil, J. D. Koalas, men and other conditioned gastronomes. In N. W. Milgram, L. Krames, & T. Alloway (Eds.), **Food aversion learning.** New York: Plenum Press, 1976, in press.

Garcia, J., Hankins, W. G., & Rusiniak, K. W. Behavioral regulation of the milieu interne in man and rat. **Science,** 1974, **185,** 824-831.

Garcia, J., & Kimeldorf, D. J. Conditioned avoidance behavior induced by low dose fast neutron exposure. **Nature,** 1960, **185,** 261.

Garcia, J., Kimeldorf, D. J., & Hunt, E. L. Spatial avoidance behavior in the rat as a result of exposure to ionizing radiation. **British Journal of Radiology,** 1957, **30,** 318-320.

Garcia, J., Kimeldorf, D. J., & Hunt, E. L. The use of ionizing radiation as a motivating stimulus. **Psychological Review,** 1961, **68,** 383-395.

Garcia, J., Kimeldorf, D. J., & Koelling, R. A. A conditioned aversion towards saccharin resulting from exposure to gamma radiation. **Science,** 1955, **122,** 157-159.

Garcia, J., & Koelling, R. A. Relation of cue to consequence in avoidance learning. **Psychonomic Science,** 1966, **4,** 123-124.

Garcia, J., McGowan, B., Ervin, F. R., & Koelling, R. A. Cues: Their relative effectiveness as a function of the reinforcer. **Science,** 1968, **160,** 794-795.

Green, L., Bouzas, A., & Rachlin, H. Test of an electric-shock analog to illness-induced aversion. **Behavioral Biology,** 1972, **7,** 513-518.

Green, K. F., & Garcia, J. Role of reinforcer in selecting and responding to cues. 78th Annual APA Convention, 1970, 251-252.

Gustavson, C. R., Garcia, J., Hankins, W. G., & Rusiniak, K. W. Coyote predation control by aversive conditioning. **Science,** 1974, **184,** 581-583.

Gustavson, C. R., Kelly, D. J., Sweeney, M., & Garcia, J. Prey-lithium aversions I: Coyotes and wolves. **Behavioral Biology,** 1976, **17,** 61-72.

Hankins, W. G., Garcia, J., & Rusiniak, K. W. Dissociation of odor and taste in baitshyness. **Behavioral Biology,** 1973, **8,** 407-419.

Hankins, W. G., Rusiniak, K. W., & Garcia, J. Dissociation of odor and taste in shock avoidance learning. **Behavioral Biology,** 1976, in press.

Harris, L. J., Clay, J., Hargreaves, F. J., & Ward, A. Appetite and choice of diet. The ability of the vitamin B deficient rat to discriminate between diets containing and lacking the vitamin. **Proceedings of the Royal Society of London,** 1933, **63,** 161-190.

Hunt, E. L., Carroll, H. W., & Kimeldorf, D. J. Humoral mediation of radiation-induced motivation in parabiont rats. **Science,** 1965, **150,** 1747-1748.

Johnson, C., Beaton, R., & Hall, D. Poison-based avoidance learning in nonhuman primates: Salience of visual cues. **Physiology and Behavior,** 1975, **14,** 403-407.

Kimeldorf, D. J., & Hunt, E. L. **Ionizing radiation: Neural function and behavior.** New York: Academic Press, 1965.

Levy, C. J., Carroll, M. E., Smith, J. C., & Hofer, K. G. Antihistamines block radiation-induced taste aversions. **Science,** 1974, **186,** 1044-1045.

Levy, C. J., Ervin, F. R., & Garcia, J. Effect of serum from irradiated rats on gastrointestinal function. **Nature,** 1970, **225,** 463-464.

18

Lieb, C. C., & Mulinos, M. G. Pigeon emesis and drug action. **Journal of Pharmacology and Experimental Therapeutics,** 1934, **51,** 321-326.

Mackintosh, N. J. **The psychology of animal learning.** New York: Academic Press, 1974.

McLaurin, W. A., Farley, J. A., Scarborough, B. B., & Rawlings, T. D. Postirradiation saccharin avoidance with non-coincident stimuli. **Psychological Reports,** 1964, **14,** 507-512.

Muller, F. *Ituna* and *Thyridia*; a remarkable case of mimicry in butterflies. (Translated by R. Meldola), **Proceedings of the Entomological Society of London,** 1879, 20-29.

Poulton, E. B. The experimental proof of the protective value of color and marking in insects in reference to their vertebrate enemies. **Proceedings of the Zoological Society of London,** 1887, 191-274.

Revusky, S. H. Aversion to sucrose produced by contingent X-irradiation: Temporal and dosage parameters. **Journal of Comparative and Physiological Psychology,** 1968, **65,** 17-22.

Riddle, O., & Burns, F. H. A conditioned emetic reflex in the pigeon. **Proceedings of the Society for Experimental Biology and Medicine,** 1931, 979-981.

Roll, D. L., & Smith, J. C. Conditioned taste aversion in anesthetized rats. In M. E. P. Seligman & J. L. Hager (Eds.), **Biological boundaries of learning.** Englewood Cliffs, N. J.: Prentice-Hall, 1972.

Rozin, P., & Kalat, J. W. Learning as a situation-specific adaptation. In M. E. P. Seligman & J. L. Hager (Eds.), **Biological boundaries of learning.** Englewood Cliffs, N.J.: Prentice-Hall, 1972.

Rzoska, J. Bait shyness, a study in rat behavior. **British Journal of Animal Behavior,** 1953, **1,** 128-135.

Rzoska, J. The behavior of white rats towards poison baits. In D. Chitty (Ed.), **Control of rats and mice Vol. 2, Rats.** Oxford: Clarendon Press, 1954.

Seligman, M. E. P., & Hager, J. L. **Biological boundaries of learning.** Englewood Cliffs, N. J.: Prentice-Hall, 1972.

Smith, J. C., & Roll, D. L. Trace conditioning with X-rays as the aversive stimulus. **Psychonomic Science,** 1967, **9,** 11-12.

Smith, J. C., Taylor, H. L., Morris, D. D., & Hendricks, J. Further studies of X-ray conditioned saccharin aversion during the postexposure period. **Radiation Research,** 1965, **24,** 423-431.

Taukulis, H. Odor aversions produced over long CS-US delays. **Behavioral Biology,** 1974, **10,** 505-510.

Thorndike, E. L. Animal intelligence. **Psychological Review Monograph Supplement,** 1897, **2.**

Wallace, A. R. Untitled. **Proceedings of the Entomological Society of London,** 1867, 80-81.

Wilcoxon, H., Dragoin, W., & Kral, P. Illness-induced aversions in rat and quail: Relative salience of visual and gustatory cues. **Science,** 1971, **171,** 826-828.

Zahorik, D., & Maier, S. Appetitive conditioning with recovery from thiamine deficiency as the unconditioned stimulus. **Psychonomic Science,** 1969, **17,** 309-310.

COMPARATIVE PERSPECTIVES

II

COMPARATIVE AND FIELD ASPECTS OF LEARNED FOOD AVERSIONS

CARL R. GUSTAVSON
Eastern Washington State College

COMPARATIVE ASPECTS OF LEARNED FOOD AVERSIONS

The most striking aspect of a comparative overview of taste aversion conditioning is the consistency of the results obtained across species with the basic conditioning procedure. Overlooking the procedural differences required for administering different flavors and illness-inducing agents to a wide variety of species, several general principles originally described for the laboratory rat are apparent. If an animal consumes a flavored food and subsequently becomes ill, that animal will avoid or drastically reduce consumption of that flavor upon later encounters. The strength of the resulting aversion is directly related to the intensity of the flavor and of the illness, and inversely related to the length of the interval between consumption of the flavor and the onset of the illness. Unlike traditional conditioning studies, the interval between the conditioned stimulus and the illness experience can be expanded from seconds to hours (Garcia, Hankins, & Rusiniak, 1974).

SIMILARITIES AMONG SPECIES

The results of a wide variety of taste aversion conditioning experiments primarily on animals other than white laboratory rats are summarized in Table 1. The 30-plus species in Table 1 are grouped by trophic feeding level.

It may be expected that since a large proportion of plant species contain toxic substances, compared to the orally toxic variety of animal prey species, carnivores may not demonstrate learned food

23

Table 1. Generality of Conditioned Food Aversions Across Trophic Feeding Levels and Species (After Garcia, Rusiniak and Brett, 1976)

Trophic Feeding Level	Species	Food/Flavor Cue	Illness Agent/ Route of Admin.	Illness Delay/ Trials	Comments
Carnivores					
	Cougar (*Felis concolor*)	Deer Meat	LiCl (or), 6.0g	0/1	No emesis during treatment. Observed conditioned emesis on posttest with plain deer meat (Gustavson, Kelly, Sweeney, & Garcia, 1976).
	Cat (*Felis domesticus*)	Chocolate Milk	X-ray, 106r/1hr	0/3	Safe food, plain milk. Weak effect after 1 trial, big effect after three (Kimeldorf, Garcia, & Rubadeau, 1960).
		Cottage Cheese	LiCl (ip)	5min/4	Gradually increasing dose. Vomiting 30-60 min after each injection (Brett & Garcia, 1975).
	Ferrett (*Mustela putorius furo*)	Beef Kidney	LiCl (ip)	5min/3	One trial effect (Brett & Garcia, 1975).
		Salt Water	.12M LiCl (or)	0/5	Reduced very high preference to water consumption level. Vomiting and diarrhea observed (Rusiniak, Gustavson, Hankins, & Garcia, 1976).
		Dog Food	LiCl (ip), 70-100 mg/kg	5-10 min/1	Big effect (Rusiniak et al., 1976).
		Mackerel	LiCl (ip), 70-100 mg/kg	5-10 min/1	Prior experience with illness did not attenuate effect (Rusiniak et al., 1976).
		Mouse	LiCl (or caps), 1.6g	5-10 min/5	Illness after killing without consumption induced aversion, no effect on killing (Rusiniak et al., 1976).
	Timber Wolf (*Canis Lupus*)	Sheep flesh in hide	LiCl (or caps)	0/1	Suppressed attack of fully grown sheep (Gustavson, Kelly, Sweeney & Garcia, 1976).
	Coyote (*Canis latrans*)	0.12 LiCl/ 0.12M NaCl	LiCl, (or)	0-30 min/3	No aversion to salt, all vomited 20-50 min after drinking lithium (Gustavson, 1974).
		Chicken flavored dog food	LiCl (ip) (0.12M) 50-250 ml	10-15 min/ 1-5	1 coyote learned in one trial following 50 ml doses; 2 required 5 trials with progressively increasing dose (Gustavson, 1974).
		Raw hamburger	LiCl (or caps), 2.7-6.0g	0/1	Vomiting occurred 2½-6hr after meat consumption (Gustavson, Garcia, Hankins, & Rusiniak, 1974).
		Minced lamb hide	LiCl (or caps), 6-0g	0/1	Vomiting 80 min after meal. Also suppressed attack of live lamb (Gustavson et al., 1974).

24

	Food	Agent	Dose/Trials	Results
	Rabbit Carcass	LiCl (or) + LiCl (ip), 5.0g + 2.5g	10-15 min/2	Suppressed attack and consumption of live rabbit (Gustavson et al., 1974).
	Rabbit Carcass	LiCl (or), 6.0g	0/1	Suppressed rabbit attack (Gustavson, Kelly, Sweeney, & Garcia, 1976).
	Dog food in rabbit hide	LiCl, 3.0g	0/2	Suppressed rabbit attack (Gustavson, Kelly, Sweeney, & Garcia, 1976).
Red-tailed Hawk (*Buteo jamaicensis*)	Black mouse, black + bitter mouse, bitter mouse	LiCl (ip), 213-320 mg/kg	5-10 min/1-3	Taste learned better than color; rapid chaining of color to taste (Brett, Hankins, & Garcia, 1976).
Garter Snakes (*Thamnophis sirtalis*)	Earthworm extract	LiCl (ip), 570 mg/kg	0.5hr/1	Apparently mediated via Jacobson's organ (Burghardt, Wilcoxon, & Czaplicki, 1973).
Atlantic Cod (*Gadus morhua L.*)	Liver, squid	LiCl (ip), 636 mg/kg	0.5 hr/1	Some sensitization effects (MacKay, 1974).
Anemone (*Aiptasia annulata*)	Shrimp	Quinine (or)	0/1	True "discriminative learning" not yet unequivocally demonstrated (Haralson, & Haralson, 1974).
Omnivores				
Man (*Homo sapiens*)	Variable, novel	Visceral upset	0-6 hr/1	Specific aversions in individuals from a survey of 969 people in six different populations—novelty and age contribute strongly (Garb & Stunkard, 1974).
	Alcoholic drink	Emetine	0/4-6	Follow-up trials 6 mo later; 44% still avoiding (Lemere & Voegtlin, 1950).
	Alcoholic drink	Many	Var	Chemical aversion therapy in alcoholics (Mottlin, 1973).
Squirrel Monkey	Red Water	LiCl	0.5 hr/1	(Gorry & Ober, 1970).
American Black Bear (*Ursus americanus*)	Marshmallows	LiCl (ip) 0.56M (100ml); LiCl 3 g (laced marshmallow)	0/15 min/1	Vomited 26 min after feeding—rejected marshmallow on 4 out of 7 posttests over a 65 day period (Gustavson, Kelly, Sweeney, & Thomas, 1976).
	Marshmallows	LiCl (caps) 3 g	0/1	No emesis—rejected marshmallow for 48 day period (Gustavson, Kelly, Sweeney, & Thomas, 1976).
	Marshmallows	LiCl (caps) + (laced) 4g, 3g, 5g	0/3	No emesis—also no aversion (Gustavson, Kelly, Sweeney, & Thomas, 1976).
	Marshmallows	LiCl (caps) + LiCl (ip) 4.5-7.5g 0.94M (100ml)	0-10 min/4	No emesis with 4.5 g—vomiting with both 7.5-8g—Emesis with ip—aversion ranging from 5-38 days with treatment (Gustavson, Kelly, Sweeney, & Thomas, 1976).

	Honey	LiCl (30g) mixed in raw honey (250ml)	0/1	No emesis—aversion lasting after 9 days (Wooldridge, 1975).
	Honey	LiCl (8g) mixed in raw honey (250ml)	0-30 min/1	No emesis—aversion lasting after 9 days (Wooldridge, 1975).
European Brown Bear—Cub A & B	Marshmallows	LiCl (caps) + raw mixed in marshmallow 8-9g	0/2	Emesis—one cub aversion after one trial. Emesis—2nd aversion after 2 trials (Gustavson, Kelly, Sweeney, & Thomas, 1976).
Brown Rat (*Rattus norvegicus*)	Grains	Common pesticides	0/many	Free consumption studies (Thompson, 1954).
Half-wild Rats & Laboratory strains	Saccharin, sucrose, NaCl, HCl, quinine, coffee, vinegar, apple juice, & others, many levels	X-ray, LiCl, apomorphine, cyclophosphamide, iv saline, many psychoactive drugs, thiamine deficiency and others, many levels	0-12hr/ 1-5	1 trial effects are common. (See appendix.)
	Mouse flesh, mouse dipped in sweet-minty fluid	LiCl (ip), 127 mg/kg	0-0.5hr/ 1-11	Mouse eating always reduced, killing sometimes, if tested in choice situation (Krames, Milgram, & Christie, 1973; Berg & Baenninger, 1974; Rusiniak et al., 1976).
Black Rat (*Rattus rattus*)	Millet seed	Zn_3P_2 (or), 2mg/ 10g food, 4mg/10g food	0/6-8 days	Free consumption over several days was reduced—anosmia does not reduce avoidance (Barnett, Cowan, Radford, & Prakash, 1975).
Mouse (*Mus musculus*, CFI)	1% saccharin	X-ray, 119r/3h	0/3	1 trial effect (Kimeldorf et al. 1960).
	Crickets	LiCl (ip), 127 mg/kg	0-30 min/1-5	Suppression of cricket eating and killing (Lowe & O'Boyle, 1976).
Wild Mice (*Microtus montanus & Peromyscus maniculatus*)	Orange Tang	LiCl (or) 0.12M	0/1, 24hr	1 trial effect and generalization to untainted Tang (Gustavson, Kelly, Sweeney, & Thomas, 1976).
White-throated Sparrow (*Zonotrichia albicollis*)	Mealworm	Tartar emetic (or)	0/6-22	Vomiting 5-10 min. after eating poison worm. Multiple trials on same day. Refused to even turn over seed covering mealworm (Alcock, 1970b).
Black-capped Chickadee (*Parus atricapillus*)	Mealworm	Quinine sulfate	0/1-8	Vomiting 5-10 min after poison worm consumption. Multiple daily trials. Avoidance of seed covers and mimics also (Alcock, 1970a).
Magpie (*Pica pica*)	Rabbit	LiCl (or) 6g	0/1	Vomiting within 30 min. Pecked meat twice on 1st posttest. Complete avoidance without pecking on 2 following tests (Gustavson, Kelly, Sweeney, & Thomas, 1976).

Harbivores				
Blue Jays (*Cyanocitta cristata bromia*)	Monarch Butterflies	Cardiac glycoside, .028-.167g	0/1-10	A 1-3 trial effect, depending on prey food containing the glycoside (Brower, 1969; Platt, Coppinger, & Brower, 1971).
Rhesus (*Macaca*)	Cherry Kool-Aid	X-ray, 30-150r/45 min	0/3	1 trial effect (Harlow, 1964).
	Apple Juice	X-ray, 30-150r	0/5	1 trial effect (Harlow, 1964).
Green Monkey (*Cercopithecus sabaeus*)	Blue/yellow tubes, water	LiCl (ip), 32 mg/kg, 64 mg/kg	1hr/1	32 mg/kg threshold effect—64 mg/kg 5 day aversion (Johnson, Beaton, & Hall, 1975).
Monkeys	Peanut, carrot, raisin, apple, bread	X-ray, 100-400r	0/12	Successive choices between 2 foods during irradiation. General anorexia followed by persistent avoidance of peanuts especially (Leary, 1955).
Guinea Pig (*Cavia porcellus*)	.05% HCl, 1% saccharin, red water, blue water (3 drops vegetable dye/100 ml) red tubes, blue tubes	LiCl (ip), 127 mg/kg	1hr/1	Aversions to both color of fluid and taste of fluid (Braveman, 1974).
(Infrequent Carnivore)				
Golden Hamster	Vaginal secretion	LiCl (ip)	0/1	Johnston, Beaton, & Hall, 1975.
Gerbils (*Tatera indica*, *Meriones hurrianae*)	Millet with ground nut oil	Zinc phosphide (Zn_3P_2) (or)	0/4 days	LD_{50} determined (approximately 64 mg/kg)—but animals allowed to free feed on poison (Prakash & Jain, 1971).
Bobwhite Quail (*Colinus virginianus*)	Blue sour water, blue water, sour water	Cyclophosphamide, 132 mg/kg	30 min/1	Both taste and color learned in one trial (Wilcoxon, Dragoin, & Kral, 1971).
(Occasionally Carnivore)				
Chicken (*Gallus gallus*)	Red mash/blue mash	10% NaCl (or), 2ml	0/6	Reduced preference (Capretta, 1961).
Pigeon (*Columba*)	Red water, saccharin water, red + saccharin water	LiCl (ip), 127 mg/kg	5-10 min/ 1-5	Both color and taste learned (Homer & Rusiniak, 1975).
Land Slug (*Limax maximus*)	Mushroom, Cucumber	CO_2, 5 min	0/multiple 1 hr/multiple 3 hr/multiple	1 trial effect Marginal effect Sensitization possible effect (Gelperin, 1975).

or caps = lithium chloride in gelatin capsules   ip = intraperitoneal injection   y = year

or = oral: ingested or by stomach tube   var = variable

aversions as readily as either omnivores or herbivores. Like the omnivores and herbivores represented in the table, however, carnivores appear to associate just as readily the results of consuming a food with its internal consequences, and a delay in illness consequences is coped with equally well. Such broad ecological divisions may be quite arbitrary, however, and of limited value in predicting specific behavior patterns. Such categorizations are based essentially on the proportion of the diet made up of a certain food type. Most animals, however, do not strictly adhere to such a dietary habit; i.e., while carnivores are primarily meat eaters, most will accept plants as food, especially when preferred foods are scarce. In general, these trophic feeding levels result from morphological adaptations and are established and maintained to reduce feeding competition across species. However, considerable behavioral plasticity remains available to the animals to adapt to fluctuating food resources.

The vertebrates represented in the table include Primates, Bears (Ursus), Canines, Felines, Mustelids, Avians, Rodents, Reptiles, and Fish. Two invertebrate groups, Molluscs and Coelenterates, are also listed. The similarity in food-aversion learning across these species attests to the evolutionary and ecological pressures that must have been and are constantly being exerted on animals to take advantage of mechanisms that allow for the rapid alternation of diet to exclude toxic foods. However, some animals do have severely restricted dietary bases, and possibly for these animals there is less necessity for dietary plasticity. The Koala bear of Australia is worth considering in this context. Of several hundred species of eucalyptus in Australia, the Koala bear will accept only about a dozen as food, and prefers only three or four as a constant diet. These varieties do not, however, remain wholesome throughout the year and lethal concentrations of prussic acid can be found seasonally with the new leaf shoots. Because of this, the Koala must rapidly change to another species of non-toxic eucalyptus and does so quite readily (Martin, 1975). In light of the feeding plasticity of even the Koala bear, it would be surprising at this point to find an animal that would not demonstrate the acquisition of food aversions. However, some consistent differences across species do exist, and in order to put these differences in perspective let us momentarily digress.

FEEDING BEHAVIORS AS SPECIFIC ADAPTATIONS

From the standpoint of species survival the role of behavior and associated sensory systems is to provide the fulfillment of a few

minimum biological requirements through reproductive maturation. In introductory biology classes these requirements are typically cited as the characteristics defining life—including locomotion,
respiration, reproduction, ingestion of nutrients, excretion of
wastes, etc. What provides for evolutionary diversity is that organisms attempting to meet these minimum biological requirements must do so in an environment that has finite, and typically
inadequate, resources. This oversimplified view of evolution is
brought into discussion because at times the comparative study of
behavior is mistakenly approached either as a search for species
differences that indicate some hierarchical description of the
evolution of behavior from "lower" to "higher" development, or as
an attempt to challenge the generality of an established
phenomenon. Rather, the role of comparative study is more pro-
ductively viewed with reference to the function that a behavior has
for the animal to meet some biological requirement in its natural
ecosystem. Consistent differences or similarities within or across
species must eventually be accounted for anatomically,
physiologically, or as the result of varied ecological requirements.
This functional view of behavior is by no means new but is presented here to put into productive perspective differences across
species that are found in the taste aversion literature.

SPECIES DIFFERENCES IN THE ACQUISITION OF FOOD AVERSIONS

As was suggested above, taste-aversion learning has been demonstrated in a wide variety of animals indicating that broad
ecological and evolutionary pressures have been exerted on
animals to avoid toxic food. However, some differences among
species have been noted.

Food Aversions in Avians. In general, most animals associate only the flavor cue of food with the subsequent illness. However,
Wilcoxon, Dragoin, and Kral, (1971; see also Wilcoxon, this
volume) with bobwhite quail, and Homer and Rusiniak (1975),
with pigeons, suggested that color cues functioned equally well as
the flavor cues in taste-aversion conditioning for these animals.
Garcia, Rusiniak, and Brett (1976) suggested that for these birds, the
environment poses a different problem than for most other animals.
The chemical elements comprising flavor are readily available to
most animals as food is placed on the tongue, or as chewing breaks
down the food for swallowing. In this way, the tongue functions as
the critical sensor for protecting mammals from poisoning and
identifying nutrient foods. For quail and pigeons, however, the diet

consists of seeds in a very hard and relatively flavorless shell, broken down only after the food is ground in the gizzard. These birds may have developed mechanisms for the visual association of non-gustatory stimulus elements of a food with illness because they cannot easily identify foods with orosensory mechanisms.

The predisposition to form a visual aversion does not appear to be characteristic of avians as a general group. Brett, Hankins, and Garcia (1976) reported a series of experiments on redtailed hawks in which some were presented with mice distinguished by color and then poisoned, while others were either given different flavored mice, or both color and flavor cues for illness. Both attack and consumptive measures of the resultant aversions indicated that birds with both stimulus cues had an obvious advantage, and that while birds receiving only the gustatory cue did not as readily suppress approach and attack behaviors, consumption of toxic mice was reduced. Finally, birds with only visual stimuli were at a definite disadvantage and tended to generalize suppression of attack and consumption of all mice. In a subsequent study two magpies were presented with LiCl-laced pieces of rabbit meat which was consumed and followed in 0.5 hr by vomiting. When subsequently tested with rabbit meat one bird stoically remained on the perch. The other bird immediately approached the meat, pecked it, and pulled off pieces which were then shaken from the mouth violently without swallowing. On a third exposure neither bird approached the meat, even though it remained in the cage for several days. Although both birds vomited on the first trial resulting in the pairing of the visual aspects of the meat with its flavor, the first bird may have learned a direct visual aversion to the meat. The second bird appears to have acquired an aversion only to the flavor of the meat initially and needed additional pairing of the now aversive flavor with the visual aspects of the meat before rejecting it on sight (Gustavson, Kelley, Sweeny, & Thomas, 1976). A similar two-phase learning system has been proposed for both coyotes and wolves by Gustavson, Garcia, Hankins, and Rusiniak (1974).

Species Differences in Emesis. A second difference that has been noted in cross-species studies is the unreliable occurrence of emesis or vomiting. Vomiting may be of significant evolutionary importance as a mechanism for emptying the contents of the stomach when a toxin has been consumed. Rats are incapable of emesis and possibly depend entirely on learning mechanisms for protection from toxic foods. Vomiting probably lessens the immediate life-threatening aspects of having consumed poison; however, the risk of death remains high in many instances and permanent damage could result. Learned aversions appear to functionally protect the animal from further exposure to risk. We have noted that the occurrence of vomiting is inconsistent even within a species that does vomit when identical doses of poison are administered. In our work with coyotes, vomiting has not been a completely reliable indicator of illness, nor has the occurrence of vomiting been necessary for the establishment of an aversion (see Gustavson, 1974). Similar results were obtained with a cougar which also did not vomit. Bears have been given up to 81 g of LiCl in a 0.5 hr period without inducing emesis. However, aversions to the honey in which the LiCl was mixed were complete and lasted for a 9-day test period (Wooldridge, 1975).

While emesis may be our most obvious indicator of illness, it is probably not a necessary component of aversion learning. Emesis is also a mechanism for feeding the young in many species, suggesting that regurgitation per se is not aversive. Rather, other aspects of toxicosis are responsible for the aversive contingency or unpleasantness associated with vomiting. The occurrence of vomiting may, however, facilitate the generalization of aversions to other sensory systems by contiguously representing the flavor with both visual and olfactory components of a food.

Species Differences in Responses to Aversive Foods. Not unexpectedly the reaction of different animals to the presentation of an aversive food also differs. Cats have shaken their paws in disgust. Coyotes have urinated on, buried, and rolled on aversive foods. Rats have been reported to empty food cups and rub their noses and mouths on the bottom of a cage to remove remnants of the food. Hawks "chitter" and flap their wings. Blue jays and coyotes have retched at the sight of an aversive food, and normally aggressive wolves have cavorted and played with a sheep as though it were a dominant member of the pack after having sheep-ingestion paired with illness. These differences are probably due in part at least to the structure of the animals. Some behaviors may be functional in the removal of an aversive item from the mouth or environment. Disgust behaviors have similar appearance to behaviors associated with illness and might be considered conditioned illness symptoms. Still other responses, such as coyotes eating grass, or rats and cougars biting the edge of a food dish, appear to be nonfunctional (displaced) activities. These may be generated when the animal, being highly motivated to engage in feeding, is confronted with an item that has in the past been edible and appetitive and has suddenly become unpalatable. In such a situation all of the sensory and motivational systems except the tongue indicate that feeding is appropriate. This confusing set of information may generate what appears to be abnormal or displaced behavior (Garcia et al., 1976).

SEPARATION OF PREDATORY AND CONSUMMATORY BEHAVIORS

Feeding behavior in general, and predatory behavior in particular, may best be conceived as having two facets. First, during the appetitive phase, food is located distally through vision, audition, and olfaction and the approach is guided by these sensory systems. The second consummatory phase of feeding begins when food enters the mouth, and the critical acceptance or rejection of the food is accomplished by the sensors of the tongue, with the possible exception of several avians described above. Since for most species the acquision of food aversions is limited to only the flavor of the food paired with illness, it should not be surprising that some differences have been noted in the extent to which a taste aversion can interfere with the earlier appetitive phase of feeding.

Brower (1969) described the acquisition of aversions and suppression of attack on monarch butterflys by blue jays following one consumption-illness episode with a toxic form of the monarch. Brett et al. (1976) demonstrated that redtailed hawks rapidly acquire aversions to the flavor of mice paired with illness and subsequently suppress attack on the conditioned aversive prey. Gustavson et al. (1974) and Gustavson, Kelly, Sweeney, and Garcia (1976) reported that both coyotes and wolves suppressed attack on sheep when fed sheep meat and wool paired with lithium-induced illness on one or two occasions.

In contrast to the above studies, Krames, Milgram, and Christie (1973) and Berg and Baenninger (1974) found that consumption of mice flesh followed by illness would not inhibit subsequent attack on mice by rats. When the consumption of mice is followed by illness, rats will continue to kill mice in the home cage and not eat them, but will learn to select a safe-flavored prey in a T-maze situation, leaving the aversive mouse completely alone (Rusiniak, Gustavson, Hankins, & Garcia, 1976). Rusiniak et al. (1976) also reported that domestic ferrets would not suppress attack on mice either in the home cage or T-maze when consumption of mice was followed by LiCl-induced illness. However, conditioning suppressed consumption of the mice and altered the form of attack from biting to killing with the feet. Possibly these domesticated rats and ferrets have lost the wisdom of their feral forefathers and will now waste precious calories killing what they will not eat. It must also be remembered that many aggressive motives exist for the rat in the home cage. Mice killing in such a situation may be a response to territorial intrusion rather than an impulse to feed.

SUMMARY OF COMPARATIVE ASPECTS

A comparative overview of taste-aversion studies suggests that in spite of large technical differences in procedures, a wide variety of animals are readily sensitive to the food-illness contingency. Categorization of studies by either broad taxonomic or ecological divisions such as trophic feeding level does not predict well the differences that exist across species. Rather, the examination of the specific feeding requirements of a species is of more value (see Zahorik & Houpt, this volume). Some avians appear to associate visual aspects of a food with illness more readily than other animals, perhaps because feeding on a resource that is largely lacking in flavor requires identification of toxic foods by other stimulus aspects. The emetic response of animals to toxicosis also differs. However, this response may be of no significant value in the establishment of learned aversions. Species-specific responses to aversive foods also differ, and appear to take three forms: (1) functional removal of either the food from the environment or the animal from the food, (2) disgust behaviors, and (3) displaced behaviors. Finally, the extent to which the establishment of an aversion to the flavor of a food will interfere with the appetitive or approach phase of feeding appears to differ across species. Feral species appear not to waste effort approaching or attacking food they will not eat. In contrast, domesticated animals are more likely to attack prey following aversive ingestional experiences.

FIELD ASPECTS OF LEARNED AVERSIONS

In the laboratory the phenomenon and associated subtleties of taste aversion conditioning has produced what is now a vast literature (see Appendix). However, only a limited number of studies exist on the functional role of learned food aversion for the free-ranging animal. Brower's (1969) laboratory investigation of the predator-prey relationship between bluejay and monarch butterflys demonstrated that aversion conditioning mechanisms can serve to protect both the predator and the prey. This is accomplished when the bluejay ingests the toxic monarch and therefore learns to reject the butterfly on subsequent encounters. The rat can also learn to avoid toxic substances in the free-ranging situation as was dramatically demonstrated in Richter's (1945) studies of rat poisoning programs. Our current research interests are to establish selected aversions to a food source to protect the interests of man, thereby leaving the feral animal to perform its more natural control functions in the ecosystem.

Factors Influencing Feeding in Natural Situations. Two sets of variables function independently and interactively to produce the dietary characteristic of a population. The first involves variables that affect the feeding of specific individuals, excluding interactions with members of its own species. These variables include: (1) the morphological, anatomical, and physiological systems of the species that determine the limits of food items available to the animal for exploitation, (2) the availability of the specific food in the environment, as determined by both density of the food, and its accessibility through ease of capture, (3) the availability of alternative foods in reference to a specific dietary item, and (4) wholesomeness of the food, both itself and with reference to other food resources (Gustavson, Brett, Garcia, & Kelly, 1976). The second set of variables involve social interaction events with conspecifics. These include: (1) the reproductive habits of the species as they affect mobility in individuals, (2) the offspring caretaking behavior as it affects mobility, and influences the diet ot the offspring (Capretta & Rawls, 1972; Galef & Clark, 1972; see also chapters by Capretta and by Galef, this volume), (3) the territorial patterns of a species, and finally, (4) the population density of the predator.

Field Modification of Diet. Of the various factors which control the dietary characteristics of a population, the variable most easily manipulated is the wholesomeness of a specific dietary item. All of the other variables require drastic modification of either the predator, prey, or ecosystem. For small areas, modification of the ecosystem by fencing, for example, may be of practical use. However, both economic and aesthetic considerations make these drastic manipulations of the environment unacceptable on a large scale. Structural changes in either the prey or the predator certainly would not be acceptable on the basis of ecological risk, even if technologies were available for such modification. Finally, drastic manipulation of population numbers has been demonstrably disastrous to natural controls on prey populations, and in the case of the coyote, of limited value as a control tool (Gustavson et al., 1976).

Partially Toxic Prey Populations as a Means of Predatory Control. Many animals reject mildly bitter flavors on contact (e.g.,

34

Brower, 1969; Garcia et al., 1974). Since bitter tastes often reflect the toxicity of a food, this rejection response is adaptive. In addition, it can also serve to protect bitter-tasting species from natural predators, as illustrated by studies in which bitter-tasting and toxic monarch butterflies were protected from a natural predator, the bluejay, by conditioning aversions in these birds (Brower, 1969). Such natural predator-prey relationships, however, pose a potential problem in the application of food aversion technology in the field. The monarchs were protected precisely because bitter taste and toxicity were characteristic of many members of this prey species. In relationships between species like coyotes and sheep, however, the prey is rarely if ever naturally toxic. Consequently, sheep-aversion learning must be established in coyotes using artificially toxic sheep. Since it is impossible to toxify all sheep in a range, a small number of toxic sheep must function to condition an aversion in coyotes which will then generalize to all other sheep.

There is suggestive evidence that all members of a class need not be toxic to be protected from predation by a food-aversion learning mechanism. Brower (1969), in his discussion of the monarch-bluejay relationship, reports that non-toxic queen butterflies are protected from their bird predators because they mimic the distinct coloration of toxic monarchs. Such findings suggest that partially toxic prey populations may be an effective technique in modifying natural predator-prey relationships in the field. The following case studies describe our attempts to apply this technique in reducing sheep predation by coyotes.

CASE STUDIES OF PREDATION CONTROL

During the latter part of January, 1975, we undertook our first application of taste aversion conditioning to free-ranging coyotes on a 3000-acre sheep ranch in southeastern Washington. Prior to putting out poison baits, coyotes were frequently observed individually or in groups of two or three. Fresh tracks and scats (excrement) were common along trails and fence lines. A trap survey found a high count of 276 rodents per acre, indicating an abundant source of alternate prey. Two large open carcass dumps appeared to be regular feeding sites for the coyotes. About 365 ewes and 160 lambs from the previous year spent the winter in the eastern section of the ranch. Two weeks prior to lambing, the pregnant ewes were released onto pastures near their winter grazing area.

Twelve bait stations were originally established throughout the ranch along fence lines, at gates, at the carcass dumps, and wherever fresh signs of coyote movement were apparent. Baits consisting of 340 g of dog food (Top Choice, General Foods, Inc.) containing 6 g of LiCl were wrapped and stapled in a fresh piece of unsheared hide. Initially, two to four baits comprised a bait station. Later, relatively fresh sheep carcasses from natural losses were moved to a bait station or left in place and treated with lithium. Carcasses were injected throughout with a solution of LiCl (82.4 g/L water) so that a coyote feeding on any part would consume at least some LiCl. When carcasses were too decomposed for injection, they were sprayed thoroughly with the LiCl solution from a commercial weed sprayer. Ultimately, all carcasses (18 ewes and 74 lambs), including those in the dump, were treated with lithium. Bait stations were checked every 24-72 hr. Missing baits were replaced and the area was examined for tracks and remains by walking out in concentric circles from the station. Coyote feeding on baits was recorded when a bait was disturbed or missing, if the remains resembled those left by our captive coyotes, or if coyote tracks, scats or vomitus were evident. Coyote feeding on LiCl-laced carcasses was determined by similar examinations and photographed. In most cases, it was impossible to determine if a carcass feeding was due to one or more coyotes. Hence, each new evidence of feeding was scored as one unit.

Figure 1 (top panel) illustrates the cumulative weekly number of dog food bait pickups and lithium carcass findings. Initially bait consumption was high, then declined. After about eight weeks, no dog food baits required replacing. The remaining baits were left in place throughout the study period.

Evaluation of predation losses proved to be somewhat controversial. A "placebo" study in which saline-treated baits were scattered on a comparable ranch would have simplified interpretation but seemed impractical. Unpoisoned baits would be likely to increase lamb predation by attracting predators and cultivating a taste for lamb. Thus, given our limited resources, we had to compare this year's losses with previous losses on the same range. These records were maintained each year on a monthly basis, since accurate records of profit and loss are essential for business and income tax purposes. By comparing the rancher's estimate of losses in 1975 to previous years, a 30% decrease was observed. Our records suggest a 62% decrease, but either estimate suggested a dramatic reduction in losses to coyotes (for further details see Gustavson, Kelly, Sweeney, & Garcia, 1976).

Our second field study of aversion conditioning in coyotes was conducted in the Turnbull National Wildlife Refuge. In order to

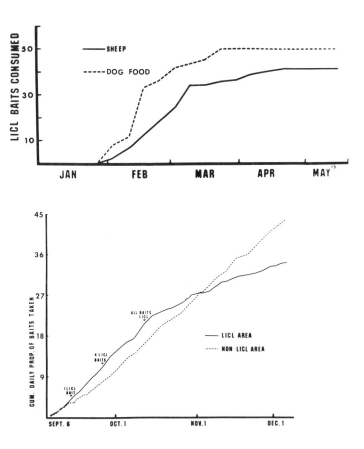

Figure 1
Coyote ranch study (upper panel). Cumulative feedings upon lithium treated sheep carcasses, and dog food-lithium baits wrapped in raw sheep hides. Note the terminal plateaus in the feeding curves. Coyote refuge study (lower panel). Cumulative daily proportion of available baits removed from two distinct baiting areas on the Turnbull National Wildlife Refuge. Note the lack of terminal plateaus on the area treated with LiCl during the fall of the year.

gain a preliminary estimate of bait consumption by the coyotes, we instigated a reduced baiting study in the fall of 1975. On August 25, three bowls of dog food were placed at each of nine stations on the western half, and at five stations on the eastern half, of the Turnbull Refuge.

These stations were checked once every twenty-four hours. Removed baits were replaced, and the type of tracks in the smoothed station was recorded and cleared. Some coyote activity was observed initially. However, signs of coyote visits to the stations quickly diminished and activity was almost strictly limited to magpies. Further, magpies were observed following our trucks and descending on the station immediately as we drove away (see Figure 2).

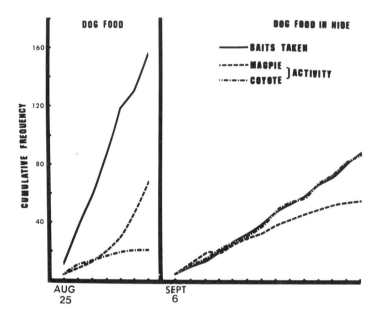

Figure 2
The cumulative number of dog food baits (left panel) and dog food in hide baits (right panel) plotted with the incidence of magpie and coyote activity at the bait stations on the Turnbull Wildlife Refuge.

Apparently, both coyotes and magpies were originally investigating and consuming the baits left at stations. Eventually, many magpies may have found these stations a source for an easy and consistent meal. Baits were probably consumed during the daylight hours by these birds, and therefore the opportunity for coyotes to consume them was non-existent during their evening activity period, so the coyotes no longer visited the station.

On September 6, all remnants of the dog baits were removed from the station and replaced with dog food wrapped and sealed in a green sheep hide at each station. These baits were exactly like the ones used previously in our sheep ranch study. Initially with these

38

new baits, coyote activity was low and magpie activity was high. However, magpies were unable to penetrate the thick wooly hide of the bait and apparently extinguished investigation of the stations. Coyote activity rapidly increased as did bait consumption (see Figure 2). These results indicate the importance of properly preparing baits for application to coyotes. In general baits should be rather large and sealed in the hide of the target prey species. Small baits seem to be inappropriate because complete consumption by birds and small mammals could rule out treatment of the coyotes.

Lithium chloride (6 g) was introduced into a single bait on the western half of the Turnbull Refuge on September 14 and four of the nine baits in this area were laced with LiCl on September 26. Finally, all baits on the western half were tainted with LiCl on October 12. The baits on the eastern half of the refuge were somewhat isolated and were never tainted with LiCl so as to serve as a control. Besides being a different location from the sheep ranch, this situation differed in two major ways from our ranch study. First, our bait density was relatively scant, and during the fall of the year young pups were dispersing from the den. Territorial arrangements may be the least binding and mobility at its highest.

Figure 1 (lower panel) shows the cumulative proportion of possible daily baits taken on both the LiCl treatment area and the non-LiCl control area. This proportion allows a comparison of areas even though the number of stations differed. In general, the most striking difference from our ranch study was that coyotes continued to pick up LiCl baits even after long term exposure to treatment (compare terminal plateaus in the upper panel of Figure 1 to the lack of plateaus in the lower panel). The greater number of coyotes on the refuge could account for some of the observed differences. Alternatively, the reduced bait density may have made location and, therefore, exposure to treatment more difficult and delayed. We suggest that continued bait removal was due to the constant fluctuation of animals through the area from pup dispersal at this time of the year. While it could be interpreted that the bait consumption was not successful in suppressing utilization, the general decrease in bait pickup after all baits contained LiCl suggests that animals were acquiring aversions.

The availability of alternative foods is probably of critical importance in determining the success of any program designed to alter the diet of free-ranging animals. In both of our field study areas the abundant rodent and small mammal populations provided alternative food sources for the coyotes. The coyotes could therefore avoid sheep without suffering food deprivation.

People have suggested to us that taste aversion conditioning may have applicability in reducing crop damage in Eastern Washington where vast wheat fields constitute the only source of plant food. Any baiting program to induce aversions in rodents to wheat in this area would be doomed to failure. The animals would be forced to either discriminate between toxic baits and wheat or die of starvation.

Any program to alter the diet of free-ranging animals must take into account the ecological situation in which manipulation is to be attempted. The predatory activities of many animals help maintain the healthy stock in prey populations. In spite of the hunting value of increased game populations, the relationship between wild animals may best be controlled by natural balances, and diet manipulation may be most desirable when wildlife is interfering with man's domestic interests.

REFERENCES

Alcock, J. Punishment levels and the response of black-capped chickadees (*Parus atricapillus*) to three kinds of artificial seeds. **Animal Behavior**, 1970, **18**, 592-599. (a)

Alcock, J. Punishment levels and the response of white-throated sparrows (*Zonotrichia albicollis*) to three kinds of artificial models and mimics. **Animal Behavior**, 1970, **18**, 733-739. (b)

Avis, H. H., & Treadway, J. T. Mediation of rat-mouse interspecific aggression by cage odor. **Psychonomic Science**, 1971, **22**, 293-294.

Barnett, S. A., Cowan, P. E., Radford, G. G., & Prakash, I. Peripheral anosmia and the discrimination of poisoned food by *Rattus rattus L.* **Behavioral Biology**, 1975, **13**, 183-190.

Berg, D., & Baenninger, R. Predation: Separation of aggressive and hunger motivation by conditioned aversion. **Journal of Comparative and Physiological Psychology**, 1974, **86**, 601-606.

Braveman, N. S. Poison-based avoidance learning with flavored or colored water in guinea pigs. **Learning and Motivation**, 1974, **5**, 182-194.

Brett, L. P., & Garcia, J. Unpublished observations, 1975.

Brett, L. P., Hankins, W. G., & Garcia, J. Prey-lithium aversions: III. Buteo hawks. **Behavioral Biology**, 1976, **17**, 87-98.

Brower, L. P., Ecological chemistry. **Scientific American**, 1969, **220**, 22-29.

Burghardt, G. M., Wilcoxon, H. C., & Czaplicki, J. A. Conditioning in garter snakes: Aversion to palatable prey induced by delayed illness. **Animal Learning and Behavior**, 1973, **1**, 317-320.

Capretta, P. J. An experimental modification of food preference in chickens. **Journal of Comparative and Physiological Psychology**, 1961, **54**, 238-242.

Capretta, P. J., & Rawls, N. H. Establishment of flavor preference in rats: Importance of early nursing and weaning experiences. Paper presented at American Psychological Association meetings, Honolulu, Hawaii, 1972.

Davenport, J. W., Bowns, J. E., Workman, J. P., & Nielson, D. B. (1973). Assessment of sheep losses. In F. H. Wagner (P.I.), **Predator control study**, 3-17. Contract FCRC No. 621-366-044, Final Report, Four Corners Regional Commission, Utah State University, Logan, Utah.

Denenberg, V. H., Paschke, R. E., & Zarrow, M. X. Killing of mice by rats prevented by early interaction between the two species. **Psychonomic Science**, 1968, **11**, 39-40.

Galef, B. G., & Clark, M. M. Social factors in the poison avoidance and feeding behavior of wild and domesticated rat pups. **Journal of Comparative and Physiological Psychology**, 1972, **78**, 220-225.

Garb, J., & Stunkard, A. Taste aversions in man. **American Journal of Psychiatry**, 1974, **131**, 1204-1207.

Garcia, J., Clarke, J. C., & Hankins, W. G. Natural responses to scheduled rewards. In P. P. G. Bateson & P. Klopfer (Eds.), **Perspectives in ethology**. New York: Plenum Press, 1973.

Garcia, J., Hankins, W. G., & Rusiniak, K. W. Behavioral regulation of the milieu interne in man and rat. **Science**, 1974, **185**, 824-831.

Garcia, J., Kimeldorf, D., & Hunt, E. The use of ionizing radiation as a motivating stimulus. **Psychological Review**, 1960, **68**, 383-394.

41

Garcia, J., Rusiniak, K., & Brett, L. Conditioning food-illness aversions in wild animals: Caveant canonici. In H. Davis & Harwitz (Eds.), **Operant-Pavlovian interactions**, in press, 1976, Lawrence Ehrlbaum Associates, New Jersey.

Gelperin, A. Rapid food aversion learning by a terrestrial mollusk. **Science**, 1975, **189**, 567-570.

Gorry, T. H., & Ober, S. E. Stimulus characteristics of learning over long delays in monkeys. Paper presented at Psychonomic Society, San Antonio, 1970.

Gustavson, C. R. Taste aversion conditioning as a predator control method in the coyote and ferret. Unpublished doctoral dissertation, University of Utah, 1974.

Gustavson, C. R., Garcia, J., Hankins, W. G., & Rusiniak, K. W. Coyote predation control by aversive conditioning. **Science**, 1974, **184**, 581-583.

Gustavson, C. R., Brett, L. P., Garcia, J., & Kelly, D. J. A working model and experimental solution to the control of predatory behavior. In H. Markowitz & V. Stevens (Eds.)., **Studies of captive wild animals**, in press, 1976.

Gustavson, C. R., Kelly, D. J., Sweeney, M., & Garcia, J. Prey-lithium aversions: I. Coyotes and wolves. **Behavioral Biology**, 1976, **17**, 61-72.

Gustavson, C. R., Kelly, D. J., Sweeney, M., & Thomas, S. Final Report to the Washington Game Department. February, 1976.

Haralson, J., & Haralson, S. Personal communication, 1974.

Harlow, H. F. Effects of radiation on the central nervous system and on behavior--general survey. In T. J. Haley & R. S. Snider (Eds.), **Response of the nervous system to ionizing radiation; Second international symposium**. Boston: Little, Brown, 1964.

Homer, A. L., & Rusiniak, K. W. Unpublished observations, 1975.

Johnson, C., Beaton, R., & Hall, K. Poison-based avoidance learning in non-human primates: Salience of visual cues. **Physiology and Behavior**, 1975, **14**, 403-407.

Johnston, R. E., & Zahorik, D. M. Taste aversions to sexual attractants. **Science**, 1975, **189**, 893-894.

Karli, P. The Norway rat's killing response to the white mouse; an experimental analysis. **Behavior**, 1956, **10**, 81-103.

Kimeldorf, D. J., Garcia, J., & Rubadeau, D. O. Radiation-induced conditioned avoidance behavior in rats, mice, and cats. **Radiation Research**, 1960, **12**, 710-718.

Krames, L., Milgram, N. W., & Christie, D. P. Predatory aggression: Differential suppression of killing and feeding. **Behavioral Biology**, 1973, **9**, 641-647.

Kuo, Z. Y. The genesis of the cat's response toward the rat. **Journal of Comparative Psychology**, 1930, **11**, 1-35.

Leary, R. W. Food-preference of monkeys subjected to low-level irradiation. **Journal of Comparative and Physiological Psychology**, 1955, **48**, 343-346.

Lemere, F., & Voegtlin, W. L. An evaluation of the aversion treatment of alcoholism. **Quarterly Journal of Studies on Alcohol**, 1950, **11**, 199-204.

Linhart, S. B., Brusman, H. D., & Balsar, D. S. An antifertility agent for inhibiting coyote reproduction. **Transactions of the 33rd North**

American Wildlife and Natural Resources Conference, 1968, **1**, 316-327.

Lowe, W. C., & O'Boyle, M. Conditioned suppression and recovery of cricket killing and eating in laboratory mice. **Animal Learning and Behavior**, in press, 1976.

MacKay, B. Conditioned food aversion produced by toxicosis in atlantic cod. **Behavioral Biology**, 1974, **12**, 347-355.

Martin, L. Tough and cuddly. **International Wildlife**, 1975, **5**, 14-18.

Meyer, J. S. Stimulus control of mouse-killing rats. **Journal of Comparative and Physiological Psychology**, 1964, **58**, 112-117.

Mottlin, J. L. Drug-induced attenuation of alcohol consumption. A review and evaluation of claimed, potential or current therapies. **Quarterly Journal of Studies on Alcohol**, 1973, **34**, 444-472.

Paul, L. Predatory attack by rats: Its relationship to feeding and type of prey. **Journal of Comparative and Physiological Psychology**, 1972, **78**, 69-76.

Paul, L., Miley, W. M., & Baenninger, R. Mouse killing by rats: Roles of hunger and thirst in its initiation and maintenance. **Journal of Comparative and Physiological Psychology**, 1971, **76**, 242-249.

Paul, L., Miley, W. M., & Mazzagatti, N. Social facilitation and inhibition of hunger-induced killing by rats. **Journal of Comparative and Physiological Psychology**, 1973, **84**, 162-168.

Paul, L., & Posner, I. Predation and feeding: Comparison of feeding behavior of killer and non-killer rats. **Journal of Comparative and Physiological Psychology**, 1973, **84**, 258-264.

Platt, A. P., Coppinger, R. P., & Brower, L. P. Demonstration of the selective advantage of mimetic Limentis butterflies presented to caged avian predators. **Evolution**, 1971, **25**, 692-701.

Prakash, I., & Jain, A. P. Baitshyness of two gerbils, *Tatera indica* Hardwicke and *Meriones hurrianae* Jerdon. **Annals of Applied Biology**, 1971, **69**, 169-172.

Richter, C. P. The development and use of alpha-naphthyl thiorea (antu) as a rat poison. **Journal of American Medical Association**, 1945, **129**, 927-931.

Rusiniak, K. W., Gustavson, C. R., Hankins, W. G., & Garcia, J. Prey-lithium aversions: II. Rats and ferrets. **Behavioral Biology**, 1976, **17**, 73-85.

Thompson, H. V. The consumption of plain and poisoned cereal baits by brown rats. In D. Chitty (Ed.), **Control of rats and mice**. Oxford: Clarendon Press, 1954.

Van Hemel, P. E., & Meyer, J. S. Satiation of mouse killing by rats in an operant situation. **Psychonomic Science**, 1970, **21**, 129-130.

Wilcoxon, H. C., Dragoin, W., & Kral, P. A. Illness induced aversions in rat and quail: Relative salience of visual and gustatory cues. **Science**, 1971, **171**, 826-828.

Wooldridge, D. Aversion conditioning in the black bear (*Ursus americanus*). Unpublished manuscript, Department of Bioscience, Simon Fraser University, 1975.

III

THE CONCEPT OF NUTRITIONAL WISDOM: APPLICABILITY OF LABORATORY LEARNING MODELS TO LARGE HERBIVORES

DONNA M. ZAHORIK
Cornell University

and

KATHERINE ALBRO HOUPT
New York State College of
Veterinary Medicine

The concept of "nutritional wisdom"—that animals select foods which optimize their nutritional well-being and reject foods which are poisonous or low in nutritional value—is an extremely old idea with a certain amount of empirical support. It would be a gross overstatement to claim that the match between the foods animals select and the nutrients they require is a perfect one, but in those species whose diets and nutritional requirements are sufficiently well documented to permit some assessment of the correspondence between the two, there is usually enough of a relationship to require some sort of explanation. How *do* animals which eat a wide variety of foods—most of them less than completely nutritious—manage to select a reasonably well-balanced diet? Can one mechanism explain all cases of nutritional wisdom, or are there many mechanisms involved in adaptive diet selection? If various mechanisms are employed, are different nutrients chosen by different methods? Are different mechanisms used by different species?

An early and extremely influential answer to these questions was offered by Curt Richter (1943), who proposed a theory of "specific hungers" as an explanation for all cases of nutritional wisdom. According to this theory, animals can recognize specific deficiency states (they can tell whether they are protein-deficient, sodium-deficient, thiamine-deficient, etc). They can also innately recognize the presence of the needed nutrient in food, and preferentially ingest those foods containing the required substance. Both Richter's own work (Richter, 1936) and more recent evidence (e.g.,

45

Nachman, 1962) suggest that the theory of specific hungers provides an accurate interpretation of the increased preferences for sodium observed in sodium-deficient rats. Adrenalectomized rats show altered food preferences which are quite specific to sodium, and they show these preferences so quickly that the "correct" food choices cannot possibly be reinforced by alleviation of sodium deficiency. The specific hunger for sodium in rats seems to be an example of innate nutritional wisdom.

In a brilliant series of studies first discussed in 1967, Paul Rozin demonstrated the limitations of Richter's theory as an explanation for the adaptive diet choices made by rats deficient in nutrients other than sodium. Like sodium-deficient rats, rats deficient in the B vitamins can be shown to select diets containing the vitamin they require, but Rozin's data clearly indicated that selection of the vitamin-rich diets does not depend on the ability to recognize either specific deficiency states or the presence of specific vitamins in food. For example, rats made vitamin deficient while eating diet A and then given a choice between diet A (lacking the needed nutrient) and diet B (containing the nutrient) immediately ate diet B; however, the same overwhelming preference for diet B over diet A occurred even when neither diet contained the required vitamin. Clearly, the choice of the vitamin-rich diet does not involve any ability to detect specific nutrients, but simply represents the rejection of a food (diet A) which has been associated with illness produced by vitamin deficiency. More recent evidence suggests that positive as well as negative internal consequences may become associated with particular foods (see Zahorik, this volume), so that vitamin-containing foods may be selected by virtue of their association with recovery from deficiency as well as being chosen in preference to foods associated with illness. But that does not alter the power of Rozin's original conclusion: nutritional wisdom can be acquired through experience with foods and their consequences.

LEARNED AVERSIONS AS A MODEL FOR NUTRITIONAL WISDOM IN THE RAT

There are a number of factors which have led to the wide acceptance of learned aversions as a model for most examples of nutritional wisdom. First, such a model simply offers the best fit for the data on rats' avoidance of nutritionally poor or toxic foods; a huge body of data on rats' responses to nutritional deficiencies and to poisoned baits becomes understandable if we accept Rozin's hypothesis. In contrast to a specific-hunger model for adaptive food selection, a learning model for nutritional wisdom does not require a large variety of special sensory mechanisms for the detection and recognition of every conceivable deficiency and its antidote nutrient, nor does it need to explain how rats could have evolved the ability to identify and avoid modern man-made poisons which bear no chemical resemblance to poisons encountered by previous generations of the species. A learning model only requires that the animal be able to distinguish between the foods it eats, that it be able to recognize that it is ill, and that it be able to form associations between food cues and illness.

A learning model of nutritional wisdom also fits well with current knowledge of learning mechanisms and feeding behavior in the rat. Rozin was not the first investigator to observe that experience seemed to play an important role in promoting adaptive food choices (for example, see Harris, Clay, Hargreaves, & Ward, 1933), but the earlier studies aroused little interest because a learning interpretation demanded that rats be capable of forming associations between food cues and internal consequences which occur minutes or hours apart—a delay which was believed to make learning impossible. By the time Rozin published his results, the work of Garcia and his colleagues (see Garcia & Ervin, 1968) had provided innumerable examples of learning over "impossibly" long delays, in experiments employing gustatory stimuli paired with various illnesses.

SPECIAL PROPERTIES OF RAT FOOD-AVERSION LEARNING

The growing literature on learned aversions not only demonstrated that associations between food cues and internal consequences can occur, but also suggested that these associations have unusual properties which appear particularly well suited to solving the diet-selection problems faced by rats in field situations. (1) The associations between food cues and illness can be formed in a single trial and can be remembered for weeks or months without further training. Such rapidly-formed, long-lasting associations seem essential if what a rat learns about foods and their consequences is to be of any real value in selecting a safe and nutritious diet, because every "trial" threatens the life of the organism. (2) Illness seems to be most readily associated with the cues rats use to recognize their food (tastes and odors) even though those cues are not readily associated with other unpleasant consequences (Garcia & Koelling, 1966). The idea that some pairs of events are more easily associated than others has been called "belongingness," and this phenomenon also makes good ethological sense. All stimulus changes are not equally good predictors of illness, and the "belongingness" feature of food aversions leads to avoidance of the most likely causes of illness. (3) The associations between food cues and illness can be formed in spite of extremely long delays between the two events (Garcia, Ervin, & Koelling, 1966; Smith & Roll, 1967), making possible learned aversions to foods which do not produce immediate symptoms of illness. In view of all these adaptive peculiarities, and evidence that rats not only learn food aversions under ideal laboratory conditions but also make use of this ability in their natural habitats (Barnett, 1963; Rzoska, 1953), it is not surprising that food aversions have been viewed as an adaptive specialization of learning (Rozin & Kalat, 1971), "prepared" (Seligman, 1970) or "constrained" (Shettleworth, 1972) by evolution to solve the food selection problems faced by the rat.

SPECIAL PROPERTIES OF RAT FEEDING PATTERNS

A learned-aversion model for nutritional wisdom in the rat is also compelling because it fits with everything we know about the rat's diet, sensory abilities, learning abilities, and general feeding behavior. Learned aversions offer a solution to dietary problems which the rat actually encounters in his natural habitat, and we know that the rat possesses all the abilities and habits which are believed to be important in forming aversions and using them adaptively. What are the properties of the rat and his diet which make learned aversions possible and useful?

1. The rat consumes an extremely varied diet. When an animal chooses its diet from a great number of foods which it finds at least marginally palatable, avoidance of a few foods on the basis of their unpleasant consequences does not greatly reduce the supply of acceptable foods. On the other hand, if we can imagine an animal whose diet consists of only one food, or a very small number of foods, learned aversions to a food paired with illness could easily lead to starvation. It is clearly maladaptive to develop long-lasting aversions to foods unless other "safe" foods are available. Moreover, food is a very unlikely cause of illness in a species with such a limited diet, because it seems impossible that a species could evolve in such a way that its members find only one or two foods acceptable unless those foods are both nutritious and non-poisonous for that species.

2. The rat can recognize and discriminate between many foods. Both abilities are obvious prerequisites for learning aversions which are specific to the foods which are the likely cause of illness and avoiding ingestion of those foods in subsequent encounters.

48

3. The rat's potential diet includes foods which are nutritionally inadequate or poisonous. In addition to avoiding a variety of man-made and naturally-occurring poisons, the rat must choose a diet containing adequate quantities of a large number of nutrients required for good health. Few foods contain all those nutrients in sufficiently large amounts. If a species did not face such hazards as poisoning and malnutrition, learned aversions to food would not be necessary.

4. The rat's feeding habits, especially its temporal patterns of feeding, are ideally suited to the formation of associations between foods and their consequences; in fact, the rat's natural feeding patterns mimic the two most common situations we set up in the laboratory when we want to demonstrate food aversions: (a) One way to produce aversions is to give the subject access to a "meal" of a single, distinctively flavored food, and then administer a fast-acting poison or radiation. Rats set up similar situations for themselves by eating discrete "meals" containing a single food; when they *fail* to eat single-food meals, they also fail to alter their food preferences adaptively in response to gastrointestinal consequences (Rozin, 1969). (b) A second way to produce aversions is to restrict the subject's diet to a single food for a period of days or weeks while the animal slowly develops a nutritional deficiency, such as thiamine deficiency. It is likely that rats face a similar situation when they are forced to subsist on a hoarded food supply in the burrow. Both situations involve a correspondence between patterns of the stimulus and consequence to be associated, and this correspondence may be an essential condition for the rapid formation of long-lasting associations (Testa, 1974; Testa & Ternes, this volume).

LEARNED AVERSIONS AS A MODEL FOR NUTRITIONAL WISDOM IN OTHER SPECIES

While taste aversions in rats are often cited as an example of "species-specific" learning, there is abundant evidence that a wide variety of species can learn to avoid ingestion of foods which have been paired with unpleasant gastrointestinal consequences: humans (Garb & Stunkard, 1974), monkeys (Gorry & Ober, 1970), coyotes (Gustavson, Garcia, Hankins, & Rusiniak, 1974), domestic pigs (Houpt & Zahorik, 1975), guinea pigs (Braveman, 1974), hamsters (Zahorik & Johnston, 1976), bats (Dunning, 1968), chickens (Capretta & Moore, 1970), quail (Wilcoxin, Dragoin, & Kral, 1971), frogs (Schaeffer, 1911), and garter snakes (Burghardt,

49

Wilcoxin, & Czaplicki, 1973) form a partial list of the species which have been claimed to show food aversions (see Gustavson, this volume, for additional examples). Recognizing the utility of a learning model for most cases of nutritional wisdom in the rat, and seeing that a large number of species as diverse as garter snakes and man are capable of forming associations between food cues and illness, it is tempting to assume that such associations are an important mechanism underlying adaptive food selection in all these species. However, there is actually very little evidence which supports such an assumption. Many species *can learn* to avoid foods which have been paired with illness under carefully controlled conditions, but there are very few examples which suggest that species other than rats *do learn* to avoid nutritionally poor or poisonous foods under field conditions.

There is strong evidence that free-ranging coyotes stop preying on sheep when their range is salted with lamb meat containing a powerful, fast-acting gastrointestinal poison (Gustavson, Garcia, Hankins, & Rusiniak, 1974; see also Gustavson, this volume). Apparently coyotes learn to avoid the poisoned baits, and the association between "lambburgers" and illness quickly generalizes to include whole, living sheep. Other evidence of food aversions formed under field conditions is provided by Garb and Stunkard (1974), who concluded from questionnaire data on hundreds of human subjects that people who become ill after ingesting a novel food often form long-lasting aversions to the taste of the food. In addition, the existence of visual mimics among butterflies which are the prey of birds (Rettenmeyer, 1970) and of auditory mimics among moths which are the prey of bats (Dunning, 1968) constitutes indirect evidence that these predators also learn to avoid unpalatable or poisonous prey on the basis of visual or auditory cues. Thus, there is field evidence that learning plays some role in the adaptive food choices of a number of species, but this evidence is sparse in comparison to the abundant data on aversions formed under restricted laboratory conditions.

In making a distinction between studies demonstrating the capacity to associate food cues with illness under laboratory conditions and studies demonstrating the *role* of such associations in altering food selection under field conditions, we do not mean to suggest that food aversions produced under carefully controlled conditions are somehow less real, less important, or less deserving of our attention than food aversions which occur in the absence of our experimental manipulations. However, we do believe that the two kinds of studies answer rather different kinds of questions, and that it is unwise to assume that every ability we can demonstrate experimentally serves some obvious adaptive function in the animal's everyday life.

We must consider the possibility that there are species whose diets, abilities, and habits are sufficiently different from those of rats to make the learned-aversion model unlikely to explain their nutritional wisdom; a species' natural history could provide important clues about the likely role of aversion learning in adaptive food selection. Among mammals whose feeding habits are reasonably well documented, varied diets, the ability to discriminate between acceptable foods, and the possibility of ingesting poisonous foods or foods which are less than completely nutritious seem to be extremely common; but there are many species which, unlike the rat, do not feed in discrete meals containing a single food and do not subsist on a single food for long periods of time under field conditions. The best known examples of such feeding patterns are found in the large generalist herbivores—grazing and browsing animals like cattle, sheep, deer, horses, and buffalo. Because many of these animals are of great economic importance, their diets, nutritional requirements, sensory abilities, and general feeding habits are documented in a vast literature stretching from Linnaeus to the present. That literature also provides a largely untapped source of information on the role of learning in the food selection of a group of species whose feeding habits are quite different from those of the rat.

FEEDING HABITS OF LARGE HERBIVORES

If the acquisition of nutritional wisdom through experience with foods and their consequences were the inevitable result of eating a varied diet, discriminating between acceptable foods, and facing many dietary hazards, then large herbivores would be the wisest of beasts.

Diversity of Dietary Selection. Grazing and browsing animals may find literally hundreds of plant species acceptable as food. For example, Linnaeus offered 618 plants to sheep and found that 449 were always eaten, 32 were sometimes eaten, and 137 were never eaten (Linnaeus, 1749, described by Tribe, 1950). Cattle and horses were somewhat more selective, and it is unlikely that any field situation would provide as many species from which to choose as Linnaeus offered in the course of his experiments, but qualitative studies of foods eaten by domestic animals grazing on pasture routinely list dozens of species which are acceptable as food growing in close proximity (Cory, 1927; Doran, 1943).

51

Sensory Factors. The existence of relatively stable preference hierarchies for acceptable food species suggests that grazing and browsing animals can discriminate between foods reliably, although the particular cues used in selecting herbage are not well understood. Some grazing animals, particularly the ruminants, have exceptionally large numbers of taste buds and low thresholds for salty, bitter, sour, and sweet tastes, whether thresholds are determined electrophysiologically or behaviorally (Bell, 1959). But factors other than taste certainly play a role in food preferences and recognition. For example, it has been suggested that while odor cues as well as taste determine the initial response of deer to forage, familiar plants are recognized by sight (Longhurst, Oh, Jones, & Kepner, 1968). Data from sheep variously deprived of smell, taste, or the sense of touch in the lips not only show that all three senses play some role in food preferences, but that the importance of each sense depends on the plant being sampled (Arnold, 1964).

Dietary Hazards. The number of poisonous plants accepted as food by grazing and browsing animals is extremely large and in many cases the chemical composition of the poison and its dosimetry, symptoms, and mechanism of action have been studied extensively. The classic text on plant poisons, Kingsbury's *Poisonous Plants of the United States and Canada* (1964), provides an incomplete bibliography of almost 2000 references on hundreds of plants known to cause illness or death in livestock. Like other mammals, large herbivores require minimum levels of various nutrients for good health (protein, sodium, calcium, etc.), and many plants accepted as forage do not meet all these requirements. Certain nutrients required by rats and men (the B vitamins) are manufactured by rumen bacteria in those herbivores which are ruminants, so that these animals have no dietary requirement for B vitamins, but the number of required nutrients is still large. There is no lack of dietary hazards for large herbivores.

Even though these species face many dangers in selecting their diets and can readily distinguish between the plants they eat, their feeding patterns seem unlikely to facilitate associations between specific foods and their consequences. Grazing animals spend an incredibly large proportion of their time ingesting food. Tyler (1972) found that wild ponies spend 5-9 hours a day grazing. Measured grazing times in cattle usually fall between 5 hours a day (Johnstone-Wallace & Kennedy, 1944) and 7 hours a day (Corbett, 1953), with grazing occurring in four to six lengthy feeding bouts (Atkinson, Shaw, & Cove, 1942) separated by periods of rumination

(Corbett, 1953). Sheep spend even more time eating and ruminating, with 9-10 hours per day devoted to such activity (England, 1954). Thus a "meal" can last for hours and includes a large number of foods. In ruminants, the meal is not only tasted sequentially, but the mixture of recently ingested foods is regurgitated and chewed again. Even if we ignore the added taste and odor cues provided during rumination, it is difficult to understand how illness could be correctly and specifically associated with a particular food when so many foods are included in each meal. It is conceivable that variables like novelty (Revusky & Bedarf, 1967) and salience (Kalat & Rozin, 1970), which influence the associability of food cues in the rat, might help to reduce the number of highly associable cues and thus reduce confusion, but the problem of correctly identifying the food which produced a particular internal consequence still seems to be far more difficult when an animal's feeding patterns fail to limit the set of possible causes.

DO LARGE HERBIVORES LEARN TO SELECT FOOD WISELY?

Relationship Between Palatability and Wholesomeness of Ingested Substances. Before addressing the issue of the role of learning in the nutritional wisdom of grazing and browsing animals, it may be instructive to review what is known about the food selections of large herbivores. The nutritional wisdom of these species is far from perfect (Tribe, 1950), but loose correlations between food palatability and such properties as digestibility, content of required nutrients, and lack of poisonous compounds have been found by many investigators. For example, Longhurst and his colleagues (1968) measured the digestibility of 39 plant species eaten by deer, relative to the digestibility of alfalfa. For the nine plants ranked *most palatable* to deer, the mean digestibility was 83% of the alfalfa standard. The mean digestibility of the nine plants ranked *moderately palatable* was 47% of the standard, and twenty-one *unpalatable* species showed a mean digestibility score of 45%. On the average, the most palatable plants were also easily digested, but one plant, Chamise (*Adenostoma fasciculatum*), was highly palatable in spite of a very low digestibility score (42%). Since palatability is also related to the nutritional value of forage for deer (Swift, 1948), we might explain the palatability of this indigestible plant on the basis of nutrient content, but Chamise also had the lowest protein content of any species in this study (i.e., only .25 to .50 the protein of the other eight highly palatable species). Palatability is related to digestibility and to levels of important nutrients, but it is not an infallible guide to nutritional value.

Summarizing similar correlational studies in sheep and cattle, Arnold (1964) suggests that palatability is loosely related to high protein content, high nitrogen content, high calorie content, and low fibre content—all nutritionally wise choices. Many poisonous plants are also unpalatable, so that poisonous species usually make up a very small proportion of the grazing animal's diet even when they are available in large quantities, However, when a range is overgrazed so that alternative foods are in short supply, increases are often noted in the amount of poisonous herbage ingested and in the number of deaths due to poisoning (Doran, 1943).

Mechanisms of Food Selection. It seems clear that large herbivores show a certain amount of nutritional wisdom, but these studies tell us nothing about the mechanisms underlying adaptive food choices. The historical sequence of popular theories about these mechanisms has paralleled the sequence of theories we discussed earlier as popular explanations for nutritional wisdom in the rat (largely because these theories have usually been based on *data* from rats, even though they were being applied to other species): following Richter's work, it was proposed that livestock possess an innate wisdom about required nutrients and about poisonous plants (Stapledon, 1947), and as in rats, there is evidence that large herbivores show a specific hunger for sodium (Denton, 1967). But some researchers have cautioned against carrying this view too far, because, ". . . the craving which many animals show for Yew (*Taxus*), for example, cannot be regarded as an inherent desire on the part of the animal to commit suicide," (Ivins, 1955, p. 78). More recently, it has been suggested that "long-delay learning" is the primary mechanism for optimizing food selection in large herbivores (Westoby, 1974), although the author shares our concerns that such learning has never been demonstrated in these species, and that "meal" patterns in large herbivores present a problem for this explanation of their nutritional wisdom.

In spite of the lack of research designed to explore the role of learning in the adaptive food selection of grazing animals, there is actually a large amount of data from the literature of animal science and veterinary medicine which relates to the question of whether nutritional wisdom in these species is the result of learning.

Effects of Varied Food Experiences. If these animals develop food preferences and aversions as the result of *experience* with foods and their consequences, anything which reduces or prevents experience with a wide variety of forage species should alter food preferences. For example, if nutritional wisdom is the product of experience, we would expect animals to become "wiser" with age.

But in fact, lambs just beginning to graze avoid nutritionally inferior species as effectively as ewes. The only obvious difference between the diets of the two age groups is that lambs eat a smaller percentage of extremely low-growing herbage, because their bodily proportions make it difficult to reach those plants (Doran, 1943). Similarly, if experience with various foods plays any role in determining the palatability of herbage, we would expect deer raised in pens on a restricted diet (a single commercial pelleted food) to show different preferences from wild-trapped deer of the same age; but when the preferences of the two groups are tested, using browse species familiar to the wild deer and totally novel for the penned deer, the two groups show virtually identical preference hierarchies (Longhurst et al., 1968).

Effects of Ingestion of Poisonous Plants. The situations which would seem to provide the most obvious tests of a learning model for nutritional wisdom are those involving ingestion of poisonous plants, but the literature on plant poisoning proves to be somewhat less informative than we would wish. Most of this literature is devoted to identifying poisonous plants, describing symptoms and dosage curves, and evaluating treatments; information on ingestion of the plant following the development of symptoms is rarely given. Because many of the plants are extremely unpalatable, the poisonous plant is often force-fed by techniques which prevent the animal from seeing, smelling, or tasting the food before it becomes ill—thus preventing associations between food cues and illness. Even when quantitative data on ingestion are available, they are often very difficult to interpret: Some poisonous plants are only palatable for a brief season during the year, so that changes in intake following illness can indicate changes in the plant, rather than learning by the animal. Other poisons produce peripheral symptoms like dermatitis which we would not expect to be readily associated with food cues, and some plants are so slow to produce symptoms that we couldn't expect them to be associated with illness unless they were eaten exclusively for a long period of time.

Given these difficulties, our attempts to find cases of poisoning which produces learned aversions in livestock have focussed on those plants and feeding situations which seem most likely to produce aversions: poisonous plants which are reasonably palatable (so that they are voluntarily eaten in amounts sufficiently large to allow accurate measurements of any decreases in consumption following illness), and which produce clear symptoms of gastrointestinal illness in a few hours (slow-acting poisons were considered only in cases where the poisonous plant was fed exclusively until symptoms developed). But even under these conditions, we found no evidence that large herbivores learn to avoid foods which have made them ill. There are reports of a number of poisonous plants which are eaten repeatedly or continue to be eaten after symptoms of poisoning develop when those plants are the only food offered. These include relatively slow-acting poisons like Napier grass (eaten by buffalo in India, reported by Dhillon, Paul, Bajwa, & Singh, 1971) and *Baileya multiradiata* (eaten by sheep in the U.S.A., reported by Mathews, 1933). Cattle and sheep also fail to avoid plants containing fast-acting gastrointestinal poisons, such as staggergrass (Marsh & Clawson, 1918) and larkspur (Marsh & Clawson, 1916) even after several episodes of illness. If any aversions were formed during these studies, they may have been obscured by the conflicting motivation of hunger, since the subjects were not offered a choice of foods and could only choose to eat the poisonous plants or nothing at all, making these studies equivalent to relatively insensitive one-bottle tests for taste aversions in rats. However, there are also cases of repeated poisonings by buttercups on pastures containing abundant "safe" forage (Forsyth, 1954). Certainly these negative findings do not imply that large herbivores never learn to avoid foods which cause illness, but if learned aversions are a common occurrence, we would certainly expect to see them under the conditions which were present in these studies.

Effects of Nutritional Deficiency. If large herbivores learn about the nutritional consequences of the foods they eat, we would expect animals deficient in some nutrient to quickly learn to prefer a food rich in that nutrient—an example of adaptive food selection which has been demonstrated in rats suffering from a variety of nutritional deficiencies (see review by Rozin, 1967), and which was often misconstrued as evidence for "specific hungers." Yet, when dairy cattle are given a choice between two forages, one containing adequate protein and the other deficient in protein, the cattle which show an initial preference for the protein deficient diet never switch their preferences even after they become protein deficient (Coppock, Everett, Smith, Slack, & Harner, 1974). Coppock, Everett, and Belyea (1976) also found that lactating cows deficient in either calcium or phosphorus often did not consume enough dicalcium phosphate supplement to cure their deficiency, although some cows ate large quantities of supplement whether or not they were deficient in either mineral.

Taken as a whole, studies of food selection in large herbivores give some evidence that these species show nutritional wisdom— selecting from forage in the field a diet which is reasonably nutritious and non-poisonous—but there is very little evidence that these adaptive diet choices are the result of associations between food cues and the consequences of ingestion, even in cases where conditions seem highly favorable for the formation of such associations.

CAN LARGE HERBIVORES FORM LEARNED AVERSIONS?

Granting that the large generalist herbivores' feeding patterns may make it difficult for them to use learned aversions adaptively under field conditions, and that evidence from the literature of animal science and veterinary medicine does not support an associative explanation of nutritional wisdom in these species, are there any circumstances under which grazing animals can learn to change their responses to foods on the basis of associations between food cues and the consequences of ingestion? While it is certainly possible that these species do not have the associative abilities which are needed to acquire learned preferences and aversions, it is also possible that these animals are capable of forming such associations, but can only form them under conditions which rarely or never occur in the field or in the feeding experiments we have described. If we forced cattle to eat a brief meal containing a single distinctive novel food and immediately administered a fast-acting gastrointestinal poison (duplicating the feeding pattern common to many species which have been shown to form aversions, and also duplicating the most widely-used experimental design for demonstrating learned aversions), would they then form long-lasting aversions?

Method. Four adult Jersey cows which had been maintained on hay, mineral supplement, and tap water were used as subjects. They weighed between 830 and 1070 pounds at the beginning of the experiment and all four had chronic rumen fistulae fitted with removable plugs which allowed easy access to the interior of the rumen. The cows continued to receive water and mineral supplement continuously throughout the experiment, and they were given hay *ad libitum* on even-numbered days. On odd-numbered days the subjects were deprived of hay for 20 hr and then presented with a highly distinctive novel food for 15 min.

Because grazing animals seem to use various sensory cues to recognize and discriminate between foods, we chose stimulus foods which differed from each other and from the cows' usual diet of hay on several stimulus dimensions: sweet feed (Agway) is a mixture of golden grains, flavored with molasses; alfalfa pellets

(Agway) are very dark green uniform pellets containing no added sweeteners. In addition to these differences in taste, texture, and appearance of the foods, the forages were presented in different colored buckets, with alfalfa pellets always presented in brilliant yellow pails and sweet feed presented in dark brown pails. The two foods were presented alternately, sweet feed on day 1, alfalfa pellets on day 3, sweet feed on day 5, etc., and intake was recorded for each 15 min trial.

At the end of 15 min, the bucket was removed and .5% body weight of either lithium chloride solution (.2 M) or a physiological saline solution was funneled directly into the rumen. Two cows were poisoned after eating sweet feed and given saline after eating alfalfa pellets, while the other two were poisoned after eating alfalfa and given saline after eating sweet feed.

Results. The results for all four cattle on six trials with sweet feed and five trials with alfalfa pellets are shown in Figures 1 and 2. The pairing of alfalfa pellets and lithium chloride poisoning produced a very dramatic reduction of intake in a single trial. After the second pairing, the animals poisoned on alfalfa pellets did not

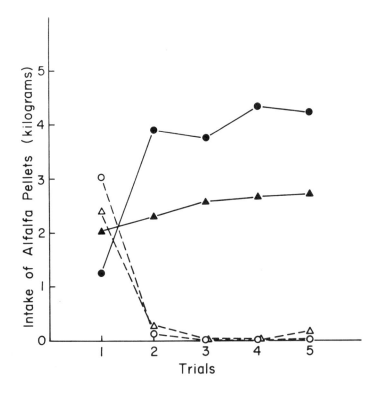

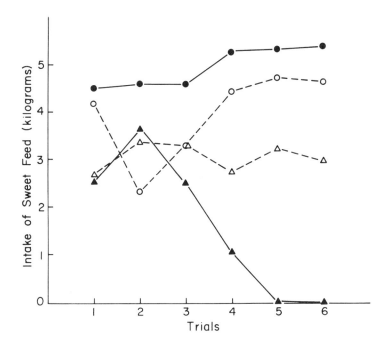

Figures 1 and 2
Intake of sweet feed and alfalfa pellets by four cows over a series of 15 minute feeding trials. The cows poisoned after eating sweet feed are represented by closed symbols and solid lines in both figures. The cows poisoned after eating alfalfa pellets are represented by open symbols and dashed lines.

even contact the pellets with tongue or muzzle, and for those cows lithium was replaced with saline for the remaining alfalfa trials. The animals poisoned after eating alfalfa pellets clearly developed a strong aversion to that food in a single trial, and that aversion was maintained throughout the experiment.

The pairing of the more palatable sweet feed with illness produced different responses in the two poisoned cows: one cow showed no reduction in intake even after five pairings, while the other cow showed some reduction after three pairings and a total avoidance of sweet feed after four pairings. Given the extremely small sample, it is not clear whether the more palatable sweet feed is somehow less associable with illness than alfalfa pellets or whether the two cows assigned to that condition learned less for other reasons, but there is no question that three of the cows developed complete aversions to the food which was followed by poisoning. The three animals which showed aversions behaved identically: On the first trial showing reduced intake (trial 2 for those poisoned on alfalfa and trial 4 for the cow poisoned on sweet feed), the cattle took the food into the mouth and chewed, but they spilled or spit most of it out. On the remaining trials, they placed their muzzles in the bucket, and before they actually touched the food, they jerked their heads back violently and retreated to the back of the stall. In contrast, none of the subjects reduced their intake of the food which was followed by saline infusion over trials.

Even though we have several sources of evidence that the nutritional wisdom of large herbivores is not dependent on experience with food cues and their consequences, this study suggests that cattle can form aversions under conditions which are optimal for producing aversions in other species. If the adaptive food choices of cattle are less dependent on learning than those of rats, this difference does not appear to stem from any associative deficit in cattle; rather, the difference may simply reflect the differential probabilites with which the two species encounter conditions which favor the association of food cues and the consequences of ingestion.

OTHER MECHANISMS OF NUTRITIONAL WISDOM

If learning does not play an important role in guiding the adaptive diet choices of grazing and browsing animals, how can their nutritional wisdom be explained? Certainly we do not believe the data support the existence of real "specific hungers" for nutrients other than sodium, so we do not advocate a return to Richter's explanation of adaptive food selection. In fact, we cannot offer a single theory which encompasses all cases of nutritional wisdom in large herbivores or in other animal groups, but we believe that mechanisms other than learned preferences and aversions and specific hungers deserve serious consideration as explanations for many peculiarities of food preferences in grazing animals. Furthermore, understanding the nutritional wisdom in these species requires some explanation of their failures as well as their successes in selecting nutritious, non-poisonous foods.

Diverse Diets Minimize Ill Effects of Poison. The choice of a varied diet even in the presence of large quantities of a particularly palatable food is a nutritionally wise feeding strategy shared by the large herbivores and many other mammals (Freeland & Janzen, 1974). Many dietary hazards can be avoided by this strategy alone, because plant species which are lacking sufficient quantities of a

60

given nutrient and even species containing potentially deadly poisons can often be eaten without ill effects as long as they do not form a very large proportion of the total food intake. For example, oak and acorns are both palatable and nutritious for livestock, and they are valuable foods as long as they form part of a varied diet. However, when drought or poor management practices reduce the availability of other food sources and acorns or oak browse begin to make up more than half the diet, the animals soon succumb to oak poisoning (Kingsbury, 1964, pp. 444-446). It is important to note that evolutionary pressure to consume a varied diet may be a more effective mechanism than learned aversions for preventing poisoning by plants which cause no symptoms unless they are eaten in very large amounts, because such plants can become very familiar (and therefore unlikely to be associated with illness) before they produce any problems. Moreover, since stock losses from such poisons rarely occur when an adequate supply of other forage is available, learned aversions to the poisonous plant would only shift the animal's problem from poisoning to starvation. The utility of innate aversions to such plants would also be questionable, since they are valuable sources of energy under normal feeding conditions.

Preference for Leaves and New Growth. While the tendency of grazing animals to eat a variety of foods every day automatically eliminates some potential hazards as long as food is plentiful, that tendency cannot explain the observed correlations between forage palatability and such desirable properties as digestibility, nutrient content, and lack of poisonous compounds, which were discussed earlier. These imperfect relationships can be explained without postulating recognition of specific nutrients or poisons and without reference to learning. For example, it is well known that livestock prefer leaves to stems and new growth to old (Arnold, 1964), and that any treatment of a pasture which encourages growth of herbage (fertilizing, watering) automatically renders the herbage on that pasture more palatable (Ivins, 1952). These preferences alone make the diet the grazing animal selects higher in protein, gross energy, nitrogen, and other limiting nutrients than the total herbage from which the selections are made. On unimproved pastures a feeding strategy which maximizes these nutrients is highly adaptive. Interestingly, cattle and sheep can become ill grazing on pastures made exceptionally lush by modern agricultural techniques, because they persist in preferring new growth on these pastures, ingesting an excess of certain leaf cytoplasmic proteins which produce bloat (Laby, 1975) and a general excess of proteins in proportion to readily fermentable carbohydrates (Arnold, 1970). In other

61

words, these preferences are consistently adaptive under the feeding conditions in which these animals evolved, but the strategy persists and becomes maladaptive under certain conditions created recently by man.

Mutual Evolution of Plants and Grazing Habits. Some consideration of the mutual evolution of herbivores and the plants on which they feed is probably a prerequisite for understanding much of the nutritional wisdom shown by large herbivores. It has been suggested that plants eaten by these species evolve toward some balance between the metabolic expense of producing various defenses (including poisonous and unpalatable secondary compounds) and the risk of being eaten, while herbivores evolve toward some balance between accommodation to the defenses (such as systems for detoxifying secondary compounds) and reduced consumption of the defended plants (Pimentel, 1968). It is unnecessary to assume that herbivores recognize and avoid poisons directly—after all, some poisonous plants are palatable and many unpalatable plants are neither poisonous nor low in nutrients; avoidance of plants on the basis of cues even loosely related to the presence of poisons or lack of nutrients would confer some adaptive advantage on the consuming herbivore and on the herbage producing those cues.

The importance of this mutual evolution in determining palatability of herbage is best illustrated by the difficulties encountered when livestock are introduced to ecological systems very different from those in which they evolved. For example, in reviewing the history of studies of livestock poisoning in the U.S.A., Kingsbury claims that European cattle and sheep thrived when introduced to the northeastern forests, because the flora of that area closely resembles the flora of western Europe; in contrast, the unfamiliar flora west of the Mississippi presented an enormous challenge for herds and herdsmen, because it contained vast numbers of poisonous plants which produced particularly severe illness (Kingsbury, 1964). One interpretation of these findings is that the poisoning problem in the American west stems not just from an unusual number of poisonous plants, but from an unusual number of poisonous plants which are *palatable* to European livestock because the herbs and herbivores evolved independently. A similar case of flora proving almost universally palatable to animals introduced from other continents was observed in New Zealand, where imported livestock and deer caused serious damage to herbage which had not evolved defenses against those herbivores (Howard, 1967).

SUMMARY AND CONCLUSIONS

We believe that innate preferences for a variety of food cues loosely associated with nutritional value and lack of deadly poisons probably accounts for most of the evidence on nutritional wisdom in large generalist herbivores—offering a very general explanation of herbivores' successes and failures in avoiding dietary hazards; but until more detailed information is available on the specific cues which cause some plants to be relished and others to be avoided, and the relationship between those cues and the nutritional quality of herbage is better understood, such an explanation will be of little predictive value. In addition to these preferences, large herbivores show at least one very specific preference for a nutrient, the specific hunger for sodium. They are also capable of learning to avoid foods on the basis of unpleasant gastrointestinal consequences, although the available evidence does not suggest that this ability is very frequently utilized. Although these mechanisms promote adaptive diet choices in herbivores, there are features of the grazing animals' feeding behavior and physiology which serve to reduce the importance of wise food selection. The ingestion of a wide variety of foods, the ability to detoxify some poisons, and (in ruminants) the harboring of bacteria whose production of vitamins removes the dietary requirements for those nutrients, are factors which render many dietary choices irrelevant.

While we have focussed our discussion on the larger generalist herbivores as an example of animals whose food choices are not highly dependent on learning, we do not mean to suggest *either* that these species are unique *or* that they should replace the rat as our model for nutritional wisdom throughout the animal kingdom. Our goal in presenting this summary of the data on nutritional wisdom in one group of animals which has been largely ignored by psychologists is twofold. First, we hope to encourage an appreciation of the complexity of the issues involved in nutritional wisdom: it is unlikely that any one theory can account for the adaptive food choices made by any species, and even less likely that all species which show nutritional wisdom achieve a safe, nutritious diet through the same selection mechanisms. Second, by focussing our attention on species which are capable of forming learned aversions, yet seem to make little use of this ability in the field, we hope to discourage the assumption that learned food aversions necessarily play an important adaptive role in the everyday life of all species which are capable of associating food cues with illness. The discoveries of Garcia, Rozin, and many other scientists studying the learned-aversion phenomenon have contributed major insights into the variety of learning processes and the role of those processes in adaptation; the importance of their discoveries is certainly not diminished by the realization that this phenomenon may not provide a model for all cases of nutritional wisdom.

ACKNOWLEDGEMENTS

The authors gratefully acknowledge the assistance of Lynn S. Morgan, Carl E. Coppock, and Mary C. Smith, who contributed ideas and source materials for this chapter, and of Barbara Susan Long, who contributed valuable editorial comments on the manuscript.

REFERENCES

Arnold, G. W. Some principles in the investigation of selective grazing. **Proceedings of the Australian Society of Animal Production,** 1964, **5,** 258-271.

Arnold, G. W. Regulation of food intake in grazing ruminants. In A. T. Phillipson (Ed.), **Physiology of digestion and metabolism in the ruminant.** Newcastle upon Tyne, England: Oriel Press Limited, 1970.

Atkinson, F. W., Shaw, A. O., & Cove, H. W. Grazing habits of dairy cattle. **Journal of Dairy Science,** 1942, **25,** 779-784.

Barnett, S. A. **The rat: A study in behavior.** Chicago: Aldine, 1963.

Bell, F. R. The sense of taste in domesticated animals. **Veterinary Record,** 1959, **71,** 1071-1079.

Braveman, N. S. Poison-based avoidance with flavored or colored water in guinea pigs. **Learning and Motivation,** 1974, **5,** 182-194.

Burghardt, G. M., Wilcoxon, H. C., & Czaplicki, J. A. Conditioning in garter snakes: Aversion to palatable prey induced by delayed illness. **Animal Learning and Behavior,** 1973, **1,** 317-320.

Capretta, P. J., & Moore, M. Appropriateness of reinforcement to cue in the conditioning of food aversions in chickens. **Journal of Comparative and Physiological Psychology,** 1970, **72,** 85-89.

Coppock, C. E., Everett, R. W., & Belyea, R. L. Effect of low calcium or low phosphorus diets on free choice consumption of dicalcium phosphate by lactating dairy cows. **Journal of Dairy Science,** 1976, **59,** 571-580.

Coppock, C. E., Everett, R. W., Smith, N. E., Slack, S. T., & Harner, J. P. Variation in forage preference in dairy cattle. **Journal of Animal Science,** 1974, **39,** 1170-1179.

Corbett, J. L. Grazing behavior in New Zealand. **British Journal of Animal Behaviour,** 1953, **1,** 67-71.

Cory, V. L. Activities of livestock on the range. **Texas Experimental Station Bulletin,** 1927, **367,** 5-47.

Denton, D. A. Salt appetite. In C. F. Code & W. Heidel (Eds.), **Handbook of physiology (Section 6). Alimentary canal (Vol. 1). Food and water intake.** Baltimore: Williams and Wilkins, 1967.

Dhillon, K. S., Paul, B. S., Bajwa, R. S., & Singh, J. A preliminary report on a peculiar type of Napier grass (*Pennisetum purpureum,* 'Pusa giant') poisoning in buffalo calves. **Indian Journal of Animal Science,** 1971, **41,** 1034-1036.

Doran, C. W. Activities and grazing habits of sheep on summer ranges. **Journal of Forestry,** 1943, **41,** 253-258.

Dunning, D. C. Warning sounds of moths. **Zeitschrift fur Tierpsychologie,** 1968, **25,** 129-138.

England, G. J. Observations on the grazing behaviour of different breeds of sheep at Pantyrhuad Farm Carmarthenshire. **British Journal of Animal Behaviour,** 1954, **2,** 56-60.

Forsyth, A. A. British poisonous plants. **Ministry of Agriculture, Fisheries, and Food** (London), Bulletin 161, 1954.

Freeland, W. J., & Janzen, D. H. Strategies in herbivory by mammals: The role of plant secondary compounds. **American Naturalist,** 1974, **108,** 269-289.

Garb, J. L., & Stunkard, A. J. Taste aversions in man. **American Journal of Psychiatry,** 1974, **131,** 1204-1207.

Garcia, J., & Ervin, F. R. Gustatory-visceral and telerceptor-cutaneous conditioning: Adaptation in internal and external milieus. **Communications in Behavioral Biology,** 1968, **1,** 389-415.

Garcia, J., Ervin, F. R., & Koelling, R. A. Learning with prolonged delay of reinforcement. **Psychonomic Science,** 1966, **5,** 121-122.

Garcia, J., & Koelling, R. A. Relation of cue to consequence in avoidance learning. **Psychonomic Science,** 1966, **4,** 123-124.

Gorry, T., & Ober, S. Stimulus characteristics of learning over long delays in monkeys. Paper presented at the 10th Annual Meeting of the Psychonomic Society, San Antonio, 1970.

Gustavson, C., Garcia, J., Hankins, W., & Rusiniak, K. Coyote predation by aversive conditioning. **Science,** 1974, **184,** 581-583.

Harris, L. J., Clay, J., Hargreaves, F., & Ward, A. Appetite and choice of diet. The ability of the vitamin B deficient rat to discriminate between diets containing and lacking the vitamin. **Proceedings of the Royal Society, London. (Series B)** 1933, **113,** 161-190.

Houpt, K. A., & Zahorik, D. M. 1975, unpublished data.

Howard, W. E. Ecological changes in New Zealand due to introduced mammals. IUCN 10th Technical Meeting, Lucerne, Switzerland. IUCN Publication No. 9 (New Series), 1967, 219-240.

Ivins, J. D. The relative palatability of herbage plants. **Journal of the British Grassland Society,** 1952, **7,** 43-54.

Ivins, J. D. The palatability of herbage. **Herbage Abstracts.** 1955, **25,** 75-79.

Johnstone Wallace, D. B., & Kennedy, K. Grazing management practices and their relationship to the behavior and grazing habits of cattle. **Journal of Agricultural Science,** 1944, **34,** 190-197.

Kalat, J. W., & Rozin, P. "Salience": A factor which can override temporal contiguity in taste-aversion learning. **Journal of Comparative and Physiological Psychology,** 1970, **71,** 192-197.

Kingsbury, J. W. **Poisonous plants of the United States and Canada.** Englewood Cliffs, New Jersey: Prentice-Hall, 1964.

Laby, R. H. Surface active agents in the rumen. In I. W. McDonald & A. C. I. Warner (Eds.), **Digestion and metabolism in the ruminant.** University of New England Publication Unit, 1975.

Longhurst, W. M., Oh, H. K., Jones, M. B., & Kepner, R. E. A basis for the palatability of deer forage plants. **North American Wildlife and Natural Resources Conference Transactions,** 1968, 181-192.

Marsh, C. D., & Clawson, A. B. Larkspur poisoning of livestock. **USDA Bulletin,** 1916, # 365, 1-90.

Marsh, C. D., & Clawson, A. B. Staggergrass (*Chrosperma muscaetoicum*) as a poisonous plant. **USDA Bulletin,** 1918, #710, 1-14.

Mathews, F. P. The toxicity of *Baileya multiradiata* for sheep and goats. **Journal of the American Veterinary Medicine Association,** 1933, **83,** 673-679.

Nachman, M. Taste preferences for sodium salts by adrenalectomized rats. **Journal of Comparative and Physiological Psychology,** 1962, **55,** 1124-1129.

Pimentel, D. Population regulation and genetic feedback. **Science,** 1968, **159,** 1432-1437.

Rettenmeyer, C. W. Insect mimicry. **Annual Review of Entomology,** 1970, **15,** 43-74.

Revusky, S. H., & Bedarf, E. W.   Association of illness with prior ingestion of novel foods. **Science,** 1967, **155,** 219-220.

Richter, C. P. Increased salt appetite in adrenalectomized rats. **American Journal of Physiology,** 1936, **115,** 155-161.

Richter, C. P.   Total self-regulatory functions in animals and human beings. **Harvey Lectures Series,** 1943, **38,** 63-103.

Rozin, P.   Thiamine specific hunger. In C. F. Code & W. Heidel (Eds.), **Handbook of physiology (Section 6). Alimentary canal (Vol. 1). Food and water intake.** Baltimore: Williams and Wilkins, 1967.

Rozin, P.   Adaptive food sampling patterns in vitamin deficient rats. **Journal of Comparative and Physiological Psychology,** 1969, **69,** 126-132.

Rozin, P., & Kalat, J. W.   Specific hungers and poison avoidance as adaptive specializations of learning. **Psychological Review,** 1971, **78,** 459-486.

Rzoska, J.   Bait shyness, a study in rat behaviour. **British Journal of Animal Behaviour,** 1953, **1,** 128-135.

Schaeffer, A. A.   Habit formation in frogs. **Journal of Animal Behavior,** 1911, **1,** 309-335.

Seligman, M. E. P.   On the generality of the laws of learning. **Psychological Review,** 1970, **77,** 406-418.

Shettleworth, S. J.   Constraints on learning. In D. S. Lehrman, R. A. Hinde, & E. Shaw, **Advances in the study of behavior.** (Vol. 4) New York: Academic Press, 1972.

Smith, J. C., & Roll, D. L.   Trace conditioning with X-rays as an aversive stimulus. **Psychonomic Science,** 1967, **9,** 11-12.

Stapledon, R. G.   The palatability and nutritive value of herbage plants. **Journal of the Ministry of Agriculture,** 1947, **53,** 427-431.

Swift, R. W.   Deer select most nutritious forages. **Journal of Wildlife Management,** 1948, **12,** 109-110.

Testa, T. J.   Causal reelationships and the acquisition of avoidance responses. **Psychological Review,** 1974, **81,** 491-505.

Tribe, D. E.   The composition of a sheep's natural diet. **Journal of the British Grassland Society,** 1950, **5,** 81-91.

Tyler, S.   The behaviour and social organization of the New Forest ponies. **Animal Behavior Monographs,** 1972, **5,** 85-196.

Westoby, M.   An analysis of diet selection by large generalist herbivores. **American Naturalist,** 1974, **108,** 290-304.

Wilcoxon, H. C., Dragoin, W. B., & Kral, P. A. Illness-induced aversions in rats and quail: Relative salience of visual and gustatory cues. **Science,** 1971, **171,** 826-828.

Zahorik, D. M., & Johnston, R. E.   Taste aversions to food flavors and vaginal secretion in golden hamsters. **Journal of Comparative and Physiological Psychology,** 1976, **90,** 57-66.

THE DEVELOPMENT
OF
FOOD PREFERENCES

───────── IV ─────────

THE ONTOGENY OF FOOD PREFERENCES IN CHICKS AND OTHER ANIMALS

JERRY A. HOGAN
University of Toronto

The purpose of this paper is twofold. First, I shall review data on the development of food preferences in newly-hatched chicks and newborn guinea pigs, and discuss the associative and non-associative mechanisms that must be postulated to account for these data. Second, I shall consider in what ways these mechanisms that determine food preferences are dependent upon developmental factors. That is, some mechanisms may be presumed to influence food preferences throughout the animal's life, whereas other mechanisms may be peculiar to an animal's first experience with food or to some specific stage of its development.

ONTOGENY OF FOOD PREFERENCES IN CHICKS

EVIDENCE FOR THE DEVELOPMENT OF FOOD PREFERENCES

Newly-hatched chicks with no prior pecking experience will peck at a large variety of small objects. In particular, such inexperienced chicks will peck at both chick crumbs (food) and sand. Their initial pecking rates to the two stimuli are about equal. If the chicks are allowed continuous access to both stimuli, by the time they are 3 days old they show a marked preference for crumbs over sand (Hogan, 1971). If the chicks are held without either food or sand until they are 3 days old, their pecking rates to the two stimuli are still about equal (Hogan, 1973a). Thus, experience with food and/or sand is necessary for a food preference to develop. It is this experience which many of the experiments reviewed in this paper were designed to investigate.

71

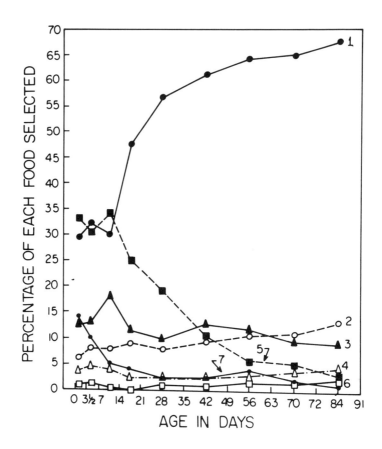

Figure 1

The relation between age and choice of food. The records are based upon the average consumption of food of 100 Rhode Island Red chicks from 0 to 91 days of age. (After 3 weeks, each point represents the average intake for a 2-week period.) The foods are numbered as follows: 1 =Yellow Attrition Corn Meal; 2 =Fish Meal (white fish and herring, vacuum dried, biologically assayed as a source of Vitamin D); 3 =Wheat Bran; 4 =Bone Meal; 5 =Oat Meal; 6 =Oyster Shell Flour; 7 =Wheat Middlings. The ratios of foods chosen during the first few weeks tended to differ strikingly from the ratios of foods chosen in the later periods of the growth cycle. (Redrawn from Dove, 1935.)

Chicks need not only distinguish food from non-food items, but must also choose among foods in order to obtain a proper nutritional balance. Dove (1935) allowed chicks to choose from a variety of foods in a cafeteria experiment. Figure 1 reproduces some data from Dove's paper. These data show that chicks distributed their intake among the foods offered, and that the relative preference for various food items changed as a function of age. From a wide range of additional evidence, Dove was able to show that these choices did provide chicks with a proper nutritional balance, and that feeding chicks with other proportions of the same food substances led to inferior growth rates. I shall not be concerned directly with these long-term changes in preference, but shall return to consider them in the last section of the paper. For the present, these data demonstrate that food selection is a problem that chicks face throughout their lifetime. It is important to inquire whether the mechanisms underlying the discrimination of food from non-food are the same as the mechanisms responsible for long-term food selection.

MECHANISMS UNDERLYING THE DEVELOPMENT
OF FOOD PREFERENCES

It seems to be the common wisdom that food preferences can be either innate or learned. Yet, in the case of chicks at least, a moment's thought makes it clear that the development of all food preferences must require some sort of experience. Chicks initiate feeding on the basis of visual stimuli, but the probability of approaching, pecking, and swallowing any particular kind of object changes according to the particular experience of an individual chick. The initial feeding responses to objects on the basis of their appearance show very little, if any, correspondence to the nutritional value of these objects, yet the feeding responses of experienced chicks correspond very well to the nutritional value of these objects. As C. Lloyd Morgan (1896) stated many years ago: "It seems, therefore, that . . . there is no instinctive discrimination; that what shall be selected for eating and what rejected is a matter of individual experience; and that by repetition of the selective process, the eating of certain materials, and not of others, passes into a more or less fixed food habit." (p. 55). We shall see that "repetition of the selective process" is only one way that experience affects the development of food preferences—but it is an important way throughout a chick's lifetime.

It is possible to look separately at food preferences that develop on the basis of immediate feedback from oral factors—that is, gustatory and tactual effects of pecking, mandibulating, and swallowing—and those that depend on postingestional factors, both short-term and long-term. One might wish to argue that preferences based on oral factors are somehow more "innate" than preferences

73

based on postingestional factors—that is, a good taste could be considered more "innate" than a good feeling after eating a nutritious meal (cf. Katz, 1937, p. 179ff). But such reasoning seems at best artificial. Taste factors do provide information about ingested substances more quickly than gastro-intestinal factors, and it is generally easier to eject a substance from the mouth than from the stomach. Yet the stimuli from a substance that initiate feeding (visual and/or olfactory, sometimes auditory) do not always bear a fixed relationship to the gustatory or gastro-intestinal qualities of that substance: In most animals, even the best-tasting foods are quickly avoided by sight or smell when the animal becomes sick after ingestion. The point is that to speak of innate recognition is to avoid some of the most interesting problems in food selection. We often eat good-tasting things that are bad for us, and sometimes eat bad-tasting things that are good for us—and so do most animals. The factors responsible for these examples of food selection are what is of interest, and it is simply not possible to classify these factors as innate or learned.

I would suggest that a more profitable way to look at the question of genetic versus environmental control of feeding preferences is to ask how much experience with factor B is necessary to overcome a preference based on factor A. For example, how many meals of a non-nutritive (factor B), but good tasting (factor A) substance are necessary before that substance is no longer preferred? Such titration methods should lead to a statement of the relative importance of all the factors (and their interactions) that influence food selection, rather than to a simple, either-or statement of innate or learned. There will be cases, of course, where no amount of experience with factor B will overcome a preference based on factor A. For example, young chicks may keep pecking aquarium gravel and ignore food until they die (Hogan, 1971, p. 191). But even in such an extreme case, it does not make much sense to talk about innate preferences. Rozin (1976) reviews a number of studies where such titration methods have been used.

In the remainder of this section, I shall first cite a few examples of food preferences that develop on the basis of oral factors (see also Capretta; Wilcoxon, this volume). Then the bulk of this section will be devoted to a review of my work on the development of food preferences based on postingestional consequences. Finally, I shall consider whether the food preferences that develop can best be characterized as learned aversions or learned preferences. A more complete review and discussion of the factors that influence pecking in young chicks can be found in Hogan (1973c).

74

Newly-hatched chicks will usually approach and peck at many small, moving, insect-like objects (if they are not too frightening, see Hogan, 1965). If such an object turns out to be a mealworm (*Tenebrio* larva), the chick will swallow it and approach subsequent mealworms with increasing alacrity and other signs of pleasure (Hogan, 1966). If the object turns out to be a cinnabar caterpillar (*Euchelia jacobiae*), the chick will reject it with clear signs of disgust and will avoid subsequent cinnabar caterpillars (Morgan, 1896). Marked changes of behavior occur in both cases after just one experience.

Objects of similar nutritional value but of different shapes or textures may be pecked at equally when first encountered, but preferences may emerge within the first few minutes. For example, pecking at round sago grains increased, and pecking at oblong spratt grains decreased during the chick's first 10-min exposure to these objects (Hellwald, 1931). The visual appearance of the grains must become associated with particular stimulus properties detected in the mouth, since the time is too short for nutritional effects to play a role (Hogan, 1973b). A very likely explanation of this discrimination invokes receptive fields of neurons responsible for tactile sensitivity in the bill that are specific to particular shapes. Such neurons have been found to innervate the bill of the pigeon (Zeigler, Miller, & Levine, 1975), and may be responsible for discrimination among different grains.

PREFERENCES DEPENDENT ON POSTINGESTIONAL FACTORS

The taste and tactile qualities of many substances do not provide sufficient information for an animal to either increase or decrease ingestion of that substance. In such instances, postingestional factors may play an important role. Two effects of postingestional factors will be considered here: (1) the association of pecking with its consequences: effects not specific to particular stimuli; and (2) stimulus-specific effects of ingestion.

As an introduction to these experiments, I shall say a few words here about the general methods I have used. Junglefowl chicks are hatched in an incubator in the laboratory and placed individually in cages about half a meter cubed when they are about 24 hr old. Water is always available, but the solid metal floor is empty. At about 72 hr of age, chicks are given certain kinds of experience and after a certain interval are tested. In the tests, chicks are usually presented with one stimulus only—either food or sand. Some tests last 2 min and others last 10 min. The food used in the tests is ordinary chick starter crumbs, which are different in color, size, and texture from the toybox sand. In some experiments a force-feeding technique is used in which the chick's bill is gently lowered into a liquid. The bill fills up, and when the chick is released, it raises its head and the swallowing reflex follows. In most cases, the liquid is a mixture of chick crumbs and water that has been put through a blender. About 8 mouthfuls of this mixture is equivalent to the amount of crumbs a chick would swallow in a 10-min exposure to food. (See Hogan, 1971, 1973a for a more complete description.) Further details and variations will be mentioned when necessary.

1. **The association of pecking with its consequences.** Two aspects of this problem have been investigated: The delayed effects of ingestion on pecking, and, using the force-feeding technique, the effects of the time interval between pecking and food ingestion on subsequent pecking.

Several experiments have looked at the effects of ingestion on pecking as a function of the time interval between experience and test. In these experiments chicks had a 10-min experience pecking at either food or sand and then, after varying time intervals, were tested for 2 min with either food or sand (Hogan, 1973b, 1977b). Some typical results are shown in Figure 2. In this graph, the change in pecking (seconds per 2 min) between the original experience and the test is plotted as a function of the interval between the 10-min experience and the 2-min test. Positive values indicate higher rates of pecking in the test, and negative values indicate lower rates of pecking.

In the upper curve in Figure 2, chicks that were allowed experience with food showed increased rates of pecking, but only if tested one or more hours after their initial experience. These delayed effects of ingestion are not motivational in nature in that the amount of food ingested in the first experience with food is not related either to the amount of increased pecking or to the time the increase occurs, except that a certain minimum amount of food must be ingested before these changes occur (Hogan, 1973b). These delayed effects of ingestion, however, are associational in nature in that pecking and ingestion must occur more or less simultaneously (Hogan, 1973a, 1977b; see below).

In the lower curve in Figure 2, chicks that were allowed experience with sand showed a mirror image effect: Decreased pecking rates were seen, but only if the chicks were tested an hour or more later.

Of particular interest in the context of the development of food recognition is the fact that the increase and decrease in pecking rate

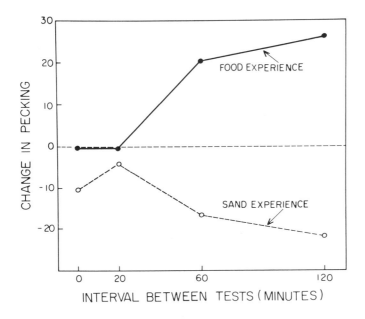

Figure 2
Delayed effects of food or sand ingestion on pecking. Solid
curve: Chicks given experience with food and tested on food.
Dashed curve: Chicks given experience with sand and tested on
sand. Each point represents data from a separate group of 12
3-day-old chicks. (See Hogan, 1977b, for more details.)

are not specific to food and sand, respectively. Pecking rate increases to both food and sand after experience pecking food; and
pecking rate decreases to both sand and food after experience pecking sand (Hogan, 1973a). This result suggests that it is the response
of pecking itself that is influenced by ingestion. A second point of
interest is that the effects of ingesting sand are delayed. One can
imagine that the effects of food are not seen for some time after ingestion since digestion is a process requiring a certain amount of
time. But if ingesting sand were merely aversive, one would expect
an immediate decrease in pecking rate. Yet the results show that
the time course of the effects of eating sand is very similar to the
time course of the effects of eating food. These considerations have
suggested to me the hypothesis that the chicks are associating the
act of pecking with the motivational system of hunger.[1] That is, it
seems quite possible that pecking is not controlled by the nutritional state of the chick until the chick learns that its nutritional
state can be affected by pecking. I shall return to this hypothesis
later with some additional evidence.

The second aspect of the association of pecking with its consequences that I have looked at is the time interval between pecking and food ingestion (Hogan, 1977b). These experiments are a control for the previous experiments in that they demonstrate that an association is really being formed. In these experiments, chicks were allowed to peck sand for 10 min and were also force-fed liquid food. Previous experiments (Hogan, 1973a) have shown that force-feeding immediately after pecking sand leads to increased pecking an hour later—the effect is of the same magnitude as occurs an hour after pecking food for 10 min. In the present experiments the variable of interest was the time interval between pecking and force-feeding; it ranged from 10 min prior to pecking sand to 60 min after. Chicks were tested for 2 min on sand about an hour and a half after force-feeding. The results are shown in Figure 3. Once again, change in pecking rate (seconds per 2 min) is plotted on the ordinate. It can be seen that force-feeding immediately before, immediately after, or 5 min after the pecking bout results in significantly increased pecking an hour later, but force-feeding at other times does not affect pecking. (Actually, since pecking sand

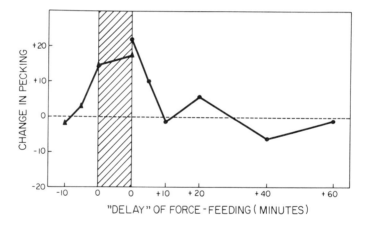

"DELAY" OF FORCE-FEEDING (MINUTES)

Figure 3
Effects of the interval between pecking experience (on sand) and force-feeding (of liquid food) on pecking sand an hour later. The hatched area represents the 10-min experience pecking sand. The triangles and circles represent two separate experiments. Each triangle represents data from a separate group of 24 3-day-old chicks; each circle represents data from a separate group of 12 3-day-old chicks. (See Hogan, 1977b for more details.)

78

for 10 min normally leads to a decrease in pecking an hour later and no decrease is seen in these results, it seems likely that simply ingesting food increased pecking rate somewhat—see below.) These results show that pecking and food ingestion must be associated in time in order for increased pecking to occur.

2. Stimulus-specific effects of ingestion. The previous experiments have given evidence that pecking rate can be influenced by the effect of pecking, but in no case have those changes been specific to particular stimuli. In this section I shall review experiments that demonstrate stimulus-specific effects.

To begin, however, I should say that for a long time we were unsuccessful in finding any stimulus-specific effects. We gave chicks experience with food or sand for periods ranging from 10 min to 67 hr, we tested with food and sand successively and simultaneously, and we gave chicks 4 separate 10-min simultaneous choice tests. In all cases, there was no evidence of any differential behavior to the two stimuli (Hogan, 1973a, 1975). We finally discovered a way to see differential behavior—and the reason for our success was that our single-stimulus test sessions were changed from 2 min in length to 10 min. The results of one experiment will serve as an example (Hogan, 1975). In this experiment, chicks were give 1 or 3 days' experience with either food or sand, or were maintained on an empty floor. At 72 hr of age, 5 hr after the stimuli were removed, they were tested with either food or sand for 10 min. The results are shown in Figure 4. In this graph the 10-min test has been divided into 5 2-min intervals. If you look at the first 2-min interval you can see that after food experience the chicks peck more than after sand experience. And, after both kinds of experience there is no significant difference in the pecking rate to the two stimuli. Over the course of the whole 10-min test, however, pecking rates to food and sand diverge; pecking at food remains constant whereas pecking at sand declines. The control groups (empty floor) showed a constant pecking rate during the entire 10-min test. (Let me remind you that each chick was tested on one stimulus only which means that each curve represents a separate group of chicks.) I have interpreted these results to mean that the discrimination is based on feedback that develops 2 to 3 min after ingestion. But, the chicks are able to make use of this feedback only if they have had previous experience with food or sand. This interpretation helps us understand why the chicks did not show signs of discrimination in the simultaneous choice tests mentioned above: Because chicks tend to peck at both stimuli within a 2-min interval, the after-effects of swallowing food and sand become mixed up.

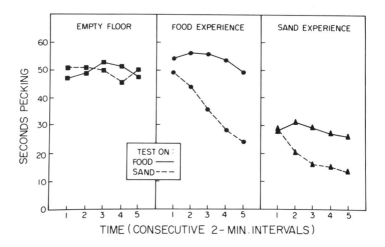

Figure 4
Mean time spent pecking the stimulus in groups with the indicated experience on either Day 3 or on Days 1-3. Each curve
represents data from a separate group of 20 3-day-old chicks
(food or sand experience) or 10 3-day-old chicks (empty floor).
[Redrawn from Hogan, 1975.]

It is worth pausing a moment to ask what is associated with what
in the present experiment. The answer to that question is not very
clear. In chicks with food experience, one might imagine that the
short-term effects of ingesting food become associated with the
long-term effects; when the chicks experience the short-term effects
of food again, they remember the good long-term effects and continue eating. But is is not immediately obvious why the short-term
effects of ingesting sand—for the first time—should lead to a
decrease in pecking (remember that in chicks with no prior pecking
experience, the response to sand is usually constant over the whole
10 min). And similar problems arise when considering the behavior
of chicks with sand experience.

In order to get more insight into this matter, a large number of experiments have been carried out in which chicks have had a variety
of ingestive experiences before being tested on food or sand. The
idea behind these experiments was to see whether the effects seen
in the previous experiment were due to certain associations being
formed or to non-associative mechanisms.

The results of these experiments are shown in schematized form
in Figure 5 (Hogan, 1977a). This chart is read as follows: In Experiment 1, chicks were given an opportunity to peck food for 10 min,

80

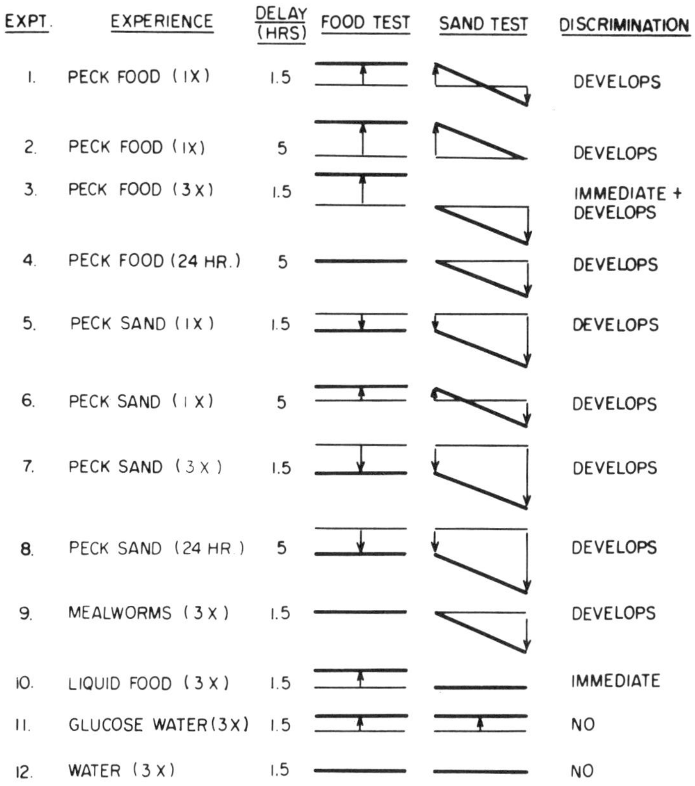

EXPT.	EXPERIENCE	DELAY (HRS)	FOOD TEST	SAND TEST	DISCRIMINATION
1.	PECK FOOD (1X)	1.5			DEVELOPS
2.	PECK FOOD (1X)	5			DEVELOPS
3.	PECK FOOD (3X)	1.5			IMMEDIATE + DEVELOPS
4.	PECK FOOD (24 HR.)	5			DEVELOPS
5.	PECK SAND (1X)	1.5			DEVELOPS
6.	PECK SAND (1 X)	5			DEVELOPS
7.	PECK SAND (3 X)	1.5			DEVELOPS
8.	PECK SAND (24 HR)	5			DEVELOPS
9.	MEALWORMS (3 X)	1.5			DEVELOPS
10.	LIQUID FOOD (3 X)	1.5			IMMEDIATE
11.	GLUCOSE WATER (3X)	1.5			NO
12.	WATER (3 X)	1.5			NO

Figure 5
Summary of experiments reported in Hogan, 1975, 1977a. Explanation given in the text.

once, and were tested 1.5 hr later either on food or on sand for 10 min. The thin lines indicate the average level of pecking, over 10 min, for chicks without any experience, and the heavy lines give the level of pecking for chicks with the indicated experience. The arrows show how much pecking increased or decreased over control levels. A discrimination is said to *develop* if the difference in pecking between food and sand was greater at the end of the 10-min test than at the beginning. A discrimination is said to be *immediate* if the pecking level at food and sand was significantly different during the first 2 min of the test. If any change from control levels is indicated on the chart, that change was statistically significant. All tests were given when the chicks were about 72 hr posthatch. When a particular experience was repeated three times, that experience was given once on the afternoon of day 2 and twice

81

on the morning of day 3 with a 2-hr interval separating the two experiences. For further details see Hogan (1975, 1977a).

This is not the place to discuss these results in detail, but I shall point to a few of the conclusions that can be drawn from them. First, in all cases in which a discrimination developed (Experiments 1 through 9), chicks had experience pecking some object—either food, sand, or mealworms. In the case where one of these objects—food—was ingested without pecking (Experiment 10), no change in pecking rate over the 10-min test occurred. Thus, pecking experience seems to be the critical factor in determining whether a discrimination will develop. But how can so many different kinds of pecking experience—i.e., pecking sand, food, or mealworms—lead to the same result? I suggest that the way to understand these data is to regard pecking experience as an indirect factor in the development of the discrimination. Specifically, I suggest that pecking experience leads the chick to associate the act of pecking with the hunger system. Once this association has been formed, effects of ingestion can serve as stimuli to control the rate of pecking. In other words, I am suggesting that the signals that arise from ingestion of nutritive and non-nutritive substances do not change as a result of experience; the inexperienced chick, however, is not able to react to these signals, whereas the experienced chick reacts by modulating its pecking rate appropriately.

A second conclusion that can be drawn from these results is that once pecking is associated with ingestion, deprivation effects are seen. If one compares pecking after 1.5-hr delay with pecking after 5-hr delay following one experience either pecking food or pecking sand (Experiment 1 with 2 and Experiment 5 with 6), it is seen that pecking rate was much higher after 5-hr delay (Hogan, 1975). In fact, pecking rate after one experience pecking sand actually increased over baseline when there was a 5-hr delay (Experiment 6). Although the pecking rate of inexperienced chicks generally rises over the course of the first 3 or 4 days (Hogan, 1973a), changes of the magnitude shown here only occur once a chick has associated pecking with ingestion. These results seem to me to provide further support for the hypothesis proposed above, namely, that chicks are associating the act of pecking with the hunger system.

A third conclusion from these results is that several experiences with a particular stimulus can lead to stimulus-specific effects. In the two cases where immediate discrimination was shown (Experiments 3 and 10), chicks had 3 separate experiences ingesting food. This discrimination is stimulus-specific rather than specific to some rapid effect of ingesting a nutritive substance in that 3 separate experiences ingesting other nutritive substances (mealworms and glucose water) is not sufficient for immediate discrimination to be shown (Experiments 9 and 11). It seems most likely that this immediate discrimination is based on taste cues that become associated with the long-term metabolic effects of food ingestion. Taste cues are implicated since this association can be formed even though, as in the case of liquid food ingestion, chicks never pecked at, or even saw, chick crumbs before their first food test. It should be noted that several experiences with a specific stimulus need not lead to immediate discrimination, as in the case of sand ingestion (Experiment 7). I shall return to this point in a moment.

Finally, there is some evidence that ingesting sufficient amounts of nutritive substances can lead to a general increase in pecking (Experiment 11 and experiments depicted in Figure 3). Such general effects of food ingestion are quite small in magnitude and large numbers of chicks are needed in order to obtain significant results (Hogan, 1977a). Further, these general effects are often masked by effects of deprivation and satiation (e.g., Experiment 4). I should stress here that the particular factors I have discussed in this section do not account for all the results shown in Figure 5, especially the absolute levels of pecking in Experiments 9, 10, and 11. Additional control experiments would be necessary before further conclusions would be justified.

PREFERENCES AND AVERSIONS

As a result of previous experience, the probability of ingesting particular objects changes. Can these changes best be characterized as preferences for certain objects, aversions to certain objects, or both? In the case of changes based on taste, it is clear that both preferences and aversions are involved. Not only do latency and frequency measures change as a function of experience, but also the entire behavior of the chick changes: Mealworms are avidly sought after (Hogan, 1971, p. 191), while cinnabar caterpillars are strenuously avoided (Morgan, 1896, p. 41). Changes based on postingestional consequences are much more subtle, yet some evidence is available that suggests an answer to the question.

Do chicks develop a preference for food (i.e., chick crumbs) on the basis of postingestional factors? The answer to this question seems to be yes, based on three lines of evidence. First, chicks with three separate experiences of ingesting food showed a stimulus-specific increase in pecking food. This preference is presumably based on taste cues (see above). The second and third lines of evidence come from experiments by Hogan-Warburg (1977). She

83

gave individual chicks a series of 9 10-min choice tests beginning on day 3 and continuing until day 6. In her tests a dish of food and a dish of sand were simultaneously present. Further, in addition to measuring pecking at each stimulus she also measured the number of each type of particle that was swallowed. She found that 9 of her 22 chicks developed a preference for food even though they never swallowed a significant amount of sand on any of the 9 tests. She also found that 16 out of 19 chicks repeated their choice for food on the test immediately following the test in which they took their first substantial food meal. Both these results support the statement that chicks develop a preference for food.

Do chicks develop an aversion to sand on the basis of postingestional factors? The answer to this question seems to be no. Once again there are three lines of evidence that lead to this conclusion. First, as mentioned above, chicks with three separate experiences of ingesting sand did not show an immediate stimulus-specific decrease in pecking sand. The second line of evidence comes, once again, from the work of Hogan-Warburg (1977). Of her 22 chicks, 11 chose sand as their first substantial meal. Of those 11, 5 chose sand as their second substantial meal. And of those 5, 2 chose sand as their third substantial meal. These data suggest that the probability of choosing a sand meal does not change as a consequence of ingesting sand. Finally, the third line of evidence comes from observation of chicks throughout their lives: all chicks continue to peck sand, even as adults (see Hogan, 1971, Figures 11 and 13).[2] It seems reasonable to conclude that chicks do not develop an aversion to ingesting sand.

It remains, of course, to inquire why the rate of pecking declines after ingesting sand the first time (Figure 2) and during the course of a 10-min test after certain kinds of experience (Figures 4 and 5). If these decreases do not reflect an aversion to sand, why do they occur? It seems not unlikely that the decrease is a direct effect of ingesting a non-nutritive substance; the delayed effects seen when a chick has sand as the stimulus during its first pecking experience would occur because pecking had not yet been associated with ingestion. The decrease in pecking might be considered an aversion to the metabolic effects of eating non-nutritive particles. Since these effects do not lead to an aversion to sand, however, it seems best to think of sand ingestion as leading to a temporary lowering of the pecking or the hunger "drive." Such a conceptualization would make understandable the fact that pecking food after sand experience (and before food becomes a "preferred" substance) remains at a low level (Figure 4).

ONTOGENY OF FOOD PREFERENCES IN GUINEA PIGS

Recognition of food is a problem all animals must solve, yet very little attention seems to have been paid to how animals learn what items in their environment are food. One reason for this lack of attention is that many newly-born (or hatched) animals are totally dependent on one or both parents for needs that seem almost impossible for an experimenter to supply. And, if parents are left to interact with their offspring, important experimental control is lost. This is especially true in mammals where the mother must supply milk, generally, for a long time before the young can manage any other food. There is now a considerable body of work, primarily by Galef and his colleagues, that shows how both the mother's behavior and the quality of her milk can influence the young rat's choice among various foods (see Galef, this volume, for review). Thus, it is especially important to separate out the influence of the mother when investigating the mechanisms that allow a young animal to discriminate food from non-food. The problem of raising young rats without interference from their mother has recently been solved by Hall (1975), and work has been started on the development of food preferences in young rats using this technique. There is also one study of the development of food recognition in a mammal in which the problem of maternal influence was met in a different way. This is Reisbick's (1973) work on guinea pigs. Young guinea pigs are precocious to the point where they can ingest some solid foods within a day after birth. This allows the experimenter to make very early manipulations with food and non-food items. I shall briefly review some of Reisbick's results and compare them with my results from the chicks.

Reisbick used guinea pig pups between 1 and 9 days of age. The pups were kept with their mother, who provided a normal milk supply. Pups received no solid food, however, except during 10-min tests. Two groups of stimuli were tested: 1) rat pellets, wooden blocks, glass stoppers and 2) lettuce, paper towels, clear plastic. In each group, the first stimulus was ingestible and nutritive, the second was ingestible but non-nutritive, and the third was neither ingestible nor nutritive. Most of her experiments used the lettuce group of stimuli since lettuce is a more natural food stimulus than rat pellets, and because it was possible to keep the mothers from any contact with lettuce or other greens during the entire nursing period.

Guinea pig pups tend to contact and bite each of the stimuli in a stimulus group about equally the first time they are tested. This is true whether the first test is on day 1, day 5, or day 9. When retested some time later, the pups direct relatively more of their bites toward the food stimulus. Thus, guinea pig pups develop a discrimination between food and non-food items and that discrimination depends on experience. Several experiments were performed to determine what kinds of experience were necessary for this discrimination to develop and what was the time course of the changes.

Reisbick's results show that guinea pig pups increase biting objects about 4 hr after first ingesting solid food, and that, at first, the increase is not specific to food. By 8 hr after first ingesting food, however, a preference for food is shown. It is not clear whether the preference is actually for food or only for the particular food used as one of the stimuli. Results from animals that had been raised on milk and guinea pig pellets and were given lettuce for the first time when they were adults suggest that the preference may be for a particular food: lettuce was contacted equally with the other stimuli on the first trial and preference for lettuce was not seen until the third trial, 16 or 48 hr later. Further experiments would be necessary to confirm this conclusion since the adult animals had so much more experience ingesting solid food than the young ones, and new factors, such a neophobia, might be expected to play a role in the adults. The discrimination that occurs seems to be based on feedback obtained after contact with the object: The number of contact initiations with the various objects in the test does not change, but rather the duration of contacts with food increases as a result of experience. The fact that the preference for food develops equally well whether the stimuli to be discriminated are presented successively or simultaneously means that the feedback on which the discrimination is based must occur more rapidly than it does in the chicks.

Some of these points can be seen in data from one of Reisbick's experiments that are shown in Figure 6. In this particular experiment pups were given experience for the first time on day 8 and were tested with the lettuce group of stimuli on day 9. The lower part of the figure shows that pups with previous experience of food show higher numbers of contacts in the test than pups with no experience of food. (The increases for both the Successive and Simultaneous groups were not significant in this experiment, but larger and significant increases were seen in other experiments.) Of some interest in connection with the chick results is the fact that experience with plastic does not result in lowered numbers of contacts. The upper part of the figure shows that experience with lettuce, whether alone or in combinations with the other stimuli, leads to an increased preference for lettuce.

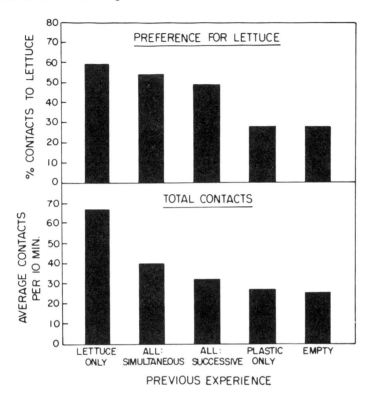

Figure 6
Effects of experience with lettuce, paper towels, and plastic on subsequent choice behavior (upper part) and total number of contacts with all stimuli (lower part) in 9-day-old guinea pigs. (Based on Reisbick, 1973, Experiment 4, and additional data supplied by the author.)

These results show a number of similarities with the chick results. First, discrimination between food and non-food items requires experience on the part of the pup, and that experience does not have its effects until some time later. These results are consistent with the hypothesis that biting and chewing must become associated with ingestion. It is possible that the reason experience with plastic has no effect on subsequent behavior is that none of the plastic is ingested. Second, the discrimination that occurs seems to be based on cues that arise as a result of biting and ingesting, rather than on learning a visual discrimination. These cues seem to be available much more rapidly than they are in the case of the chicks and may, therefore, be of a different kind. More detailed experiments with easily swallowed, non-nutritive stimuli would be necessary to discover what these cues are.

Thus, the results of Reisbick's studies are consistent with a number of the suggestions I have made above concerning the mechanisms underlying the development of food recognition in the chicks. It is well to remember, however, that functionally similar results may be based on completely different mechanisms. A closer look at the mechanisms will be necessary before firm conclusions can be drawn.

ROLE OF DEVELOPMENTAL FACTORS
IN DETERMINING FOOD PREFERENCES

We have now seen that the development of food recognition in chicks and guinea pigs depends on several different mechanisms that operate together to produce an adaptive outcome. In this section I shall pose the question: Are these mechanisms available to the animal throughout its lifetime, or are they peculiar in some way to a specific stage of the animal's development? Four topics will be discussed: (1) Critical periods; (2) Permissive changes; (3) Primacy versus recency; (4) Behavioral expression of changing nutritional needs.

CRITICAL PERIODS

There are many examples of behavioral changes that occur with especial ease at a particular stage of an animal's development, but occur with difficulty or not at all either before or after that particular stage. Such a stage in development is often called a critical or sensitive period (see Hinde, 1970, pp. 563-566). The most widely known example of behavioral change that occurs most readily during such a critical or sensitive period is probably the phenomenon of imprinting (Lorenz, 1935; Sluckin, 1972). Hess (1964, 1973) has suggested that a process akin to imprinting also underlies the development of food recognition in young chicks. There are several reasons to believe that the development of food recognition does not normally involve an imprinting process (Hogan, 1973c; Brown, 1975). The most important reason is that chicks continue eating a wide variety of foods throughout their lives. Nevertheless, there is substantial evidence that critical periods play an important role in the development of food recognition. In particular, the association of pecking with its consequences does not occur before the chicks are about 3 days old (Hogan, 1973a, 1975). It is for this reason that all the experiments reported above used chicks that were 72 hr posthatch.

It is still open to question whether there is an end to this critical period. The most straightforward way to investigate this question would be to withhold pecking experience until the chicks are 4, 5, 6 or more days old. Unfortunately, chicks need to eat after they are 3 days old, so special procedures are needed. An early study by Padilla (1935) showed that chicks that had been kept in the dark for 14 days, but had been force-fed, did not peck at grains when brought into the light. Further, a number of chicks so treated actually starved to death when allowed normal access to food at the end of the experiment. Chicks deprived for 8 days showed only minor deficits in pecking. It is usual to see these results cited in support of the statement that deprivation of the pecking response for two weeks or more leads to disintegration of pecking. In fact, Padilla reported further experiments with other chicks also deprived of pecking for 14 days. These chicks also did not peck when exposed to grains; however, by using a laborious training procedure, Padilla was able to teach these chicks to peck within two weeks. Control experiments ruled out malnutrition or retinal deterioration as factors responsible for the results. Padilla's observations of the chicks' behavior suggest that the pecking response itself was intact in the deprived chicks; the deficit in behavior was that the chicks did not orient their pecking at small objects. These results suggest that the sensitive period for learning to associate pecking with ingestion ends about 8 to 14 days posthatch.

In a more recent study, Kovach (1969) reported that he was unable to replicate Padilla's results. There were a number of differences between the two studies, including the breed of the animals and the color of the background on which the chicks were tested, which may have accounted for the discrepant results. But a close examination of the two sets of results shows that the differences between them are much smaller than Kovach suggests. It is true that, after deprivation, Kovach's chicks did not need any special training to learn to peck at food. However, groups of chicks with similar experience to Padilla's chicks did require 1 to 3 days of experience before the initiation of effective ingestive behavior, whereas control chicks required less than 3 hr of experience. Observations of the chicks' behavior after deprivation were also very similar in the two studies. Thus, the differences between the two studies seem to be, at most, quantitative in nature. And the conclusion is still valid that a given amount of experience has much greater effects between 3 and 14 days than it has either before or after that time. According to the present analysis, what is learned in the sensitive period is that pecking leads to ingestion.

PERMISSIVE CHANGES

A second developmental factor that plays a role in the ontogeny of food preferences can be called a permissive change. Permissive is used in the sense that a particular change in behavior must occur before the normal functioning of another behavior is apparent. A simple example is that young mammals cannot make visual discriminations until their eyes have opened. The important point here is that whatever factors cause the permissive change (eye opening), those factors have no direct effect on the development of the other behavior (seeing). A second example is that young male chicks must experience normal agonistic (i.e., attack and escape) interactions with their peers in order to perform adequate sexual behavior when adult. Attack and escape have no direct effect on the development of the ability to copulate but effective copulation requires a particular relationship between the tendencies to attack and escape. This relationship does not occur unless the chicks have had normal social experience early in their lives (Kruijt, 1964). A final example is provided by Hebb's (1946) analysis of fear: Fear is a reaction to "the disruption of temporally, and spatially organized cerebral activities"—that is, a reaction to something unfamiliar. In many instances, an animal must build up such cerebral organization through experience. Thus, fear cannot be expressed until the animal has learned what is familiar. These three examples show that the permissive change can depend on different degrees and kinds of experience. In all these cases, however, the development of seeing, sexual behavior, or fear responses is not directly dependent on these same factors.

The development of the discrimination between food and nonfood items in chicks seems to be still another example of behavior dependent on a permissive change. The chicks must first learn to associate pecking with ingestion before the effects of ingesting food or sand are reflected in the pecking response. In previous publications I have called this factor a switching mechanism (Hogan, 1971) and a priming mechanism (Hogan, 1973c, 1975). The term switching mechanism now seems inappropriate because, if the present analysis is correct, the discrimination mechanism is not switched on by experience, but rather certain experience is necessary before the discrimination mechanism can be manifest.

The term priming also seems inappropriate because this term is normally used to denote a reversible, motivational process (e.g., van Iersel, 1953; Noirot, 1969; Gallistel, 1969), whereas in the chicks we are dealing with a non-reversible, associational process. Strictly speaking, a permissive change should not be considered a developmental factor unless the change is essentially non-reversible.

PRIMACY VERSUS RECENCY

It seems to be generally true that, all else being equal, recent experiences have a more profound effect on an animal's behavior than earlier experiences. When the reverse is true, however, the earlier experiences can be shown to have a more profound effect, developmental factors can be said to play a role. Primacy effects are often associated with critical periods and non-reversible changes in behavior, but such effects could logically occur independently.

There is some evidence that primacy effects play a role in the development of food recognition in chicks (Capretta, 1969; see also Capretta, this volume, for review). However, the fact that chicks continue to eat a wide variety of foods throughout their lives means that primacy effects cannot normally play a very important role in the choice of food items. Evidence discussed in the next section on changes in food preferences throughout life also supports this conclusion. There is somewhat stronger evidence that primacy effects play a role in the development of preferences for places in the environment (see Hess, 1973, p. 310ff; but see also discussion of this point in Hogan, 1973c). Preferences for particular places in the environment could, of course, indirectly influence the choice of food items.

BEHAVIORAL EXPRESSION OF
CHANGING NUTRITIONAL NEEDS

Early in this paper I presented some data from Dove (1935) that showed that the choice of food items ingested by chicks changed as a function of age. I then asked whether the mechanisms responsible for this long-term food selection were the same as the mechanisms underlying the original discrimination of food from non-food. The answer to this question seems to be primarily yes.

The data presented in Figure 1 show that the percentage of each food selected from the various foods offered changed gradually over the course of 12 weeks. For example, the percentage of corn increased, while the percentages of bran, wheat middlings, and oatmeal decreased. But, these changes were not the result of gradually learning about the consequences of ingesting these foods. Dove reports that chicks that were permitted free selection of foods for the first time at 3 weeks tended "to consume foods in ratios in keeping with their age or stage of development. Thus chicks seem not to be required to learn from experience or else learn very rapidly."

In the light of what we now know, Dove's conclusion seems essentially sound. It seems likely that the same mechanisms that lead chicks to discriminate between food and sand operate to lead chicks to discriminate among various foods. Thus, the feedback that develops during the first minute or two of ingesting one food could regulate the amount of pecking and swallowing of that food, and, "by repetition of the selective process" (Morgan, 1896) stimulus-specific preferences could develop during the first few meals. The changes in preference that occur over time would be the result of these mechanisms operating on a changing physiological substrate.

It may be useful to point out here that the formation of stimulus-specific associations probably proceeds in the manner suggested by Hull (1943, pp. 98-99) and by Testa and Ternes (this volume). Hogan-Warburg's (1977) results show that chicks are able to make a discrimination between food and sand after 9 simultaneous choice tests. Although most of her chicks pecked at both food and sand during most tests, her analysis indicates that chicks were able to associate the long-term consequences of ingestion with the particle they had swallowed most. This was a gradual process that seemed first to involve an association between long-term consequences and taste cues, and later an association between the taste and the visual and/or tactile properties of the particle.

Maturational changes in the physiological substrate certainly occur, and animals respond appropriately. For example, Kruijt and I raised a number of Black Grouse *(Lyrurus tetrix tetrix)* chicks from hatching to maturity in isolation from adult members of the species. The chicks were offered a choice of insects, grains, and greens at all ages. When newly-hatched and for the first few weeks, the chicks ate insects almost exclusively; when they were about 6 weeks old, within a few days, all the chicks switched to eating the typical adult diet of grains and greens. A dramatic example of the same kind of change in some human groups and in other mammals is the disappearance, after infancy, of the enzyme lactase, which digests milk sugar. Ingestion of milk stops after the disappearance of the enzyme. This example is discussed in detail by Rozin (1976). Maturational changes in physiological substrates must be a normal occurrence in many animals. Such animals must be sensitive to these changes, and must be able to respond quickly and effectively. The mechanisms I have described that are available to young chicks would be quite suitable for coping with changing demands as the chicks grow older.

CONCLUSIONS

There are three processes that seem to be involved in the development of food recognition.

First, chicks (and, very likely, guinea pigs) must learn to associate the act of ingestion with the hunger system. On the one hand, this means that the young animal must learn what behavior to perform in order to achieve ingestion. It is not clear why experience should be necessary for this association to be formed. About the best that can be said is that it seems to be a general developmental principle that behavior patterns often appear in ontogeny before they serve their normal function. As the animal grows older these simple behavior patterns become integrated into more complex systems (Kruijt, 1964; Hogan, 1971). The fact that experience is necessary for integration to occur in this case raises the interesting question of whether behavior patterns other than pecking *could* become associated with the hunger system.

Another aspect of learning to associate ingestion with its consequences is the delayed change in pecking rate. The length of the delay corresponds well to the natural rhythm of feeding and resting seen in young chicks (Hogan, 1973c). Ingestion of nutritive substances leads to increases in pecking rate, whereas ingestion of non-nutritive substances leads to decreases in pecking rate. In both cases the changes in pecking rate are not stimulus-specific. This means that chicks will keep pecking at all objects in a place where a substantial part of their intake is nutritive, but will reduce pecking if their intake is primarily non-nutritive. Since a decrease in pecking at non-nutritive particles is correlated with an increase in moving (Hogan, 1971), chicks will tend to move elsewhere when ingesting sand, but will keep sampling particles at a low rate until they begin ingesting food. This is a fairly primitive mechanism for selecting food, and is similar in many ways to the indirect orientation mechanism, kinesis (see, e.g., Hinde, 1970, Ch. 7). Nonetheless, this mechanism does function to provide a wide range of food items for the chicks.

The second process involved in the development of food recognition is specific to nutritive feedback and is able to modulate the rate of ingestion. It is this process that is responsible for the development of the discrimination between food and sand seen in many of the experiments. No direct experience seems to be necessary for the operation of this process, but the association of pecking with the hunger system must occur before it becomes apparent. At the moment, this process can only be inferred from the behavioral evidence. Physiological experiments would be needed to determine its nature.

The third process involves the development of stimulus-specific, visual recognition of food. This process seems to conform to the standard discrimination learning paradigm. As with the modulation of ingestion rate, discrimination based on visual cues cannot occur until the chicks have first learned to associate pecking with the hunger system. The second and third mechanisms involved in food recognition solve the problem of food selection directly and are thus analogous to the direct orientation mechanism, taxis. These mechanisms are also used to solve the problem of food selection throughout life.

FOOTNOTES

[1] I use the term 'hunger system' to refer to "all the perceptual mechanisms that affect the hunger coordinating mechanism and all the behavior mechanisms affected by the hunger coordinating mechanism, as well as the hunger coordinating mechanism itself." (Hogan, 1971, p. 132.) The hunger coordinating mechanism is that part of the central nervous system responsible for coordinating the internal messages that arise from metabolic deficit and ingestion. In the present context, I am suggesting that pecking and the hunger system may develop independently, and that pecking *becomes* a 'behavior affected by the hunger coordinating mechanism' only after particular experiences.

[2] It is commonly assumed that chicks require sand or other grits for proper digestion. Although ingestion of grits does not seem to have any detrimental effects on chicks, beneficial effects are generally small or non-existent. In one study (Fritz, 1937), the presence of grits had essentially no effect on the digestibility of an all-mash diet, and led to a slightly increased digestibility (about 15%) of a coarse-grained diet of southern field peas. Thus, it cannot be argued that chicks *need* to ingest sand.

ACKNOWLEDGEMENTS

I am grateful to Baylor University for providing me with this opportunity to summarize my work on food recognition, and for their gracious hospitality during the Symposium. I would like to thank Margaret Jackson for assistance in collecting data over the past 6 years and for keeping my lab in running order, and Lidy Hogan-Warburg, Sara Shettleworth, Martin Daly, and David Sherry for helpful comments on the manuscript. Preparation of this paper, as well as the research reported herein, was supported by a grant from the National Research Council of Canada.

REFERENCES

Brown, R. T. Modification of chick's pecking preferences: Food imprinting or instrumental conditioning? **Animal Learning and Behavior,** 1975, **3,** 217-220.

Capretta, P. J. The establishment of food preferences in chicks *Gallus gallus.* **Animal Behaviour,** 1969, **17,** 229-231.

Dove, W. F. A study of individuality in the nutritive instincts and of the causes and effects of variations in the selection of food. **American Naturalist,** 1935, **69,** 469-544.

Fritz, J. C. The effect of feeding grit on digestibility in the domestic fowl. **Poultry Science,** 1937, **16,** 75-79.

Gallistel, C. R. The incentive of brain-stimulation reward. **Journal of Comparative and Physiological Psychology,** 1969, **69,** 713-721.

Hall, W. G. Weaning and growth of artificially reared rats. **Science,** 1975, **190,** 1313-1315.

Hebb, D. O. On the nature of fear. **Psychological Review,** 1946, **53,** 259-276.

Hellwald, H. Untersuchungen über Triebstärken bei Tieren. **Zeitschrift für Psychologie,** 1931, **123,** 94-141.

Hess, E. H. Imprinting in birds. **Science,** 1964, **146,** 1128-1139.

Hess, E. H. **Imprinting: Early experience and the developmental psychobiology of attachment.** New York: Van Nostrand Reinhold, 1973.

Hinde, R. A. **Animal behaviour, 2nd ed.** New York: McGraw-Hill, 1970.

Hogan, J. A. An experimental study of conflict and fear: An analysis of behavior of young chicks toward a mealworm. I. The behavior of chicks which do not eat the mealworm. **Behaviour,** 1965, **25,** 45-97.

Hogan, J. A. An experimental study of conflict and fear: An analysis of behavior of young chicks toward a mealworm. II. The behavior of chicks which eat the mealworm. **Behaviour,** 1966, **27,** 273-289.

Hogan, J. A. The development of a hunger system in young chicks. **Behaviour,** 1971, **39,** 128-201.

Hogan, J. A. The development of food recognition in young chicks: I. Maturation and nutrition. **Journal of Comparative and Physiological Psychology,** 1973a, **83,** 355-366.

Hogan, J. A. The development of food recognition in young chicks: II. Learned associations over long delays. **Journal of Comparative and Physiological Psychology,** 1973b, **83,** 367-373.

Hogan, J. A. How young chicks learn to recognize food. In R. A. Hinde & J. Stevenson-Hinde (Eds.), **Constraints on learning.** London: Academic Press, 1973c. Pp. 119-139.

Hogan, J. A. Development of food recognition in young chicks: III. Discrimination. **Journal of Comparative and Physiological Psychology,** 1975, **89,** 95-104.

Hogan, J. A. Development of food recognition in young chicks: IV. Associative and non-associative effects of experience. **Journal of Comparative and Physiological Psychology,** in press, 1977a.

Hogan, J. A. The association of pecking with ingestion in newly-hatched chicks. (In preparation, 1977b.)

Hogan-Warburg, A. J. Feeding strategies in young chicks. (In preparation, 1977.)

Hull, C. L. **Principles of behavior.** New York: Appleton-Century-Crofts, 1943.

Iersel, J. J. A. van. An analysis of the parental behavior of the male three-spined stickleback *(Gasterosteus aculeatus* L.). **Behaviour Supplement 3,** 1953.

Katz, D. **Animals and men: Studies in comparative psychology.** London: Longmans, Green, 1937.

Kovach, J. K. Development of pecking behavior in chicks: Recovery after deprivation. **Journal of Comparative and Physiological Psychology,** 1969, **68,** 516-523.

Kruijt, J. P. Ontogeny of social behavior in Burmese Red Junglefowl *(Gallus gallus spadiceus).* **Behaviour Supplement 12,** 1964.

Lorenz, K. Der Kumpan in der Umwelt des Vogels. **Journal für Ornithologie,** 1935, **83,** 137-213; 289-413.

Morgan, C. L. **Habitat and instinct.** London: Arnold, 1896.

Noirot, E. Changes in responsiveness to young in the adult mouse: V. Priming. **Animal Behaviour,** 1969, **17,** 542-550.

Padilla, S. G. Further studies on the delayed pecking of chicks. **Journal of Comparative Psychology,** 1935, **20,** 413-443.

Reisbick, S. H. Development of food preferences in newborn guinea pigs. **Journal of Comparative and Physiological Psychology,** 1973, **85,** 427-442.

Rozin, P. The selection of foods by rats, humans and other animals. In J. S. Rosenblatt, R. A. Hinde, E. Shaw, & C. Beer (Eds.), **Advances in the study of behavior.** Vol. 6. New York: Academic Press, 1976. Pp. 21-76.

Sluckin, W. **Imprinting and early learning.** London: Methuen, 1972.

Zeigler, H. P., Miller, M., & Levine, R. R. Trigeminal nerve and eating in the pigeon *(Columba livia)*: Neurosensory control of the consummatory responses. **Journal of Comparative and Physiological Psychology,** 1975, **89,** 845-858.

V

ESTABLISHMENT OF FOOD PREFERENCES
BY EXPOSURE TO INGESTIVE STIMULI
EARLY IN LIFE

PATRICK J. CAPRETTA
Miami University

Few would be surprised to learn that an animal's diet is subject to its experiences with foods and feeding situations as a growing organism. The problem arises in specifying what these experiences are and their relative importance for the species in question. It might be argued that while such experiences may occur at any time in the life of an animal, those occurring when the organism is young and impressionable are especially important. A young animal may be influenced in what it eats by what its parents feed it, by what it observes other (adult) animals of its kind eating, and by its own trial and error experiences of pleasure and discomfort with specific foods. My own research over the past decade has dealt with the question of whether the food (flavor) choices of chickens and rats are influenced by what they were exposed to as very young animals. I will concentrate on a description of this research as it has evolved chronologically, in addition to related work bearing directly on my own concerns in the area.

ESTABLISHMENT OF FOOD PREFERENCES
IN PRECOCIAL BIRDS

Although committed early in my career to the theoretical views of Clark Hull (Hull, 1943; Hull, Livingston, Rouse, & Barker, 1951) on the feeding response, I took rather naturally to the suggestion of the ethologists (e.g., Hess, 1962; Thorpe, 1956) that something akin to "imprinting" might be involved in the development of food preferences, especially in the precocial bird. The possibility that

99

such an attachment-like process is working in the early learning of food habits led us (Bronstein & Capretta, 1970; Capretta & Bronstein, 1967) to study the interrelationship between imprinting to a moving object and the development of feeding preferences in the young chicken. Lest it be misunderstood at the outset, I prefer to think of such "attachments" (assuming for the moment they exist) as experientially influenced inclinations to select one food over another. Of course, preferences induced in this manner are subject to change as the chicken enlarges upon its initial encounters with foods.

Specifically, Bronstein and I explored the possibility that one of the functions of an attachment by juveniles to a conspecific adult is the finding of food and the development of an attachment (albeit a temporary one) to that food or to some obvious features of the food. [Domestic fowl do seem to engage in a special form of feeding enticement, whereby the hen, say, in discovering food lures her chicks to her side by clucking. In addition, she may also peck conspicuously at the ground, gather pieces of food and let them fall to the ground again near the chicks (Wickler, 1972).] It was expected that domestic chicks given their initial exposure to a food while exhibiting approach/follow responses would display a greater preference for that food than would subjects experiencing their first meal in the absence of approach/follow behavior. Groups of Leghorn chicks were given 25 min exposure to colored foods of identical nutritional value 30 hr after hatching. Half of the chicks were individually exposed to a moving trough, and the other half to a stationary trough. One-third of the subjects in each of these two movement conditions had the trough filled with red food, green food, or no food, respectively.[1] Birds in the three mobile-trough groups displayed the expected approach/follow behavior; pecking at the trough, the food, or both was observed in all of these chicks. The subjects confronted with an immobile trough were, on the whole, less active than the chicks in the mobile-trough groups. After exposure training, and following a 10-hr interim without food, each chick received three preference tests when they were about 40, 110, and 185 hr posthatch. Each test consisted of presenting both red and green foods in a stationary trough for 20 consecutive hr (the position of the foods varied from left to right every 5 hr).

The significant interaction of the foods with the motion of the trough, presented in Figure 1, is interpreted as showing that approach/follow responses did facilitate the development of a food preference. Only those chicks exposed to green mash in the moving

100

trough demonstrated an absolute preference for the green food, or aversion to the red (on the radian scale a mean score of 1.5708 is equivalent to a random selection of foods).

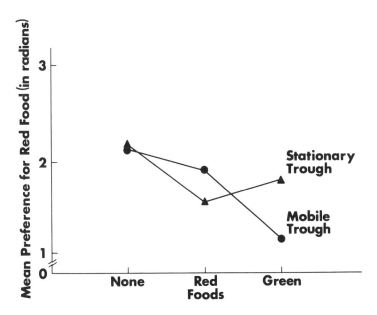

Figure 1
The proportion of red food ingested by chicks as a function of the kinds of food and the motion of the trough during training. (From Bronstein & Capretta, unpublished observations.)

The selection of foods of a particular hue and brightness among chickens would seem to interact with strain; Capretta (1969) found that chicks of the Cornish Rock variety, when presented with both red and green foods, chose the latter. Red food was never preferred by these birds, although the strength of the preference for green was subject to manipulation. Burghardt (1970) has noted similar variability in the prey preferences of young garter snakes. The potentiation of the preference for only green mash by the use of a moving trough in the present study remains a puzzle.

About this time—the mid 1960s—Burghardt and Hess (1966) reported on their studies with a snapping turtle, in a design meant to determine the relative importance of *primacy* and *recency* factors in the establishment of food preferences in a precocial species. I initiated a similar study with the chicken (Capretta, 1969), though beginning training at an earlier age than others had and would be doing. In one experiment, chicks of a Cornish Rock variety were taken in their first day posthatch and some were exposed to a dyed mash of one color, others to a dyed mash of a second color, and still others to an undyed starter mash in what was referred to earlier as "stationary trough" conditions.[2] The birds were allowed to eat these foods undisturbed in individual cages for 24 hr. This was followed by a reversal in the colored mashes, such that chicks started on the red mash were then given plain undyed mash or green mash for an additional 24 hr. The controls continued eating plain mash throughout the 48-hr training period. After 3 days maintenance under conditions of dim illumination and ad-lib access to plain mash, all of the chicks were given a 5-hr test to determine individual preferences for the red or green mash. Two additional preference tests were given about 8 days and 12 days posthatch. In this way I hoped to ascertain the relative effectiveness of the different periods of exposure, and determine whether the chicks would show a preference for the first colored mash they had eaten or the one they had ingested most proximal to the tests.

Although none of the groups preferred red over green mash (top portion of Table 1), the overall mean proportions were significantly

Table 1. Amount of Red Mash (or Rice) Consumed Divided by Total Amount of Colored Mash (or Rice and Oats) Eaten by All Groups for All Tests

Training condition		Preference tests				Mean amount food eaten in training period (in g)	
Group	N	1	2	3	All tests	0-24 hr	25-48 hr
Experiment 1							
Red-Plain	4*	0.30	0.35	0.39	0.35(27.2)**	3.8	9.9
Red-Green	5	0.46	0.42	0.40	0.43(35.2)	3.1	8.3
Plain-Plain	6	0.16	0.12	0.19	0.16(30.6)	3.8	8.8
Experiment 2							
Rice-Oats	6	0.30	0.27	0.23	0.27(23.6)	3.2	4.8
Oats-Rice	6	0.26	0.21	0.22	0.23(20.1)	2.3	3.0
Plain-Plain	4	0.06	0.10	0.07	0.08(21.0)	2.2	5.3

*One subject died late in training.
**Numbers in parentheses represent the mean amount (in g) of the two test foods eaten during all testing trials. Group variability was not large enough to warrant a breakdown of the data into proportions for individual chicks. (From Capretta, 1969.)

higher for the two experimental groups than for the control group. The data of the group first given red and then green mash in training underscore the importance of the initial food experienced on later preferences. This was so even though these chicks ate more than twice as much green as red mash (8.3 g versus 3.1 g) in training. In this same study an attempt was also made to influence the consumption of different kinds of foods by a similar procedure. Each subject in one group of newly hatched White Link chicks was given ground rice for the first 24 hr, followed by an additional 24 hr of feeding on ground oats. A second group of chicks received oats for 24 hr and then rice for another 24 hr. A third group of controls was given the plain starter mash for the entire 48-hr training period. Three separate preference tests, each 5 hr in duration, were conducted at about 5, 8, and 12 days after hatching. As shown in the bottom portion of Table 1, both of the groups of experimental subjects ate considerably more of the nonpreferred ground rice than did the control chicks that had had neither rice nor oats in

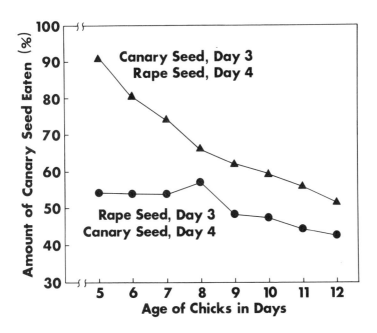

Figure 2
Food choices by weight for chicks given both rape and canary seeds for 8 days after being fed only one kind of seed on Day 3 and the other kind on Day 4. Eight chicks in each condition (redrawn from Burghardt, 1969).

103

training. The small difference between the two experimental groups, though in the expected direction, was not significant.

In a related study Burghardt (1969) used a different breed of chicken, different foods, and an exposure period beginning on the third day posthatch. The chicks were given rape or canary seed on an alternating schedule, and then tested on both types of seeds on 8 consecutive days. As shown in Figure 2, subjects initially fed canary seed showed a strong preference for canary seed when both seeds were first offered and the chicks first fed rape seed showed no clear preference. With continued testing on the two foods, the preference of both groups (especially the canary seed group) shifted toward rape seed, though differences in favor of the food first eaten existed throughout most of the testing period.

Although my own findings and Burghardt's are in general agreement, it should be noted that in both of the studies I outlined earlier, the food choices of young fowl were subject to manipulation prior to the age of 3-5 days, described by Hess (1962) as a critical or sensitive period when experiences with particular foods are *most* effective in influencing later food preferences in the chicken. That this is the case with regard to the actual consumption of food is supported by Hogan's (1973) research on the ontogeny of food recognition. He found that chicks can learn about the consequences of ingested food by a long-delay learning mechanism similar to that described for rats (Revusky & Garcia, 1970). Furthermore, such learning starts on or about the third day posthatch, when the yolk sac reserves are depleted by approximately half and the need for an external food supply is becoming imperative. Studies of other species of birds have also provided evidence that early experience with particular foods may be of greatest influence during certain sensitive periods of development (Rabinowitch, 1968, 1969).

ESTABLISHMENT OF PREFERENCES FOR NON-CALORIC SOLUTIONS IN THE RAT

Our initial research along these lines was inspired in part by the appearance of contradictory evidence in the literature. The failure of Gordon Bronson (1966), for example, to train the adult laboratory rat to prefer a diet it had eaten in infancy appeared to be at odds with other findings, especially those of Zing-Yang Kuo (1967) who, working decades earlier, had reported success in markedly influencing the diets of adult cats and dogs by controlling their food intake over the first few months of life. Because of problems we saw in Bronson's study and the cursory account of Kuo's research available to us, my students and I decided on similar work with rats as subjects using various flavored solutions instead of solid foods.

Bronson (1966) gave preweaned rats special diets including gelatin encapsulated Mynah bird pellets and a mash made from such pellets mixed with wine vinegar. The rats received these foods from age 16 to 25 days; they were then given preference tests at 48 days of age, having been fed an alternate food during the interim between training and testing. Little, if any, support was found for the hypothesis that the type of food eaten in infancy is preferred by adult laboratory rats.

Our (Capretta & McClellan, 1970) design and summary of procedures are shown in Table 2. Two training solutions were used: one consisted of peppermint extract and tap water dyed red, and the other of white vinegar and water dyed yellow.[3] Thus, we used two training solutions which were distinct in taste, odor, and brightness. Results of preliminary efforts indicated that these non-caloric solutions were about equally preferred by mildly thirsty adult rats, though both were rejected when plain water was also available.

Table 2. Summary of Design and Procedure of Peppermint-Vinegar Experiment

Age (in days)	Peppermint Condition	Vinegar Condition	Water Control
Preweaning			
0-23	water	water	water
Training			
24-27			
(habituation)	water	water	water
28-34			
(early exper.)	peppermint	vinegar	water
35-44			
(interim)	water	water	water
45-51			
(late exper.)	vinegar	peppermint	water
52-61			
(interim)	water	water	water
Testing			
62-67	peppermint & vinegar	peppermint & vinegar	peppermint & vinegar

The rats were weaned at 23 days of age and placed in separate cages where they were kept for the duration of the study. Littermates were divided among the 3 conditions of the experiment. Standard lab chow was available at all times. All of the solutions— whether plain water, peppermint, or vinegar—were left in the cages throughout the designated periods. Each rat received both flavors in the test phase, with the position of the bottles reversed every day.

Judging from body weights and liquid consumption, all of the rats adjusted to the different experimental conditions. Our main concern was with the relative amounts of flavored water consumed during the preference tests. Table 3 shows the percentage of peppermint solution ingested over the entire 6 days of testing.

Table 3. Percentage of Peppermint Ingested for Six-Day Test Period

Rat	Peppermint Condition	Vinegar Condition	Water Control
1	.53	.79	.17
2	.17	.18	.19
3	.03	.11	.17
4	.10	.03	.19
5	.17	.05	.15
6	.64	.06	.23
7	.15	.30	.07
8	.76	.34	.12
9	.03	.29	.21
10	.68	.68	.62
11	.60	.22	.32
12	.83	.28	.75
13	—	—	.14
Means	.39	.28	.26

Although the breakdown of test results for each day indicated certain fluctuations of possible interest, a simple and revealing comparison is the number of rats in each group showing a preference for peppermint water (that is, scores of 51 percent or higher). In the peppermint group there were 6 out of 12 rats that preferred peppermint, whereas only 2 out of 12 in the vinegar group and 2 out of 13 in the water group showed such a preference. One curious feature about these results is the "either-or" nature of the percentages. For many of the rats not showing a peppermint preference, including several animals in the peppermint group itself, relative intake of vinegar was very high, accounting in part for the lack of significant mean differences across conditions. Be this as it may, these results provide some support for the hypothesis that early exposure to a distinctive flavor predisposes *some* rats at least (those without strong natural preferences, perhaps) to prefer such flavors later in life.

As to whether there was a primacy effect—that is, a prepotency of initial taste experience—occurring in this study is unclear. This seemed to be true for (some) rats in the peppermint group, that first received peppermint and then (in the "late experience" phase) vinegar water. Their average consumption over the two consecutive exposure periods increased, as might be expected of growing animals, from 24 g of peppermint to 37 g of vinegar solution. Yet, despite this greater intake of the naturally more palatable vinegar water at a point closer in time to the actual tests, a significantly greater number of these rats showed a preference for peppermint than was the case in either the water control or the vinegar groups. Unfortunately, our pilot work was misleading since the flavors, in the concentration we used, turned out to be markedly different in palatability as evidenced by the percentages for the water group.

ESTABLISHMENT OF A FLAVOR PREFERENCE IN RATS: IMPORTANCE OF NURSING AND WEANING EXPERIENCE

Up to this point in our research, we had labored on the assumption that one could not introduce the training flavors very conveniently until after the rats are normally weaned in the laboratory at some three weeks of age. The work to which we had access indicated that success with some species and not with others was due in some small part at least to the fact that one could impose the experimental feeding regimen at an earlier age in the case of precocial animals such as the chicken and turtle than was possible in the later maturing rat. Bronson (1966), in commenting on his lack of success with the rat, cited Barnett (1963, p. 38), who noted the absence of any kind of maternal behavior in rats which might guide the young in their earliest selection of solid foods. Additional evidence was also cited in support of this conclusion: for example, Barnett (1956), who reared rats on bitter-tasting foods, and Warren and Pfaffman (1959), who exposed the precocial guinea pig to bitter liquids, were unable to produce any enduring preferences for these innately aversive substances. So it was gratifying to read about Bennett Galef's mother's milk research (Galef & Henderson, 1972; Galef & Sherry, 1973) in which the food preferences of young rats appeared to be affected by what flavor cues they had been exposed to in the very act of nursing.

107

The conjecture that food cues (more palatable foodstuffs than had been used previously) may be transmitted in this way, from lactating mother to nursing pup, was consistent with the commonplace observation that the milk of dairy cows often takes on the "off-flavor" of their food, and by laboratory research (Dougherty, et al., 1962; Shipe, et al., 1962) showing conclusively that flavors from certain substances such as wild leek leaves, onion bulbs, and garlic can be carried to the milk via either the digestive or respiratory system. [Various materials suspected of influencing the milk flavors were introduced either by the lung route (pumping air through a chamber containing odoriferous gases) or the rumen route (by means of cannulas inserted in ruminal fistulas). Substances causing off-flavors were detectable in milk much sooner when given by the respiratory route. Flavors imparted by esters (methyl acetate, ethyl acetate, etc.) and alcohols were judged pleasant, while those flavors given by acetone and 2-butanone resembled the more unpleasant features of feedy flavors. An interesting finding was that the effect of ethanol introduced by both lung and rumen produced a flavor described by the judges as "sweet, vanilla like, ester-like."] Given such information, we (Capretta & Rawls, 1974) wished to compare the relative importance of nursing versus postweaning exposure to a strong flavor such as garlic and the acceptance of this flavor later in the animal's life.

The basic plan of the study is given in Table 4. Of 4 rats late in pregnancy, 2 received plain tap water and 2 a strong solution of garlic water[4] to drink with their breeder chow. This feeding regimen was continued throughout the 21 days of nursing, with the pups being prevented from gaining direct access to the liquids given their mothers. On or about the twenty-second day of age, the pups were weaned and half of each treatment group was continued on the same liquid given their mothers or changed to the one not ingested earlier by their mothers. Thus, from the pups nursed by garlic-imbibing mothers, 9 chosen at random received 5 days of direct access to garlic solution (the Garlic-Garlic rats), while the other 9 had tap water with their chow (the Garlic-Water rats). Likewise of those pups nursed by water-imbibing mothers, half were given garlic water (the Water-Garlic rats) and half tap water (the Water-Water rats) as their only liquids for the 5 days of the postweaning phase of the experiment. Then, all 36 pups were placed in individual cages and maintained on lab chow and water for 2 days. Finally, all were given 12 daily 2-bottle tests, each lasting 8 hr, to determine whether tap water or garlic solution was preferred. The rats were deprived of all liquids for the 16 hours between tests, though they had dry food at all times. A second series of daily tests was given 1 month later, the rats being kept on chow and tap water during the interim.

Table 4.   Summary of Design and Procedure of Garlic Experiment

	GROUPS			
	GG	GW	WG	WW
Days 3-21 (nursing)	(Nursing Garlic Mother)		(Nursing Water Mother)	
Days 22-26 (weaning)	Garlic Water	Tap Water	Garlic Water	Tap Water
Days 27-28 (Interim A)	— — — ad libitum food and tap water — — —			
Days 29-40 (Test 1)	— — — 8-hr choice of garlic or tap water — — —			
Days 41-72 (Interim B)	— — — ad libitum food and tap water — — —			
Days 73-78 (Test 2)	— — — 8-hr choice of garlic or tap water — — —			

Note. Abbreviations: GG = garlic water during nursing and weaning; GW = garlic water during nursing, tap water during weaning; WG = tap water during nursing, garlic water during weaning; WW = tap water during nursing and weaning. Data for an additional group of 9 pups, which had neither tasted nor smelled garlic before testing were not included since they did not differ from those for WW rats.

There was no appreciable difference in fluid intake by the dams in the nursing phase of the study. Ingestion during the postweaning period showed that when the solution received during this time was the same as that drunk by the mother during nursing, consumption was relatively high, especially for the Garlic-Garlic pups. Conversely, when the pups were switched from one substance to the other, intake was relatively low.

The main results, depicted in Figure 3, show the mean percentage of garlic solution consumed in each of the initial tests (Days 1 to 12) and in the second series given 1 month later (Days I to VI). It was our expectation that the Garlic-Garlic rats would drink the most garlic solution (at least in the early tests) and that decreasing levels would be shown by the Garlic-Water, Water-Garlic, and

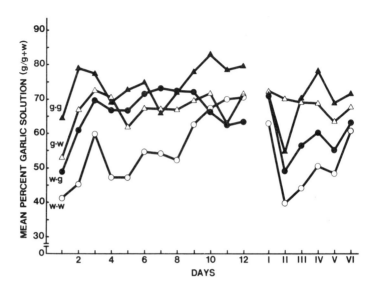

Figure 3
Mean percentage of garlic water ingested by each group for both the initial series of tests (Days 1-12) and the delayed series conducted 1 month later (Days I-VI). (The actual amounts of fluid consumed during each series was appreciable, averaging some 29 g per rat per test. The mean percentages garlic water ingested for the first 3 days of testing were: GG, 73.5%; GW, 64.2%; WG, 59.7%; and WW, 48.8%. Mean percentages for all 12 tests in the first series for this same ordering of groups were: 74.5%, 66.8%, 66.2%, and 56.1%. Similarly, the mean percentages for the 6 days of the second series of tests were: 68.8%, 67.3%, 62.3%, and 51.4%. Abbreviations: GG—garlic water during nursing and weaning; GW—garlic water during nursing and tap water during weaning; WG—tap water during nursing and garlic water during weaning; WW—tap water during nursing and weaning.) (From Capretta & Rawls, 1974.)

Water-Water groups, in that order. The predictions for the Garlic-Water and Water-Garlic conditions followed, we thought, from an acceptance of a primacy effect. That such was the case for the first few days of testing was borne out by statistical analysis.

An additional control group was used in this study to find out whether exposure to the garlic odor alone was sufficient to affect preferences. Since the Water-Water controls were housed in the same room as the other groups, a litter of pups nursed by a water-imbibing mother and weaned in an environment free of garlic odor was tested in the same manner as were all of the other rats. Data for

110

these animals over 12 days of tests were not reliably different from those of the Water-Water pups, and so are not included in Figure 3.

Our own experiment (and replications using not only garlic but peppermint extract as the experimental flavors) demonstrates that neonate experience with certain pungent flavors appears to be at least as effective as postweaning experience in the development of preferences for such flavors later in the life of the altricial rat. A more guarded conclusion, one bearing on the primacy effect, is that consumption of garlic milk during nursing results in slightly more marked garlic preferences in the first few days of testing than does consumption of actual garlic solution following weaning. Considering the results of the first series of tests separately, the overall impression is that at whatever age garlic is experienced (from birth to 40 days), it becomes more acceptable with repeated exposure. Support for this is given by the fact that the 24 percent spread in scores between the Garlic-Garlic and Water-Water groups at the beginning of testing converged to 10 percent or so by the last day of the initial test series.

However, this account does not fit as well with what was found in the tests given a month later, where it is clear (see Figure 3) that after 1 or 2 days of somewhat jumbled ordering, the groups sort themselves out in the final four tests into the original rankings, viz., Garlic-Garlic > Garlic-Water > Water-Garlic > Water-Water. Apparently, prolonged early experience (especially the combination of garlic milk and garlic water received by the Garlic-Garlic rats) makes for strong and lasting preferences, something which is not reported by others using differently flavored solid foods—though probably not so pungently flavored as garlic—restricted to the period of nursing.

In a replication of our experiment, Rawls and I tried not only garlic again but peppermint extract as the training solutions. Though I cannot report on the details of this experiment, the outcome was similar to that of the present study except that the results in the second test series were not as supportive of a long-lasting effect for the peppermint flavoring (Rawls, Personal Communication).

Though olfaction alone was not enough to enhance garlic consumption in our study, a recent experiment by Bronstein and Crockett (1976) suggests a different conclusion. They subjected some nursing rat litters to a garlic-free environment, others to one in which their mothers were fed a garlic-laced Purina chow (a nonpreferred diet for rats not previously exposed to this flavoring), and still others to the smell but not the taste of garlic. Soon after wean-

111

ing, each pup was given a 6-hr choice between plain Purina chow and chow containing 0.5% garlic powder. As shown in Figure 4, the pups reared by Purina-fed mothers ate relatively less of the garlic-laced Purina chow than did their counterparts who had had garlic flavor or garlic odor during nursing. The latter two groups did not differ reliably from one another. Bronstein and Crockett concluded that exposure of rat pups and their dams to the odor of garlic is sufficient to cause a temporary tolerance for this flavoring when encountered at weaning.

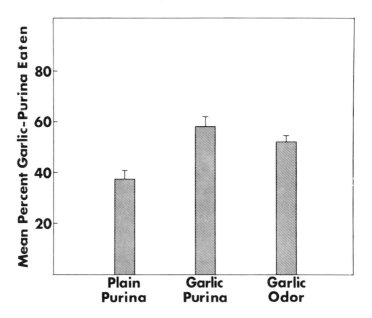

Figure 4
Mean percentage of garlic-purina consumed by newly weaned rats as a function of their nursing experiences with a plain- or garlic-purina-fed mother. The third group was exposed, along with their dams, to the odor of garlic alone. (Redrawn from Bronstein & Crockett, 1976.)

[It is interesting to note that the effect they reported was transient, i.e., little evidence that the garlic tolerance persists beyond 1 day of testing. But the garlic powder they used seems different from the garlic extract employed by us. In our study, the liquid garlic was only weakly rejected by the water controls at the start of testing, becoming increasingly preferred as the rats received more experience in the test situation. Conversely, the McCormick's

Garlic Powder used by Bronstein and Crockett is a tastant to which naive rats show an aversion which becomes more pronounced as the animals are exposed to repeated two-food choices.]

EXPERIENCE WITH FLAVOR DIVERSITY AND LATER ACCEPTANCE OF FLAVOR NOVELTY

The hypothesis that the more an animal is exposed to different flavors at one time in life the more it will accept new flavors later on gained credibility for this investigator from something Zing-Yang Kuo (1967) observed nearly 40 years ago. Reporting on a series of experiments on cats, dogs, and mynah birds, Kuo concluded that such animals raised on restricted diets for extended periods avoided new foods, while their counterparts reared on varied diets ate novel foods readily. Kuo certainly was not an extreme environmentalist on this issue, since he did stress the fact that preferences, once "established" by early training, could be more easily modified provided the animal's diet was being changed from a food low in natural palatability (hedonic quality) for that species to one high in such palatability. In dogs, for instance, Kuo found it easier to effect preference changes from the accustomed soybean meal to meat than in the opposite direction.

In keeping with Kuo's approach, Daniel Stewart and I gave newly weaned rats either a single flavored lab chow mash or several differently flavored mashes to eat for a 2-week period, and then tested them for the acceptance of a flavored mash none of the animals had been exposed to previously. Specifically, the rats who experienced flavor diversity received 3 containers of pulverized chow, one laced with banana flavor, another with lemon flavor, and the third mash contained imitation rum. The rats could eat freely from any of the 3 flavored mashes during the 2-week training period. Each of 3 additional groups of rats was restricted to just one of the experimental foods. After a brief interval on plain chow, each rat was given a choice between plain mash and one mixed with vanilla extract, a flavor to which none of the rats had been previously exposed. The results of these tests, continued for several days, were inconclusive. There was some evidence that the varied group ate a greater proportion of the novel food on the first day of tests than did those rats having a restricted fare but the effect was very weak and short-lived. We (Capretta, Petersik, & Stewart, 1975) then decided to change from solid foods to liquids because of the problems we were having with food spillage and with the selection of flavors that would give us distinctly different mashes.

113

Table 5. Summary of Design and Procedure of Diversity Experiment

	(Immature)	25-36	37-38	39-48	49-79	80-85
Age (d)						
	(Mature)	65-76	77-78	79-88	89-119	120-125
Group	n	Training	Interim	Test 1	Interim	Test 2
Restricted	10/9	Black Walnut	T	24-hr choice	T	24-hr choice
Restricted	10/9	Rum	a	of novel***	a	of chocolate
Restricted	10/9	Vanilla	p	chocolate	p	solution or
Varied*	10/9	All three	w	solution or	w	tap water
Control**	10	Tap water	a	tap water	a	
			t		t	
			e		e	
			r		r	

*The flavor solutions for this group were varied every 2 training days, such that some rats received black walnut for the first 2 days, then 2 days each with rum and vanilla; others were given rum, vanilla and black walnut; and still others, vanilla, black walnut and rum, each order repeated for the duration of training. Each of the other groups was restricted to a single flavor (either black walnut, rum or vanilla) or tap water for the entire training period.[5]

**This condition was included after the main study was completed. It serves as an additional comparison group (the most restricted of all) from which to gauge the effects of training. A comparable group of mature rats was not used because of the general ineffectiveness of training for these animals.

***A 'novel' flavor is operationally defined here as one to which the animal had not been exposed before. Of course, it may well taste like something the rat previously had, and this is the reason for the design used here. Since all the flavors experienced by the varied group are represented in separate experimental conditions, any differential effects found relating to the dimensions of diversity and restriction should reflect something more than a simple generalization (or summation of generalization) from training flavor(s) to test flavor(s).

The experimental plan, shown in Table 5, consisted of exposing both juvenile and adult rats to either 1 or 3 flavors in the training phase of the study. Thus, for mature and immature rats alike, each of 3 groups was restricted to a single flavored water to drink with its lab chow for the 12 days of training, while a fourth group received all 3 of the same flavors, one at a time in 2-day intervals, during the same exposure period. An additional group of juvenile rats was given tap water during this time. The appropriate solutions and chow were available 24 hours a day throughout the study. After a 2-day interim on water following training, the rats received a choice between tap water and a novel chocolate solution for 10 days. A series of identical preference tests, lasting 6 consecutive days, was conducted 1 month after the first block of tests, the rats having been given tap water beween the test series.

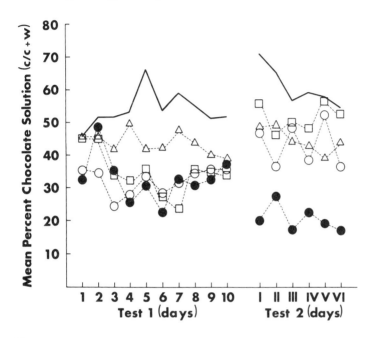

Figure 5
Mean percentage of chocolate solution consumed by immature rats (10 per group). Mean percentages of chocolate drunk over all test days: test 1, tap water (●) = 0.33; rum (□) = 0.35; black walnut (O) = 0.36; vanilla (△) ⊂ 0.44; varied (—) = 0.56: test 2, tap water = 0.21; black walnut = 0.44; vanilla = 0.45; rum = 0.53; varied = 0.62. (Symbols are the same for both tests.) Mean amount (g) of solution consumed in training (given first) and test 1: black walnut (23.7, 46.7); rum (21.7, 49.9); vanilla (25.7, 44.2); varied (26.8, 49.6); tap water (24.8, 39.8). (From Capretta, Petersik, & Stewart, 1975.)

The main results for the immature rats are given in Figure 5, which presents the mean percentage of chocolate solution consumed in each of the 2 test periods. Basic to the design was our belief that relative consumption of the novel solution, at least in the early tests, would be greatest by the varied group trained on 3 flavors. Statistical analysis indicated that all of the restricted

115

groups, including the water controls, drank less chocolate than did the rats trained on a variety of flavors, and this was the trend throughout many of the test days. With 51 percent or higher indicating a preference for chocolate, only the varied group showed a slight to moderate preference for this flavor in several days of Test 1. Overall mean percentages of chocolate consumed ranged from a high of 55 percent for the varied group to a low of 33 percent for the water controls, with the vanilla trained rats at an intermediate mean of 44 percent.

A similar difference between conditions, at least for the first several days, is observed in the second series of tests occurring a month later. No reasonable explanation is given for the uniformly low consumption of chocolate in the water condition, except to suggest that it may reflect the impact of even a modest degree of diversity (be it a single training flavor) on later retention or augmentation of such preferences. The experiment was repeated with immature rats using maple rather than chocolate as the test flavor. A 30/1 solution of Kroger's imitation maple proved to be too palatable, with all of the groups, restricted and varied alike, drinking large proportions of the novel flavor. When the concentration of maple was luᴜᵣₑₐꜱcd to 10/1 midway through the first test series, the curves separated, with the varied group holding at a high level of maple consumption and all of the restricted groups declining noticeably for the duration of the tests. This illustrates the importance of using test flavors of only moderate to low "natural" palatability so as not to obscure any training effects which might otherwise be there.

The results for the mature rats (shown in Figure 6) are unlike those for the younger animals. Most importantly, these groups of rats trained at an older age did not differ from one another in Test 1, though they all showed, more or less, a steady decline in percentages of chocolate solution consumed over the 10-day test period. When tested again a month later, chocolate consumption of all groups increased from that at the conclusion of Test 1, approaching levels attained by rats trained when immature. As in the initial test period, however, the mature groups did not differ from one another in any reliable manner.

Findings in this study appear to show that young rats will accept an unfamiliar flavor more readily if their early taste experiences are varied rather than restricted. Furthermore, the effect seems to persist into maturity, at least for the conditions described here. A comparable effect was not found for rats who were older at the start of training. An interpretation of these results in terms of (stimulus)

116

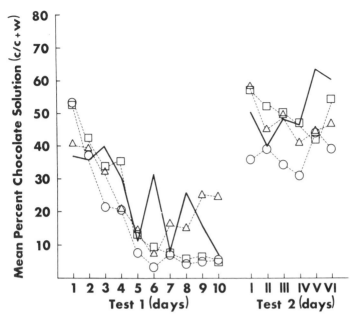

Figure 6
Mean percentage of chocolate solution consumed by mature
rats (9 per group). Mean percentages of chocolate drunk over
all test days: test 1, black walnut = 0.16; rum = 0.21; varied =
0.25; vanilla = 0.29: test 2, black walnut = 0.38; vanilla =
o.49; rum = 0.52; varied = 0.52. Mean amount (g) of solution
consumed during training (given first) and test 1: black walnut
(43.3, 51.8); rum (43.2, 49.5); vanilla (49.1, 46.7); and varied
(49.8, 48.4). The symbols are as in Figure 5. (From Capretta,
Petersik, & Stewart, 1975.)

"flavor generalization" alone seems implausible for two reasons:
the effect was found only with juvenile rats (thus it is probably age-
dependent), and second, none of the flavor-restricted juveniles
reached the high levels of chocolate consumption shown by those
animals trained on all three flavors—either during the immediate
tests or a month later. In some sense, more liquid flavors were
familiar to these latter animals than to their taste-sheltered counterparts. A tentative interpretation is offered for these results, one
based on the notion of *transfer of diversity*, whereby the animal's early experiences—perhaps at some sensitive period in life—either do
or do not prepare it for diversity or unfamiliarity later on. [In a recently completed study, an attempt was made to test the robustness
of the diversity effect by using not only different training flavors,
but also, more importantly it was thought, more than one test

117

flavor. In brief, newly weaned laboratory rats received almond, chocolate, and lemon flavors under restricted or varied conditions of training. This was followed by preference tests in which half of each training condition was given rum as the novel flavor, while the other rats received vanilla. The only reliable difference to emerge was a litter effect, suggesting that certain non-experiential (i.e., genetic) factors might be important determinants in such research.]

Experimental support for a diversity effect of a different kind has also been reported. In one line of research having both practical application (i.e., development of a major rat poison) and theoretical import, Richter (1950, 1953) demonstrated the extent to which the *wild* rat's aversion to novel foods (neophobia) can be increased by encounters with poisons. By repeated poisonings, Richter was able to make some rats (though not all) so suspicious of new foods that they starved to death rather than try additional novel foods. Here, it appears, we have evidence for a "transfer of diversity" of a negative kind. As Rozin (1976) points out, this work and that of Barnett (1956, 1963) and Rzoska (1953) ". . . raised fundamental issues regarding the psychology of learning and suggested the critical importance of neophobia and responses to novel vs. familiar stimuli in the rat world." [Rozin argues that such findings were not assimilated into psychology because wild rats had been used as subjects (and I suspect that the diversity effect as we found it in the laboratory rat would have been more pronounced had we used wild rats), because the ideas were not compatible with the prevailing beliefs in learning theory, and finally because the research was not published in "mainstream" psychology journals.]

A second line of support also deals with the relationship between neophobia and the conditioning of flavor aversions, but in a different manner. Braveman (1976) found that preexposing rats to flavors different from the test solution serves to reduce neophobia without subsequently interfering with the formation of a conditioned aversion. These results—in addition to the findings of Siegel (1974), that consumption of coffee flavored water increases a rat's intake of vinegar water and *vice versa,* and Domjan (1976), that mere exposure to a flavored solution is sufficient to increase its subsequent intake—lead Braveman to agree with my conclusion that a rat's early experiences may indeed prepare it for diversity or novelty later in life. The actual nature of such "preparation" could be one in which the animal learns to be more trusting of flavor novelty by prior (safe) exposure to any novel flavor (Kalat & Rozin, 1973).

FOOTNOTES

[1]Dyeing consisted of mixing 2.3 kg of dry starter mash with 33.9 l of tap water and 62.5 ml of either red or green Kroger food coloring containing 2.5% propylene glycol.

[2]The light brown commercial starter mash was dyed either deep red or light green with 15 parts of tap water to 1 part bright red or apple green Rayner's food colour (purchased in Scotland). The undyed starter mash used in the control condition was mixed in a similar proportion of white vinegar and tap water to approximate the taste of the acetic acid based colors.

[3]Eight drops of red Kroger food coloring was added to 2cc Kroger Brand peppermint extract in 215 cc of tap water. The vinegar solution was made of 6cc Heinz brand distilled white vinegar in 215cc tap water to which 2 drops of yellow Kroger food coloring was added.

[4]The garlic solution in all phases of the experiment consisted of 1 part Frank's brand (Frank Foods, Inc., Cincinnati, OH) garlic juice to 15 parts tap water, by weight.

[5]All flavors consisted of 30 parts tap water to 1 part flavor, by volume. All flavors were an imitation variety (Kroger Brand), except for the test flavor which was a pure chocolate extract, also Kroger Brand.

ACKNOWLEDGEMENT

The research described in this paper was supported by grants from the National Institute of Mental Health and the National Science Foundation. I thank Anthony Cooper, John Jahnke, Donald Parker, J. Timothy Petersik, Randall Potter, and Raymond White for helpful comments on the manuscript.

REFERENCES

Barnett, S. A. Behavior components in the feeding of wild and laboratory rats. **Behaviour,** 1956, **9,** 24-43.

Barnett, S. A. **The rat: A study in behavior.** Chicago: Aldine Press, 1963.

Braveman, N. S. Independence of neophobia and aversion formation: Implications for learned safety. Unpublished manuscript, Department of Psychology, Memorial University of Newfoundland, St. John's, Newfoundland, Canada, 1976.

Bronson, G. W. Evidence of the lack of influence of early diet on adult food preferences in rats. **Journal of Comparative and Physiological Psychology,** 1966, **62,** 162-164.

Bronstein, P. M., & Capretta, P. J. The "imprinting" of food preferences in chicks. Unpublished manuscript, Department of Psychology, Brooklyn College, New York, 1970.

Bronstein, P. M., & Crockett, D. P. Odor adaptation determines the food preference of weanling rats. Unpublished manuscript, Department of Psychology, Brooklyn College, New York, 1976.

Burghardt, G. M. Effects of early experience on food preference in chicks. **Psychonomic Science,** 1969, **14,** 7-8.

Burghardt, G. M. Intraspecific geographical variation in chemical food cue preferences of newborn garter snakes. **Behaviour,** 1970, **36,** 246-257.

Burghardt, G. M., & Hess, E. H. Food imprinting in the snapping turtle, *Chelydra serpentina.* **Science,** 1966, **151,** 108-109.

Capretta, P. J. The establlshment of food preferences in chicks, *Gallus gallus.* **Animal Behaviour,** 1969, **17,** 229-231.

Capretta, P. J., & Bronstein, P. M. Effects of first food ingestion on tthe later food preferences of chicks. **Proceedings of the 75th Annual Convention of the American Psychological Association,** 1967, **2,** 109-110.

Capretta, P. J., & McClellan, T. E. Establishment of preferences for a non-caloric solution in the rat. Unpublished manuscript, Department of Psychology, Miami University, Oxford, Ohio, 1970.

Capretta, P. J., Petersik, J. T., & Stewart, D. J. Acceptance of novel flavours is increased after early experience of diverse tastes. **Nature,** 1975, **254** (5502), 689-691.

Capretta, P. J., & Rawls, L. H. Establishment of a flavor preference in rats: Importance of nursing and weaning experience. **Journal of Comparative and Physiological Psychology,** 1974, **86,** 670-673.

Domjan, M. Determinants of the enhancement of flavored-water intake by prior exposure. **Journal of Experimental Psychology: Animal Behavior Processes,** 1976, **2,** 17-27.

Dougherty, R. W., Shipe, W. F., Gudnason, G. V., Ledford, R. A., Peterson, R. D., & Scarpellino, R. Physiological mechanisms involved in transmitting flavors and odors to milk. I. Contribution of eructated gases to milk flavors. **Journal of Dairy Science,** 1962, **45,** 472-476.

Galef, B. G., Jr., & Henderson, P. W. Mother's milk: A determinant of the feeding preferences of weaning rat pups. **Journal of Comparative and Physiological Psychology,** 1972, **78,** 213-219.

Galef, B. G., Jr., & Sherry, D. F. Mother's milk: A medium for transmission of cues reflecting the flavor of mother's diet. **Journaal of Comparative and Physiological Psychology,** 1973, **83,** 374-378.

Hess, E. H. Imprinting and the "critical period" concept. In E. L. Bliss (Ed.), **Roots of behavior.** New York: Harper, 1962. Pp. 254-267.

Hogan, J. A. How young chicks learn to recognize food. In R. A. Hinde & J. Stevenson-Hinde (Eds.), **Constraints on learning: Limitations and predispositions.** New York: Academic Press, 1973. Pp. 119-139.

Hull, C. L. **Principles of behavior.** New York: Appleton-Century, 1943.

Hull, C. L., Livingston, J. R., Rouse, R. O., & Barker, A. N. True, sham, and esophageal feeding as reinforcements. **Journal of Comparative and Physiological Psychology,** 1951, **44,** 236-245.

Kalat, J. W., & Rozin, P. "Learned safety" as a mechanism in long-delay taste-aversion learning in rats. **Journal of Comparative and Physiological Psychology,** 1973, **83,** 198-207.

Kuo, Z. Y. **The dynamics of behavior development: An epigenetic view.** New York: Random House, 1967.

Rabinowitch, V. E. The role of experience in the development of food preferences in gull chicks. **Animal Behaviour,** 1968, **16,** 425-428.

Rabinowitch, V. E. The role of experience in the development and retention of seed preferences in zebra finches. **Behaviour,** 1969, **33,** 222-236.

Revusky, S., & Garcia, J. Learned associations over long delays. In G. H. Bower & J. T. Spence (Eds.), **Psychology of learning and motivation: Advances in research & theory** (Vol. 4). New York: Academic Press, 1970. Pp. 1-83.

Richter, C. P. Taste and solubility of toxic compounds in poisoning of rats and man. **Journal of Comparative and Physiological Psychology,** 1950, **43,** 358-374.

Richter, C. P. Experimentally produced behavior reactions to food poisoning in wild and domesticated rats. **Annals of the New York Academy of Sciences,** 1953, **56,** 225-239.

Rozin, P. The selection of foods by rats, humans, and other animals. In J. S. Rosenblatt, R. A. Hinde, E. Shaw, & C. Beer (Eds.), **Advances in the study of behavior** (Vol. 6). New York: Academic Press, 1976. Pp. 21-76.

Rzoska, J. Bait shyness, a study in rat behavior. **British Journal of Animal Behaviour,** 1953, **1,** 128-135.

Shipe, W. F., Ledford, R. A., Peterson, R. D., Scanlen, R. A., Geerken, H. F., Dougherty, R. W., & Morgan, M. E. Physiological mechanisms involved in transmitting flavors and odors to milk. II. Transmission of some flavor components of silage. **Journal of Dairy Science,** 1962, **45,** 477-480.

Siegel, S. Flavor pre-exposure and "learned safety." **Journal of Comparative and Physiological Psychology,** 1974, **87,** 1073-1082.

Thorpe, W. H. **Learning and instinct in animals.** London: Methuen, 1956.

Warren, R. P., & Pfaffmann, C. Early experience and taste aversion. **Journal of Comparative and Physiological Psychology,** 1959, **52,** 263-266.

Wickler, W. **The sexual code: The social behavior of animals and men.** Garden City, New York: Doubleday, 1972. Translated from **Sind Wir Sünder?** Munich: Droemar Knaur, 1969.

VI

MECHANISMS FOR THE SOCIAL TRANSMISSION OF ACQUIRED FOOD PREFERENCES FROM ADULT TO WEANLING RATS

BENNETT G. GALEF, JR.
McMaster University

This paper is concerned with the role of social interaction in the determination of diet selection by weanling wild rats (*Rattus norvegicus*). Discussion of the subject is presented in three parts: The first is intended to place the role of social factors in food preference determination within the context of other determinants of dietary selection. The second presents evidence concerning mechanisms by which adult rats may bias their young at weaning toward initiation of feeding on a particular food, and the third discusses neophobia as a factor in the maintenance of socially transmitted diet preferences in weanlings.

DETERMINANTS OF DIET SELECTION

INNATE TASTE FACTORS

It is a commonplace observation that the members of any species exhibit a tendency to select similar foods for ingestion. It seems reasonable to propose, as P. T. Young did many years ago, that such consistency in the pattern of food acceptance exhibited by conspecifics is determined, in part, by genetically encoded and transmitted propensities to experience some gustatory sensations as more pleasurable than others (Young, 1959, 1966, 1968). According to this hypothesis, primary responses to potential food items reflect the biological organization of sensory-affective processes and are assumed to have evolved as an adaptive response to constancies in the food resource base of the ecological niche of each species (Young, 1968).

Of course, the existence of genetically influenced consistencies in the flavor preference hierarchy of a species does not preclude the possibility that experiential factors may produce differences in the food preferences of conspecific individuals. It is, for example, well established that populations of laboratory animals which have experienced aversive gastro-intestinal events in association with the ingestion of normally preferred food will subsequently exhibit a profound aversion to that food. Conversely, there is preliminary evidence that groups of laboratory animals having a history in adolescence of prolonged ingestion of a normally nonpreferred food item may show a preference for that food or similar foods when subsequently offered such familiar but normally unpalatable items in a choice situation (Kuo, 1967).

Social Influences on Food Selection. Comparison, in the natural environment, of the feeding patterns of individuals belonging to distinct subpopulations reveals similar examples of within-species, intergroup differences in diet selection. In uncontrolled situations the causes of such between-group variability in resource exploitation are, of course, difficult to ascertain. However, a number of field workers have reported observations suggesting that to understand subpopulation differences in food selection in natural situations one has to take into account the social context within which feeding behavior occurs, as well as other food-related experiential variables more frequently considered by laboratory investigators. For example, it has been reported that a variety of species of British birds have acquired the habit of removing or puncturing the caps of milk bottles and eating cream from the surface of the milk. The fact that many birds in some localities, and none in other areas with similar milk bottles, have acquired the milk-bottle opening behavior strongly suggests a social transmission of this feeding habit from individual to individual in the localities where it is common (Fisher & Hinde, 1949; Hinde & Fisher, 1951, 1972. See also Galef, 1976, for other such examples). In laboratory situations, an observer normally will not see the effects of such social processes on diet selection, unless he intentionally looks for them, because most experimental paradigms are explicitly arranged so as to keep the behavior of individual subjects independent of one another. However, examples of feeding patterns which apparently require explanation in terms of the intraspecific social context in which the feeding occurs are not uncommon in the ethological literature.

The capacity of freely interacting natural subpopulations to socially transmit patterns of food resource utilization among themselves would be of obvious advantage. The mechanism of differential reproductive success responsible for the natural selection process [which, in turn, underlies the evolution of sensory affective processes of the type hypothesized by Young (1968)], is only sufficient to produce genetically coded and transmitted food preference patterns in a population adaptive with respect to the mean properties of that population's ecological niche (Williams, 1966). Adaptive behavior with respect to the special demands of an individual's particular home range can only develop as a result of individual behavioral plasticity in response to the demands and contingencies of a particular environment. In the natural situation, social transmission could function to facilitate individual acquisition of information concerning the exploitable resource base of a particular area (Mainardi, 1973), by reducing the cost to an individual organism, in both energy and risk, of the usual direct trial and error learning about a particular ecological situation (Galef, 1976). To the extent that an individual can utilize the experience of sympatric conspecifics in selecting or rejecting items for ingestion, it increases its probability of rapidly locating new sources of food already discovered by conspecifics and reduces its risk of ingesting noxious novel food items.

Importance of Social Influences During Weaning. If, as suggested above, the function of social transmission of information is to reduce the cost to the individual inherent in acquiring information about its individual ecological situation, then it seems reasonable to hypothesize that social influence would be particularly important in mammals during the weaning process. It is during the weaning stage that the demands on the individual to rapidly acquire appropriate behavior with respect to its individual ecological niche are most acute. With respect to dietary selection, it is weanling young which are ignorant of the location and identity of nutritious foodstuffs to be found in the vicinity of the nest-site and which have to seek out food at a stage of development during which they are particularly vulnerable to environmental stress. Adults rearing young have learned the identity and location of necessary foods during their own explorations in the area in which they reproduce, and it would clearly be advantageous to the young (and, hence, to the reproductive advantage of their parents) if the young could make use of the experience of adult conspecifics in locating solid foods.

In the case of wild rats, which have been the subject species in my own work on social transmission processes, the ability of weanlings

125

to make use of the acquired feeding patterns of adult conspecifics might be particularly important because weanling rats not only have to locate and identify safe foods but also often need to avoid ingesting palatable poison baits introduced into their home ranges by humans seeking to exterminate commensal rodent populations. Because successful poison avoidance by rats depends in considerable measure on discrimination of familiar from unfamiliar foods (Galef & Clark, 1971), the weanling rat, to which all solid foods are unfamiliar, is in particular need of some source of information other than its personal experience if it is to avoid ingesting potentially lethal baits. There is, in fact, field data suggesting that adult rats can protect their young against the ingestion of toxic substances. Von Fritz Steiniger (1950), an ecologist working on problems of rat extermination, reported some years ago that if a given poison bait is used in one area for an extended period, despite initial success, later acceptance of that bait is very poor. He noted, in particular, that the offspring of animals surviving initial poisoning rejected the bait without sampling it themselves and continued to do so for so long as animals which had survived initial poison ingestion remained in the area. Steiniger attributed such avoidance of contact with potentially toxic baits by naive animals to the behavior of experienced individuals, which he believed, dissuaded the inexperienced young from ingesting poisoned food. For the past several years, my students and I have been examining the social interactions of both wild and domesticated rats under controlled conditions to determine the mechanisms by which such social transmission of feeding preferences might proceed.

MECHANISMS FOR THE SOCIAL TRANSMISSION
OF FOOD PREFERENCES

BASIC EXPERIMENTAL PARADIGM

In our basic experimental paradigm (Galef & Clark, 1971), colonies consisting of two male and four female wild rats are established in enclosures like the one diagrammed in Figure 1a. Water is continuously available and food is presented to the colony for 3 hr daily in two ceramic food bowls located approximately 2.5 ft apart. Each of these bowls contains one of two nutritionally adequate diets, discriminable from one another in color, texture, taste, and smell. I will refer to these diets as Diets A and B. Diet A is powdered Purina Laboratory Chow, and Diet B, compounded by Teklad Mills, consists mainly of sucrose and casein and is highly preferred to Diet A by rats in a simple choice situation.

126

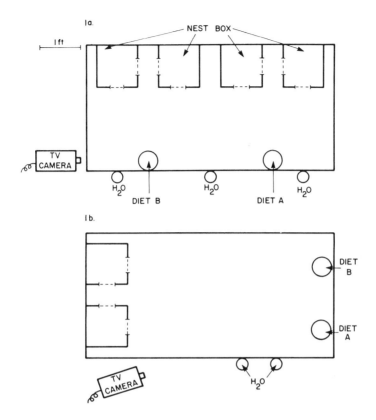

Figure 1
Enclosures in which rat pups were observed prior to (a) and after
removal from (b) their adult clan in the "Basic Experimental
Paradigm."

The adult members of the colony are trained to eat one diet and to
avoid the other by introducing sub-lethal concentrations of a toxin,
lithium chloride, into samples of one of the diets offered to the adult
colony during daily 3-hr feeding periods. Under these conditions,
members of our adult colonies rapidly learn to avoid ingesting the
lithium-contaminated diet and continue to avoid it for some weeks
even if subsequently offered samples of the once-poisoned diet free
from contaminants.

The experiment proper begins when litters of pups born to trained
adult colony members leave their nest site to feed on solid food for
the first time. We observe both adults and pups throughout daily
3-hr feeding periods via closed circuit television and record the
number of times the pups approach to within 4 in of each food bowl,

127

each containing uncontaminated samples of diet, and the number of times they eat from each food bowl.

After the pups have been feeding on solid food for a number of days, they are transferred to new enclosures (illustrated in Figure 1b), where, without the adults of their colony, they are again offered the choice of uncontaminated samples of Diets A and B for 3 hr daily. The amount of each diet eaten by the pups in this situation is determined by weighing food bowls before and after each feeding session.

Typical results of such studies are presented in Figures 2a, 2b, and 3. Figure 2a presents data describing the food choices of a litter of

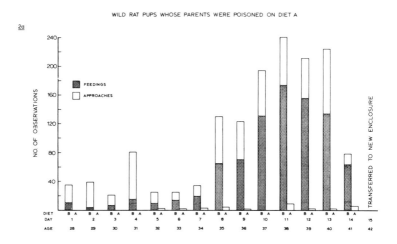

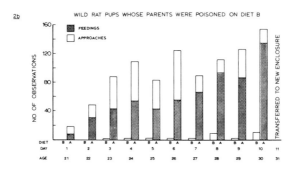

Figure 2
Number of observed approaches to and feedings from bowls containing Diets A and B by wild rat pups, the adults of whose colonies had been poisoned on Diet A (a) or Diet B (b). (From Galef & Clark, 1971.)

128

wild rat pups born to a colony of adults trained to avoid ingesting the normally non-preferred Diet A, while Figure 2b presents data describing the feeding behavior of a litter of pups born to a colony of adults trained to avoid ingesting the normally preferred Diet B. It is clear from comparison of the data presented in these figures that the learned feeding preferences of adult colony members profoundly affect the feeding preferences of their young. As Steiniger (1950) observed, in the presence of adult rats avoiding a diet, weanling colony members also avoid ingesting that diet. Furthermore, as illustrated in Figure 3, the learned dietary preferences of adults continue to affect the feeding preferences of their young for some 8 to 10 days following transfer of the pups to enclosures separate from the adult colony members.

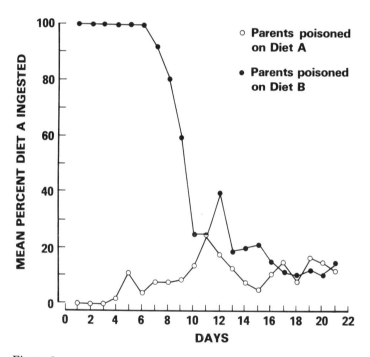

Figure 3
Percentage intake of Diet A by pups on the days following removal from adult influence. (Redrawn from Galef & Clark, 1971.)

WEANLINGS LEARN TO EAT WHAT ADULTS EAT

It is not possible to determine from the data described above whether the pups learn to ingest the diet consumed by the adults of

129

their colony or to avoid the diet rejected by the adults. It is, however, important to determine the precise nature of the behavior being transmitted from adults to young before attempting an analysis of underlying mechanisms.

If pups learn to avoid the diet which the adults of their colony avoid, as a result of interaction with them, then it should be important that the pups experience that diet during the time they are with the adults. Conversely, if the pups learn only to eat what the adults of their colony eat, then the presence of the adult-avoided diet during the period of adult-young interaction should be of no importance.

The experimental design used to determine whether pups learn to eat the adult-ingested diet or to avoid the adult-avoided diet was

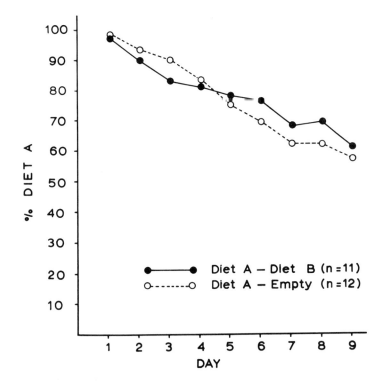

Figure 4
Mean percentage of Diet A eaten by pups following their transfer to individual enclosures. For one group the second food bowl contained Diet B; for the other group the second food bowl was empty. (From Galef & Clark, 1971.)

130

very similar to the "Basic Experimental Paradigm." Colonies of adults were again trained to avoid the normally preferred Diet B and to eat Diet A. Pups were allowed to feed with the adults for 10 days and were then moved to individual enclosures and offered the choice of uncontaminated samples of Diets A and B. While in the enclosure with the adults for 10 days of feeding, pups of one colony and their adults were offered the choice of Diets A and B (and ate only Diet A) while pups and adults in another colony were offered the choice between Diet A and an empty bowl placed in the location in which Diet B was usually available. If pups in the "Basic Experimental Paradigm" learned to avoid the diet that the adults of their colony avoided, then one would expect pups which had Diet B available while with the adults to show a more profound avoidance of Diet B, when offered the choice of Diets A and B in individual enclosures, than pups which had not previously seen Diet B.

Figure 4 illustrates the percentage of Diet A eaten by pups in the two groups when offered the choice of Diets A and B in individual enclosures. As is clear from examination of the figure, there is no difference between the two groups in their acceptance of Diet B. The simplest interpretation of these data is that pups learn to eat the diet that the adults eat rather than to avoid the diet the adults avoid.

POSSIBLE MECHANISMS FOR
TRANSMISSION OF FOOD PREFERENCES

Any of a wide range of mechanisms might be responsible for the observed transfer of an acquired feeding preference from adult rats to pups. For example, adults may mark either the diet they are eating or the diet they are avoiding with residual chemical cues which attract or repel the pups and thereby influence their feeding site selection. Alternatively, adults may carry samples of the diet they ingest back to the nest site and ingestion of these samples may influence pups' subsequent choice of diet. Or, the physical presence of adults at a feeding site may attract pups to that site and influence their choice of diet for early ingestion. Each of these possibilities has been examined.

Effects of Chemical Cues on Feeding Site Selection. If adults deposit attractive chemicals in or near the food they are eating or mark the food they are avoiding, or its surrounding area, with some warning chemical and these residual chemicals are responsible for adult influence on pups' initial choice of diet, then it should be fairly easy to disrupt the apparent influence of the adults on the food choices of their young. All that would be needed would be to disturb the

131

chemicals deposited by the adults. We have conducted the following experiment in order to determine the importance of such chemical cues for the behavior of the pups. The experimental situation was similar to the "Basic Experimental Paradigm" except that sheet metal trays (2 x 2 ft) covered with sawdust were placed under both food bowls during both the training of the adults (to eat Diet A) and the observation of the pups. When pups in each of the litters we used had been observed to eat solid food 20 times, we performed the following manipulations: (1) The two food bowls were emptied. (2) The food bowls and the trays of sawdust they were sitting on were reversed in position. (3) Finally, new samples of Diets A and B were placed in their initial positions in the now-reversed food bowls. Thus, all chemical cues located within 1 ft of the food bowls had been reversed in position within the experimental enclosure. These manipulations had absolutely no effect on the feeding behavior of the pups. Without exception, the pups continued to eat Diet A and avoid Diet B, as did the adults.

While the above result suggests that the deposition of residual chemical cues is not a necessary condition for the observed transmission of a preference for the diet of colony adults, more recent research indicates that such cues may be sufficient to influence pup choice of feeding site (Galef & Heiber, 1976). A lactating female rat and her litter were left undisturbed in the left-hand portion of the enclosure diagrammed in Figure 5 from Day 1 to Day 17 post-partum. Starting on Day 17, and for the subsequent 6 days, the female and her litter were removed from the enclosure for 3 hr daily. During the period when the enclosure was vacated, experimental pups of the

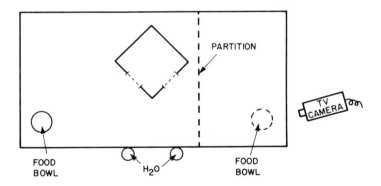

Figure 5
Enclosure in which effects of residual olfactory cues on pup behavior were ascertained.

132

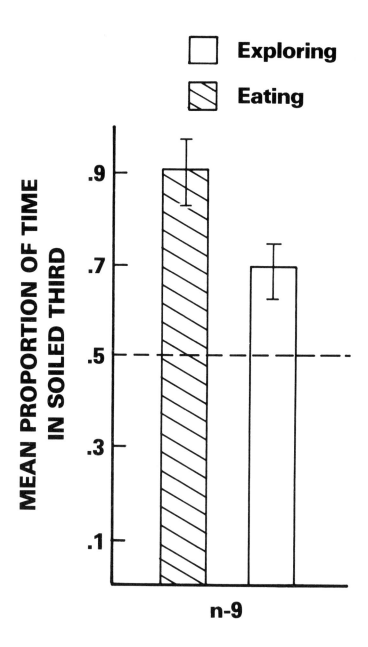

Figure 6
Mean proportion of time spent by individual pups exploring and feeding in the end of the enclosure previously occupied by a lactating female rat and her litter. (Redrawn from Galef & Heiber, 1976.)

same age as the pups just removed were placed individually in the enclosure and the partition indicated in Figure 5 was removed, allowing the experimental pups to choose between two food bowls containing Diet A. Each experimental pup was observed on closed circuit television for 50 min daily for 7 consecutive days. The observer recorded the amount of time each pup spent feeding from each food bowl and the amount of time each pup spent exploring in the previously occupied and unoccupied end thirds of the enclosure. The results are presented in Figure 6. It is clear from the figure that residual chemical cues deposited by a lactating rat are sufficient to affect the feeding locations selected by pups during weaning.

Taken together the results of the preceding two studies indicate that rat pups can utilize residual olfactory cues to select a feeding site previously visited by conspecifics. However, the data also indicate that the manipulation of such cues does not disrupt adult influence on pup food choice. Alternative mechanisms for the transmission of food selection must exist.

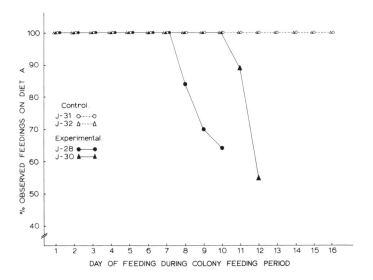

Figure 7
Percentage of observed feeding responses directed to the bowl containing Diet A during colony feeding periods by litters of pups offered in the nest site samples of Diet A eaten by adult colony members (Control) or samples of Diet B avoided by adult colony members (Experimental). (From Clark & Galef, 1972.)

134

Effects of Food Present in the Nest Site. To look at the effects of the ingestion of food stuffs at the nest site on subsequent food choices, one can offer the pups in the nest site, at some time other than the 3-hr colony feeding period, samples of the food the adults of their colony have been trained to avoid. The pups' food preferences during colony feeding periods can then be observed. The results of such an experiment (Clark & Galef, 1972) are presented in Figure 7. There are two interesting aspects of the data. First, sampling by the pups in the nest site of the adult-avoided diet did not produce an initial preference for that diet. Second, such sampling did affect the later rate of acceptance by pups of the adult-avoided diet. I will be returning to the second point later in discussion of the role of neophobia in the maintenance of socially transmitted feeding preferences in rats.

Effects of Physical Presence of Adults. If ingestion of food samples in the nest site is not sufficient to explain the pups' strong dietary preferences in the "Basic Experimental Paradigm," what is? The

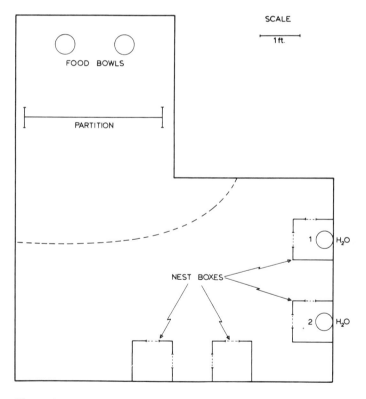

Figure 8
Enclosure for continuous observation of a wild rat colony.

135

evidence indicates that the most important factor influencing pups' choice of initial diet is the presence of adults at a food site at the time the pups are ready to begin feeding on solid food (Galef & Clark, 1971, 1971a). To examine this possibility, we established a colony of adult wild rats in the enclosure illustrated in Figure 8. Diet A was constantly available in the two food bowls located behind the partition (the adults ate at both bowls) and the area above the dotted line was continuously monitored via closed circuit television. We marked pups individually and looked to see under what conditions each pup ingested its first meal of solid food. We observed 9 pups in all, and all 9 ate their first meal under exactly the same circumstances: in the presence of a feeding adult and at the same food bowl as that feeding adult, not at the other bowl 1.5 ft away. Given the temporal distribution of adult meals, the probability of this occurring by chance was less than .001. The presence of an adult at a feeding site seems to attract pups to that site and to cause pups to initiate feeding on the diet present there. Our further observations and experiments within this enclosure indicated that the pups tend to approach adults outside the nest area rather than to follow them from the nest site to food, and that visual cues are necessary to guide this approach. Blinded pups showed no tendency to eat their first meal of solid food in the presence of a feeding adult (Galef & Clark, 1971a).

DIRECT ADULT INFLUENCE
ON PUP FOOD SELECTION

The mechanisms by which adult rats may influence the food choice of their young discussed thus far are rather indirect. The adults bias their offspring to a feeding site rather than to a food. However, examination of the possibility of direct transfer of food preference from adults to young has revealed that this too can occur. We conducted an experiment which was similar to the "Basic Experimental Paradigm" except for one very important feature (Galef & Clark, 1972). Colonies of adult rats were again housed in 3 x 6 ft enclosures of the type illustrated in Figure 1a. However, in this experiment the adults were removed to a separate cage where they were fed either Diet A or Diet B for 3 hr daily, depending on the experimental condition to which their colony was assigned. While the adults were out of the colony enclosure, the pups were presented with two standard food bowls, one containing Diet A and the other Diet B. We weighed the food bowls before and after each 3-hr feeding session to determine the amount of each diet eaten by the pups. The results are presented in Figure 9. As is apparent from the figure, the diet eaten by the adults affects the food choices of the pups even though, under the conditions of the present experiment, the adults and young have no opportunity to interact directly in the feeding situation and the adults have no opportunity to influence pups' choice of feeding site. Similar results have been reported by Capretta and Rawls (1974) and Bronstein, Levine, and Marcus (1975).

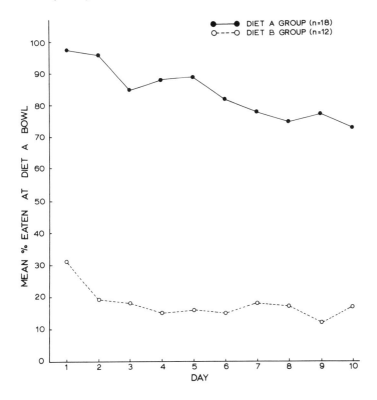

Figure 9
Mean percentage of Diet A eaten by pups, the adults of whose colony are eating Diet A or Diet B, when adults and pups have no opportunity to interact in a feeding situation. (From Galef & Clark, 1972.)

Again there are a number of possible explanations of the observed ability of the adults to influence pups' choice of diet. The flavor of the diet ingested by an adult rat may directly affect the flavor of its feces, and ingestion of adult feces may cause pups to preferentially ingest diets of a similar flavor during weaning. Alternatively, particles of food may cling to an adult's fur and vibrissae and pups

137

could ingest these and become familiar with the adult's diet. Finally, the flavor of the diet ingested by a lactating female rat during the nursing period may directly affect the flavor of her milk and cause pups to prefer similar-tasting diets during weaning.

Effects of Mother's Milk on Pup Food Preference. The available evidence suggests that the most likely direct adult influence on pup food selection occurs through the flavor of the mother's milk (Galef & Henderson, 1972). The milk of a lactating female appears to contain gustatory cues reflecting the taste of her diet with sufficient accuracy to enable her pups to identify that diet during weaning. In one of our experiments which supports this conclusion (Galef & Sherry, 1973), rat pups nursing from a lactating female eating Diet A were force fed 0.5 ml of milk manually expressed from a second lactating female eating Diet B. Following this force feeding, the pups were poisoned by intraperitoneal injection of lithium chloride. A test session subsequently conducted at weaning revealed that this milk-lithium pairing conditioned an aversion to Diet B. Despite these results, however, we have not been entirely successful in producing a preference for a diet in pups at weaning by feeding the pups milk manually expressed from a female eating that diet. Although the outcome of such studies, involving a wide variety of parameters, have consistently been in the direction predicted by the milk-flavor hypothe is, we have not found a procedure which reliably produces acceptable levels of significance. The search continues. Thus, although there is reason to believe that there are cues present in maternal milk sufficient to enable pups to identify maternal diet, there is not yet sufficient evidence to justify the conclusion that such cues actually play a role in determining pups' diet preference at weaning.

Effects of Maternal Excreta on Pup Food Preference. Further work is also needed before firm conclusions may be reached concerning the adequacy of cues associated with the anal excreta of lactating female rats to influence weanling food choices. Leon (1974) presented data indicating that 20-day-old rat pups may ingest anal excreta produced by their mother. It is possible, as Leon has suggested, that cues influencing pup food choice may be transferred from mother to young via the smell or taste of the dam's excreta. This possibility has not, however, been directly tested. Data from my laboratory indicate that pup access, throughout the nursing period, to the anal excreta of a nulliparous female rat eating a diet different from that of their mother is not sufficient to modify pup food choice toward a preference for the diet of that nullipara (Galef & Henderson, 1972). However, given the known differences in the attractiveness of the anal excreta of nulliparous and lactating rats (Leon, 1974), such results are not adequate to permit conclusions concerning the importance of maternal excreta in the determination of weanling diet preference. Thus, the issue remains without satisfactory resolution at the present time.

Effects of Particles of Food Clinging to an Adult's Fur. Results of experiments in which lactating female rats were fed separately from their young, brushed clean, and then dusted with a diet other than the one they were eating following each feeding session and prior to being returned to their litters revealed no effect of this manipulation on initial pup food preferences. The pups continued to exhibit a normal preference at weaning for the diet their mother was eating (Galef & Henderson, 1972). Thus, explanations of the transfer of feeding preferences from adult to young rats via particles of food clinging to the fur of adults seem fairly well excluded.

SUMMARY

The results of our research to date indicate the existence of at least three mechanisms by which adult rats may bias the choice of diet by conspecific young at weaning. Both the physical presence of adults at a feeding site and residual olfactory cues deposited by adults in the vicinity of a food source influence pups' choice of place of weaning and thereby their choice of diet at weaning. There is very strong evidence that a further mechanism exists whereby adults can directly influence pup food choice as a result of interaction with them outside the feeding situation. Cues contained in maternal milk may play a role in this interaction.

ROLE OF NEOPHOBIA IN THE MAINTENANCE OF SOCIALLY TRANSMITTED DIET PREFERENCES

The ability of adults to influence the diet chosen for initiation of feeding is only part of the total phenomenon exhibited by wild rat pups in the "Basic Experimental Paradigm" described above. Young wild rat pups not only initiate feeding on an adult-exploited diet in preference to an adult-avoided one; they continue to ingest only that diet so long as they remain with the adults and for some 8-10 days following removal from interaction with adults. A question remains as to the cause of the wild pups' continued avoidance of the diet which the adults of their colony have learned to avoid. The results of our studies suggest a three-stage process adequate to account for the observed behavior of the weanling wild rats in our experiments.

139

First, as discussed in the preceding section, we have evidence that adult rats can bring their young to initiate feeding on one diet rather than another as a result of interaction with them. Second, it seems reasonable to suppose that, as a result of ingesting the diet to which the adults introduce them, the young become familiar with its taste and smell. Third, as we will see below, there is reason to believe that once wild rat pups become familiar with one diet, they avoid alternative diets because of the relative novelty of those alternatives. Wild rats are strongly neophobic organisms: they show a pronounced avoidance of novel foods or other novel objects in their environment (Barnett, 1958; Galef, 1970). It seems likely that this neophobia contributes to the tendency of wild rat pups to continue avoiding diets other than the one to which the adults of their colony introduce them.

Maintenance of Adult-Determined Food Selection in Wild and Domesticated Pups. If, in fact, neophobia is at least in part responsible for prolonged avoidance by wild rat pups of the adult-avoided diet, then one would expect domesticated rat pups, which are only mildly neophobic in comparison with their wild conspecifics (Barnett, 1958; Galef, 1970; Mitchell, 1976; Rozin, 1968), to behave quite differently from the wild pups in the "Basic Experimental Paradigm." Domesticated pups should follow adults to the diet which the adults were trained to eat (Galef, 1971), but the domesticated pups should then transfer feeding to the adult-avoided alternative diet at the time when neophobia becomes responsible for continued avoidance by wild rat pups (Galef & Clark, 1971). Figure 10 presents data describing the behavior of two typical litters of domestic rat pups tested in the "Basic Experimental Paradigm." Adult colony members were trained to eat the normally less preferred Diet A, and the food choices of their young were observed. As can be seen in Figure 10, although domesticated pups initially fed on the same diet as the adults of their colony, the pups began to ingest the adult-avoided alternative after some 3 to 5 days. In contrast, wild rat pups fail to ingest the adult-avoided alternative for at least 10 days (see Figures 2 and 3). These findings are consistent with an hypothesis implicating neophobia as an important factor in maintenance of wild rat pup ingestion of the diet to which the adults introduce them.

Novelty of Alternative Foods as a Factor in Pup Food Selection. If weanling wild rats do not ingest the adult-avoided diet because of its novelty, they should show less reluctance in feeding at the location avoided by the adults if the diet positioned there is familiar rather than novel. In a test of this prediction (Galef & Clark, 1972), we of-

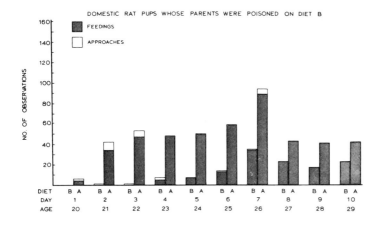

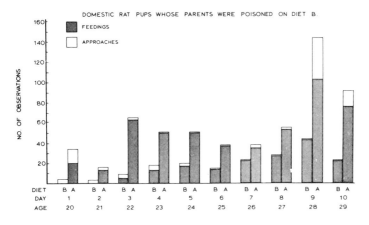

Figure 10
Number of observed approaches to and feedings from the bowls
containing Diets A and B by domesticated rat pups, the adults of
whose colony had been poisoned on Diet B. Each panel displays
data for one litter of pups. (From Galef & Clark, 1971.)

fered adult colony members Diet A in two locations and trained
them, using electric shock, to eat in one location but not the other.
Independent litters of pups were then tested with samples of familiar
Diet A or unfamiliar Diet B in the adult-avoided bowl. Figure 11
shows the proportion of pup feedings directed toward the adult-
utilized food bowl (containing Diet A) by the two groups. Wild
weanlings clearly transfer feeding to the adult-avoided site more
rapidly if offered the same diet there that is available at the adult-
utilized site. This finding provides additional evidence that the

neophobia of wild rat pups in response to a novel food is, at least in part, responsible for prolonging avoidance of alternative diets once pups have become familiar with the diet to which the adults of their colony introduce them.

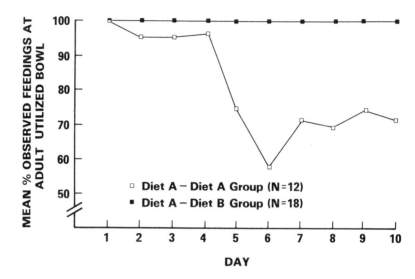

Figure 11
Mean percentage of observed feeding bouts by wild rat pups at the food bowl from which the adults of their colony were feeding when Diet A was present in both bowls (Diet A-Diet A group) and when Diet A was presented in the adult-utilized food bowl and Diet B in the adult-avoided food bowl (Diet A-Diet B Group). (Redrawn from Galef & Clark, 1972.)

Social Influence and Individual Experience in Determination of Pup Food Preference. A major effect of interaction between adults and young appears to be to familiarize the young with one diet rather than another, a result which can obviously be achieved experimentally by means other than social interaction. For example, Crockett (1975) has shown that exposure of pre-weaning rats to the smell of garlic in the general environment will produce an increased acceptance of garlic-adulterated food at weaning. Leon, Behse, and I are engaged in comparable studies, results of which indicate that exposure of pre-weaning rats to the smell of peppermint produces a tendency in the pups to approach the odor of peppermint as well as a preference for peppermint-flavored food. Our interpretation of these data, taken together with our findings on social transmission pro-

142

cesses, is that rats will approach or ingest familiar-smelling objects in their environment regardless of whether this familiarity is achieved by social or other processes. Thus, the transmission of adult feeding preferences to the young wild rat depends, first, on an ability of adults to bias the young toward experience of a specific food, as a result of social interaction with them, and, second, on an independent predisposition on the part of the young to prefer an experienced food to unfamiliar ones.

Evidence of the independence of social influence and individual experience in the determination of pup food preference is provided by an experiment (Clark & Galef, 1972), the results of which are presented in Figure 7. The pups' experience of eating the adult-avoided diet in the nest site affected their choice of diet following 5-10 days of colony feeding, but not their choice of diet early in weaning. Thus, it seems reasonable to conclude that the response of wild rat pups seeking their first meals of solid food is initially a social one, with individual feeding history influencing later food selection.

DISCUSSION

If one looks across species at the role of social interaction in the development of feeding behavior, a similar pattern emerges with considerable regularity. Adult individuals introduce young ones to a subset of the class of potential food items to which the young might have been introduced and, for a limited time following exposure, the young exhibit a tendency to ingest the items experienced as a result of social interaction in preference to unfamiliar items (Galef, 1976).

The means of introduction clearly varies considerably from species to species. Mother hens, for example, use a specific food call to attract their young to a food source, and, as Hogan (1966) has shown, a food-calling hen can induce her chicks to ingest mealworms which they might otherwise avoid. A female meerkat (*Suricata suricatta*) with weaning young will run to and fro in front of her offspring, evoking a food snatching response in her kits and inducing them to ingest food such as banana, which they would normally ignore (Ewer, 1969). And, as discussed above, adult wild rats, as a result of their presence at a food site, can induce pups to feed there on a relatively unpalatable diet.

Although such social interaction may play a role in the initiation of a particular pattern of food selection at weaning, it is the response of the young animal to its early diet, in relation to other available foods, which is critical in determining whether or not the socially transmitted pattern of food selection is maintained to become a permanent feature of the recipient individual's feeding behavior. If it were the case that adult mammals showed an abiding preference for food items ingested at weaning, a sort of "food imprinting," then one might consistently observe relatively permanent effects of social influence at weaning on adult feeding patterns. However, young mammals tend to independently sample available foods in their environments and arrive at a stable pattern of food selection reflecting their species-typical palatability hierarchy (Figure 3; Bronson, 1966; Warren & Pfaffman, 1959). As a general rule, the observable effects of biases in food preference induced by social interaction occuring early in life appear transitory and become obscured as the maturing individual gains experience of the variety of foods available within its home range.

There are, however, important exceptions to this generalization, instances in which presumably socially transmitted feeding patterns (Galef, 1975, 1976) have permanent effects on the diet selection of individuals exposed to social transmission. It has been reported, for example, that many members of some colonies of wild rats (*R. norvegicus*) living along the banks of the Po river, dive for and feed on bivalve molluscs living on the river bottom, while members of neighboring colonies, which have molluscs available within their home ranges, do not exploit them as a food source (Gandolfi & Parisi, 1972, 1973). Similarly, members of some colonies of rats in Germany have been observed to stalk, kill, and eat sparrows, while most colonies do not, even though sparrows are present within their clan territories (Steiniger, 1950). Such examples, and there are numerous others, in which the effects of social interaction appear to be of sufficient duration to serve as the basis of distinctive feeding traditions in certain populations, require some explanation.

It seems reasonable to suppose that two necessary conditions must be met if the results of social interaction are to be observable in the feeding behavior of an individual or population over extended periods of time. First, the transmitted behavior must be one which any individual has a very low probability of acquiring independently. If the transmitted behavior is one which an individual has a high probability of acquiring on its own, the majority of species members will, by definition, acquire that behavior, even if not socially induced to do so. Although socially influenced individuals may acquire the transmitted behavior sooner than those acquiring it independently, differences between the observable feeding behavior of socially influenced and independent individuals will soon disappear. Second, in the absence of any "imprinting" on food ingested early in life, it would appear necessary that the transmitted food preference be for a relatively highly palatable food item, if it is to be maintained. As discussed above, the recipient of a transmitted preference for a relatively unpalatable food will soon find alternatives and abandon the diet to which it was socially introduced. In summary, it seems most consistent with available data to suggest that in the majority of cases the observable effects of biases in food preference induced by social interaction occurring early in life will be transitory and play their major role in vertebrates during thee weaning or fledging period. There are, however, special circumstances in which food preferences established as a result of social interaction may be maintained to maturity.

The importance attributed to the absolute duration of socially influenced patterns of food selection depends on one's theoretical position. Many of those who study the behavior of juvenile organisms do so with the view that the primary goal of such work is the understanding of the ontogenetic processes resulting in the development of an adult behavioral phenotype. The research program described here has proceeded from the view that to survive organisms must exhibit adaptive behavior with respect to their environment at each stage of development (Williams, 1966). Consequently, we have been more concerned with the role of social factors in diet selection as an adaptation during weaning than with the investigation of parameters affecting the duration of food preferences developed as the result of social interaction early in life. The particular case of social transmission of dietary selection we have investigated may well be of little importance in the determination of adult feeding patterns but it gives every indication of being an important adaptation of young mammals undergoing the transition from maintenance on mother's milk to independent acquisition of solid food in the general environment. Our data indicate that social interaction can facilitate the weaning process by reducing the time spent by weanlings in locating needed nutrients and reducing the probability that they will ingest toxic foods which the adults of their social group have learned to avoid. Study of the factors influencing the duration of socially influenced behaviors is clearly important, both from the developmental point of view and for the understanding of the maintenance of traditions in animal populations in natural situations, and we plan to turn our attention to these issues in the immediate future.

145

ACKNOWLEDGEMENTS

The research described here was supported by National Research Council of Canada Grant AP307 and grants from the McMaster University Research Board. I would like to thank Mertice Clark and Abe Black for their helpful discussions of the manuscript and my students: Mertice Clark, David Sherry, Jefrey Alberts, Patricia Henderson, and Rod Pelchat, without whose support this research program would never have come to fruition.

REFERENCES

Barnett, S. A. Experiments on "neophobia" in wild and laboratory rats. **British Journal of Psychology,** 1958, **49,** 195-201.

Bronson, G. Evidence of the lack of influence of early diet on adult food preference in rats. **Journal of Comparative and Physiological Psychology,** 1966, **62,** 162-164.

Bronstein, P. M., Levine, M. J., & Marcus, M. A rat's first bite: The nongenetic, cross-generational transfer of information. **Journal of Comparative and Physiological Psychology,** 1975, **89,** 295-298.

Capretta, P. J., & Rawls, L. H. Establishment of a flavor preference in rats: Importance of nursing and weaning experience. **Journal of Comparative and Physiological Psychology,** 1974, **86,** 670-673.

Clark, M. M., & Galef, B. G., Jr. The effects of forced nest-site feeding on the food preferences of wild rat pups at weaning. **Psychonomic Science,** 1972, **28,** 173-175.

Crockett, D. P. Rats' food preferences are determined by maternal diet. Paper presented at meetings of the Eastern Psychological Association, New York, April, 1975.

Ewer, R. F. The "instinct to teach." **Nature** (London), 1969, **222,** 698.

Fisher, J., & Hinde, R. S. The opening of milk bottles by birds. **British Birds,** 1949, **42,** 347-357.

Galef, B. G., Jr. Aggression and timidity: Responses to novelty in feral Norway rats. **Journal of Comparative and Physiological Psychology,** 1970, **70,** 370-381.

Galef, B. G., Jr. Social effects in the weaning of domestic rat pups. **Journal of Comparative and Physiological Psychology,** 1971, **75,** 358-362.

Galef, B. G., Jr. The social transmission of acquired behavior. **Biological Psychiatry,** 1975, **10,** 155-160.

Galef, B. G. Jr. The social transmission of acquired behavior: A discussion of tradition and social learning in vertebrates. In J. S. Rosenblatt, R. A. Hinde, E. Shaw, & C. Beer (Eds.), **Advances in the study of behavior** (Vol. 6). New York: Academic Press, 1976.

Galef, B. G. Jr., & Clark, M. M. Social factors in the poison avoidance and feeding behavior of wild and domesticated rat pups. **Journal of Comparative and Physiological Psychology,** 1971, **75,** 341-357.

Galef, B. G. Jr., & Clark, M. M. Parent-offspring interactions determine time and place of first ingestion of solid food by wild rat pups. **Psychonomic Science,** 1971a, **25,** 15-16.

Galef, B. G. Jr., & Clark, M. M. Mother's milk and adult presence: Two factors determining initial dietary selection by weanling rats. **Journal of Comparative and Physiological Psychology,** 1972, **78,** 220-225.

Galef, B. G., Jr., & Heiber, L. The role of residual olfactory cues in the determination of the feeding site selection and exploration patterns of domestic rats. **Journal of Comparative and Physiological Psychology,** 1976, **90,** 727-739.

Galef, B. G., Jr., & Henderson, P. W. Mother's milk: A determinant of the feeding preferences of weaning rat pups. **Journal of Comparative and Physiological Psychology,** 1972, **78,** 213-219.

Galef, B. G. Jr., & Sherry, D. F. Mother's milk: A medium for the transmission of cues reflecting the flavor of mother's diet. **Journal of Comparative and Physiological Psychology,** 1973, **83,** 374-378.

147

Gandolfi, G., & Parisi, V. Predazione su *Unoi pictorum* L. da parte del Ratto, *Rattus norvegicus* (Berkenhout). **Acta Naturalia,** 1972, **8,** 1-27.

Gandolfi, G., & Parisi, V. Ethological aspects of predation by rats, *Rattus norvegicus* (Berkenhout) on bivalves *Unio pictorum,* L. and *Cerastoderma lamarcki:* (Reeve). **Bollettino di Zoologia,** 1973, **40,** 69-74.

Hinde, R. A., & Fisher, J. Further observations on the opening of milk bottles by birds. **British Birds,** 1951, **44,** 392-396.

Hinde, R. A., & Fisher, J. Some comments on the republication of two papers on the opening of milk bottles by birds. In P. H. Klopfer & J. P. Hailman (Eds.), **Function and evolution of behavior.** Reading, Massachusetts: Addison-Wesley, 1972.

Hogan, J. A. An experimental study of conflict and fear: An analysis of behavior of young chicks toward a mealworm. Part II. The behavior of chicks which eat the mealworm. **Behaviour,** 1966, **27,** 273-289.

Kuo, Z. Y. **The dynamics of behavior development.** New York: Random House, 1967.

Leon, M. Maternal pheromone. **Physiology & Behavior,** 1974, **13,** 441-453.

Mainardi, D. Biological basis of cultural evolution. **Atti Academia Nazionale dei Lincei,** 1973, **182,** 177-188.

Mitchell, D. Experiments on neophobia in wild and laboratory rats: A reevaluation. **Journal of Comparative and Physiological Psychology,** 1976, **90,** 190-197.

Rozin, P. Specific aversions and neophobia resulting from vitamin deficiency or poisoning in half-wild and domestic rats. **Journal of Comparative and Physiological Psychology,** 1968, **66,** 82-88.

Steiniger, von F. Beitrage zur Soziologie und sonstigen Biologie der Wanderratte. **Zeitschrift Fur Tierpsychologie,** 1950, **7,** 356-379.

Warren, R. P., & Pfaffman, C. Early experience and taste aversion. **Journal of Comparative and Physiological Psychology,** 1959, **52,** 263-266.

Williams, G. C. **Adaptation and natural selection: A critique of some current evolutionary thought.** Princeton: Princeton University Press, 1966.

Young, P. T. The role of affective processes in learning and motivation. **Psychological Review,** 1959, **66,** 104-125.

Young, P. T. Hedonic organization and regulation of behavior. **Psychological Review,** 1966, **73,** 59-86.

Young, P. T. Evaluation and preference in behavioral development. **Psychological Review,** 1968, **75,** 222-241.

VII

ATTENUATION AND ENHANCEMENT OF NEOPHOBIA FOR EDIBLE SUBSTANCES

MICHAEL DOMJAN
University of Texas at Austin

Ingestive behaviors represent one of the most intimate interactions between animal and environment. Substances consumed not only provide olfactory, gustatory, tactile, and other sensory stimulation but also activate the complex and elaborate sequence of events involved in digestion and absorption. Therefore, ingestion may have a variety of consequences including hunger and thirst reduction, alleviation of illness, vitamin deficiency, temporary toxicosis, rapid death, or no change in the state of well-being. With the exception of certain materials such as water, oxygen, sodium, and possibly sugars, animals confronted with a novel substance have no way to predict its postingestional consequences. Given that these postingestional consequences may be lethal, it is not surprising that animals typically consume less of novel than familiar substances. This suppression in the consumption of novel edibles is referred to as neophobia.

The neophobia of animals for edible substances was first observed by exterminators attempting to kill rats by distributing poisoned bait. Robert Smith, the rat-catcher to Princess Amelia of England, noted in 1768 that a certain amount of exposure may be necessary before rats will accept a new food (Shortens, 1954). Subsequent experimental investigations have confirmed that rats tend to eat less of novel than familiar substances (Barnett, 1956; Barnett & Spencer, 1953; Capretta & Rawls, 1974; Domjan & Bowman, 1974; Gentile, 1970; Green & Parker, 1975; Nachman & Jones, 1974; Navarick & Strouthes, 1969; Sheffield & Roby, 1950; Siegel, 1974; Singh, 1974; Shortens, 1954; Young, 1944). Food neophobia has also been observed in dogs (Maslow, 1932), guinea pigs (Warren & Pfaffmann, 1959), turtles

151

(Burghardt & Hess, 1966), fish (Mackay, 1974; Miller, 1963), birds (Capretta, 1969; Capretta & Bronstein, 1967; Coppinger, 1969, 1970; Morell & Turner, 1970; Rabinowitch, 1968, 1969), and humans (Hollinger & Roberts, 1929; see also Rozin, 1976, and this volume). The suppression in the intake of novel edibles is noteworthy not only because it occurs in many different species but also because the behaviors involved are sometimes quite striking. For example, Coppinger (1970) reports that blue jays given new butterflies to eat raise their crests, make alarm calls, retreat from the new food source, and frantically fly from side to side banging loudly against the cage walls. Such agitation in response to a novel edible has been also noted in young Burmese jungle fowl by Hogan (1965). Rats given a novel 2% solution of saccharin to drink have been observed to rattle the drinking tube and bite parts of their cage (Domjan, 1976). If the novel saccharin solution is infused directly into the oral cavity through a fistula, the rats sometimes attempt to escape the taste exposure by jumping out of the infusion cages (Domjan, 1976)—a reaction which is almost never observed when water is presented through the fistula.

As with other behavioral phenomena, neophobia for edibles is influenced by numerous factors. The present chapter describes some of the recent efforts to identify what experiences attenuate and enhance food neophobia and the mechanisms involved in these effects. Other aspects of the food neophobia phenomenon are discussed in subsequent chapters by Capretta, Galef, and Rozin. Given the focus of the present volume on plasticity in food selection, experiments on neophobia for nonedible stimuli (e.g., Barnett, 1958; Mitchell, 1976) will not be reviewed.

BASIC EXPERIMENTAL METHODS

All of our research on neophobia for edibles has involved 50-70-day old male Sprague-Dawley rats maintained in individual wire-mesh cages with continual access to Purina Laboratory or Rat Chow. Novel edibles were provided by flavored solutions of saccharin, vinegar, or casein hydrolysate mixed with tap water and presented at room temperature. The amount consumed in relation to control levels was used as the measure of neophobia. In each experiment, subjects were initially adapted to a daily 23.5-hr water-deprivation schedule to confine their drinking to a time of day convenient for behavioral observations. On days with experimental treatments, the daily 30 min access to water was always presented following the experimental procedures.

ATTENUATION OF NEOPHOBIA FOR EDIBLES

As the term neophobia implies, the suppression of drinking observed with novel fluids becomes attenuated as subjects gain familiarity with the substances. The following discussion describes how various factors related to the conditions of familiarization influence the attenuation of neophobia.

EFFECTS OF CHOICE VS. SINGLE-STIMULUS EXPOSURE ON THE ATTENUATION OF NEOPHOBIA

The amount consumed of a particular edible often depends on what alternative edibles are simultaneously available. Subjects given a choice between a novel and a familiar fluid may be expected to drink less of the novel substance than comparably-deprived subjects given the novel substance as their only liquid. If the attenuation of neophobia is primarily determined by exposure to the novel substance, single-stimulus exposure should result in greater attenuation of neophobia than choice exposure. To evaluate this prediction, Domjan and Gregg (1976) assigned subjects to four groups of a 2 x 2 factorial design in which differences in the procedures used to reduce neophobia (single-stimulus vs. choice) were factorially combined with differences in the procedures used to assess the loss of neophobia (single-stimulus vs. choice). A 2% solution of sodium saccharin was used as the novel edible. The single-stimulus procedure consisted of presenting this saccharin solution as the only fluid for 30 min following 23.5 hr water deprivation. The choice procedure consisted of a similar 30-min access to saccharin, but with tap water also available during this period. Each group received two such 30-min periods of access to the saccharin solution prior to the test session, which was conducted two days later. The groups were identified by two symbols, the first designating the type of pre-test exposure to the novel edible (1 =single-stimulus, 2 =choice) and the second designating the type of test procedure administered subsequently (1 =single-stimulus, 2 =choice).

The amount of saccharin subjects drank during the two pre-test familiarization sessions as well as the subsequent test session is presented in Figure 1. As expected, subjects drank more saccharin during the training sessions if the novel saccharin solution was the only available fluid (single-stimulus procedure) than if tap water was also present (choice procedure). Saccharin consumption during the subsequent test session confirmed that single-stimulus training results in greater loss of neophobia than choice exposure. Groups 1-1 and 1-2 drank more than Groups 2-1 and 2-2 even though the two pairs of groups were equally water deprived before the test session.

153

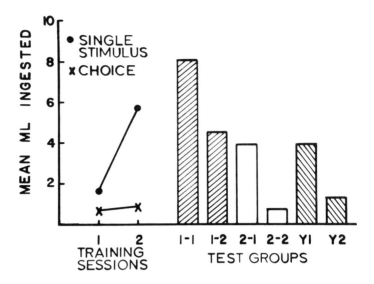

Figure 1
Amount of saccharin ingested by choice and single-stimulus pre-exposure groups during Training Sessions 1 and 2 as well as amount consumed by the various groups during the subsequent test session. (See text for group designations.)

The results of this experiment also demonstrate that single-stimulus procedures are more effective than choice procedures in revealing the loss of neophobia. Regardless of their type of prior saccharin exposure, subjects showed greater increases in consumption with the single-stimulus test than with the choice test. This superiority of the single-stimulus procedure in providing evidence of the attenuation of neophobia contrasts with the relative superiority of choice procedures in providing evidence of learned aversions to edibles (Dragoin, McCleary, & McCleary, 1971; Grote & Brown, 1971).

The choice procedure in the present experiment may have been less effective in reducing neophobia because subjects did not drink much saccharin during such exposure. To evaluate this possibility, two additional groups were allowed to drink as much saccharin during the training sessions as the mean intake of the choice groups. However, for these subjects the saccharin was presented as the only available fluid. During the subsequent test session, one of these yoked-intake groups was given the single-stimulus procedure (Group Y1) while the other was tested with the choice procedure

154

(Group Y2). The right panel of Figure 1 shows that the test-session saccharin intakes of these yoked groups were very similar to the intakes of the choice preexposure Groups 2-1 and 2-2. This finding indicates that the relative ineffectiveness of the choice procedure in reducing neophobia was a result of the limited novel-fluid intakes during training associated with this procedure rather than a direct result of the simultaneous availability of other fluids.

The findings of this experiment suggest that the attenuation of neophobia is directly related to the extent of prior exposure to the edible. The experiment also illustrates that single-stimulus procedures are more effective than choice procedures in both producing and detecting attenuations in neophobia. Single-stimulus procedures were therefore employed in all of our subsequent research.

EFFECTS OF STIMULUS CONCENTRATION AND
NUMBER OF DAILY STIMULUS EXPOSURES
ON THE ATTENUATION OF NEOPHOBIA

The experiment described above suggested that the attenuation of neophobia is directly related to the extent of prior exposure to the edible. To investigate this relationship over a broader range of exposures, the saccharin consumption of subjects was measured during 20 consecutive daily 30-min single-stimulus test sessions (Domjan & Gillan, 1976). So that subjects could satisfy their fluid needs even if they did not drink much saccharin, tap water was available for 30 min each day following the saccharin exposure. Saccharin concentrations ranging from .15 to 3.0% were tested with independent groups.

The daily saccharin consumption of each group of subjects is presented in the left panel of Figure 2, while the right panel shows how much water each group consumed following the saccharin exposure each day. As has been often reported previously (e.g., Beebe-Center, Black, Hoffman, & Wade, 1948), subjects generally drank less of the more concentrated saccharin solutions. Those tested with the .15% solution initially drank more than 19 ml during the 30-min test session, whereas groups tested with the 2.0 and 3.0% solutions drank less than 1 ml. As subjects were repeatedly exposed to the saccharin solutions, their neophobia was attenuated and their consumption increased. This effect was apparent as early as the second day and was quite prominent by the end of the experiment. The greatest increase in intakes occured with the intermediate .5 and 1.0% solutions, with smaller increases evident in subjects tested with the most dilute solution (.15%) and the two highest concentrations (2.0 and 3.0%).

155

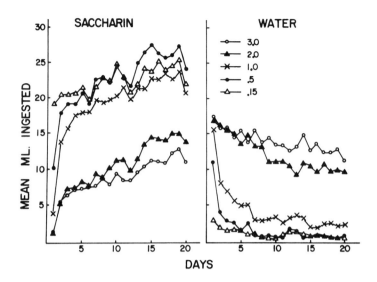

Figure 2
Saccharin (left panel) and water (right panel) intakes of independent groups given daily access to .15%, .5%, 1.0%, 2.0%, and 3.0% saccharin for 30 min followed by water for 30 min. (From Domjan & Gillan, 1976.)

Consumption of the .5 and 1.0% saccharin solutions increased to such an extent that as early as Day 4, differences among the intakes of .15, .5, and 1.0% saccharin were no longer statistically significant, even though earlier in the experiment subjects drank less of the .5 and 1.0% solutions than of the .15% solution. This finding suggests that the initial suppression in consumption of the .5 and 1.0% solutions was largely due to the novelty of these substances. Ingestion of the 2.0 and 3.0% solutions increased only moderately, and subjects drank less of these solutions than of the more dilute concentrations throughout the experiment. This result indicates that the initial suppression in the drinking of 2.0 and 3.0% saccharin was only partially a response to stimulus novelty.

The right panel of Figure 2 shows that daily water consumption was generally inversely related to the amount of saccharin subjects drank. Groups exposed to higher concentrations of saccharin tended to drink more water, and while saccharin intakes increased with repeated testing, water intakes decreased. This finding, as well as the fact that subjects maintained normal increases in weight during the experiment, is evidence that the daily saccharin presentations did not create a disturbance in fluid balance.

156

EFFECTS OF THE DURATION OF DAILY STIMULUS EXPOSURES ON THE ATTENUATION OF NEOPHOBIA

Additional evidence of the direct relationship between the loss of neophobia and the extent of prior exposure to an edible is provided by experiments which manipulated the duration of daily exposures to the edible. In one such study (Domjan, 1976, Experiment 3), independent groups received access to a 2.0% solution of saccharin for 0, 5, 30, 120, or 240 min on each of two occasions prior to a 30-min single-stimulus test session with the saccharin solution conducted two days later. Each of Groups 5, 30, 120, and 240 given prior exposure to saccharin drank more of this substance during the test session than Group 0 which had not encountered the solution before. This finding demonstrates that as little as 5-min exposure to a novel edible on two occasions produces some reduction in neophobia. Comparison of the amounts of saccharin ingested by Groups 5, 30, 120, and 240 during the test session revealed a direct relationship between the loss of neophobia and the duration of prior saccharin exposure. Thus, neophobia reduction was a function of not only the presence or absence of exposure to saccharin but also the duration of this exposure.

ROLE OF VOLUNTARY INGESTION AND CONDITIONED REINFORCEMENT IN THE ATTENUATION OF NEOPHOBIA

In all of the experiments discussed so far, neophobia was reduced by permitting subjects to consume the novel flavored solutions. It was assumed that the critical aspect of this procedure was exposure to the novel substances. However, this exposure was often accompanied by repeated approach and withdrawal responses to the drinking tube, particularly during the first time the solution was presented, and this pattern of voluntary ingestion also may have contributed to the resultant attenuation of neophobia. In addition, subjects were always water deprived during their exposure to the novel fluids and received their daily 30-min access to tap water shortly afterward. Since their food source was dry pellets of Purina Chow, most of their daily food intake was probably also limited to the periods of fluid availability. Therefore, the novel fluid could have become a conditioned reinforcer through association with hunger and thirst reduction, (e.g., Revusky, 1967, 1968, 1974), and this conditioning may have been responsible for the loss of neophobia rather than mere exposure to the novel substances.

To determine whether approach and withdrawal behaviors and the possibility for conditioned reinforcement are necessary for the attenuation of neophobia, Siegel (1974) exposed rats to novel solutions after their daily access to water by infusing these fluids directly into the oral cavity using a fistula technique we developed earlier (Domjan & Wilson, 1972). Despite the fact that these subjects did not have the opportunity to either associate the novel solutions with hunger and thirst reduction or engage in voluntary ingestive behaviors, exposure to the novel flavors resulted in some loss of neophobia. This finding indicates that voluntary ingestion and conditioned reinforcement are not necessary for neophobia reduction.

Although voluntary ingestion and conditioned reinforcement appear not to be necessary for the loss of neophobia, these factors may contribute to the phenomenon. This possibility was evaluated in an experiment which compared the effectiveness of four different procedures in attenuating neophobia (Domjan, 1976, Experiment 5). One group (Si-D: saccharin-infused deprived) was exposed to a novel 2% solution of saccharin by having this fluid infused directly into the oral cavity through a fistula on 13 occasions while it was water deprived. During each saccharin presentation 1 ml of solution was infused over an 80-sec period. Twelve and a half min elapsed between successive presentations, and subjects were given access to water for 1 hr immediately after the session. Thus, subjects in Group Si-D had the opportunity to associate the novel saccharin solution with subsequent thirst reduction but could not engage in voluntary ingestive behaviors. Group Si-ND (saccharin-infused nondeprived) received the same saccharin exposures as Group Si-D except its contacts with the novel solution occurred 1 hr after access to tap water. Therefore, this group could not associate the saccharin solution with subsequent thirst reduction and also could not engage in voluntary ingestive behaviors. Groups FI-home and FI-app were allowed to ingest the saccharin freely in either the home cage or the infusion apparatus over the same period as the other groups received the saccharin infusions. These subjects drank a mean of 12.0 ml saccharin during this pre-test exposure and were given access to water for 1 hr immediately afterward. A fifth group (Group Wi) served as the control group and received oral infusions of water instead of saccharin during the treatment session.

Two days after these various treatments, each group received a 60-min single-stimulus test with the 2% saccharin solution. The cumulative amount consumed during successive 10-min periods of this test is displayed in Figure 3 for each group. As expected, subjects encountering the saccharin solution for the first time (Group Wi) drank very little. In contrast, each of the other groups, which had previous contacts with saccharin, drank more than Group Wi, indi-

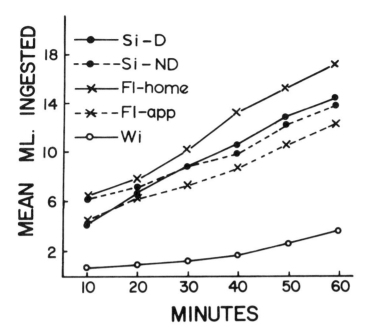

Figure 3
Mean cumulative intake of saccharin during a 60-min test for independent groups that previously had either no prior exposure to the saccharin solution (Group Wi), prior exposure to saccharin through free ingestion in the infusion apparatus (Group FI-app) or in the home cage (Group FI-home), or prior exposure to saccharin through infusions into the oral cavity while water deprived (Group Si-D) or in the absence of deprivation (Group Si-ND). (From Domjan, 1976.)

cating that their neophobia had been somewhat reduced. More importantly, however, all of the various saccharin preexposed groups drank comparable amounts, whether or not they freely ingested the saccharin during the prior exposure and whether or not they had the opportunity to associate the saccharin solution with hunger and thirst reduction. These findings confirm that voluntary ingestion and conditioned reinforcement are not necessary for neophobia reduction and indicate that in the present experiment these factors also did not contribute to the effect.[1]

POSTEXPOSURE VARIABLES AND
THE ATTENUATION OF NEOPHOBIA

The loss of neophobia produced by exposure to a novel edible is a function of not only the parameters of stimulus exposure but also

159

variables related to the postexposure period. Green and Parker (1975) found that the attenuation of neophobia is disrupted by exposure to other novel solutions following presentations of the novel target edible, with the disruption more pronounced if the interfering stimulus is presented sooner following the target edible. This finding appears to be related to the fact that the loss of neophobia produced by exposure to a novel stimulus gradually increases with time following the stimulus presentation (Green & Parker, 1975; Nachman & Jones, 1974). Subjects tested within minutes of their first contact with a novel edible show less neophobia reduction than those tested several hours later, and the full attenuating effects of a stimulus exposure on neophobia may not be evident until 6-8 hr following the stimulus presentation (Green & Parker, 1975; Nachman & Jones, 1974). It may be that reduction of neophobia is subject to disruption by exposure to other edibles only if the interfering stimuli are presented before neophobia reduction has completely developed following a stimulus presentation.

STIMULUS GENERALIZATION OF
THE ATTENUATION OF NEOPHOBIA

As other processes of behavioral plasticity, neophobia loss produced by exposure to a specific edible generalizes to other similar edibles, with progressively less generalization apparent if subjects are tested with increasingly different stimuli. In one experiment (Domjan & Gillan, 1976, Experiment 2), for example, extensive exposure to .5% saccharin also increased the subsequent intakes of .15% and 1.0% saccharin but not of 2% and 3% saccharin. Familiarization with 2% saccharin generalized to 1% and 3% saccharin but not to .15% or .5% saccharin. Furthermore, some of the evidence indicated that the attenuation of neophobia is more likely to generalize from low to high concentrations of saccharin than vice versa. While extensive exposure to 1% saccharin enhanced the subsequent consumption of a 3% solution, comparable familiarization with 3% saccharin did not reduce neophobia for the 1% solution.

RETENTION OF THE ATTENUATION OF NEOPHOBIA

Subjects appear to remember their loss of neophobia for edibles for long periods. Perfect retention has been reported over 17-day (Domjan, 1976) and 24-day (Siegel, 1974) intervals. However, some forgetting does occur over longer durations. In a recent unpublished experiment, we found that subjects tested with 2% saccharin 75 days after their initial contacts with the solution drank more than they consumed during the first exposure, but less neophobia loss was apparent with this 75-day retention interval than with retention intervals of 30 and 1 days. Others have also noted that the effects of exposure to edibles may be forgotten over long periods of time (e.g., Warren & Pfaffman, 1959). Additional research is necessary to identify variables which determine the nature of the retention function.

ASSOCIATIVE CONSEQUENCES OF
THE ATTENUATION OF NEOPHOBIA

Increased exposure to a novel edible not only reduces neophobia but also decreases the associability of that edible with subsequent postingestional consequences (e.g., Garcia & Koelling, 1967; McLaurin, Farley, & Scarborough, 1963; Revusky & Bedarf, 1967; Wittlin & Brookshire, 1968). Furthermore, every tested manipulation has comparable effects on neophobia reduction and this loss of associability. For example, just as increased stimulus exposure produces increased neophobia loss, increased stimulus exposure also produces greater decrements in associability (e.g., Domjan, 1972; Elkins, 1973; Fenwick, Mikulka, & Klein, 1975). Similarly, just as voluntary ingestion and the opportunity for conditioned reinforcement are not necessary for the reduction of neophobia, these factors are also not necessary of the loss of associability (Domjan, 1972). Finally, neither the attenuation of neophobia (Domjan, 1976) nor the decrease in associability (Domjan, 1972) is influenced by the subjects' drive state during the stimulus exposure.

The functional similarity of neophobia reduction and decreased stimulus associability has encouraged consideration of these phenomena as manifestations of a common process (Kalat & Rozin, 1973; Siegel, 1974). Kalat and Rozin (1973) suggested that both neophobia reduction and loss of associability occur because subjects learn that the edible is safe to eat as a result of being exposed to it in a nonaversive context. However, since familiar edibles are not comparable to other safety signals (Best, 1975), it seems inappropriate to refer to the effects of stimulus exposure as learned safety (see also Best & Barker; and Kalat, this volume). Other concepts such as learned non-correlation (Kalat, this volume), learned inattention (Lubow, Alek, & Arzy, 1975), or loss of salience (Rescorla, 1971; Mackintosh, 1975) may be useful in considering the associative consequences of stimulus exposure but fail to characterize the attenuation of neophobia. Without additional assumptions, it is not clear why subjects should consume more of non-correlated, unattended, or low-salient edibles.

The evidence reviewed indicates that neophobia for flavored solutions is attenuated by repeated exposure to these solutions, with the loss of neophobia directly related to the extent of stimulus exposure. Other factors such as voluntary ingestion or the opportunity to associate the novel solution with thirst and hunger reduction are not necessary for the attenuation of neophobia and probably make only a minor, if any, contribution to the effect ordinarily. Although neophobia reduction may be observed with both dilute and concentrated novel solutions, the greatest loss of neophobia occurs with intermediate concentrations. The attenuation of neophobia is more evident in single-stimulus than choice test procedures, is retained for at least several weeks without forgetting, and generalizes to other novel fluids along a solution-concentration gradient. Rather than being evident immediately, the attenuating effects of a stimulus exposure on neophobia gradually increase over several hours following the stimulus presentations, provided other novel edibles are not presented during this interval. Finally, the loss of neophobia is accompanied by a reduction of the associability of the edible with consequent unconditioned events.

On first exposure to a novel edible, subjects not only suppress their consumption but also display indications of arousal, such as rattling and biting the drinking tube. The suppression of intake may occur because contacts with the novel edible increase arousal above some optimal level (cf. Hebb, 1955; Leuba, 1955). With repeated exposure to the substance the arousing effects of novelty become habituated and the intake suppression is reduced. If it is further assumed that a stimulus has to be somewhat arousing to be conditionable, such a traditional formulation can explain not only why stimulus exposure produces loss of neophobia but also why such neophobia reduction is accompanied by a decrement in stimulus associability.

It is important to note that the above hypothesis does not assume that ingestion is directly suppressed by high levels of arousal. Rather, the intake suppression is attributed to an ingestion-produced increase in arousal which is aversive because it elevates arousal above some preferred level. This suggests that if the level of arousal is decreased by the absence of novel stimulation, subjects may prefer to ingest a slightly novel edible which increases arousal somewhat but not above the preferred level. The arousal hypothesis also predicts that neophobia will be enhanced in subjects which are already aroused above the preferred level. Both of these implications have some empirical support. Rats given one of two solutions to drink before a preference test usually prefer the other relatively more novel substance (Holman, 1973; Morrison, 1974). Water-deprived rats appear to be more neophobic toward edibles than nondeprived rats (Peck & Ader, 1964), and rats suffering from aversive drug treatments are more neophobic than normal rats (see discussion of illness-mediated neophobia below).

ENHANCEMENT OF NEOPHOBIA FOR EDIBLES

Early in the research on learned modifications in food selection, it was observed that neophobia for edibles can be substantially enhanced by repeated poisoning experiences (Richter, 1953; Rzoska, 1953). Although the behavioral manifestations of this increased finickiness were unmistakable, the early observations failed to specify the variables and mechanisms involved in the phenomenon. Our recent research has identified several of these variables and suggests that two different mechanisms operate to enhance neophobia. One of these, referred to as conditioned-aversion-mediated neophobia, involves the novelty-dependent stimulus generalization of conditioned taste aversions and increases neophobia for a considerable period following poisoning (Domjan, 1975). The second mechanism, referred to as illness-mediated neophobia, increases neophobia for only a limited period following administration of a toxic agent and probably reflects direct effects of the poison administration (Domjan, in press).

CONDITIONED-AVERSION-MEDIATED NEOPHOBIA

Effects of Conditioning Taste Aversions. The increased food finickiness observed in the early experiments (Richter, 1953; Rzoska, 1953) was produced by repeatedly giving subjects access to poisoned baits. The phenomenon may have been a reaction to either the repeated illness experiences or the repeated pairings of ingested substances (poisoned bait) with subsequent illness. In order to decide between these alternatives, we compared the neophobia-enhancing effects of four different treatments in domesticated rats (Domjan, 1975, Experiment 1). Intraperitoneal injections of lithium chloride were used to provide temporary toxicosis. Group Sacc-Li received access to a .2% saccharin solution before being injected with lithium. Group Sacc-Na received the same saccharin exposure but was injected with physiological saline instead of lithium, and Group H_2O-Na was injected with saline after exposure to water. The fourth group (Li) did not receive access to any solution for 23.5 hr before being in-

163

jected with lithium. These treatments were executed four times with a 3-4-day interval between successive administrations. Subjects then received two 15-min single-stimulus test sessions, each following 23 hr water deprivation. During one test, a novel 5% solution of casein hydrolysate was available; during the other test, tap water was provided. Cumulative intakes during each of these tests were obtained at 1-min intervals, and these values are presented in Figure 4.

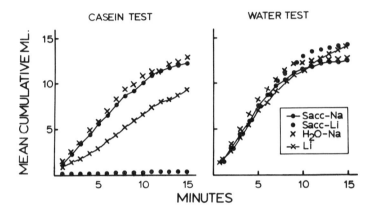

Figure 4
Mean cumulative intake of casein hydrolysate and water in subjects previously poisoned after access to saccharin (Group Sacc-Li), poisoned in the absence of edibles (Group Li), not poisoned after access to saccharin (Group Sacc-Na), or neither poisoned nor exposed to saccharin (Group H_2O-Na). (From Domjan, 1975.)

No significant differences in water consumption were observed among the groups. In contrast, the various group treatments resulted in differential consumption of the novel casein solution. The two nonpoisoned groups (Sacc-Na and H_2O-Na) drank the most casein and did not differ from each other. Group Li, which had been poisoned in the absence of edibles, drank slightly less than the nonpoisoned groups, this difference being statistically significant only at the end of the first 5 min of the test. The greatest suppression of casein intake occurred in Group Sacc-Li which had been poisoned after access to saccharin. Subjects in this group drank less than 1 ml of the casein solution. These results demonstrate that a prominent increase in neophobia for edibles occurs several days after repeated lithium injections only if these injections are administered in conjunction with exposure to some other ingested substance. Lithium administrations in the absence of edibles produced only slight and transitory enhanced neophobia in the test session conducted several days later. In other experiments (e.g., Domjan, 1975, Experiment 3B) we have failed to find even such small effects of lithium-alone treatments.

Effects of Extinguishing Conditioned Taste Aversions. Subjects in Group Sacc-Li of the experiment described above not only experienced the aversive lithium effects but also learned an aversion to a saccharin solution as a result. Our next experiment (Domjan, 1975, Experiment 2) was designed to determine whether the casein neophobia of these subjects was mediated by their learned aversions to saccharin. The learned saccharin aversions of half the subjects in Group Sacc-Li were extinguished by providing *ad libitum* access to saccharin for two days (Extinction sub-group), while the remaining subjects received access to tap water (Control sub-group). The water deprivation schedule was then reinstituted, and each sub-group received two test sessions, one with saccharin and the other with casein. Cumulative intakes during each of these tests are displayed in Figure 5.

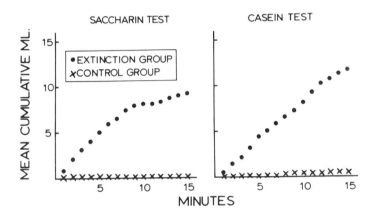

Figure 5
Mean cumulative intake of saccharin and casein for control subjects and subjects whose saccharin aversions were partially extinguished before the test sessions. (From Domjan, 1975.)

Extinction of the conditioned aversion to saccharin also reduced the suppression in consumption of the novel casein solution. Even though the Control and Extinction sub-groups received the identical lithium injections, only the Control sub-group which maintained its aversion to saccharin also retained its suppression of casein consumption. This outcome demonstrates that avoidance of a novel casein solution in subjects repeatedly poisoned after saccharin exposure is mediated by the extent to which these subjects avoid the saccharin solution. Therefore, the casein avoidance may represent the stimulus generalization of this conditioned saccharin aversion (cf. Nachman, 1963).

Novelty-Dependent Stimulus Generalization of Conditioned Taste Aversions. If the suppression of casein intake following saccharin-lithium treatment reflects the stimulus generalization of a learned saccharin aversion, one would not expect suppressions in the intake of all novel solutions following saccharin-aversion conditioning. Subsequent experiments (Domjan, 1975, Experiments 3 and 4) confirmed this prediction. Following saccharin-lithium pairings, subjects again avoided the novel casein solution but did not suppress their intakes of a novel vinegar flavor, even though other evidence indicated that the vinegar solution was just as unfamiliar as the novel casein. Thus, novelty was not a sufficient condition for the avoidance of test solutions following saccharin-aversion conditioning. However, these experiments also indicated that test-stimulus novelty was necessary for such avoidance. Increased familiarity with the casein solution substantially reduced the suppression in casein intake observed following saccharin-lithium treatments.

The present findings encourage the conclusion that the enhanced neophobia observed several days after repeated poisonings administered in conjunction with an edible represents the novelty-dependent stimulus generalization of a conditioned food-aversion. The phenomenon is therefore referred to as conditioned-aversion-mediated neophobia. This associative interpretation of the enhanced neophobia produced by repeated post-ingestional poisonings is consistent with not only the results described above but also the previous observations of Richter (1953) and Rzoska (1953) as well as the more recent reports of Rozin (1968) and Carroll, Dinc, Levy, and Smith (1975).

ILLNESS-MEDIATED NEOPHOBIA

Evidence of learned-aversion-mediated neophobia is usually obtained several days after toxicosis, at a time when presumably subjects are entirely recovered from the malaise. A different type of enhanced neophobia may be observed if subjects are tested shortly following poisoning when they are probably still suffering from the toxin effects.

Basic Demonstration. Like the experiments on aversion-mediated neophobia, our studies of this illness-mediated neophobia (Domjan, in press) also involved lithium chloride as the aversive agent. The first experiment was designed to evaluate effects of the amount of

166

lithium administered on consumption of a novel .5% solution of saccharin. Independent groups were injected with various doses of lithium ranging from .3 to 3.0 mEq/kg, while a control group received an injection of physiological saline. Thirty min after this treatment, subjects were given either water or a .5% saccharin solution to drink for 60 min. The total amount of each solution consumed is presented in Figure 6. Control subjects not injected with lithium drank slightly more water than saccharin. As the dose of lithium was increased, a dose-related decrement in saccharin consumption occurred. However, increasing amounts of lithium had no detectable effect on water drinking.

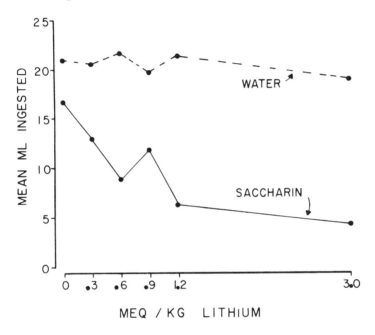

Figure 6
Amount of water and .5% saccharin ingested during a 60-min test started 30 min after the injection of various amounts of lithium chloride. (From Domjan, in press.)

Injections of lithium not only produced suppressions in the total amount of saccharin consumed, but also altered the pattern of saccharin drinking during the 60-min test session. Figure 7 illustrates the within-session cumulative saccharin intakes of each group. The control Group Na drank some saccharin during each successive 10-min period of the test session. This was also true for subjects injected with .3 mEq/kg lithium. In contrast, each of the other lithium-treated groups showed a suppression of intake following some drinking during the first 10 min of the test. This suppression of consumption was temporary in subjects injected with .6, .9, and 1.2 mEq/kg of lithium but persisted during the entire session in subjects injected with 3.0 mEq/kg.

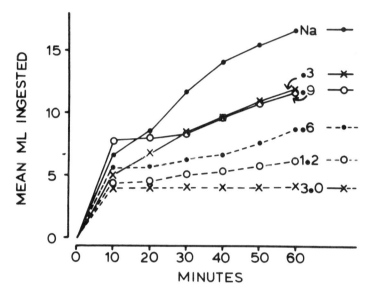

Figure 7
Mean cumulative intake of .5% saccharin during a 60-min test started 30 min after the injection of saline (Na) or .3, .6, .9, 1.2, and 3.0 mEq/kg lithium chloride. (From Domjan, in press.)

Limitation of the Intake Suppression to Novel Solutions. Since the lithium injections presumably create a certain degree of discomfort, it is not surprising that the injections also disrupt consummatory behavior. However, the suppression of saccharin intake described above does not reflect a nonspecific disturbance of drinking since a comparable disruption of water intake was not observed. Lithium injections appear to suppress consumption of only certain types of edibles. Subsequent experiments demonstrated that the effect occurs with both palatable and unpalatable novel solutions (Domjan, in press, Experiment 2). However, lithium-induced suppressions are not observed with highly familiar substances. This result was obtained in an experiment which involved raising independent groups of subjects with either a 3% solution of vinegar or a .15%

168

solution of saccharin as their only fluid (Domjan, in press, Experiment 5). When the subjects reached 55-65 days of age, their consumption of the vinegar and saccharin solutions was measured starting 30 min after injections of lithium or physiological saline. Figure 8 shows the cumulative intakes of each solution for the saccharin-reared rats. Treatment with lithium suppressed consumption of the novel vinegar solution but did not disrupt drinking of the familiar saccharin flavor. Test results obtained from the vinegar-reared subjects confirmed these findings in that lithium-induced suppressions of intake were observed when subjects were tested with the novel solution (saccharin) but not when consumption of the familiar substance (vinegar) was measured. The fact that suppressions in the intake of edibles shortly following lithium toxicosis occur for novel but not highly familiar edibles justifies considering this phenomenon as an example of increased neophobia.

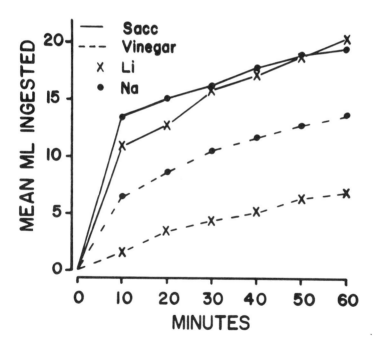

Figure 8
Mean cumulative intake of .15% saccharin and 3% vinegar in saccharin-reared rats tested starting 30 min after the injection of lithium (Li) or physiological saline (Na). (From Domjan, in press.)

169

Limitation of the Intake Suppression to the Presumed Illness Period. Our next experiment (Domjan, in press, Experiment 3) was designed to determine how long the enhancement of neophobia persists following lithium treatment. Independent groups received a 60-min drinking test with a novel 1.0% solution of saccharin starting at various periods after the injections of 1.8 mEq/kg lithium chloride. An additional group was tested after an injection of physiological saline. The results are presented in Figure 9. Subjects drank more if the start of their drinking session was delayed a longer period following the lithium injection. In fact, the saccharin intakes of groups tested starting 45, 75, 90, and 120 min after lithium treatment were not significantly less than the consumption of saline-injected controls. In contrast, significant suppressions of drinking were observed in groups tested starting 5, 15, 25, 35, and 55 min after lithium injection. These results demonstrate that lithium administered in the absence of the edibles increases neophobia for only

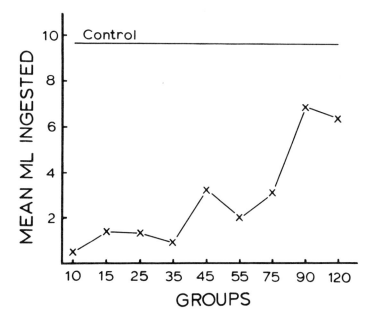

Figure 9
Amount of 1.0% saccharin ingested during a 60-min test session administered to independent groups starting 10, 15, 25, 35, 45, 55, 75, 90, and 120 min following the injection of lithium. The control level indicates the intakes of saline-injected subjects. (Redrawn from Domjan, in press.)

170

a limited period and suggest that the effect is observed only if subjects are presumably still experiencing the lithium malaise. Therefore, this enhancement of neophobia is referred to as illness-mediated rather than conditioned-aversion-mediated neophobia.

Generality of Illness-Mediated Neophobia. Investigators focussing on somewhat different problems have also observed suppressions in the intake of saccharin solutions but not of water in water-reared rats following exposure to radiation (Carroll & Smith, 1974; Smith & Schaeffer, 1967) and injections of cyclophosphamide (Barker, Suarez, & Gray, 1974; Green, McGowan, Garcia, & Ervin, 1968). Although it was not demonstrated that these effects were a function of the novelty of the saccharin solutions, these findings suggest that illness-mediated neophobia also may be produced by a variety of aversive agents other than lithium chloride.

COMPARISON OF CONDITIONED-AVERSION-MEDIATED AND ILLNESS-MEDIATED NEOPHOBIA

Conditioned-aversion-mediated and illness-mediated neophobia differ in numerous procedural and functional respects. Conditioned-aversion-mediated neophobia occurs only if subjects acquire and retain an aversion because of the poisoning experience, and this aversion generalizes to other novel substances. The increased neophobia thus produced is evident for at least several days after toxicosis. In contrast, illness-mediated neophobia does not depend on the consumption of a conditionable edible prior to toxicosis, and the increased neophobia is evident for only a limited period following the toxin administration. Since conditioned-aversion-mediated neophobia involves the stimulus generalization of a learned aversion, the increased neophobia occurs only with novel solutions which presumably are sufficiently similar to the conditioned edible to permit such generalization. In contrast, no such stimulus limitation appears to exist for illness-mediated neophobia. We have observed illness-mediated neophobia with every novel solution we tested, including various concentrations of casein, vinegar, and saccharin.

In addition to the above-mentioned differences between conditioned-aversion-mediated and illness-mediated neophobia, the two types of increased neophobia are also differentially influenced by increased familiarity with the test solution and produce different patterns of consumption. These findings are illustrated by one of our previously unpublished experiments in which a 5% mixture of casein hydrolysate served as the test solution. The casein was novel for half the subjects and slightly familiar for the remaining rats, with

171

familiarization accomplished by giving the latter subjects access to the casein solution for 30 min daily for 8 days as their only fluid. Treatments designed to produce conditioned-aversion-mediated neophobia, illness-mediated neophobia, and control levels of casein intake were compared in both the casein-novel and casein-familiarized subjects. Several days before the 60-min single-stimulus casein test, SLi groups received a 16 ml/kg injection of .15 M lithium chloride after drinking a .2% saccharin solution for 10 min. Li groups also received 10 min access to saccharin on this day but did not get injected with lithium until 30 min before the casein test. The Control groups received the same procedure as the SLi groups except for receiving injections of physiological saline instead of lithium following saccharin exposure. The SLi treatment was considered to produce conditioned-aversion-mediated neophobia for casein since the lithium injections were administered immediately after saccharin exposure and presumably conditioned a saccharin aversion. The Li treatment was considered to produce illness-mediated neophobia for casein since the lithium injections were administered in the absence of edibles, and subjects were tested with casein at a time when they were presumably still suffering from the lithium malaise.

Mean cumulative intakes of the casein solution are displayed in Figure 10 for each group. The left panel of the figure shows that among subjects for which the casein solution was novel, both the SLi and Li treatments produced marked suppressions of consumption. The conditioned-aversion-mediated neophobia associated with the SLi treatment resulted in a suppression of intake during the first part of the test session, with a gradual recovery thereafter. In contrast, the illness-mediated neophobia associated with the Li treatment resulted in almost normal drinking during the first part of the test session, with the intake-suppression apparent only later. The right panel of Figure 10 illustrates that limited familiarization with the casein solution entirely eliminated the conditioned-aversion-mediated neophobia associated with the SLi treatment. However, suppressions of casein intake were still apparent with the Li treatment. Analysis of these findings confirmed that while the reduction in casein novelty eliminated conditioned-aversion-mediated neophobia, this manipulation did not have a statistically significant effect on illness-mediated neophobia.

Limited familiarity with the test solution has also failed to reduce illness-mediated neophobia in other situations (Domjan, in press, Experiment 4). In contrast, as we noted earlier, raising subjects with a flavored solution as their only fluid does eliminate illness-mediated neophobia (Domjan, in press, Experiment 5). These find-

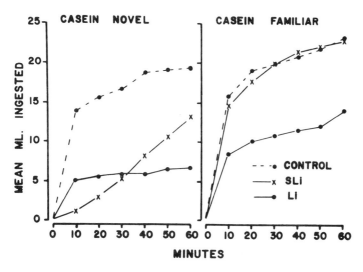

Figure 10
Mean cumulative intake of 5% casein hydrolysate among subjects never before exposed to casein and subjects previously exposed to casein on 8 occasions. Several days before the casein test all subjects were exposed to saccharin for 10 min. This saccharin exposure was immediately followed by a lithium injection for the SLi groups, while the control groups were injected with physiological saline. The Li groups were injected with lithium 30 min before the casein test.

ings may reflect the fact that illness-mediated neophobia is attenuated only by extensive familiarity with the test solution. However, an alternative and more intriguing possibility is that subjects have to experience a flavored solution during a critical stage in life in order to learn to consume normal amounts of it when they are suffering from temporary malaise (see Capretta; and Hogan, this volume, for further discussion of possible critical-period effects in food selection).

ENHANCEMENT OF NEOPHOBIA:
SUMMARY AND DISCUSSION

The effects of a poisoning experience on the subsequent consumption of novel edibles depends on how and when the poison is administered. If the poison is administered in such a way that subjects acquire an aversion to a particular food, a persistent increased neophobia will be observed to novel edibles which are somehow similar to the conditioned aversive food. If the poison is administered in the absence of prior exposure to a conditionable substance, increased neophobia will be observed only as long as subjects

173

are presumably suffering from the toxin malaise. However, this latter increased neophobia will be evident with a wide variety of novel edibles. The conditioned-aversion-mediated neophobia results in a suppression of intake of novel edibles which is very similar to what is observed with conditioned-aversive substances: subjects hesitate to drink initially but consume increasing amounts as their aversion is extinguished. In contrast, the illness-mediated neophobia is usually not observed until subjects have consumed several milliliters of the novel edible during the test session.

Associative mechanisms are clearly responsible for conditioned-aversion-mediated neophobia since this phenomenon is not observed following repeated poisonings administered without exposure to a conditionable edible and because the effect is dramatically attenuated by extinguishing food aversions which may have been conditioned by the poisonings. Illness-mediated neophobia may also reflect an associative process, i.e., association of the test solution with the malaise presumably present during the test session. However, several aspects of the phenomenon are unexpected on the basis of such an interpretation: (1) Taste-aversion conditioning is easily disrupted by as little as a single nonpoisoned preconditioning exposure to the taste stimulus (Kalat & Rozin, 1973; Siegel, 1974). In contrast, as many as 8 30-min exposures to casoin (see experiment described above) and 25 30-min exposures to .15% saccharin (Domjan, in press, Experiment 4) have been noted not to attenuate significantly illness-mediated neophobia to these solutions. (2) Illness-mediated neophobia is not observed with lithium doses as low as .3 mEq/kg (Domjan, in press, Experiment 1) even though such doses have been found to condition taste aversions (Nachman & Ashe, 1973). (3) Studies specifically designed to investigate taste aversions conditioned as a result of exposure to the taste following drug injection have generally found a low correspondence between the suppression of intake observed shortly following drug injection and the degree of aversion subjects display during test sessions conducted one or more days later (Barker et al., 1974; Barker & Smith, 1974). Consistent with these findings, we have failed to find successful backward taste-aversion conditioning with a .15% saccharin solution presented 30 min after lithium treatment, even though illness-mediated neophobia to .15% saccharin is evident with such a lithium-to-saccharin interval (Domjan, in press, Experiments 4 and 5). Given that several aspects of illness-mediated neophobia are inconsistent with an associative interpretation, we are encouraged to regard the phenomenon as a sensitization effect of poisoning rather than as a special case of taste-aversion conditioning.

174

FOOTNOTES

[1]It is important to note that in both the present experiment as well as in the study by Siegel (1974), subjects were adapted to the oral infusion procedure before novel solutions were presented with the infusion technique. As was noted earlier, the oral infusion of novel fluids appears to be aversive. We have found that if subjects are not sufficiently adapted to the infusion procedure, the aversiveness of the infusions may become associated with the flavor of the infused fluid, with the result that such exposure to novel substances does not elevate subsequent intakes.

ACKNOWLEDGEMENTS

Preparation of the manuscript and original research reported in this chapter were supported by funds from the Spencer Foundation, the Public Health Service (Grant No. MH 25007-O1A1), and the National Science Foundation (Grant No. BMS 74-17829) to M. Domjan and a Biomedical Sciences Support Grant to the University of Texas. The thoughtful assistance of numerous students including D. Gillan, B. Gregg, and J. Lewis is gratefully acknowledged.

REFERENCES

Barker, L. M., & Smith, J. C. A comparison of taste aversions induced by radiation and lithium chloride in CS-US and US-CS paradigms. **Journal of Comparative and Physiological Psychology,** 1974, **87,** 644-654.

Barker, L. M., Suarez, E. M., & Gray, D. Backward conditioning of taste aversions in rats using cyclophosphamide as the US. **Physiological Psychology,** 1974, **2,** 117-119.

Barnett, S. A. Behaviour components in the feeding of wild and laboratory rats. **Behaviour,** 1956, **9,** 24-43.

Barnett, S. A. Experiments on "neophobia" in wild and laboratory rats. **British Journal of Psychology,** 1958, **49,** 195-201.

Barnett, S. A., & Spencer, M. M. Experiments on the food preferences of wild rats *(Rattus Norvegicus Berkenhout).* **Journal of Hygiene,** 1953, **51,** 16-34.

Beebe-Center, J. G., Black, P., Hoffman, A. C., & Wade, M. Relative per diem consumption as a measure of preference in the rat. **Journal of Comparative and Physiological Psychology,** 1948, **41,** 239-251.

Best, M. R. Conditioned and latent inhibition in taste-aversion learning: Clarifying the role of learned safety. **Journal of Experimental Psychology: Animal Behavior Processes,** 1975, **1,** 97-113.

Burghardt, G. M., & Hess, E. H. Food imprinting in the snapping turtle, *Chelydra serpentina.* **Science,** 1966, **151,** 108-109.

Capretta, P. J. Establishment of food preferences in the chicken *(Gallus gallus).* **Animal Behaviour,** 1969, **17,** 229-231.

Capretta, P. J., & Bronstein, P. M. Effects of food ingestion on later food preferences in chicks. **Proceedings of the 75th Annual Convention of the American Psychological Association,** 1967, **2,** 109-110.

Capretta, P. J., & Rawls, L. H. Establishment of a flavor preference in rats: Importance of nursing and weaning experience. **Journal of Comparative and Physiological Psychology,** 1974, **86,** 670-673.

Carroll, M. E., Dinc, H. I., Levy, C. J., & Smith, J. C. Demonstrations of neophobia and enhanced neophobia in the albino rat. **Journal of Comparative and Physiological Psychology,** 1975, **89,** 457-467.

Carroll, M. E., & Smith, J. C. Time course of radiation-induced taste-aversion conditioning. **Physiology and Behavior,** 1974, **13,** 809-812.

Coppinger, R. P. The effect of experience and novelty on avian feeding behavior with reference to the evolution of warning coloration in butterflies. I: Reactions of wild-caught blue jays to novel insects. **Behaviour,** 1969, **35,** 45-60.

Coppinger, R. P. The effect of experience and novelty on avian feeding behavior with reference to the evolution of warning coloration in butterflies. II: Reactions of naive birds to novel insects. **The American Naturalist,** 1970, **104,** 323-335.

Domjan, M. CS preexposure in taste-aversion learning: Effects of deprivation and preexposure duration. **Learning and Motivation,** 1972, **3,** 389-402.

Domjan, M. Poison-induced neophobia: Role of stimulus generalization of conditioned taste aversions. **Animal Learning and Behavior,** 1975, **3,** 205-211.

Domjan, M. Determinants of the enhancement of flavored-water intake by prior exposure. **Journal of Experimental Psychology: Animal Behavior Processes,** 1976, **2,** 17-27.

Domjan, M. Selective suppression of drinking during a limited period following aversive drug treatment in rats. **Journal of Experimental Psychology: Animal Behavior Processes,** in press.

Domjan, M., & Bowman, T. G. Learned safety and the CS-US delay gradient in taste-aversion learning. **Learning and Motivation,** 1974, **5,** 409-423.

Domjan, M., & Gillan, D. Role of novelty in the aversion for increasingly concentrated saccharin solutions. **Physiology and Behavior,** 1976, **16,** 537-542.

Domjan, M., & Gregg, B. Comparison of choice and single-stimulus procedures in the production and detection of learned increases in flavored-water intake. In preparation, 1976.

Domjan, M., & Wilson, N. E. Contribution of ingestive behaviors to taste-aversion learning in the rat. **Journal of Comparative and Physiological Psychology,** 1972, **80,** 403-412.

Dragoin, W., McCleary, G. E., & McCleary, P. A comparison of two methods of measuring conditioned taste aversions. **Behavior Research Methods and Instrumentation,** 1971, **3,** 309-310.

Elkins, R. L. Attenuation of drug-induced bait shyness to a palatable solution as an increasing function of its availability prior to conditioning. **Behavioral Biology,** 1973, **9,** 221-226.

Fenwick, S., Mikulka, P. J., & Klein, S. The effect of different levels of preexposure to sucrose on the acquisition and extinction of a conditioned aversion. **Behavioral Biology,** 1975, **14,** 231-235.

Garcia, J., & Koelling, R. A. A comparison of aversions induced by x-rays, toxins, and drugs in the rat. **Radiation Research Supplement,** 1967, **7,** 439-450.

Gentile, R. L. The role of taste preference in the eating behavior of the albino rat. **Physiology and Behavior,** 1970, **5,** 311-316.

Green, K. F., McGowan, B. K., Garcia, J., & Ervin, F. R. Onset of bait-shyness. **Proceedings of the 76th Annual Convention of the American Psychological Association,** 1968, **3,** 295-296.

Green, K. F., & Parker, L. A. Gustatory memory: Incubation and interference. **Behavioral Biology,** 1975, **13,** 359-367.

Grote, F. W. Jr., & Brown, R. T. Conditioned taste aversions: Two-stimulus tests are more sensitive than one-stimulus tests. **Behavior Research Methods and Instrumentation,** 1971, **3,** 311-312.

Hebb, D. O. Drives and the C.N.S. (conceptual nervous system). **Psychological Review,** 1955, **62,** 243-254.

Hogan, J. A. An experimental study of conflict and fear: An analysis of behaviour of young chickens toward mealworm. I: The behaviour of chicks which do not eat the mealworm. **Behaviour,** 1965, **25,** 45-97.

Hollinger, M., & Roberts, L. J. Overcoming food dislikes: A study with evaporated milk. **Journal of Home Economics,** 1929, **21,** 923-932.

Holman, E. W. Temporal properties of gustatory spontaneous alternation in rats. **Journal of Comparative and Physiological Psychology,** 1973, **85,** 536-539.

Kalat, J. W., & Rozin, P. "Learned safety" as a mechanism in long-delay taste-aversion learning in rats. **Journal of Comparative and Physiological Psychology,** 1973, **83,** 198-207.

Leuba, C. Toward some integration of learning theories: The concept of optimal stimulation. **Psychological Reports,** 1955, **1,** 27-33.

Lubow, R. E., Alek, M., & Arzy, J. Behavioral decrement following stimulus preexposure: Effects of number of preexposure, presence of a second stimulus, and interstimulus interval in children and adults. **Journal of Experimental Psychology: Animal Behavior Processes,** 1975, **1,** 178-188.

Mackay, B. Conditioned food aversions produced by toxicosis in Atlantic cod. **Behavioral Biology,** 1974, **12,** 347-355.

Mackintosh, N. J. A theory of attention: Variations in the associability of stimuli with reinforcement. **Psychological Review,** 1975, **82,** 276-298.

Maslow, A. H. The "emotion" of disgust in dogs. **Journal of Comparative Psychology,** 1932, **14,** 401-407.

McLaurin, W. A., Farley, J. A., & Scarborough, B. B. Inhibitory effect of preirradiation saccharin habituation on conditioned avoidance behavior. **Radiation Research,** 1963, **18,** 473-478.

Miller, H. C. The behavior of the pumpkinseed sunfish *Lepomis gilbosus* (Linneaus), with notes on the behavior of other species of *Lepomis* and pigmy sunfish, *Elassoma everglade.* **Behaviour,** 1963, **22,** 88-151.

Mitchell, D. Experiments on neophobia in wild and laboratory rats: A reevaluation. **Journal of Comparative and Physiological Psychology,** 1976, **90,** 190-197.

Morrell, G. M., & Turner, J. R. G. Experiments on mimicry, I. The response of wild birds to artificial prey. **Behaviour,** 1970, **36,** 116-130.

Morrison, G. R. Alterations in palatability of nutrients for the rat as a result of prior tasting. **Journal of Comparative and Physiological Psychology,** 1974, **86,** 56-61.

Nachman, M. Learned aversion to the taste of lithium chloride and generalization to other salts. **Journal of Comparative and Physiological Psychology,** 1963, **56,** 343-349.

Nachman, M., & Ashe, J. H. Learned taste aversions in rats as a function of dosage, concentration, and route of administration of LiCl. **Physiology and Behavior,** 1973, **10,** 73-78.

Nachman, M., & Jones, D. R. Learned taste aversions over long delays in rats: The role of learned safety. **Journal of Comparative and Physiological Psychology,** 1974, **86,** 949-956.

Navarick, D. J., & Strouthes, A. Relative intake of saccharin and water on a restricted drinking schedule. **Psychonomic Science,** 1969, **15,** 158-159.

Peck, J. H., & Ader, R. Illness-induced taste aversion under states of deprivation and satiation. **Animal Learning and Behavior,** 1974, **2,** 6-8.

Rabinowitch, V. The role of experience in the development of food preferences in gull chicks. **Animal Behaviour,** 1968, **16,** 425-428.

Rabinowitch, V. The role of experience in the development and retention of seed preferences in zebra finches. **Behaviour,** 1969, **33,** 222-236.

Rescorla, R. A. Summation and retardation tests of latent inhibition. **Journal of Comparative and Physiological Psychology,** 1971, **75,** 77-81.

Revusky, S. H. Hunger level during food consumption: Effects on subsequent preference. **Psychonomic Science,** 1967, **7,** 109-110.

Revusky, S. H. Effects of thirst level during consumption of flavored water on subsequent preference. **Journal of Comparative and Physiological Psychology,** 1968, **66,** 777-779.

178

Revusky, S. Retention of a learned increase in the preference for a flavored solution. **Behavioral Biology,** 1974, **11,** 121-125.

Revusky, S. H., & Bedarf, E. W. Association of illness with prior ingestion of novel foods. **Science,** 1967, **155,** 219-220.

Richter, C. P. Experimentally produced behavior reactions to food poisoning in wild and domesticated rats. **Annals of the New York Academy of Sciences,** 1953, **56,** 225-239.

Rozin, P. Specific aversions and neophobia resulting from vitamin deficiency or poisoning in half-wild and domestic rats. **Journal of Comparative and Physiological Psychology,** 1968, **66,** 82-88.

Rozin, P. The selection of food by rats, humans, and other animals. In J. Rosenblatt, R. A. Hinde, C. Beer, & E. Shaw (Eds.), **Advances in the study of behavior** (Vol. 6). New York: Academic Press, 1976.

Rzoska, J. Bait shyness, a study in rat behaviour. **British Journal of Animal Behaviour,** 1953, **1,** 128-135.

Sheffield, F. D., & Roby, T. B. Reward value of non-nutritive sweet taste. **Journal of Comparative and Physiological Psychology,** 1950, **43,** 471-482.

Shortens, M. The reaction of the brown rat toward changes in its environment. In D. Chitty (Ed.), **Control of rats and mice** (Vol. 2). Oxford: Clarendon Press, 1954.

Siegel, S. Flavor preexposure and "learned safety." **Journal of Comparative and Physiological Psychology,** 1974, **87,** 1073-1082.

Singh, D. Role of preoperative experience on reaction to quinine taste in hypothalamic hyperphagic rats. **Journal of Comparative and Physiological Psychology,** 1974, **86,** 674-678.

Smith, J. C., & Schaeffer, R. W. Development of water and saccharin preferences after simultaneous exposures to saccharin solution and gamma rays. **Journal of Comparative and Physiological Psychology,** 1967, **63,** 434-438.

Warren, R. P., & Pfaffmann, C. Early experience and taste aversion. **Journal of Comparative and Physiological Psychology,** 1959, **52,** 263-266.

Wittlin, W. A., & Brookshire, K. H. Apomorphine-induced conditioned aversion to a novel food. **Psychonomic Science,** 1968, **12,** 217-218.

Young, P. T. Studies of food preference, appetite, and dietary habit. I. Running activity and dietary habit of the rat in relation to food preference. **Journal of Comparative Psychology,** 1944, **37,** 327-370.

179

VIII

ASSOCIATIVE AND NON-ASSOCIATIVE FACTORS IN LEARNED FOOD PREFERENCES

DONNA M. ZAHORIK
Cornell University

Most of the literature dealing with the role of learning in food selection focusses on the formation of associations between food cues and the unpleasant gastrointestinal consequences of X-irradiation, poisoning, and vitamin deficiencies—the "learned aversions" which are discussed in many chapters in this volume. In spite of the enormous body of data suggesting that many species can learn to avoid foods which have been paired with illness, there has been relatively little research on changes in food preferences due to association between food cues[1] and the *positive* consequences of recovery from illness. Yet it seems reasonable to suppose that animals which can learn about the deleterious effects of ingestion may also be able to learn about its beneficial effects, and that learning about both kinds of consequences could serve an adaptive function in food selection.

It has been known for many years that thiamine deficient rats will ingest large quantities of foods containing the required nutrient and that these foods continue to be eaten in large amounts even after recovery from deficiency is complete. Such observations led several investigators to conclude that learned preferences for food cues associated with recovery from deficiency might play some role in producing the apparent "specific hunger" for thiamine (Harris, Clay, Hargreaves, & Ward, 1933; Scott & Verney, 1947; Rodgers, 1967). While these studies and other more recent experiments clearly show that the procedure of pairing a distinctive food with recovery from illness increases the preference for that food (relative to baseline consumption of the distinctive substance and relative to consumption of other available foods), none of these studies offers unequivocal evidence that the observed changes in preference are due to associations between food cues and the physiological changes which constitute recovery from illness.

To understand the controversies surrounding the role of associative learning in altering responses to foods paired with recovery from illness, it is convenient to consider a classification of foods first proposed by Rozin and Kalat (1971). These authors suggested that foods fall into three categories, based on the amount and nature of the animal's experience with each food: (1) Foods which have been paired with illness are categorized as *familiar-aversive*. (2) Foods which have never been sampled are classified as *novel*. (3) Foods which have been ingested previously but without any unpleasant consequences are classified as *familiar-safe* (Figure 1). There is abundant evidence that rats respond differently to these three categories of ingested substances. The literature on neophobia indicates that rats prefer familiar-safe foods to novel foods (Barnett, 1963; Rozin, 1968), and many studies of taste aversions indicate that rats prefer novel foods to familiar-aversive ones (see Rozin, 1967; Garcia & Ervin, 1968, for numerous examples). Thus, the three categories show clear differences on a dimension of preference, ranging from familiar-aversive foods (least preferred) to familiar-safe foods (most preferred).

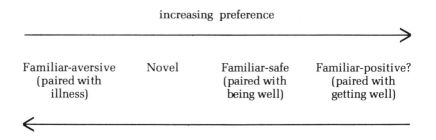

Figure 1
Classification of foods on the basis of the amount and consequences of the previous experience.

Given these categories, is there any evidence for the existence of a fourth category of foods which we might call *familiar-positive*? Are foods which have been paired with *recovery* from illness treated any differently than foods presented in the *absence* of illness? If rats associate food cues with relief from symptoms of illness and subsequent responses are altered by such associations, we would expect foods paired with *getting well* to be preferred to foods paired with *being well,* and we might also expect foods paired with getting well to be even less readily associated with illness than are other familiar foods. In fact, most studies of responses to foods which have been paired with recovery from illness simply do not offer any convincing evidence that these foods are treated any differently from familiar-safe foods (Rozin & Kalat, 1971; McFarland, 1973). Nevertheless, these experiments provide some information relevant to the place of recovery flavors in Rozin and Kalat's classification of foods, and they point out some of the methodological problems encountered in trying to resolve the issue of the need for a familiar-positive category.

FLAVORS PAIRED WITH RECOVERY ARE PREFERRED
TO FLAVORS PAIRED WITH ILLNESS

One of the earliest experiments investigating responses to flavors explicitly paired with recovery from illness was reported by Garcia, Ervin, Yorke, and Koelling (1967). These investigators found that rats made thiamine deficient while drinking tap water and recovered from deficiency while drinking saccharin solution drank more saccharin in a one-bottle test than rats which became deficient while drinking saccharin and recovered drinking tap water. Because only flavors paired with recovery or deficiency were tested in this experiment, it is not clear whether the rats developed a preference for the recovery flavor, an aversion to the deficiency flavor, or both. Recovery flavors are ingested in greater quantities than familiar-aversive flavors, but that only tells us that recovery flavors do not belong in the familiar-aversive category. Even though this study fails to answer all our questions about the effects of pairing a taste with recovery from illness, it does provide a convenient and reliable method for producing that pairing. The time course of recovery from the various symptoms of thiamine deficiency following injection of thiamine HCl is reasonably well documented, and this technique allows us to produce repeated cycles of recovery from illness with confidence that tastes presented at the time of the thiamine injection will be followed by dramatic changes in the symptoms of deficiency within a few hours. Figure 2 illustrates the changes in one symptom of thiamine deficiency (food intake) when thiamine is removed from the diet and then administered in a series of four injections, each containing one day's minimum daily requirement of the vitamin.

Recognizing that the comparison of recovery and deficiency flavors tells little about associations between tastes and positive gastrointestinal consequences, Seward and Greathouse (1973) used a method similar to Garcia's for producing cycles of illness and recovery, but attempted to compare a recovery flavor with a familiar-safe flavor. Experimental rats drank saccharin solution before each thiamine injection and drank tap water on the other days of each cycle; control rats received the saccharin solution two days after the injection in each cycle and water on the other days. Thus the two groups differed only in the temporal location of the saccharin exposure relative to the thiamine injection in each cycle. The result of this treatment was that the experimental rats came to drink more saccharin in a fixed period of time than did the controls.

Although Seward and Greathouse intended to pair saccharin with *getting well* in the experimental group and with *being well* in the control group, their own data suggest that saccharin presentations may have been paired with recurring thiamine deficiency in the control group. When we compare saccharin intake with the baseline of water intake on the preceding day, we find that consumption of saccharin actually decreased relative to consumption of water in the control group (as we would expect if the rats were developing an aversion to saccharin), rather than increasing (as we would expect if saccharin were becoming familiar-safe over trials). Thus, as in Garcia's experi-

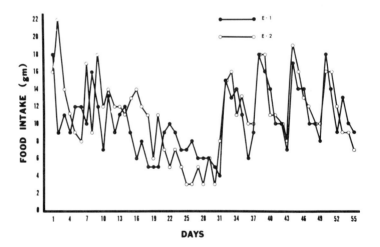

Figure 2
Changes in mean fluid intake for two groups of rats (E-1 and E-2) during 30 days of increasing thiamine deficiency followed by four cycles of recovery from deficiency. Both groups ate thiamine-deficient diet throughout the experiment and received injections containing one day's minimum daily requirement of thiamine on days 31, 37, 43, and 49. Saline injections were given on all other days marked on the abscissa. (From Zahorik, 1972)

ment, it is unclear whether the group differences in saccharin intake should be attributed to a learned preference in the experimental group, a learned aversion in the control group, or to both effects. A more recent experiment by Parker, Failor, and Weidman (1973) uses a different method for producing cycles of illness and recovery, but is subject to the same criticisms.

FLAVORS PAIRED WITH RECOVERY ARE PREFERRED TO NOVEL FLAVORS

In another early investigation of the effects of pairing tastes with recovery from illness, rats were offered a choice between a flavor previously paired with recovery from thiamine deficiency, a second flavor paired with thiamine deficiency, and a third flavor which was novel at the time of testing. In this three-bottle test, rats clearly preferred the recovery flavor to both novel and familiar-aversive tastes (Zahorik & Maier, 1969). However, this finding also fails to provide evidence for associations between flavors and illness because the comparison of the recovery and novel flavors is confounded with a difference in familiarity of the flavors. Obviously a flavor paired with recovery must be more familiar than a novel taste, and because rats generally prefer familiar-safe flavors to novel ones, the preference for the recovery flavor in this experiment could be explained by differences in familiarity, rather than by appetitive conditioning.

At first glance, it seems that there are several obvious ways to deal with the problem of familiarity differences between the flavor paired with recovery and the control flavors used for comparison. For example, one could take a group of rats trained like the subjects in the Zahorik and Maier experiment and compare them with a second group of animals receiving exactly the same sequence of flavors without ever becoming thiamine deficient or recovering from deficiency. The two groups should then be identical in their *familiarity* with the recovery and novel flavors, but the controls should not show any preference for the recovery flavor due to associations between that flavor and positive gastrointestinal consequences. If in a choice test with a novel flavor the experimental animals show a *larger* preference for the recovery flavor than the controls, it might seem reasonable to conclude that the difference between the groups is due to appetitive conditioning in the experimental group. In fact, experimental rats trained in this way do show a larger recovery/novel preference than do controls which have experienced the same sequence of flavors without ever becoming thiamine deficient (Zahorik, 1972).

185

OTHER EFFECTS OF
PAIRING FLAVORS WITH RECOVERY

The preceding argument requires the assumption that rats which have recently been thiamine deficient and rats which have never been ill are equally affected by the novelty-familiarity of flavors presented to them. A study by Rozin (1968) suggests that this may be a bad assumption. Rozin tested the preference for familiar vs. novel flavors (neophobia) in several different groups of rats and found that the preference for familiar foods is partially dependent on the subject's previous experience with gastrointestinal illness. Rats that had experienced illness produced by poisoning or thiamine deficiency showed a stronger preference for familiar foods than rats that had never been sick. Thus the experimental animals' greater preference for the recovery flavor (Zahorik, 1972) could be explained by their increased neophobia following experience with thiamine deficiency, rather than by their opportunity to associate the recovery flavor with recovery from illness. This criticism can also be applied to experiments in which intake data collected prior to the pairing of flavors with illness or recovery are used as a baseline from which learned aversions and preferences are measured (e.g., Green & Garcia, 1971; Green, Holmstron, & Woolman, 1974); if mere experience with illness can alter responses to familiar and novel flavors, none of these studies offers conclusive evidence that flavors paired with getting well are preferred because they are associated with recovery from illness.

DEMONSTRATING A LEARNED PREFERENCE
FOR RECOVERY FLAVORS

This brief review of studies exploring the effects of pairing flavors with recovery from illness helps to identify the kinds of comparisons and controls which would be required to demonstrate learned preferences for foods produced by the association of food cues with positive gastrointestinal consequences. We would have to show that foods paired with recovery are preferred to foods paired with the absence of illness. Furthermore, in making this comparison, we should control for both differences in familiarity of the foods being compared as well as differences in history of illness prior to the time of making our comparison. All the studies discussed earlier failed to meet at least one of these requirements: comparing recovery flavors with familiar-aversive ones, comparing flavors which were not equally familiar, or failing to hold history of illness constant.

While recognizing these methodological difficulties in earlier studies, we must also recognize a logical impasse in attempting to design an experiment which would make the desired comparison (recovery vs. familiar-safe) while holding both flavor familiarity and history of illness constant: if groups are exactly matched in amount and recency of experience with illness and experience with tastes, a taste cannot be differentially paired with getting well and being well.

In spite of this difficulty, it is still possible to make a meaningful comparison of preferences for recovery flavors vs. preferences for familiar-safe flavors. After all, the earlier experiments failed to give us a definitive conclusion not just because familiarity and history of illness were not held *constant*, but because those factors varied in ways which could produce preferences for the recovery flavor even if no associations between recovery flavors and recovery from illness had been formed. All the inequalities and possible artifacts in these studies led to *overestimation* of the preference for the recovery flavor over other familiar flavors, providing alternative explanations for all the positive findings. Even though we cannot hold both flavor familiarity and history of illness constant simultaneously, we can at least arrange that any necessary inequalities work *against* finding a preference for the recovery flavor. By purposely erring on the side of underestimating this preference, we run the risk of failing to identify weak associations between flavors and recovery, but at least any preference for the recovery flavor observed under these circumstances is a preference produced by associations between that flavor and recovery from illness.

A recent experiment by Zahorik, Maier, & Pies (1974) made use of this reasoning to create a comparison between a recovery flavor and a familiar-safe flavor in which any preference for the recovery flavor could only be explained by appetitive conditioning involving the recovery taste and its positive consequences. This study also included groups designed to replicate the phenomena of neophobia and increased neophobia following experience with illness—the effects which caused problems in interpreting the results of earlier experiments.

Four experimental groups were made thiamine deficient and then given cycles of recovery induced by injections of thiamine hydrochloride, with the last of the thiamine injections followed by complete and permanent recovery from deficiency. Each group had distinctive novel flavors paired with various phases of this procedure. Flavors presented for four days before the beginning of the deficiency period are labelled OF (old familiar); flavors paired with the thiamine injections which initiated each recovery period are labelled R (recovery); the label NF (new familiar) indicates flavors presented for four days *following* the last recovery day, while recovery

187

was maintained; and flavors which had never been presented are labelled N (novel). The experimental design is summarized in Table 1. As shown in this table, the particular tastes which were paired with the various conditions in the four groups were assigned in such a way that when all groups were given the *same* two-bottle preference test (saccharin solution vs. a very weak acetic acid solution), those two flavors represented a different comparison for each of the four groups. Half of the subjects in group R-N had saccharin paired with recovery from deficiency and had never tasted acetic acid at the time of the test; the other animals in group R-N had no previous experience with saccharin, but had acetic acid paired with recovery from deficiency. For half of the rats in group R-OF, saccharin was paired with recovery and acetic acid was presented during the pre-deficiency period, etc. In addition, each of the four experimental groups shown in Table 1 had a corresponding control group which received exactly the same sequence of flavors, but never experienced deficiency or recovery.

Table 1: EXPERIMENTAL DESIGN: FLAVORS PAIRED WITH THE
VARIOUS DEFICIENCY STATES FOR THE FOUR GROUPS
(Reprinted from Zahorik, Maier, & Pies, 1974)

Group	Deficiency States					
	Predefi-ciency	Defi-ciency	Re-covery	Post-re-covery	Novel	Test
R-N						
Subjects 1-5	—	Q	S	—	A	S vs. A
Subjects 6-10	—	Q	A	—	S	S vs. A
R-OF						
Subjects 11-15	A	Q	S	—	—	S vs. A
Subjects 16-20	S	Q	A	—	—	S vs. A
OF-N						
Subjects 21-25	A	Q	V	—	S	S vs. A
Subjects 26-30	S	Q	V	—	A	S vs. A
R-NF						
Subjects 31-35	—	Q	A	S	—	S vs. A
Subjects 36-40	—	Q	S	A	—	S vs. A

Note. Abbreviations: Q =.2g quinine HCl/ liter tap water; S =2g sodium saccharin/ liter tap water; A =2ml glacial acetic acid/liter tap water; V =50ml McCormick's vanilla extract/ liter tap water.

The mean absolute intakes for all groups during the choice test are presented in Table 2. With regard to our question about associations between flavors and positive gastrointestinal consequences, the most interesting experimental group is R-NF. The rats in this group showed a significant preference for the flavor presented on the four recovery days over a flavor presented for four days following recovery. It is clear from data on body weight and fluid intake recorded throughout the experiment that the presentations of the recovery flavor were always accompanied by dramatic improvement in the symptoms of deficiency, and that recovery continued at a slower rate

188

during the four-day presentation of the new familiar flavor; the new familiar flavor was not paired with illness, and there is no reason to believe that it became familiar-aversive. The two flavors may have differed in familiarity at the time of the test, but any differences in familiarity would favor a stronger preference for the new familiar flavor, because both tastes had been presented for equal periods of time, with the new familiar flavor presented closer in time to the test. Because intake of both solutions was measured simultaneously for each rat, the same history of illness preceded the test for both solutions. Thus, the inequalities which may have been present in this preference test worked against finding any preference for the recovery flavor, but that flavor was still preferred. Other comparisons among the groups in this study confirm the validity of several criticisms of earlier experiments. For all groups given a choice between a familiar flavor and a novel flavor, the familiar flavor was preferred (neophobia), and those preferences for the familiar taste were always larger in the experimental groups than in the coresponding control groups (increased neophobia following experience with illness).

Table 2. MEAN ABSOLUTE INTAKE OF RECOVERY, FAMILIAR, AND NOVEL LIQUIDS IN TWO-BOTTLE TESTS FOLLOWING RECOVERY

(After Zahorik, Maier, & Pies, 1974)

	Experimental		Control	
Group R-N	Recovery 67ml	Novel 3ml	Recovery 43ml	Novel 27ml
Group R-OF	Recovery 61ml	Familiar 8ml (Old)	Recovery 45ml	Familiar 36ml
Group OF-N	Familiar 23ml (Old)	Novel 8ml	Familiar 45ml	Novel 31ml
Group R-NF	Recovery 51ml	Familiar 40ml (New)	Recovery 33ml	Familiar 39ml

These data strongly suggest that rats can associate flavors with recovery from illness and that these associations are one of the factors producing stronger preferences for recovery flavors than for other familiar tastes. In terms of the categories proposed by Rozin and Kalat to describe the influence of experience on flavor preferences, foods paired with recovery from illness seem to belong in a familiar-positive category rather than familiar-safe (cf. Figure 1).

189

Up to this point, we have focussed on the amount and nature of the rat's experience with food as factors determining food preferences, with preferences increasing in sequence from familiar-aversive to novel, familiar-safe, and familiar-positive foods. However, preference may not be the only variable altered by ingestion and its consequences. If rats prefer flavors paired with recovery to other familiar foods, are recovery flavors also more resistant to association with illness? We know that rats develop smaller aversions to familiar flavors than to novel flavors when both tastes are paired with illness (Maier, Zahorik, & Albin, 1971; Revusky & Bedarf, 1967), as if familiarity somehow "immunizes" flavors against subsequent association with unpleasant gastrointestinal consequences. Will they develop still smaller aversions to flavors first paired with recovery from illness and later paired with a second illness?

A recent study by Zahorik and Bean (1975) assessed the strength of aversions produced by pairing a familiar-positive flavor or a familiar-safe flavor with lithium chloride poisoning. Three groups of rats were familiarized with saccharin solution under different circumstances: the *recovery* group received saccharin on four days when they were showing rapid recovery from thiamine deficiency; the *familiarity* group received the same sequence of flavors as the recovery group, including four days of exposure to saccharin, but the animals never experienced deficiency or recovery; the *recovery-familiar* group had the same history of thiamine deficiency and recovery as the recovery group, but their four days of exposure to saccharin solution came after their last recovery from deficiency rather than being paired with recovery.[2] After the fourth day of experience with saccharin, the subjects were allowed to drink tap water for four days. All groups were then poisoned immediately following five minutes of access to the familiar saccharin solution.

Figure 3 shows the three groups' consumption of saccharin in a one-bottle test beginning two hours after poisoning; baseline consumption of saccharin (established on the fourth day of exposure to saccharin for each group, prior to poisoning) is also represented. There are striking and highly significant differences between the groups, both in absolute intake of saccharin during the test and in intake relative to baseline. The familiarity and recovery-familiarity groups show large depressions of intake even at the end of the 22-hr test period, but the recovery group begins to drink saccharin in large quantities within a few hours and continues to drink throughout the

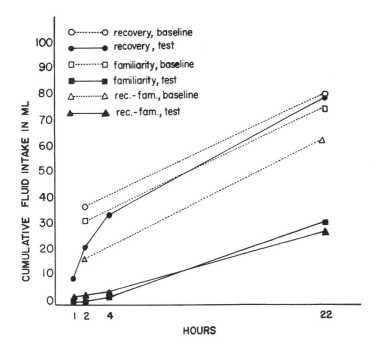

Figure 3
Mean cumulative intake of saccharin solution for the three groups during the baseline period and during the test following the pairing of saccharin with lithium chloride poisoning. (From Zahorik & Bean, 1975)

test period. It is not clear whether the recovery group's initial reduction in intake should be attributed to a weak aversion or to the continuing effects of the poison, but the recovery group certainly responds very differently from the other two groups. Pairing a recovery flavor with illness produced a far smaller aversion than pairing either familiar-safe flavor with illness.

This resistance of recovery flavors to later association with illness is not limited to flavors which have been paired with recovery from thiamine deficiency. Like thiamine deficient animals, parathyroidectomized rats learn to prefer solutions containing the nutrient they require (calcium), and once that preference has been learned it becomes very difficult to produce an aversion to the preferred solution by pairing it with lithium chloride injections (Frumkin, 1975).

191

Taken as a whole, the studies reviewed here offer strong evidence that rats can associate flavors with the physiological changes which represent recovery from illness. Although I have emphasized studies in which rats learn to prefer foods paired with administration of the specific nutrient required to alleviate an existing nutritional deficiency, there are several other examples of learned food preferences which may also involve associations between food cues and positive gastrointestinal consequences. For example, there are a number of studies demonstrating an increased intake of foods paired with morphine administration in morphine addicted rats (Parker, Failor, & Weidman, 1973; Ternes, 1975; Riley, 1976). It is also possible that associations between food cues and the filling of caloric requirements may play some role in the development of food preferences in young chicks (see Hogan, this volume).

On the basis of these studies, it is tempting to speculate about the adaptive role of appetitive conditioning in guiding food selection, and it is easy to imagine situations in which the capacity to associate food cues with beneficial gastrointestinal consequences would be advantageous. But these speculations are no substitute for data. Rozin and Kalat argued against the existence of a familiar-positive category of foods not only because they found alternative explanations for the results of laboratory studies of flavors paired with recovery, but because their three categories alone (familiar-aversive, novel, and familiar-safe) could account for a large variety of changes in food preferences seen in field situations (Rozin & Kalat, 1971). Field data on learning mechanisms in food selection are so sparse that it would be unreasonable to claim on the basis of lack of evidence that rats never make use of their ability to associate food cues with positive gastrointestinal consequences. However, it is equally unreasonable to assume that every ability we can demonstrate in the laboratory plays an important role in normal feeding behavior.

In assessing the research reported in this chapter, it is important to consider the possibility that those effects and mechanisms which are of greatest interest to learning theorists are not invariably of equal importance in producing ongoing behavior outside the laboratory. To provide a definitive answer to the questions about whether rats can associate flavors with relief from the symptoms of illness, it was necessary to control for preferences produced by neophobia and poison-induced neophobia. It would be foolish, however, to assume that changes in food preferences due to flavor familiarity or to experience with illness are either less important or less interesting than the changes produced by associations between flavors and recovery from illness. Indeed, these factors caused serious problems in interpreting the results of earlier experiments precisely because their effects on food preferences can be extremely powerful, and because they are known to alter food preferences in a wide variety of feeding situations. Several lines of research illustrate the importance of neophobia in determining rats' food choices.

In a fascinating series of studies summarized in another chapter of this volume, Bennett Galef and his colleagues have shown how the rat's natural reluctance to sample new foods combines with normal social behaviors to produce adaptive food preferences in rat pups. These authors provide evidence that the rat mother's milk contains flavor cues which reflect the flavor of her own diet, so that the pups become familiar with foods which are familiar-safe to their mother even before they begin to eat solid food (Galef & Sherry, 1973). When the pups do begin to eat solid food, they are strongly attracted by the presence of adult colony members at feeding sites, so that their first meals are likely to contain the same foods being eaten by those adults (Galef & Clark, 1971). Thus weanling rats need not go through a dangerous sequence of trial and error to discover a few safe foods; nursing and social interaction with colony adults increase familiarity with foods already found safe by other colony members, and the pups' neophobia guarantees that they will prefer those safe foods to novel (and potentially dangerous) substances.

The role of neophobia in producing some of the findings of greatest theoretical importance in the taste aversion literature is well illustrated by the recent experiments of Mitchell, Kirschbaum, and Perry (1975). These authors noted that many investigators who have reported difficulty in producing aversions to exteroceptive stimuli paired with illness had unintentionally minimized the novelty of those stimuli by presenting them in situations filled with many other relatively novel exteroceptive cues. By thoroughly habituating their subjects to the cages in which the experimental pairings were to occur and then pairing food presented in novel containers with gastrointestinal illness, Mitchell's group was able to show large aversions to the novel food containers after only one or two pairings. These data do not argue against the popular view that illness is less readily associated with exteroceptive cues than with tastes; rather, they suggest that it is impossible to make fair comparisons of the associability of different cues unless the novelty of the cues is carefully equated.

193

Taste novelty is such an important factor in laboratory studies of food preferences and aversions that it seems prudent to examine the possibility that standard methods of rearing rats in laboratories may maximize the salience of novel taste cues. Compared with novel cues presented in other sense modalities, there is something unique about the context in which novel flavors are presented in typical taste experiments: laboratory-reared rats have extremely limited experience with flavors of food and water prior to the experiment—mother's milk, lab chow, and tap water may provide the total dietary history of taste experience for the laboratory animal. In the context of this limited taste experience, the presentation of a novel flavor could be a far more powerful and aversive stimulus event than the presentation of the same novel taste to a rat with a more varied dietary history. However, several recent experiments argue against the hypothesis that limited taste experience plays a major role in producing laboratory rats' neophobia or their strong tendency to associate illness with novel foods. In another chapter of this volume, Capretta presents evidence that previous experience with other novel food flavors does not greatly reduce neophobia; and even when rats are raised from birth on a diet containing a wide variety of distinctively flavored solids and liquids, they still develop far larger aversions to a novel taste than to a familiar taste when both tastes have been followed by illness (Zahorik, 1976). Neophobia and the tendency to associate illness with novel foods cannot be dismissed as effects seen only in animals whose taste experiences have been artificially limited by the laboratory environment.

Clearly, the pairing of specific flavors with positive gastrointestinal consequences is only one type of experience which can increase the preference for a flavor; other experiences (including simple exposure to a taste) also increase preferences and promote the ingestion of foods which are unlikely to cause illness.

ARE NEOPHOBIA AND POISON-INDUCED
NEOPHOBIA ASSOCIATIVE EFFECTS?

Neophobia, poison-induced neophobia, and associations between flavors and recovery from illness are empirically separable effects of experience on flavor preferences, and a casual inspection of the standard procedures for producing these phenomena might convince the reader that neophobia and poison-induced neophobia are perfectly analagous to certain non-associative effects which are routinely controlled in traditional conditioning experiments. In assessing increases in the strength of CS-US associations over trials, it has been considered important to control for changes in the criterion response

194

caused by repeated presentations of either the CS or the US, rather than by the *temporal pairing* of the two. Learning theorists have disagreed about whether these effects of stimulus presentations (habituation, sensitization, pseudoconditioning) should be considered examples of learning, but they have generally agreed that such effects are not the products of *associative* learning. However, changes in food preferences due to increasing familiarity with the food and changes due to poison-induced neophobia may not fit these non-associative models.

Kalat and Rozin (1973) have proposed that the increased preference for a taste produced by increasing familiarity represents the association of the taste with the *absence* of negative gastrointestinal consequences. Their theory of *learned safety* offers compelling explanations for many food selection phenomena. When ingestion of a novel substance is not followed by illness, the animal learns that the food is safe to eat and therefore ingests it in larger amounts on subsequent exposures, demonstrating the preference for familiar foods which we have called neophobia. Associations between a food and the absence of negative consequences interfere with the formation of *new* associations, so that familiar-safe foods are not readily associated with illness. Moreover, the CS-US delay gradient in taste-aversion learning can be attributed to increasing association of the taste with safety (increasing interference with association of the taste with illness), rather than to decay of the stimulus trace. (See Kalat, this volume, for a summary of the evidence supporting the theory of learned safety). Following this line of reasoning, familiar-safe and familiar-positive flavors are both preferred by virtue of their association with gastrointestinal consequences; familiar-safe flavors have been associated with *being well* and familiar-positive flavors have been associated with getting well.

The work of Domjan (1975; see also Domjan, this volume) suggests that part of the increases in neophobia seen after experience with poison are also the result of associative learning. First, Domjan's findings imply that in certain situations the term "poison-induced neophobia" may be a misnomer: experience with poison *in the absence of ingestion of distinctive foods or liquids* does not produce a long-lasting increase in the strength of neophobia. However, reluctance to ingest novel substances *does* increase following the pairing of a novel substance with illness, but the size of this effect depends on the particular *combination* of foods used to test for the neophobia and to produce the aversion. Apparently a large part of this "non-specific" increase in neophobia is *quite* specific—specific to novel substances which are similar to foods recently made familiar-aversive. Thus

195

poison-induced neophobia is in part the result of associative learning, produced by the generalization of learned aversions to similar novel foods.

On the basis of existing research, there is no compelling evidence that any of the increases in food preferences produced by experience—preferences for flavors paired with recovery, preferences for familiar flavors, or increased neophobia following the pairing of a novel flavor with illness—are the result of non-associative mechanisms. Perhaps all three effects are examples of similar associative learning mechanisms; but the different effects are experimentally separable because they represent the associations of different events.

FOOTNOTES

[1]In another chapter in this volume John Garcia discusses evidence suggesting that rats avoid novel foods primarily on the basis of odor, while they avoid foods which have been paired with illness on the basis of taste. Because the studies reported in this chapter employ stimuli which provide both kinds of cues, it is impossible to separate the roles of taste and olfaction in the effects discussed here. While I have referred to the cues in these experiments as "tastes" and "flavors," I recognize that taste and olfactory stimuli are confounded and that either type of stimulus (or some combination of the two) could be of primary importance in each of the results I discuss.

[2]The procedures used to produce familiarity with saccharin in these three groups are similar to the procedures described earlier in the study by Zahorik, Maier, and Pies (1974): Saccharin in the *recovery* group had the same history as the recovery flavor in the experimental groups of the earlier experiment; saccharin in the *familiarity* group was treated like the recovery flavor in the control groups of that study; the *recovery-familiarity* group had saccharin treated like the new familiar flavor in the experimental groups of Zahorik et al.

ACKNOWLEDGEMENTS

The author gratefully acknowledges the assistance of Steven Maier, Carol Bean, Richard Albin, and Ronald Pies in the studies reported in this chapter. Jack Catlin provided many helpful criticisms of the manuscript.

REFERENCES

Barnett, S. A. **The rat: A study in behavior.** Chicago: Aldine, 1963.

Domjan, M. Poison-induced neophobia in rats: Role of stimulus generalization of conditioned taste aversions. **Animal Learning & Behavior,** 1975, **3,** 205-211.

Frumkin, K. Failure of sodium and calcium-deficient rats to acquire conditioned taste aversions to the object of their specific hunger. **Journal of Comparative and Physiological Psychology,** 1975, **89,** 329-339.

Galef, B. G., Jr., & Clark, M. M. Social factors in the poison avoidance and feeding behavior of wild and domesticated rat pups. **Journal of Comparative and Physiological Psychology,** 1971, **75,** 341-357.

Galef, B. G., Jr., & Sherry, D. F. Mother's milk: A medium for transmission of cues reflecting the flavor of mother's diet. **Journal of Comparative and Physiological Psychology,** 1973, **83,** 374-378.

Garcia, J., & Ervin, F. R. Gustatory-visceral and telerceptor-cutaneous conditioning: Adaptation in internal and external milieus. **Communications in Behavioral Biology,** 1968, **1,** 389-415.

Garcia, J., Ervin, F. R., Yorke, C. H., & Koelling, R. A. Conditioning with delayed vitamin injections. **Science,** 1967, **155,** 716-718.

Green, K. F., Holmstron, L. S., & Woolman, M. A. Relation of cue to consequence in rats: Effect of recuperation from illness. **Behavioral Biology,** 1974, **10,** 491-503.

Harris, L. J., Clay, J., Hargreaves, F. J., & Ward, A. Appetite and choice of diet: The ability of the vitamin B deficient rat to discriminate between diets containing and lacking the vitamin. **Proceedings of the Royal Society, London, Series B,** 1933, **113,** 161-190.

Kalat, J. W., & Rozin, P. "Learned safety" as a mechanism in long-delay taste-aversion learning in rats. **Journal of Comparative and Physiological Psychology,** 1973, **83,** 198-207.

McFarland, D. J. Stimulus relevance and homeostasis. In R. A. Hinde & J. Stevenson-Hinde (Eds.), **Constraints on learning.** New York: Academic Press, 1973.

Maier, S. F., Zahorik, D. M., & Albin, R. W. Relative novelty of solid and liquid diet during thiamine deficiency determines development of thiamine-specific hunger. **Journal of Comparative and Physiological Psychology,** 1971, **74,** 254-262.

Mitchell, D., Kirschbaum, E. H., & Perry, R. L. Effects of neophobia and habituation on the poison-induced avoidance of exteroceptive stimuli in the rat. **Journal of Experimental Psychology: Animal Behavior Processes,** 1975, **1,** 47-55.

Parker, L., Failor, A., & Weidman, K. Conditioned preferences in the rat with an unnatural need state: Morphine withdrawal. **Journal of Comparative and Physiological Psychology,** 1973, **82,** 294-300.

Revusky, S. H., & Bedarf, E. W. Association of illness with prior ingestion of novel foods. **Science,** 1967, **155,** 219-220

Riley, A. L. Personal communication. 1976.

Rodgers, W. L. Specificity of specific hungers. **Journal of Comparative and Physiological Psychology,** 1967, **64,** 49-58.

Rozin, P. Thiamine specific hunger. In C. F. Code & W. Heidel (Eds.), **Handbook of physiology,** Sect. 6, **Alimentary canal.** Vol. 1, **Food and water intake.** Baltimore: Williams and Wilkins, 1967.

198

Rozin, P. Specific aversions and neophobia resulting from vitamin deficiency or poisoning in half-wild and domestic rats. **Journal of Comparative and Physiological Psychology**, 1968, **66**, 82-88.

Rozin, P., & Kalat, J. W. Specific hungers and poison avoidance as adaptive specializations of learning. **Psychological Review**, 1971, **78**, 459-486.

Scott, E. M., & Verney, E. L. Self selection of diet: VI. The nature of appetites for B vitamins. **Journal of Nutrition**, 1974, **34**, 471-480.

Seward, J. P., & Greathouse, S. R. Appetitive and aversive conditioning in thiamine-deficient rats. **Journal of Comparative and Physiological Psychology**, 1973, **83**, 157-167.

Ternes, J. W. Induced preferences for morphine in rats. **Bulletin of the Psychonomic Society**, 1975, **5**, 315-316.

Zahorik, D. M. Conditioned physiological changes associated with learned aversions to tastes paired with thiamine deficiency in the rat. **Journal of Comparative and Physiological Psychology**, 1972, **79**, 189-200.

Zahorik, D. M. The role of dietary history in the effects of novelty on taste preferences and aversions. Unpublished manuscript, 1976.

Zahorik, D. M., & Bean, C. A. Resistance of "recovery" flavors to later association with illness. **Bulletin of the Psychonomic Society**, 1975, **6**, 309-312.

Zahorik, D. M., & Maier, S. F. Appetitive conditioning with recovery from thiamine deficiency as the unconditioned stimulus. **Psychonomic Science**, 1969, **17**, 309-310.

Zahorik, D. M., Maier, S. F., & Pies, R. W. Preferences for tastes paired with recovery from thiamine deficiency in rats: Appetitive conditioning or learned safety. **Journal of Comparative and Physiological Psychology**, 1974, **87**, 1083-1091.

IX

LEARNING TO INITIATE AND TERMINATE MEALS: THEORETICAL, CLINICAL AND DEVELOPMENTAL ASPECTS

RAYMOND C. HAWKINS, II
University of Texas at Austin

LEARNING INFLUENCES ON MEAL INITIATION AND TERMINATION

Previous reviews of the perception of satiety and the control of food intake in man (e.g., Stellar & Jordan, 1970) have stressed the role of physiological regulatory mechanisms for the control of meal initiation and meal termination. Their aim was to analyze hunger and satiety with experimental methods derived from animal research and to isolate the sensory factors controlling neurological mechanisms involved in food-intake regulation. According to Stellar (1974), this approach has sought the common underlying brain structures for physiological regulation of energy balance and the control of food intake, motivated behavior, and subjective experiences of hunger and satiety. These investigations have yielded compelling evidence for the role of gastric distension in controlling meal termination in human subjects. Systematic manipulation of the volume and caloric density of liquid preloads (Walike, Jordan, & Stellar, 1969; Spiegel, 1973) and of intragastric (IG) meals (Jordan, 1969) have shown convincingly that volume, not calories, determines meal size.

These studies have an important limitation, however. Since orosensory factors were usually minimized or eliminated, the role of learning mechanisms involving the association of orosensory cues with postingestive consequences was not emphasized. The importance of oral cues was strongly suggested by findings that the perception of hunger and satiety was dissociated from the

201

volumetric or postabsorptive control of amount ingested. For example, although human subjects could learn to control meal size on the basis of gastric cues alone, they reported less satisfaction and less satiety during voluntary IG feeding (Jordan, 1969). Moreover, in clinical studies of intravenous hyperalimentation, human subjects reported the persistence of hunger in spite of the infusion of sufficient calories to maintain body weight (Jordan, Moses, Mac-Fayden, & Dudrick, 1974).

One case in which unconditioned physiological mechanisms for hunger and satiety may not provide a sufficient explanation for the control of food intake is the challenge to caloric regulation of increasing or decreasing the caloric density of the diet. Spiegel (1973) investigated the caloric regulation of food intake in fifteen normal-weight human subjects. The subjects were given *ad libitum* access to a standard liquid food (Metrecal) diet (1.0 Kcal/ml) for 4-9 days followed by 4-14 days on a dilute diet (0.5 Kcal/ml). Nine subjects failed to regulate their caloric intake in the time permitted, while six subjects compensated for the caloric dilution by increasing both meal size and meal frequency. However, this regulation was sluggish, requiring 2-5 days to develop. Furthermore, the mean level of compensation was only 87%. In agreement with these findings, Snowdon (1970) observed that rats do not immediately adjust meal size to caloric requirements. McHugh, Moran, and Barton (1975), however, demonstrated that rhesus monkeys given intragastric preloads immediately showed nearly perfect behavioral compensation for the extra calories, in sharp contrast to human subjects' failure to reduce meal size as a function of increasing caloric density of the liquid preloads (Spiegel, 1973). The relative sluggishness and imprecision of caloric regulation in man seems to implicate a process of "learning" to detect internal hunger and satiety cues associated with nutrient depletion and repletion—not the operation of innate, unconditioned physiological hunger and satiety reflexes controlling meal size and meal frequency. In this chapter we shall not be concerned with determining the relative influence of unconditioned alimentary reflexes vs. conditioning mechanisms in the control of food intake. The necessary experimental procedures for isolating the effects of early rearing experiences have only recently been developed for the study of feeding and growth in rats (Hall, 1975). Instead, we shall present an overview of the empirical evidence for the conditioning of meal initiation and meal termination in animals and humans, suggest theoretical learning mechanisms for these effects, and finally, discuss the clinical and developmental implications for human obesity.

SATIETY AS A CONDITIONED RESPONSE:
THEORIES OF STUNKARD AND LeMAGNEN

Stunkard (1975) has proposed that meal size is adjusted to changes in caloric density via a Pavlovian mechanism. Orosensory stimuli and especially gastric filling serve as the conditioned stimuli (CSs) for meal termination. The unconditioned stimuli (USs), which occur perhaps two hours later, consist of nutrients absorbed from the gastrointestinal tract or their metabolic products which are conveyed to the satiety area of the brain through the blood stream. Stunkard points out that under stable conditions of food intake, eating is terminated by these CSs, resulting in the maintenance of a relatively constant meal size from meal to meal. When the caloric density of the diet or the meal interval changes, the new postingestional US thus produced indicates either excess or deficiency of food intake, and, through association, the CSs decrease or increase the size of the subsequent meal as a function of the nature of the new US. Stunkard claims that this Pavlovian response sequence can account for both the termination of eating early in the process of food absorption from the intestines as well as the long-term adjustment of meal size to the changing caloric needs of the organism.

The speculation that gastrointestinal distension may serve as a CS for satiety and meal termination is intriguing, and has some empirical support. Razran (1961) cites demonstrations in dogs and humans in which gastric filling served as a satiety-eliciting CS. For example, in one experiment gastric distension produced by 300-500 ml of a 3-5% sodium chloride solution was used to evoke an unconditioned reduction of dogs' salt appetite when these animals were free to choose a range of NaCl concentrations in a "cafeteria" situation. Subsequently, gastric distension by an equivalent volume of water produced a conditioned reduction of salt appetite.

Nevertheless, there are problems with Stunkard's conditioned reflex theory of satiety. Because his theory de-emphasizes the role of orosensory food conditioning relative to the conditioned stimulus effects of gastric filling, it fails to fully account for phenomena such as specific satiety or partial satiety. These terms refer to the fact that satiety may be limited to the specific orosensory properties of the ingested food, and that meal size markedly increases with successive presentation of different orosensory cues (e.g., LeMagnen, 1971; Cabanac & Duclaux, 1973).

LeMagnen (1971) proposed a theory for the control of meal size which can better explain orosensory specific satiety and partial satiety effects. According to this theory, an oral satiety mechanism acts in coordination with negative gastrointestinal feedback to determine meal size specific to orosensory cues of the food substances. The mechanism involves the appropriate adjustment of the relative palatabilities of the food choices according to the nutritional postingestive consequences which had been associated (after a delay) with these specific orosensory cues. The orosensory stimuli function as CSs and the postingestive effects correlated with caloric repletion serve to condition these CSs. LeMagnen likens this food conditioning process to the long-delay learning observed for the acquisition of taste aversions in flavor-toxicosis experiments (Garcia, Hankins, & Rusiniak, 1974).

SOME EMPIRICAL EVIDENCE FOR
THE CONDITIONING OF SATIETY

Cravens and Renner (1970) reviewed the research literature on conditioned appetitive drive states and found the evidence for such conditioning to be inconclusive. Nevertheless, several studies have yielded findings consistent with LeMagnen's (1971) food conditioning theory. Revusky (1967) examined what effects the hunger level of rats during food consumption has on subsequent preference and found that rats consume less of an edible substance if that substance was previously paired with satiation. Kurtz and Jarka (1968) found that rats in a T-maze avoid the side where they had previously been fed while satiated in favor of the side where they had previously been fed while deprived. Russek (1970) demonstrated conditioned anorexia (satiety) to a testing cage and light compound CS using intraportal vein glucose infusion as the US. Additional evidence of conditioned satiety was reported by LeMagnen (1959, 1971) and Capretta (1962) who also found reduced intake of substances following association with nutritional repletion.

Although the above evidence is consistent with a conditioned satiety interpretation, the data can also be explained in terms of a conditioned aversion acquired to stimuli paired with repletion (Deutsch, Molina, & Puerto, 1976). To decide between these alternatives, Booth (1972) suggested that conditioned reductions in meal size be considered evidence of conditioned satiety only if the meal size reductions occur because of decelerated intake toward the end and not the beginning of the meal. Much of Booth's data on conditioned satiety satisfies this criterion.

In one series of experiments designed to demonstrate the acquisition of conditioned oral satiety in the rat, Booth (1972) used liquid or solid foods in which the caloric density of the test diet was varied and a distinctive olfactory or gustatory cue was paired with each caloric concentration. One study involved two groups of rats which were food deprived for 4.5 hr daily and presented with 10% carbohydrate (dextrin suspension) and 50% carbohydrate liquid test meals on alternate days, each caloric concentration being paired with a different odor. By the second block of 4 meals greater ingestion of the 10% diet had already begun to develop. After this "differential reinforcement" phase, "extinction" trials were initiated. The rats were presented with foods of the same intermediate caloric composition but having different odor cues, either the odor previously paired with 50% carbohydrate or that paired with the 10% concentration. As expected, rats satiated more quickly to the 50%-paired odor than to the 10%-paired odor. This difference in meal size under olfactory stimulus control was attributable to a difference in the suppression of intake in the later stages of the meal rather than differences in initial acceptability of the odor-paired foods (i.e., there were no differences in initial eating rate).

NATURE OF THE ALIMENTARY REINFORCER (US)

Booth (1972) and his colleagues (Booth, Lovett, & McSherry, 1972) obtained compelling evidence for conditioned meal termination in which oral cues were associated with the different postingestive effects of various carbohydrate loads. Assuming, then, that satiety becomes conditioned to oral cues, what is the specific nature of the reinforcer (US) in this process? Stunkard (1975) considers the primary alimentary reinforcer to be nutrients absorbed from the gastrointestinal tract or other metabolic products which are carried by the blood stream to the glucoreceptors in the satiety areas of the brain. More recently, however, attention has been directed to gastrointestinal controls of ingestive behavior, i.e., the nutritive/osmotic, humoral, and neural postingestive consequences which are related to rate of gastric emptying (Snowdon, 1970, 1975; Booth & Davis, 1973). Of particular interest is a recent theory for explaining intestinal satiety in rats (Smith, Gibbs, & Young, 1974; Liebling, Eisner, Gibbs, & Smith, 1975; Antin, Gibbs, Holt, Young, & Smith, 1975). According to this theory, the entry of nutrients into the duodenum elicits "a behavioral sequence of satiety" that includes not only the termination of eating but also grooming, exploration, and subsequent sleep. This satiety sequence is assumed to result from the action of an endogenous hormone cholecystokinin (CCK), which is released in response to nutrients entering the duodenum (Meyer & Grossman, 1972), or stimulation

205

of stretch receptors in the walls of the duodenum (Antin et al., 1975; Liebling et al., 1975). Like duodenal infusion, CCK inhibits sham-feeding in the rat (Gibbs, Young, & Smith, 1973) and also elicits the complete behavioral sequence of satiety (Antin et al., 1975). Liebling et al. (1975) argue that these parallel effects strongly suggest that emptying food into the duodenum elicits a satiety reflex mediated by the release of CCK (the US), although they have no evidence that the quantity of endogenous CCK released by food in the intestine is necessary and sufficient to evoke satiety. Moreover, this peripheral humoral mechanism may likely be supplemented by other satiety signals of a neural nature arising from the intestine (Sharma & Nasset, 1962), or from portal vein glucoreceptor stimulation (Russek, 1970).

THEORETICAL LEARNING MECHANISMS
FOR MEAL INITIATION AND TERMINATION

In this section the conditioned satiety effects previously described are considered within the context of a more general conceptual framework for meal initiation and termination which will integrate the orosensory stimulus control mechanisms emphasized by LeMagnen (1971) and Booth (1972) and the gastrointestinal satiety cues postulated by Stunkard (1975). First of all, let us consider the role of learning in establishing meal patterns.

Konorski (1967) noted that the hunger drive and the satiety "antidrive" reflexes may be conditionable to the time and place of eating. He speculated that the constancy of meal schedules displayed by human beings reflects classical conditioning in which the individual who eats at definite times of the day and in particular situations develops a hunger CR to these times and situations and thus repeats meals at the same time and place on subsequent days. This leads to alimentary CRs becoming more strongly established to these CSs. Konorski further suggested that satiation is easily conditionable, noting the common experience of how overeating a particular food in a particular place may evoke satiation when encountering this food and situation on subsequent occasions. Pavlov (1927) reported an empirical demonstration of temporal conditioning in dogs who learned to salivate (CR) only at 30-min intervals (the temporal CS) as a result of the food US being presented according to this temporal schedule. He also showed that an external CS (e.g., a light) could be compounded with the temporal CS to evoke the CR. Such conditioning effects might account for human specific hungers (and satiety) evoked by specific food presented at specific time intervals in specific situations.

Konorski (1967) also commented upon the selectivity of the association between the external food CS and the hunger drive or the satiety anti-drive reflex. He noted that if we become accustomed to a "heavy meal" consisting of a number of dishes, we are not satisfied if the meal is light. This observation brings us to the second area of speculation regarding learning mechanisms in food selection: the role of interoceptive and exteroceptive Pavlovian conditioning in controlling feeding behavior.

Razran (1961) made the distinction between interoceptive and exteroceptive classical conditioning, pointing out that CSs and USs may be differentiated by whether they involve external stimulus events or internal stimuli. Two sub-categories of Razran's system are most relevant for our understanding of learning mechanisms involved in food selection and satiety:

(1) **Exteroceptive-interoceptive conditioning.** In this category a food-related external CS is associated with an internal US to elicit the CR, as illustrated by the following diagram.

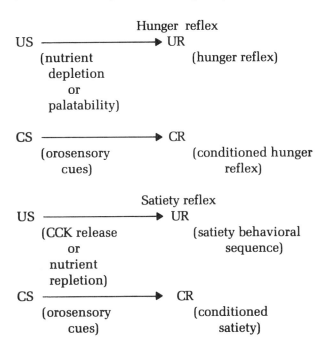

Such exteroceptive-interoceptive conditioning describes the learning mechanism for flavor-toxicosis food-aversion learning, and also accounts for the role of orosensory control of ingestion mentioned previously in the work of LeMagnen (1971) and Booth (1972).

207

(2) Interoceptive-interoceptive conditioning. Stunkard's (1975) view of satiety as a conditioned reflex seems to be best fitted by this category, in which an internal stimulus event (CS) comes to elicit a CR through association with an internal unconditioned stimulus.

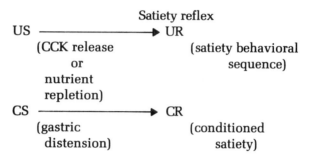

Satiety reflex

US ⟶ UR
(CCK release   (satiety behavioral
   or   sequence)
nutrient
repletion)

CS ⟶ CR
(gastric   (conditioned
distension)   satiety)

SATIETY AS THE CONDITIONED SUPPRESSION OF
THE HUNGER REFLEX BY GASTRIC DISTENSION CUES

One problem with the above Pavlovian models for conditioned hunger and satiety reflexes is that there is an isolation of the exteroceptive orosensory control of ingestion from the interoceptive controls. One possible way to integrate orosensory cues and gastrointestinal cues in the conditioning of satiation is shown in the following modification of the above two conditioning processes.

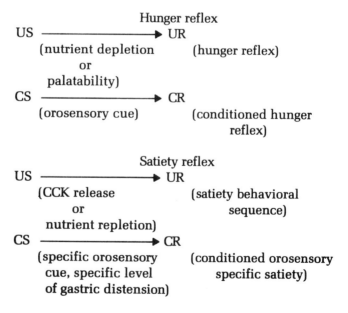

Hunger reflex

US ⟶ UR
(nutrient depletion   (hunger reflex)
   or
palatability)

CS ⟶ CR
(orosensory cue)   (conditioned hunger
                                reflex)

Satiety reflex

US ⟶ UR
(CCK release   (satiety behavioral
   or   sequence)
nutrient repletion)

CS ⟶ CR
(specific orosensory   (conditioned orosensory
cue, specific level   specific satiety)
of gastric distension)

208

In this model, conditioned satiety is hypothesized to be evoked by a specific level of gastrointestinal filling or distension in combination with a specific taste or other orosensory cue. This formulation appears to account for the orosensory specific satiety effect discussed by LeMagnen (1971) and Cabanac and Duclaux (1973). The phenomenon of partial satiety or the "dessert effect" in humans can be viewed as the release from conditioned satiety brought about by the presentation of a different orosensory cue (especially a more palatable taste), disinhibiting the consummatory response until specific satiety occurs to this second orosensory cue and level of gastric distension.

CLINICAL IMPLICATIONS FOR THE TREATMENT OF OBESITY

The preceding theoretical discussion of conditioned hunger and satiety yields practical suggestions for the assessment and modification of inappropriate eating behavior contributing to human obesity. Jordan and Levitz (1975a) have proposed a behavioral classification system for problematic eating behavior which includes the following categories: inappropriate habits of food selection (e.g., preference for highly palatable, "empty calorie" foods), meal initiation problems (e.g., excessive snacking), and problems in meal termination (e.g., tendency for overeating resulting in large meals and snacks). This review will not be concerned with metabolic or emotional factors, nor with inactivity, which also contribute to the development and maintenance of excessive adipose tissue.

Several studies have compared obese persons with non-obese persons on the above-listed behavioral parameters. For example, Gates, Huenemann, and Brand (1975) observed that in a cafeteria setting, obese subjects not only chose larger quantities of food than non-obese controls, but also selected more servings classified as "high in calories" in proportion to their nutrient composition. Findings such as these suggest the value of gradually modifying food selection of obese persons to increase preference for lower calorie foods. This indeed has been the aim of traditional dietary treatments for obesity. More recently, this goal has also led to clinical applications of conditioned-aversion procedures to alter food selection habits of obese persons.

209

In their recent self-report survey of taste aversions, Garb and Stunkard (1974) suggest the utility of conditioned-aversion approaches for treating alcoholism and obesity. Several studies have attempted to modify inappropriate food selection in obese persons by pairing the sight, smell, taste, or thought of the target food with various aversive events, including noxious odors (Foreyt & Kennedy, 1971), smoke (Morganstern, 1974), electric shock applied to the arm (Meyer & Crisp, 1964), and even vivid nausea-inducing images evoked by covert sensitization techniques (e.g., Elliott & Denney, 1975). These procedures involve both classical conditioning to attach a negative valence to the sensory cues of the target food, and the punishment of approach behaviors toward these foods.[1]

It is difficult to demonstrate that these acquired taste aversions for target foods generalize beyond the treatment setting and provide a necessary and sufficient explanation for the maintenance of weight loss. However, aversive procedures may prove useful when incorporated in an overall treatment plan which provides for reduction of caloric intake through training in self-monitoring skills (Foreyt & Kennedy, 1971). Such a plan should ultimately enable the obese person to select low-calorie foods which will facilitate weight reduction. Training clients to choose low rather than high calorie foods might also minimize the overgeneralization of negative affect sometimes associated with inappropriately implemented aversion conditioning procedures (Bandura, 1969). In addition to learning appropriate food selection habits, the obese individual should learn to reduce anxiety by performing some behavior other than the maladaptive eating of the problem food.

ANALYSIS AND MODIFICATION
OF PROBLEMATIC PATTERNS OF
MEAL/SNACK INITIATION IN OBESE PERSONS

Clinical observations suggest that many obese individuals, particularly young adults living in less structured college settings, overeat by ingesting frequent "snacks." Schachter's (1971) "stimulus binding" theory of obesity makes the prediction that in obese persons snack initiation is more likely to be elicited by external stimuli such as the sight, smell, and/or taste of foods than by internal hunger cues, which exert more control over eating behavior in non-obese individuals. Therefore, it would follow that to decrease snack frequency obese persons should avoid contacting external food-related cues. However, neither the "abstinence" approach of traditional diet programs nor aversion therapy to alter food selection habits seem to be appropriate or effective in decreasing the frequency of ingestions.

A different approach for conceptualizing and modifying excessive meal/snack frequency is to train obese individuals to decide upon the number of daily meals and snacks, and then to schedule these eating events for specific times and settings. The goal is for meal initiation to become controlled by a limited number of discriminative stimuli, i.e., particular times of the day and particular settings associated with these times. If this technique of meal/snack scheduling leads to regular ingestive patterns, the designated times and places for meals and snacks may become CSs for "hunger" and the initiation of ingestive behavior, while intermeal times become CSs for the absence of hunger reflex and the suppression of eating (e.g., Konoski, 1967). Accordingly, an obese person eating meals and snacks at designated times should begin to report stronger hunger sensations when eating according to the meal/snack schedule. Therefore, control of meal/snack initiation may be transferred from external cues (i.e., "clock time" and special eating settings) to internal physiological hunger cues occurring at the designated temporal intervals, and overeating due to excessive frequency of ingestion may be decreased.

OVEREATING RELATED TO OBESE PERSONS' DIFFICULTY IN MEAL/SNACK TERMINATION

Anecdotally, obese persons are said to "wolf down their food" (Stuart & Davis, 1972; Mahoney, 1975), i.e., they spend less time eating a meal (Wagner & Hewitt, 1975), eat faster (Hill & McCutcheon, 1975), and take more bites and spend less time chewing (Gaul, Craighead, & Mahoney, 1975) than do non-obese individuals, and therefore eat larger meals. Some recent empirical studies (Mahoney, 1975; Warner & Balagura, 1975) yield findings in contradiction with this assumption, however.

Warner and Balagura (1975) for example, studied the intrameal patterns of obese and non-obese college students in both a cafeteria and a laboratory setting. In contrast to previous reports (Schachter, 1971; Nisbett, 1972), these investigators found significant group differences for only one of seven behavioral parameters, the duration of eating. Obese subjects tended to spend a longer time eating their meals, but did not differ from the non-obese in number of bites or number of bites per minute. These findings are reminiscent of Meyer and Pudel's (1972) observation that the cumulative intake curves of obese subjects ingesting liquid food through a straw show

211

a linear slope, unlike the negatively accelerating cumulative intake curves from non-obese persons. Thus, although the evidence is inconclusive, it may be the case that many obese persons actually eat at the same rate as do non-obese persons, but they eat longer and, consequently, ingest more calories in a given meal.

There are at least three possible explanations for the overeating displayed by these obese persons. First, according to Schachter's (1971) theory, obese subjects have learned to eat until external cues for meal termination occur (e.g., until all food has been consumed from the plate). This tendency has been called "the clean plate syndrome." Schachter contends that obese subjects pay relatively less attention to internal physiological satiety cues and more attention to these external stimuli for meal termination. Singh (1973, 1974) has proposed an alternative interpretation that the basic deficit shown by obese persons is their difficulty inhibiting prepotent reflexive and instrumental responses. Thus, Singh accounts for overeating and increased meal size on the basis of a failure to inhibit eating behavior. Yet another explanation for increased meal duration of obese persons is Solomon's theory that obese individuals' taste craving overrides physiological satiety cues, which usually terminate eating in non-obese persons (Solomon, this volume). Training obese subjects to leave increasing portions of uneaten food on the plate at meal termination would be called for by both Schachter's and Singh's theories. This would enable the obese individual to learn to inhibit overeating responding and to remove or modify external stimulus cues (i.e., the clean plate) as conditioned or discriminative stimuli for meal termination. Solomon's hypothesis suggests that one should train the obese person to pause perhaps two thirds of the way through a meal or snack to allow the taste craving to diminish while increasing the strength or probability of appropriate behavior incompatible with overeating. This would place meal termination under the internal stimulus control of physiological satiety cues rather than external food-related cues.

INCREASING THE PERCEPTION OF GASTRIC
MOTILITY AND DISTENSION AS CUES FOR
MEAL INITIATION AND TERMINATION

Despite research calling into question the validity of Schachter's (1971) stimulus binding theory (e.g., Wooley & Wooley, 1975), there are indications that obese persons are somewhat less accurate in perceiving internal satiety cues and that this relative inaccuracy may be clinically important. Coddington and Bruch (1970), for example, observed a trend, which approached statistical significance, for fasted obese subjects to be less accurate than non-obese controls in discriminating a gastric intubation of one ounce of liquid food (Metrecal) from a control intubation of zero ounces.

Stunkard and Fox (1971) found a weak relationship between gastric motility and subjective reports of hunger in normal-weight and obese persons. The records of a group of obese individuals defined as "neurotic" based upon disturbances in body image and the presence of deviant eating patterns (binge eating or night eating syndrome) showed two distinctive characteristics: more frequent decrease in hunger over the 4-hr test period despite continued gastric motility, and impaired perception of individual gastric contractions. Training resulted in improved accuracy in detecting gastric contractions, but did not strengthen the relationship of hunger to gastric motility or improve the ability of obese subjects to control body weight. A possible explanation for these negative training effects is that Stunkard and Fox apparently did not specifically instruct their obese subjects to experience hunger and eat during periods of increased gastric motility. If intensity or frequency of gastric motility is associated with nutrient depletion, then increased accuracy in detecting gastric contractions, experienced as hunger and signalling eating, might facilitate more appropriate meal initiation and weight loss in obese persons.

Apart from the clinical utility of increasing the accuracy of detecting gastric contractions as a hunger cue for meal initiation, we might consider the value of enhancing the perception of gastric distension (or other interoceptive cues related to satiety) and placing these cues in discriminative control of meal termination. For example, we might compare the perception of gastric distension in obese and non-obese persons under conditions of voluntary intragastric feeding (Jordan, 1969). Inaccurate utilization of gastric distension cues by obese persons would be inferred from several indices: 1) variability in voluntary IG meal size (underfeeding or overfeeding), 2) weak association between amount ingested and subjective satiety ratings at meal termination, and 3) inaccurate estimates of amount consumed intragastrically. If these predictions obtain, then, as in the Stunkard and Fox (1971) study, a signal detection or biofeedback paradigm might be instituted to train the obese persons to attend to gastric cues to control the amount of food they ingest. This training procedure might utilize the technique of Coddington and Bruch (1970) with experimenter-controlled parametric manipulation of amount of liquid food intubated, or the voluntary IG feeding approach of Jordan (1969). Empirical support for this strategy comes from the interoceptive animal and human condi-

213

tioning studies using gastric and bladder distension summarized by Razran (1961) and mentioned previously. In addition, Jordan (1969) has demonstrated that human subjects can control their liquid meal size on the basis of gastric volume cues.

Thus, it seems clinically feasible to utilize biofeedback technology to enhance the salience of gastric distension cues and thereby train obese subjects to control meal size. However, the use of nasogastric measuring catheters and IG liquid feedings is inconvenient and requires close medical supervision. Consequently, the search for other satiety cues is called for. For example, directing the subject's attention to the decrease in taste pleasure of a food substance as a function of amount ingested (negative alliesthesia) (Cabanac, Minaire, & Adair, 1968; Cabanac, 1971; Cabanac & Duclaux, 1973) or utilizing biofeedback to inform the subject of the increase of peripheral skin temperature which follows 30-60 min after the beginning of a meal (Stunkard, Clovis, & Free, 1962) would appear to be useful alternative satiety cues. In each case, attention to these sensory correlates of short-term satiety would be enhanced through application of behavioral techniques to slow down the rate of eating (e.g., Jordan & Levitz, 1975) since the peak of negative alliesthesia as well as the maximum peripheral vasodilatation tend to occur 30 min or more after the initiation of ingestion (Cabanac & Duclaux, 1973; Stunkard et al., 1962). The aim of these clinical methods is to train obese persons to attend to changes in orosensory cues from pleasant to unpleasant during the course of a meal, and, more importantly, to increase awareness of internal satiety cues, thereby bringing meal termination under internal stimulus control.

DEVELOPMENTAL ASPECTS OF LEARNING INFLUENCES ON MEAL INITIATION AND TERMINATION

In deriving clinical applications of learning theory for the treatment of obese persons, we should not make the logical error of affirming the consequent and too hastily conclude that the accumulation of excessive adipose tissue is the result of faulty learning experiences. Attention has recently been focussed on prevention or early treatment of infantile or childhood obesity (Winick, 1975). Some provocative evidence exists that the accumulation of an excessive number of adipose "fat" cells early in life in both rats (Knittle & Hirsch, 1968) and possibly human infants (e.g., Brook, Lloyd, & Wolff, 1972) may result in a permanent increase in the number of fat cells in adulthood. This could account for the predisposition of

214

obese children to remain obese in adulthood regardless of subsequent attempts to remove fat through weight loss (Stunkard, 1974). To what extent is this early increase in number of fat cells attributable to genetic causes or to early learning?

Genetic metabolic factors clearly are involved in predisposing certain people to become obese (Seltzer & Mayer, 1965). Moreover, there is recent evidence for innate taste preferences in human newborns and young infants (e.g., Nisbett & Gurwitz, 1970; Desor, Maller, & Turner, 1973; Nowlis & Kessen, 1976), with some indication that newborns with heavier weight show a stronger preference for more concentrated sweet taste solutions than do low birth weight infants (Nisbett & Gurwitz, 1970; Desor et al., 1973). There are also indications that innate differences in temperament may be implicated, since inactive, "placid" babies show a more rapid relative weight gain in the first few months of life (Mack & Kleinhenz, 1974; Ainsworth & Bell, 1969).

There are interesting developmental changes in preferences for sweet and salty tastes which may involve modification of innate taste preferences by learning experiences. Desor, Greene, and Maller (1975) observed that 9-15 yr old subjects preferred greater sweetness and saltiness than did adults. Their cross-sectional study did not investigate the specific relationship between body weight and this developmental shift to preferences for less sweet tastes. Grinker, Price, and Greenwood (1976) recently reported that obese children as young as age eight show an aversion for concentrated sucrose solutions which are preferred by non-obese controls. Grinker and Hirsch (1972) previously found that adult obese subjects displayed a stronger aversion to concentrated sucrose solutions, which was correlated with adipose cell number. Further developmental studies of human taste preferences related to learned dietary intake patterns are required to clarify these puzzling developmental differences between obese and non-obese persons' hedonic reactions to concentrated sucrose solutions.

IMPORTANCE OF PARENT-CHILD INTERACTIONS

It seems likely that careful scrutiny of parent-child interactions may yield a key to understanding the development of food selection habits of children who become obese. Bruch (1973) has proposed that faulty caregiver-infant feeding interactions may also explain how infants learn inappropriate meal initiation and termination patterns resulting in developmental obesity. She suggested that because the caregiver fails to discriminate the infant's signals of hunger from its cues of other internal aversive states, feeding does not occur specifically in response to the infant's biological needs for food, but instead occurs in response to the infant's cues of negative affective states in general. Thus, overfeeding develops as a learned response to general distress. Bruch contends that as a result of this learning process, the infant (and child) confuses hunger and satiety with other internal unpleasant sensations. This confusion persists in adulthood, accounting for the life-long maintenance of obesity and secondary personality disturbances (e.g., negative body image and feelings of personal ineffectiveness) which are more frequently found among juvenile-onset obese (Stunkard & Mendelson, 1967; Stunkard & Burt, 1967) than among adult-onset obese persons. It is tempting to speculate that the adult neurotic obese person's relative inaccuracy in perceiving gastric motility (Stunkard & Fox, 1971) may have its origin in such a faulty learning process, acquired during the early caregiver-infant feeding interaction.

Ainsworth and Bell's (1969) longitudinal study of feeding interactions of 26 white middle-class Baltimore mothers and their infants during the period from birth to age three months provides some case study data consistent with Bruch's learning theory for the development of obesity. For example, two mother-infant dyads were characterized as showing "demand feeding with overfeeding to gratify the baby." These mothers appeared to treat too broad a spectrum of their infants' cues as hunger. They coaxed their infants to overeat at a given feeding and to take meals too frequently. Perhaps as a result, these two infants became relatively overweight and began to oversleep. In two other mother-infant dyads, characterized as showing "scheduled feeding with overfeeding to gratify the baby," the infants slept excessively, requiring their mothers to awaken them to be fed, at which point they coaxed their infants to overeat, with obesity resulting. In this latter case, not only did these two mothers appear to respond inappropriately to their infants' satiety cues, but also the infants' cues were inappropriate—perhaps because of innate temperamental differences in activity and sleeping (i.e., they slept until feeding time rather than signalling mother when hungry).

There is also another potentially important variable to consider in this context. These four obese infants described by Ainsworth and Bell (1969) were bottle-fed. Jordan and Levitz (1975b) suggest that an important biological feedback system for the control of meal size is completely disrupted when the breast is replaced by a bottle. This occurs because with a bottle the mother can use visual

216

cues to control how much formula the infant has to consume. According to Jordan and Levitz, the mother's attitudes can then affect how much the baby is allowed to eat. The likelihood of the mother overfeeding or underfeeding her infant is consequently increased.

It is clear that there is a need for more longitudinal studies of caregiver-infant interactions during feeding over the first three months of the infant's life to attempt to delineate the interaction between innate biological determinants of obesity and proposed early learning mechanisms. One such attempt is currently being undertaken by this investigator. Feeding interactions of a sample of obese and non-obese mothers and their bottle-fed first-born infants will be videotaped during the first three months of life, with periodic follow-up throughout the rest of the first year. These mothers will also keep a simple, yet systematic daily diary of infant sleeping and feeding times and amount of food ingested per feeding. Weekly measures of each infant's length and body weight changes will also be made. Hopefully, these videotapes of caregiver-infant feeding interactions will permit identification of those behavioral cues by which the infant signals his mother that he is hungry or satiated and the mother's response to these infant signals. Perhaps overfeeding and relative rate of weight gain in early infancy may be specifiable as a function of the infant's inappropriate hunger or satiety cues and/or maternal inappropriate responses to these infant signals.

CONCLUSION

In this review of clinical and developmental applications of learning mechanisms in food selection and satiety in obese and non-obese persons, there is a recognition of the importance of considering the "appropriateness of cues to consequences" (Garcia et al., 1974), but also an appeal for more studies delineating the learning processes and physiological substrates involved in the conditioning of meal initiation and termination.

Clinical applications focus on the nature of the postingestive consequences and the ways of increasing the salience of internal satiety cues, shifting control of the initiation and termination of ingestions from external food-related cues to interoceptive stimuli. Clinical treatments for modifying inappropriate food selection habits of obese individuals via conditioning aversions to the taste, smell, and sight of food may be useful when combined with training in self-monitoring and appropriate food selection. Additional behavioral techniques, however, are required to alter inappropriate

217

patterns of meal/snack initiation and problems with meal/snack termination.

Developmentally, there is a need for the longitudinal study of the interaction of innate genetic determinants of obesity (e.g., innate sweet taste preferences, inactivity, and metabolic individual differences contributing to early increase in fat cell number) with early learning in the context of the caregiver-infant feeding interaction. By this approach, overfeeding and rapid weight gain in early infancy should be specifiable as a function of infant inappropriate hunger or satiety cues (innate or acquired) and/or caregiver inappropriate responses to these infant signals. Predictive measures for identifying infants at risk for childhood and adult obesity and learning strategies for early intervention and prevention of developmental obesity should thereby obtain.

FOOTNOTE

[1]It is interesting to note that "stimulus relevance" and "preparedness" of certain food-related cues to aversive consequences appears to be involved in aversion therapy. For example, nausea induced by drugs (e.g., Lemere & Voegtlen, 1950), and by noxious odors (Foreyt & Kennedy, 1971; Morganstern, 1974) is a more effective US for conditioning aversions to alcoholic beverages and to the taste and smell of food than is electric shock. In contrast, for aversion therapy for sexually deviant behavior, electric shock is a more effective US (MacCulloch, Feldman, Orford, & MacCulloch, 1966). [See also Wilson and Davison (1969), Revusky (1973), and Garb and Stunkard (1974) for a further discussion of this issue.]

219

REFERENCES

Ainsworth, M. D. S., & Bell, S. M. Some contemporary patterns of mother-infant interaction in the feeding situation. In A. Ambrose (Ed.), **Stimulation in early infancy.** New York: Academic Press, 1969.

Antin, J., Gibbs, J., Holt, J., Young, R. C., & Smith, G. P. Cholecystokinin elicits the complete behavioral sequence of satiety in rats. **Journal of Comparative and Physiological Psychology,** 1975, **89,** 784-790.

Bandura, A. **Principles of behavior modification.** New York: Holt, Rinehart & Winston, 1969.

Booth, D. A. Conditioned satiety in the rat. **Journal of Comparative and Physiological Psychology,** 1972, **81,** 457-471.

Booth, D. A., & Davis, J. D. Gastrointestinal factors in the acquisition of oral sensory control of satiation. **Physiology and Behavior,** 1973, **11,** 23-29.

Booth, D. A., Lovett, D., & McSherry, G. M. Postingestive modulation of the sweetness preference gradient in the rat. **Journal of Comparative and Physiological Psychology,** 1972, **78,** 485-512.

Brook, C. G. D., Lloyd, J. K., & Wolff, O. H. Relation between age of onset of obesity and size and number of adipose cells. **British Medical Journal,** 1972, **2,** 25-27.

Bruch, H. **Eating disorders: Obesity, anorexia nervosa, and the person within.** New York: Basic Books, 1973.

Cabanac, M. Physiological role of pleasure. **Science,** 1971, **173,** 1103-1107.

Cabanac, M., & Duclaux, R. Alliesthésie olfacto-gustative et prise alimentaire chez l'homme. **Journal de Physiologie** (Paris), 1973, **66,** 113-135.

Cabanac, M., Minaire, Y., & Adair, E. R. Influence of internal factors on the pleasantness of a gustative sweet sensation. **Communications in Behavioral Biology,** 1968, (Part A), **1,** 77-82.

Capretta, P. J. Saccharin consumption and varied conditions of hunger drive. **Journal of Comparative and Physiological Psychology,** 1962, **55,** 656-660.

Coddington, R. D., & Bruch, H. Gastric perceptivity in normal, obese, and schizophrenic subjects. **Psychosomatics,** 1970, **11,** 571-579.

Cravens, R. W., & Renner, K. E. Conditioned appetitive drive states: Empirical evidence and theoretical status. **Psychological Bulletin,** 1970, **73,** 212-220.

Desor, J. A., Greene, L. S., & Maller, O. Preferences for sweet and salty in 9- to 15-year-old and adult humans. **Science,** 1975, **190,** 686-687.

Desor, J. A., Maller, O., & Turner, R. E. Taste in acceptance of sugars by human infants. **Journal of Comparative and Physiological Psychology,** 1973, **84,** 496-501.

Deutsch, J. A., Molina, F., & Puerto, A. Conditioned taste aversion caused by palatable nontoxic nutrients. **Behavioral Biology,** 1976, **16,** 161-174.

Elliott, C. H., & Denney, D. R. Weight control through covert sensitization and false feedback. **Journal of Consulting and Clinical Psychology,** 1975, **43,** 842-850.

Foreyt, J. P., & Kennedy, W. A. Treatment of overweight by aversion therapy. **Behavior Research and Therapy,** 1971, **9,** 29-34.

Garb, J. L., & Stunkard, A. J. Taste aversions in man. **American Journal of Psychiatry,** 1974, **131,** 1204-1207.

Garcia, J., Hankins, W. G., & Rusiniak, K. W. Behavioral regulation of the milieu interne in man and rat. **Science,** 1974, **185,** 824-831.

Gates, J. C., Huenemann, R. L., & Brand, R. J. Food choices of obese and non-obese persons. **Journal of the American Dietetic Association,** 1975, **67,** 339-343.

Gaul, D. J., Craighead, W. E., & Mahoney, M. J. Relationship between eating rates and obesity. **Journal of Consulting and Clinical Psychology,** 1975, **43,** 123-125.

Gibbs, J., Young, R. C., & Smith, G. P. Cholecystokinin decreases food intake in rats. **Journal of Comparative and Physiological Psychology,** 1973, **84,** 488-495.

Grinker, J., & Hirsch, J. Metabolic and behavioral correlates of obesity. In **Physiology, emotion & psychosomatic illness,** (CIBA Foundation Symposium 8), 1972.

Grinker, J. A., Price, J. M., & Greenwood, M. R. C. Studies of taste in childhood obesity. In D. Novin, W. Wyrwicka, & G. Bray (Eds.), **Hunger: Basic mechanisms and clinical implications.** New York: Raven Press, 1976.

Hall, W. G. Weaning and growth of artificially reared rats. **Science,** 1975, **190,** 1313-1315.

Hill, S. W., & McCutcheon, N. B. Eating responses of obese and non-obese humans during dinner meals. **Psychosomatic Medicine,** 1975, **37,** 395-401.

Jordan, H. A. Voluntary intragastric feeding: Oral and gastric contributions to food intake and hunger in man. **Journal of Comparative and Physiological Psychology,** 1969, **68,** 498-506.

Jordan, H. A., & Levitz, L. S. A behavioral approach to the problem of obesity. In T. Silverstone & J. Fincham (Eds.), **Obesity: Pathogenesis and management.** Lancaster: Medical and Technical Publishing Co., 1975 (a).

Jordan, H. A., & Levitz, L. S. Behavior modification in the treatment of childhood obesity. In M. Winick (Ed.), **Childhood obesity.** New York: Wiley, 1975 (b).

Jordan, H. A., Moses, H. III, MacFayden, B. V. Jr., & Dudrick, S. J. Hunger and satiety in humans during parental hyperalimentation. **Psychosomatic Medicine,** 1974, **36,** 144-155.

Knittle, J. L., & Hirsch, J. Effect of early nutrition on the development of rat epididymal fat pads: Cellularity and metabolism. **Journal of Clinical Investigation,** 1968, **47,** 2091-2098.

Konorski, J. **Integrative activity of the brain.** Chicago and London: University of Chicago Press, 1967.

Kurtz, K. H., & Jarka, R. G. Position preference based on differential food privation. **Journal of Comparative and Physiological Psychology,** 1968, **66,** 518-521.

LeMagnen, J. Effets des administrations post-prandiales de glucose sur l' éstablissement des appétits. **Comptes Rendus des Séances de la Société de Biologie,** 1959, **153,** 212-215.

LeMagnen, J. Advances in studies on the physiological control and regulation of food intake. In E. Stellar and J. M. Sprague (Eds.), **Progress in physiological psychology,** New York: Academic Press, 1971.

Lemere, G., & Voegtlen, W. L. An evaluation of the aversion treatment of alcoholism. **Quarterly Journal for the Study of Alcohol,** 1950, **11,** 199-204.

Liebling, D. S., Eisner, J. D., Gibbs, J., & Smith, G. P. Intestinal satiety in rats. **Journal of Comparative and Physiological Psychology,** 1975, **89,** 955-965.

MacCulloch, M. J., Feldman, M. P., Orford, J. F., & MacCulloch, M. L. Anticipatory avoidance learning in the treatment of alcoholism: A record of therapeutic failure. **Behavior Research and Therapy,** 1966, **4,** 187-196.

Mack, R. W., & Kleinhenz, M. E. Growth, caloric intake, and activity levels in early infancy: A preliminary report. **Human Biology,** 1974, **46,** 345-354.

Mahoney, M. J. Fat fiction. **Behavior Therapy,** 1975, **6,** 416-418.

McHugh, P. R., Moran, T. H., & Barton, G. N. Satiety: A graded behavioral phenomenon regulating caloric intake. **Science,** 1975, **190,** 167-169.

Meyer, J., & Grossman, M. I. Release of secretin and cholecystokinin. In L. Demling (Ed.), **Gastrointestinal hormones.** Stuttgart: Georg Thieme Verlag, 1972.

Meyer, J. E., & Pudel, V. Experimental studies on food-intake in obese and normal weight subjects. **Journal of Psychosomatic Research,** 1972, **16,** 305-308.

Meyer, V., & Crisp, A. H. Aversion therapy in two cases of obesity. **Behavior Research and Therapy,** 1964, **2,** 143-147.

Morganstern, K. P. Cigarette smoke as a noxious stimulus in self-managed aversion therapy for compulsive eating: Techniques and case illustration. **Behavior Therapy,** 1974, **5,** 255-260.

Nisbett, R. Hunger, obesity, and the ventromedial hypothalamus. **Psychological Review,** 1972, **79,** 433-453.

Nisbett, R. E., & Gurwitz, S. B. Weight, sex, and the eating behavior of human newborns. **Journal of Comparative and Physiological Psychology,** 1970, **73,** 245-253.

Nowlis, G. H., & Kessen, W. Human newborns differentiate differing concentrations of sucrose and glucose. **Science,** 1976, **191,** 865-866.

Pavlov, I. P. **Conditioned reflexes.** Cambridge: Oxford University Press, 1927.

Razran, G. The observable unconscious and the inferable conscious in current Soviet psychophysiology: Interoceptive conditioning, semantic conditioning, and the orienting reflex. **Psychological Review,** 1961, **68,** 81-147.

Revusky, S. H. Hunger level during food consumption: Effects on subsequent preference. **Psychonomic Science,** 1967, **7,** 109-110.

Revusky, S. H. Some laboratory paradigms for chemical aversion treatment of alcoholism. **Journal of Behavior Therapy and Experimental Psychiatry,** 1973, **4,** 15-17.

Russek, M. Demonstration of the influence of an hepatic glucosensitive mechanism on food-intake. **Physiology and Behavior,** 1970, **5,** 1207-1209.

Schachter, S. Some extraordinary facts about obese humans and rats. **American Psychologist,** 1971, **26,** 129-144.

Seltzer, C. C., & Mayer, J. A review of genetic and constitutional factors in human obesity. **Annals of the New York Academy of Science,** 1965, **134,** 688-695.

Sharma, K. N., & Nasset, E. S. Electrical activity in mesenteric nerves after perfusion of gut lumen. **American Journal of Physiology,** 1962, **202,** 725-730.

Singh, D. Role of response habits and cognitive factors in determination of behavior of obese humans. **Journal of Personality and Social Psychology,** 1973, **27,** 220-238.

Singh, D. Psychology of obesity: Failure to inhibit responses. **Obesity/Bariatric Medicine,** 1974, **3,** 160-165.

Smith, G. P., Gibbs, J., & Young, R. C. Cholecystokinin and intestinal satiety in the rat. **Federation Proceedings,** 1974, **33,** 1146-1149.

Snowdon, C. T. Gastrointestinal sensory and motor control of food intake. **Journal of Comparative and Physiological Psychology,** 1970, **71,** 68-76.

Snowdon, C. T. Production of satiety with small introduodenal infusions in the rat. **Journal of Comparative and Physiological Psychology,** 1975, **88,** 231-238.

Spiegel, T. A. Caloric regulation of food intake in man. **Journal of Comparative and Physiological Psychology,** 1973, **84,** 24-37.

Stellar, E. Brain mechanisms in hunger and other hedonic experiences. **Proceedings of the American Philosophical Society,** 1974, **118,** 276-282.

Stellar, E., & Jordan, H. A. Perception of satiety. In **Perception and its disorders,** Research Publication of the Association for Research in Nervous and Mental Disease, Vol. XLVIII, 1970.

Stuart, R. B., & Davis, B. **Slim chance in a fat world.** Champaign, Ill.: Research Press, 1972.

Stunkard, A. J. Obesity. In **The American handbook of psychiatry,** 2nd Edition, S. Arieti (Ed.), Vol. IV. Organic Disorders and Psychosomatic Medicine. New York: Basic Books, 1974.

Stunkard, A. J. Satiety is a conditioned reflex. **Psychosomatic Medicine,** 1975, **37,** 383-387.

Stunkard, A. J., & Burt, V. Obesity and body image: II. Age at onset of disturbances in the body image. **American Journal of Psychiatry,** 1967, **123,** 1443-1447.

Stunkard, A. J., Clovis, W. L., & Free, S. M. Skin temperatures after eating: Evidence bearing upon a thermostatic control of food intake. **American Journal of the Medical Sciences,** 1962, **244,** 126-130.

Stunkard, A. J., & Fox, S. The relationship of gastric motility and hunger. **Psychosomatic Medicine,** 1971, **33,** 123-134.

Stunkard, A. J., & Mendelson, M. Obesity and body image: I. Characteristics of disturbances in the body image of some obese persons. **American Journal of Psychiatry,** 1967, **123,** 1296-1300.

Wagner, M., & Hewitt, M. I. Oral satiety in the obese and non-obese. **Journal of the American Dietetic Association,** 1975, **67,** 344-346.

Walike, B. C., Jordan, H. A., & Stellar, E. Preloading and the regulation of food intake in man. **Journal of Comparative and Physiological Psychology,** 1969, **68,** 327-333.

Warner, K. E., & Balagura, S. Intrameal eating patterns of obese and non-obese humans. **Journal of Comparative and Physiological Psychology,** 1975, **89,** 778-783.

Wilson, G. T., & Davison, G. C. Aversion techniques in behavior therapy: Some theoretical and metatheoretical considerations. **Journal of Consulting and Clinical Psychology,** 1969, **33,** 327-329.

Winick, M. (Ed.). **Childhood obesity.** New York: Wiley, 1975.

Wooley, O. W., & Wooley, S. C. The experimental psychology of obesity. In T. Silverstone and J. Fincham (Eds.), **Obesity: Pathogenesis and management.** Lancaster: Medical and Technical Publ. Co., 1975.

FOOD AVERSION
LEARNING

X

SPECIFICITY OF CONDITIONING MECHANISMS IN THE MODIFICATION OF FOOD PREFERENCES

THOMAS J. TESTA
University of Pennsylvania
and
Veterans Administration Hospital
(Philadelphia)

and

JOSEPH W. TERNES
Monell Chemical Senses Center
University of Pennsylvania

Those interested in the formation of food aversions sometimes wonder whether or not the conditioning mechanism responsible for such aversions is specific to the taste-visceral system or represents a more general process. Our intention in this chapter is to examine some of the similarities and differences which exist between food-aversion learning and other forms of laboratory conditioning. We will then assess more general mechanisms of conditioning for their ability to explain such differences.

SIMILARITIES BETWEEN LEARNING ABOUT FOODS AND OTHER FORMS OF CONDITIONING

Reward and Punishment. When some neutral stimulus becomes associated with a reward, that stimulus is often approached. In contrast, when some stimulus becomes associated with punishment, the stimulus is avoided. Like these conventional effects of positive and negative incentive, ingestional conditioning also has its analog of reward and punishment. If a food is paired with illness,[1] it is later avoided (see Revusky & Garcia, 1970, for review). If a food is paired with recovery from illness or some other reward, it is approached and ingested (see Zahorik, this volume, for review).

Conditioned Stimulus (CS) and Unconditioned Stimulus (US) Intensity. Classical conditioning occurs more rapidly both as the intensity of the CS is increased and as the intensity of the US is increased. Similarly, food-aversion learning varies directly as a function of CS intensity (e.g., Dragoin, 1971; Nowlis, 1974) and US intensity (e.g., Dragoin, 1971; Garcia, Kimeldorf, & Koelling, 1955; Nachman & Ashe, 1973; Revusky, 1968).

Extinction. When a conditioned stimulus, which has become capable of eliciting a conditioned response, is presented repeatedly without being followed by the unconditioned stimulus, extinction takes place and the conditioned stimulus ceases to elicit the conditioned response. Conditioned aversive tastes also extinguish when they are repeatedly presented without aversive consequences (Garcia et al., 1955). Grote and Brown (1970) have shown that taste aversions will extinguish more rapidly when rats which have been severely deprived of water are given the aversive taste solution as compared to rats which have been mildly deprived. The severely deprived subjects drank more to relieve their thirst, and this greater exposure to the taste CS presumably resulted in the more rapid extinction, in accordance with the expectations from traditional Pavlovian conditioning.

Generalization. When conditioning has occurred to one stimulus and other similar stimuli are subsequently presented, conditioned responses of varying strength occur to these test stimuli. The more similar the test stimulus is to the original conditioning stimulus, the stronger the conditioned response. Taste aversions also appear to display such generalization gradients. For example, Nachman (1963) reported that a conditioned aversion to the taste of lithium chloride also reduced the consumption of sodium chloride, and to lesser degrees, of ammonium chloride, potassium chloride, and water. Repeated tests with these solutions, particularly with sodium chloride, were found to extinguish the aversion not only to the test solution but also to lithium chloride. Apparently generalization occurred between the taste of lithium chloride and these other safe solutions. Domjan (1975) has also demonstrated generalization in the taste-aversion procedure.

Novelty. When an animal first experiences a novel stimulus, that stimulus evokes a strong orienting response, suppresses ongoing behavior, and often causes withdrawal from or avoidance of the stimulus. As the stimulus is repeated, the orienting response becomes habituated and the stimulus no longer interferes with ongoing activity. Additional presentations of the stimulus typically result in investigatory or approach responses. Reactions to taste

230

stimuli appear to be similar. Novel tastes usually suppress ongoing behavior (which by necessity is the drinking response) and cause withdrawal from the stimulus. Subsequent reduction of this neophobic response is directly related to the frequency and duration of taste exposure (see Domjan, this volume, for review).

Sensitization. If a noxious stimulus is presented to an animal, the animal will react with increased vigor to any subsequently presented novel stimulus in that situation. Carroll, Dinc, Levy, and Smith (1975) and Rozin (1968) have reported that rats which were poisoned demonstrate an enhanced neophobia. That is, the prior noxious illness presentation results in a more vigorous reaction to subsequent novel tastes. Domjan (1975; see also Domjan, this volume) reports that the degree of such enhanced neophobia is a function of the similarity of the taste which was paired with illness and the novel test flavor. He found that enhanced flavor neophobia is not evident several days after an illness experience unless the illness was preceded by the ingestion of edibles. Hence, it appears that a persistent enhanced neophobia only occurs to stimuli which share some properties in common with the noxious event itself or stimuli associated with that event. Razran (1971) discusses similar issues with respect to the associative components of sensitization to more traditional stimuli.

Conditioned Inhibition. Many procedures will make a stimulus a conditioned inhibitor. For example, if stimulus A is paired with shock many times and then the simultaneous presentation of stimulus A and a different stimulus B is not followed by shock, the B stimulus will become a conditioned inhibitor (Pavlov, 1927). Recently, Best (1975) reported that a taste solution will acquire inhibitory properties if it is presented without aversive postingestional consequences shortly after exposure to a conditioned aversive taste. This training procedure results in an enhanced preference for the conditioned inhibitory flavor. Taukulis and Revusky (1975) have reported similar results using an odor as the conditioned inhibitory stimulus.

Delay of Reinforcement Gradient. Increases in the interval between a conditioned stimulus and the subsequent presentation of the unconditioned stimulus typically decrease the strength of the resulting association. Such a CS-US delay gradient has been repeatedly observed in taste-aversion learning following initial demonstrations of the phenomenon with apomorphine (Garcia, Ervin, & Koelling, 1966), irradiation (Smith & Roll, 1967), and lithium chloride (Nachman, 1970) serving as the unconditioned stimulus.

Latent Inhibition. If a stimulus is presented to an animal many times before it is first paired with an unconditioned stimulus, it takes many more pairings for that stimulus to become conditioned (Lubow, 1973; Siegel, 1969). Studies which vary the number of taste preexposures prior to the first taste-illness pairings have similarly shown that such CS preexposure markedly retards the development of subsequent taste aversions (e.g., Domjan, 1972; Elkins, 1973; Farley, McLaurin, Scarborough, & Rawlings, 1964; McLaurin, Farley, & Scarborough, 1963; Revusky & Bedarf, 1967).

US Preexposure. If an unconditioned stimulus is presented many times before it is paired with a CS, the formation of an association between the CS and US is retarded. The taste-aversion phenomenon is also strongly affected by preconditioning illness exposure. If the illness US is presented several times before the first taste-illness pairing little aversion develops to the taste (see Braveman, Gamzu, this volume, for reviews).

DOES LEARNING ABOUT FOODS INVOLVE UNIQUE MECHANISMS?

The similarities between characteristics of traditional conditioning phenomena and learning about foods underscore the assumption that associative processes are indeed involved in the formation of taste aversions (cf. Revusky & Garcia, 1970). However, it is also of interest to note that because many have considered the association of a taste with an illness to be a unique form of conditioning, they have often approached certain characteristics of the phenomenon as being equally unique. Consider some examples.

Neophobia has been discussed repeatedly in the literature as an adaptive specialization which prevents animals from ingesting potentially harmful substances (e.g., Rozin & Kalat, 1971). It is difficult to understand why this characteristic of feeding behavior has been treated as though unique to ingestive responses. As Domjan (1976) has recently suggested, neophobia for edibles is similar to the reaction to novelty which is characteristic for nearly all stimuli and most organisms. In some way, poison-enhanced neophobia has also been attributed to specializations of the feeding system (Rozin, 1968). However, there is an obvious analogy between this phenomenon and the one more traditionally known as sensitization. The characteristics of the poison-enhanced neophobic reaction (see Domjan, this volume) are very similar to those of sensitization (detailed by Razran, 1971). When a noxious US is presented in some situations, the animal is effectively energized and set to react much more vigorously to other stimuli (particularly novel ones). The greater the similarities which exist between the

232

context of the US presentation and the test stimuli, the greater the sensitization. Domjan reports that (1) when the illness is preceded by a taste, the greatest neophobia occurs to similar tastes, and (2) a persistent enhanced neophobia occurs to ingestive stimuli only when ingestion occurs prior to poisoning. Apparently the new concept of poison-enhanced neophobia is a combination of three more traditional traits: the reaction to novelty, stimulus generalization, and sensitization. *Novel* stimuli are always avoided. When a situation is considered dangerous (as it is when poisoning has been experienced), the animal is *sensitized* to such novelty, and when any similarities exist between the poisoning experience and the test situation such that *generalization* might occur, the reaction to novelty is further sensitized.

Similarly, the latent inhibition effect noted in taste-aversion conditioning can also be attributed to conventional concepts, rather than notions such as learned safety or learned noncorrelation (Kalat, this volume). Preconditioning taste exposures may retard later taste-aversion formation because the preexposures affect the taste-illness contingency. Rescorla (1967) has argued that the formation of an association is determined by the degree of contingency which exists between the to-be-associated events. A contingency in turn is determined by the conjoint probabilities of occurrence of the unconditioned stimulus given the conditioned stimulus and the unconditioned stimulus given no conditioned stimulus. Establishment of associations among more traditional stimuli has been shown to be a function of these conditional probabilities (Rescorla, 1968). According to this definition of a contingency, taste preexposures lower the conditional probability of illness given the occurrence of that particular taste. If the first taste presentation is paired with illness, the probability of the US given the CS is free to approach one. However, if for example, three taste presentations have preceded the first taste-illness pairing, the conditional probability of the US given the CS would become .25 rather than one.[2,3]

In order to preserve the taste-toxicosis association as a special case, many authors have also ignored the more conventional explanations of the US preexposure effect. For example, if the illness preexposure effect is treated like the more traditional conditioning situation, we might assume that such a procedure affects the CS-US contingency as does the latent inhibition prodedure. In this case the prior exposure to the US should function to increase the conditional probability of the US in the absence of the CS. In fact, such US exposure might raise this inhibitory probability to one and greatly reduce subsequent excitatory conditioning. However, as Rescorla and Wagner (1972) have concluded, it is much more reasonable to assume that US preexposure interferes with subsequent conditioning because it results in an association of non-CS background situational cues with the US. Such exteroceptive conditioning has been reported by several authors. For example, Mitchell, Kirschbaum, and Perry (1975) observed that rats develop an avoidance response to food containers paired with illness when the relative novelty of apparatus cues is controlled. (For further discussion of exteroceptive conditioning, see Best, Best, & Henggeler; Braveman; and Nachman, Rauschenberger, & Ashe, this volume.) More directly, Krane (1975) has shown that toxicosis preexposure will differentially affect subsequent taste-aversion formation depending on the novelty of the exteroceptive cues which are present at the time of US preexposure and subsequent taste-illness pairing. He demonstrated that US presentation in a very novel environment will attenuate the subsequent formation of a taste aversion to a greater degree than US presentations which occur in a more familiar environment. Presumably, the greater novelty of these exteroceptive cues permitted stronger conditioning to background cues, and this in turn had a greater effect on the subsequent taste-aversion conditioning.

The food-aversion learning phenomenon has often been described as an example of adaptive specialization of learning (Garcia, McGowen, & Green, 1972; Seligman, 1970; Rozin & Kalat, 1971). The preceding examples suggest that this label has frequently influenced the nature of explanatory concepts which have been employed to aid our understanding of certain characteristics of the phenomenon. Often perfectly acceptable concepts employed in other areas of learning were overlooked. At times these concepts were abandoned in favor of evolutionary arguments. At other times new terminology was invoked when in fact the more traditional nomenclature was appropriate. Thus, it appears that many characteristics of traditional conditioning phenomena are present in food-illness conditioning, although these characteristics have been given new names or explained in different ways.

DIFFERENCES BETWEEN THE FOOD-AVERSION PHENOMENON AND OTHER FORMS OF CONDITIONING

Although many similarities exist between traditional conditioning and food-toxicosis conditioning, this is not sufficient evidence that identical mechanisms are involved. In fact, the differences which exist between food-aversion learning and other forms of learning have led some to conclude that the food-toxicosis association is a specialized form of learning aided by specialized genetic foundations. The critical distinctions which support such a position are that (1) food aversions can form within only one trial, (2) food aversions can form even though a long delay occurs between the taste and subsequent illness, and (3) tastes will become readily associated with illnesses but lights and sounds will not. Our intention is to discuss several attributes inherent in the food-toxicosis procedure which could produce these unique features of the phenomenon in accordance with traditional theoretical principles. We will speak of traditional theoretical principles when referring to those rules of event covariation which are silent with respect to the indigenous nature of the events themselves. It should be noted that although each attribute of the food-toxicosis procedure may not be critical by itself, when taken together as a group all may contribute to large effects on the observed conditioning rate parameters. These attributes fall into five categories: (1) novelty, (2) preexperimental associations, (3) competing stimulus paradigms, (4) learning about objects, and (5) indicant response requirements.

NOVELTY

The preexperimental environmental history of the laboratory rat may be such that biases on a dimension of novelty will be involved when the conditioning of auditory and visual stimuli is compared to the conditioning of tastes. Rats are typically fed one type of solid food and unflavored water throughout most of their preexperimental lives. In contrast, they hear many sounds of differing intensities, durations, and frequencies and are exposed to countless varying visual events. The use of auditory and visual stimuli thus ensures a low degree of novelty of such stimuli when employed in a conditioning paradigm. This should, as previously discussed, reduce the maximal conditional probability of the US given the CS which can be attained on the first CS-US pairing. The relatively greater novelty of flavors should, conversely, permit the conditional probability of the US given a flavor CS to approach one on the first taste-illness pairing.

PREEXPERIMENTAL ASSOCIATIONS

Although most laboratory rats only experience a limited variety of flavors, they do repeatedly engage in eating and drinking. These preexperimental experiences with eating and drinking and their accompanying stimuli are always followed by interoceptive consequences of the sort discussed by Revusky and Garcia (1970). When eating or drinking occurs, proprioceptive stimulation as well as oral receptor stimulation such as wetness, coldness, texture, and viscosity reliably precedes natural gastric and other interoceptive stimuli. Such experiences are repeated several thousand times in the life of the typical rat, and this preexperimental history should provide the regular conditions for the association of oral stimulation with interoceptive changes.

Although tastes and other oral stimuli are correlated with gastric stimuli, lights and sounds which are seen and heard in the colony room are not. They bear little relationship to gastric events. Independence between these events should lead to future associative interference.

There is some data which supports the contention that preexperimental associations are critical to the formation of toxicosis-induced aversions. Lucy Sullivan (personal communication) has demonstrated that when rats are raised in an environment in which visual cues are made predictive of ingestive consequences and taste cues are made irrelevant, conditioning of taste aversions and visual aversions occur at the same rate and to the same degree. Certainly, more of these developmental studies should be attempted. It appears that although prior experience should provide positive transfer for oral-event gastric-event associations, the same experience might retard, due to associative interference, the association of auditory or visual events with the same gastric events.

Preexperimental associations between orosensory and postingestional stimuli probably occur not only because these two types of cues are repeatedly paired during normal ingestive activity. Orosensory and postingestional stimulation are also similar in location and temporal intensity patterns. The contribution of these variables to food-aversion learning is described further below.

COMPETING STIMULUS PARADIGMS

Studies which have assessed the relevance of taste cues to illness consequences have employed a special variant of the double-dissociation procedure. Garcia and Koelling's (1966) study provides the prototype. Rats were permitted to drink from a vessel which provided taste as well as audiovisual stimulation contingent on drinking. Half the subjects had this drinking paired with illness; the remaining rats had this drinking paired with foot-shock. The subjects were then separately tested with the taste and audiovisual CSs. Poisoned rats displayed an aversion to only the taste CS, whereas shocked rats showed an aversion to only the audiovisual CS.

As Schwartz (1974) has noted, a double-dissociation procedure of the type used by Garcia and Koelling (1966) is essential to the demonstration of stimulus-specific associations. But, there is nothing in the double-dissociation strategy which demands that both audiovisual and taste cues be presented simultaneously in a within-group design. It is possible that such simultaneous-CS procedure introduces a bias into the results. As Kamin (1969) and Rescorla and Wagner (1972) have shown, when two CSs of differing associability are presented simultaneously, the one which is more highly associable with the US will take the majority of associative strength and overshadow or block the conditioning of the second stimulus. Because one stimulus is slightly more associable with the US, the second becomes redundant and gathers little associative strength. Therefore, it is somewhat presumptive to conclude that when two CSs such as audiovisual cues and tastes are made to compete with one another for association with toxicosis, that one stimulus is more specific for rapid conditioning to the US because there is a difference between the magnitude of the conditioned reactions subsequently elicited by each stimulus. One stimulus may only be slightly more conditionable. When taste and exteroceptive stimuli are made to compete with one another, as in the Garcia and Koelling study, the taste stimulus may take a major portion of the associative strength, leaving the other exteroceptive stimulus redundant and unconditioned. Thus, the associability difference might not be very great if conditioning to tastes alone was compared to conditioning to audiovisual cues alone.

LEARNING ABOUT OBJECTS

Although the difference in associability of tastes and audiovisual cues with toxicosis may be very exaggerated when the two types of stimuli are made to compete for associative strength, one may still conclude that tastes are somewhat more associable with toxicosis than are audiovisual events. We must then explain this real, albeit smaller, discrepancy. Two possible explanations have been offered: (1) tastes are usually more novel and thus more associable and (2) tastes have been subjected to a preexperimental conditioning set in which a taste-toxicosis association is readily generalizable from the familiar prior experience in which tastes are followed by normal interoceptive effects.

However, there is another characteristic of the taste-aversion conditioning procedure which we believe facilitates the rapid learning despite long CS-US intervals. Taste-aversion conditioning probably has something to do with learning about objects. Assume that when an aversion is formed, the subject does not associate a taste with an illness but instead associates an ingested liquid or solid *object* with illness and only identifies that object by its taste. This is not a trivial distiction because it leads to several new conclusions. Most notably, it suggests that more than one association is always formed in such a procedure. A liquid is associated with illness and some discriminative cue, the taste, is associated with the liquid.

How do we come to know the attributes of an object or that an event originates from, or is caused by, an object? Suppose you have noticed a box in front of you which emits a glow and a hum. In order to learn more about the object you might approach it. As you do, several things will happen. First, the size of the retinal image of the object will gradually grow larger as you approach, the intensity of the glow will become greater, and the hum will grow louder. Most important is the fact that the temporal intensity patterns and the location of each of these stimulus changes will be identical. This identity will promote the rapid formation of multiple associations among these attributes, the result of which will be the formation of a mental representation of the object (Testa, 1974, 1975). It is suggested that such event covariations, and their accompanying microcontingencies, are responsible for the many basic associative perceptual processes constituting object learning.

Consider a case from the shock-avoidance paradigm. A very important *object* in the escape-avoidance procedure is the grid floor. Learning about this object should be rapid, as associations are formed between the tactile stimuli of hardness, coldness, smoothness, and so on. All of these have the same location and vary with the same temporal intensity pattern as contact is made and broken with the grid object. When shock is presented via the grids, this quality also varies as a function of the others, and "shockness" becomes a trait of the object. Later, the previously neutral qualities can function as cues for the more important shock attribute (Testa, 1974).

Assuming that taste-aversion formation requires object learning, the object which is most important is the ingested substance. It, like the grids, has certain attributes such as taste and one most important attribute, toxicity. Consider how these traits vary with each other:

Association of the Taste with the Ingested Object. The taste becomes associated with the ingested object for the same reason that the hardness becomes associated with the grids. Every lick

238

produces a complex of stimulus attributes, all of which covary as functions of the others. Each contact with the edible causes an intensification of the taste quality as well as the quality of wetness, coldness, texture, viscosity, and so on. The similarity of the temporal intensity patterns and locations of these stimuli will cause rapid association of the taste with the ingested object. It should be noted that we are not in fact suggesting that hardness becomes associated with grids or that taste becomes associated with some edible. More correctly we assume that an associative network is formed among all the traits of the physical object. The important fact is that the physical constraints placed on these stimuli require that they covary similarly in time and space. This reduces to a similarity in temporal intensity patterns and locations when considered psychologically. It is also interesting to note that tactile and taste receptors (the proximal senses) maintain this correlation of attributes most closely. These are not trivial distinctions. We will argue that tastes are ideal stimuli for association with toxicosis because they also are ideal stimuli for association with ingested objects. It is suggested that the illness is associated with previously-ingested substances. Therefore, *any* cue which is made to be associated with or is an attribute of the ingested object will be capable of entering into a quick association with illness. In order to understand how the edible is ultimately associated with illness we must first consider how the ingested object becomes associated with the normal interoceptive gastric consequences of ingestion.

Association of the Ingested Object with its Interoceptive Effects. Two factors promote the formation of this association. First, a great deal of preexperimental conditioning has occurred. Ingestion has typically been followed by interoceptive effects on numerous occasions. Secondly, even without a great deal of pretraining, associations of oral stimulation with postingestional changes should still form rapidly. All eating and drinking provides a temporal pattern of oral stimulation which is a function of the rat's rate of consumption. These oral stimuli are always followed by gastric stimulation, the temporal pattern of which is also a function of the rate of consumption. The faster the rat eats or drinks, the faster its stomach fills. The consistent pairing of oral stimuli with normal gastric stimuli which have the same temporal intensity patterns and similar locations should promote the formation of strong associations between the two events (Testa, 1974, 1975). Figure 1 schematically represents the intensity patterns which may be experienced by rats while drinking. The curve on the left represents the cumulative drinking patterns. The curve on the right represents

239

the patterns of interoceptive stimulation which should follow such a drinking pattern. It should be noted that patterns of stimulus change may be substituted for intensity. That is, during the continued bout of drinking the nature of the oral stimulation is assumed to change as a function of preceding oral stimuli (hence the cumulative curve for taste stimulation).

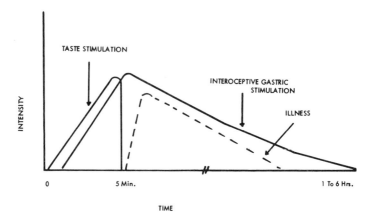

Figure 1
Theoretical functions representing the patterns of stimulation experienced by rats in the typical food-aversion conditioning trial.

Association of the Illness with the Interoceptive Gastric Consequences of Ingestion. Although the location and temporal pattern of oral stimulation is similar to the pattern of normal consequent interoceptive stimulation while the subject is ingesting, when consumption stops the two forms of stimulation become very different. Oral stimulation ceases abruptly but interoceptive stimulation continues to change following one exposure to an edible until the next exposure, rising to some maximum shortly after one exposure and decreasing slowly and continually until the next exposure. It is this extended pattern of changing interoceptive stimulation which may become associated with the extended pattern of toxicosis stimulation. The location and temporal intensity pattern of interoceptive effects due to ingestion may be similar to the location and temporal intensity pattern of the illness stimulation. This may provide for the rapid association of the illness with the interoceptive effects of the ingested substance. The association of the taste with the edible then provides the proper bridging association by which the taste

240

becomes aversive and is subsequently avoided. In this way, the extended stimulation arising from the interoceptive effects of ingestion permits associations to form over long delays because even though there is a long delay between the taste and the illness, the delay is not necessarily long between the interoceptive effects of ingestion and the illness. In fact, these two events may very well coincide. For instance, some emetic drugs which have been used to induce illness actually work on the digestive process and thus presumably follow a time course which approximates that process. Other drugs, although they may not affect digestion, are injected in such a way that their rate of absorption approximates that of edibles. The temporal intensity patterns of these illnesses should therefore be similar to the temporal intensity patterns of the interoceptive consequences of ingestion; the locations should be identical (see Figure 1).

INDICANT RESPONSE REQUIREMENTS

We have mentioned several ways in which the taste-aversion paradigm differs from other more traditional conditioning procedures. There is another factor deserving our attention, the nature of the indicant response. In any conditioning procedure, the experimenter usually wishes to assess the formation of an association. The association itself may involve two events which are completely controlled by the experimenter, as in Pavlovian conditioning. The formation of an association is usually inferred by some response which is likely to occur if the to-be-associated events have indeed become associated. Often this indicant response is a natural or reflexive consequence of the association. However, in many procedures the critical association will affect behavior only after a second association between the indicant response and some other outcome has developed. This learning-performance distinction is most obvious in the avoidance procedure. The typical avoidance response will occur only after a CS-US association has been formed and a response-CS termination association has been formed. Hence, the speed of acquisition of the avoidance response is a function of the speed of acquisition of two associations.

In the same way, the speed of acquisition of a taste aversion is a function of two associations: one which makes the taste aversive, and one which enables the subject to demonstrate its aversion. In this case, the second association provides the basis for the passive avoidance response of no ingestion. This must be an association of the ingestive response with the production of the flavor CS. It may be that the rapidity with which taste aversions can develop is a

241

function of the subject quickly learning what to do in order *not* to taste the aversive CS. One trial learning might therefore be a more common phenomenon if the development of the indicant response did not slow the revelation of the important association. One-way avoidance responding seems to be a case in which the indicant avoidance response is quickly acquired. Taste aversions appear to be another. While the association between flavor and illness may occur rapidly for the reasons discussed previously, the association between the ingestive response and the production or termination of the aversive flavor should also occur rapidly. This is because the proprioceptive stimulation which arises from the ingestive response has the same pattern and location as the stimulation of the flavor CS. The response and the CS should thus be quickly associated and the taste-illness association should be demonstrated as rapidly as the second association forms.

EXPERIMENTAL PREDICTIONS AND EVIDENCE

ASSOCIATION OF TASTE AND INGESTED OBJECT

Tastes are ultimately associated with illness because they are associated with the ingested object. Association of the taste with the edible object is assumed to occur because the location and temporal intensity pattern of the taste stimulation is identical to the location and temporal intensity patterns of all other aspects of oral stimulation provided by the ingested object. We conclude from this that only stimuli which bear this special relationship with the edible will permit aversions to develop rapidly. Typically lights and sounds are undifferentiated with respect to such objects, especially when distantly located.

Certain aspects of this prediction have been studied. For example, in an odor-aversion conditioning experiment, Taukulis (1974) maximized the similarity in the location and temporal intensity pattern of the odor CS and a liquid object (water) and found substantial conditioning with CS-US intervals as long as 8 hr.[4] This contrasts with previous investigators who failed to obtain long-delay odor aversion learning using a more diffuse olfactory stimulus (e.g., Hankins, Garcia, & Rusiniak, 1973). Perhaps any stimulus which is made to bear similarities with the ingested substance will become associated with that object and will therefore become associated with illness.

It is interesting to note that odor CSs which are not restricted in such a way that they become attributes of the ingested liquid are capable of directing exploratory motor responses and can be conditioned to shock (Hankins, Rusiniak, & Garcia, 1976).

ASSOCIATION OF INGESTED OBJECT
AND INTEROCEPTIVE STIMULATION

The oral attributes of the ingested object become associated with the interoceptive effects of ingestion, particularly early gastric stimulation, because the temporal pattern and location of oral stimulation is similar to that of gastric stimulation. Pretreatment with stomach loading to dissociate the patterns of interoceptive gastric stimulation and oral stimulation would provide a test of this hypothesis. Holman (1968) reported work along these lines. He demonstrated in several ways that associations are definitely formed between the oral attributes of a substance and interoceptive events. Rats which have had a certain taste paired with intragastric feeding of a nutritive substance come to prefer that taste over a taste which was paired with intragastric infusion of water. He also demonstrated that only rats which receive both oral stimulation and intragastric feeding will learn to bar press for intragastric feeding. This implies that oral stimulation acts as a good secondary reinforcer which bridges the gap between bar pressing and the delayed interoceptive consequences. Studies which assess the influence of developmental factors (i.e., preexperimental experiences in which oral stimulation is followed by interoceptive stimulation) have yet to be reported. It is also of interest to ask whether exteroceptive cues which are contingent with intragastric infusion and which follow similar temporal intensity patterns with the rate of stomach loading during infancy might not make lights or other exteroceptive cues prepotent as associates with illness and the like. Holman's work clearly implies that many stimuli become associated with interoceptive gastric events and that rats can readily discriminate these gastric occurrences. His rats often licked and gnawed the bar which delivered intragastric infusion. This indicates that such exteroceptive cues can become associated with interoceptive effects.

ASSOCIATION OF INTEROCEPTIVE STIMULATION AND ILLNESS

The location and temporal intensity patterns of the changes in interoceptive stimulation which follow the cessation of ingestive behaviors and which are normal consequences of ingestion are the same or very similar to the location and temporal intensity patterns of most illnesses. This similarity causes an association to develop

243

rapidly between these events. If this hypothesis is correct, we would expect that taste-aversion conditioning would be affected by the presence or absence of interoceptive stimulation. That is, subjects which tasted but did not ingest a substance would be expected to learn a weaker aversion. Bradley and Mistretta (1971) reported that rats will form an aversion to saccharin if the flavor is followed by illness, even if the saccharin has been experienced via intravascular administration. Clearly little intragastric stimulation followed as a direct consequence of this taste experience (although rats were permitted continuous access to food and water following injection of the sodium saccharin and prior to illness onset). Unfortunately, the authors did not report the degree of aversion found in a group which experienced the flavor as a function of normal fluid ingestion. They did report, however, that the saccharin concentration which was necessary to yield positive results with intravascular CS presentation was many times higher than the normal saccharin concentration commonly used when the CS is ingested. Likewise the degree of their conditioned aversion was much less severe than what is commonly found with an ingested CS. Domjan and Wilson (1972) directly measured the strength of an aversion formed without mediating gastric stimuli and found that "rats tasting but not ingesting a flavored solution prior to toxicosis acquired *weaker* aversions to the flavor than subjects that actively consumed the CS during conditioning" (p. 403). A similar finding was later reported in odor-toxicosis conditioning (Domjan, 1973).

Taste-aversion formation has also been reported to be, within limits, an increasing function of the volume of liquid ingested (e.g., Barker, 1976). Although one may interpret this relationship to be a result of increased exposure to the flavor CS, we interpret it to be a function of interoceptive stimulation. Without enough ingested liquid, there is insufficient interoceptive stimulation and thus a lesser association of this stimulation with illness.

Studies of "backward" taste-aversion conditioning motivated by radiation exposure (see Barker, Smith, & Suarez, this volume for review) can also be interpreted in this context. It has been shown that the optimal placement of the liquid ingestion period is sometime after irradiation. We suggest that such a placement moves the pattern of ingested liquid interoceptive stimulation more in phase with the illness pattern of radiation.

The importance of covariation between interoceptive gastric stimulation and illness is also implicated by research comparing various routes of administration of aversive agents. Lester, Nachman, and Le Magnen (1970) evaluated the aversion-inducing effects of intraperitoneal injection (IP), intracardiac injection (IC), and stomach intubation (ST) of ethanol administration. They found a significant difference between the IP and IC routes on the one hand and ST on the other hand. They concluded that the aversion-inducing effects of ethanol are mediated systemically and depend on the speed, intensity and duration of intoxication. Since the duration of intoxication did not differ after equal doses by different routes, the speed of onset of intoxication appeared to be the most important factor. However, duration does appear to be important when other aversive agents are used. Coussens (1975; see also Coussens, Crowder, & Davis, 1973) reported that while IP injections of amphetamine sulphate and morphine sulphate were adequate USs for taste-aversion formation, the same drugs, when injected intravenously (IV) resulted in substantially less aversion. He suggested that this finding occurred because with IV administration the action of the drugs was too brief to produce an aversion. Additional support for this contention was provided by an experiment demonstrating that cocaine administered alone (either IP or IV) does not motivate taste-aversion learning unless the subjects are pretreated with alphamethyltyrosine, a drug which is believed to increase the duration of action of cocaine. Findings such as these fit well with the notion that the illness stimulation must be similar in temporal pattern to the normal interoceptive stimulation which follows liquid ingestion. Such interoceptive stimulation usually has a long duration, because it decays slowly in time.[5]

Nachman and Hartley (1975) reported data which might also be interpreted as a temporal patterning effect. These investigators compared the ability of several rodenticides with that of lithium chloride in producing learned taste aversions and found that highly toxic poisons which have onset delays and durations of action which are very different from lithium chloride are less likely to produce aversions. The effects of these rodenticides, like IV injected drugs, may decay *too* quickly or act with inappropriate temporal patterns.

We should note that according to this explanation, the ideal conditions for forming a taste aversion occur when the temporal pattern and location of illness are very similar to the pattern and location of interoceptive stimuli, which in turn are very similar to the pattern and location of taste stimulation. As we suggested previously, this situation is approximated when an injection of poison follows a period of ingestion. However, the various patterns are not identical in this case because only the onset and duration of taste stimulation are similar to the onset of interoceptive effects stimula-

245

tion, and only the decay pattern of the interoceptive effects is similar to the decay pattern of illness (see Figure 1). According to our model, aversion conditioning should occur most rapidly when the poison is actually dissolved in the taste solution. Here the onset of poison effects will begin at a rate proportional to the drinking rate, which itself will determine the rate of growth of interoceptive effects. Nachman (1963) has shown that this procedure produces very rapid and stable taste aversions. As few as 200 licks of the liquid poison may be sufficient (J. C. Smith, personal communication).

The results of Coussens (1975), Lester et al. (1970) and possibly of Nachman and Hartley (1975) imply that a drug which either starts too slowly or decays long before the decay of the normal interoceptive stimulation caused by liquid ingestion will be less likely to become associated with such an interoceptive stimulus pattern. This conclusion is very similar to those of Krane and Wagner (1975). They tested various CS-US intervals in taste-aversion conditioning with shock serving as the unconditioned stimulus and found better conditioning with 30- and 210-sec CS-US intervals than with a 5-sec CS-US interval delay. They explained these results by assuming that taste stimulus traces are slow to decay. Therefore, when the shock was delayed (in the 30- and 210-sec groups) the taste CS trace did not outlast the shock. The authors argued that with the 5-sec CS-US interval extension of the CS trace into the postshock interval interfered with learning. This explanation is in agreement with Coussens' and Lester et al.'s data and with the similarity in temporal patterning argument. The distinction between the two explanations is that, according to Krane and Wagner, the longer decay of the CS trace appears to be a decay in the actual taste stimulus trace. The present argument assumes that the slowly decaying trace which permits long delay learning is the interoceptive stimulation which results from the ingestion of the flavored liquid.

CONCLUSION

We have made an attempt in this paper to enumerate the important aspects of the food-aversion learning phenomenon. We feel that these factors should be studied carefully before the phenomenon is deemed a strong biological predisposition. In closing we wish to emphasize two points.

First, the arguments presented in this paper are to be contrasted with other mediational positions. For example, the after-taste explanation of food-aversion learning is very different from the explanation offered in this paper. No appeal is made to an extended or prolonged taste stimulus. In fact, our discussion of the Krane and Wagner research details our theoretical position regarding the nature and role of the taste stimulus. The taste event itself is not assumed to persist long after the cessation of drinking. Rather, we assume that the taste becomes associated with the interoceptive consequences of ingestion which do last long after drinking stops. This assertion is most similar to the mediational hypothesis offered by Revusky and Garcia (1970). They note that one might postulate the association of the after-effects of ingestion with illness. However, they discount this position citing the work of Smith and Roll (1967) who demonstrated an aversion when poisoning occurred as long as 12 hr after ingestion. We do not feel that this data is critical to our argument. When an animal is placed on a restricted feeding or watering schedule, it is reasonable to assume that the interoceptive state changes continually between each period of ingestion. A pattern of illness occurring several hours after ingestion may still approximate the delayed interoceptive changes which are a consequence of ingestion and which mediate the formation of an association between food and illness.

The second point we wish to emphasize in conclusion is the possible importance of interactions. Too often the effect of some variable "y" will be measured in one experimental procedure and shown to have little effect on the conditioning of a taste aversion. Later, another procedure is undertaken but because the variable "y" was shown to be unimportant in the first study, it is subsequently not controlled for. However, variable "y" may become critical in combination with the new procedures. The recent exchange between Garcia and his colleagues and Bitterman (Garcia, Hankins, & Rusiniak, 1976; Bitterman, 1976) illustrates this point. Garcia et al. note several empirical demonstrations which make their case for taste-toxicosis associative predispositions while Bitterman underscores several weaknesses in the methodology of these experiments, preferring to reserve judgment on the issue until less controversial evidence is presented. This problem is an important feature of this chapter.

Many of the factors which were discussed have been found to be ineffective in determining food aversions individually. However, we suggest that these factors may interact at certain levels of each variable to contribute to large effects on the observed conditioning rate parameters. Consider the example of overshadowing. It was suggested that simultaneously presenting a taste stimulus with a light-noise stimulus during conditioning might result in over-shadowing or blocking of the light-noise cue by the taste cue, leading to the erroneous conclusion that the taste was far more easily conditioned than the light and noise. Domjan and Wilson (1972a) tested this possibility. Using a buzzer as the CS for one group without any taste and a taste as the CS for the other group without a buzzer, rats always associated the taste with illness but not the buzzer. This shows that the blocking effect cannot be responsible for the original data reported by Garcia and Koelling (1966). However, suppose one then wished to test the role of similar location and temporal intensity patterns in the association of exteroceptive cues and illness. It would be a mistake to ignore the blocking factor at this point since it may very well be important in this other context. More obviously, if one wished to test the effects of experience during development it would be unfortunate if one neglected to prevent simultaneous exposures of taste and light-contingent interoceptive stimuli in the same subjects. It might be equally unfortunate if one overlooked the influence of temporal patterning and location in such a case merely because such factors are not important in adulthood (e.g., Green, Bouzas, & Rachlin, 1972). As we noted earlier, by providing a learning set in which visual cues rather than taste cues were predictive of interoceptive consequences Sullivan was able to eliminate the usual discrepancy in the rate with which taste cue aversions and visual cue aversions occurred. In combination with such developmental studies the contribution of overshadowing or locations and temporal intensity patterns could be critical.

The possible importance of interactions should also be considered, for example, in connection with the contribution of taste novelty to the selective association of taste as compared to exteroceptive cues with illness. One cannot dismiss this variable by simply equating the relative novelty of taste and exteroceptive cues. It is also necessary to equate these stimuli with respect to the other factors we discussed earlier, such as preexperimental associations and similarity of location and temporal intensity patterns to the consequence. We recognize that novelty of taste stimuli alone cannot account for the speed and selectivity of food-aversion learning. However, when these other factors are controlled, the novelty of tastes may become a critical variable. In fact, it is possible that only when all of these factors work additively in the same situation will an association form between non-food CSs and non-illness USs as rapidly as the typical food aversion.

FOOTNOTES

[1]Although we use the term illness or toxicosis throughout this chapter, we are referring to any ionizing radiation, toxin or drug effect which produces a taste aversion. Levy, Carroll, Smith, and Hofer (1974) suggest that histamine release is the basis of such conditionable interoceptive states. Braveman (this volume) suggests that stress is a common component of these states. At any rate the terms illness or drug effect are interchangeable for our purposes.

[2]It should be noted that this account of latent inhibition is orthogonal to that for the development of conditioned inhibition, and thus the findings of Reiss and Wagner (1972) and Best (1975) which indicate that latent and conditioned inhibition are two different phenomena are not at all contradictory.

[3]The concept of latent inhibition is important in this context because the role of novelty versus familiarity is easily analyzed. When a novel CS is paired with some US, the conditional probability of the US given the CS will immediately be one. This is one reason why novel stimuli may permit optimal conditioning. One should note at this point that Kalat (1974) has shown that rats form stronger aversions to solutions which are more concentrated not because such a solution is more salient but because it is more novel (i.e., unlike the familiar solutions). Kalat raised rats on a very concentrated solution and found that they formed greater aversions to the least concentrated of two test solutions. Thus, the conditionability of a CS and US appears to be a function of the novelty of the CS, which in turn is a function of that CS's generalizability to other familiar CSs.

[4]Taukulis's results may reflect a taste and not an odor aversion since the animals might have tasted the odor molecules in the airstream which was directed at the animals' faces.

[5]It should be noted that Nachman and Ashe (1973) found no differences in aversive taste conditioning when they varied route of administration. However, they did not test the intravascular route.

ACKNOWLEDGEMENT

The authors wish to acknowledge the helpful comments and criticisms of Drs. R. L. Solomon, M. E. P. Seligman, S. F. Maier and R. Rosellini and are thankful for the support of Dr. C. O'Brien. We also wish to thank Barbara Wells for her technical assistance.

REFERENCES

Barker, L. M. CS duration, amount and concentration effects in conditioning taste aversions. **Learning and Motivation,** 1976, **7,** 265-273.

Best, M. R. Conditioned and latent inhibition in taste-aversion learning: Clarifying the role of learned safety. **Journal of Experimental Psychology: Animal Behavior Processes.** 1975, **1,** 97-113.

Bitterman, M. E. Flavor aversion studies. **Science.** 1976, **192,** 266-267.

Bradley, R. M., & Mistretta, C. M. Intravascular taste in rats as demonstrated by conditioned aversion to sodium saccharin. **Journal of Comparative and Physiological Psychology.** 1971, **75,** 186-189.

Carroll, M. E., Dinc, H. I., Levy, C. J., & Smith, J. C. Demonstration of neophobia and enhanced neophobia in the albino rat. **Journal of Comparative and Physiological Psychology,** 1975, **89,** 457-467.

Coussens, W. R. Route of administration and conditioned taste aversion. Paper presented at the meeting of the American Psychological Association, Chicago, 1975.

Coussens, W. R., Crowder, W. F., & Davis, W. M. Morphine induced saccharin aversion in alpha-methyltyrosine pretreated rats. **Psychopharmacologia,** 1973, **29,** 151-157.

Domjan, M. Determinants of the enhancement of flavored-water intake by prior exposure. **Journal of Experimental Psychology: Animal Behavior Processes.** 1976, **2,** 17-27.

Domjan, M. Role of ingestion in odor-toxicosis learning in the rat. **Journal of Comparative and Physiological Psychology,** 1973, **84,** 507-521.

Domjan, M. Poison-induced neophobia in rats: Role of stimulus generalization of conditioned taste aversions. **Animal Learning and Behavior,** 1975, **3,** 205-211.

Domjan, M. CS preexposure in taste-aversion learning: Effects of deprivation and preexposure duration. **Learning and Motivation,** 1972, **3,** 389-402.

Domjan, M., & Wilson, N. E. Contribution of ingestive behaviors to taste-aversion learning in the rat. **Journal of Comparative and Physiological Psychology,** 1972, **80,** 403-412.

Domjan, M., & Wilson, N. E. Specificity of cue to consequence in aversion learning in the rat. **Psychonomic Science,** 1972a, **26,** 143-145.

Dragoin, W. B. Conditioning and extinction of taste aversion with variations in intensity of the CS and US in two strains of rats. **Psychonomic Science,** 1971, **22,** 303-305.

Elkins, R. L. Attenuation of drug-induced bait shyness to a palatable solution as an increasing function of its availability prior to conditioning. **Behavioral Biology,** 1973, **9,** 221-226.

Farley, J. A., McLaurin, W. A., Scarborough, B. B., & Rawlings, T. D. Pre-irradiation saccharin habituation: A factor in avoidance behavior. **Psychological Reports,** 1964, **14,** 491-496.

Garcia, J., & Koelling, R. A. Relation of cue to consequence in avoidance learning. **Psychonomic Science,** 1966, **4,** 123-124.

Garcia, J., Ervin, F. R., & Koelling, R. A. Learning with prolonged delay of reinforcement. **Psychonomic Science,** 1966, **5,** 121-122.

Garcia, J., Hankins, W. G., & Rusiniak, K. W. Flavor aversion studies. **Science,** 1976, **192,** 266-267.

Garcia, J., Kimeldorf, D. J., & Koelling, R. A. Conditioned aversion to saccharin resulting from exposure to gamma radiation. **Science,** 1955, **122,** 157-158.

Garcia, J., McGowen, B. K., & Green, K. F. Biological constraints on conditioning. In A. H. Black & W. F. Prokasy, (Eds.), **Classical conditioning II. Current research and theory.** New York: Appleton-Century-Crofts, 1972.

Green, L., Bouzas, A., & Rachlin, H. Test of an electric shock analog to illness-induced aversion. **Behavioral Biology,** 1972, **7,** 513-518.

Grote, F. W., Jr., & Brown, R. T. Deprivation level affects extinction of a conditioned taste aversion. **Learning and Motivation,** 1973, **4,** 314-319.

Hankins, W. G., Garcia, J., & Rusiniak, K. W. Dissociation of odor and taste in bait shyness. **Behavioral Biology,** 1973, **8,** 407-419.

Hankins, W. G., Rusiniak, K. W., & Garcia, J. Taste, odor and shock: Further evidence for associative bias in rats. Manuscript submitted for publication, 1976.

Holman, G. L. Intragastric reinforcement effect. **Journal of Comparative and Physiological Psychology,** 1968, **69,** 432-444.

Kalat, J. W. Taste salience depends on novelty, not concentration, in taste-aversion learning in the rat. **Journal of Comparative and Physiological Psychology,** 1974, **86,** 47-50.

Kamin, L. J. Predictability, surprise, attention and conditioning. In B. A. Campbell & R. M. Church (Eds.), **Punishment and aversive behavior.** New York: Appleton-Century-Crofts, 1969.

Krane, R. V. Exteroceptive CS novelty and attenuation of flavor-aversion learning (or) "Flavor-aversion" as a function of the similarity between exteroceptive test stimuli and exteroceptive training stimuli. Paper presented as the meeting of the American Psychological Association, Chicago, 1975.

Krane, R. V., & Wagner, A. R. Taste-aversion learning with a delayed-shock US: Implications for the "generality of the laws of learning." **Journal of Comparative and Physiological Psychology,** 1975, **88,** 882-889.

Lester, D., Nachman, M., & Le Magnen, J. Aversive conditioning by ethanol in the rat. **Quarterly Journal of Studies on Alcohol,** 1970, **31,** 578-586.

Levy, C. J., Carroll, M. E., Smith, J. C., & Hofer, K. G. Antihistamines block radiation-induced taste aversions. **Science,** 1974, **186,** 1044-1046.

Lubow, R. E. Latent inhibition. **Psychological Bulletin,** 1973, **79,** 398-407.

McLaurin, W. A., Farley, J. A., & Scarborough, B. B. Inhibitory effect of pre-irradiation saccharin habituation on conditioned avoidance behavior. **Radiation Research,** 1963, **18,** 473-478.

Mitchell, D., Kirschbaum, E. H., & Perry, R. L. Effects of neophobia and habituation on the poison-induced avoidance of exteroceptive stimuli in the rat. **Journal of Experimental Psychology: Animal Behavior Processes,** 1975, **1,** 47-55.

Nachman, M. Learned taste and temperature aversions due to lithium chloride sickness after temporal delays. **Journal of Comparative and Physiological Psychology,** 1970, **73,** 22-30.

Nachman, M. Learned aversion to the taste of lithium chloride and generalization to other salts. **Journal of Comparative and Physiological Psychology,** 1963, **56,** 343-349.

251

Nachman, M, & Ashe, J. H.   Learned taste aversions in rats as a function of dosage concentration and route of administration of LiCl. **Physiology and Behavior,** 1973, **10,** 73-78.

Nachman, M., & Hartley, P. L.   The role of illness in producing learned taste aversion in rats: A comparison of several rodenticides. **Journal of Comparative and Physiological Psychology,** 1975, **89,** 1010-1018.

Nowlis, G. H.   Conditioned stimulus intensity and acquired alimentary aversions in the rat. **Journal of Comparative and Physiological Psychology,** 1974, **86,** 1173-1184.

Pavlov, I. P.   **Conditioned reflexes.** London: Oxford University Press, 1927.

Razran, G.   **Mind in evolution. An East-West synthesis of learned behavior and cognition.** Boston: Houghton Mifflin Co., 1971.

Reiss, S., & Wagner, A. R.   CS habituation produces a "latent inhibition effect" but no active "conditioned inhibition." **Learning and Motivation,** 1972, **3,** 237-245.

Rescorla, R. A.   Pavlovian conditioning and its proper control procedures. **Psychological Review,** 1967, **74,** 71-80.

Rescorla, R. A.   Probability of shock in the presence and absence of CS in fear conditioning. **Journal of Comparative and Physiological Psychology,** 1968, **66,** 1-5.

Rescorla, R. A., & Wagner, A. R.   A theory of Pavlovian conditioning: Variations in the effectiveness of reinforcement and non-reinforcement. In A. H. Black & W. F. Prokasy (Eds.), **Classical conditioning II. Current research and theory.** New York: Appleton-Century-Crofts, 1972.

Revusky, S. H.   Aversion to sucrose produced by contingent x-irradiation: Temporal and dosage parameters. **Journal of Comparative and Physiological Psychology,** 1968, **65,** 17-22.

Revusky, S. H., & Bedarf, E. W.   Association of illness with prior ingestion of novel foods. **Science,** 1967, **155,** 219-220.

Revusky, S. H., & Garcia, J.   Learned associations over long delays. In G. H. Bower & J. T. Spence (Eds.), **Psychology of learning and motivation: Advances in research and theory** (Vol. IV). New York: Academic Press, 1970.

Rozin, P.   Specific aversions and neophobia resulting from vitamin deficiency or poisoning in half-wild and domestic rats. **Journal of Comparative and Physiological Psychology,** 1968, **66,** 82-88.

Rozin, P., & Kalat, J. W.   Specific hungers and poison avoidance as adaptive specializations of learning. **Psychological Review,** 1971, **78,** 459-486.

Seligman, M. E. P.   On the generality of the laws of learning. **Psychological Review,** 1970, **77,** 400-418.

Siegel, S. Effect of CS habituation on eyelid conditioning. **Journal of Comparative and Physiological Psychology,** 1969, **68,** 245-248.

Smith, J. C.   Personal communication, April 10, 1976. Florida State University, Tallahassee.

Smith, J. C., & Roll, D. L. Trace conditioning with X-rays as an aversive stimulus. **Psychonomic Science,** 1967, **9,** 11-12.

Sullivan, Lucy.   Personal communication, April 22, 1976. Macquarie University, North Ryde, New South Wales.

Schwartz, B. On going back to nature: A review of Seligman and Hager's **Biological boundaries of learning. Journal of the Experimental Analysis of Behavior,** 1974, **21,** 183-198.

Taukulis, H. K. Odor aversions produced over long CS-US delays. **Behavioral Biology,** 1974, **10,** 505-510.

Taukulis, H. K., & Revusky, S. H. Odor as a conditioned inhibitor: Applicability of the Rescorla-Wagner model to feeding behavior. **Learning and Motivation,** 1975, **6,** 11-27.

Testa, T. J. Casual relationships and the acquisition of avoidance responses. **Psychological Review,** 1974, **81,** 491-505.

Testa, T. J. Effects of similarity of location and temporal intensity pattern of conditioned and unconditioned stimuli on the acquisition of conditioned suppression in rats. **Journal of Experimental Psychology: Animal Behavior Processes,** 1975, **104,** 114-121.

XI

AN OPPONENT-PROCESS THEORY OF MOTIVATION
V. AFFECTIVE DYNAMICS OF EATING

RICHARD L. SOLOMON
University of Pennsylvania

The attention of this symposium has been almost exclusively focused on the associative or conditioning variables which influence eating. Animals can be conditioned to avoid the tastes, sights, and odors of food temporally associated with the aversive consequences of being poisoned or made ill. They may prefer the tastes and odors of food associated with getting well after an illness. They learn, early in life, what is edible, even though they may not be as clever in learning to avoid what is inedible. Eventually, animals may choose food on the basis of distance perception as well as the more proximal stimuli of taste and odor. This control at a distance is accomplished by mechanisms of Pavlovian conditioning. Here, when the tastes and smells are UCSs, the distance stimulations compose the compound CSs. The known empirical laws of Pavlovian conditioning satisfactorily describe this kind of transfer of control across stimulus modalities. Note that in this case tastes and odors are not CSs. They are Pavlov's original UCSs.

ASSOCIATIVE PROCESSES AND UCSs

In most of the popular interpretations of the conditioning of food preferences and food aversions, the taste and smell of food (and sometimes the sight of it) is referred to, or treated interpretively, as the CS. The stimuli of illness, or recovery from illness, are referred to as UCSs. This is, conceptually (if you are a Pavlovian theorist) and psychologically (if you are a motivation theorist) quite inappropriate and misleading. Because it can be shown that the taste and smell (perhaps also sight for some animals) of food functions well as a Pavlovian UCS in many conditioning experiments, an appropriate conceptualization of a conditioned taste, or odor, or sight aversion experiment is that a food-attribute UCS is being used, in a trace or delayed conditioning paradigm, "as though" it were a CS. Therefore, the empirical laws for associating UCSs with each other, rather than the laws of CS-UCS conditioning, will be applicable to the case of conditioned food aversion. This possibility has been consistently overlooked, partly because the major interests of those working on acquired food aversions have been focused on adaptive functioning, not on associative mechanisms. A notable exception is Richter (1953).

UCS-UCS CONDITIONING

Actually, we know a lot about the association of UCSs with UCSs. Of course, Pavlov was the first to think about the problem, and his ideas were, as usual, very clever. He had to postulate a principle that would enable one to predict whether forward or backward conditioning would occur when two UCSs were paired in a temporal sequence. Which of the two would function as the CS? (1) If the second UCS should function as a CS, then we have a backward conditioning process and, with a long intertrial interval, the outcome should be inhibitory: the second UCS would be expected to inhibit the reflex skeletal and autonomic nervous system (ANS) patterns normally evoked by the first UCS. (2) If the first UCS should function as a CS, then we have a forward conditioning process and, with a long intertrial interval, the outcome should be excitatory: the first UCS should eventually acquire the capacity to elicit those reflex, skeletal and ANS patterns evoked originally only by the second UCS. It was important for Pavlov to understand which way the conditioning would go, because Krasnogorski (1909) had already used a pin-prick as one UCS and milk as the second UCS, in conditioning infant human Ss. The pin-prick eventually elicited conditioned sucking. Why did this result occur (rather than the milk becoming a fear-inhibitor and being unable to elicit conditioned sucking)?

Pavlov solved this problem to his own satisfaction. Pavlov's *prediction rule* should have appealed to a behavioral biologist, but instead it was ignored. He induced a concept of biological prepotency or survival importance as an attribute of all UCSs (which, after all, are the releasers of many innate behavior patterns). Some UCSs are qualitatively more prepotent than others, but their intensities are capable of reversing the prepotency relationship. Thus, a biologically-prepotent UCS presented at a low intensity would have a much better chance to function as an excitatory CS if it is presented first in a temporal sequence with another, more intense UCS. If it is presented second in the sequence, and if its intensity is low relative to that of the other UCS, then backward, inhibitory conditioning would result, and the low-intensity UCS would become able to inhibit those reactions normally elicited by the more intense UCS.

These theoretical predictions work remarkably well, once we have agreed on how to rank-order the prepotencies and roughly compare the intensities across UCS modalities. For example, a weak shock UCS, if it regularly precedes a strong food UCS, will come to elicit conditioned alimentary and vegetative behaviors. (For a general review of these matters, a good secondary source is Konorski, 1967). A strong food UCS, if it regularly precedes a strong shock UCS, will come to elicit very intense conditioned fear in the presence of the food, resulting in self-starvation (see Masserman & Pechtel, 1953; Lichtenstein, 1950, for dramatic evidence of this in cats and dogs). This would demonstrate the prepotency of pain. In such cases, the effective UCS-UCS time interval can be very long, provided that both UCSs occur in the same environmental context. A monkey shown a toy snake, in a familiar eating place and many hours after the last feeding, may thereafter avoid the particular food it was last fed. This aversion may persist in the home cage. The toy snake functions as a very intense, prepotent, fear-evoking UCS. The food UCS functions as though it was a CS. Such "feeding inhibitions" are frequent occurrences in the study of "experimental neuroses" in the laboratory (see Solomon, Turner, & Lessac, 1968 for a direct examination of the role of the food-punishment time interval in feeding inhibitions in dogs). Almost all examples of "experimental neurosis" involve the juxtaposition of two, biologically-significant UCSs (see Masserman, 1943).

FOOD-AVERSION LEARNING AS
UCS-UCS CONDITIONING

A careful consideration of the discussion up to this point should have convinced one that the conditioning of a specific food aversion via toxicosis is but a special case of the Pavlovian UCS-UCS conditioning paradigm. It is not a case of CS-UCS conditioning. The best examples of how the UCS-UCS paradigm works can be found in "experimental neurosis" experiments, but there are many other examples too. The UCS-UCS time interval can be very long and still produce a conditioned reaction. This is not a typical finding with CS-UCS relations, unless the background stimulation is constant and there are no intervening events.

Indeed, there is a good rule of thumb that the laboratory conditioner can go by. There is an ascending order of ease of conditioning when we choose the stimulus categories of the stimuli being paired. It is quite difficult to demonstrate a CS-CS association, or sensory pre-conditioning. The arrangements have to be just right. Next most difficult is a UCS-CS association, or backward, inhibitory conditioning. This usually requires many trials. Then, much easier, is the CS-UCS association, and under the right conditions the temporal spacing can be long and we still may see forward conditioning. Finally, the UCS-UCS association seems to be the easiest, when the second UCS is prepotent over the first. No one has given us an adequate theory about this ordering of conditioning difficulty. Perhaps Pavlov's prepotency concept is the best, but there are others, such as stimulus intensity, novelty, surprisingness and orienting-reflex arousal value.

The outcomes of most recent conditioned food-aversion experiments are quite in harmony with the findings of the earlier experiments on UCS-UCS conditioning and "experimental neurosis." Indeed, Richter (1953) wrote a detailed account of the reactions of wild and domesticated rats to food poisoning in a volume on "Comparative conditioned neuroses." He was struck by the "catatonic" postures of some of the poisoned rats. The intriguing problem is the mechanism which enables UCSs to be successfully associated with each other more readily than are CSs associated with UCSs. We have very little understanding about this beyond Pavlov's original biological prepotency hypothesis. We do know that it is important to distinguish CSs from UCSs whenever possible, in trying to understand what will happen in a conditioning experiment. UCSs are important. This is not to state that all of the most dramatic cases of adaptive specificity are but special cases of UCS-UCS associations. But some of them are, and this needs to be taken into account if we are to understand better the associative mechanisms involved in conditioned food aversions.

ARE CONDITIONED FOOD AVERSIONS
INTEROCEPTIVE OR EXTEROCEPTIVE?

Another aspect of the conditioned food aversion experiment is the *modality* of the UCS. The Russian psychophysiologists have demonstrated the importance of the distinction between interoceptive and exteroceptive CSs and interoceptive and exteroceptive

UCSs. Without reviewing all of the major empirical findings here, we can summarize by stating that the most easily established and longest-lasting CRs are those involving interoceptive CSs and UCSs. When both stimuli are UCSs, and both are interoceptive, Pavlov's prepotency law holds.

Thus, a new question arises, one that stems from a Pavlovian frame of reference: are tastes or odors of food, which can function as UCSs, also interoceptive? Or are they exteroceptive? The answer would be important for a Pavlovian psychophysiologist (see Bykov, 1957, and Razran, 1961, for reviews of interoceptive conditioning). One would expect much faster conditioning if all of the important stimuli in a taste-aversion experiment were not only UCSs but also were interoceptive. The criteria for deciding about the interoceptive or exteroceptive distinction for tastes and odors are not too clear. Anatomically, the taste and odor systems may be considered to be exteroceptive, part of the skin sense system. The mouth, nose, and skin are derived from the same germ layer. However, one can also label the taste and odor systems as visceral afferents and consider them to be interoceptive. One can even turn the tables on the UCSs for illness and claim that gastritis, for example, is a skin inflammation, because the gut and skin are continuous. That would render the illness UCSs into the exteroceptive category. Obviously, more thinking and analysis needs to be done before one can accept the seemingly reasonable notion that tastes, odors and illness-related stimuli are somehow in the same psychophysiological category, whereas tastes and shocks to the skin are not. The intuitively obvious becomes, on analysis, not very obvious at all, in the case of the assumed modality-relatedness of tastes and illnesses, on the one hand, and sounds and skin shocks, on the other. What are the relatedness criteria?

OPPONENT-PROCESSES AND UCSs

Unconditioned stimuli have non-associative effects, in addition to their capacity to enter into associations with other stimuli. These non-associative effects are motivationally significant. They can help us to understand some of the affective dynamics of eating itself, and enable us to specify more precisely when it is that an animal will start to eat and when it will stop eating after it has started. First we will need to describe the opponent-process theory of motivation (Solomon & Corbit, 1973; Hoffman & Solomon, 1974; Solomon & Corbit, 1974) in order to pursue our analysis.

The opponent-process theory argues that most Ucss, whether pleasant or aversive, arouse affective reactions. These affective reactions are actively opposed by an open-loop, negative feedback mechanism which serves to reduce the magnitude of the affective reaction to the UCS. Opponent-processes exist for both pleasurable (appetitive) and aversive (defensive) affects, and they serve to reduce the magnitude of reactions of both kinds. As will be seen, opponent-processes provide a mechanism for affective habituation, the "getting used to" a variety of Ucss.

The formal theoretical model (Solomon & Corbit, 1974) postulates that certain Ucss, at their onset and during their maintenance, will produce an affective arousal called an *a-process*. This results in an A-state which has either motivational or reinforcing attributes. The occurrence of an *a-process* causes an opponent loop to be aroused, and it generates a *b-process* which opposes the a-process and reduces the A-state intensity and changes its quality. The b-

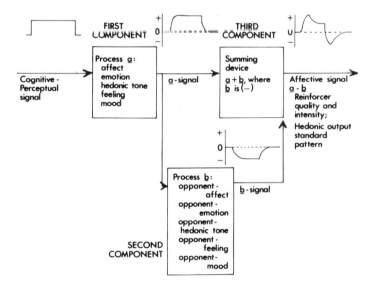

Figure 1
An analysis of the three components of the affective mechanism. (In the first component the *a-process* is aroused. The second component, the *b-process*, is aroused via the arousal of *a*. Then the third component, a summing device, combines the *a* and *b* signals to generate the standard pattern of affective dynamics.) (From Solomon & Corbit, 1974)

260

process itself is affectively the opposite to the a-process. If the a-process is pleasant, the b-process is aversive, and vice versa.

The b-process, relative to the quick and phasic a-process, is sluggish, and so it has a long latency, and recruits or builds up slowly while the stimulation is present. It dies out slowly as a function of passage of time after stimulus termination. The b-processes (which are the defensive opponents for affect) are strengthened through use and weakened through disuse, similar to a typical immunity system.

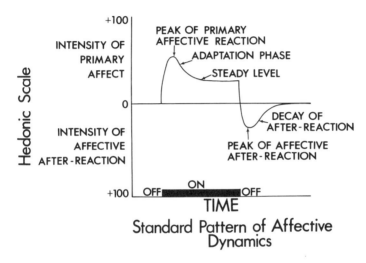

Standard Pattern of Affective Dynamics

Figure 2
The manifest temporal dynamics generated by the opponent-process system during the first few stimulations. (The five features of the affective response are labeled.) (From Solomon & Corbit, 1974)

Figure 1 shows a block diagram of the opponent-process system, taken from Solomon and Corbit (1974). It shows two stages of information processing, a cognitive-perceptual stage that converts the stimulus input to an informational signal, and an affective or hedonic stage that converts the informational signal to an affective signal. The affective system in turn has three components which convert the square-wave informational input to the complex affective signal seen in Figure 2. It does this by means of the second component, the opponent-loop, process b, in interaction with the first component, the primary process a, the interaction taking place by means of the summing device, the third component. The affective output, even though there has been a square wave (on-off) in-

261

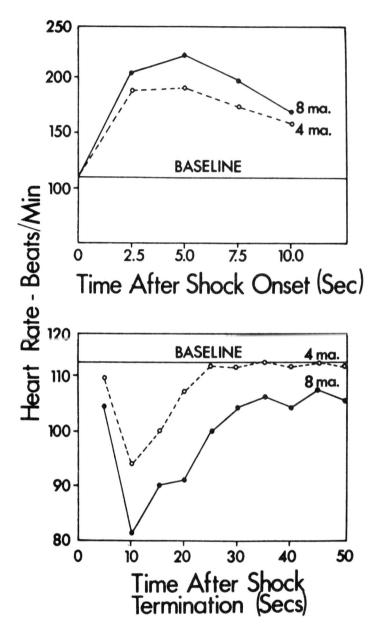

Figure 3 (Top Panel) and Figure 4 (Bottom Panel)
Heart rate changes as a function of shock onset, maintenance, and termination. (There is a decline following the initial peak reaction to shock onset. There is a deceleratory "overshoot" following shock termination, and then the heart rate slowly re-

262

turns to baseline rate. Note that the eight-milliampere shock produces a bigger heart rate increase and a bigger deceleration than does the four-milliampere shock.) (From Solomon & Corbit, 1974)

put, has, because of the sluggishness of the b-process, five distinctive features. They compose what Solomon and Corbit (1974) call "the standard pattern of affective dynamics."

We can illustrate the standard pattern first with an example using aversive stimulation. A dog is in a Pavlov harness, and we present it with a series of 10-second, 4 ma. shocks (a series of square-wave UCS inputs) each separated by at least three minutes. When we turn the shock on, the dog screeches and struggles; its eyes bulge out, its pupils dilate, its hair stands on end; it expulsively defecates and urinates; and its heart rate doubles (see Figure 3). Call this syndrome state A. Or, call it "terror." When we look closely at the component reactions of state A, we see that the peak reaction magnitude occurs during the first few seconds after shock onset and then the magnitude slowly declines even while the shock is still on. When we turn the shock off, the behavioral components abruptly change. Vocalization is gone, the pupils constrict, hair lies down. The heart rate descends below baseline rate, then slowly recovers over a two-minute period. The dog appears to be relieved. It may wag its tail. We call this reaction, State B. These features are shown in Figure 4. State B is postulated to be the affective opposite of State A. If one is "bad," the other is "good."

If we repeat the shocks over a long session (30-60 minutes), it becomes apparent that States A and B are not remaining constant in their magnitudes and attributes. There is a peak of A, just as there was during the first few shocks, but it is less intense than it was. Furthermore, State B is now quite changed. The dog wags its tail, looks around, pricks up its ears, seems to relax completely. Furthermore, the heart rate deceleration increases in magnitude and duration (see Katcher et al., 1969). If we now let the dog out of the harness, it will romp around, tail wagging, jumping up on people and looking very happy. After several minutes, this euphoric episode will end, and the dog will return to its original, baseline affective state. It will look "normal." The postulated interaction of a-processes and b-processes for new UCSs, and UCSs after many repetitions, is shown in Figure 5. The quantity (a-b) is decreased as b is strengthened with use.

Three principles of the action of a UCS have been exemplified. First, there is affective habituation or adaptation. Second, there is

263

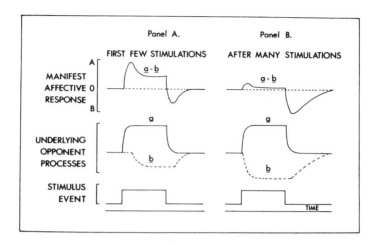

Figure 5
Panel A: The operation of the summing device for the first few
stimulations. (The summation of the underlying opponent processes, *a* and *b,* yields the manifest affective response.) Panel B:
The operation of the summing device after many repeated
stimulations. (From Solomon & Corbit, 1974)

an after-reaction, state B, revealing itself when the UCS is terminated; and this after-reaction becomes stronger and longer-lasting with
repetitions of the UCS. Third, the after-reaction appears to be
hedonically opposite to that of state A.

These three principles apply to pleasant UCSs, too. The best example is opiate use. It is a very powerful reinforcer of a pleasurable
sort. With repeated doses, however, the affective reaction in the
presence of the drug will decline in magnitude. In addition, the after-reaction will increase in magnitude and duration. The opponent-process model generates these outcomes with no additional
assumptions, and it also deduces that the after-reaction will be
highly aversive. Of course, these affective events are the substrate
for addiction. When the drug user is in the throes of the B-state, he
is faced with a momentous choice. He can let the B-state decay and
disappear, which involves long hours of suffering. Or, he can re-
dose, thereby wiping out the B-state and supplanting it with the A-
state which is pleasurable. If redosing becomes the pattern, there
will be more and more habituation (tolerance) as the b-process is
strengthened, and the after-reaction will become more intense and
longer-lasting.

264

We think that the affective dynamics of the typical addiction process may tell us a great deal about the process of eating, even though painful shocks and pleasurable drugs seem to be a far cry from eating. First, note that we are dealing with processes aroused by UCSs. Eating is accompanied by pleasurable taste and odor UCSs whenever a preferred diet is being eaten. These UCSs elicit alimentary and vegetative reflexes but, in addition, they arouse affective processes. We can deduce from the opponent-process theory what to expect of the UCSs in their moment-to-moment influences on eating behavior.

The mechanisms controlling food intake have been studied extensively by psychologists and physiologists. The problem is complex, and most of the major questions are still unanswered. Nevertheless, we now have the vague outlines of the mechanisms of control at the physiological and behavioral levels. There is a postulated hunger process and a satiety process. They are partly interrelated by homeostatic control circuitry. However, they are also partly orthogonal to each other; for example, an empty stomach is not sufficient to precipitate eating, but a stuffed stomach is often sufficient to cause eating to cease.

The hunger process is influenced by several variables, among which are blood sugar level, body temperature, body fat deposits, hormones correlated with time since the last meal, and insulin secretion. Other things constant, an animal is more likely to start eating, given that a palatable food is at hand, when its body temperature is low, its blood sugar level is low, its current fat deposits are lower than they have been, it is relatively rested, and its insulin output is high. There are other variables of importance, too, but just the few above suggest the great complexity of the eating-initiation control system.

The satiety process also is influenced by many variables, among which are body temperature, stomach loading, blood sugar level, the secretion of cholecystokinin in the small intestine, protracted physical exercise, and body fat deposits. The constant interaction of the hunger and satiety mechanisms produces long-term body weight control within rather narrow limits.

On the other hand, the short-term control of eating is much more haphazard. Huge meal-to-meal variations in caloric intake can be seen in animals which are nevertheless maintaining a long-term, narrow weight envelope. These intake variations often are related to variables other than those normally conceived to influence

265

hunger and satiety mechanisms. Among these are the taste, odor and textural qualities of the available foods. Despite general acceptance of the fact that such factors ought to influence eating, very little systematic work has been carried out to relate them to the hunger and satiety mechanisms. Until recently, most theorists assumed that good-tasting, highly preferred foods will enhance eating and that bad tasting, non-preferred foods will suppress eating. We also know that foods associated with bad events like poisoning or electric shocks will suppress eating. But to what extent? In what specific attributes of eating? We can't yet state whether the influences of such sensory and affective qualities of food will be on the initiation of eating, or its rate, or its cessation. Nor do we know how the sensory and affective qualities will interact with a given momentary state of either the hunger or the satiety mechanism.

The first comprehensive theoretical analysis of the relationships between the hunger and satiety systems, on the one hand, and taste quality factors, on the other, was worked out by Konorski (1967) and elaborated by Konorski and Gawronski (1970), then was further developed by Soltysik (1975). The models conceive of a hunger system and satiety system existing in a homeostatic, reciprocally-inhibiting arrangement. The model further postulates a UCS, food-in-the-mouth system and a no-food system which reciprocally inhibit each other. In addition, the food system inhibits the hunger system, and the no-food system inhibits the satiety system. There are "rebound" effects whenever an inhibitor is suddenly deactivated. Thus, if the food-in-the-mouth system is suddenly deactivated, the hunger system will show rebound excitation, and the eater will look hungrier and give alimentary CRs to background stimuli (CSs).

A moment's thought will convince one that the latter deduction is also a feature of the opponent-process theory. The opponent-process theory of motivation assumes that an effective positive reinforcer (UCS), when suddenly terminated, will be followed by a negatively-reinforcing state (B state) which quickly peaks in intensity and then decays as a function of time. In the case of pleasant tastes, the negatively-reinforcing state is called *taste-craving*. Taste-craving is an aversive motivator. The decay of this aversive opponent-process is probably rapid, a matter of 15 to 180 seconds, depending on prior stimulus quality, intensity and duration.

Assume that hunger is an aversive motivator and satiety is a pleasant reinforcer. Assume further that taste-pleasure and taste-craving summate algebraically with hunger and satiety. Then we would have the following four processes at work in controlling eating behavior at *any given moment* in time:

PROCESS	HEDONIC QUALITY
Hunger	aversive
Satiety	pleasant
Taste-pleasure	pleasant
Taste-craving	aversive

A simple theoretical behavior rule is that eating will persist only when the sum of all four quantities is aversive. If the sum is pleasant, then eating will stop, and the organism will relax and "enjoy" its state.

During a meal, hunger will of course decline slowly and satiety will grow slowly as a function of post-ingestional events. However, taste-pleasure and taste-craving will be highly variable and phasic, constantly interacting with hunger and satiety. For example, the first bite of a meal will be motivated by hunger. However, if the food is preferred, and if it is tasted, swallowed, and its taste quickly fades, then the opponent-process, taste-craving, will be manifest. The taste-craving will summate with hunger, because both are aversive. Thus, in the few seconds during which taste-craving reaches its peak in time, the total motivation for eating will be stronger than it was prior to the first taste, assuming, of course, that post-ingestional events have not yet activated the satiety system significantly. However, if a time elapse is imposed between the disappearance of the first taste and the next opportunity to taste the food, and if this time lapse is longer than the decay time for the taste-craving process, then motivation to eat will be determined only by the strengths of hunger and satiety.

This model for viewing the eating process leads us to several simple predictions. Remember that cessation of eating will occur only when the sum of the four processes is pleasant. Therefore, if anything is done to increase taste-craving, eating will be prolonged. This is the *dessert effect*. At a time when satiety has overtaken hunger, and eating would be expected to cease, the alteration of the taste of the food to a more pleasant quality will then make the peak of taste-craving more intense than it was. At the peak, the aversiveness of taste-craving will then exceed the pleasure of satiety, and therefore eating will continue.

However, if a long time delay were to be imposed after the first taste of dessert, then eating would cease. Only one bite of dessert would be consumed, because the taste-craving would have decayed to zero, and satiety would control the behavior, producing relaxation.

The interaction of the four processes also leads us to predict that a normal meal, consisting of one type of food, would be prematurely terminated if a long interruption (say, 3 min) could be imposed late in the meal, at a time when eating would normally be expected to cease in but a few minutes' time. Late in a meal, hunger and satiety are close to the same strength, and only the peak of taste-craving, coming with the cessation of the prior pleasant taste, keeps the eating behavior in a motivated state. If the peak is allowed to occur and then decay to zero, there should be no resumption of eating. The interruption technique should be capable of lowering the total calories taken in any meal.

When pleasant tastes become less pleasant or somewhat aversive, due either to conditioning or to adulteration, the phasic effects in eating should disappear. A standard meal should be terminated sooner, *not* because of any change in the hunger or satiety processes, but because the taste-craving process will be weak or absent.

These deductions are illustrative. They are presented in order to start the members of this symposium thinking about the eating process itself and the UCSs correlated with it. We should not ignore the possibility that the perceptual and affective attributes of an acceptable food constitute a positively-reinforcing UCS, or that the perceptual correlates of an unacceptable food constitute a less effective UCS, or an aversive one. We should not deny to the field of acquired food preferences the theoretical richness it deserves. To do so can lead to important conceptual errors.

In summary, we have pointed out that most conditioned taste preference and aversion experiments contain associative contingencies between two types of UCSs. Furthermore, the UCSs may serve a motivational and reinforcement function during eating, in ways suggested by an opponent-process theory of motivation.

REFERENCES

Bykov, K. M. **The cerebral cortex and the internal organs.** New York: Chemical Publishing Company, 1957.

Hoffman, H. S., & Solomon, R. L. An opponent-process theory of motivation: III. Some affective dynamics in imprinting. **Learning and Motivation,** 1974, **5,** 149-164.

Katcher, A. H., Solomon, R. L., Turner, L. H., LoLordo, V., Overmier, J. B., & Rescorla, R. A. Heart rate and blood pressure responses to signaled and unsignaled shocks: Effects of cardiac sympathectomy. **Journal of Comparative and Physiological Psychology,** 1969, **68,** 163-174.

Konorski, J. **Integrative activity of the brain.** Chicago: University of Chicago Press, 1967.

Konorski, J., & Gawronski, R. An attempt at modelling of the central nervous system in higher animals. I. Physiological organization of the alimentary system. **Acta Neurobiologiae Experimentalis,** 1970, **30,** 313-331.

Krasnogorski, N. I. Uber die bedingungsreflexe im kindersalter. **Jb. Kinderheilk,** 1909, **69,** 1-24.

Lichtenstein, P. E. Studies of anxiety: II. The effect of lobotomy on the feeding inhibition in dogs. **Journal of Comparative and Physiological Psychology,** 1950, **43,** 419-427.

Masserman, J. H. **Behavior and neurosis: An experimental psycho-analytic approach to psychobiologic principles.** Chicago: University of Chicago Press, 1943.

Masserman, J. H., & Pechtel, C. Neuroses in monkeys: A preliminary report of experimental observations. **Annals of the New York Academy of Science,** 1953, **56,** 253-265.

Razran, G. The observable unconscious and the inferable conscious in current Soviet psychophysiology: Interoceptive conditioning, semantic conditioning, and the orienting reflex. **Psychological Review,** 1961, **68,** 81-147.

Richter, C. P. Experimentally produced behavior reactions to food poisoning in wild and domesticated rats. **Annals of the New York Academy of Science,** 1953, **56,** 225-239.

Solomon, R. L., & Corbit, J. D. An opponent-process theory of motivation: I. Temporal dynamics of affect. **Psychological Review,** 1974, **81,** 119-145.

Solomon, R. L., & Corbit, J. D. An opponent-process theory of motivation: II. Cigarette addiction. **Journal of Abnormal Psychology,** 1973, **81,** 158-171.

Solomon, R. L., Turner, L. H., & Lessac, M. S. Some effects of delay of punishment on resistance to temptation in dogs. **Journal of Personality and Social Psychology,** 1968, **8,** 233-238.

Soltysik, S. S. Post-consummatory arousal of drive as a mechanism of incentive motivation. **Acta Neurobiologiae Experimentalis,** 1975, **35,** 447-474.

LONG-DELAY
LEARNING

XII

STATUS OF "LEARNED SAFETY" OR "LEARNED NONCORRELATION" AS A MECHANISM IN TASTE-AVERSION LEARNING

JAMES W. KALAT
Duke University

The pioneers in the field of animal learning, principally Pavlov and Thorndike, bequeathed to their successors not only a wealth of phenomena and theories, but also some fundamental, often unstated, assumptions. Some of these assumptions, though hallowed by tradition, deserve to be challenged. One assumption which has already been challenged is that CS-US contiguity, or response-reinforcer contiguity, is the basis for learning. It was first demonstrated that contiguity is not a sufficient condition for learning (Kamin, 1969; Egger & Miller, 1962, 1963), and later that it is not a necessary condition for learning (Garcia, Ervin, & Koelling, 1966).

There are two more assumptions I wish to challenge in this paper. The first is that a necessary condition for learning is the presence of an explicit "reinforcer." I shall contend that the *absence* of any unusual event, or the absence of any change in the usual course of events, can also be the basis for associative learning. The second assumption to be challenged is that of "trace decay." When CS and US, or response and reinforcer, are temporally separated, less learning occurs than when the two are contiguous. The traditional interpretation has been that the CS sets up a trace somewhere in the brain, which passively decays over time. If the US occurs before the CS trace has decayed to zero, the US is associated with whatever is left of the trace. Clearly, this hypothesis can account for the decrease in learning with increased delays. It has the advantage that it suggests a plausible, though non-demonstrated, physiological mechanism. I shall argue, however, that this advantage is not enough; and that an admittedly less physiological, less scientific-sounding hypothesis accords better with the behavioral data.

IS AN EXPLICIT REINFORCER
NECESSARY FOR LEARNING?

The necessity of reinforcement for learning is often actually incorporated into the definition of learning (e.g., Kimble, 1967). Typically, the lack of any change in the world is not accepted as an instance of "reinforcement." Consequently, "habituation" and "latent inhibition" are often excluded by definition from being associative learning (see critique by Rhoad, Kalat, & Klopfer, 1975); many sources describe habituation as a phenomenon similar to learning but simpler or different by virtue of being non-associative (e.g., Thompson, 1976). Note the underlying assumption that the formation of an association requires an explicit second stimulus and that "no change in the environment" does not qualify as such a stimulus. If this assumption is accepted as an a priori postulate, then there can be no basis to challenge it. However, it is not clear what empirical evidence supports the assumption. For instance, contrary to the assumption, there is general acceptance that extinction is a legitimate learning process (see even Pavlov, 1927). In extinction, as in habituation, a change in behavior results from repeated presentation of a stimulus eliciting a response but followed by no change in the environment. The only apparent difference between extinction and habituation is that extinction decreases a learned response, while habituation decreases an unlearned response. The conditions for producing these two phenomena are the same, and the resulting behavioral changes can be very similar. Figure 1 presents an extinction curve from Sheffield (1949) and a habituation curve, from Kinastowski (1963). To paraphrase B. F. Skinner, extinction, habituation: which is which? Perhaps it really doesn't matter. If extinction is a matter of learning that a stimulus predicts nothing, why not the same interpretation for habituation and latent inhibition?

Besides habituation and latent inhibition there are several other instances in which a relatively permanent change in behavior results from an animal's experiencing a noncorrelation between some stimulus or behavior and subsequent changes in the environment. Mackintosh (1973) and Baker (1976) found that random, uncorrelated presentations of CS and US produce later retardation in learning when CS and US are subsequently paired. Maier, Seligman, and Solomon (1969) found that repeated unavoidable shocks retard an animal's later ability to learn to avoid shocks. Baker (1976) similarly demonstrated that an initial experience with unpredictable, inescapable shocks retards subsequent punishment learning based on shocks—an effect not explainable in terms of competing responses.

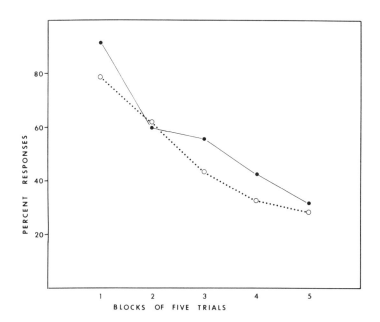

Figure 1
Habituation of contraction response to mechanical stimulation in *Spirostomum* (5 trials per min), after Kinastowski (1963); and extinction of alley-running in rats for food reinforcement after massed training on 100% reinforcement, after Sheffield (1949).

Also, Hein, Held, and Gower (1970) demonstrated that passive visual experience noncorrelated with paw movement in kittens retards later acquisition of eye-paw coordination, worse than having no previous visual experience at all. In taste-aversion learning, it has been demonstrated that initial exposure to a taste not followed by poison (Revusky & Bedarf, 1967; Kalat, 1974) or to a poison not preceded by a particular taste (see chapters by Braveman and Gamzu, this volume) can interfere with the later association of the taste with the poison. In each of these cases an experience with noncorrelation among events produced profound effects on later behavior. In short, apparent learning occurred on the basis of a stimulus which predicted no change in the environment.

IS TRACE DECAY RESPONSIBLE FOR THE CS-US DELAY GRADIENT?

Given that rats can readily associate tastes with poisons over unusually long CS-US delays, and that the association does not seem to

275

depend on peripheral aftertastes (see reviews by Rozin & Kalat, 1971; Revusky & Garcia, 1970), it would be possible to speculate that "trace decay" is slower for tastes than for other stimuli. However, the only basis for the "trace decay" assumption has been that it accounts for learning over a delay without abandoning the concept of temporal contiguity. But close temporal contiguity seems to be of little importance in taste-aversion learning. A poison is readily associated with something tasted an hour or more previously, and not necessarily with the most recent taste at that (Kalat & Rozin, 1970). If temporal contiguity is not critical for learning, perhaps trace decay is not what mediates learning over a delay.

Consequently, taste-aversion learning has inspired two non-trace-decay interpretations of the CS-US delay gradient, both involving an interference process. Revusky's (1971; see also this volume) concurrent-interference interpretation could be described as a CS_1 - CS_2 - US interference process. An increased delay between CS_1 - US provides increased opportunity for unscheduled CS_2 to get in the way. If the US is preferentially associated with the most recent possible CS, then increased delay means increased association with CS_2 and therefore decreased association with CS_1. According to this interpretation, long-delay taste-aversion learning can occur because only ingested substances serve readily as CSs for gastrointestinal USs, and thus little relevant interference occurs between a taste and a delayed poison. Kalat and Rozin (1971) have argued that this cannot be the whole story, but it is certainly part of the story.

A second interpretation, not incompatible with the first, is what Kalat and Rozin (1973) referred to as "learned safety." Briefly, this proposal is as follows: (1) A stimulus, in this case a food or liquid, which is followed by no unusual consequences, can produce a type of learning, as discussed in the section above. Basically, the rat learns that the taste predicts little or no change in its internal state, i.e., that the taste is "safe" or "noncorrelated." (2) It is proposed, and must be demonstrated, that this learning depends on the passage of an uneventful period of time after consumption of the food or liquid, and not just on the consumption itself. (3) It is assumed that an association between a taste CS and a no-event US interferes with an association between the taste and a poison. If the no-event US comes between the taste and poison, we have CS - US_1 - US_2 interference. The greater the association between the CS and US_1 (which consists of an uneventful period of time), the less the association between the CS and the US_2. In other words, as time passes after the animal tastes something, the animal gradually learns that the taste is "safe" or "un-

276

correlated." The greater this learning, the less the taste can be associated with a delayed poison.

EVIDENCE FOR THE LEARNED SAFETY OR LEARNED NONCORRELATION INTERPRETATION

In this section six lines of evidence are discussed which tend to support the learned noncorrelation interpretation.

(1) The CS-US delay gradient depends on some active process, not just the passage of time. Rozin and Ree (1972) poisoned rats 9 hr after the rats drank a novel solution. One group of rats was anesthetized with halothane during most of the 9-hr delay; this group acquired a strong aversion to the solution. A second, non-anesthetized group acquired little if any aversion. Evidently whatever process mediates the CS-US delay gradient depends on the animal's being awake and actively processing information, not on a passive decay process requiring only the passage of time.

(2) Rats tend to show a higher preference for familiar foods than for novel foods (see Domjan, this volume). Since the behavior toward familiar tastes is greatly different from behavior toward novel tastes, and since it depends on an experience the animal had, clearly the transfer from the category "novel" to the category "familiar" is a learning process of some type. The reclassification from "novel" to "familiar" may require only a single trial (Siegel, 1974; Nachman & Jones, 1974).

(3) A familiar taste is less associable with poison than a novel taste. This was first clearly documented by Revusky and Bedarf (1967), and has been replicated repeatedly since then. Even a single previous experience with a taste can greatly decrease the associability of the taste with poison (Kalat & Rozin, 1973), though the effect may be greater after repeated preexposures (Elkins, 1973). Evidently, learning that a solution predicts nothing unusual can interfere with later learning that it predicts poisoning.

(4) Familiarization with a taste can decrease the associability of the taste with poison even if the familiarization took place 21 days before the pairing of the taste with poison (Kalat & Rozin, 1973). Regarding the CS-US delay gradient, when a rat fails to associate a taste with poison over, say, an 8-hr delay, the trace-decay interpretation assumes that the trace was in some sense lost during the 8-hr delay. However, one-trial familiarization over a 21-day period implies that the memory "trace" is still present for at least 21 days. What happens during an 8-hr CS-US delay is not that the trace is lost, but that it is reclassified from an associable state to an unassociable state.

277

(5) Neophobia—the avoidance of novel foods compared to familiar foods—seems to reflect the same process that is involved in the increased associability of novel foods with poisons, as compared to familiar foods. After lesions to either the basolateral amygdala (Nachman & Ashe, 1974; Rolls & Rolls, 1973a, 1973b) or the gustatory cortex (Kiefer & Braun, Reference note 1), rats show decreased neophobia and decreased taste-aversion learning. Also, they acquire equal aversions to novel and familiar solutions, based on poisoning. Thus it is reasonable to suppose a single learning process underlying both the reduction of neophobia by familiarization and the decreased associability with poison as a result of familiarization.

(6) The final line of evidence was designed as a direct test of the learned-safety interpretation. If various groups of rats are poisoned at various times after drinking a solution—e.g., ½ hr, 4 hr, and 24 hr—there is less acquired aversion after longer delays. This, of course, is what one would expect on the basis of either trace decay or learned safety. However, the two views make different predictions for a group which drinks the solution 4 hr before poisoning and again half an hour before the poisoning. This group should have at least as strong a "trace" as the ½ hr group; however, it has had a much longer time in which to learn "safety." The results, shown in Figure 2, support the learned-safety prediction. Two presentations of the solution prior to poisoning produce less learned aversion than just the second presentation (Kalat & Rozin, 1973).

This "two-presentation" effect occurs with the non-nutritive substance saccharin (Bolles, Riley, & Laskowski, 1973) as well as the solutions used for the experiments illustrated in Figure 2. The effect has also been replicated with slightly different procedures by Domjan and Bowman (1974) and Bond and DiGiusto (1975).

IS LEARNED SAFETY/LEARNED NONCORRELATION A LEARNING PROCESS?

The preceding section documents the ways in which the experience of an unfamiliar taste, followed by an uneventful period, affects an animal's later behavior toward that taste. It is essential to the learned safety interpretation that this change in behavior be regarded an associative learning. That is, the familiarization process consists of associating the taste with an uneventful period. The alternative would be that the familiarization effect depends merely on the presentation and consumption of a flavored substance and not on the subsequent uneventful period. In other words, this alternative is to

278

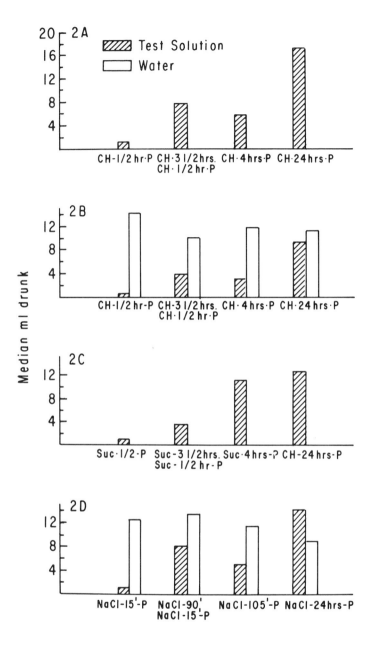

Figure 2
Learned aversions after one or two presentations of a solution.
(From Kalat & Rozin, 1973).

279

attribute the effects of familiarization to a non-associative process. The question, then, is whether the effects of familiarization on behavior can be seen immediately after the animal consumes a novel substance, or whether they increase during the next several hours.

It has been shown that the decrease in "neophobia" by a single exposure to a taste depends not simply on tasting something, but also on the uneventful period subsequent to tasting it. Nachman and Jones (1974) offered rats a novel, concentrated saccharin solution for 2 min. After varying delays, rats were offered the saccharin solution again. Within the range from a 4-min delay to an 8-hr delay, the greater the delay, the greater the intake of saccharin was on the second test. This gradually increasing preference was not demonstrable if the rats had already been familiar with the saccharin solution. Similar results were reported by Green and Parker (1975). These findings suggest that the reduction of neophobia by familiarization with the flavor is a learning process.

The following experiment was designed to test whether the passage of time following the first exposure to a solution is essential for the "two-presentation effect" of Kalat and Rozin (1973). One group of rats drank 5% casein hydrolysate for 2½ min and were poisoned 30 min later. Other groups drank casein hydrolysate for 10 min, and after varying delays drank casein hydrolysate again for 2½ min; 30 min later they too were poisoned. A control group drank casein hydrolysate twice, and were poisoned 24 hr later. Eight days later (with brief access to water on intervening days) the rats were offered casein hydrolysate for 30 min.

A similar experiment was conducted with 10% sucrose, using 5-min presentations of sucrose on both the first and second presentations, using a 1-hr delay between the final sucrose presentation and poison, and using a 2-bottle test. Results for both experiments are presented in Figure 3. Clearly, when the interval between two presentations of the solution is short, rats learn as much aversion as with just the second presentation. However, as the delay between the two presentations increases, the learned aversion decreases. That is, the "two-presentation effect" depends on the delay between the two presentations (cf. Best & Barker, this volume). The effect of familiarization seems to depend on the uneventful period following consumption, and therefore seems to be a learning process.

If learned safety (or learned noncorrelation) is a learning process, it should be possible to interfere with that process by physiological or other manipulations, just as one can block other types of learning. Kalat (1975) found that exposure of neonatal guinea pigs (age 0-4 days) to sucrose produced very little reduction of neophobia, as

280

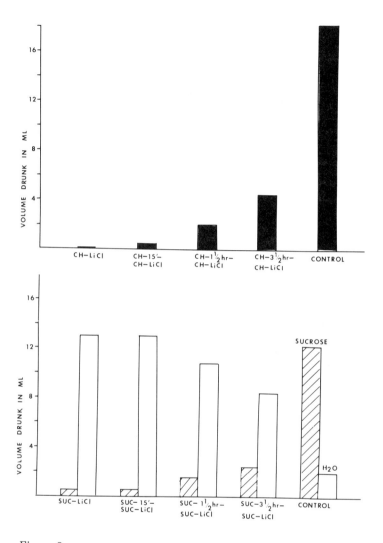

Figure 3
Learned aversions as a function of delay between the first and
second presentations of a solution. Delay between the second
presentation and poison was 30 min for casein hydrolysate
groups, 60 min for sucrose groups.

compared to similar treatment of guinea pigs aged 7-11 days. Also,
pairing sucrose with poison produced somewhat stronger aversions
in the younger group than in the older group, as if the neonatal
guinea pigs were somewhat deficient in learning "safety." Recently,
Pearlman (1976) found that injecting various drugs into rats which

281

just drank a novel solution seemed specifically to block learned safety. Rats drank a sucrose solution one day, then the next day drank it again and were poisoned 30 min later. Ordinarily, such rats acquired significantly weaker aversions than rats which had not drunk sucrose before the second day. However, rats injected with imipramine, pentobarbital, chlordiazepoxide, or several other drugs after drinking sucrose on the first day failed to show the reduced association effect, and acquired nearly as much aversion as rats which drank no sucrose before the second day. The explanation does not seem to be that the first-day drugs produced mild aversions to the sucrose. First, no such aversion could be demonstrated for many of the effective drugs. Furthermore, chlorpromazine, which by itself produced a stronger aversion than imipramine, produced considerably less "impairment of learned safety."

Neither Kalat's (1975) results with the neonatal guinea pigs nor Pearlman's results with the drugs were predicted in advance, and it would clearly be wise to interpret these results cautiously, pending further investigation.

One further test of whether "learned safety" is really "learned" makes use of the finding (Domjan & Wilson, 1972) that rats neither swallow a rapidly force fed solution nor learn strong aversions to such a solution based on subsequent poisoning. (If force-fed slowly enough, the solution is swallowed and readily associated with poison.) Thus, by rapidly force-feeding a solution to rats, one can provide them with the taste stimulation, and presumably an opportunity for any non-associative effects, without providing the requisite basis for associative learning. This technique has been applied to the "two-presentation" phenomenon. Subjects were 92 rats, mean weight 189 grams, mostly pigmented, bred in the author's laboratory. All were given Purina lab chow ad lib; they had access to water 2 hr per day for seven days prior to the experiment. One group of rats (n=10) drank 10% sucrose for 5 min and were poisoned an hour later with 1 ml/30 g 0.15M LiCl. Three other groups drank sucrose for 5 min, then drank sucrose again for 5 min after a delay of 15 min (n=10), 1½ hr (n=10), or 3½ hr (n=11); one hour after the second sucrose presentation these rats were poisoned. Another three groups (n=10, 10 and 11, respectively) were treated similarly except that for their first presentation of sucrose, instead of drinking sucrose for 5 min, they were force-fed sucrose in six 1-ml doses, at a rate of about 1 ml per 4 sec, with 10 sec between doses. Thus these groups were force-fed approximately the same amount that the first three groups drank on their first presentation, but the latter groups did not swallow it. One control group (n=10) drank sucrose twice (with subgroups having inter-presentation intervals of 15 min, 1½ hr, and 3½ hr), and was poisoned 24 hr later. A force-fed control group (n=10) was treated the same as the first control group except that the first presentation was force-fed. All rats were given water for 2 hr on the third day. On the fourth day, all rats were offered 10% sucrose and water simultaneously for 35 min. The question is, would the force-fed sucrose, though not associable with poison, produce a learned-safety effect?

Figure 4 presents the results. All experimental groups acquired strong aversions compared to the control groups. The top part of the figure shows the groups which drank the solution twice (the same groups as the sucrose portion of Figure 3): for rats which drank the sucrose twice before poison, the learned aversion decreased as the delay increased between the first and second presentations of the solution. The bottom part of the figure shows that this effect was absent in the force-fed rats. There were no significant differences among the three force-fed groups, nor between any of them and the group which had only the one exposure to sucrose, drinking it 1 hr before poisoning. That is, the learned-safety effect (decreased associability of a previously tasted solution) seems to depend on the same conditions as learned aversions require—the swallowing of the

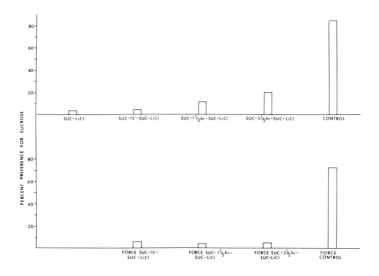

Figure 4
Learned aversions as a function of delay between the first and second presentations of a solution, and as a function of whether the first presentation was drunk normally, or forcefed.

283

solution. This result further supports an analysis in terms of associative learning rather than some non-associative process.

LEARNED SAFETY OR LEARNED NONCORRELATION?

Kalat and Rozin (1973) proposed that when a rat drinks something which produces no unusual consequences, the rat learns that the solution is "safe." They acknowledged, however, the related possibility that the rat does not specifically learn that the solution predicts nothing bad, but rather that it predicts nothing at all. That is, the rat may learn that the solution is "meaningless," "irrelevant," or "not correlated with subsequent events." To decide between "learned safety" and "learned noncorrelation" we must discover whether a familiar solution, in addition to having a lowered association with poison, also has a lowered association with particularly favorable consequences.

To do so, one must first demonstrate that rats *can* learn an enhanced preference for a solution based on association with some favorable event. Only recently has this possibility been confirmed unambiguously (Best, 1975; Zahorik, this volume). Best (1975) paired one solution with poison. Later he offered thirsty rats the same solution, followed by a second solution, followed by no poisoning. This procedure generated a particularly strong preference for the second solution. He found, furthermore, that this effect was reduced if the rats had previous uneventful experience with that second solution.

Since familiar solutions are evidently less associable with good consequences as well as bad, the term "learned safety" is no longer satisfactory; it would be better to use some broader term, such as "learned noncorrelation."

"LEARNED NONCORRELATION" OR
"LEARNED GOODNESS" (POSITIVE REINFORCEMENT)?

The learned noncorrelation interpretation insists that a solution followed by nothing is specifically associated with the absence of consequences. An alternative way to account for some of the results described above would be to assume that rats associate a novel solution with its beneficial metabolic effects, and thereby learn a preference for the solution. This assumption could account for the decrease of neophobia and for the decrease of associability after familiarization with a solution.

There are several lines of evidence against this interpretation. First, the decrease in associability with poison is demonstrable after a brief exposure to an isotonic saline solution (Kalat & Rozin, 1973) or to a saccharin solution (Bolles et al., 1973). The post-ingestive consequences of either should be minimally rewarding at best.

Second, it is not clear that rats readily associate solutions with their metabolic consequences; certainly they have great difficulty calibrating meal size based on caloric density (Le Magnen & Tallon, 1966; Snowdon, 1969). If they did associate an ingested substance with its metabolic consequences (see Hawkins, this volume), and if this association interfered with associating the substance with poison, then the more the animal drank of a solution, the greater would be the positive reinforcement, and therefore the less should be the associability with a given amount of poison. In fact, however, increased consumption of a solution before a constant dose of poison may produce either increased aversion or no change in aversion (Barker, 1976; Bond & DiGiusto, 1975; Bond & Harland, 1975; Kalat, 1976); there is certainly no evidence that it produces a decrease in aversion.

Third, if a solution were associated with metabolic consequences, this association would presumably reach asymptote in the time it required to digest the solution fully. It is not clear exactly how long it should take a rat to digest 5 ml of 10% sucrose. Nevertheless, one would hardly expect it to take long enough that there should be more reward from 4½ hr of digestion time than from 2½ hr, or even from 1¼ hr. Yet the two-presentation effect does increase with delays in this range between the first presentation and poison (see Figure 3).

Fourth, if one force-feeds a solution very slowly to a rat, the rat does swallow it and (unless poisoned) later shows reduced neophobia for the solution. Domjan (1972, 1976) has shown that this effect occurs even in rats which were satiated on food and water before the solution was infused. In fact, the effect was about as large for these rats as for rats which were hungry and thirsty during the infusion, for whom the solution should have been much more "positively reinforcing."

Finally, Best (1975) demonstrated that familiarization reduces a solution's associability with favorable as well as unfavorable consequences. This can hardly be explained in terms of familiarization as a "positive reinforcement" experience.

PROBLEM: IF "LEARNED NONCORRELATION" IS LEARNING, WHERE IS THE CONTINGENCY?

Recently it has become widely accepted that the necessary condition for classical conditioning is not simply temporal contiguity between CS and US, but the presence of a contingency between them (Rescorla, 1967). If so, there is a problem with learning "safety" based on non-consequences, since there is as much "safety" before the taste as after it, and therefore no contingency.

There are two possible answers. One possibility is that contingencies are less critical in taste-aversion learning than in other situations. Perhaps when the rat tastes something novel it asks, in effect, "What happens now?" It is then particularly alerted to gastrointestinal events of the next few hours, and associates the taste with whatever happens. In agreement with this proposal, it has been found that a rat can learn an aversion to a solution by drinking it while already ill, provided that the rat does not recover from the illness soon after drinking the solution (Scarborough, Whaley, & Rogers, 1964; Barker & Smith, 1974). Also, rats which eat or drink something while thiamine-deficient and which *remain* thiamine-deficient learn an aversion to the substance (Rodgers & Rozin, 1966). In each of these cases rats rapidly associate a taste with whatever happened in the subsequent period, despite the absence of a contingency. Indeed, there is evidence in a shock-avoidance paradigm that non-contingent learning may be possible whenever there is one-trial learning (Keith-Lucas & Guttman, 1975).

A second possible resolution to the problem is as follows: it is no longer claimed that rats learn specifically that the food is safe; rather, rats learn that a food is not correlated with any later event, favorable or unfavorable. That is, the acquisition of a CS-US association does depend on a contingency between them. However, in the absence of a contingency, the rat does not simply fail to learn anything at all; it learns, in fact, the absence of a contingency (see also Mackintosh, 1973; Baker, 1976).

A closely related objection to the learned-safety position has been that it requires the animal to associate a taste with the absence of illness, even though the animal may not have experienced illness before. Typically, "safety signals" in shock-related situations can be established only after giving the rat experience with shocks (Rescorla & LoLordo, 1965; Moscovitch & LoLordo, 1968). While I would not care to rule out the possibility that rats approach new flavors with an "innate pessimism," this problem may be somewhat beside the point. The re-description of learned safety as learned noncorrelation suggests that the rat does not specifically associate a taste with the absence of poison, but with a period of time during which nothing unusual of any type occurs.

286

ANOTHER PROBLEM: LEARNED AVERSION IS
MORE THAN THE ABSENCE OF LEARNED SAFETY

With increasing delays between taste and poison, rats learn decreasing aversions. This decrease has been attributed to an increase in learned noncorrelation during the interval. However, it is clear that poisoning, after a several hour delay, does more than merely stop the learning of noncorrelation. The learning of noncorrelation, it is held, regulates the amount of learned aversion, but clearly there are two separate things an animal can learn.

There are several possible ways to describe the interaction between learned noncorrelation and learned aversion. Perhaps the simplest version, conceptually, is to analyze a single trial as if it were a series of discrete events. Suppose a rat drinks some novel solution. It is then prepared to associate the solution with whatever happens in, say, the next six hours. The time scale would probably be distorted, of course, such that one minute early after drinking the solution might be the equivalent of several minutes later. At any rate, the rat associates the solution with whatever happens in the first n time bins after tasting it. If, for example, the first three time bins represent "no event," and the rest represent "poison," there will be a small amount of learned noncorrelation and a strong learned aversion (dependent also, obviously, on the intensity of the poison). If the first 60 time bins represented "no event" and the remainder "poison," the learned noncorrelation would be stronger and the learned aversion weaker. And so on.

The above is not the only possible analysis of the interaction between learned noncorrelation and learned aversion. It does, however, have the advantage that it suggests a testable prediction. According to the above analysis, a delayed poisoning has something in common with partial reinforcement. That is, a solution is associated with a certain number of "no event" intervals plus a certain number of "poison" intervals. Might one obtain something like the partial reinforcement effect in this situation? Suppose one group of rats had learned a mild aversion based on a delayed poison, while a second group had learned an aversion of equal strength, based on an immediate but weaker poison. Would the first group have greater resistance to extinction? No evidence is currently available on this point.

ANOTHER PROBLEM: HOW DOES AN ANIMAL LEARN AN AVERSION TO A FAMILIAR TASTE?

If an animal is poisoned many hours (the exact figure depends on several parameters) after drinking some solution, it may learn no aversion. The learned noncorrelation interpretation asserts that by the time of poison the animal has already re-classified the solution as "noncorrelated" and therefore does not associate it with poison. However, no matter how familiar a solution is, if the rat drinks it again and is poisoned fairly promptly, it does learn some aversion. Is there a contradiction here?

There is a problem here only if one assumes that the first presentation of the solution is the only one that counts. The problem is minimized if we assume that on a single trial a rat learns merely something to the effect that "this stimulus predicted nothing." To learn "this stimulus *never* predicts anything" would require a cumulation over many trials. On the first presentation, the rat may associate the solution with a prolonged uneventful period, until learned noncorrelation has reached some asymptotic limit. On later presentations the rat's behavior toward the solution is changed: it shows a greater preference for the solution than it did the first time, and less tendency to associate it with poison, especially with significant delays. Nevertheless, the new presentation is a new trial, and the rat can associate the solution anew with whatever happens. There is even the possibility of increased learned noncorrelation if the solution is again followed by nothing unusual (Domjan, 1976; Elkins, 1973).

Given the above analysis, a new problem arises. Does familiarization with a solution actually decrease its associability with poison? That is, suppose a rat drinks some solution, followed by an uneventful period, and several days later drinks the solution again, followed by poison. It shows less aversion than a rat which drank it only once, followed by poison. Did the first rat actually associate the solution less than the second rat, or did it acquire an equal aversion *on that trial*, which was partially cancelled by the earlier learning?

The best test of this question is an indirect one. If a rat drinks solutions A and B prior to poison, its aversion to A should be a decreasing function of its aversion to B because of concurrent interference (see Revusky, this volume). Suppose, then, two groups of rats drink A and B before poison. Solution A is novel for both groups whereas B is familiar for one group and novel for the other. The amount of aversion which the rats acquire to A should provide an unambiguous measure of how much aversion they acquired to B *on that trial,* never mind competition with previous trials. Revusky (1971) demonstrated that the learned aversion to the first of two solutions preceding poisoning was greater if the second solution was familiar than if it was novel. That is, familiarization with a solution really does decrease its associability with poison.

IN CONCLUSION

The scheme which Pavlov and Thorndike gave us depicts learning as a rather passive process. A stimulus occurs, or a response is emitted; if something else happens quickly, the animal may learn something. However, if nothing else happens, the animal learns nothing. The view of learning which I am proposing implies a more active role for the animal as an information processor: whenever it experiences any salient stimulus it asks, in effect, what does this stimulus mean? The animal will always learn something. Either it associates the stimulus with some subsequent event, or it associates it with "nothing happening." If the stimulus is followed by some important second event, but the delay is great, the association will be weak or absent only because the animal had already associated the stimulus with the prolonged uneventful period. Although this proposal grew out of the taste-aversion phenomenon, it is intended to apply to other situations as well, including most of what we call "habituation."

In the last several years the learned safety proposal, now re-named learned noncorrelation, has received a variety of reactions. Clearly, the proposal faces a variety of unanswered questions. However, the unanswered but potentially answerable questions may not be the main problem. There is also the problem of a certain degree of vagueness—perhaps inevitable for a still-new conception, and perhaps no worse than the vagueness of most other theories about learning—but a problem nonetheless when one wishes to test the conception. There is also the problem of what could be regarded as mentalistic implications, particularly of the term "learned safety." Furthermore, there are some basic theoretical issues at stake. One's attitudes about an animal's learning that a stimulus predicts "nothing" are necessarily linked to one's definition of learning and to one's orientation toward S-R or S-S conceptions of learning.

At times, the various a priori assumptions about the nature of learning may seem to be an obstacle in the way of evaluating something like the learned noncorrelation proposal. Yet, in a sense, a re-evaluation of these assumptions is the whole point. In the long run the most important contribution of our investigation of taste-aversion learning may not be what we discover about taste-aversion learning itself—after all, as an isolated phenomenon it would be of only limited significance—but rather the main contribution may be the challenge our investigations offer to basic assumptions, and the opportunity they provide to re-open some fundamental questions.

REFERENCES

Baker, A. G. Learned irrelevance and learned helplessness: Rats learn that stimuli, reinforcers, and responses are uncorrelated. **Journal of Experimental Psychology: Animal Behavior Processes**, 1976, **2**, 130-141.

Barker, L. M. CS duration, amount, and concentration effects in conditioning taste aversions. **Learning and Motivation**, 1976, **7**, 265-273.

Barker, L. M., & Smith, J. C. A comparison of taste aversions induced by radiation and lithium chloride in CS-US and US-CS paradigms. **Journal of Comparative and Physiological Psychology**, 1974, **87**, 644-654.

Best, M. R. Conditioned and latent inhibition in taste-aversion learning: Clarifying the role of learned safety. **Journal of Experimental Psychology: Animal Behavior Processes**, 1975, **1**, 97-113.

Bolles, R. C., Riley, A. L., & Laskowski, B. A. A further demonstration of the learned safety effect in food-aversion learning. **Bulletin of the Psychonomic Society**, 1973, **1**, 190-192.

Bond, N., & DiGiusto, E. Amount of solution drunk is a factor in the establishment of taste aversion. **Animal Learning and Behavior**, 1975, **3**, 81-84.

Bond, N., & Harland, W. Effect of amount of solution drunk on taste-aversion learning. **Bulletin of the Psychonomic Society**, 1975, **5**, 219-220.

Domjan, M. CS preexposure in taste-aversion learning: Effects of deprivation and preexposure duration. **Learning and Motivation**, 1972, **3**, 389-402.

Domjan, M., & Bowman, T. G. Learned safety and the CS-US delay gradient in taste-aversion learning. **Learning and Motivation**, 1974, **5**, 409-423.

Domjan, M. Determinants of the enhancement of flavored-water intake by prior exposure. **Journal of Experimental Psychology: Animal Behavior Processes**, 1976, **2**, 17-27.

Domjan, M., & Bowman, T. G. Learned safety and the CS-US delay gradient in taste-aversion learning. **Learning and motivaâtion**, 1974, **5**, 409-423.

Domjan, M., & Wilson, N. E. Contribution of ingestive behaviors to taste-aversion learning in the rat. **Journal of Comparative and Physiological Psychology**, 1972, **80**, 403-412.

Egger, M. D., & Miller, N. E. Secondary reinforcement in rats as a function of information value and reliability of the stimulus. **Journal of Experimental Psychology**, 1962, **64**, 97-104.

Egger, M. D., & Miller, N. E. When is a reward reinforcing?: An experimental study of the information hypothesis. **Journal of Comparative and Physiological Psychology**, 1963, **56**, 132-137.

Elkins, R. L. Attenuation of drug-induced bait shyness to a palatable solution as an increasing function of its availability prior to conditioning. **Behavioral Biology**, 1973, **9**, 221-226.

Garcia, J., Ervin, F. R., & Koelling, R. A. Learning with prolonged delay of reinforcement. **Psychonomic Science**, 1966, **5**, 121-122.

Green, K. F., & Parker, L. A. Gustatory memory: Incubation and interference. **Behavioral Biology**, 1975, **13**, 359-367.

Hein, A., Held, R., & Gower, E. C. Development and segmentation of visually controlled movement by selective exposure during rearing. **Journal of Comparative and Physiological Psychology**, 1970, **73**, 181-187.

Kalat, J. W. Taste salience depends on novelty, not concentration, in taste-aversion learning in the rat. **Journal of Comparative and Physiological Psychology,** 1974, **86,** 47-50.

Kalat, J. W. Taste-aversion learning in infant guinea pigs. **Developmental Psychobiology,** 1975, **8,** 383-387.

Kalat, J. W. Should taste-aversion learning experiments control duration or volume of drinking on the training day? **Animal Learning and Behavior,** 1976, **4,** 96-98.

Kalat, J. W., & Rozin, P. "Salience": A factor which can override temporal contiguity in taste-aversion learning. **Journal of Comparative and Physiological Psychology,** 1970, **71,** 192-197.

Kalat, J. W., & Rozin, P. Role of interference in taste-aversion learning. **Journal of Comparative and Physiological Psychology,** 1971, **77,** 53-58.

Kalat, J. W., & Rozin, P. "Learned safety" as a mechanism in long-delay taste-aversion learning in rats. **Journal of Comparative and Physiological Psychology,** 1973, **83,** 198-207.

Kamin, L. J. Predictability, surprise, attention, and conditioning. In B. A. Campbell & R. M. Church (Eds.), **Punishment and aversive behavior.** New York: Appleton-Century-Crofts, 1969.

Keith-Lucas, T., & Guttman, N. Robust single trial delayed backward conditioning. **Journal of Comparative and Physiological Psychology,** 1975, **88,** 468-476.

Kiefer, S. W., & Braun, J. J. Absence of differential associative responses to novel and familiar gustatory stimuli in rats lacking gustatory neocortex. Unpublished manuscript, Arizona State University, 1976.

Kimble, G. A. The definition of learning and some useful distinctions. In G. A. Kimble (Ed.), **Foundations of conditioning and learning.** New York: Appleton-Century-Crofts, 1967.

Kinastowski, W. Der einfluss der mechanischen reize auf die kontraktilitaet von Spirostomum ambiguum Ehrbg. **Acta Protozool.,** 1963, **1,** 201-222.

LeMagnen, J., & Tallon, S. La periodicite spontanee de la prise d'aliments ad libitum du Rat blanc. **Journal de Physiologie** (Paris), 1966, **58,** 323-349.

Mackintosh, N. J. Stimulus selection: Learning to ignore stimuli that predict no change in reinforcement. In R. A. Hinde & J. Stevenson-Hinde (Eds.), **Constraints on learning.** London: Academic Press, 1973.

Maier, S. F., Seligman, M. E. P., & Solomon, R. L. Pavlovian fear conditioning and learned helplessness: Effects on escape and avoidance behavior. In B. A. Campbell & R. M. Church (Eds.), **Punishment and aversive behavior.** New York: Appleton-Century-Crofts, 1969.

Moscovitch, A., & LoLordo, V. M. Role of safety in the Pavlovian backward fear conditioning procedure. **Journal of Comparative and Physiological Psychology,** 1968, **66,** 673-678.

Nachman, M., & Ashe, J. H. Effects of basolateral amygdala lesions on neophobia, learned-taste aversions, and sodium appetite in rats. **Journal of Comparative and Physiological Psychology,** 1974, **87,** 622-643.

Nachman, M., & Jones, D. Learned taste aversions over long delays in rats: The role of learned safety. **Journal of Comparative and Physiological Psychology,** 1974, **86,** 949-956.

Pavlov, I. P. **Conditioned reflexes.** Oxford: Oxford Univ. Press, 1927.

Pearlman, C. A. Learned safety for taste impaired by several drugs in rats. Unpublished manuscript, Boston V. A. Hospital, 1976.

Rescorla, R. A. Pavlovian conditioning and its proper control procedures. **Psychological Review,** 1967, **74,** 71-80.

Rescorla, R. A., & LoLordo, V. M. Inhibition of avoidance behavior. **Journal of Comparative and Physiological Psychology,** 1965, **59,** 406-412.

Revusky, S. H. The role of interference in association over a delay. In W. Honig & H. James (Eds.), **Animal memory.** New York: Academic Press, 1971.

Revusky, S. H., & Bedarf, E. W. Association of illness with prior ingestion of novel foods. **Science,** 1967, **155,** 219-220.

Revusky, S. H., & Garcia, J. Learned associations over long delays. In G. H. Bower & J. Spence (Eds.), **Psychology of learning and motivation: Advances in research and Theory (Vol. IV).** New York: Academic Press, 1970.

Rhoad, K. D., Kalat, J. W., & Klopfer, P. H. Aggression and avoidance by *Betta splendens* toward natural and artificial stimuli. **Animal Learning and Behavior,** 1975, **3,** 271-276.

Rodgers, W., & Rozin, P. Novel food preferences in thiamine-deficient rats. **Journal of Comparative and Physiological Psychology,** 1966, **61,** 1-4.

Rolls, B. J., & Rolls, E. T. Effects of lesions in the basolateral amygdala on fluid intake in the rat. **Journal of Comparative and Physiological Psychology,** 1973, **83,** 240-247.

Rolls, E. T., & Rolls, B. J. Altered food preferences after lesions in the basolateral region of the amygdala in the rat. **Journal of Comparative and Physiological Psychology,** 1973, **83,** 248-259.

Rozin, P., & Kalat, J. W. Specific hungers and poison avoidance as adaptive specializations of learning. **Psychological Review,** 1971, **78,** 459-486.

Rozin, P., & Ree, P. Long extension of effective CS-US interval by anesthesia between CS and US. **Journal of Comparative and Physiological Psychology,** 1972, **80,** 43-48.

Scarborough, B. B., Whaley, D. L., & Rogers, J. G. Saccharin-avoidance behavior instigated by x-irradiation in backward conditioning paradigms. **Psychological Reports,** 1964, **14,** 475-481.

Sheffield, V. F. Extinction as a function of partial reinforcement and distribution of practice. **Journal of Experimental Psychology,** 1949, **39,** 511-526.

Siegel, S. Flavor pre-exposure and "learned safety." **Journal of Comparative and Physiological Psychology,** 1974, **87,** 1073-1082.

Snowdon, C. T. Motivation, regulation, and the control of meal parameters with oral and intragastric feeding. **Journal of Comparative and Physiological Psychology,** 1969, **69,** 91-100.

Thompson, R. F. The search for the engram. **American Psychologist,** 1976, **31,** 209-227.

XIII

THE NATURE OF "LEARNED SAFETY" AND ITS ROLE IN THE DELAY OF REINFORCEMENT GRADIENT

MICHAEL R. BEST
Southern Methodist University

LEWIS M. BARKER
Baylor University

We have been interested for some time in applying the classical conditioning paradigm and its concepts to taste-aversion learning phenomena. While the conditioned taste-aversion paradigm can be construed as one involving both Pavlovian and instrumental aspects, the classical conditioning paradigm has been critical in establishing the framework within which taste-aversion learning is conceptualized. Indeed, the classic work of Garcia and his colleagues was largely responsible for the introduction of Pavlovian principles into the analysis of conditioned taste aversions (e.g., Garcia, Kimeldorf, & Koelling, 1955; Garcia, Ervin, & Koelling, 1966; Garcia & Koelling, 1966).

One relatively recent theory purporting to account for a number of phenomena in taste-aversion learning is the learned safety theory of Kalat and Rozin (1973; see also Kalat, this volume). This theory, while certainly not the only one attempting to account for these phenomena, has stimulated considerable research (see Bolles, Riley, & Laskowski, 1973; Domjan & Bowman, 1974; Nachman & Jones, 1974; Siegel, 1974) and is very intriguing when treated within the context of several classical conditioning concepts. This paper will explore the relationships between learned safety and these concepts as well as consider its possible interaction with other less permanent processes in accounting for the delay of reinforcement gradient in taste-aversion learning.

LEARNED SAFETY AS AN INSTANCE
OF LATENT INHIBITION

The learned safety theory assumes that rats attend especially carefully to the consequences of an ingestional experience. If the consequences are aversive, an aversion is learned; if an aversive gastrointestinal consequence does not ensue, the animal learns safety. This safety, it is hypothesized, then interferes with aversion learning if the flavor is subsequently paired with toxicosis. Learned safety has been proposed as a mechanism mediating the decrement in aversion conditioning which is observed as the interval between ingestion and toxicosis is increased. It is also one possible interpretation of the stimulus preexposure or latent inhibition effect which is reflected in the relative difficulty of conditioning aversions to familiar flavors (e.g., Domjan, 1972; McLaurin, Farley, & Scarborough, 1963; Revusky & Bedarf, 1967).

Ambiguity of the Term "Safety." Using the term "safety" to refer to the process which occurs when a rat consumes an edible followed by no aversive gastrointestinal consequences, however, is inherently ambiguous (for a more detailed treatment of the following analysis see Best, 1975). Briefly, there are at least two separate procedures which may result in the learning of safety. One involves establishing a stimulus as a safety signal in an aversive conditioning procedure. In this process, known as conditioned inhibition (for a review, see Rescorla, 1969), a stimulus, A, is paired with an aversive US (e.g., shock) and, subsequently, a compound stimulus, AX, is presented and followed by no aversive consequences. In the presence of the excitatory context created by A, rats come to treat X as a predictor of safety. This is evidenced by the fact that stimulus X comes to control behavior in a direction opposite to that of A. In a conditioned emotional response (CER) procedure, for example, a conditioned inhibitor will reduce suppression, or accelerate barpressing (e.g., Hammond, 1966), while the stimulus paired with footshock will reduce this response. Similarly, performance of a Sidman shock avoidance response will increase to a stimulus predicting shock and decrease to an event signaling safety (Rescorla & LoLordo, 1965). Likewise, in flavor-aversion learning, stimuli explicitly signaling safety come to be preferred (Best, 1975; Taukulis & Revusky, 1975). Such conditioned inhibitors are psychologically meaningful, salient events which have come to control behavior via an associative process.

A second procedure which might be construed as learned safety is the stimulus preexposure or familiarization manipulation (this procedure is generally known as latent inhibition; see Lubow, 1973 for a general review). In this procedure, animals receive nonreinforced preexposure to a stimulus prior to its pairing with reinforcement. Such preexposure comes to reduce the general associability of the familiar stimulus, i.e., it becomes more difficult for this event to enter into an association of any kind. One interpretation of this effect is that the animal learns that the preexposed event predicts no reliable change in reinforcement and, consequently, comes to ignore or disregard the stimulus (Mackintosh, 1973). The similarity between latent inhibition and habituation procedures has been recognized, and a number of investigators prefer to construe the latent inhibition process as nonassociative (e.g., Halgren, 1973; Rescorla, 1971; Reiss & Wagner, 1971). As yet, however, there is no systematic work which identifies latent inhibition as a process independent from learning; the evidence merely indicates that a familiar event is subsequently less associable with reinforcement.

Learned Safety vs. Conditioned Inhibition. One way of determining which type of "safety" (conditioned inhibition or latent inhibition) rats develop as a consequence of benign ingestional experiences is to determine the extent to which the establishment of conditioned inhibition to a flavor is disrupted by familiarization with this stimulus. If learned safety is conditioned inhibition, then familiarization with a nonaversive solution should either facilitate or have no effect on subsequent conditioned inhibition training to that stimulus. If learned safety is compatible with latent inhibition, on the other hand, solution familiarization should reduce the ability of a flavor stimulus to acquire conditioned inhibitory properties. Its general associability should be disrupted.

In the conditioned inhibition procedure, a flavor is presented following exposure to an aversive solution without adverse postingestional consequences. Rats come to prefer this solution as conditioned inhibition develops, presumably because the flavor predicts an illness-free period. For example, in one demonstration of conditioned inhibition, an aversion to a .15 saccharin solution was first created by twice following its ingestion with an injection of apormorphine, an emetic. When the saccharin was presented for a third time, the rats merely sampled the solution. This brief exposure was followed immediately by exposure to a second, novel, fluid (saline or casein hydrolysate) with no subsequent poisoning. The animals developed a significant preference for the second substance relative to control animals in which saccharin was not rendered aversive (see Figure 1 for the results and Table 1 for a more detailed description of the procedure).

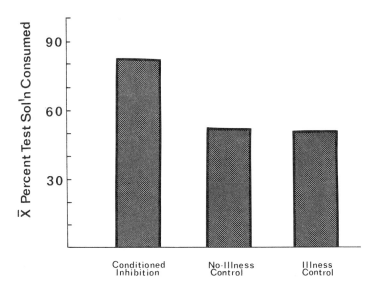

Figure 1
Mean preference ratios (test fluid / test fluid + water) on the
Day 6 test. Test fluids either .9 saline (sodium chloride) or 5
casein hydrolysate. See Table 1 for procedural details. (After
Best, 1975).

In contrast to the above findings, when rats were familiarized
with the flavor prior to conditioned inhibition training, an
enhanced preference was not conditioned. In this experiment, an
isotonic saline solution was presented several times before saccharin aversion conditioning. The saline solution was then presented without poisoning shortly after exposure to the aversive saccharin. The animals did not learn a preference for the saline in
comparison to other animals in which saline was not preexposed
(see Figure 2 for the results and Table 2 for a more detailed description of the procedure). Previous familiarization with the solution,
then, apparently reduced its associability, thereby preventing the
flavor from entering into an association when it explicitly predicted
the absence of illness. These findings support the conclusion that
learned safety in taste-aversion learning is an instance of latent inhibition, not the establishment of a flavor as a conditioned inhibitor. With this in mind, a more appropriate and certainly less
ambiguous term for the learned safety effect would be *learned
familiarity*.[1]

Learned Safety as Nonassociative Learning. Granted that the
"safety" established following nonaversive exposure to an edible is

TABLE 1

Procedure: Conditioned Inhibition in Taste-Aversion Learning

Day	CS		US	
	Solution	Cond Inhib (n =18)	No-Ill Cont (n =18)	Ill Cont (n =18)
1				Apomorphine (Noncontingent)
2				Apomorphine (Noncontingent)
3	Saccharin (20 min)	Apomorphine	Iso Sal	Iso Sal
4	Saccharin (20 min)	Apomorphine	Iso Sal	Iso Sal
5	Saccharin (2 min) Saline (or Casein) (10 min)			

TESTING

6	CHOICE (all groups):	Saline (or Casein)	+ Water (20 Min)

Stimuli:

CS
Saccharin (.15)
Saline (.9)
Casein Hydrolysate (5)

US
Apomorphine (15 mg/kg)
Isotonic Saline (.15 M)

compatible with a latent inhibition rather than a conditioned in-hibition interpretation, it is still unclear whether the process of learned safety should be construed as associative or nonassociative. Some might suggest that if learned safety is not associative, the term "learned" has no place in its description. But this would be true only if a distinction between "associative" and "non-associative" learning were impossible—a distinction which does not seem to us to be unreasonable. Associative learning is typically inferred from long-term or relatively permanent changes in behavior resulting from an experimental relationship established between two or more events explicitly defined by the experimental procedure (cf. Rescorla, 1967). Conditioned excitation and condi-

TABLE 2

Procedure: Latent Inhibition of Conditioned Inhibition in Taste-Aversion Learning

Groups

	COND INHIB (n = 9)	NO-ILL CONT (n = 8)	LATENT INHIB OF COND INHIB (n = 9)	NO-ILL CONT (n = 8)
Phase I (Preexpose)				
Day				
1	Vanilla (20 min)	Vanilla (20 min)	Saline (20 min)	Saline (20 min)
2	Vanilla (20 min)	Vanilla (20 min)	Saline (20 min)	Saline (20 min)
Phase II (Conditioning)				
Day				
1	Saccharin/Apo (20 min)	Saccharin/Iso (20 min)	Saccharin/Apo (20 min)	Saccharin/Iso (20 min)
2	Saccharin/Apo (20 min)	Saccharin/Iso (20 min)	Saccharin/Apo (20 min)	Saccharin/Iso (20 min)
3		All Groups: Saccharin (2 min) Saline (10 min)		

Phase III (Testing)

Day

1

CHOICE (all groups):   Saline + Water
                       (20 min)

Stimuli:

CS
Saccharin (.15%)
Vanilla (.08%)
Saline (.9%)

US
Apomorphine (15 mg/kg)
Isotonic Saline (.15 M)

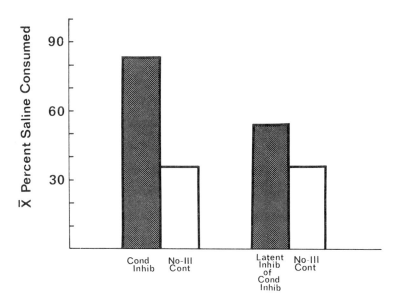

Figure 2
Mean saline preference ratios (saline / saline + water) for each
group on the Phase III, Day 1 test. See Table 2 for procedural
details. (Redrawn from Best, 1975).

tioned inhibition are both unambiguous examples of associative
learning. Nonassociative learning would include those durable
changes in behavior resulting from procedures in which the above
conditions have not been met. Habituation and latent inhibition or
learned safety, among other behavioral phenomena, would be
possible candidates for this latter learning category. Within this
framework, latent inhibition could be classified as a nonassociative
instance of learning. The evidence merely indicates that a familiar
event is subsequently less associable when this stimulus becomes
an element in an excitatory or inhibitory contingency; it does not
imply that learning of some sort cannot mediate this alteration in
associability.

   Evidence for Learned Safety. While learned safety has been proposed as the mechanism mediating a number of flavor-aversion
phenomena, much of the evidence used to reflect its operation is
presently indirect. It has been hypothesized, for example, that the
associability of flavors with toxicosis decreases as the ingestion-
illness interval is increased because longer intervals allow for more
learned safety before toxicosis (Kalat & Rozin, 1973). Similarly, it
has been proposed that flavors lose their associability with tox-

302

icosis following nonaversive preexposure because learned safety competes with the learning of aversion. However, in none of these arguments is learned safety measured directly; the process is inferred from the effects such manipulations have on taste-aversion learning.

Several recent attempts, however, have looked at this hypothesized process of learned safety more directly. Siegel (1974) has shown that nonaversive exposure to a novel flavor creates a substantial and relatively durable preference for this solution in a two-bottle test. The single-bottle intake of such flavors is also increased by prior nonaversive exposure. Similarly, Nachman and Jones (1974) and Green and Parker (1975) have shown that increasing the interval between successive exposures to a novel flavor increases intake of that fluid. Domjan (1976; also see Domjan, this volume) has shown this enhancement of intake to be primarily a function of the number and duration of prior exposures to the flavored solution. Such accelerating intake of familiar solutions suggests that the animals are learning something about these substances as the result of their experience with them. Indeed, the fact that the initial reluctance rats show to ingest most novel edibles (neophobia) dissipates following the initial exposure, further supports this interpretation.

LEARNED SAFETY AS AN EXPLANATION OF THE DELAY OF REINFORCEMENT GRADIENT

It is apparent from the above analysis that the effects of learned safety and its interaction with other processes are far from simple. This is especially true when considering its role in the delay of reinforcement gradient in conditioned taste aversions.

THE TWO-PRESENTATION EXPERIMENT: EVIDENCE FOR LEARNED SAFETY

Kalat and Rozin (1973) were the first to investigate the role of learned safety in the delay of reinforcement gradient and did so by introducing a special procedure hereafter referred to as the "two-presentation" design. In this experiment, one group of rats was presented with a novel sucrose solution 30-min prior to illness (Group ½-Li). This group was compared to groups receiving the novel flavor either 4 hr (Group 4-Li) before toxicosis or 4 hr and again 30 min prior to illness (Group 3½-½-Li). If learned safety depends on the time since a novel fluid is first encountered, as Kalat and Rozin suggest, Groups 3½-½-Li and 4-Li should have equal opportunity to acquire safety. Provided that learned safety is the primary determinant of the delay gradient, groups 4-Li and 3½-½-Li should also not differ in amount of learned aversion. These groups, however, should both show reduced aversion when compared to Group ½-Li which had little opportunity to acquire safety prior to the induction of illness. This, indeed, is what Kalat and Rozin found, and the results were interpreted within the context of the learned safety hypothesis. This pattern of results was later replicated and similarly interpreted by Bolles et al. (1973) and by Bond and DiGiusto (1975).[2] A traditional trace-decay model would have difficulty handling these findings since the second sucrose presentation in group 3½-½-Li, a presentation which should reinstate the fading trace, failed to increase the associability of sucrose with poison.

THE TWO-PRESENTATION EXPERIMENT:
EFFECTS OF THE SECOND PRESENTATION

Domjan and Bowman Study. Domjan and Bowman (1974) partially replicated the Kalat and Rozin experiment with two important control groups. In addition to the 3½-½-Li and ½-Li groups, they included identical groups which were not poisoned (3½-½-Na and ½-Na). Like Kalat and Rozin, they found that the 3½-½-Li group showed significantly less aversion than the ½-Li group. They discovered, however, that the 3½-½-Na group also evidenced significantly greater intake of the test solution than the ½-Na group. Apparently, the second exposure 30 min prior to the control injection served to reduce the animals' reluctance to consume the relatively novel flavor. This resulted in greater consumption when compared to that of animals receiving the fluid only once 30 min before the control injection. These findings indicate that the reduced aversion shown by the animals in Kalat and Rozin's 3½-½-Li group may at least partially reflect effects of the second flavor exposure, not simply safety acquired by virtue of the exposure 4 hr prior to the illness experience.

Indeed, when using a flavor which left preference unaffected after a second exposure (.2 saccharin), Domjan and Bowman were able to reduce the difference between the 3½-½-Li and ½-Li groups. Using this flavor, the 3½-½-Li group also developed a significantly greater aversion than the 4-Li group. This difference stresses still further the important impact of a second flavor exposure. In fact, in the last experiment of this series, Domjan and Bowman were able virtually to eliminate a learned safety effect by

304

reinstating a flavor 20 min prior to toxicosis. In this experiment, rats were exposed to the flavor 6 hr and again 20 min prior to receiving lithium chloride injections (Group 5 2/3-1/3-Li). This group showed an aversion of comparable magnitude to that of rats receiving a single exposure to the flavor 20 min prior to toxicosis (Group 1/3-Li). In this case, reinstating the flavor served to disrupt or mask any safety acquired prior to the second exposure.

Barker Study. It would seem, then, that the interval between the first and second exposures to a novel flavor as well as that between the second presentation and illness, are critical in determining the extent to which a learned safety mechanism is able to influence taste-aversion learning over a delay. In a recent series of experiments, Barker took a systematic look at this relationship. In one of these experiments, independent groups of rats were presented with a 15 sucrose solution 30 min prior to lithium chloride-induced toxicosis. This exposure was preceded by sucrose at varying intervals prior to the second drinking period. Group ¼-½-Li received their first sucrose period 15 min prior to the second exposure. Likewise, groups 1½-½-Li, 3½-½-Li, 7½-½-Li, and 23½-½-Li received their second exposure 1.5, 3.5, 7.5, and 23.5 hr, respectively, after their initial contact with sucrose. Aversion learning in these groups was compared to that of single exposure groups which received sucrose once either 45 min (¾-Li), 2 hr (2-Li), 4 hr (4-Li), 8 hr (8-Li), or 24 hr (24-Li) prior to toxicosis. Figure 3 shows the stimulus sequencing of these 10 groups as well as the other relevant procedural details from the experiment.

In the form proposed by Kalat and Rozin (1973), the learned safety hypothesis predicts no differences between the groups which received their initial exposure to sucrose at comparable first-taste-to-toxicosis intervals (i.e., the ¼-½-Li and ¾-Li groups, the 1½-½-Li and 2-Li groups, etc. should learn comparable aversions). Indeed, the ¼-½-Li and ¾-Li and the 1½-½-Li and 2-Li groups did show comparable aversions (see Figure 4). Furthermore, the aversions in the 1½-½-Li and 2-Li groups were somewhat less than those shown in the ¼-½-Li and ¾-Li groups, a prediction compatible with the operation of learned safety. At 2-hr intervals and less, then, the single-stimulus and double-stimulus manipulations had comparable effects on the level of aversion learning. At 4, 8, and 24 hr, however, a completely different picture emerged. At these first-taste-to-toxicosis intervals, the second exposure dramatically affected the level of conditioned sucrose aversion. The 3½-½-Li, the 7½-½-Li, and the 23½-½-Li groups learned aversions at least as strong as those shown by the ¾-Li group. The 4-Li group, on the other hand, showed only a

305

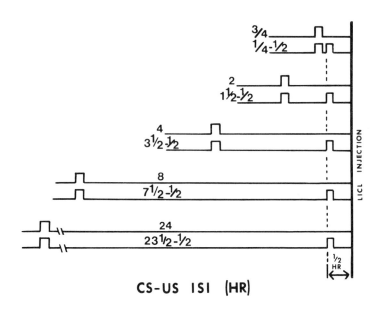

CS-US ISI (HR)

Figure 3
Stimulus sequencing for 10 independent groups of rats (ns =6) that were allowed access to 15 sucrose for either 10 min at 3/4, 2, 4, 8, and 24 hr prior to a 20ml/kg, 0.15M LiCl I.P. injection, or for 5 min at these same intervals with a second 5 min access ½ hr prior to LiCl.

slight sucrose aversion, and the 8-Li and 24-Li groups showed virtually no aversion to the sucrose solution.

These results suggest that the relatively brief (about 5 min) re-instatement of a previously experienced flavor 30 min prior to lithium chloride-induced illness constituted such a potent conditioning experience that the effects of the initial presentation were either lost or masked. It is reasonably well established, however, that a single, lengthy exposure to a novel flavor literally weeks prior to pairing that same fluid with toxicosis reduces the rate at which a learned aversion is acquired (e.g., Kalat & Rozin, 1973; McLaurin, Farley, & Scarborough, 1963; Siegel, 1974). What, then, determines whether a safe ingestional experience has a detectable effect on the associability of a flavor with toxicosis?

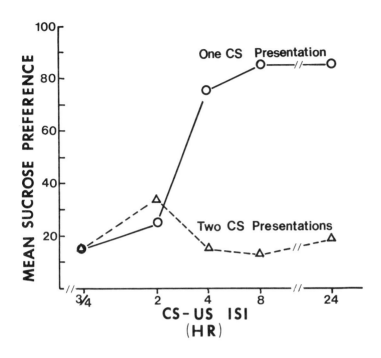

Figure 4
Mean sucrose preference in a 10-min, two-bottle test (one containing tap water) initiated 48 hr postconditioning as a function
of the interval between first CS presentation and toxicosis (CS-
US ISI) for groups having a single CS presentation (circles) and
for groups that also had a second CS presentation 30 min prior
to the US event (triangles). (See Figure 3 for stimulus sequencing for these groups). Analysis of variance indicated that the
one-CS vs. two-CS treatment was significant (p < .01), and
pairwise comparisons further revealed that the one-CS and two-
CS groups differed significantly at 4, 8, and 24 hr CS-US intervals (all p < .01).

THE EFFECTS OF EXTENSIVE PREEXPOSURE
ON THE DELAY OF REINFORCEMENT GRADIENT

Nachman and Jones Study. Nachman and Jones (1974) reported
several experiments which were designed to separate the permanent
effects of learned safety from other more transient determinants of
the delay gradient in conditioned taste aversions. In one of these experiments, they attempted to establish asymptotic learned safety to a

307

.3 saccharin solution prior to observing the delay gradient obtained when this familiar flavor was then paired with lithium over various CS-US intervals. The rats first received five days of *ad libitum* saccharin interspersed with five days of water. These animals were then given a 2-min saccharin period followed at intervals of 4 min, 2 hr, or 8 hr with a 10-min saccharin test. Whereas intake of saccharin was shown to be an increasing function of the taste intervals for animals in which the saccharin was novel, the interval separating the two saccharin exposures on test day had no differential effects on the amount of the familiar saccharin ingested. This finding suggested to the authors that maximal learned safety had developed as a function of the previous exposure of saccharin. When the same saccharin solution was subsequently paired with toxicosis at various taste-toxin intervals, however, a delay of reinforcement gradient was observed; asymptotic learned safety did not prevent animals from developing gradually decreasing aversions to familiar flavors as the taste-toxin interval was systematically increased. This is further evidence that the learned safety hypothesis is unable to account completely for the delay gradient. While prior exposure clearly reduces the associability of an ingestional stimulus, the interval between trace reinstatement and toxicosis is an important factor in the learning of taste aversions. It may be that a permanent process (learned safety?) and a transient process (trace decay?) operate concurrently to determine the extent to which a flavor will become associated with toxicosis over a delay.

Barker and Best Study. Recently, in a preliminary investigation of this question, we observed the effects of flavor preexposure on conditioning in the procedure used previously (see Figure 3). One group of rats (8-Li) was given 10 min of sucrose 8 hr prior to receiving a lithium chloride injection. Another group was treated in the same fashion except the animals in this condition received 10-min exposures to sucrose on each of the five preceding days (Group 5—/8-Li). When tested 48, 96, and 144 hr following lithium administration, neither group consumed significantly different amounts of sucrose. Three additional groups, however—one receiving sucrose for 10-min periods 8 hr and again ½ hr prior to toxicosis (Group 7½-½-Li), a second receiving sucrose 45 min and again 30 min prior to lithium injections (¼-½-Li), and a third which received one sucrose exposure 45 min prior to the induction of illness (¾-Li)— showed strong and virtually identical aversions to sucrose on the initial test day. As noted before, the brief exposure to sucrose 30 min prior to toxicosis conditioned a strong aversion in the 7½-½-Li group even though it had received a 10-min preexposure trial 7½ hr earlier

(Figure 5, left panel). On the other hand, all animals preexposed to sucrose for 5 days (10 min/day) prior to the conditioning day, consumed substantial amounts of sucrose on the test day regardless of their respective stimulus sequencing (cf. Groups ¾, ¼-½, 7½-½ in Figure 3). In fact, these groups consumed sucrose on all test days in amounts comparable to that of group 8-Li (see Figure 5, right panel).

These data demonstrate that five brief preexposures to a sucrose solution substantially reduce its associability with toxicosis. It is reasonable to conclude from such an outcome that the effects of these nonreinforced preexposures were stored in a relatively permanent form, one which influenced subsequent reclassification of the flavor. This contrasts with the effects of a single brief preex-

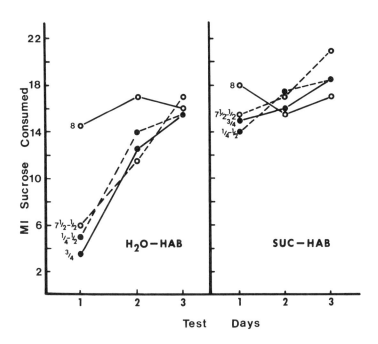

Figure 5
Median sucrose intake for 8 independent groups (ns = 7) is plotted for 10-min extinction tests initiated 48, 96, and 144 hr postconditioning. The treatment of each group in the left panel was identical to those so designated in Figure 3; the right panel results are also for similarly-treated groups except that they had 10 min per day access to 15 sucrose for the five days prior to conditioning. The overall sucrose habituation effect was significant (p < .01). The left panel results replicated the previous experiment (see legend, Figure 4).

309

posure. If the exposure preceded a conditioning trial by more than several hours (e.g., Group 7½-½-Li), it had no deleterious influence on a conditioned taste aversion; it is as if the animal had no prior experience with the preexposed flavor.

The data reported above raise at least two general questions. First, why do several exposures, or a single extensive one, have a relatively permanent effect on intake of a flavor and/or its subsequent associability with toxicosis? It has been suggested that familiarization merely reduces the novelty of a flavor, thereby habituating the neophobia reaction to the taste (Domjan, 1976). The relative difficulty of this latently inhibited stimulus to subsequently enter into an association might then reflect the importance of the orienting reflex for learning. It must still be recognized, however, that such an effect is dependent on the animal's memory of its previous experience with the flavor. Learning which results from stimulus preexposure, in other words, mediates the behavioral phenomena (i.e., increase in preference and reduced associability).

The second question is more problematic. Why does a single brief exposure to a flavor have little or no deleterious effect on subsequent taste-aversion conditioning under certain conditions (i.e., Groups 7½-½-Li and 23½-½-Li)? The results of our experiments described above do not allow us to give an unequivocal answer. One possibility is that the representation of the single, brief sucrose exposure was fragile and dissipated rapidly. Consequently, this presentation exerted a functional impact for only a short period of time following exposure. A second, equally likely interpretation of these experiments is that the second presentation shortly before toxicosis facilitated conditioning to such an extent that it masked any effects from the first exposure several hours earlier.

THE TWO-PRESENTATION EXPERIMENT: INTERACTIONS

In order to distinguish between the possibilities discussed above, the two-presentation experiment was again replicated with the interval between the two CS exposures systematically varied (Gemberling, 1976). Six groups of eight Sprague-Dawley rats were placed on a fluid deprivation schedule, receiving water for a 10-min period daily. On the conditioning day, each group was allowed to drink 5 ml of a casein hydrolysate solution 30 min prior to receiving lithium chloride injections (.15M, 2 ml/100 g, i.p.). For one group (½-Li), this was their only casein exposure. Each of the other groups had received one previous 5 cc exposure to casein at various intervals preceding the second presentation. Group ¼-½-Li

310

received this presentation 15 min prior to the second presentation. Groups 3½-½-Li, 7½-½-Li, 23½-½-Li, and 1 wk-½-Li received their initial 5 cc exposure 3.5 hr, 7.5 hr, 23.5 hr, and 1 week, respectively, prior to the second exposure. To assure that thirst levels did not differ systematically among the various groups at the time of second exposure, animals in the ½-Li, 7½-½-Li, 23½-½-Li and 1 wk-½-Li groups received 5 cc of water at the same time the 7½-½-Li group received their initial casein exposures. Animals from all groups received water for 20 min on the day following the lithium exposure and were given single-bottle casein tests 24, 48, and 72 hr later. All rats received 10 min of water following the casein test on each day.

Figure 6 summarizes the results from the initial test day. The animals in the ½-Li group showed virtually complete suppression to the casein solution.[3] Animals in the ¼-½-Li group, while manifesting a strong aversion, consumed significantly more casein than the rats in the ½-Li group and the 3½-½-Li groups consumed significantly more casein than either the ½-Li or the ¼-½-Li

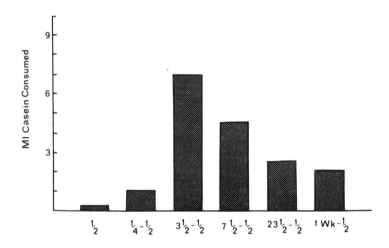

Figure 6
Median intake of casein hydrolysate for each group on the initial test day. Group ½ drank 5 ml of casein hydrolysate 30 min prior to lithium injections on the conditioning day. The other 5 groups drank 5 ml of casein twice prior to lithium, with the first number and/or fraction under each bar representing the interval (in hours) between the first and second drinking periods and the last fraction representing the interval (in hours) between the second period and lithium administration.

311

groups. This pattern of results is consistent with the results of Kalat and Rozin (1973) as well as those of Bolles et al. (1973) and is quite compatible with a learned safety interpretation which predicts a systematic decrease in conditioning as the interval separating two presentations is increased.

The learned safety hypothesis, however, would also predict continued reduction in the conditioned aversion to casein as the interval between the two casein presentations increases beyond 3.5 hr. As Figure 6 shows, this is not what happened. The 7½-½-Li group demonstrated a significantly stronger casein aversion than the 3½-½-Li group as did the 23½-½-Li and 1 wk-½-Li groups. Whereas the initial stimulus presentation systematically reduced the associability of casein with toxicosis up to and including a 3.5 hr interval between the two presentations, the deleterious effects of the initial presentation were reduced at 7.5 hr. It should be noted that some loss in associability remained even at the one-week interval (the 1 wk-½-Li and the 23½-½-Li groups both differed significantly from the ½-Li group but not from the ¼-½-Li group or from each other), but to a far lesser degree than in the 3½-½-Li animals. Also, since the initial presentation systematically retarded

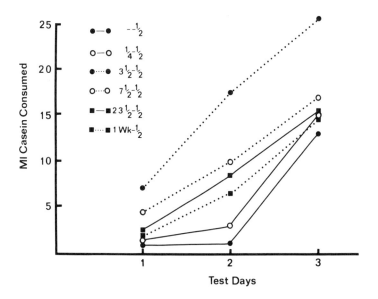

Figure 7
Median intake of casein hydrolysate for each group on the three test days. Refer to Figure 6 for description of group labels.

312

conditioning for at least 3.5 hr, the argument cannot be made that conditioning to the second presentation overshadowed all the pre-exposure effects of the first presentation.

Figure 7 presents the results of the three casein tests. This graph shows that the differential effects observed on the initial test day were not spurious; the results on the subsequent two casein extinction trials reflect a pattern of extinction consistent with the results of the first test day.

It would appear, then, that the two-presentation experiment—a prototype for the demonstration of learned safety—is not a procedure which reflects the operation of a single process. In the absence of extensive familiarization with a flavor, two presentations of the stimulus over variable intervals have non-linear effects on the conditioning of taste aversions when the second presentation precedes illness by a fixed duration. If the flavor exposures occur within several hours of each other, the initial presentation has a progressively more disruptive effect on conditioning. This is the phenomenon which has generally been interpreted as evidence for the operation of learned safety. The present findings, however, indicate that a large portion of the loss in associability observed with taste-to-taste intervals of 3.5 hr and less is due to transient rather than permanent effects of the initial presentation. As the interval is systematically expanded, the short-term effects of the initial exposure begin to dissipate and associability of the flavor with toxicosis returns. This suggests that the graded loss in associability observed over the shorter intervals is due primarily to processes other than the permanent influences implied by learned safety and contrast with the long-term loss in associability which results from more extensive non-aversive preexposure.

Why associability begins to recover when the interval separating two presentations to a flavor reaches a critical point is presently unclear. It may be that the initial exposure remains active in a short-term system for several hours during which a second presentation does not constitute the onset of a conditioning trial for the animal; the initial presentation, while active, may reduce the salience, or functional impact, of subsequent exposures to that stimulus. Conditioning in such cases is predicted better from the interval between the initial presentation and illness than from that between the second exposure and toxicosis. As the initial presentation loses its active properties, however, the second presentation becomes progressively more functional as an associable event. Conditioning is then predicted better by the interval between the second presentation and illness.

313

The present results also have broader implications for the delay of reinforcement gradient in taste-aversion learning. If, as the above data suggest, the processes operating over relatively short delays are primarily short-term in nature, the delay gradient is probably not best characterized by concepts like learned safety which postulate the operation of relatively long-term, associative processes operating during the taste-toxin interval. The more traditional trace-decay model is compatible with the findings reported here as are several of the more recent information processing models (e.g., Wagner, Rudy, & Whitlow, 1973; see also Wagner, 1976; Terry, 1976; and Whitlow, 1975).

SUMMARY

The results of experiments described in this chapter indicate several things. First, learned safety as a concept accounting for the reduced associability resulting from nonaversive preexposure to a flavor is compatible with latent inhibition rather than conditioned inhibition. Hence, the concept is more accurately termed learned familiarity. Second, while the operations used to demonstrate learned safety do not meet the criteria typically required for the demonstration of associative processes, there is little doubt that the long-term changes in behavior resulting from these operations reflect a learning process of some type. Third, much of the delay of reinforcement gradient observed in taste-aversion learning is due to the operation of short-term processes. Consequently, the applicability of a concept like learned safety toward explaining the delay gradient is less obvious than previous work indicated. In light of this, the concept of learned safety is probably most appropriately applied as an explanation of the stimulus preexposure effect in learned taste aversions rather than of the delay of reinforcement gradient.

FOOTNOTES

Support for this project was provided by a Faculty Research Grant from Southern Methodist University and Public Health Service Grant MH 28141 to M. R. Best and an Encouragement of Scholarship Award by Baylor University to L. M. Barker.

[1]While recognizing its restricted applicability, the term *learned safety* will be retained in this manuscript for the sake of convenience and continuity.

[2]While obtaining a two-presentation learned safety effect using a .25 saccharin solution, Bond and DiGiusto (1975) noted that a significant enhancement of conditioning was obtained if intake on the second exposure was greater than that on the first—a finding not strictly compatible with learned safety.

[3]Significance levels are $p < .05$ as computed by the Mann-Whitney U test, two-tailed.

REFERENCES

Best, M. R. Conditioned and latent inhibition in taste-aversion learning: Clarifying the role of learned safety. **Journal of Experimental Psychology: Animal Behavior Processes,** 1975, **1,** 97-113.

Bolles, R. C., Riley, A. L., & Laskowski, B. A further demonstration of the learned safety effect in food-aversion learning. **Bulletin of the Psychonomic Society,** 1973, **1,** 190-192.

Bond, N., & DiGiusto, E. Amount of solution drunk is a factor in the establishment of taste aversion. **Animal Learning and Behavior,** 1975, **3,** 81-84.

Domjan, M. CS preexposure in taste-aversion learning: Effects of deprivation and preexposure duration. **Learning and Motivation,** 1972, **3,** 389-402.

Domjan, M. Determinants of the enhancement of flavored-water intake by prior exposure. **Journal of Experimental Psychology: Animal Behavior Processes,** 1976, **2,** 17-27.

Domjan, M., & Bowman, T. G. Learned safety and the CS-US delay gradient in taste-aversion learning. **Learning and Motivation,** 1974, **5,** 409-423.

Garcia, J., Ervin, F. R., & Koelling, R. A. Learning with prolonged delay of reinforcement. **Psychonomic Science,** 1966, **5,** 121-122.

Garcia, J., Kimeldorf, D. S., & Koelling, R. A. Conditioned aversion to saccharin resulting from exposure to gamma radiation. **Science,** 1955, **122,** 157-158.

Garcia, J., & Koelling, R. A. Relation of cue to consequence in avoidance learning. **Psychonomic Science,** 1966, **4,** 123-124.

Gemberling, G. A. Learned safety and the delay of reinforcement gradient in taste-aversion learning: Evidence for other processes. Unpublished manuscript, 1976. (Available from G. A. Gemberling, Department of Psychology, Southern Methodist University, Dallas, Texas, 75275).

Green, K. F., & Parker, L. A. Gustatory memory: Incubation and interference. **Behavioral Biology,** 1975, **13,** 359-367.

Halgren, C. R. Latent inhibition in rats: Associative or nonassociative? **Journal of Comparative and Physiological Psychology,** 1974, **86,** 74-78.

Hammond, L. J. Increased responding to CS- in differential CER. **Psychonomic Science,** 1966, **5,** 337-338.

Kalat, J. W., & Rozin, P. "Learned safety" as a mechanism in long-delay taste-aversion learning in rats. **Journal of Comparative and Physiological Psychology,** 1973, **83,** 198-207.

Lubow, R. E. Latent inhibition. **Psychological Bulletin,** 1973, **79,** 398-407.

Mackintosh, N. J. Stimulus selection: Learning to ignore stimuli that predict no change in reinforcement. In R. A. Hinde & J. Stevenson-Hinde (Eds.), **Constraints on learning: Limitations and predispositions.** New York: Academic Press, 1973.

McLaurin, W. A., Farley, J. A., & Scarborough, B. B. Inhibitory effect of preirradiation saccharin habituation on conditioned avoidance behavior. **Radiation Research,** 1963, **18,** 473-478.

Nachman, M., & Jones, D. R. Learned taste aversion over long delays in rats: The role of learned safety. **Journal of Comparative and Physiological Psychology,** 1974, **86,** 949-956.

Reiss, S., & Wagner, A. R. CS habituation produces a "latent inhibition effect" but no active "conditioned inhibition." **Learning and Motivation,** 1972, **3,** 237-245.

Rescorla, R. A. Summation and retardation tests of latent inhibition. **Journal of Comparative and Physiological Psychology,** 1971, **75,** 77-81.

Rescorla, R. A. Pavlovian conditioned inhibition. **Psychological Bulletin,** 1969, **72,** 72-94.

Rescorla, R. A. Pavlovian conditioning and its proper control procedures. **Psychological Review,** 1967, **74,** 71-80.

Rescorla, R. A., & LoLordo, V. M. Inhibition of avoidance behavior. **Journal of Comparative and Physiological Psychology,** 1965, **59,** 406-412.

Revusky, S. H., & Bedarf, E. W. Association of illness with prior ingestion of novel foods. **Science,** 1967, **155,** 219-220.

Siegel, S. Flavor preexposure and "learned safety." **Journal of Comparative and Physiological Psychology,** 1974, **87,** 1073-1082.

Taukulis, H. K., & Revusky, S. H. Odor as a conditioned inhibitor: Applicability of the Rescorla-Wagner model to feeding behavior. **Learning and Motivation,** 1975, **6,** 11-27.

Terry, W. S. Effects of priming unconditioned stimulus representation in short-term memory on Pavlovian conditioning. **Journal of Experimental Psychology: Animal Behavior Processes,** 1976, **2,** 354-369.

Wagner, A. R. Priming in STM: An information processing mechanism for self-generated depression of performance. In T. J. Tighe & R. N. Leaton (Eds.), **Habituation: Perspectives from child development, animal behavior, and neurophysiology.** Hinsdale, N.J.: Erlbaum, 1976.

Wagner, A. R., Rudy, J. W., & Whitlow, J. W. Rehearsal in animal conditioning. **Journal of Experimental Psychology,** 1973, **97,** 407-426.

Whitlow, J. W. Short-term memory and dishabituation. **Journal of Experimental Psychology: Animal Behavior Processes,** 1975, **1,** 189-206.

317

XIV

THE CONCURRENT INTERFERENCE APPROACH
TO DELAY LEARNING

SAM REVUSKY
Memorial University of Newfoundland

In a delay learning experiment, an animal is required to learn that two events separated by time occur in sequence. In the traditional animal learning literature, delay learning experiments have been divided into at least three categories as follows: (1) In delayed reward (or punishment) learning, the prior event is an animal's motor response and the later event is a reward (or punishment). (2) In delayed reaction learning, the prior event is a cue which supplies information about whether a later response will be rewarded. (3) In conditioning over an interstimulus interval, the prior event is a Pavlovian CS and the later event is usually a US.

Traditionally, there has been a tendency to treat these categories of delay learning as separate effects to be explained in different ways. The present chapter is based on the different supposition that the associative process underlying all instances of delay learning is similar. This makes it desirable to describe all these instances in terms of a single theoretical language. For this reason, the prior event is called E-pre in this chapter regardless of whether it is a response emitted by the animal or a cue or CS supplied by the experimenter. The later event is called E-post, also regardless of what it is.

Although the traditional approach was to explain different categories of delay learning in different ways, prior to the acceptance of long-delay food-aversion learning, all explanations had a common theme. This was, quite simply, that delay learning did not really exist; the underlying associative process was always supposed to involve events that overlap in time. Where this overlap

319

was not obvious, it was hypothesized as a theoretical construct. For instance, if an E-pre terminated before the onset of an E-post and the animal still learned, it often was hypothesized that sensory aftereffects of the E-pre lingered until E-post; hence, the real association involved not E-pre itself but an aftereffect of E-pre which was temporally contiguous with E-post. Alternatively, it was hypothesized that the real E-post was not the ostensible E-post; the real E-post was supposed to be a mediating event which was associated by contiguity with E-pre and also was associated by contiguity with the ostensible E-post. Still another theoretical device was to invoke behaviors occurring during the delay to supply indirect temporal contiguity between E-pre and E-post.

This type of theorizing was validated by many experiments in which all potential sources of indirect temporal contiguity between E-pre and E-post were removed. With such experiments, it was found that indeed animals could not associate over delays of greater than a minute or two if E-pre was a response (Perkins, 1947) or over a few seconds if E-pre was a visual cue (Grice, 1948). These instances of associations over short delays were easily explicable in terms of sensory aftereffects of the ostensible E-pre. In general, these experiments were conducted rigorously and they have since been confirmed in a variety of ways.

Thus, the theory that delay learning was impossible without indirect temporal contiguity seemed firmly established. When long-delay flavor-aversion learning was first reported in the psychological literature, those indoctrinated in traditional theories kept to their strategy of looking for an explanation in terms of indirect temporal contiguity. An extreme example is from a review of a paper I submitted to the *Psychological Review* in 1968: In reference to a finding that X-irradiation could follow consumption of sugar solution by seven hours and still produce an aversion to the sugar solution in a single trial (Revusky, 1968), the reviewer wrote: "However, before concluding that the principle of temporal contiguity between stimulus and consequence is violated, one should make sure that X-irradiation does not cause persistence of the stimulus, perhaps by altering cell permeability." Rather than admit the existence of delay learning, the reviewer preferred to hypothesize that time could run backward: that is, X-irradiation could produce persistence of a stimulus that had been administered hours earlier. Although mediation by time-warping (Garcia's term) was selected as an example here because it is funny, in fact, it is not an extreme example of the refusal to consider alternatives to contiguity theory.

It occurred to me that if psychologists were so irrational in dealing with irrefutable instances of long-delay food aversions, perhaps they had also been irrational in their interpretation of the results of traditional delay-learning experiments. With this possibility in mind, I reviewed the purported evidence that delay learning was impossible in traditional learning situations and found that it was really evidence that animals cannot solve insoluble problems. Psychologists had erroneously acted as if an E-pre and an E-post which had been designated as elements in a reference association by an experimenter were the only things the animal was experiencing. An animal removed from his home cage and placed in a novel and unnatural experimental apparatus is being subjected to a buzzing booming confusion of sense impressions if only as a result of its own exploratory behaviors. In this confusion, animals were required to associate between two apparently unrelated events separated by a delay. Consider for example, how a rat in a Skinner Box might be trained to depress a lever for delayed reward: When it happens to press the lever, the lever is removed and a few minutes later the rat is rewarded with food. The known failure of such a procedure to produce learning readily was attributed to the lack of temporal contiguity between the response and the reward. However, from the present viewpoint the main reason the rat does not learn is that it is bound to emit many behaviors during the delay. It is more reasonable for the rat to associate one of these intervening behaviors with the reward than the earlier lever depression. According to traditional analyses, devices that might give the rat a logical criterion by which to associate between the lever press and the reward, such as secondary reinforcements, were defined as artifacts in the experiments. While all of this seemed reasonable from the vantage points of traditional learning theories, in retrospect conventional delay procedures look like a deliberate attempt to make the animal seem stupid by confusing it.

As an imaginary analogy to these traditional delay-learning experiments, consider a prisoner taken every day to a chamber where he is subjected to a variety of Kafkaesque experiences at the rate of five or six experiences per minute; these include exposure to pictures, brief snatches of various tunes played over a loudspeaker, and so on. After 40 min of this confusion, the prisoner is fed. Every day the prisoner is subjected to the same sequence of experiences followed by feeding. Unknown to the prisoner, his salivation is being monitored by psychologists studying his ability to associate over a delay; they are interested in salivation to the picture of an automobile battery presented 20 min before the food as a test of the prisoner's capacity to associate over a 20 min delay. The psychologists had selected the picture of an automobile battery because they wanted a cue for the food reward which would not in any way be thematically related to the food; for instance, if the cue were the picture of a sandwich, there would be artificial aids to association over a delay to contaminate the experiment. Despite dozens of experimental sessions, the prisoner does not learn to salivate to the picture of the automobile battery. The psychologists are not surprised because many similar experiments had shown that prisoners cannot associate over delays far shorter than 20 min.

There were no statistical or routine methodological defects in these imaginary experiments with the Kafkaesque prisoner. Indeed, it is quite certain that the empirical conclusion was correct; if a prisoner (or anybody else) is subjected to 5 or 6 experiences per minute, he will not associate the appearance of the automobile battery with food over a delay greater than a minute or so. The question is whether such experiments really show that prisoners do not have the capacity to associate over delays greater than a minute or so. The prisoner would not be able to solve such a problem even if the delay were not a factor; if he were allowed access to the automobile battery and 100 other objects just prior to feeding, he would not associate the automobile battery with the food in preference to some other object. It seemed apparent to me that exactly the same analysis was applicable to the traditional experiments with delay learning in animals. If so, the traditional assumption that temporal contiguity was necessary for associative learning in animals was without a valid basis.

The concurrent interference approach to delay learning (Revusky, 1971) began in an attempt to develop these intuitive ideas into a useful theory. The traditional belief that association of an E-pre with a delayed E-post requires some sort of indirect temporal contiguity may be alternatively expressed as the assumption that animals cannot remember E-pres for purposes of association. The contrary assumption of concurrent interference theory is that animals can remember E-pres for periods far longer than the delays used in traditional experiments. If so, the failure of memory cannot be considered the main limiting factor in delay learning. Instead, the usual failure of delay learning to occur is attributed to what is called concurrent interference; this is mainly interference by events which occur during the delay, but will be described more exactly in the following section.

322

OUTLINE OF CONCURRENT INTERFERENCE THEORY

According to the concurrent interference approach, any learning situation is overloaded with events which the animal experiences. Some of these events are under the control of the experimenter, and others, such as extraneous sights and sounds in the laboratory and the animal's own behaviors, are relatively uncontrolled. It is the nature of an animal to associate pairs of events, just as it is its nature to breathe. Thus, any situation is almost certain to result in associative learning, but this learning may be very different from the learning upon which the experimenter focusses. The experimenter chooses two events from the learning situation as reference events and determines through observation of behavior if the animal has associated them. However, if either or both events in the reference association become associated with extraneous events, there is interference with the development of the reference association. Hence, such associations are called interfering associations. Thus, the problem of the concurrent interference theorist is not the traditional problem of whether the animal will learn or not, but whether it will learn the reference association or interfering associations.

Although it is central to the concurrent interference analysis, the distinction between the reference association and interfering associations is arbitrary. For example, if both a tone and a light precede shock, the tone-shock association may be designated as the reference association while the light-shock association is designated as an interfering association or vice versa. In much of the experimental work to validate concurrent interference theory, an interfering event is deliberately brought into the situation in order to determine what effect the resultant interfering association will have on the strength of the reference association. The presumed effects of unknown interfering associations are inferred from the effects of this controlled interfering association. In other experimental work, devices which are presumed to change the opportunity for interference are introduced in order to determine their effects on delay learning.

To implement this approach, a vocabulary which distinguishes between reference events and interfering events is necessary. "E-pre-ref" and "E-post-ref" designate events in the reference association. An "E-pre-X" is an interfering event which tends to usurp the role of E-pre-ref; it produces interference with learning of the reference association by becoming associated with E-post-ref. Thus, an E-pre-X must precede E-post-ref. Logically, E-pre-X may also precede E-pre-ref, but because the main theoretical concern is with the detrimental effects of events which occur during a delay on the reference association, E-pre-Xs relevant to the interference analysis of delay learning tend to occur between E-pre-ref and E-post-ref. Similarly, an E-post-X can be any event which follows E-pre-ref so that it can usurp the role of E-post-ref.

Using this terminology, the concurrent interference principle can be stated explicitly as follows. *The strength of a reference association is an inverse function of the number and strength of two types of interfering associations:* (1) *between E-pre-Xs and E-post-ref; and* (2) *between E-pre-ref and E-post-Xs.* Since the distinction between a reference association and interfering associations is arbitrary, a reference association must affect interfering associations in the same way interfering associations affect the reference association. Thus, a strong reference association can protect itself by weakening interfering associations. In other words, interference and association are concomitant aspects of the same associative process.

ASSOCIATIVE NATURE OF THEORY

The concurrent interference principle describes interrelationships among learned associations; it does not describe behavior. Of course, the strength of learned associations must be inferred from behavior, but this is to be regarded as an unfortunate practical necessity. Although by contemporary definitions this makes concurrent interference theory a cognitive approach, the only cognitive process postulated is association. The freewheeling postulation of cognitive structures and processes usually characteristic of cognitive theories is avoided and, for this reason, I prefer to call the theory associationistic rather than cognitive.

Regardless of how the concurrent interference principle is to be characterized, it is such an abstract analysis of the associative process that it does not specify anything about the natures of the events which are to be associated. Even the distinction between E-pre and E-post does not specify anything about the events themselves other than their temporal relationships; E-pre is that event of a pair which happens to occur first. In practice, E-pre-ref will usually be a cue or a response and E-post-ref will be an event of great biological importance to the animal, but this is only a practical device to permit the learning to be measured. E-post-ref can occasionally be an ordinary cue, as in the sensory preconditioning procedure; E-pre-ref can occasionally be a reward, as in cases where the animal learns to use the type of reward as a cue. In fact,

324

the same event can be either an E-pre or an E-post depending on the association of interest to the experimenter. For instance, if a rat presses a lever for saccharin solution and then is made sick, saccharin solution is an E-post relative to its association with lever-pressing and an E-pre relative to its association with sickness.

As indicated at the beginning of this chapter, this abstract approach ignores the distinction between types of associative learning which traditionally have been considered very different, such as classical conditioning and instrumental learning. A thorough defense of this abstract approach to learning theory has been presented elsewhere (Revusky, in press). Here it is only necessary to defend such an approach as it applies to the analysis of concurrent interference. The approach would be justified if the traditional distinctions between different types of learning were irrelevant to the analysis of concurrent interference. This would be true if, for instance, classically conditioned associations and instrumental associations interfered with each other. Unfortunately, there is little direct evidence to bear on this question, but one recent study, described below, suggests that they do interfere with each other.

St. Claire-Smith (1970; described by Mackintosh, 1974, pp. 220-221) first trained rats to press a lever for food so that there would be a baseline level of lever pressing. Then, the rats were intermittently punished for lever pressing with shock. For an experimental group, a light or noise CS was paired with each shock in additon to the lever press; this CS was absent for a control group. The reduction in lever pressing produced by shock was less marked for the experimental group than for the control group. This may be regarded as a demonstration that a classical association between a CS and shock can interfere with an instrumental association between a lever press and shock. More specifically, in terms of the present vocabulary, both groups were subjected to a reference association between a lever press E-pre-ref and a shock E-post-ref. In traditional language, this reference association involves instrumental learning. The experimental group was also subjected to an extraneous E-pre-X, the CS, whose association with E-post-ref was an interfering association. In traditional language, this interfering association involved classical conditioning. The fact that the classically conditioned interfering association actually did interfere with the instrumentally learned reference association shows that concurrent interference can cut across traditional experimental paradigms.

St. Claire-Smith also had a third group which was treated like the experimental group except that the interfering association was

325

strengthened before it was used to interfere with the reference association. This was accomplished by pairing the CS with shock prior to using it as an E-pre-X to interfere with the punishment of lever pressing. For this third group, interference with the punishment of lever pressing was even more marked than in the experimental group. Thus, the amount of interference produced by the classical association was increased when its strength was increased. This finding is also in agreement with the concurrent interference principle.

Although St. Claire-Smith's findings are from only a single experiment which cannot be considered definitive by itself, they suggest strongly that the distinction between classical conditioning and instrumental learning is irrelevant to concurrent interference. If so, it would be gratuitous to incorporate this distinction into a vocabulary to be used to analyze concurrent interference.

DETERMINANTS OF ASSOCIATIVE STRENGTH ARE NOT SPECIFIED

The concurrent interference principle specifies that the strength of one association is reduced as a function of the strength of interfering associations, but it does not specify the factors which underlie the strength of association. To specify these factors, it is necessary to make use of facts about learning which are not subsumed by the concurrent interference principle itself. For instance, suppose E-pre-ref is a light and E-pre-X is a tone, while E-post-ref is a shock. The concurrent interference principle indicates that the stronger the tone-shock association, the more it will interfere with the light-shock association, but it does not indicate which factors strengthen or weaken the tone-shock association. It is known, however, that if the tone is made louder, the tone-shock association will be strengthened; given this knowledge, the concurrent interference principle predicts increased interference with the light-shock association. Similarly, if the tone is paired with shock prior to introduction of the light, the tone-shock interfering association will also be strengthened; given this knowledge, the concurrent interference principle predicts increased interference with the light-shock association.

The determinants of associative strength other than interference are not specified in a deliberate attempt to further an abstract analysis of interference. This is similar to the analysis of force in mechanics, which considers only its magnitude and direction, not how it is produced. In theory, the amount of concurrent interference depends only on the strength of the interfering association, not on the way in which the interfering association is strengthened or weakened. Presumably, if the strength of an interfering association is changed by the same amount by two different methods, each method will produce the same change in interference. I hasten to add that although cruder implications of the concurrent interference principle are testable, this very precise statement of it is not now testable. Experimental methods are too crude, our knowledge of possible extraneous factors is too meager, and the way in which associative strength is to be measured has not been made exact enough. I offer the precise statement only for heuristic purposes.

DIFFERENCE FROM TRADITIONAL INTERFERENCE THEORIES

The difference between the present interference approach and traditional interference approaches to forgetting is both in the subject matter and in the source of the interference. The subject matter of the present theory is the effects on learning of a delay between elements of an association; this leads to a concern with interference produced by events which occur during the delay—concurrent interference. The subject matter of traditional interference theories of forgetting is the effect of a delay between training and testing on the retention of a learned association; thus, the main concern is with interfering associations that are learned during the delay between training and testing, a process called retroactive interference. Later in the development of interference theories of forgetting, there was also a concern with interfering associations acquired prior to training, a process called proactive interference.

There are many differences between the types of interference traditionally studied and concurrent interference. In the case of proactive and retroactive interference, an interfering event is directly paired with one reference event while the other reference event is absent. In contrast, concurrent interference develops while both E-pre-ref and E-post-ref are available for the association. In most proactive and retroactive interference experiments involving animals, the interfering association is between E-pre-ref and E-post-X; in most concurrent interference experiments with animals, the interfering association is between E-pre-X and E-post-ref, for reasons to be explained below. Although associations between E-pre-X and E-post-ref produce powerful concurrent interference, it is my strong impression that they produce little or no proactive and retroactive interference in the absence of concurrent interference. As a result of all these differences, there is little practical similarity between concurrent interference theory and traditional interference theories of forgetting.

However, there is one way in which a procedure resembling proactive interference can enter into the present analysis of the effects of concurrent interference. An interfering association can be strengthened (or weakened) proactively, before the concurrent interference phase begins. There was an example of this earlier in this chapter, i.e., St. Claire-Smith's experiment in which an interfering association of a tone E-pre-X with a shock E-post-ref was strengthened prior to the concurrent interference phase. In this case, proactive interference was a determinant of the strength of an interfering association. It is emphasized, however, that proactive interference, like all determinants of the strength of association other than concurrent interference itself, is outside of the scope of the concurrent interference principle. It is a factor to be used occasionally in the application of the theory but is not itself part of the theory. As for retroactive interference, it is irrelevant to the study of the effects of a delay on learning because it does not occur until after the learning is completed.

Finally, it is only fair to indicate that the concurrent interference approach to delay learning has a family resemblance to various competing response theories of the 1950's (Estes, 1958; Spence, 1956; Weinstock, 1958). These explained decrements in the rate of a measured reference response in terms of the usurpation of the role of the reference response by a competing response. This parallels the way in which an interfering event in concurrent interference theory usurps the role of a reference event. But although competing response theories may have influenced me personally, they differ substantially from concurrent interference theory in its present form.

CONCURRENT INTERFERENCE PRODUCES SELECTIVE ASSOCIATION

Concurrent interference weakens weak associations more than it weakens strong associations. As a demonstration of this, consider an imaginary situation in which there are only two associations which interfere with each other; one is strong and the other is weak. The amount of interference to which each association is subjected is an increasing function of the strength of the other association. Hence the weak association is subjected to more interference than the strong association.

Since learning is an adaptive biological process, the strength of an association is, on the average, directly related to its usefulness to the animal. The net effect of concurrent interference is to weaken further those weak associations which probably are not very useful. In effect, this process selects out the more useful associations. Elsewhere (Revusky, in press), it has been argued that the concurrent interference process results in animals essentially comparing all potential causes of an effect to determine which is most likely to be the true cause. Concurrent interference should not be considered a defect in the animal, but as an adaptive mechanism to prevent it from becoming overwhelmed by too much information.

TYPES OF CONCURRENT INTERFERENCE AND THE DELAY GRADIENT

The distinction between interference produced by associations of E-pre-Xs with E-post-ref and the interference produced by associations of E-pre-ref with E-post-Xs is not simply an exercise in pedantry. These two types of interference differ in the evidence available for them and in the ways in which they may produce a delay gradient, as will be explained below.

Experimental Evidence. It is a fact that E-pre-Xs produce interference when they become associated with E-post-ref. As far as I know, no experimental attempt to demonstrate such interference has failed, provided the interfering associations were made reasonably strong relative to the reference association. One such experiment by St. Claire-Smith has been described earlier in this chapter and a few others will be described later. Revusky (1971) and Rescorla and Wagner (1972) review many other such experiments.

Although interference produced by associations of E-pre-ref with E-post-Xs is intuitively compelling, it has not been demonstrated in a rigorous way. The difficulty is methodological. Suppose a tone E-pref-ref is followed by a food E-post-X and then by a shock E-post-ref. It is quite certain that any fear reaction to E-pre-ref will be less marked than in a control case in which the food E-post-X is omitted (Fowler, 1976). However, although interference by a food E-post-X with a fear reaction is in agreement with the hypothesis of concurrent interference produced by E-post-Xs, it does not prove it. The same effect also is explicable in terms of a competition between the fear reaction and the anticipatory reaction to food. It is very difficult, but probably not impossible, to find a test for interference by E-post-Xs which avoids this problem.

It is possible to have a concurrent interference analysis of delay learning which relies only on interference by E-pre-Xs, but it would be conceptually less elegant than one which includes interference by E-post-Xs. I have chosen to mention interference by E-post-Xs here because, as far as I know, there is no evidence against it and there is ample precedent to include unproven assumptions in learning theories. However, there will be more emphasis on interference by E-pre-Xs than on interference by E-post-Xs.

Explanations of the Delay Gradient. Below, a number of approaches to the explanation of the delay gradient in terms of concurrent interference theory will be discussed. We begin with an explanation of the delay gradient in terms of associations of E-pre-ref with E-post-Xs because it is conceptually straightforward. Consider a long-delay reference association and suppose E-pre-ref has just occurred. As time elapses, more and more E-post-Xs occur and insofar as these become associated with E-pre-ref, E-pre-ref becomes unavailable for association with a still later E-post-ref. It is noteworthy that this account of the delay gradient has the same end result as the model of long-delay taste-aversion learning suggested by Kalat and Rozin (see Kalat, this volume). They suggest that as time elapses, E-pre-ref increasingly becomes classified as "safe" and hence becomes less available for association with E-post-ref. Here it is suggested that a similar unavailability of E-pre-ref for association develops over the delay due to interfering associations with E-post-Xs.

The explanation of the delay gradient in terms of interference by E-pre-Xs is far more cumbersome because it involves some sort of "mental reflection" at the time E-post-ref occurs. That is, because nothing can become associated with E-post-ref until E-post-ref actually occurs, the competition between E-pre-Xs and E-pre-ref for association must begin then. There are two ways in which it is possible to visualize what happens when E-post-ref occurs.

The first way is to suppose that the animal scans backward in time in strict reverse chronological order when E-post-ref occurs. Metaphorically speaking, the animal has a motion picture camera in its head and runs the film backward. If the delay between E-pre-ref and E-post-ref is long, the animal is likely to have scanned a number of E-pre-Xs before it gets to E-pre-ref, and, as a result, there are already a number of interfering associations. However, if the delay between E-pre-ref and E-post-ref is short, there are few interfering associations by the time the animal gets to E-pre-ref, and thus the reference association is not weakened as markedly.

The assumption that animals scan backward in time in strict reverse chronological sequence is too reminiscent of mediation by time warping and overimaginative cognitive theories to appeal to me. It is mentioned here only for logical completeness. It is more reasonable to suppose that when E-post-ref occurs, all potential E-pres simultaneously compete to become associated with it. Unfortunately, such a process by itself does not account for a delay gradient because it does not explain why more recent E-pres tend to become more strongly associated than earlier E-pres. One way around this problem is to abandon the goal of explaining delay effects *only* in terms of concurrent interference. This does not imply a retreat to the traditional temporal contiguity theory because long-delay flavor aversions and other long-delay learning effects to be described later in this chapter disprove this theory. However, it is not unreasonable to suppose that even though delays of several hours do not prevent associative learning, they may weaken it even in the absence of concurrent interference. If so, the net effect of concurrent interference when E-pres compete to become associated with E-post-ref will be to weaken weak associations more than relatively strong associations and thus sharpen the delay gradient by the principle described earlier. The same principle also should sharpen any possible gradient resulting from interference by E-post-Xs.

In summary, there are a number of ways concurrent interference can be largely responsible for the delay gradient. The possibility I consider most reasonable is that both interference by E-pre-Xs and interference by E-post-Xs interact to produce the gradient. Probably, there is also a detrimental effect of a delay itself on learning which is not due to interference, but this alone is not able to prevent learning unless it is amplified by the concurrent interference process. Admittedly, it would be desirable to be more specific, but this does not seem possible at present. However, there will be ample evidence in the remainder of this chapter that some type of concurrent interference has an important role in the delay gradient and that the traditional temporal contiguity theory is untenable.

RELEVANCE PRINCIPLES

So far, it has been shown that concurrent interference can account for the usual failure of long-delay learning to occur. In this respect its implication is the same as that of traditional theories. However, in contrast to traditional theories, concurrent interference theory also implies that long-delay learning ought to develop if the strength of the reference association is great enough to overcome the effects of interference.

331

There are four classes of operations which conceivably can strengthen a long-delay reference association relative to interfering associations and hence facilitate delay learning of the reference association: (1) Direct strengthening of the reference association between E-pre-ref and E-post-ref. (2) Weakening of interfering associations between E-pre-Xs and E-post-ref. (3) Weakening of interfering associations between E-pre-ref and E-post-Xs. (4) Strengthening of associations between E-pre-Xs and E-post-Xs; the stronger these are, the less available E-pre-Xs and E-post-Xs are to become associated with events in the reference association.

This identification of four factors which can contribute to long-delay learning leaves a great deal unspecified. It does not specify how the strengthening or weakening of different types of associations is to be accomplished. Nor does it specify the relative importance of these four factors. It is conceivable that there might be instances of long-delay learning attributable entirely to strengthening of the reference association; weakening of interfering associations might have no role. It will be shown below that long-delay associations in runways and T-mazes depend only upon weakening of interfering associations and not upon direct strengthening of the reference association. Thus, the concurrent interference analysis is actually a general statement of a variety of ways in which long-delay learning might occur through selective association. Regardless of this, we define those selective association principles which produce the conditions for long-delay learning as relevance principles; these can operate either by strengthening the reference association, weakening interfering associations, or both. The role of relevance principles in the present explanations of long-delay learning is just as central as the role of interference. Indeed, in a sense, relevance principles may be said to have the main explanatory role and concurrent interference is a means of describing how relevance principles operate to produce the learning. The present theory is called a concurrent interference theory rather than a relevance theory because it is the only theory of delay learning which emphasizes interference, but not the only theory which emphasizes relevance.

The most famous relevance principle is stimulus relevance, the relevance principle responsible for long-delay food-aversion learning. The paradigm demonstration of stimulus relevance was by Garcia and Koelling (1966). They showed that if saccharin solution was consumed in the presence of audiovisual stimulation, only the saccharin E-pre would become associated if E-post was toxicosis, and only the audiovisual E-pre would become associated if E-post

332

was electrical shock. Later, Garcia, McGowan, Ervin, and Koelling (1968) showed that motor responses emitted by the animal have the same associative properties as audiovisual stimuli. It may be extrapolated from these results that events related to the feeding system tend to be selectively associated with each other, and that events related to the external world also tend to be selectively associated with each other (Garcia, McGowan, & Green, 1972).

Revusky (1971) explained long-delay flavor aversions by combining the stimulus relevance principle with the assumption that events related to the feeding system occur far less frequently than events related to the external world. Thus, he conjectured that stimulus relevance tends to enhance long-delay food aversions in each of the four ways suggested by the concurrent interference principle: (1) It strengthens the reference association between feeding stimuli and toxicosis; (2) it weakens interfering associations between feeding stimuli and E-post-Xs not related to the feeding system (these presumably constitute all but a few of the potential E-post-Xs); (3) it weakens interfering associations between E-pre-Xs not related to the feeding system and toxicosis (all but a small proportion of potential E-pre-Xs are presumed to be unrelated to the feeding system); and (4) it strengthens associations between E-pre-Xs and E-post-Xs not related to the feeding system (presumably this means that the greater proportion of potential interfering events which occur during the delay will not be available to interfere with the reference association because they will be part of other associations).

FOOD-AVERSION EXPERIMENTS

The analysis of long-delay learning in terms of four factors may seem more complex than necessary. The most parsimonious strategy is to try to explain long-delay learning of food aversions in terms only of the strengthening of the associability of feeding stimuli and toxicosis. If so, feeding stimuli and toxicosis are associated over long delays only because of the unusual relationship between them, and considerations of interference are redundant and hence unnecessary. However, such extreme parsimony is not usually applicable to the analysis of biological processes such as learning. Furthermore, there is evidence that interference with learned food aversions can occur and hence that considerations of interference are not irrelevant to the explanation of long-delay food aversions.

333

This role of interference in flavor-aversion learning was demonstrated by Revusky (1971) through experiments in which rats drank a second flavored solution (E-pre-X) either before or after the E-pre-ref solution and prior to the E-post-ref toxicosis. For instance, instead of drinking only a saccharin E-pre-ref solution prior to toxicosis, the rats might drink the saccharin solution and then drink a vinegar E-pre-X solution prior to toxicosis. The hypothesis was that the stronger the association of the E-pre-X solution, the weaker would be the association of the E-pre-ref solution with toxicosis. Three lines of evidence confirmed this hypothesis:

(1) It is known that an increase in the concentration of flavoring results in a stronger association of the flavored solution with toxicosis (Dragoin, 1971; Garcia, 1971). Revusky (1971) found that if the concentration of the flavoring in an E-pre-X solution was increased there was a decreased aversion to the E-pre-ref solution. This effect occurred regardless of whether the E-pre-X solution was consumed prior to the E-pre-ref solution or after it and corresponds to the traditional overshadowing effect (Pavlov, 1927).

(2) It is known that an increase in the familiarity of a flavored solution reduces the strength of its association with later toxicosis (Revusky & Bedarf, 1967). Revusky, Lavin, and Pschirrer (reported by Revusky, 1971) found that a familiar E-pre-X solution produced less interference with an aversion to an E-pre-ref solution than a novel E-pre-X solution. Similar effects have been obtained in other, more traditional, learning situations (Carr, 1974; Lubow, 1973).

(3) If the E-pre-X solution had already been associated with the E-post-ref toxicosis prior to the experiment, it tended to block association of the E-pre-ref solution with the toxicosis. For instance, if consumption of vinegar had repeatedly been paired with toxicosis and then both saccharin solution and vinegar solution were consumed prior to toxicosis, the resultant aversion to saccharin was relatively weak. This corresponds to the blocking effect in traditional learning experiments (Kamin, 1969).

These three lines of evidence showed that when E-pre-Xs strongly associable with toxicosis were added to the food-aversion learning situation, learning of the reference association was weakened as an increasing function of the strength of the interfering association. Since experimental introduction of concurrent interference weakened the aversion to the E-pre-ref solution, Revusky (1971) conjectured that interfering events which normally occur during a delay might similarly weaken a long-delay reference association.

Revusky (1971) interpreted his demonstration that interference would weaken long-delay food-aversion learning as evidence that the usual delay gradient could be accounted for in terms of interference. In traditional learning experiments, the events in the reference association were readily associable with most uncontrolled events, and so the delay gradient was short. In flavor-aversion experiments, there were relatively few events which could become associated with events of the reference association, and so the delay gradient was long. This analysis implicitly denied that any other difference between feeding stimuli and other types of E-pre-refs might be responsible for long-delay food aversions.

OBJECTIONS BY KALAT AND ROZIN

Kalat and Rozin (1971) strongly disagreed with Revusky's interpretation of the fact that introduction of an E-pre-X solution would weaken a reference flavor aversion, although they confirmed his results. They illustrated their objection with an experiment in which rats consumed three E-pre-X solutions between consumption of an E-pre-ref solution and toxicosis. When tested, the subjects exhibited a weakened aversion to the E-pre-ref solution. Kalat and Rozin felt that the occurrence of an aversion to an E-pre-ref in spite of three intervening E-pre-X flavors showed that concurrent interference was not a sufficiently powerful factor to account for the usual delay gradient in flavor-aversion learning. The basis of their argument was a claim that a normal delay of many hours in which animals were left alone without food or water could not include interfering events equivalent in associative strength to the consumption of three E-pre-X solutions. Their conclusion was that while interference might well be a factor in some delay gradients, it could not account for the flavor-aversion delay gradient when no interference was artificially added to the situation.

Kalat and Rozin would be correct if the only important sources of interference in the feeding situation were taste and olfactory experiences. However, I consider it likely that physiological changes in the animal are another major source of interference. Recently, Revusky, Taukulis, and Peddle (in press) and Revusky, Parker, Coombes, and Coombes (unpublished) have shown that physiological changes produced by small doses of pentobarbital, alcohol, chlordiazepoxide, or amphetamine can become associated with toxicosis produced by large doses of lithium or amphetamine. It is conceivable that normal physiological changes which are bound to occur during a long delay after ingestion might also become associated with toxicosis and produce interference. It is also conceivable that such physiological changes might also become associated with the E-pre-ref flavor and thus produce in-

335

terference in their roles as E-post-Xs. Although the invocation of physiological events which produce interference to answer Kalat and Rozin's objections may seem like an *ex-post-facto* alibi, it really is not. Revusky and Garcia (1970) discussed the possible role of physiological stimuli in the regulation of caloric intake before Kalat and Rozin (1971) objected to Revusky's (1971) interpretations.

Although Kalat and Rozin (1971) have not disproven the hypothesis that interference is the only factor in the delay gradient, I do not seriously maintain that the burden of proof should be upon them. After all, it is very seldom that an effect in biology or psychology as complex as the delay gradient is explicable in terms of a single underlying process. What I do seriously maintain (for the time being) is that factors other than interference have a relatively minor role in the delay gradient. In the next section I will briefly compare concurrent interference theory with the "learned safety" theory preferred by Kalat and Rozin (1973).

LEARNED SAFETY THEORY

As Kalat indicates (Kalat, this volume), "learned safety" is not an ideal term by which to describe the theory which he and Rozin have proposed to explain the delay gradient; the term "information processing" will be used here to describe its actual operation. Their main assumption is that after an E-pre occurs, there is a time during which the animal processes information about it. As this processing continues without the occurrence of a significant E-post, the event becomes classified as unrelated to important E-posts and thus increasingly becomes unavailable for association with a later E-post. The theory is called "learned safety" theory as a result of its origin as an explanation of long-delay food aversions; in such situations, it is heuristic to say that the animal learns that the flavor is safe. However, if the term "information processing" is substituted for learned safety, the theory becomes applicable to the association of a flavor E-pre with beneficial aftereffects, such as repletion of nutrient deficiencies (see Zahorik, this volume). Kalat and Rozin suppose that information processing occurs over a much longer period of time for feeding stimuli than for other E-pres; hence, it takes more time for a feeding E-pre to become classified as irrelevant to later E-posts, and, as a result, the delay gradient is longer for feeding E-pres than for other E-pres.

The hypothesis that information processing is related to the delay gradient has become increasingly attractive since it was first proposed by Kalat and Rozin. There is the evidence from flavor-aversion experiments summarized by Kalat in this volume. There is also recent independent evidence that new experiences lead to information processing (Green & Parker, 1975; Wagner, Whitlow, & Rudy, 1973). At the present time, it would be foolhardy to flatly deny that the processing of information about E-pre can be a factor in the delay gradient. Nevertheless, the role of information processing has not been proven. It was pointed out earlier in this chapter that any loss over time of the capacity of E-pre to become associated can also be accounted for in terms of associations of E-pre with E-post-Xs which occur prior to E-post-ref. It is not easy to decide on experimental grounds between this possibility and information processing. The best guess is that both of these processes are involved, as well as some others.

The net result is that the present position regarding learned safety theory is an exact counterpart of Kalat and Rozin's position regarding concurrent interference theory. I do not deny that information processing can be a factor in the delay gradient but do deny that it is the main factor, just as Kalat and Rozin (1971) have not denied that concurrent interference can be a factor in the delay gradient but do deny that it is the main factor. Furthermore, the experimental strategy to be used here to buttress the present position parallels the strategy used by Kalat and Rozin to buttress their position against concurrent interference theory. As explained in the preceding section, they supplied evidence (disputed by me) that a delay gradient can occur in the absence of concurrent interference. In the following section, I will describe evidence that long-delay learning can occur under conditions not predictable from learned safety theory. Long-delay learning involving conventional E-pre-refs predictable from concurrent interference theory will be shown to occur in runways and T-mazes. According to Kalat and Rozin, long-delay learning is a result of the slow processing of information about E-pre-refs in the feeding system and hence ought not to occur with other types of E-pre-refs.

RUNWAY AND T-MAZE EXPERIMENTS

For an overview of the reasoning which led to the extension of concurrent interference theory to runway and T-maze learning, it is useful to consider the correspondence of the present emphasis on selective association in learning to the emphasis on selective association in gestalt psychology. According to the gestalt analysis of perception, visual events separated in space can become selectively associated through various innate principles of organization. The

337

present position is similar in that events separated in time can become associated through various principles of selective association. Indeed, early on, the gestalt psychologists did apply their methods of analysis to learning, and one result was the early delayed reaction experimentation by Tinklepaugh (1932). But, somehow, gestalt psychology became more influential in perception than in learning.

Of course, the present analysis of delay learning is hardly traditional gestalt psychology, but this may really be due to the intellectual background of its author rather than due to a difference in the basic scientific strategy. Whenever there is a long-delay learning effect not easily explicable in terms of indirect temporal contiguity, the present approach is to look for an explanation in terms of innate principles of selective association. As in gestalt psychology, it is conceivable that there are a variety of such selective association principles. After a selective association principle is detected, its detailed operation can be studied in terms of interference.

Our runway and T-maze experiments were stimulated by the observation that two effects obtained in runway and T-maze learning situations might conceivably be instances of long-delay discrimination learning:

(1) Alternate reward in a runway. Tyler, Wortz and Bitterman (1953) rewarded rats in a runway on odd trials, but not on even trials. The rats gradually began to run more slowly on even trials than on odd trials, suggesting that during any trial, they could use the reward outcome of the preceding trial as a discriminative cue for whether reward would be obtained. A reward on the preceding trial indicated that reward would not be obtained on the present trial, and a failure to receive reward on the preceding trial indicated that reward would be obtained. Capaldi (1967, 1971) has replicated this basic effect in a large number of ways, and it is very robust when the intertrial interval is many minutes long.

(2) Response alternation in a T-maze. Petrinovich and Bolles (1957) rewarded rats in a T-maze only if the rats ran in the direction opposite to that of the preceding run. The rats performed this discrimination with delays of up to several hours. Thus, the rats seemed to have learned that if the previous run had been to the left, only a run to the right would be rewarded, and vice versa. This suggested that the rats used their own behavior as discriminative cues. Petrinovich, Bradford, and McGaugh (1965) found this effect robust enough to use in the study of drugs which affect memory.

The obvious traditional explanation of these effects is that they are not ordinary instances of discrimination learning despite their apparent adherence to the discrimination learning paradigm. For instance, the reward and response cues used in these two situations might be far more salient than the cues used in traditional experiments. However, the contrary possibility preferred here is that long-delay learning occurred in both of these situations because the events to be associated were separated by an intertrial interval rather than the type of delay interval used in traditional experiments. In traditional experiments, the animal remains in the learning situation during the delay; during an intertrial interval, however, the animal is absent from the learning situation. The difference between these two types of intervals is where potentially interfering events of the delay occur. In traditional delay experiments, the potentially interfering events occur in the experimental apparatus, while in intertrial association experiments, they occur in a holding chamber or in the home cage. Thus, it seemed possible that the place in which an event occurs might provide the criterion for selective association to permit long-delay learning. If so, selective association might be responsible for long-delay intertrial associations rather than the supposed high salience of response or reward cues.

The hypothesis that a principle of selective association might be responsible for long-delay intertrial associations was translated into language similar to that used earlier to analyze long-delay food aversions. It will be recalled that stimulus relevance was presumed to permit long-delay food aversions by favoring selective association between pairs of events related to feeding. An analogous principle, called situational relevance, in which events are classified according to the environmental situation in which they occur, is hypothesized to be responsible for long-delay intertrial associations. Presumably, animals are far more likely to associate two events that occur in the same situation than two events that occur in different situations. Hence, pairs of events which occur in the same apparatus can become associated with each other even if they are separated by a delay during which the animal experiences a variety of events outside of the experimental apparatus.

Earlier, a distinction was made between the direct strengthening of an association between E-pre-ref and E-post-ref by a selective association principle and three ways in which interfering associations might be weakened. These three ways to weaken interfering associations were (1) weakening of associations between E-pre-ref and E-post-Xs, (2) weakening of associations between E-pre-Xs and E-post-ref, and (3) strengthening of associations between E-pre-Xs and E-post-Xs. Suggestive evidence was offered that weakening of interfering associations was involved in long-delay food-aversion learning, but it still remained possible to explain long-delay food-aversion learning only in terms of the direct strengthening of the food-sickness reference association by stimulus relevance. However, if the situational relevance analysis is correct, reduction of interference with the reference association must have the major role in long-delay intertrial associations. The reason is that both in intertrial associations and in traditional delay experiments, E-pre-ref and E-post-ref occur in the same experimental apparatus; thus, the direct strengthening of the reference association by situational relevance is bound to be similar. Hence, if long-delay intertrial discriminations are to be explained in terms of concurrent interference theory, it is because situational relevance weakens potential interfering associations produced by events which occur during the delay. If so, this adds to the suggestive evidence that similar weakening of interference by stimulus relevance might have an important role in long-delay food aversions.

EXTENSION TO THE ALTERNATE REWARD EXPERIMENT

The experiments to be described in this section were designed to exclude alternatives to the theory that the absence of the animal from the apparatus during the intertrial interval is responsible for long-delay intertrial associations. For the alternate reward situation, the most obvious possibility from traditional points of view was that it was not discrimination learning at all. Rats simply might innately tend to run faster after nonrewarded trials than after rewarded trials because of the long-lasting emotional aftereffects of frustrative nonreward (Amsel, 1967) or of reward. However, Bloom and Capaldi (1961) quickly disposed of this possibility when they showed that the effect disappeared when the pattern of nonreward was changed so that reward or nonreward was not a valid cue for the outcome of the following trial. They used a repeating sequence of four trials in which the first two were rewarded and the second two were not rewarded (RRNN) so that half the rewarded trials signalled nonrewarded trials and the other half signalled rewarded trials; in this experiment, the rats ran at the same speed after both rewarded and nonrewarded trials. However, this result did not exclude the related possibility that the emotional aftereffects of reward or nonreward might make reward and nonreward more salient cues, so that such cues might be remembered for a longer period than conventional cues.

Triple Discrimination Experiments. Pschirrer (1972) showed that the difference between emotional reactions produced by a re-

340

ward and a presumably frustrating nonreward could not be entirely responsible for the ability of rats to use them as cues when they were obtained on alternate trials in a runway. He found that a similar discrimination could be learned when two different types of food rewards were differential discriminative stimuli for intertrial associations. Pschirrer's procedure was a modification of the alternate reward procedure to a repeating cycle of three runway trials in which the first trial is rewarded with milk, the second trial is rewarded with chow pellets, and the third trial is unrewarded. In this milk→pellets→nonreward cycle, the cue functions of chow pellets and nonreward in the cycle are identical to the respective functions of reward and nonreward in the alternate reward cycle, i.e., pellets indicate that reward will not be obtained on the following trial, while nonreward indicates that reward (milk) will be obtained on the following trial. The innovation in Pschirrer's procedure is in the cue function of the milk reward: it indicates that reward (pellets) will be obtained on the following trial. Thus, the cue function of the milk reward is opposite to that of the pellet reward, which indicates that no reward will be obtained on the following trial. (Of course, Pschirrer interchanged the sequence of milk and pellets for half the rats.)

With an interval of 15 min, Pschirrer's rats learned to run equally quickly on each of the rewarded trials and more slowly on the unrewarded trials. Thus, they successfully learned, for instance, that the milk reward was followed by another reward on the next trial and that the pellet reward was followed by nonreward. If the emotional aftereffect of reward was an important factor in the discrimination, there would have been generalization of the milk cue with the pellet cue. As an example, consider the sequence milk→ pellets→nonreward, in which milk and nonreward each were positive cues (S+) that reward would be obtained on the following trial and the pellets were a negative cue (S-) that reward would not be obtained on the following trial. Had there been generalization between milk and pellets, milk on the preceding trial would have produced slower running speeds than nonreward on the preceding trial because the milk S+ cue would have generalized with the pellets S- cue. No such generalization occurred. Thus, the emotional aftereffect of the goal outcome was not an important factor.

Pschirrer (1972) also subjected five rats to a variant of the basic triple discrimination procedure, which, although horribly complex, further clarifies what happens in the alternative reward procedure. In this variant, the rats were first trained on the alternate reward procedure and then were switched to the triple discrimination. In one subgroup, the alternative reward procedure involved pellets and nonreward on alternate trials; after some learning, the triple discrimination, milk→pellets→nonreward, was instituted; thus the pellets and nonreward retained their earlier cue functions (S- and S+ respectively) and the new milk reward had an S+ function. It would be expected that if there was generalization between the

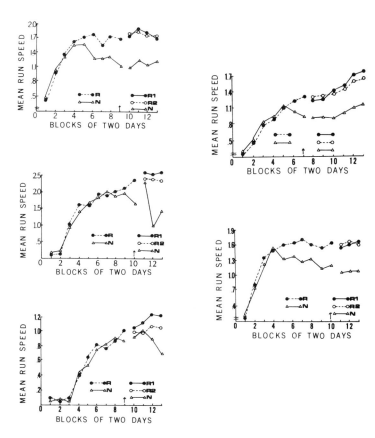

Figure 1
Mean runway speeds for individual rats. The left portion of each graph shows speeds on rewarded (R) and nonrewarded (N) trials, when the two types of trials were alternated. The right portion shows speeds on each trial of a triple discrimination cycle; R_1 and R_2 are the first and second rewarded trials, while the nonrewarded (N) trial follows the R_2 trial. The minimum intertrial interval was 15 min. (From Pschirrer, 1972.)

342

milk and the pellets, immediately after transition to the triple discrimination, the new milk S+ would tend to act like the pellet S- and lower running speeds on the following trial. For two or three other rats, the roles of milk and pellets were interchanged.

Figure 1 shows mean running speed during each type of trial for each individual rat. The break in each curve marks the changeover from alternate reward to the triple discrimination. Prior to the break, N designates unrewarded trials and R designates rewarded trials. After the break, N continues to designate unrewarded trials, R_1 designates rewarded trials where S+ from the preceding trial was nonreward, and R_2 refers to rewarded trials where S+ from the preceding trial was the reward first introduced in the triple discrimination phase.

Figure 1 shows gradual learning of the alternate reward discrimination prior to the break in the curves and no noticeable decrement in discrimination performance immediately after the triple discrimination was introduced. In other words, just after the triple discrimination was introduced, the rats ran just as quickly on R_2 trials as on R_1 trials; this is surprising because R_2 trials were preceded by the novel reward while R_1 trials were preceded by the nonreward which had been paired with reward on the following trial during the entire first phase. These results show that although the rats performed the triple discrimination successfully, they did so only on the basis of learning one fact: that a *particular* food reward (either milk or pellets) was S- for reward on the following trial. It is the failures of some potential factors to have much of a role in the discrimination which is of theoretical significance as follows.

(1) Nonreward did not have an important role in the discrimination because the substitution of a novel reward for nonreward did not affect running speed. Capaldi (1967) hypothesized that nonreward was the stimulus complex to which running was conditioned; this does not seem to be so. Nor is it tenable to suppose that frustration induced by nonreward (Amsel, 1967) had any important role.

(2) If any satisfaction (or drive reduction) produced by reward were to have amplified the cue salience of rewards, one would expect generalization between the novel reward at the beginning of the triple discrimination and the familiar reward which had functioned as S- during the earlier phase. There was no sign of any such generalization either in Figure 1 or in Pschirrer's first experiment. This suggests that it was the cue properties of a particular reward which had the role of S-, not its emotional properties.

343

Thus, Pschirrer's results in Figure 1 contradicted those explanations of the alternate reward effect which were relatively compatible with traditional approaches to delay learning.

Extension to the T-maze. Pschirrer's next step was to show that response selection in a T-maze could be made to depend upon the type of food reward obtained on the preceding trial, just as Petrinovich and Bolles (1957) had shown that response selection could depend upon the response emitted on the preceding trial. Thus, in Pschirrer's second experiment, the right goalbox of a T-maze contained reward if the preceding reward had been milk and the left goalbox contained reward if the preceding reward had been pellets or vice versa. Otherwise, the sequence of correct responses was quasi-random. After about 700 trials with an intertrial interval of over 3 min, the rats were correct on over 80% of the trials.

Extension to Arbitrary Cues. Revusky (1974) modified the alternate reward runway experiment by using cues that are more like the cues conventionally used in discrimination learning experiments. The rat's task was to use the type of goalbox on the preceding trial as the cue for the goal outcome of the current trial. A trial was rewarded if the preceding trial had terminated in a black goalbox, but not if it had terminated in a white goalbox (or vice versa). More specifically, the goalboxes of the runway were removable so that a large, black, wooden goalbox could be used on half the trials and a smaller, white, plastic goalbox could be used on the remaining trials. There were nine trials per day with a minimum intertrial interval of 4 min. The sequence of black and white trials was quasi-random and different for each rat. The reward outcomes of the preceding trial were not useful for prediction because the sequence was so arranged that half the rewarded trials were preceded by reward, while the other half were preceded by nonreward; the same was true for the nonrewarded trials. Furthermore, half of each rat's rewards were received in the black goalbox and the other half were received in the white goalbox; the same was true for failures to receive reward. Consequently, the only possible cue for reward or nonreward was the type of goalbox on the preceding trial.

Figure 2 shows mean running speeds on rewarded and unrewarded trials in the course of the experiment. The learning was very slow, not being apparent until over 300 trials, but eventually each of the four rats learned the discrimination. The slow learning, by the way, need not be attributed to the 4-min delay over which association occurred. The intertrial association procedure necessarily involves handling the rat at the beginning and at the

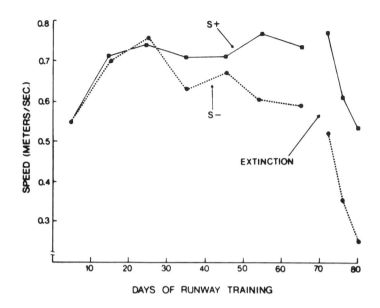

Figure 2
Mean runway speeds on rewarded (S+) and unrewarded (S-)
trials, where the discriminative stimulus was the type of
goalbox used on the preceding trial over 4-min earlier. (From
Revusky, 1974.)

end of the intertrial interval. This distracting experience alone
might explain why learning was slower than in other black-white
discrimination experiments. The repeated handling, however, also
has an advantage: it excludes any reasonable possibility that the
rats could have maintained a muscular set to mediate the long-
delay association (Spence, 1956).

According to the present interpretation, Figure 2 shows that rats
can associate directly between conventional E-pres and E-posts that
occur minutes later. It may be objected that there is no evidence
from these results alone that it is the absence of the animal from
the apparatus during the delay which is responsible for the long-
delay learning. However, there have been 50 years of experimentation in which rats which remained in the apparatus during a delay
were not able to learn similar discriminations with delays of only a
number of seconds. Later in this chapter (Figure 5 and 6) direct
evidence that long-delay associations of a related type depend on
absence from the apparatus during the delay will be offered.[1]

345

According to classical S-R theory, delayed reward learning does not involve association of the response with a delayed reward and hence is not an instance of association between temporally separated events. The S-R position is that the learned association is always between a stimulus and a response; the reward strengthens the association but is not an element of the association. In terms of the S-R position, it is naive to treat delayed reward learning in the way we will treat it, as mainly involving the association of a response E-pre-ref with a reward of E-post-ref. Although few if any contemporary investigators explicitly advocate the classical version of S-R theory, its influence still lingers in a tendency to use different theoretical frameworks for different types of delay learning. By obliterating distinctions between different types of delay learning, the present analysis in terms of association of E-pre-ref with a delayed E-post-ref permits a general description of delay learning. It will be shown below that delayed reward learning can be explained in the same theoretical framework as intertrial associations between a cue and the reward contingency on the following trial.

According to the present point of view, the rules of concurrent interference determine whether a response E-pre-ref will become associated with a delayed reward or nonreward E-post-ref. These rules are the same rules which were alleged in the preceding section to govern learning that a goalbox E-pre-ref is to be associated with reward or nonreward of a response on the following trial (E-post-ref). If so, removal of an animal from the apparatus during the delay between a response and a reward ought to facilitate delayed reward learning in the same way it facilitated intertrial discriminations as shown, for instance, in Figure 2.

On the basis of this conjecture, Lett (1973) took upon herself the task of finding a variant of the intertrial discrimination procedure which might yield learning in a T-maze with long delays of reward. This was different from Pschirrer's (1972) demonstration of long-delay learning in the T-maze when milk and pellet rewards were discriminative cues for different responses on the following trial. In Pschirrer's experiment, the delay was between the cue and the response, while Lett was interested in obtaining learning with a delay between the response and the reward.

For quite a while, it seemed as though technical difficulties would make Lett's task impractical because the obvious way to adapt the intertrial discrimination procedure to delayed reward learning would yield uninterpretable results. The obvious way is to allow the rat to select one of two goalboxes in a T-maze and remove

346

it immediately without reward regardless of whether it selected the correct goalbox or the incorrect goalbox; if correct, the rat could be returned to the correct goalbox after a delay and then rewarded. According to an analysis in terms of interference and situational relevance, the rat would learn because the events occurring outside of the apparatus would not enter into strong interfering associations with events that occur inside the apparatus. However, learning with such a procedure could also be attributed to secondary reinforcement. The correct goalbox is bound to become secondarily reinforcing because the rat is rewarded in it, and, of course, the rat prefers a secondarily reinforcing goalbox to one which is not secondarily reinforcing. It would have been possible to circumvent secondary reinforcement by having both paths in the T-maze lead to a common goalbox; but this would have made the problem difficult for rats and introduced frustration as a factor since the rat would have to run into an empty goalbox in which reward sometimes was received.

Lett (1973, 1974, 1975) avoided the secondary reinforcement artifact in a unique way: when a rat made the correct response, she rewarded it in the startbox after a delay spent outside of the apparatus. Since the startbox also functioned as a goalbox, no separate goalbox was needed; the rat had a choice of entering one of two endboxes, and if it selected the correct endbox, it was later rewarded in the startbox. The correct endbox could not become secondarily rewarding except through association over a delay because the rat was never fed in it. Figure 3 shows the simplified

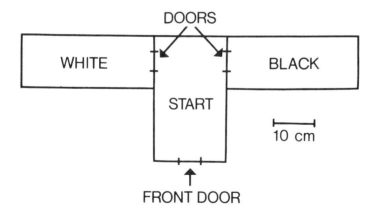

Figure 3
The simplified T-maze used by B. T. Lett; a gray wooden startbox flanked by two endboxes opposite in color.

347

T-maze which Lett used; each of two endboxes could be entered directly from the startbox. The white endbox was always on the left and the black endbox was always on the right, so that the rats could use both visual and positional cues.

Lett subjected rats to one trial per day with a very simple procedure. The rat was placed head first in the startbox and could enter either endbox through one-way doors. Immediately after it entered an endbox, the rat was returned to its home cage. After a delay, it was returned to the startbox; the side doors to the endboxes were now locked. If the rat had previously selected the correct endbox (left-white for half the rats and right-black for the other half), it found a small cup of 25% weight/volume sucrose solution. If the rat had previously selected the incorrect endbox, it was confined in the empty startbox for 1 min and then was returned to its home cage.

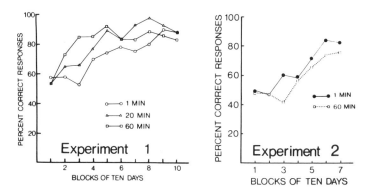

Figure 4
Mean percentage of correct responses with various delays of reward. The delay was spent in the home cage. (From Lett, 1975.)

Figure 4 shows the results of two experiments (Lett, 1975) in which groups of 11 or 12 rats were trained with reward delayed either by 1, 20, or 60 min. Each of the five groups in Figure 4 learned, but neither experiment yielded a statistically significant delay gradient. The absence of a significant delay gradient is reminiscent of McLaurin's (1964) early failure to obtain a delay gradient for saccharin aversions induced by radiation sickness when the delays ranged from 3 to 180 min. Smith and Roll (1967) were later to show that McLaurin's range of delays was too small to yield a gradient under his experimental conditions; the minimum delay that noticeably interfered with aversion learning was greater than 6

348

hr. If it turns out that Lett's failure to obtain a delay gradient is also due to too small a range of delays, then her procedure ought to yield learning with delays of at least several hours.

In the procedure Lett used to obtain the data in Figure 4, a rat was returned to its home cage immediately after it entered an endbox. The purpose of this immediate removal from the endbox was to minimize the number of delay events in the endbox which would follow the rat's response. Such delay events were expected to enter into associations that would interfere with development of an association between the response and the reward. The theoretical reasoning underlying this expectation involved both situational relevance and interference. According to the situational relevance principle, delay events in the endboxes are likely to enter into association with the response and the reward because they occur in the same apparatus. According to interference theory, these extraneous associations ought to hinder development of the association between the response and the reward. Hence, the longer the animal remains in the endbox after a response, the poorer learning ought to be.

Lett (1975) tested this analysis in her next experiment. Three groups were trained in the two-choice delayed reward task used in the preceding experiment, but differed in how long they remained in the endbox after a response. Group Stay-O was removed to the home cage immediately after entry into an endbox, Group Stay-15 was removed 15 sec after entry, and Group Stay-60 was removed 60 sec after entry. All rats were removed from the home cage to the startbox 120 sec after they had first entered an endbox so that if the delay is calculated from initial entry to the endbox, all groups were subjected to the same 120-sec delay. However, an alternative definition of the delay might be from the time the rats were returned to the home cage until they were replaced in the startbox; by this criterion, Group Stay-0 was subjected to a 120-sec delay, Group Stay-15 was subjected to a 105-sec delay (since it spent 15 of the 120 sec in the endbox), and Group Stay-60 was subjected to a 60-sec delay.

Other details of the experiment were as follows. If the rat had previously selected the correct endbox, it was rewarded with 2.5 ml of 25% sucrose solution. However, if it had previously selected the incorrect endbox, the method was different from that of Lett's earlier experiments described here. The rat simply was subjected to another trial in which it again could select one of the two endboxes; the procedure was identical with that of the previous trial in all respects. The day's training did not end until the correct response

349

was made, no matter how many incorrect responses there were. This actually was the original version of Lett's delayed reward procedure and had repeatedly been shown to be effective (Lett, 1973, 1974; Denny, 1974).

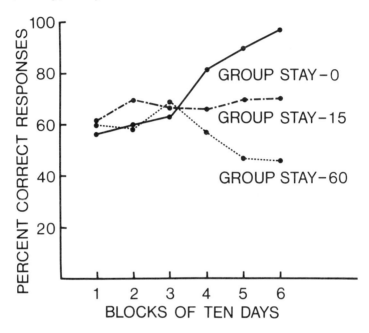

Figure 5
Mean percentage of correct responses with a 2-min delay of reward for groups which differed in the number of seconds they stayed in the endbox prior to return to the home cage. (From Lett, 1975.)

Figure 5 shows the percentage of correct responses on the first trial of each day in blocks of ten days for each group. The longer the rats remained in the endbox after their initial selection, the poorer was their performance; if the delay is calculated from initial entry into the endbox, all groups were subjected to the same 120-sec delay, but if the delay is calculated from removal from the goalbox, the performance was actually an inverse function of the delay of reward. The only known theory which can account for these results is the present concurrent interference theory.

G. Barnes (unpublished) conjectured that if extra time in the endbox interferes with delayed reward learning by increasing the number of interfering events experienced in the apparatus, extra time in the startbox must have a similar effect. The Barnes's experiment involved three groups. A home cage delay group was subjected to approximately the same procedure by which Lett had obtained her 1-min delay data in Figure 4. A startbox delay group was transferred to the startbox for a 1-min delay immediately after selecting an endbox and then was briefly handled and replaced in the startbox, which now contained a dish of sugar water if its earlier choice response had been correct. A third group (called "other box") was delayed in a box that resembled the startbox but was in a different location and oriented differently; like the home cage delay group, this other box delay group was transferred to the startbox for feedback after the delay. The group delayed in the other box had been expected to learn more quickly than the startbox delay group because it was absent from the apparatus during the delay, but more slowly than the home cage group because the resemblance of the other box to the startbox would strengthen concurrent interference.

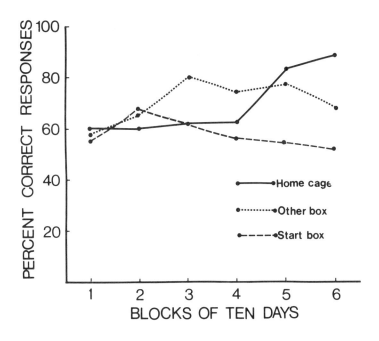

Figure 6
Percentage of correct responses for rats subjected to a 1-min delay of reward as a function of where the delay was spent. (Data courtesy of G. Barnes.)

Figure 6 shows that the rats delayed in the startbox did not learn. The rats detained in the home cage and those detained in the other box do not seem to have performed very differently as far as can be determined from visual inspection of Figure 6. However, statistical analysis indicated that learning by the home cage group was highly reliable while the learning by the other box group was marginal. Overall, the results are in excellent agreement with concurrent interference theory.[2]

PROBLEMS FOR CONCURRENT INTERFERENCE THEORY

Denny (1974) obtained learning with delays of 1.5 to 2.0 min with a modification of Lett's procedure in which he rewarded the rats in a wastebasket instead of in the startbox of the apparatus. According to a straightforward situational relevance analysis, his rats should not have learned because the reward was obtained in a different situation from the response. However, there seemed to be two ways in which to reconcile this learning with concurrent interference theory:

(1) Denny's rats might not have learned an association between the correct response and reward, but rather an association between the incorrect response and placement in the startbox of the apparatus on the following trial. Denny (1974) had used Lett's (1973) original procedure in which the rat was subjected to repeated training trials on each day until it finally made a correct response. Since the rats received feedback in the apparatus after incorrect responses, they might have associated the incorrect response with the presumably aversive replacement in the startbox and learned nothing else. A precedent for learning based only on nonreward is Pschirrer's triple discrimination (Figure 1) in which the only apparent association was between one food E-pre-ref and a failure to obtain reward on the following trial.

(2) Another possible way to account for Denny's result in terms of the present theory is to suppose that there was generalization between the apparatus and the wastebasket. Both were novel and differed from the rat's usual home cage environment.

However, Lett's (in press) next experiment was to exclude both of these explanations of Denny's effect: rats learned the delayed reward task without any specific feedback after incorrect responses and when delayed reward was administered in the home cage itself. Her experimental group received one trial per day; 1 min after being returned to the home cage following a correct response, the rat received a dish of sugar water in its home cage, and there was no replacement in the startbox after an incorrect response. The control group was rewarded in the startbox 1 min after a correct response and spent the delay in its home cage; as in the experimental group, there was no feedback after an incorrect response.

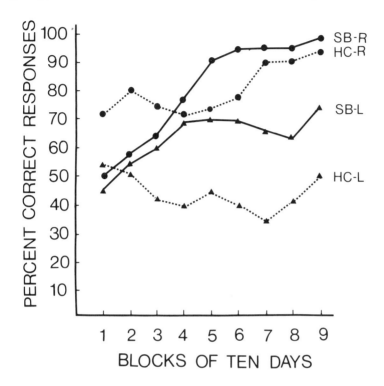

Figure 7
Percentage of correct responses for rats subjected to a 1-min delay of reward. The delay was spent in the home cage. Separate curves are shown depending on whether reward was obtained in the startbox (SB) or in the home cage (HC) and on whether the right or the left response was correct. (From Lett, in press.)

Figure 7 shows Lett's results as a function of whether the rats were rewarded in the home cage or in the startbox and as a function of whether the left or right response was correct. (It was desirable to show left and right S+ groups separately because of an overall preference for running to the right.) It is apparent from Figure 7 that the rats rewarded in the home cage learned, although not as well as the rats rewarded in the startbox. This was damaging to the explanation of such delayed reward learning in terms of concurrent interference and situational relevance since there ought not

353

to be any situational relevance between the apparatus and the home cage.

Since learning by the rats rewarded in the home cage (Figure 7) was marginal, Lett (in press) considered it likely that a small increase in the length of the delay would eliminate it entirely. However, this also turned out not to be true. Figure 8 shows the results of a second experiment in which all rats were treated like the home cage reward rats in Figure 7, but the delay was varied for different groups: 0, 15, 60, and 120 sec. Each of the groups learned, but the learning was markedly superior for the 0 and 15 sec delay groups.

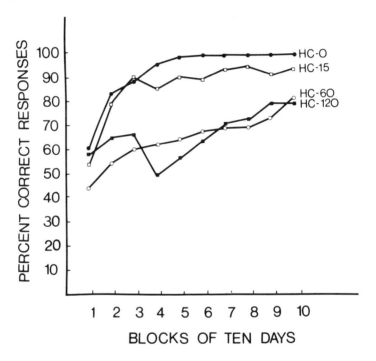

Figure 8
Percentage of correct responses for rats rewarded in the home cage after various delays (in sec). (From Lett, in press.)

On the surface, the clear evidence that delayed reward learning can occur if the rats are rewarded in their home cages is extremely damaging to concurrent interference theory. However, since this result is equally damaging to every other conceivable theory except for association by black magic, it seems worthwhile to try to stretch concurrent interference theory so as to accommodate Lett's results.

It might be that, in casual language, the experimental situation begins for the rat when the experimenter approaches it. If so, the delayed placement of the reward in the home cage by the experimenter may have produced learning because the experimenter was a source of situational relevance. If this is true, delayed reward learning ought not to occur if an automated device is used to supply reward in the home cage.

There is some anecdotal evidence suggesting that rats do associate between experimenters and the experimental situation. Capaldi (personal communication, 1970) has noticed that in the alternate reward procedure, rats picked up by the experimenter prior to a rewarded trial are lively and eager, while rats picked up prior to an unrewarded trial are lethargic. Denny (1974) has made a similar comment. Lett (personal communication, 1974) found the influence of the experimenter in the situation to be so great that she noticed a decrement in performance when relief experimenters were substituted on a weekend. Given the eagerness of many people to deny the existence of long-delay learning, I hasten to add that all of these competent experimenters have excluded the possibility that the difference in the experimenter's behavior on rewarded and unrewarded trials is responsible for intertrial associations. Capaldi (personal communication, 1970) actually tried to use the way rats were handled as a discriminative cue with no success, and Lett (1973) introduced double-blind procedures during testing.

ROLE OF TEMPORAL CONTIGUITY

The preceding material definitively disproves the traditional theory that learning is impossible without temporal contiguity between E-pre-ref and E-post-ref. At one time (Revusky, 1971) in an overreaction against this traditional theory, I implied that all facilitory effects of temporal contiguity on learning were due to an indirect reduction in concurrent interference. I now think that this earlier position was wrong and that, in fact, temporal contiguity does facilitate learning, although it certainly is not a necessary condition for it. One influence has been my belated awareness of Kamin's (1965) demonstration that rats learn conditioned suppression of bar pressing far better with a 0-sec CS-US gap than with a 0.5-sec gap. It would be churlish to try to attribute this difference to the concurrent interference produced by events which occur during the 0.5-sec delay. Another influence has been exploratory observations by Lett suggesting that learning with her delay procedure is facilitated by temporal contiguity. She finds that no delay results in markedly better learning of a spatial discrimination than

355

a 15-sec delay. Furthermore, if the delay is under 30 sec or so, the learning is markedly superior than if the delay is 1 min even though there is no apparent delay gradient from 1 to 60 min (Figure 4); indeed, there is a trace of this effect in Figure 8.

Recently, Lett (in press) has obtained new suggestive evidence that temporal contiguity improves learning when her delayed reward procedure is used. Two groups of rats were trained to run to the left (unpreferred) side of her T-maze with a 1-min delay of reward. Each rat received as many trials as were necessary for it to make one correct choice per day. Group Stay, the experimental group, stayed in the endbox during the 1-min delay of reward and was transferred to the startbox immediately afterward. If its earlier response had been correct, it found reward there, and if its earlier response had been incorrect, it was subjected to another trial. To

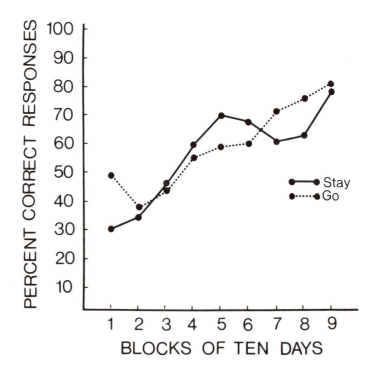

Figure 9
Percentage of correct responses for rats rewarded in the startbox after a 1-min delay. Group Stay was delayed in the endbox but was allowed to see the reward toward the end of the delay. Group Go spent the delay in its home cage. (From Lett, in press.)

356

insure temporal contiguity between the endbox and the reward in Group Stay, the dish of sugar water reward was placed in the startbox a few seconds before a rat in Group Stay was transferred there; since the barrier between the startbox and the endbox was of clear plastic, the rat could see the reward while still in the endbox. Group Go, the control group, was subjected to the standard procedure in which the rat spent the delay in its home cage and was rewarded in the startbox.

Figure 9 shows that the rats in Group Stay, which stayed in the endbox during the delay, learned just as well as the rats in Group Go, which were in the home cage during the delay. To interpret these results, the data for Group Stay-60 in Figure 5 must be utilized. These rats were delayed for 60 sec in the endbox and then removed to the home cage for another 60 sec before they were returned to the startbox. As Figure 5 shows, they failed to learn. Group Stay of Figure 9, which did learn, differed from Group Stay-60 of Figure 5, which did not learn, in two respects: (1) There was temporal contiguity between the endbox cues and the startbox cues in Group Stay but not in Group Stay-60. (2) The delay of reward was 60 sec for Group Stay and 120 sec for Group Stay-60. Since the effects of a 60-sec delay on learning are similar to those of a 120-sec delay with Lett's procedure (Figure 4), it seems unreasonable to attribute the difference in learning of the two groups to the difference in the delay of reward. Thus, by elimination, the learning of Group Stay in Figure 9 seems attributable to temporal contiguity. Admittedly, this line of reasoning contains more conjectures than are desirable.

EVALUATION OF CONCURRENT INTERFERENCE THEORY

If integration of old information and discovery of new information are to be the criteria for measuring the success of a theory, few theories have been as successful as concurrent interference in so short a space of time. Within a few years after its origin as a theory of food-aversion learning, it subsumed delay learning in traditional learning situations and led to the discovery of new and important effects which traditional learning theorists had considered impossible. Nevertheless, it is possible to make a case against the theory, and I will do so here in order to defend it.

The theory can be considered overgeneral and vague at a time when there is a strong reaction against traditional learning theories for being overgeneral. It certainly obscures important differences. There is, in fact, little resemblance between long-delay food-aversion learning and long-delay learning in the runway and T-maze. These two quite different types of delay learning are subsumed under the same rubric with the very vague statement that neither would develop if there was too much interference produced by the events which occur during the delay. The theory defines whatever overcomes this interference as a relevance principle, but does not in any way indicate what kind of relevance principle is likely to be responsible for a particular instance of long-delay learning. It simply directs the investigator to go look for a relevance principle whenever there is a puzzling instance of long-delay learning. This approach is almost tautological. Furthermore, the two relevance principles which have been used extensively in this chapter, situational relevance and stimulus relevance, are quite different. It may be that, following Lett (in press), situational relevance is best understood in terms of cued recall of memories, while stimulus relevance is a more direct form of selective association. From the vantage point of concurrent interference theory as explained here, such a distinction is not critical; but the very fact that such an obviously important distinction is not critical may be considered very damaging to the theory.

Such objections to concurrent interference theory reflect a lack of appreciation of how an abstract scientific analysis often works. As an analogy, consider a physicist who states that force is equal to mass multiplied by acceleration and ignores differences between different forces and masses. He is not claiming that a mass of diamonds is the same thing as an equal mass of lead. What he is claiming is that such a difference is irrelevant to his analysis of force in terms of mass and acceleration. Similarly, I am not denying the difference between stimulus relevance and situational relevance when I claim that the difference is unimportant for an abstract analysis of delay learning in terms of interference. This claim is a positive statement, not an oversight, and it is upon such statements that abstract scientific theories depend.

There is also a precedent for the lack of exact predictions in concurrent interference theory: the existence theorems in certain branches of mathematics. For instance, in differential equations, an existence theorem is a proof that a solution to a certain type of differential equation exists, but it does not indicate what the solution is. Instead, it encourages the investigator's trial and error efforts to find a solution. Similarly, concurrent interference theory led to Lett's discovery of an effective way to train a rat in a T-maze with delayed reward. According to the theory, an association between a response and a delayed reward follows the same principles as other types of associations over a delay. This suggested that delayed reward learning could be obtained if a relevance principle were available to overcome interference. Thus, the theory suggested the existence of a solution to the delayed reward problem. By itself, it did not suggest a particular solution (or relevance principle), although it did suggest that one might be obtained by extrapolation from intertrial association experiments. Furthermore, the theory did not by itself suggest the apparatus shown in Figure 3 nor the strategy of rewarding the animal in the startbox; these were developed by Lett through trial and error guided by a general knowledge of animal learning. Lett worked like a physicist looking for the solution to a differential equation rather than like an algebraist developing the implications of a set of axioms.

Although a variety of factors had a role in Lett's discovery of learning with prolonged delay of reward, I would like to make the self-serving claim that her discovery would have been delayed by many years without concurrent interference theory. There is a bit of suggestive evidence for this. Lett's methodology was described by me in a 1970 grant proposal to the National Science Foundation and thus was considered by some of the most distinguished psychologists of that time. The NSF panel was friendly; they recommended funding of my flavor-aversion work and spoke very flatteringly of it. However, they regarded the suggestion that delayed reward learning could be obtained by removal of the animal from the apparatus during the delay as evidence that both Lett and I were incompetent in runway and T-maze research; they specifically mandated that no NSF money be wasted on Lett's work. In looking over that grant proposal now, I realize that by all conventional standards, the NSF panel was right. We reported a great deal of unsuccessful pilot work and discounted it all on the basis of novel theoretical conjectures. The point is that Lett's entire experimental program simply made no sense except on the basis of a strong faith in concurrent interference theory. Of course, Lett's delayed reward effect would eventually have been discovered without concurrent interference theory, but I think it would have taken the better part of a decade.

If concurrent interference theory is to be given credit for Lett's discovery, its prediction of a major counterintuitive result is unique for learning theories. During the last fifty years, the role of prediction in other learning theories, no matter how distinguished, has been to uncover minor effects or to describe major effects more accurately than before. No other learning theory has yielded a specific successful a priori prediction as important and counterin-

359

tuitive as the prediction that without interference, "manipulative and locomotor operants would also be susceptible to delays of reinforcement of several hours." (Revusky & Garcia, 1970, p. 44). This success of concurrent interference theory is an adequate defense against the charge that it is too vague and general.[3]

AFTERWORD

Although the concurrent interference theory of delay learning is an explanation of how animals associate between feeding stimuli and delayed physiological aftereffects, the strongest evidence for it comes from runway and T-maze experiments. The net result is that the experiments described extensively here integrate poorly with the food-selection theme of this volume. Since I have stretched the bounds of academic freedom given to me by the editors of this volume by going so far afield, I would like to explain why it was necessary.

If I had attempted to validate concurrent interference only in terms of feeding experiments, my case would have been very weak. This chapter would have ended essentially just before the description of the runway and T-maze studies. It would have consisted mainly of the definitions and ideological statements and some evidence that interference occurs in flavor-aversion learning situations. However, there would be no strong basis for a claim that concurrent interference has any marked advantages over learned safety theory or even over the simple statement that long-delay learning occurs in feeding situations simply because of the relevance of feeding stimuli to toxicosis.

The present necessity to validate a theory of long-delay learning of feeding behavior by means of runway and T-maze experiments indirectly makes a point which has been made more directly elsewhere (Revusky, in press): it is useful and often necessary to understand learning mechanisms in food selection in terms of general principles of learning rather than in terms of specific adaptations.

[1]There is another class of objections to the result in Figure 2 which I consider to be mainly a reflection of strong cultural beliefs with no scientific merit. However, I will answer them here because I am obviously in a minority. Three journals rejected the paper which included Figure 2, and indeed it was only due to the existence of an unrefereed journal that the scientific community finally had access to it. The objections are nicely epitomized by the claim of a reviewer for *Learning and Motivation* that the result is in agreement with the theory that temporal contiguity is necessary for learning: "All that needs to be assumed is that some representation of events which occur with a particular context (goalbox brightness) becomes associated with that context (runway apparatus) through contiguity. When that context is reinstated, memory of the preceding event is reactivated."

There is some scientific content in this comment. In the present terms, it is an explanation of why situational relevance occurs. The reviewer claims that it occurs because return to the apparatus results in retrieval of previous apparatus cues. So, if the preceding trial terminated in a black goalbox, the rat remembers the black goalbox on the following trial because the black goalbox was associated with the apparatus. Such a theory has, in fact, been developed in an intelligent way by Lett (in press), but the reviewer was simply emitting a culturally predetermined verbal reaction. He did not consider that the rats had a history of hundreds of trials when learning finally occurred in Figure 2. Half of these trials terminated in the black goalbox and the other half terminated in the white goalbox. Why then does the rat remember the black goalbox of the immediately preceding trial instead of the white goalbox of some earlier trial? To do this according to the reviewer's hypothesis, the rat must forget all that it has learned on earlier trials and learn the association of the black goalbox with the apparatus on the immediately preceding trial. Few experienced students of animal learning would consider such a hypothesis reasonable except possibly in order to defend a sacred dogma. This is not a problem for the concurrent interference view because interference is assumed to increase with time spent in the apparatus; hence, the immediately preceding goalbox cue has not been subjected to as much interference as cues from earlier trials.

However, the main point to be made here is that the reviewer's comments are absurd as a defense of temporal contiguity theory. Since it is undeniable that learning is impossible unless E-pre-ref is in some sense remembered at the time E-post-ref occurs, the reviewer's approach leaves no logically conceivable instance of long-delay learning not explicable in terms of indirect temporal contiguity. For instance, long-delay food aversions can be explained in terms of temporal contiguity between the memory of a food and toxicosis. Theories designed so that there is no conceivable scientific result which can disprove them are metaphysical dogmas. In contrast, the traditional invocations of indirect temporal contiguity through lingering stimulus traces, secondary reinforcement, and mediating chains of behaviors were within the realm of scientific discourse. They were not immediately testable due to technical difficulties, but eventually they were, in fact, disproven as the sole cause of long-delay learning. Temporal contiguity through memories is different because it can never be disproven. It is annoying to find that perfectly good experiments, such as that summarized in Figure 2, are not published because editors and reviewers are unable to distinguish between scientific theories and metaphysical dogmas.

²The experimental results summarized in Figures 1-6 have been obtained by investigators who have strongly influenced each other. Thus, it is comforting to know that Denny (1974) successfully replicated Lett's basic effect with delays of 1.5 to 2.0 min in spite of his strong theoretical predilection for temporal contiguity theory. However, there has been a report that one of Lett's results is not replicable. This involved a brightness discrimination with a 1.0-min delay of reward; after a great deal of training, Lett's (1974) rats were correct about 70% of the time. Roberts (1976) tried four variants of her procedure and reported completely negative results using the same measure of learning as Lett (increase in percent correct over five blocks of 20 days each). However, Roberts showed his mean results for each block and each variant, and percentage correct was higher than the 50% chance level in 17 of 20 blocks (five blocks per variant). This led Lett and me to reanalyze Roberts's data, which he was kind enough to supply, to see if there was any evidence for learning. First, data from the six rats subjected to an exact replication of Lett's procedure were analyzed alone instead of in a combined analysis with rats subjected to a variant of her procedure (the method used by Roberts). Learning was demonstrated at the two-tail .05 level by the criterion of learning used by Roberts and also by Lett. By a more sensitive criterion, the rats subjected to Roberts's variants of Lett's procedure also learned; those rats for which black was S+ tended to select the black side more frequently than those rats for which white was S+ ($p < .05$, F test), but this tendency did not change over blocks. Hopefully, *Learning and Motivation* will see fit to publish a note by Lett which includes more details.

³The question then arises as to whether the rather sloppy and imprecise "existence theorem" strategy contributed to the success of concurrent interference theory or impeded it. Conceivably, a more rigorous traditional approach might have led to a still better analysis of the delay problem. Of course, we cannot know the answer to this question because history does not include control experiments. However, it is possible to compare concurrent interference theory with the basically similar approach of Rescorla and Wagner (1972). They developed the idea of concurrent interference independently in a more rigorous manner than it is presented here to account for the effects of compound CSs in discrimination learning and Pavlovian conditioning. Their analysis made it possible to extend their version of the theory to problems of inhibition in a very elegant manner (Wagner & Rescorla, 1972); concurrent interference did not score points in this direction. Further, partly because the

362

Rescorla-Wagner model yields less equivocal predictions than concurrent interference theory, it became far more influential in the animal learning literature. However, I immodestly feel that the very general "existence theorem" approach of concurrent interference theory made it possible to extrapolate from CS-US associations to response-reward associations; this resulted in more spectacular discoveries than those produced by the Rescorla-Wagner model. If so, this might be taken as suggestive evidence that a sloppy imprecise approach also has its advantages. Probably, the fairest conclusion is that the very general approach of concurrent interference theory was appropriate for a general analysis of the delay problem, while the more rigorous approach of Rescorla and Wagner was more appropriate for analysis of the multiple CS problem.

ACKNOWLEDGEMENTS

I thank Bow Tong Lett for carefully editing this manuscript and Margaret Crawford for typing it. This work was partly supported by Grant A8271 from the National Research Council of Canada.

REFERENCES

Amsel, A. Partial reinforcement effects on vigor and persistence. In K. W. Spence & J. T. Spence (Eds.), **The psychology of learning and motivation.** Vol. I. New York: Academic Press, 1967.

Bloom, J. M., & Capaldi, E. J. The behavior of rats in relation to complex patterns of partial reinforcement. **Journal of Comparative and Physiological Psychology,** 1961, **54,** 261-265.

Capaldi, E. J. A sequential hypothesis of instrumental learning. In K. W. Spence & J. T. Spence (Eds.), **The psychology of learning and motivation.** Vol. I. New York: Academic Press, 1967.

Capaldi, E. J. Memory and learning: A sequential viewpoint. In W. K. Honig & P. H. R. James (Eds.), **Animal memory.** New York: Academic Press, 1971.

Carr, A. F. Latent inhibition and overshadowing in conditioned emotional response conditioning in rats. **Journal of Comparative and Physiological Psychology,** 1974, **86,** 718-724.

Denny, M. R. Recent explorations in a T-maze: Women's lib, long delays and all that. Paper delivered at the 46th annual meeting of the Midwestern Psychological Association, Chicago, 1974.

Dragoin, W. B. Conditioning and extinction of taste aversions with variations in intensity of the CS and UCS in two strains of rats. **Psychonomic Science,** 1971, **22,** 303-305.

Estes, W. K. Stimulus-response theory of drive. In M. R. Jones (Ed.), **Nebraska symposium on motivation.** Lincoln: University of Nebraska Press, 1958.

Fowler, H. Blocking and counterblocking (enhancement) effects across appetitive and aversive reinforcers. Paper delivered at Conference on cognitive aspects of animal behavior at Dalhousie University, Halifax, Nova Scotia, 1976.

Garcia, J. The faddy rat and us. **New Scientist and Science Journal,** 1971, **49,** 254-256.

Garcia, J., & Koelling, R. A. Relation of cue to consequence in avoidance learning. **Psychonomic Science,** 1966, **4,** 123-124.

Garcia, J., McGowan, B. K., Ervin, F. R., & Koelling, R. A. Cues: Their effectiveness as a function of the reinforcer. **Science,** 1968, **160,** 794-795.

Garcia, J., McGowan, B. K., & Green, K. F. Biological constraints on conditioning. In M. E. P. Seligman & J. L. Hager (Eds.), **Biological boundaries of learning.** New York: Appleton-Century-Crofts, 1972.

Green, K. F., & Parker, L. A. Gustatory memory: Incubation and interference. **Behavioral Biology,** 1975, **13,** 359-367.

Grice, G. R. The relation of secondary reinforcement to delayed reward in visual discrimination learning. **Journal of Experimental Psychology,** 1948, **38,** 1-16.

Kalat, J. W., & Rozin P. Role of interference in taste-aversion learning. **Journal of Comparative and Physiological Psychology,** 1971, **77,** 53-58.

Kalat, J. W., & Rozin, P. "Learned safety" as a mechanism in long-delay taste-aversion learning in rats. **Journal of Comparative and Physiological Psychology,** 1973, **83,** 198-207.

364

Kamin, L. J. Temporal and intensity characteristics of the conditioned stimulus. In W. F. Prokasy (Ed.), **Classical conditioning: A symposium.** New York: Appleton-Century-Crofts, 1965.

Kamin, L. J. Predictability, surprise, attention and conditioning. In B. A. Campbell & R. M. Church (eds.), **Punishment and aversive behavior.** New York: Appleton-Century-Crofts, 1969.

Lett, B. T. Delayed reward learning: Disproof of the traditional theory. **Learning and Motivation,** 1973, **4,** 237-246.

Lett, B. T. Visual discrimination learning with a 1-min delay of reward. **Learning and Motivation,** 1974, **5,** 174-181.

Lett, B. T. Long delay learning in the T-maze. **Learning and Motivation,** 1975, **6,** 80-90.

Lett, B. T. Long delay learning: Implications for learning and memory theory. In N. S. Sutherland (Ed.), **Tutorial essays in experimental psychology.** Vol. II, in press.

Lubow, R. E. Latent inhibition. **Psychological Bulletin,** 1973, **79,** 398-407.

Mackintosh, N. J. **The psychology of animal learning.** London: Academic Press, 1974.

McLaurin, W. A. Postirradiation saccharin avoidance in rats as a function of the interval between ingestion and exposure. **Journal of Comparative and Physiological Psychology,** 1964, **57,** 316-317.

Pavlov, I. P. **Conditioned reflexes.** Oxford: Oxford University Press, 1927.

Perkins, C. C. The relation of secondary reward to gradients of reinforcement. **Journal of Experimental Psychology,** 1947, **37,** 377-392.

Petrinovich, L., & Bolles, R. Delayed alternation: Evidence for symbolic processes in the rat. **Journal of Comparative and Physiological Psychology,** 1957, **50,** 363-365.

Petrinovich, L., Bradford, D., & McGaugh, J. C. Drug facilitation of memory in rats. **Psychonomic Science,** 1965, **2,** 191-192.

Pschirrer, M. E. Goal events as discriminative stimuli over extended intertrial intervals. **Journal of Experimental Psychology,** 1972, **96,** 425-432.

Rescorla, R. A., & Wagner, A. R. A theory of Pavlovian conditioning: Variations in the effectiveness of reinforcement and nonreinforcement. In A. H. Black & W. F. Prokasy (Eds.), **Classical conditioning II.** New York: Appleton-Century-Crofts, 1972.

Revusky, S. H. Aversion to sucrose produced by contingent X-irradiation: Temporal and dosage parameters. **Journal of Comparative and Physiological Psychology,** 1968, **65,** 17-22.

Revusky, S. H. The role of interference in association over a delay. In W. K. Honig & P. H. R. James (eds.), **Animal memory.** New York: Academic Press, 1971.

Revusky, S. H. Long-delay learning in rats: A black-white discrimination. **Bulletin of the Psychonomic Society,** 1974, **4,** 526-528.

Revusky, S. H. Learning as a general process with an emphasis on data from feeding experiments. In N. W. Milgram, L. Krames, & T. M. Alloway (Eds.), **Food aversion learning.** New York: Plenum Press, in press.

Revusky, S. H., & Bedarf, E. W. Association of illness with ingestion of novel foods. **Science,** 1967, **155,** 219-220.

Revusky, S. H., & Garcia, J. Learned associations over long delays. In G. H. Bower & J. T. Spence (Eds.), **The psychology of learning and motivation.** (Vol. 4). New York: Academic Press, 1970.

Revusky, S. H., Taukulis, H. K., & Peddle, C. Learned associations between pentobarbital sedation and later lithium sickness in rats. **Pharmacology, Biochemistry and Behavior,** in press.

Roberts, W. A. Failure to replicate visual discrimination learning with a 1-min delay of reward. **Learning and Motivation,** 1976, **7,** 313-325.

Smith, J. C., & Roll, D. L. Trace conditioning with X-rays as an aversive stimulus. **Psychonomic Science,** 1967, **9,** 11-12.

Spence, K. W. **Behavior theory and conditioning.** New Haven, Connecticut: Yale University Press, 1956.

St. Claire-Smith, R. Blocking of punishment. Paper presented at Eastern Psychological Association, Atlantic City, 1970.

Tinklepaugh, O. L. Multiple delayed reactions with chimpanzees and monkeys. **Journal of Comparative and Physiological Psychology,** 1932, **13,** 207-243.

Tyler, D. W., Wortz, E. C., & Bitterman, M. E. The effect of random and alternating partial reinforcement on resistance to extinction in the rat. **American Journal of Psychology,** 1953, **66,** 57-65.

Wagner, A. R., & Rescorla, R. A. Inhibition in Pavlovian conditioning: Application of a theory. In R. A. Boakes & M. S. Halliday (Eds.), **Inhibition and learning.** New York: Academic Press, 1972.

Wagner, A. R., Rudy, J. W., & Whitlow, J. W. Rehearsal in animal conditioning. **Journal of Experimental Psychology,** 1973, **97,** 407-426.

Weinstock, S. Acquisition and extinction of a partially reinforced running response at a 24-hour intertrial interval. **Journal of Experimental Psychology,** 1958, **56,** 151-158.

NON-GUSTATORY ASPECTS
OF
FOOD AVERSION
LEARNING

XV

THE CONTRIBUTION OF ENVIRONMENTAL NON-INGESTIVE CUES IN CONDITIONING WITH AVERSIVE INTERNAL CONSEQUENCES

PHILLIP J. BEST
University of Virginia

MICHAEL R. BEST
Southern Methodist University

SCOTT HENGGELER
Memphis State University

The experiments discussed in this chapter differ from the majority of experiments on toxicosis conditioning in several respects. First, the conditioned stimuli used were non-ingestive environmental (visual and tactile) as opposed to gustatory and olfactory. Second, the cues were not always presented to the animals during consummatory behavior and, hence, the extent of conditioning was measured on the basis of changes in locomotor behavior, or indirectly by measuring the effects of these stimuli on conditioned aversion of taste stimuli in higher-order conditioning and blocking paradigms.

The experiments were carried out specifically to determine under what conditions the rat could learn aversions to non-ingestive environmental cues, such as tactile and visual stimuli paired with toxicosis. However, at a more fundamental level, the studies formed part of a research program designed to determine the extent to which Pavlovian conditioning principles could be applied to the toxicosis conditioning paradigm.

SELECTIVITY OF ASSOCIATIONS

One traditional principle of classical conditioning holds that "any agent in nature which acts on any adequate receptor apparatus of an organism can be made into a conditioned stimulus for that organism" (Pavlov, 1927, p. 38). Pavlov demonstrated that many fac-

371

tors affected the ease with which one or another stimuli could be conditioned. Such factors include the strength of the conditioned stimulus (CS), the strength of the unconditioned stimulus (UCS), temporal contiguity, the animal's past history, and other parameters of the conditioning procedures. However, it appears that Pavlov did not recognize the possibility that one stimulus may be more readily conditioned (or more salient) than another stimulus when paired with one UCS but less associable when paired with another UCS. Although Pavlov did not explicitly discuss the issue of the selective associability of certain CSs with specific UCSs, his writing implies the absence of such selectivity. This is especially surprising when one considers that Pavlov worked with a variety of CSs and UCSs. For example, he reported on apomorphine- and morphine-induced retching responses and their ability to condition aversive and retching behavior toward food and toward the appearance and touch of the experimenter (Pavlov, 1927, p. 36).

BELONGINGNESS: THE RELATIONSHIP OF CUE TO CONSEQUENCE

The issue of the selectivity of associations between stimuli was introduced by Thorndike (1932) with regard to the "belongingness" of certain words and sentences in human learning and memory. However, the issue was simply not addressed in the animal learning literature until very recently. In fact, a theme running through the Pavlovian conditioning literature is that some stimuli are inherently more salient than others, independent of the particular UCS employed during conditioning. For example, modern mathematical formulations of the laws of classical conditioning use a single parameter for the salience of the CS, ignoring the possibility that the value of the salience parameter may indeed be dependent on the nature of the UCS employed (e.g., Mackintosh, 1975; Rescorla & Wagner, 1972).

The first clear demonstration that the salience of a particular cue is related to the nature of the UCS with which it is paired was reported by Garcia and Koelling (1966). In this classic study, rats were given the opportunity to drink "bright-noisy-tasty" fluid. Each lap of the fluid was accomplished by a flash of light, a click, and the taste of saccharin. Animals which were given footshock following consumption showed aversion to the visual and auditory cues but not to the taste cues. Animals experiencing toxicosis following consumption showed aversion to the taste but not to the visual and auditory cues. The results were quite striking. The animals did not merely show stronger conditioning to one or the other set of cues, dependent on the UCS; rather, they showed no aversion at all to taste cues if they experienced footshock and no aversion to audio-visual cues if they experienced toxicosis. It thus appeared that the relationship between cue and consequence was all-or-none. Certain cues could easily be conditioned with certain consequences whereas other cues could not be so conditioned.

Overshadowing. One possibility for the apparent all-or-none nature of these results is that the more salient cues simply overshadowed the less salient cues in each UCS condition. The principle of overshadowing was introduced by Pavlov (1927, p. 141) and has been shown to operate in taste-toxicosis conditioning (Lindsey & Best, 1973). When two cues of markedly different salience are presented in compound in a conditioning procedure, the less salient stimulus shows much weaker conditioning than it would if the more salient cue was absent. However, the more salient event can show the same speed and strength of conditioning in compound as it would in the absence of the less salient stimulus. In fact, the more salient cue can so strongly overshadow the weaker stimulus that the latter might show no evidence of conditioning under the most sensitive tests, even if it would readily condition in the absence of the other cue.

In order to determine if the all-or-none results of Garcia and Koelling (1966) resulted from overshadowing, Domjan and Wilson (1972) replicated this study with one important change. During conditioning they presented the animals with either auditory or taste cues, individually. They thus eliminated the possibility of overshadowing. The results were virtually identical to those reported by Garcia and Koelling (1966). Even in the absence of taste cues during conditioning, the animals showed no aversion to auditory stimuli paired with toxicosis, but showed strong conditioning of the auditory cues when paired with electric shock. Likewise, in the absence of auditory stimuli the animals showed no aversion to taste events paired with electric shock, but showed strong conditioning of the taste cues when paired with toxicosis. The results were again all-or-none. Therefore, the strong specificity of the relationship of cue to consequence could not be attributed to overshadowing. Clearly, the rat's ability to withhold consummatory behavior in the presence of certain cues was significantly determined by the specific UCS employed.

PREPAREDNESS

The results of experiments such as those described above led to a reapplication of Thorndike's principle of belongingness to the animal literature, most notably by Seligman (1970). According to

373

Seligman, rats are evolutionarily "prepared" to associate gastrointestinal distress, or other toxic postingestional cues, with the taste and odor properties of ingested substances, and are likewise prepared to associate peripheral pain with immediately preceding auditory, visual and tactile cues. But they are "contraprepared" to associate "external" cues with "internal" consequences, and likewise contraprepared to associate internal cues with external consequences. Although the concept of preparedness can be considered as a continuum, with different CS-UCS combinations showing different degrees of preparedness to become associated, the compelling all-or-none nature of the above studies has led some to conclude that it is a dichotomy: cues are either prepared or contraprepared to be associated with particular UCSs (e.g., Garcia, Hankins, & Rusiniak, 1974).

The apparent all-or-none nature of the relationship of cue to consequences has also led to the speculation that taste-toxicosis conditioning is of a diffeent form and hence cannot be incorporated into the general laws of learning (e.g., Rozin & Kalat, 1971; Seligman, 1970). Clearly, Pavlov did not entertain the possibility of the nature of the UCS differentially affecting the associability of the various CSs, and modern formulations of laws of classical conditioning do not consider the effects of such preparedness. However, one need only add a new parameter to the laws of classical conditioning to accommodate the concept. The salience parameter has to be replaced with, or multiplied by, a variable. Salience, then, would be determined by not only the physical strength of the CS, but also the preparedness of that CS to be associated with the UCS in the experiment. If preparedness were a dichotomy, the salience parameter would be multiplied by a certain value (say 1) for prepared conditions and by zero for contraprepared conditions. If stimuli of intermediate saliences are found, the salience variable would be multiplied by a value between 0 and 1.[1]

THE CONDITIONABILITY OF NON-INGESTIVE CUES WITH TOXICOSIS

Our initial concern with the conditionability of exteroceptive cues with toxicosis came about quite by accident. In some of our early studies we used injections of apomorphine to induce toxicosis. We chose apomorphine because its action on brainstem emetic centers was well known (Wang & Borison, 1952), and because injected animals showed obvious signs of toxicosis. In one study, we gave control saline injections interspersed with

374

apomorphine injections and noticed that some of the animals showed signs of toxicosis following the saline injections. It appeared that the cues associated with handling and immobilization of the animals as well as the discomfort of the injection were being conditioned to the apomorphine-induced toxicosis. Certainly, these cues are quite intense and somewhat noxious in their own right. Could innocuous cues not normally associated with ingestion be so conditioned as well, and if so, under what conditions? It occurred to us that the previous difficulty of demonstrating associations between exteroceptive cues and toxicosis could have been due to overshadowing by oral cues present at some point in the experiments. Domjan and Wilson (1972) had been careful not to present taste cues together with auditory cues, but their animals did experience a host of stimuli normally associated with ingestion during the presence of the auditory CS. If the ingestive cues present during conditioning were familiar to the animal, they should be reduced in salience and perhaps be less likely to overshadow the exteroceptive cues. [Such latent inhibition has been shown to operate in classical conditioning (e.g., Lubow & Moore, 1959; Reiss & Wagner, 1972) and in taste-toxicosis conditioning (e.g., Ahlers & Best, 1971; Best, 1975; Kalat & Rozin, 1973; Revusky & Bedarf, 1967).] However, the oral ingestive cues may be inherently so much more salient than the exteroceptive cues that even after extensive familiarization they could still overshadow the auditory cues. Further, there was sufficient precedent in the literature suggesting that conditions existed whereby external cues could become associated with toxicosis. Garcia, Kimeldorf, and Hunt (1957) noted, for example (see also Garcia, Kimeldorf, & Hunt, 1961), that rats could learn to avoid a distinct environmental compartment if these cues were concomitant with x-irradiation-induced illness. Such conditioning, however, was relatively slow in developing compared to the rapidity of learning shown to taste cues paired with toxicosis.

CONDITIONING AVERSIONS TO DISTINCT
ENVIRONMENTS WITH APOMORPHINE

Our first study investigated the degree to which rats could form conditioned aversions to environmental visual-tactile cues presented prior to apomorphine-induced toxicosis, and the degree to which oral and taste cues and drinking behavior interfered with such conditioning (Best, Best, & Mickley, 1973). Since rats normally show a high preference for a black compartment over a white one (Allison, Larson, & Jensen, 1967), we chose to investigate con-

375

ditioning to a compartment with black walls and a grid floor. The adjoining compartment had white walls and a solid white floor.

Method. On Days 1, 2, and 3, five groups of 10 male Sprague-Dawley rats were restricted to the white compartment for 30 min. They had access to a drinking tube containing water but had no access to the black compartment. On Day 4 each animal was placed in the white compartment for 2 min, followed immediately by placement in the black compartment for 2 min. The rats were then removed from the black compartment, injected with apomorphine (15 mg/kg, intraperitoneal), and returned to their home cages. One group received access to water in drinking tubes in both compartments on the conditioning trials. Two groups received access to a saccharin-sodium solution (.15%) in both compartments. One group received no fluid. (A Control group received access to water in both compartments, but was injected with an equivalent-by-volume dose of saline instead of apomorphine.) All five groups had a second conditioning trial 6 hr later. On Day 5 the partition

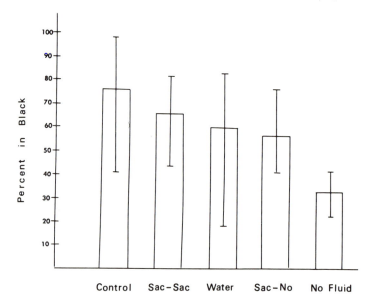

Figure 1
Median and total range of percent of time spent in black compartment for unpoisoned control animals and poisoned animals that were given saccharin, water or no fluid in black and white compartments during training and testing. (Note that the Sac-No group received saccharin during training and no fluid during testing.) (From Best, Best, & Mickley, 1973)

separating the compartments was removed and each animal was given 30 min access to both compartments. The No-fluid group and one of the saccharin groups (Sac-No) received no fluid on the test day. The Water and Control groups received access to water in both compartments, and the other saccharin group (Sac-Sac) received access to saccharin in both compartments.

Results. All experimental groups spent significantly less time in the black compartment than the unpoisoned Control group. Further, the No Fluid group spent significantly less time in the black compartment than the other experimental groups. The Water, Sac-Sac, and Sac-No groups did not differ (see Figure 1).

The Control group consumed slightly (but not significantly) more total fluid than the Sac-Sac and Water groups during the Day 5 test. Since each animal spent different amounts of time in each compartment, comparisons of drinking rates required that the total amount consumed in each compartment be divided by the amount of time spent there. Figure 2 shows the number of ml consumed

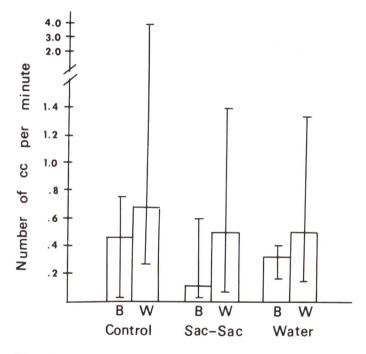

Figure 2
Median and total range of the rate of consumption (cc/min) for groups in the black (B) and white (W) compartments during testing. (From Best, Best, & Mickley, 1973)

377

per min in each compartment. All three groups showed higher drinking rates in the white compartments than in the black. This difference was not significant for the Control group, but was significant for the Sac-Sac and Water groups. The groups did not differ in drinking rate in the white compartment, but the Control group drank at a significantly higher rate in the black compartment than the Sac-Sac group. The Water group drank at an intermediate rate in the black compartment, not quite significantly different from the other groups.

The results of this experiment indicate that rats can associate visual and tactile environmental cues with toxicosis and can demonstrate that aversion by modifying their locomotive behavior. Although previous studies have shown that rats can learn to avoid a place (Garcia, Kimeldorf, & Hunt, 1957) or drinking vessel (Rozin, 1969) paired with toxicosis, in these experiments the animals either experienced toxicosis in the presence of the to-be-conditioned cues or required a large number of trials to demonstrate conditioning. In the present study, the animals were injected with apomorphine following removal from the black compartment (i.e., they did not experience toxicosis in the presence of the CS) and learned an aversion following only two conditioning trials.

The Role of Ingestion. The results also show that the presence of oral or taste cues and concomitant drinking behavior interfere with the avoidance of the black compartment. This interference is not due to performance variables operating in the testing session since the Sac-No group, which had no opportunity to drink during the test session, showed the same willingness to enter the black compartment as the Sac-Sac and water groups. This interference occurred even though the same oral and taste cues were present in both compartments, and therefore could not operate as discriminative stimuli. We would guess that if the taste and oral cues had served as discriminative stimuli, they would have caused even more interference with visual-tactile avoidance behavior and might have totally masked it.

Previous investigators may have had difficulties conditioning rats to avoid visual, auditory, and tactile cues paired with toxicosis because the cues were presented to the animals while they engaged in consummatory behavior. It is possible that a rat experiencing toxicosis is more biased to backscan in memory for cues normally related to ingestion. Alternately, during consummatory behavior, a rat may be more attentive to cues normally related to ingestion, and therefore more likely to hold them in memory, ready to become as-

378

sociated with significant consequences. Clearly, the act of drinking does not totally bias the rat's attention toward taste and smell and away from visual and auditory cues. Garcia and Koelling's animals attended to all the cues of the bright-noisy-tasty water. If they had not, they would not have been able to form an aversion to the audio-visual cues when given electric shock. It appears that the nature of the UCS determines selection of specific events in memory with which to become associated. But it also appears that the nature of the recent memories scanned is affected by the particular responses the animal has made prior to the UCS. We are suggesting that an animal experiencing toxicosis scans memory first for cues which are normally related to consummatory behavior. If the rat has recently engaged in ingestion, it will be less likely to scan cues related to other behaviors, such as locomotion. On the other hand, if the animal has not recently engaged in consummatory behaviors, it is more able to scan in memory for cues normally related to other responses that it has recently made.

Interaction of UCS and CR. It can be inferred from much of the literature in classical conditioning that the degree of success one finds in conditioning and the apparent speed of conditioning are dependent on the particular conditioned response (CR) one chooses to investigate. This principle has also been demonstrated in avoidance learning (Bolles, 1970). The more similar the required avoidance response is to the animal's repertoire of species-specific defense reactions, the easier it is for the animal to learn that response. However, we are suggesting something different: that an interaction between the UCS and the CR determines which cues are selected to become CSs. With few exceptions (Domjan, 1973; Shettleworth, 1972), this particular role of the CR has received little attention in the classical conditioning literature, the operant conditioning literature, or in discussion of preparedness. The cues which are processed by the animal during conditioning may be selected as a function of the responses occurring at the time of conditioning. Consummatory behavior is most readily associated with changes in taste, and with tactile and temperature changes on the tongue, and to a lesser degree to smells (cf. Testa & Ternes, this volume). Since changes in illumination and sound are not strongly related to consummatory behavior in the rat, the animal is less likely to form strong associations with these cues when poisoned after drinking.[2]

LONG-DELAY CONDITIONING WITH NON-INGESTIVE CSs AND TOXIN UCSs.

Although the concept of preparedness has provided some difficulty for treating taste-toxicosis conditioning under several traditional principles of classical conditioning, another issue has contributed even more to the isolation of the taste-toxicosis conditioning literature from the rest of the literature in classical conditioning. The observation that taste aversions can be learned even if toxicosis is delayed for several hours after taste exposure seems to contradict the Pavlovian principle of temporal contiguity. According to Pavlov (1927), "a first and most essential requisite for the formation of a new conditioned reflex lies in the coincidence in time of action of any previously neutral stimulus with some definite unconditioned stimulus" (p. 27). Although Pavlov demonstrated that the to-be-conditioned stimulus did not have to be physically present at the time of onset of the UCS, he found that the longer the delay between CS termination and UCS presentation, the weaker the resultant conditioning. In fact, any delay between CS termination and UCS onset (i.e., trace conditioning) resulted in substantially weaker conditioning than when the CS terminated with UCS onset or persisted during UCS presentation. Trace conditioning in traditional tone-shock paradigms is virtually impossible to establish with traces of several minutes (e.g., Kamin, 1965). Clearly, then, the ability of rats to learn aversions to tastes presented hours before toxicosis in only one conditioning trial demonstrates a qualitative difference between such conditioning and classical conditioning. Or does it? A number of investigators (e.g., Garcia, Ervin, & Koelling, 1966; Kalat & Rozin, 1971; Smith & Roll, 1967) have convincingly shown that a delay of reinforcement gradient exists in taste-toxicosis conditioning (i.e., the longer the delay between taste experience and toxicosis, the weaker the resultant aversion to those tastes). The only major difference between their data and the predictions from classical conditioning theory was a parametric one: the time scale was greatly lengthened.

Since the differences in the delay of reinforcement gradient might be merely parametric, it seems reasonable to investigate the source of the difference. Perhaps taste stimuli can be conditioned with longer delays than auditory, visual, and tactile cues regardless of the UCS, and, similarly, perhaps toxicosis can support conditioning of more distal traces than electric shock regardless of the nature of the CSs. Conditioning of auditory, visual, and tactile cues with electric shock would then require close temporal contiguity; conditioning of tastes with toxicosis would be possible with very long interstimulus intervals; and conditioning of tastes with electric shock or of external cues with toxicosis would be possible with intermediate intervals.

380

Method. We designed the present experiment to determine if conditioned aversions of environmental tactile-visual cues could be established with lithium-induced toxicosis under delay conditions longer than those normally found in studies using electric shock as the UCS but shorter than those found in taste-toxicosis conditioning (Henggeler, 1974). Eight groups (n = 9) of male Sprague-Dawley-derived rats were trained in an apparatus similar to the one used in the previous study. The walls and ceiling of the chamber were of clear acrylic plastic. Either compartment could be made dark or light by placing black posterboard or white translucent acrylic outside the clear plastic walls. The dark compartment had a smooth black acrylic floor and served as the poison chamber. The safe, light chamber had a grid floor. Each physical compartment served as a different cue compartment on different trials by rearrangement of the exterior black or white panels.

On Days 1, 3, 5, 7, 9, and 11, each animal was placed in the light compartment, and its latency to enter the dark compartment was measured. If the animal did not enter the dark compartment in 600 sec, it was placed there by hand. The rat was then confined to the dark compartment for 2 min and returned to its home cage. Six independent groups were given injections of lithium (20 cc/kg isotonic, intraperitoneal) ½ min, 2 min, 5 min, 10 min, 20 min, or 4 hr following removal from the dark compartment. A Saline group received injections of saline (equivalent-by-volume, isotonic) ½ min after removal from the dark compartment, and a -4 hr group received lithium four hr before each trial. On Days 2, 4, 6, 8, and 10 the animals were placed in the dark compartment and their latencies to enter the light compartment were recorded.

Results. All groups receiving lithium injections within 20 min of removal from the dark compartment showed some evidence of conditioning. The response latencies are shown in Figure 3. The ½ min, 2 min, and 5 min groups showed strong conditioning. The latencies of the ½ min, 2 min and 5 min groups to enter the dark compartment on Day 11 were, (a) significantly longer than their latencies on Day 1, (b) significantly longer than their latencies to exit the dark compartment on Day 10, and (c) significantly longer than the latencies of the 10 min, 20 min, 4 hr, -4 hr, and Saline groups to enter the dark compartment on Day 11.

The 10 min and 20 min groups showed much weaker conditioning. Following an initial decrease in latency to enter the dark compartment on Days 3 and 5, they showed an increase in latency. Their latency to enter the dark compartment on Day 11 was, (a) significantly longer than their latency on Day 3 and on Day 5, (b)

381

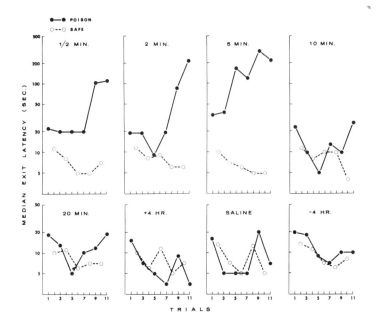

Figure 3
Median latency to enter the black compartment on poison days
(0———0) and the white compartment on safe days (0 - - 0) for
each group.

significantly longer than the latency of the Saline group on Day 11,
and (c) significantly longer than their latency to exit the dark compartment on Day 10. There was no difference among groups in
latency to enter the dark compartment on Day 1 or to exit on Day 2,
and there was no difference in latency between Day 1 and Day 2 for
any group. The -4 hr, Saline, and 4 hr groups all showed reduced
latencies to enter the dark compartment over training but these reductions were not significant. Further, they showed no difference
between latency to enter the dark compartment on Day 11 and to
exit on Day 10. All groups showed a reduced latency to exit the
dark compartment during training. However, the differences
between Day 2 and Day 10 latencies were significant only for the 2
min, 5 min, 10 min, and 20 min groups.

The pattern of results shows clear evidence for strong conditioning in groups that received lithium injections within 5 min of removal from the dark chamber and much weaker evidence of conditioning in the groups receiving injections 10 and 20 min later.
Perhaps if we had continued the training for a few additional trials,
the 10 and 20 min groups would have shown stronger condition-

ing. The intermediate latencies of the 10 min and 20 min groups on Days 9 and 11 were due, in part, to the fact that some of the animals were well conditioned, but others showed virtually no evidence of conditioning. With the exception of the 5 min group, no group had longer latency to enter the dark compartment on Day 7 than on Day 1. In fact, the trend was in the opposite direction. That is, with the exception of the 5 min group, no group showed any evidence of conditioning until Day 9, following four lithium injections.

Predicting Conditioning Over a Delay. It seems, then, that long-delay conditioned avoidance of tactile-visual environmental cues with toxicosis is much more difficult to establish than conditioned aversions to tastes with toxicosis, requires more trials, closer temporal contiguity, and the absence of consummatory behavior.[3] Further, we should note that we have never been able to find any evidence of conditioned avoidance of the dark compartment in animals given intense footshock in a different chamber, even if the animals were shocked immediately following removal from the dark compartment. Nor have we been able to find evidence of such conditioning in the literature. Should we therefore conclude that traces of tactile-visual cues are more prepared to be associated with toxicosis than with footshock? Rats can easily learn to withhold approach behavior to an environment with distinct tactile and visual cues if shocked immediately following that approach behavior. They also seem more prepared for this association than for the association of tactile-visual cues and immediate toxicosis. But if the animals are confined to the distinct chamber for 2 min and suffer noxious consequences upon removal from that environment, they are better able to associate the tactile-visual cues with toxicosis than with footshock. The apparent preparedness of certain cues to become associated with certain consequences, then, appears to be dependent not only on the nature of the cues and the consequences, but also on the interval separating them.

Since avoidance of tactile-visual environmental cues can be conditioned with toxicosis over delays intermediate between those found in environmental cue-shock conditioning and taste-toxicosis conditioning, it might be interesting to examine the possibility of establishing taste aversions with electric shock and looking at the effects of different UCS delays. Such an experiment has been reported by Krane and Wagner (1975). They presented rats with 30 sec access to fluids with different cue properties, either saccharin, light-tone, or no cue. One of the cues was presented on each of three consecutive days, in counterbalanced order. On the third day, fluid access was followed by a 4 ma footshock. The footshock was delayed either 5 sec, 30 sec, or 210 sec following consumption. So each of the nine groups received footshock at one of three delays following one of the three cue conditions. The animals were then tested for suppression of licking during presentation of the light-tone cue or saccharin. On the light-tone test, suppression of licking was greatest in animals which received shock 5 sec following light-tone licking, less in the 30 sec delay condition, and least in the 210 sec group. On the saccharin test, no greater suppression occurred for animals given shock 5 sec after saccharin licking than for the animals given shock 5 sec after light-tone licking or in the no-cue condition. However, the animals in the 30 sec and 210 sec delay conditions showed strong conditioning. Taken together, these results indicate that the light-tone cues are better prepared to be associated with 5 sec delayed shock than is saccharin, but saccharin is better prepared to be associated with 210 sec delayed shock than are the light-tone cues. Whereas our study showed that contiguity affects the preparedness of a specific set of cues to be conditioned with different UCSs, Krane and Wagner showed that contiguity affects the preparedness of different sets of cues to be conditioned with one specific UCS. The long taste-toxicosis intervals which initially seemed contrary to classical conditioning principles are explained, then, by the ability of taste CSs to extend the functional CS-US interval beyond that provided by visual or tactile CSs, and by the ability of toxicosis to support conditioning with delays longer than those supported by electric shock.

TESTING THE STRENGTH OF EXTERNAL CUE-TOXIN CONDITIONING

Our success in conditioning non-ingestive CSs with toxin UCSs led us to consider other ways in which conditioning of these exteroceptive cues with toxicosis could affect behavior. Two problems we investigated in this context were the effectiveness of non-ingestive cues in conditioning higher-order taste aversions and in establishing "blocking," the phenomenon first described by Kamin (1969). This work and that of Mitchell and his colleagues (e.g., Mitchell, Kirschbaum, & Perry, 1975) on the contribution of non-ingestive cues in the conditioning of aversions to food are summarized in the following sections as examples of applications of this paradigm.

Since visual-tactile cues are not as easily conditioned with toxicosis as taste cues, one might wonder if they are ever very strongly conditioned. One test of the strength of conditioning is to determine if a stimulus can serve as a conditioned reinforcer for another stimulus in a higher-order conditioning paradigm. Pavlov (1927, p. 33) held that such secondary conditioned reflexes could be established with strongly conditioned stimuli. The next experiment investigated the capacity of non-ingestional environmental tactile-visual cues to modify the ingestion of saccharin or saline solutions in a higher-order conditioning paradigm (Best, Best, & Mickley, 1973).

Method. Ten male Sprague-Dawley rats were trained in an apparatus identical to that used in the first experiment with the exception that both the black and white compartments had solid floors. On each day the animals received 20 min access to water in a familiar drinking cage approximately 6 hr after the experimental manipulation. On Day 1 the animals were allowed to explore both compartments for 15 min, and their time in each was recorded. On Days 2-6 each animal was confined to the black compartment for 2 min, injected with apomorphine (15 mg/kg, i.p.), and returned to the black compartment for one hour to assure stong conditioning. On Day 7 the rats were given a saline injection and placed in the black compartment for 10 min with water available. The amount consumed was recorded and the water was then removed. Finally, the animals were injected with apomorphine and confined to the black compartment for an additional hour.

During second-order conditioning, the animals were first given access to saccharin (n = 5) or saline (n = 5) for 2 min in a familiar drinking cage, placed in the safe white compartment for 10 min, and returned to their home cage. On the following day, the rats were given access to the other fluid for 2 min in the familiar drinking cage, placed in the black compartment for 10 min, and returned to their home cage. On the next day all subjects were given a 15 min two-bottle choice test between saline and saccharin followed by a 15 min preference test for the black and white compartments.

Results. Initially the animals showed a preference for the black compartment, spending 60% of their time there. Following conditioning every animal showed a reduction in time spent in the black compartment (mean time = 29%) indicating that a conditioned avoidance of the black compartment had been established. Second, following initial conditioning, every animal showed reduced drink-

385

ing in the black compartment. Further, when the black compartment was employed as a conditioned reinforcer in the taste-aversion paradigm, the taste associated with the black was never preferred. There was no overlap in taste preference between groups. These data indicate that apomorphine-induced toxicosis is effective in creating a learned toxiphobia for environmental tactile-visual cues which is potent enough for these cues to operate as conditioned reinforcers in a one-trial taste-aversion procedure. Another point made by these results is that our initial concern about the possible somatic pain of apomorphine causing the aversions in our first study was ill-founded, unless one wishes to assume that such pain can be effective in establishing higher-order taste aversions through environmental conditioned reinforcers.

BLOCKING

Another test of the strength of conditioning of visual-tactile cues with toxicosis would be to determine if such conditioning could block subsequent taste-toxicosis conditioning. The phenomenon of blocking was first described by Kamin (1969). He showed that in a conditioned suppression task a well-conditioned stimulus (such as light), when presented on later conditioning trials in compound with a new stimulus (such as a tone), would prevent or block the new stimulus from acquiring conditioned properties. He reasoned that when the UCS was reliably predicted by the light it lost the capacity to endow the new stimulus with conditioned properties. Successful blocking depends on the strength of conditioning of the first stimulus. The more strongly that stimulus is conditioned, the more reliably it predicts the presentation of the UCS and consequently blocks the conditioning of any new stimulus. Blocking has been demonstrated in a variety of conditioning situations (e.g., Vom Saal & Jenkins, 1970; Marchant & Moore, 1973), including taste-toxicosis conditioning (Best, Best, & Rudy, 1975; Revusky, 1971).

Since blocking requires strong conditioning of the first stimulus, it provides a good test for the strength of conditioning of tactile-visual cues with toxicosis. In a recent study we asked if the pairing of tactile-visual cues with toxicosis could block future saccharin toxicosis conditioning (Rudy, Iwens, & Best, in press). The study is a complex one and, in the interest of space, will not be described in detail here. However, to illustrate the thrust of the study, we will briefly review one of the experiments. Rats were given two trials, each consisting of placement in a black, smooth-floor compartment for 5 min, followed by an injection of lithium chloride and replacement in their home cages. A control group received equivalent lithium injections. All animals were then placed in the black compartment, removed and given a brief exposure to saccharin, injected with lithium, and returned to their home cages. When later given a two-bottle saccharin water choice test, the experimental rats showed a significantly reduced aversion to the saccharin compared to the controls. Thus, conditioning of the tactile-visual cues blocked conditioning of the saccharin.

Interestingly, the control condition in this study closely follows a procedure that has previously been found to retard saccharin conditioning. There are reports in the literature that prior lithium injections, supposedly in the absence of distinct cues, retard subsequent taste-toxicosis conditioning (e.g., Braveman, 1975; Cannon, Berman, Baker, & Atkinson, 1975). This toxicosis preexposure retardation effect has been attributed to pharmacological causes, such as drug tolerance (e.g., Riley, Jacobs, & LoLordo, 1976; for other explanations see Gamzu, Braveman, this volume). However our current study suggests that the toxicosis preexposure effect may be due in large part to blocking of taste-toxicosis conditioning by prior exteroceptive conditioning. We feel that when the animals experience a novel taste followed by lithium injections, they also experience handling, immobilization, and brief pain associated with the injection. Since these cues have already been experienced prior to toxicosis, they reliably predict it and therefore block association of the toxicosis with the new taste cues.

TOXICOSIS-INDUCED AVERSIONS TO FOOD CONTAINERS

The external cue-toxin paradigm has also been extensively analyzed in investigations of toxin-induced aversions to food containers (e.g., Mitchell, Kirschbaum, & Perry, 1975; Nachman, Rauschenberger, & Ashe, this volume; Revusky & Parker, 1976). Mitchell, Scott, and Williams (1973) showed that rats are reluctant to consume familiar food from a novel container, much like rats hesitate to consume novel foods (see Domjan, this volume, for a review of several issues concerning ingestional neophobia). In addition, Mitchell, Kirschbaum, and Perry (1975) demonstrated that rats poisoned after eating from a novel food container in a highly familiar environment will avoid familiar food from the novel source on a subsequent test. These animals will not, however, avoid the familiar food in the novel container if ingestion occurred in a less familiar environment prior to the induction of illness. This result is consonant with the repeated demonstration of the importance of novelty in taste-toxicosis conditioning in the rat (e.g.,

Ahlers & Best, 1971; Revusky & Bedarf, 1968). In fact, the effect of familiarization on the willingness of rats to consume previously novel tastes and on the salience of those tastes in a taste-toxicosis paradigm has led to the conclusion that during safe exposure to a novel taste, the animal actively learns that the solution is safe (Kalat & Rozin, 1973). However, this "learned safety" has been shown to be a passive process, much like the "latent inhibition" that results from nonreinforced preexposure of a conditioned stimulus in classical conditioning (Best, 1975; see also Best & Barker, this volume).

Mitchell et al. (1975) also demonstrated that rats given different amounts of familiarization to two containers will form an aversion to the more novel container even if poisoned following eating at the more familiar. This indicates that nonassociative (sensitization) as well as associative processes may be critical to a thorough understanding of the external cue-toxin paradigm in particular and the flavor-aversion phenomenon in general (see Domjan, this volume).

SUMMARY AND CONCLUSIONS

The results of the experiments reported here demonstrate that conditioned aversions to non-ingestional environmental-tactile-visual cues can be formed when these stimuli are paired with toxicosis. Such conditioning is less robust than taste-toxicosis conditioning and ingestional cue-toxicosis conditioning. It requires repeated trials, closer temporal contiguity between cue and toxicosis, and the absence of ingestional-related stimuli. Once established, however, the conditioned aversion to visual-tactile cues is robust enough for these cues to block conditioned taste aversion and to support second-order conditioning of taste aversions.

The results also have important implications for the concept of preparedness or belongingness and emphasize the importance of a preparedness dimension in classical conditioning. However, the dimension is a continuum and not all-or-none. Although non-ingestional environmental cues may be weakly prepared to become associated with toxicosis, they are not totally contraprepared, as had been suggested (Seligman, 1970). Also, ingestive, non-gustatory cues are intermediate in preparedness to become associated with toxicosis (see Footnote 1). The notion that preparedness is an all-or-none dimension also requires that stimuli can be reliably categorized into discrete, mutually exclusive classes. Such an assumption is difficult to justify, especially in the case of noxious

UCSs. Intense footshock no doubt causes many changes in the internal state of the animal, and many of the toxic agents used might cause strong stomach contractions resulting in pain. Further, the results indicate that the relative salience or preparedness of certain cues to become associated with specific UCSs is not an immutable consequence of the inherent properties of the cues and UCSs but can be affected by the past history of the animal at the time of an experiment, the responses the animal makes and consequent feedback, the temporal contiguity of the stimuli, and perhaps other parameters of the experiment.

Finally, we argue that taste-toxicosis conditioning is neither unique, nor different in kind from classical Pavlovian conditioning, but follows the same laws and principles governing classical conditioning, with slight modifications. First, the salience parameter must be multiplied by a preparedness variable dependent upon the CS, UCS, and CR, and the animal's past history with these stimuli and responses. Second, the functional relationship between temporal contiguity and strength of conditioning requires a different decay parameter for different types of CSs, UCSs, and perhaps CRs.

FOOTNOTES

[1]There is evidence that intermediate levels of preparedness exist. The chapter by Nachman, Rauschenberger, and Ashe in this volume shows that fluid temperature and tongue-tactile cues are less salient than tastes but more salient than visual cues when paired with toxicosis. Odor cues also appear to have intermediate levels of salience when paired with toxicosis (e.g., Hankins, Garcia, & Rusiniak, 1973; Kalat & Rozin, 1970; Lindsey & Best, 1973). Further, odor and taste cues can summate to form stimuli even more salient than taste alone (Best, Best, & Lindsey, 1976). Perhaps the intermediate levels of salience of these cues are due to intermediate levels of preparedness.

[2]Another issue that deserves mention is the applicability of the principles of operant conditioning to taste-toxicosis conditioning. We do not wish to dwell on that issue here, but it is important to recognize that, although the animal may first become classically conditioned to form negative or defensive emotional responses to stimuli associated with negative consequences, it has these stimuli under operant control during testing (Mowrer, 1947).

[3]Revusky and Parker (1976) have reported conditioned aversions to the appearance of a drinking cup in two trials during which the animals received lithium-induced toxicosis 30 min after drinking from the cup. Why, then, did we have such difficulty conditioning animals with a 20 min delay after five conditioning trials in the absence of drinking, especially when our first study showed that drinking behavior interfered with conditioning of visual-tactile cues? The answer is perhaps provided by the discussion of Nachman, Rauschenberger, and Ashe (this volume). They also were able to show conditioned aversions to a drinking cup as opposed to a drinking spout, with up to a 1 hr delayed toxicosis. They further showed that rats could not show an aversion to a white or black drinking cup but could show an aversion to drinking spouts with different size apertures. Their results indicate that rats learn aversions to a drinking source if the source provided differential tongue-tactile cues but could not learn an aversion if the source provided differential visual cues. Apparently, then, the successful long-delay conditioning found by Revusky and Parker was due to the differences in tongue-tactile cues between the cup and the spouts and not due to differences in visual cues.

For an analysis of the role of taste in mediating a light-lithium association within an operant procedure, see Morrison and Collyer (1974).

ACKNOWLEDGEMENTS

This research was supported primarily by U.S.P.H.S. grant MH 16478 to Phillip J. Best.

We would like to thank John Batson and Douglas Mook for their helpful comments on preliminary versions of the manuscript.

REFERENCES

Ahlers, R. H., & Best, P. J. Novelty and temporal contiguity in learned taste aversions. **Psychonomic Science,** 1971, **25,** 34-36.

Allison, J., Larson, D., & Jensen D. D. Acquired fear, brightness preference and one-way shuttlebox performance. **Psychonomic Science,** 1967, **8,** 269-270.

Best, M. R. Conditioned and latent inhibition in taste-aversion learning: Clarifying the role of learned safety. **Journal of Experimental Psychology: Animal Behavior Processes,** 1975, **1,** 97-113.

Best, P. J., Best, M. R., & Lindsey, G. P. The role of cue additivity in salience in taste aversion conditioning. **Learning and Motivation,** 1976, **7,** 254-264.

Best, P. J., Best, M. R., & Mickley, G. A. Conditioned aversion to distinct environmental stimuli resulting from gastrointestinal distress. **Journal of Comparative and Physiological Psychology,** 1973, **85,** 250-257.

Best, P. J., Best, M. R., & Rudy, J. W. Blocking in conditioned toxiphobia. Paper presented at the Sixteenth Annual Meeting of the Psychonomic Society, 1975.

Bolles, R. C. Species specific defense reactions and avoidance learning. **Psychological Review,** 1970, **77,** 32-48.

Braveman, N. S. Formation of taste aversions in rats following prior exposure to sickness. **Learning and Motivation,** 1975, **6,** 512-533.

Cannon, D. S., Berman, R. F., Baker, T. B., & Atkinson, C. A. Effects of preconditioning unconditioned stimulus experience on learned taste aversion. **Journal of Experimental Psychology: Animal Behavior Processes,** 1975, **1,** 270-284.

Domjan, M. Role of ingestion in odor-toxicosis learning in the rat. **Journal of Comparative and Physiological Psychology,** 1973, **84,** 507-521.

Domjan, M., & Wilson, N. E. Specificity of cue to consequence in taste-aversion learning in the rat. **Psychonomic Science,** 1972, **26,** 143-145.

Garcia, J., Ervin, F. R., & Koelling, R. A. Learning with prolonged delay of reinforcement. **Psychonomic Science,** 1966, **5,** 121-122.

Garcia, J., Hankins, W. G., & Rusiniak, K. W. Behavioral regulation of the milieu interne in man and rat. **Science,** 1974, **185,** 824-831.

Garcia, J., Kimeldorf, D. J., & Hunt, E. L. Spatial avoidance in the rat as a result of exposure to ionizing radiation. **British Journal of Radiation,** 1957, **30,** 318-322.

Garcia, J., Kimeldorf, D. J., & Hunt, E. L. The use of ionizing radiation as a motivating stimulus. **Psychological Review,** 1961, **68,** 383-395.

Garcia, J., & Koelling, R. A. Relation of cue to consequence in avoidance learning. **Psychonomic Science,** 1966, **4,** 123-124.

Hankins, W. J., Garcia, J., & Rusiniak, K. W. Dissociation of odor and taste in baitshyness. **Behavioral Biology,** 1973, **8,** 407-419.

Henggeler, S. Conditioned aversion to external stimuli resulting from delayed malaise. Paper presented at the proceedings of the Forty-fifth annual meeting of the Eastern Psychological Association, Philadelphia, 1974.

Kalat, J. W., & Rozin, P. "Learned safety" as a mechanism in long-delay taste-aversion learning in rats. **Journal of Comparative and Physiological Psychology,** 1973, **83,** 198-207.

Kalat, J. W., & Rozin, P. Role of interference in taste-aversion learning. **Journal of Comparative and Physiological Psychology,** 1971, **77,** 53-58.

Kalat, J. W., & Rozin, P. "Salience": A factor which can override temporal contiguity in taste-aversion learning. **Journal of Comparative and Physiological Psychology,** 1970, **71,** 192-197.

Kamin, L. J. Temporal and intensity characteristics of the conditioned stimulus. In W. F. Prokasy (Ed.), **Classical conditioning: A symposium.** New York: Appleton-Century-Crofts, 1965.

Kamin, L. J. Predictability, surprise, attention, and conditioning. In B. A. Campbell & R. M. Church (Eds.), **Punishment and aversive behavior.** New York: Appleton-Century-Crofts, 1969.

Krane, R. V., & Wagner, A. R. Taste aversion learning with delayed shock US: Implications for the "generality of the laws of learning." **Journal of Comparative and Physiological Psychology,** 1975, **88,** 882-889.

Lindsey, G. P., & Best, P. J. Overshadowing of the less salient of two novel fluids in a taste-aversion paradigm. **Physiological Psychology,** 1973, **1,** 13-15.

Lubow, R. E. Latent inhibition. **Psychological Bulletin,** 1973, **79,** 398-407.

Lubow, R. E., & Moore, A. U. Latent inhibition: The effect of non-reinforced preexposure to the conditional stimulus. **Journal of Comparative and Physiological Psychology,** 1959, **52,** 415-419.

Mackintosh, N. J. A theory of attention: Variations in the associability of stimuli with reinforcement. **Psychological Review,** 1975, **82,** 276-298.

Marchant, H. G., & Moore, J. W. Blocking of the rabbit's conditioned nictitating membrane response in Kamin's two-stage paradigm. **Journal of Experimental Psychology,** 1973, **101,** 155-158.

Mitchell, D., Kirschbaum, E. H., & Perry, R. L. Effects of neophobia and habituation on the poison-induced avoidance of exteroceptive stimuli in the rat. **Journal of Experimental Psychology: Animal Behavior Processes,** 1975, **1,** 47-55.

Mitchell, D., Scott, D. W., & Williams, K. D. Container neophobia and the rat's preference for earned food. **Behavioral Biology,** 1973, **9,** 613-624.

Morrison, G. R., & Collyer, R. Taste-mediated conditioned aversion to an exteroceptive stimulus following LiCl poisoning. **Journal of Comparative and Physiological Psychology,** 1974, **86,** 51-55.

Mowrer, O. H. On the dual nature of learning—a reinterpretation of "conditioning" and "problem solving." **Harvard Educational Review,** 1947, **17,** 102-148.

Pavlov, I. P. **Conditioned reflexes.** Oxford: Oxford University Press, 1927.

Reiss, S., & Wagner, A. R. CS habituation produces a "latent inhibition effect" but no active "conditioned inhibition." **Learning and Motivation,** 1972, **3,** 237-245.

Rescorla, R. A., & Wagner, A. R. A theory of Pavlovian conditioning: Variations in the effectiveness of reinforcement and nonreinforcement. In A. H. Black & W. F. Prokasy (Eds.), **Classical conditioning, II. Current research and theory.** New York: Appleton-Century-Crofts, 1972.

Revusky, S. H., & Bedarf, E. W. Association of illness with prior ingestion of novel foods. **Science,** 1967, **155,** 219-220.

Revusky, S., & Parker, L. A. Aversions to drinking out of a cup and to unflavored water produced by delayed sickness. **Journal of Experimental Psychology: Animal Behavior Processes,** 1976, **2,** 342-353.

Riley, A. L., Jacobs, W. J., & LoLordo, V. M. Drug exposure and the acquisition and retention of a conditioned taste aversion. **Journal of Comparative and Physiological Psychology,** 1976, **90,** 799-807.

Rozin, P. Central and peripheral mediation of learning with long CS-US intervals in the feeding system. **Journal of Comparative and Physiological Psychology,** 1969, **67,** 421-429.

Rozin, P., & Kalat, J. W. Specific hungers and poison avoidance as adaptive specializations of learning. **Psychological Review,** 1971, **28,** 459-486.

Rudy, J. W., Iwens, J., & Best, P. J. Pairing novel exteroceptive cues and illness reduce illness-induced taste aversions. **Journal of Experimental Psychology: Animal Behavior Processes,** in press.

Seligman, M. E. P. On the generality of the laws of learning. **Psychological Review,** 1970, **77,** 406-418.

Shettleworth, S. J. Constraints on learning. In D. S. Lehrman, R. A. Hinde, & E. Shaw (Eds.), **Advances in the study of behavior.** New York: Academic Press, 1972.

Smith, J. C., & Roll, D. L. Trace conditioning with x-rays as an aversive stimulus. **Psychonomic Science,** 1967, **9,** 11-12.

Sutherland, N. S., & Mackintosh, N. J. **Mechanisms of animal discrimination learning.** New York: Academic Press, 1971.

Thorndike, E. L. **Fundamentals of learning.** New York: Teachers College, 1932.

Vom Saal, W., & Jenkins, H. M. Blocking the development of stimulus control. **Learning and Motivation,** 1970, **1,** 52-64.

Wang, S. C., & Borison, H. L. A new concept of organization of the central emetic mechanism: Recent studies on the sites of action of apomorphine, copper sulfate, and cardiac glycosides. **Gastroenterology,** 1952, **22,** 1-11.

XVI

STUDIES OF LEARNED AVERSIONS
USING NON-GUSTATORY STIMULI

MARVIN NACHMAN and JOAN RAUSCHENBERGER
University of California, Riverside

JOHN H. ASHE
University of California, Irvine

Almost all of the research in food-aversion learning has focused on gustatory cues. So accustomed are we to this fact that this area of research is more often called taste-aversion learning than food-aversion learning. In a sense, this is as it should be. There is no doubt of the overwhelming role that the sense of taste normally plays in such conditioning (Nachman, Rauschenberger, & Ashe, in press), and nothing we say in this paper is meant to detract from that fundamental fact. However, in this paper we wish to focus on non-gustatory stimuli and to examine whether or not a non-gustatory stimulus can be used as the CS in learned aversions and particularly in long-delay learned aversions.

Our interest in taste-aversion learning has tended to focus on a study of neural mechanisms. There are two main reasons why the possible role of non-gustatory cues has important implications for an understanding of neural mechanisms. First, if it is true that aversion learning is restricted to gustatory cues, then there is a clear implication that there may be something special about the anatomical connections or possibly the neurophysiological responses to the gustatory stimuli which are directly responsible for this kind of learning. Such an anatomical hypothesis was clearly formulated by Garcia and Ervin (1968) and forms a hypothetical neural basis for concepts such as preparedness or stimulus relevance. Second, if it is indeed the case that long-delay learning, as found in the taste-aversion literature, occurs only with gustatory cues, we are again led in the direction of searching for anatomical-physiological substrates in the gustatory system to account for the fact that gustatory cues are in a transient state of associability for a number of hours. However, even if long-delay learning is limited to gustatory cues, this does not necessarily require the postulation of a special neural mechanism for the gustatory system. To be sure, there are also hypotheses which stress non-neural explanations to account for the special role of gustatory stimuli in long-delay learning. For example, some of the basically non-neural explanations which have been postulated to account for long-delay learning in the gustatory system are after-taste (discussed by Revusky & Garcia, 1970) and stimulus interference (Revusky, 1971). With that as a background, we would now like to examine some of the experimental work from our laboratory using various non-gustatory stimuli.

TEMPERATURE

The first experiments involved water temperature as a cue. Rats were tested for their ability to learn to avoid drinking hot (43°C) or cold (0-1°C) distilled water. Essentially, the same results were obtained with either hot or cold water, and we shall briefly summarize only the hot water study (Nachman, 1970). Distilled water was used throughout the study to avoid any possibility of taste changes due to temperature changes. Groups of rats were given daily 10 min trials with room temperature water (27°C). Then, the rats received a single acquisition trial in which they drank 43°C water and after various time delays, were injected with lithium chloride. All rats then received two additonal trials of 10 min a day room temperature water, and on the next day they were again tested with 43°C water. As can be seen in Figure 1, there is a temporal delay gradient of learned aversion to the temperature cue of 43°C water. The one min and 15 min delay groups showed a significant learned aversion to the hot water. While longer delay times were not significantly different from controls after a single trial, there was a tendency for an aversion, and subsequent experiments using other cues suggest that longer delays would have been effective if multiple trials had been given. A further point which should be made, however, is that while the non-gustatory temperature cue could serve as an effective stimulus in aversion learning, this stimulus was not nearly as effective as a taste cue, either in the amount of aversion learned or the length of the effective CS-US delay.

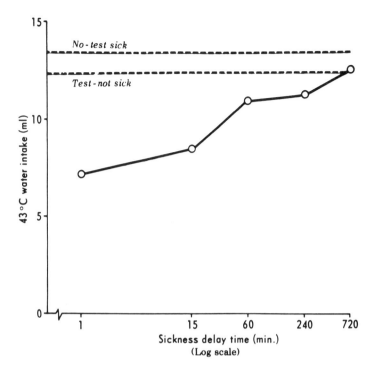

Figure 1
Mean intake of 43°C water in groups which had previously been made sick at various times after drinking 43°C water. (The no-test sick-control group had not drunk 43°C water before but had been made sick. The test not-sick control group had drunk 43°C water before but had not been made sick.) (Reprinted from Nachman, 1970)

AIR LICKING

The next experiment (Nachman, unpublished) investigated whether rats could learn an aversion to licking at a stream of compressed air which served as the non-gustatory cue. Rats were first adapted to drinking water for 10 min daily. On acquisition day, the same drinking spouts were used but this time the rats were allowed to lick at a stream of compressed air coming from these spouts, and were then injected with 20 ml/kg .15M LiCl after different temporal delays. On the next day, the rats were given a water trial and on the following day they were again tested with the air stream. Figure 2 shows the ratio of the number of test-day licks to acquisition-day licks for each group. The one-min and 15-min delay groups

397

showed a clear aversion to air licking while there was no evidence of an aversion with longer delays. Thus, this experiment found that rats were able to learn in a single trial a strong aversion to what is presumably a tasteless stimulus. We have no information on whether longer delay times would have been effective if multiple trials had been given.

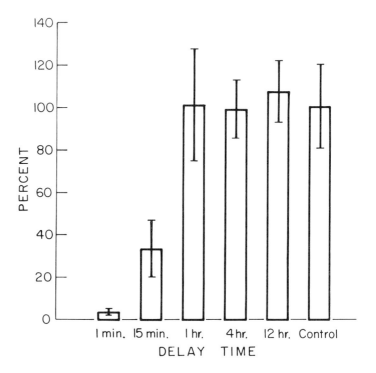

Figure 2
Mean ratio (expressed as percent) of the number of test-day licks to acquisition-day licks at an air stream for groups injected with lithium at various times after licking. The control group was injected with 20 ml/kg of .15M NaCl. The vertical bars represent ± 1 S.E.

A second air-licking study was done which was essentially the same as the first except for the fact that odorized air was used as the CS in the single acquisition trial. To odorize the air, the compressed air was first sent into a flask where it was passed over a warm amyl acetate solution before reaching the rat. Thus, in this study, the rats licked at air which was highly concentrated with amyl acetate in their single acquisition trial and were then injected with LiCl. They were tested two days later for licking amyl acetate odorized air. In contrast to the clean-air-licking experiment, strong single trial aversions to the odorized air were acquired even with a 4-hr delay. Because the rats were licking the amyl acetate air, it seems appropriate to assume that this provided a gustatory as well as an olfactory cue. This experiment, therefore, cannot be considered as an example of a learned aversion using a non-gustatory cue.

JAR VS. SPOUT

In studies of conditioning using non-gustatory cues, a typical experimental design has been to put rats in a distinctive place for the acquisition trial and to pair drinking in that place with an aversive treatment (see Best, Best, & Henggeler, this volume). Relatively little in the way of learned aversions has been reported with this experimental design, presumably because of the problem of changing many stimuli at the same time, i.e., the distinctive place may differ in visual, tactual, and olfactory cues. In our recent experiments to be described below, we have conducted all trials of a study in the same cage and varied only the type of glass container from which the rat drinks. The rats in these experiments are Sprague-Dawley albino males, which were born and reared in our laboratory. The home cages are equipped with an automatic watering system so that prior to any experiment, the rats had always obtained water by licking at a stainless steel nipple which displaces slightly to release water.

The first experiment of this series involved having rats drink from either of two types of drinking containers, a glass jar or a glass drinking tube. The glass jar was a 2 oz wide mouth jar measuring 47 mm in diameter and 45 mm high. The glass drinking tube consisted of a 25 ml graduated cylinder fitted with a bent glass drinking spout that was about the same dimensions as the typical commercially available stainless steel drinking spout.

Drinking was restricted to a single 10-min period each day. On non-conditioning days, the rats received access to water for 10 min from the glass drinking spouts whereas on conditioning-test trials, a glass jar (containing 25 ml of water) was placed in the cage for 10 min. Six groups of eight rats each were used. One group served as a non-injected control while the remaining five groups were injected with 20 ml/kg of .15M LiCl at 2 min, 15 min, 1 hr, 4 hr, or 8 hr after drinking water from the glass jars on each of days 7, 10, 13, and 16. For each rat, an aversion score was obtained by calculating the ratio of intake from the jar to the intake from the spout the day before.

On Day 7, the first conditioning trial, rats consistently drank somewhat less (about 15-20% less) from the jars than they did from the spout the day before. This presumably reflects a neophobia to drinking from the jar (or perhaps, difficulty in finding the water) since with repeated trials, the control group drank about as much from the jar as it did from the spout. The groups injected with lithium, particularly those injected after short time intervals, showed increasing aversions with repeated conditioning trials. Two types of aversions were seen, both in this study and in subsequent studies using non-gustatory cues. One was a generalized aversion to drinking from both the spout and the jar and the other was the specific aversion to drinking from the jar. The generalized aversion was evidenced by the fact that the amount of water intake from both the spout and the jar was well below control levels. That this was not simply a result of lithium sickness is clear from the

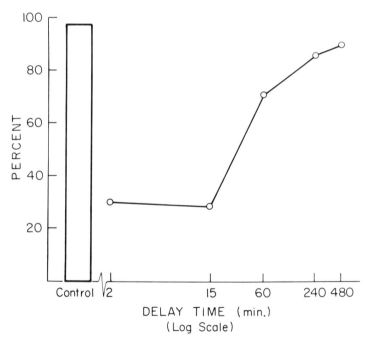

Figure 3
Mean ratio (expressed as percent) of water intake from the jar on Day 19 to water intake from the spout on Day 18 for groups injected with lithium at various times after drinking from the jar. The control group was not injected.

400

fact that the 8 hr lithium group showed little sign of this generalized aversion, and the degree of aversion in the other groups was systematically a function of the delay time of lithium injection. It was possible to separate out the specific aversion to drinking from the jar from the generalized aversion to drinking, by calculating the ratio of the intake from the jar to the intake from the spout the day before. Figure 3 shows the results for the last trial, which is the ratio of Day 19 intake from the jar to the Day 18 intake from the spout. A significant aversion was found in the 2 min, 15 min, and 1 hr groups, while no aversion was seen in the 4 hr and 8 hr groups. Figure 4 shows the trial by trial data for the same groups.

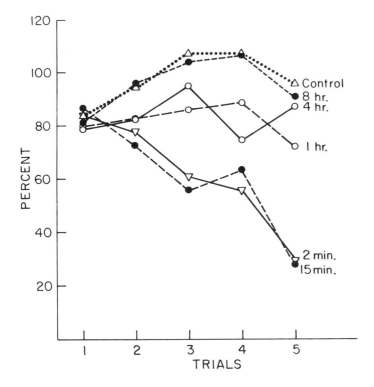

Figure 4
For each trial, mean ratio (expressed as percent) of water intake on a conditioning-test trial with a jar to the water intake on the non-conditioning trial of the day before with the spout. Groups were injected with lithium at various temporal delays after drinking from the jar.

In order to be sure that there was nothing unique about the experimental design in which the "safe" trial was drinking from the spout and the conditioning trial was drinking from the jar, we reversed the stimuli in a subsequent experiment (using new rats), and injected the rats with lithium after drinking from the spout. The same design was used except that only two groups were tested; one given lithium injections 2 min after drinking from the spout, and the other group not injected. The results of the five trials are presented in Figure 5. As can be seen by comparing the 2 min groups in Figures 4 and 5, the rats, if anything, learned much better when the spout was the CS than when the jar was the CS. There was a remote possibility that the water in the glass spout condition could have had an added taste stimulus because of the rubber stop-

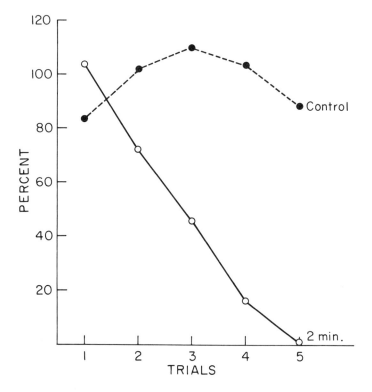

Figure 5
For each trial, mean ratio (expressed as percent) of water intake on a conditioning-test trial with a spout to the water intake on the non-conditioning trial of the day before with the jar. The 2 min group was injected with lithium after drinking from the spout.

per connecting the glass spout to the graduated cylinder. Control experiments in which a rubber stopper was added to the glass jar condition indicated that the stopper had no influence on the learning of the aversion.

Thus, these studies indicate that rats can readily learn to selectively avoid drinking from a jar or a spout. With short delays, there is some learning which appears to occur in a single trial. With multiple trials, long-delay learning is found. In a recent experiment, Revusky and Parker (1976) used a similar experimental design with a stainless steel cup and a glass spout as stimuli and obtained results similar to those reported here with glass jar versus glass spout.

ANALYSIS OF JAR VS. SPOUT DISCRIMINATION

We have attempted to analyze the stimulus difference between drinking from the glass jar versus drinking from the glass spout in order to understand why rats are able to learn this discrimination more successfully than the discriminations in other place learning experiments. There are two major classes of stimuli in the jar vs. spout discrimination: (1) the visual and other noningestional stimuli associated with the fact that the jar and spout have a different appearance, are located in different positions in the cage, and must be approached with different bodily positions while drinking, and (2) the tongue-tactile stimuli which are associated with drinking in the two situations. When drinking from the jar, the rat laps at the water in the center of the jar and the tongue does not touch the glass. Occasionally, some rats also dip their paws in the water and lick their paws. When drinking from the spout, the rat licks at the spout, making repeated tongue contacts both with the water and the glass end of the spout. It is our hypothesis that the difference in tongue stimulation between the lapping of water in the jar and the licking at the glass spout are the significant stimuli which the rat is able to discriminate and use for aversion learning. All of the remaining experiments which we will be reporting here were attempts to test this hypothesis by manipulating the stimuli present during drinking.

VISUAL CUES

Two experiments were conducted in which lapping water from a jar was held as a constant, and visual features of the jar were manipulated. In both experiments it was found that the rats could not learn to avoid drinking from the distinctive visual stimulus. In the first of these experiments, black and white jars were used and rats were injected with lithium in a repeated trials design at various temporal delays after drinking from the black jar. The rats learned a generalized aversion and suppressed drinking from either the black or white jar but showed no greater aversion to the black than to the white jar. These results for the various temporal delays are shown in Figure 6. In the second experiment two 4 oz jars with screw-on black bakelite caps were used; each jar had a different size hole cut in the bakelite cap. In one condition, the hole in the

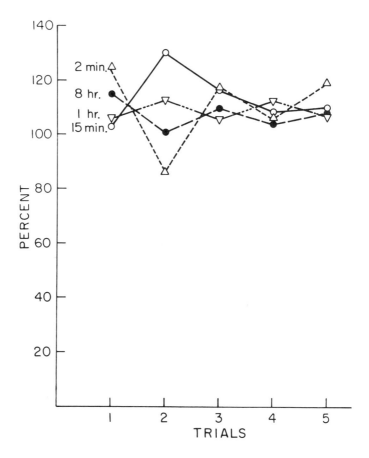

Figure 6
For each trial, mean ratio (expressed as percent) of water intake on a conditioning-test trial with a black jar to the water intake on the non-conditioning trial of the day before with the white jar. Groups were injected with lithium at various temporal delays after drinking from the black jar.

cap was 55 mm. Rats had no difficulty putting their heads into his hole and lapping the water in the jar. In the other condition, the hole in the bakelite cap was 27 mm which meant that the rats' snouts fit fairly snugly into the hole although there was no change in the way in which they lapped water from the jar. One control group was used and one experimental group was run. The experimental group was injected with lithium, in a repeated trials design, 15 min after drinking from the jar with the small hole in the cap. The experimental group showed a decrease in water intake from either jar but did not learn to selectively avoid drinking from one jar more than the other.

The next experiment used drinking from the glass jars versus drinking from glass Richter tubes. It was expected that the lapping movements in drinking from the jars would be the same as those used in drinking from the Richter tubes. The rats would therefore not be able to learn a selective aversion to drinking from one of these even though the containers had distinctive visual cues. However, the results were inconclusive. Some learning occurred, but it was also clear that rats showed individual differences in the way in which they drank from the two containers. When drinking from Richter tubes, many rats licked against the glass side of the tubes whereas when drinking from jars, the rats never appeared to make tongue contact with the glass. Similarly, studies in which we compared drinking from glass spouts with drinking from Richter tubes also proved to be inconclusive because of individual patterns of drinking.

TONGUE-TACTILE CUES

The final set of experiments attempted to focus specifically on the role of tongue-tactile stimulation by using stimuli which were highly similar in all characteristics except the tactile stimulation provided to the tongue while drinking.

Small vs. large spouts. In the first of these experiments, the two stimuli were glass spouts made from 9 mm diameter glass tubing. One of the spouts was only slightly fire polished so that there was a large diameter (7mm) opening at the end from which the rat licked to obtain water. This was about the largest opening possible; with larger openings, the water would spontaneously or very easily flow out. With the 7 mm opening, water flowed easily with each lick and in some cases would start to spill out when the rat drank. The other glass spout was fire polished until the opening at the tip was very small, approximately 2.5 mm. Drinking from these spouts was very difficult, particularly for some rats. We tested many rats

405

using spouts with the small openings and found that approximately 75% of the rats "worked" at drinking during the initial 10-min period and obtained fairly large, and in most cases, near normal, amounts of water. Once experienced, these rats were able to obtain amounts of water in 10 min which were about the same as when they drank from spouts with large openings. The remaining 25% of the rats drank very little (usually less than 1.0 ml) in the initial trial with the small-opening spouts, and were eliminated from the experiment because even though many of them would have subsequently learned to drink from a small-opening spout, their first conditioning trial would have occurred with very little CS experience.

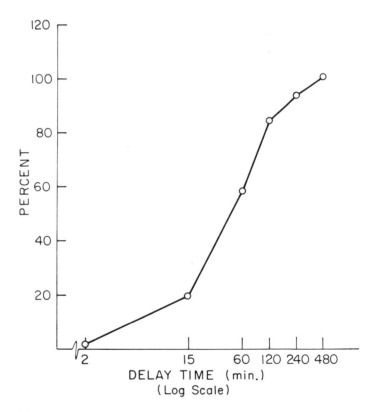

Figure 7
Mean ratio (expressed as percent) of water intake from the small-opening spout on the last trial (Day 22) to the water intake from the large-opening spout on the day before (Day 21). Groups were injected with lithium at various temporal delays after drinking from the small-opening spout.

Six groups of 12 rats each started the experiment, but after elimination based on the above considerations, the groups ended up with about 9 rats each. The procedure consisted of 10-min daily water trials in which the rats drank from the spouts with the 7 mm opening on all non-conditioning trials and from the spout with the 2.5 mm opening on conditioning-test trials. Conditioning-test trials were given on Days 7, 10, 13, 16, 19, and 22, and on the first five of these days, the six groups were injected with lithium at delay times of 2 min, 15 min, 1 hr, 2 hr, 4 hr, or 8 hr after drinking.

Figure 7 shows the amount of learned aversion to the small-opening spout after five conditioning trials, as a function of delay time. This aversion was expressed as the ratio of Day 22 to Day 21 intake (i.e., the ratio of intake from the small-opening spout on the day before). As can be seen, the rats were able to learn a strong aversion to drinking from the spout with the small opening, and the amount of aversion learned was a direct function of the delay time of the lithium injection. The 2-min, 15-min, and 1-hr groups all differed significantly from the 8-hr group. The aversion scores of the 2-hr and 4-hr groups, while also in the same direction, did not differ significantly from the 8-hr group.

Presenting the ratio of small-opening spout to large-opening spout intake gives a measure of the specific aversion to drinking from the spout with the small opening. In addition, there was the generalized aversion to drinking from the large-opening spout. The generalized aversion was greatest on trials which followed a conditioning-test trial and, thus, the generalized aversions were most readily seen on Days 8, 11, 14, 17, and 20. Because on those days the rats did not receive a conditioning trial, the drinking served as an extinction experience which lessened the aversion which was seen on the next trial, Days 9, 12, 15, 18, and 21. When the CS was again given, on Days 10, 13, 16, 19, and 22, a stronger aversion, specific to the CS, was seen. Figure 8 presents a sample of these phenomena by showing the absolute amounts of intake by each group on Days 20 and 21, the last two trials with the large-opening spout, and on Day 22, the last trial with the small-opening spout. As can be seen in this figure, there is a specific aversion to the small-opening spout on Day 22 as a function of delay time, but there is also a generalized aversion to the large-opening spout as a function of delay time, and this generalized aversion is greater on Day 20 than on Day 21. It should again be noted that what we are referring to as the generalized aversion to the large-opening spout is not simply a consequence of possible lithium illness since all groups received the same number of lithium injections. After we have presented all of the experimental data in this paper, we shall return to a discussion of the issue of the generalization of aversion.

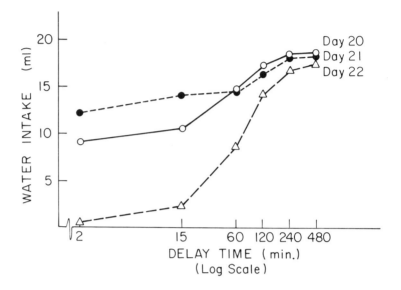

Figure 8
Mean absolute amounts of water intake (ml) by each group on Days 20, 21, and 22. Days 20 and 21 were non-conditioning trials with the large-opening spouts. On Day 22, rats were tested with the small-opening spout which was previously paired with lithium following various delays.

Figure 9 shows the trial by trial learning of the aversion to drinking from the small spout for the same groups of rats. It can be seen that a clear indication of learning the aversion occurs after a single trial in groups which received lithium injections after short delays. As before, each point in this graph represents the ratio of intake on a conditioning-test trial (small-opening spout) to the intake on the non-conditioning trial of the day before (large-opening spout).

Rats clearly learned an aversion to drinking from the spout with the small opening. Was this learning somehow specific to the difficulty of drinking from the small-opening spout or would they have been able to learn an aversion to drinking from a large-opening spout? To answer this question, a seventh group had been included as part of the above experiment and was tested at the same time and on exactly the same schedule as the other six groups. The seventh group received the spout with the 2.5 mm opening on all non-conditioning days, while on each of the condi-

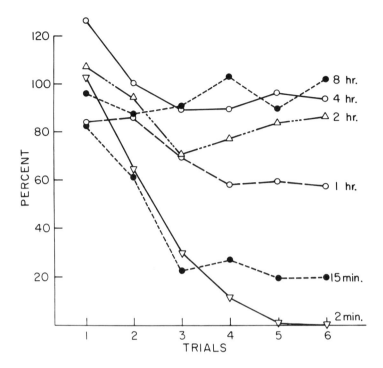

Figure 9
For each trial, mean ratio (expressed as percent) of water intake on a conditioning-test trial with a small-opening spout to the water intake on the non-conditioning trial of the day before with the large-opening spout. Groups were injected with lithium at various temporal delays after drinking from the small-opening spout.

tioning-test days (Days 7, 10, 13, 16, 19, and 22), it received the spout with the 7 mm opening and was injected with lithium 2 min after the drinking period. Figure 10 shows, for each trial, the ratio of intake from the large-opening spout to the intake from the small-opening spout on the day before. It is apparent that rats learn quite well the aversion to the large-opening spout, but they do not learn as well as the comparable 2-min delay group which had learned the aversion to the small-opening spout.

Visual Place Cues and Lapping vs. Licking. The experimental data presented so far suggest that rats in a drinking situation have great difficulty in using visual cues but that they can use tongue-tactile stimuli as cues in long-delay aversion learning. The last experiments to be reported were designed to further test this finding by using a different example of a tongue-tactile cue as well as dif-

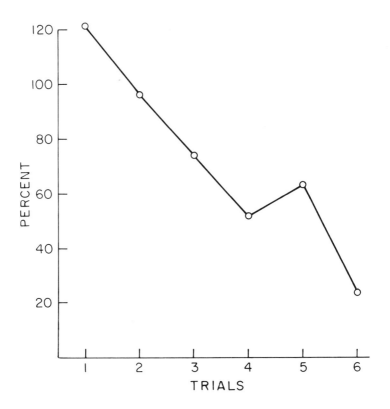

Figure 10
For each trial, mean ratio (expressed as percent) of water intake on conditioning-test trial with the large-opening spout to the water intake on the non-conditioning trial of the day before with the small-opening spout. Rats were injected with lithium 2 min after drinking from the spout with the large opening.

ferent visual-place cues. The tongue-tactile cue to be discriminated was lapping at water from a half-full petri dish versus licking water off the bottom of a nearly empty petri dish. The visual-place cue to be discriminated was lapping water from a petri dish versus lapping water from a jar located at different positions in the cage.

The drinking container in the tongue-tactile cue part of the experiment was a large diameter (150 mm by 20 mm high) petri dish. Rats were given the same petri dish on non-conditioning and on conditioning-test trials. On non-conditioning trials, the petri dish contained approximately 100 ml of water (Deep condition) which meant that the depth of the water was about 10 mm in the dish and the rat's tongue did not touch the glass while it drank. On condi-

410

tioning-test trials, the petri dish contained 10 ml of water (Shallow condition) when it was presented to the rat. Ten ml of water did not cover the bottom of the dish and usually existed in puddles about 1-2 mm deep. In order to obtain the water, the rats had to lick the bottom of the petri dish with their tongues. To provide the rats with access to more than 10 ml of water in a 10-min trial, while still keeping the water level shallow, an additional 10 ml of water was added to the dish during the 10-min trial, 5 ml at 3 min, and 5 ml at 6 min into the trial. The water could be added from the outside of the cage without disturbing the rat because the position of the petri dish was on the floor of the cage, half inside and half outside, protruding through an opening which had been cut in the solid wall of the cage to fit the dish.

For the visual-place discrimination, rats drank from a 2 oz glass jar (47 mm in diameter by 45 mm high) on the non-conditioning trials. The jar was located on the floor along one of the walls of the cage, and to drink from it the rat had to lift its head up and then down into the jar while typically standing on its hindpaws and resting its forepaws on the edge of the jar. The jar contained about 30 ml of water which meant that the depth was about 20 mm. On the conditioning-test trials, the glass jar was not placed in the cage but, instead, the petri dish (with 100 ml of water) was located one-half in the cage along an adjacent wall. The rats drank from the petri dish with their heads down and all four paws on the floor (sometimes the front two paws were in the dish). In setting up this discrimination task, it was our intention that the rats would have two distinctly different containers in different places, but that the tongue-tactile stimuli involved in drinking from each would be the same because they both involved lapping from a "deep" pool of water without the tongue touching any part of the container. We tried to monitor the rats' behavior but were not able to determine their exact drinking patterns. In some cases, some of the rats may have licked at one of the containers, and they most certainly did lick at their forepaws when they occasionally placed a paw in either the jar or dish.

Three experimental groups were used. Group 1 was a Deep-Shallow petri dish discrimination in which the rats drank from the Deep condition on non-conditioning trials and from the Shallow condition on conditioning-test days 7, 10, 13, 16, 19, and 22 and were injected with lithium 2 min after drinking. Group 2 was tested in the same way except that their lithium injections were given after an 8-hr delay. Group 3 was tested for the Jar-Petri Dish discrimination. They followed the same schedule as groups 1 and 2

411

except that they drank from the jar on non-conditioning days and from the petri dish on conditioning-test days. They were injected with lithium 2 min after drinking from the petri dish on conditioning-test days. At the conclusion of the experiment, an additional trial was given (trial 7 on Day 25), in which all three groups were tested with the shallow dish. This extra trial was given to rule out the possibility that the observed group differences in amount of learned aversion could be attributed to a performance difference in ease of drinking from the shallow vs. deep petri dish.

The results, presented in Figure 11, show that Group 1 clearly learned the Deep-Shallow discrimination and avoided drinking from the petri dish in the Shallow condition. Group 2, the Deep-

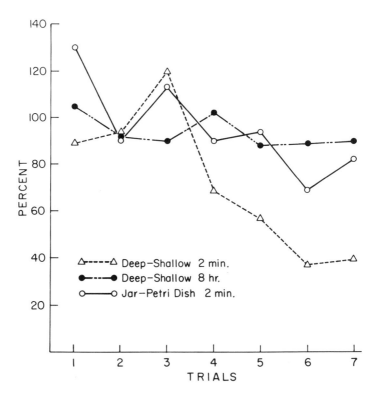

Figure 11
For each trial, mean ratio (expressed as percent) of water intake on conditioning-test trial to the water intake on the non-conditioning trial of the day before for Deep-Shallow discrimination training with 2-min and 8-hr delays and Jar-Petri Dish discrimination training with a 2-min delay.

412

Shallow 8-hr group, demonstrated that rats had little difficulty in obtaining the water in the Shallow condition, drinking almost as much each trial as they did in the Deep condition. In the last few trials of the Shallow condition the rats drank a mean of about 16 ml (of the 20 ml which was the maximum available for any one rat). In the Deep condition they drank a mean of about 18 ml.

Group 3, which was tested for their ability to utilize the visual-place cues involved in the jar-petri dish discrimination, did not show a significant learned aversion. There was a strong suggestion of an aversion, particularly on Trial 6, but this was largely due to only three of the eight rats in the group. Although we observed the rats, there was nothing obvious about the drinking patterns of these rats.

The fact that Group 1, the Deep-Shallow discrimination, learned to avoid drinking water in the Shallow condition, while Group 3, the jar-petri dish discrimination, did not learn to avoid drinking from the petri dish, was not simply due to any performance difference in the difficulty of drinking from a shallow vs. a deep petri dish. When both groups were tested on Trial 7 with the Shallow condition, the difference between the two groups in amount of learned aversion was still seen.

DISCUSSION

To summarize, we have reported results from five experiments in which long-delay aversion learning occurred without the use of gustatory stimuli. The discriminations learned in these five studies were (1) a temperature discrimination, (2) air licking vs. water licking, (3) licking water from a spout vs. lapping water from a jar, (4) licking water from a spout with a large vs. small opening, and (5) lapping water from a dish vs. licking the water from the bottom of the dish. In all five experiments, the cues to be discriminated involved somatosensory stimuli to the tongue. All of these stimuli are mediated by afferent neural activity of the trigeminal nerve.

In three other experiments, rats were apparently unable to learn the discriminations for long-delay aversion learning even in those cases when only 2-min delays were used. The discriminations which they did not acquire were (1) drinking from a black vs. white jar, (2) drinking from a jar with a wide mouth vs. narrow mouth cap, and (3) drinking from a jar vs. a petri dish. In these three experiments, the cues to be discriminated were visual and/or place cues.

413

In attempting to account for these results, we propose two types of explanations. The first focuses on the discriminability of the stimuli, while a second set of explanations focuses on the anatomical connections and physiological interactions of the afferent neural input.

DISCRIMINABILITY OF STIMULI

We have summarized the results of these eight experiments into two groups; those five which used somatosensory stimulation of the tongue and produced learning, and those three which used visual stimuli and did not result in learning. However, it is perfectly possible that these results were due to differences in discriminability of the stimuli and not to their sensory modality. It may be, for example, that various attention-getting or arousing properties of a stimulus such as intensity, novelty, or hedonic tone may have been the predominant factors in determining whether or not an aversion was learned. It is conceivable, and even reasonable, that the somatosensory stimuli used in these experiments were more novel, attention-getting or discriminable than were the visual stimuli. Thus, the inability of the rats to learn an aversion such as that involved in drinking from a black vs. white jar may be because the differences in these stimuli were not sufficiently discriminable, while the differences between drinking from a large vs. small opening spout were much more obvious. While we may speculate regarding the relative discriminability of the various stimuli used, there are clearly no a priori criteria by which we can be certain of the salience of the stimuli for the rat.

An indication of the discriminability of the various stimuli may be obtained by an examination of the data showing the presence or absence of generalized aversions. For example, rats given LiCl after drinking a saccharin solution show very little generalized aversion to drinking water in the same situation on the next day but do show a very strong specific aversion to drinking saccharin. Thus, there is no doubt of the fact that they have clearly discriminated the saccharin from water. In contrast, rats injected with lithium after drinking water from a black jar do not show an aversion which is specific to the black jar but show an equal aversion to drinking from the black or white jar, indicating an absence of discriminating between these stimuli in this situation. The results with somatosensory stimuli appear to fall somewhere between those with gustatory and visual stimuli. With somatosensory stimuli, such as those produced by drinking from large vs. small opening spouts, rats learned an aversion which was specific to the

414

small-opening spout but also showed a generalized aversion to the large-opening spout. We have consistently found throughout this series of studies that there has been an inverse relationship between the strength of the specific aversion learned to the conditioned stimulus and the strength of the generalized aversion shown to non-conditioned stimulus. These findings suggest that the stimuli may be aligned on a gradient of discriminability which may form the basis for differences in the acquisition of the aversion.

ANATOMICAL AND PHYSIOLOGICAL INTERACTIONS
OF AFFERENT NEURAL INPUT

An alternative approach to account for the effectiveness of gustatory and somatosensory stimuli in learned-aversion experiments is to focus on the special neural characteristics of these sensory systems. Garcia and Ervin (1968) suggested a specific anatomical hypothesis to account for the fact that gustatory cues are readily associated with visceral cues, while telereceptive cues are more easily associated with cutaneous cues. They stressed the idea that there is a separation of neural mechanisms subserving responses within the internal milieu from those subserving responses within the external milieu. For the internal milieu, of special significance is the fact that gustatory and visceral systems both send afferent fibers directly to the solitary nucleus. It is presumably this direct convergence of the inputs from the CS and US to the same locus which facilitates the learning of associations involving these stimuli.

Given the hypothesis that anatomical convergence of input forms the basis of predispositions favoring gustatory-visceral associations, it is of particular interest to note the anatomical similarity between somatosensory projections from the tongue and gustatory projections. *Nucleus Solitarius* in the medulla receives direct projections from the trigeminal nerve in addition to receiving direct projections from visceral afferents and from the chorda tympani and glossopharyngeal nerves. Anatomical evidence indicates that section of the trigeminal and the facial nerve, which contains the chorda tympani, both result in extensive and comparable degeneration in the solitary nucleus (Torvik, 1956). Neurophysiological recording experiments have confirmed the existence of the trigeminal projections to the solitary nucleus (Blomquist & Antem, 1965). Thus, the same type of anatomical evidence which is hypothesized to account for gustatory-visceral associations exists for associations between somatosensory information from the tongue and visceral afferents.

415

While these anatomical facts are well documented and clearly not in dispute, it should be pointed out that they are not an explanation of conditioning. There is at present no knowledge regarding how anatomical convergence, or for that matter, whether anatomical convergence on the same nucleus is converted into a physiological facilitation of conditioning. Also, it should be noted that the existence of anatomical convergence does not provide any satisfactory explanation for the long-delay learning which is well documented in gustatory-visceral conditioning and which is reported here for orosomatic-visceral conditioning.

OTHER POSSIBILITIES

While the facts of anatomical convergence certainly offer a plausible hypothesis to account for the formation of favored associations, there are of course additional hypotheses which may be considered. It may be, for example, that a principle of stimulus relevance applies in which stimuli that are intimately part of the ingestive process are readily associated with each other. Thus, the tactile, as well as the taste, components of ingesting or mouthing foods or liquids may be readily associated with aversive visceral consequences. However, an explanation using a principle of stimulus relevance, in a sense, begs the question if it does not specify a definition of relevant stimuli or provide a way of determining which stimuli are, or are not, relevant to forming an association. Also, a principle of stimulus relevance does not by itself suggest any particular neural basis for the facilitation of associations between the relevant stimuli. It is certainly possible that particular systems which are relevant to each other may have inherent physiological properties which increase the likelihood of their association. It is also possible that as a function of experience, neural change may occur which results in a facilitation of conditioning for relevant stimuli. The neural basis for favoring certain associations may involve physiological and/or chemical processes of diverse types such as special transmitter interactions, structural changes, or special membrane properties facilitating synaptic efficacy.

416

REFERENCES

Blomquist, A. J., & Antem, A. Localization of the terminals of the tongue afferents in the nucleus of the solitary tract. **Journal of Comparative Neurology,** 1965, **124,** 127-130.

Garcia, J., & Ervin, F. R. Gustatory-visceral and telereceptor-cutaneous conditioning: Adaptation in internal and external milieus. **Communications in Behavioral Biology,** 1968, **1,** 389-415.

Nachman, M. Learned taste and temperature aversions due to lithium chloride sickness after temporal delays. **Journal of Comparative and Physiological Psychology,** 1970, **73,** 22-30.

Nachman, M., Rauschenberger, J., & Ashe, J. H. Stimulus characteristics and food aversion learning. In N. W. Milgram, L. Krames, & T. M. Alloway (Eds.), **Food aversion learning.** New York: Plenum Press, in press.

Revusky, S. The role of interference in association over a delay. In W. K. Honig & P. H. R. James (Eds.), **Animal memory.** New York: Academic Press, 1971, 155-213.

Revusky, S., & Garcia, J. Learned association over long delays. In G. H. Bower (Ed.), **The psychology of learning and motivation.** New York: Academic Press, 1970, 1-84.

Revusky, S., & Parker, L. A. Aversions to drinking out of a cup and to unflavored water produced by delayed sickness. **Journal of Experimental Psychology: Animal Behavior Processes,** 1976, **2,** 342-353.

Torvik, A. Afferent connections to the sensory trigeminal nuclei, the nucleus of the solitary tract and adjacent structures. An experimental study in the rat. **Journal of Comparative Neurology,** 1956, **106,** 51-141.

417

LONG-DELAY LEARNING OF INGESTIVE
AVERSIONS IN QUAIL

HARDY C. WILCOXON
George Peabody College for Teachers

INTRODUCTION

Investigations of birds learning to avoid ingesting things that do not agree with them have been going on for a very long time and published reports have been numerous. Since diurnal birds generally have very good vision, it is not surprising to find that many of them, as adults at least, appear to avoid disagreeable things on sight. But the question of how this comes about, whether through inborn predispositions or through learning (and, if learning, under precisely what conditions), has long been the subject of investigation.

So far as I have been able to determine, the first detailed report of avian species *learning* to avoid *on sight* those substances that are distasteful, injurious, or both occurs in the book, *Habit and Instinct* by C. Lloyd Morgan in 1896. Morgan's main interest was in whether young birds showed any "instinctive" avoidance of insects, etc., which were known to be avoided on sight by older, more experienced birds. He reported a number of observations he had made with young domestic chicks, pheasants, guinea-fowl, and moorhens. The following passage is both entertaining and instructive:

> They pecked at everything of suitable size they could lay bill on. There does not seem to be any congenital discrimination between nutritious and innutritious objects, or between those which are nice and those which are nasty. This is a matter of individual acquisition. They soon learn, however, what is good for eating, and what is unpleasant, and rapidly associate

the appearance with the taste. A young chick two days old, for example, had learnt to pick out pieces of yolk from others of white of egg. I cut little bits of orange-peel of about the same size as the pieces of yolk, and one of these was soon seized, but at once relinquished, the chick shaking his head. Seizing another, he held it for a moment in the bill, but then dropped it and scratched at the base of his beak. That was enough; he could not again be induced to seize a piece of orange-peel. The obnoxious material was now removed, and pieces of yolk of egg substituted, but they were left untouched, being probably taken for orange-peel. Subsequently, he looked at the yolk with hesitation, but presently pecked doubtfully, not seizing, but merely touching. Then he pecked again, seized, and swallowed. (Morgan, 1896, pp. 40-41)

Notice what Morgan had observed in that one, two-day-old chick, all in a pleasant little garden, probably within a span of just a few minutes!

1. *Visual discrimination* of bits of yolk from bits of white, with a preference for yolk.

2. *Learned rejection* of bits of orange peel, almost certainly on the basis of chemical cues, either taste or odor, probably taste; and after only two such experiences, avoidance of orange peel on sight.

3. *Generalization* from disliked orange peel to previously preferred yolk of egg. This makes it even more certain that orange peel really had been rejected on sight (as opposed to, say, odor) after the two "distasteful" experiences.

4. *Extinction* of the generalized avoidance of egg yolk after a few tentative tries at it which were not followed by noxious consequence.

Morgan reported many other observations, all of which convinced him that several species of young birds can readily *learn* "to discriminate by sight between . . . nice and . . . nasty caterpillars." None of his observations provided any evidence that the species he studied had an inherited tendency to avoid the noxious creatures at first sight, even though some of them were quite distinctively marked. He was careful, however, to avoid a sweeping generalization. Some species, he conjectured, might require an inherited tendency in order to survive. He even suggested some of the characteristics such species might have in order for inherited avoidance to be maximally adaptive. If we may jump ahead almost a century, those species have characteristics in common with the turquoise-browed motmot (*Eumomota superciliosa*), which Susan M. Smith (Smith, 1975) has recently found to display an innate avoidance reaction to the aposematically colored coral snake which is abundant in the tropical habitat of these jay-like birds. The birds nest underground, the young do not emerge for some time, and their first appetitive interest in a coral snake would almost certainly lead to their undoing. Clearly, then, a tendency to avoid the coral snake on first sight would have great adaptive value.

From Morgan's time until the present, most of the work on ingestive behavior of birds has been done by zoologists, and most of that by persons mainly interested in mimicry. The best known examples of mimicry occur in insects whose primary predators are birds. Thus, although the focus of the work has been on the evolution of protective visual patterns and coloration in insects which are themselves quite palatable (but which look like others that are not), birds nearly always come into the picture because it is they who must be fooled. This work has gone on in the field, in the laboratory, and, again, in quiet English gardens. For example, Miriam Rothschild has called to my attention some of her own observations along this line. Had I known of them (Rothschild, 1967) when we began our work with quail, I would have cited her paper in our first publication on this subject.

Rothschild saw the nature of the learning theory problems very clearly, and her speculations regarding their solution have turned out to be remarkably accurate in light of our later experimental findings. She noted that it was obviously easy for a bird to associate a brilliant color with a "vile" taste when both impinge on the senses simultaneously. But, she asked, "if a bird makes a meal of several butterflies, how does it know which one produced the vomiting and disagreeable sensations that follow?" She describes having fed a tame crow two meals of brown noctuid moths, each meal garnished with one specimen of the brilliantly colored garden tiger moth and separated from the other meal by a few hours. The crow ate the whole meal each time. Yet, the following day the crow would accept only the brown moths, having developed "a violent and, as it proved later, a permanent aversion to garden tiger moths. . . ." She supposed that the crow had become ill an appreciable time after the two meals, "but by what means could it associate this with the real culprit?" She speculated, apparently quite correctly, that the cue for avoidance of the tiger moth was its distinctive appearance even though a long interval had separated sight of the moth and eventual malaise.

It was another line of investigation, however, that prompted us to use birds and visual cues in the long-delay, illness-induced aversion paradigm pioneered by Garcia and his colleagues. This was the work of Lincoln Brower (e.g., Brower, Ryerson, Coppinger, & Glazier, 1968) which showed that bluejays could learn to avoid toxic Monarch butterflies on sight after a limited number of experiences in eating them. He suggested a very plausible mechanism for such learning, the familiar one of higher-order conditioning. Brower observed that bluejays first peck at toxic Monarch butterflies on sight, tearing at them and then ingesting them. Later, the bird vomits. The taste of the regurgitated butterfly is now simultaneous with whatever distress the bird is experiencing and provides excellent conditions for learning an association between the taste of a Monarch and gastrointestinal malaise. On the next visual encounter with the distinctively colored butterfly, the bluejay pecks and tears at it but, upon tasting it, rejects it. This encounter provides the conditions for learning an association between the *mere sight* of the insect and what is by now a noxious taste. Subsequently, the bird avoids the Monarch on sight.

While Brower's observations are unquestioned, and his interpretation of the probable learning mechanisms certainly plausible, it occurred to us that diurnal birds might not require the mediating link provided by emetic reinstatement of taste during illness in order for them to learn to avoid on sight distinctive-looking things whose ingestion is followed by delayed illness. If the highly gustatory rat could form an unmediated association between a distinctive taste and an illness whose onset is delayed for many minutes, or even hours (Smith & Roll, 1967), perhaps the highly visual bird could somehow manage the same feat with a distinctive visual cue and a delayed-illness consequence.

Thus, our first experiment in this area was aimed primarily at answering the question of whether a diurnal bird could use a purely visual cue as a signal for avoidance in the long-delay, illness-induced aversion paradigm. We quickly found that bobwhite quail learned in one trial to reduce drastically their intake of presumably tasteless dyed water when ingestion of it was followed ½ hr later by a toxic injection (Wilcoxon, Dragoin, & Kral, 1971). Rats were run in the same experiment for comparative purposes, and a taste cue was also included for the same reason. Both the rats and quail readily learned to avoid the taste (mildly sour water, ½ ml hydrochloric acid per liter), but only the quail learned to avoid the distinctively darkened water (3 drops of blue food coloring per 100 ml of water). In a second experiment of the same study, quail also learned in one trial to avoid drinking from a tinted glass tube filled with plain water, even though they drank from it readily on first

422

encountering it, and the toxic injection which followed drinking was delayed for ½ hr.

The above findings were first reported in November 1969 at the meeting of the Psychonomic Society, but not before we had done a toxicosis control experiment. We recognized the real possibility that lowered ingestion of relatively novel substances might be a direct result of illness, rather than in any way dependent upon the birds' association of the novel color with delayed illness, and we wished to treat our finding with proper skepticism. Accordingly, we did a number of experiments between the summer of 1969 and spring of 1970 (Wilcoxon, Abernathy, Daly, Dragoin, Dwyer, & Kral, 1970) which convinced us that, although sensitization or "heightened neophobia " can and sometimes does contribute to the effect, there is a significant associative learning component as well. The most extensive and best-designed of these experiments will be reported below for the first time in published form.

In the following section, I shall describe a number of experiments from our laboratory which seem to provide quite convincing evidence that two avian species, bobwhite quail (*Colinus virginianus*) and Japanese quail (*Coturnix coturnix japonica*), (a) readily learn to associate a purely visual cue with a long-delayed illness consequence, (b) that mediation via peripheral cues such as emetic reinstatement of the cue during illness is not required for such learning, (c) that such learned aversions to colored water can last for months if alternative sources of drinking water are made available to the birds, and (d) that the aversions can be learned when the delay involved between exposure to the visual cue and onset of illness is as long as 2 hr.

LEARNED AVERSIONS TO COLORED WATER IN QUAIL

Of the two major, recurrent issues in this area of research (differential associability of cues, responses, and consequences of responding being one of them), our own research has concentrated mainly on the question of whether the long delay between the ingestive cue and consequent illness is a real delay. By real delay I mean one that is not mediated by lingering sensory aftereffects of the ingestive cue, and one which must be handled by associative learning theory rather than ignored on grounds that what appears to be associative learning is in fact mere sensitization.

423

All of the studies to be reported here were conducted in a large, air-conditioned, humidity-controlled room maintained at approximately 25° C and 50% relative humidity. Lighting was from evenly distributed, ceiling mounted fluorescent units which were on between 0400 and 1800 hr daily.

Unless otherwise mentioned, all of the studies had the following general characteristics in common. The subjects were adult male quail housed in individual wire cages and allowed free access to Purina game bird chow at all times. A few days prior to each experiment, water troughs were removed from the cage racks, and the birds were gradually habituated to drinking all of their water from 30 ml, clear glass Richter tubes within a 10-min session given at the same time each day. Individual drinking tubes were always placed in sequence along the front of the cage racks according to a prearranged schedule designed to insure that no birds would have to be removed from their cages and injected while other birds were still in the 10-min, measured drinking session. Often this meant that subjects in an experiment having a large N had to be run in squads, with staggered schedules for treatment days, recovery days, and test days for the different squads. In such cases, each squad represented a replication of the experiment with equal numbers of birds representing the various experimental and control conditions.

Birds were held as gently as possible for administration of the intraperitoneal injections and, interestingly, never gave any indication that they felt insertion of the needle, provided it was placed in the spot we always tried to put it, i.e., approximately 1 cm to one side of the lower tip of the sternum. They did, however, tend to struggle against the restraint of being held and would occasionally regurgitate some water if they struggled vigorously and the experimenter squeezed them too hard in his effort to hold them. Most of the few birds that died during the course of our several experiments did so as the result of choking on regurgitated water. A few deaths occurred for unknown reasons; since we have lost approximately equal numbers of saline- and toxin-injected birds, the most likely reason would seem to be misplacement of the needle. In no experiment was there ever any indication that birds which regurgitated during injection, and yet survived, showed more or less learning than birds which did not. Moreover, no bird in our experiments has ever been seen to regurgitate following the injection of either cyclophosphamide or lithium chloride. The most characteristic symptom of illness following toxic injection is crouching, with feathers ruffled and eyes closed or half-closed.

As mentioned earlier, our first report indicating that quail could use a visual cue in long-delay aversion learning did not include data to indicate that the effect was an instance of true associative learning rather than an effect ascribable to sensitization from recent illness per se. The study to be described now was run, however, before we submitted our basic finding for publication and is included here primarily because the earlier study has recently been criticized on the ground that it did not include a sensitization control (Bitterman, 1976). The study is of additional interest, however, because it shows a clear-cut trials effect (our earlier experiments had been designed around only one learning trial), and it showed us for the first time that quail can learn to discriminate one color of dyed water from another.

The subjects were 48 naive adult male bobwhite quail obtained from a local game bird farm. After habituation to our laboratory, and to the drinking regimen previously described, they were randomly divided into four groups of 12 birds each. For the first 6 days of the experiment, all groups received plain tap water in their regular, 10-min daily drinking sessions in order to establish an even baseline. During the next 8 days, all groups drank distilled water made red by the addition of commercial food coloring (1.5 cc per liter). The following day was the first day of experimental treatment, the treatments for each of the four groups being as follows.

Two groups were run according to a conditioning paradigm, i.e., a paradigm in which a different color of water was offered during the regular drinking period, with an IP injection administered ½ hr later. The different-colored water for these two groups was distilled water made green by the addition of food coloring (1.5 cc per liter). The IP injection for one of these conditioning-paradigm groups was cyclophosphamide (132 mg/kg body weight) but was normal saline for the other, as a control for possible effects of injection per se. The remaining two groups were treated according to a sensitization paradigm, i.e., they drank the same red water they had been drinking over the previous 8 days, but were nevertheless given injections ½ hr later. Here, too, one sensitization-paradigm group received the cyclophosphamide injection and the other an injection of normal saline. All four groups then drank the familiar red water during the next two daily drinking sessions to allow the birds which had received toxic injections to recover. A second treatment was administered on the following day, each group receiving exactly the same treatment it had received on the initial treatment day. Two recovery days on familiar red water again followed the treatment day, after which all groups received green water for five successive 10-min daily drinking sessions.

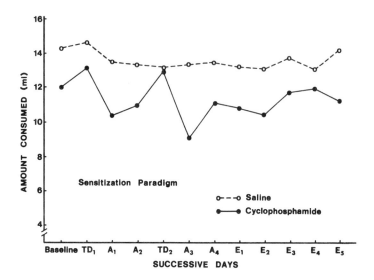

Figure 1
Mean amounts of water drunk by two groups of 12 birds run in the sensitization paradigm. The water was red each day throughout 8 days of baseline drinking (the last day of which is shown) and on all succeeding days until E_1 through E_5, on which green water was presented. IP injections were given ½ hr after the 10-min drinking sessions on days TD_1 and TD_2, one group receiving a toxic injection and the other an equivalent volume of normal saline.

The results are shown in Figures 1 and 2. Figure 1 gives the mean drinking scores of the two groups run in the sensitization paradigm on each day of the experiment from the final day of baseline drinking of red distilled water through the 5 successive days (E_1-E_5) of 10-min tests with green distilled water. As expected, the saline control group showed practically no fluctuation in drinking scores from day to day. They were, of course, drinking familiar red diistilled water each day until the tests with green began on E_1. The sensitization control groups, on the other hand, did show some depression in drinking scores following the first and second toxic injections associated with familiar red water, probably as a direct effect of illness (see below). When offered strange green water for the first time on E_1, however, they did not

426

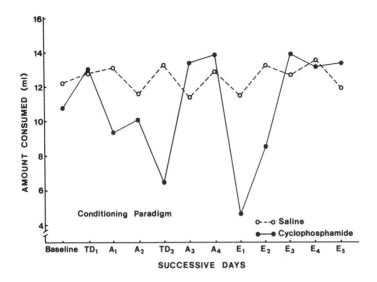

Figure 2
Mean amounts of water drunk by two groups of 12 birds run in the conditioning paradigm. The water was red throughout 8 days of baseline drinking (the last day of which is shown) but green on the first and second treatment days (TD_1 and TD_2) and on days E_1 through E_5. Treatment consisted of an IP injection administered ½ hr after the green-water drinking sessions, the injection being toxic for one group and an equivalent volume of normal saline for the other. Water of the familiar, red baseline color was drunk on the alternate days, A_1-A_2 and A_3-A_4.

show avoidance of it to any significant degree. Their drinking scores on green water, while a bit lower than those of the saline control group, are not significantly different from them on any day during the five tests with green water (E_1-E_5). Although possibly still suffering some ill effects from the two toxic injections administered during the past week, they did not show a significant "heightened neophobia" of the strange-colored green water.

Figure 2, which shows the drinking scores of the two conditioning paradigm groups, depicts a very different outcome. When first encountering strange green water on the first treatment day (TD_1) both groups drank normal amounts of it. The saline control group continued to drink normal amounts of water, regardless of its color, over the entire course of the experiment. The group which received cyclophosphamide ½ hr after drinking green water on the first and second treatment days (TD_1 and TD_2) showed, in contrast, quite radical fluctuations in amount of water consumed on subsequent

427

days, depending upon whether it was red or green. Their drinking of green water at TD_2 (after the one delayed-illness trial at TD_1) was significantly depressed ($p < .01$), and their drinking of green water at E_1 (after two conditioning trials) is even further depressed as compared to what they drank of green following one trial. The drinking of red water on the alternate days between treatments (A_1 and A_2) and between the second treatment and the beginning of extinction tests at E_1 (A_3 and A_4) is of interest in comparison to the drinking scores of birds in the sensitization group that received similar toxic injections, but after drinking red water. Drinking of red was depressed on A_1 and A_2, just as it was in the sensitization group, probably as a direct result of lingering illness. The dramatic rise in consumption of red water by these birds on alternate days A_3 and A_4 seems to have resulted in part from very strong thirst (they had drunk so little green water on TD_2) and in part from their having learned a discrimination between the two colors. The very rapid extinction of aversion to green water (E_1-E_5) almost certainly resulted from the fact that the birds were extremely water-deprived at that stage in the experiment and, with no alternative source of water, were forced to drink or die of thirst. This circumstance provided them with the opportunity to learn very quickly that drinking green water was no longer followed by an aversive consequence. As will be shown later, birds that are conditioned to avoid a given color will continue to avoid that color for a very long time if an alternative water supply is available.

TASTE VS. COLOR

In none of our work with quail up to this point had we ever had reason to suspect that they might be tasting the dyed water we had been using. Rats presumably could not taste it since they formed no aversion to it when it was paired with delayed illness (Wilcoxon et al., 1971), not even when the water was made opaque black by addition of relatively large amounts of green, blue, and red dye (Wilcoxon et al., 1970). Nevertheless, we aimed one study at the specific question of whether quail could form an association between delayed illness and whatever taste a vegetable dye might have for them.

The basic strategy was to allow one group of birds to drink all of their daily water throughout the entire course of the experiment from tubes that had been painted black. We had found that we could not detect what color the water was when we looked at the surface of it at the J-shaped end of a black Richter tube, and we surmised that the quail couldn't either. Thus, the plan was to put dyed water in the black tubes on treatment and test days to see whether the birds would learn to avoid drinking dyed water when they were unable to see what color it was. For comparison, a second group was run with clear glass tubes throughout, so that when dyed water was in the tubes on treatment and test days its color was clearly visible.

Subjects were 24 adult male bobwhite quail obtained from the Department of Poultry Science, Auburn University. All had been run in a pseudoconditioning study approximately one month prior to the present study and had experienced two injections of cyclophosphamide in the earlier experiment (Wilcoxon et al., 1970) during which half of them received their toxic injections after

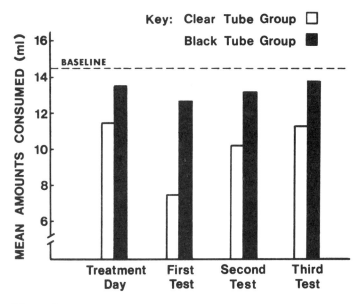

Figure 3
Mean amounts of yellow water drunk by two groups of birds on four occasions which were separated by 2 intervening days (not shown) of baseline drinking of plain distilled water. The Clear Tube Group (N=12) was able to see the yellow-dyed water on all of these four occasions. Birds in the Black Tube Group (N=12) were not expected to be able to see that the water in the tube was in fact yellow; they were expected to form an aversion to it only if it had any appreciable taste, which apparently it did not. The dashed baseline across the figure shows the mean amount consumed by all birds on the day prior to treatment.

429

drinking plain water, and half of them after drinking from blue-tinted tubes. The birds were systematically assigned (rather than randomly) to two groups of 12, therefore, in order to achieve two groups that were exactly balanced with respect to prior experimental history.

Following a week of baseline drinking in which 12 birds drank plain distilled water from black tubes and 12 drank the same from clear tubes, yellow water (1.5 cc commercial food dye per liter) was placed in all tubes for both groups. IP injections of cyclophosphamide (132 mg/kg) were then given to all birds in both groups ½ hr after the 10-min drinking session.

Results are shown in Figure 3. It is quite clear from these results that the quail readily learned an aversion to yellow-dyed water that they could see, but not to the same dyed water when drunk from a black tube which prevented their seeing its color ($p < .01$).

COLOR PREFERENCES OF BOBWHITE AND COTURNIX

The question of what color of water quail prefer to drink when offered a variety of colors is interesting in its own right. It was of special interest to us, however, because of the possibility that some particular color or colors might tend to be avoided more than others prior to any aversive conditioning. In the study described below (Fulmer, 1970), unconditioned preferences for a variety of colors of water were investigated in two species of quail, bobwhite (*Colinus virginianus*) and Japanese quail (*Coturnix coturnix japonica*).

Twenty naive adult males of each species served as subjects. The bobwhites were hatched and reared at a local gamebird farm where they had spent the last few months of maturation in large, outdoor enclosures. Coturnix subjects, on the other hand, had been hatched and reared to maturity indoors at the Department of Poultry Science, Auburn University.

Following habituation to our laboratory, and to the regimen of drinking all of their daily water supply from clear glass Richter tubes, all birds were given 10-min preference tests each day for 20 days. Five colors were used in the tests, one of them being plain tap water to which the quail were already accustomed. The other four colors (red, yellow, green, blue) were made by adding 1.5 ml of commercial food coloring to each liter of tap water. Daily preference tests consisted of placing two tubes on the front of each bird's cage. In every case the bird had a choice between water of two different colors presented simultaneously. Each bird received each of the 10 possible pairs of colors twice (left and right positions of pair members counterbalanced) in an otherwise random se-

430

quence over the 20-day course of the experiment. This was accomplished by first assigning a random number from 1 to 20 to each of the 10 possible pairs and the 10 mirror images of those pairs, and then placing the randomly selected pairs on the individual cages which, for each species, had already been numbered sequentially from 1 to 20. The random placement thus obtained served for day 1 of preference testing. Placement of the pairs on the remaining 19 days of preference testing was determined by shifting all pairs one cage to the left each day. This assured that each subject was tested on the two instances of each pair (e.g., red left - green right, and green left - red right), and in a random order that was determined once and for all for each bird on the first test day.

The first analysis of the data was in terms of the average daily consumption of each color. For bobwhite the mean daily amounts consumed (ml) were, in order of preference, blue 8.1, green 8.0, yellow 6.6, red 6.5, plain 5.9. The differences were not large and the exact order of preference could hardly be expected to hold up on replication. It is interesting, however, that the obtained order was perfectly correlated with wave length of the hues, blue through red. Only the difference between blue and plain was significant by separate t-test ($p < .01$).

The main importance of the above finding for us was that we now knew that none of the colors we had used in our earlier work with bobwhites had been a color to which the birds had any appreciable unlearned aversion.

A parallel analysis of coturnix drinking scores showed a different and steeper order of preference. Their mean daily amounts consumed (ml) of each color were, again in order of preference, yellow 8.7, green 7.0, blue 7.0, plain 6.0, red 4.0. The difference between most-preferred yellow and least-preferred red was striking and significant beyond the .01 level. All other mean differences of 1.7 ml or greater were significant at the .05 level or better.

We can only speculate as to reasons for the different preferences shown by bobwhite and coturnix. Differences in early rearing conditions cannot be ruled out, however, since as previously mentioned the bobwhites had been reared in outdoor pens (under blue skies?) and the coturnix indoors under artificial illumination.

The data were also analyzed for differences in preference for each of the five colors as compared to the remaining four colors with which it had been presented as a pair. Since each bird had been tested twice on each pair of colors (position of colors counterbalanced), the two tests were averaged for each bird to eliminate any bias which might have resulted from position preferences.

Table 1

PREFERENCE SCORES IN THE 10 PAIRS OF COLORS
FOR EACH SPECIES

Bobwhite

	Blue	Green	Yellow	Red	Plain
Blue		.53	.60	.58	.62
Green			.59	.61	.60
Yellow				.52	.55
Red					.57
Plain					

Coturnix

	Yellow	Green	Blue	Plain	Red
Yellow		.60	.59*	.67**	.74**
Green			.50	.58	.64*
Blue				.64**	.67**
Plain					.64*
Red					

The 5 colors entering into the pairs are tabulated in rows and columns in the order of preference shown for them by each species in the previous analysis of overall average daily consumption of each color. The preference scores in the table were calculated by dividing the amount consumed of the row color by the total amount consumed when row and column colors were presented as pairs.

* p < .05
** p < .01

Preference scores in the 10 different pairs of colors are shown for each species in Table 1. As in the analysis of overall average daily consumption, bobwhites failed to show a strong preference for any particular color although the obtained preference scores for blue were slightly higher in each case wherein it was paired with another color. In general, however, bobwhite preferences for particular colors over others were not statistically significant. Coturnix, on the other hand, did show several fairly strong and statistically significant preferences within the various pairs. Their preference for yellow, especially when it was paired with red, was quite strong. Indeed, red was clearly the least-preferred color. Not only yellow, but green, blue, and plain were each significantly preferred when paired with red.

CONDITIONING OF AVERSION TO PREFERRED, FAMILIAR COLORS

Since familiarity and preference both seem to work against the learning of aversions, we took it as a challenge to see whether the birds used in the study just described could be conditioned to avoid the colored water for which they had shown the greatest preference, even though they had been exposed to it on numerous occasions along with the other four colors. In anticipation of the possibility that this might be difficult, we designed the study so as to include four conditioning trials, and to provide for 2-tube preference tests as the measure, rather than the less sensitive 1-tube tests employed in our previous studies. The experiment began 4 days after completion of the 20-day preference study described above.

During the first 4 days, all birds of a given species were offered two tubes filled with water of the same color on a given day. On the first day, the least preferred color was offered in the two tubes. Thus, bobwhites received plain water and coturnix received red water. On days 2, 3, and 4, each species received two tubes of water having the color next on the rank of preferences for that species until finally, on day 5, the most-preferred color for each species was presented. One-half hr after the 10-min drinking of most-preferred water, all 20 birds of each species were injected IP with a 2% body weight dose of .15 molar lithium chloride solution. Three additional such conditioning trials on the previously-preferred water were given at 3-day intervals. On intervening recovery days, all birds were offered water of one of the other four colors in two tubes, with the colors appearing from day to day in the same sequence as described above for the days prior o the first conditioning trial.

Two-tube preference tests began on the day following the fourth conditioning trial and continued for 4 successive days. The first 2-tube preference test was between the previously most-preferred color (which had by that time been paired with four, ½ hr-delayed illnesses) and the previously least-preferred color. The second, third, and fourth preference tests were between the conditioning color and the remaining colors, the latter appearing on each successive day in ascending order of the previously determined preference for them. Placement of the conditioning color was alternated from left to right daily.

Data were first analyzed to determine whether a significant reduction in drinking of the previously preferred water had occurred over the course of the four conditioning trials, and before the introduction of 2-tube preference tests. Such was, indeed, the case for bobwhites. Their drinking of blue water showed a gradual and statistically significant reduction ($p < .01$), the means (ml) on the 4 treatment days being 14.3, 13.1, 9.8, and 8.8 respectively. Their drinking of the other colors on the days intervening between conditioning trials was above baseline after the second and third illnesses. But again the coturnix behaved differently. They showed no significant reduction in drinking their preferred color (yellow) over the course of the four conditioning trials in which the drinking of yellow had been followed ½ hr later by lithium injection. Although showing a trend in the direction of indicating some conditioned avoidance, the means (ml) of 15.6, 14.2, 13.6, and 12.8 were not significantly different from one another. Drinking of the other colors by coturnix on the days intervening between conditioning trials on yellow was at normal baseline levels.

Results of the preference tests for bobwhites following the four conditioning trials are shown in Figure 4. Bobwhites showed a strong avoidance of blue water when it was offered along with plain on the first day, with red on the second day, with yellow on the third day, and with green on the fourth day. The differences between the mean amount of blue consumed in comparison to the mean consumption of each of the other colors are in every case large and highly significant statistically ($p < .01$).

Post-conditioning preference tests for coturnix were not so clearcut as those for bobwhite. For example, on the first day of preference testing, they drank essentially equal amounts of the yellow and red water offered to them (7.1 and 6.8 ml, respectively). Thus, their previous strong preference for yellow as against red appeared to interfere with their learning to avoid yellow to the degree that bobwhites had learned to avoid their previously preferred blue

434

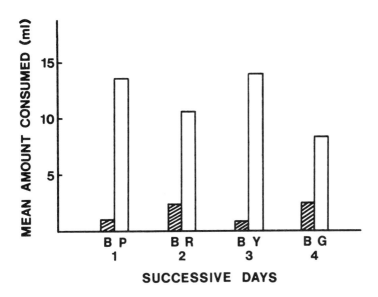

Figure 4
Mean amounts of water of different colors consumed on 4 successive days of 2-tube preference tests following four delayed-illness conditioning trials with blue water. On each successive day, B (lue) water was offered along with a different one of the other four colors, P (lain), R (ed), Y (ellow), or G (reen).

water. Recall, however, that pre-conditioning preferences among the various colors were not strong for bobwhites, whereas they had been strong for coturnix. An appropriate analysis of the post-conditioning preferences in coturnix, therefore, would be one in which their drinking of yellow versus the other colors was compared to their drinking scores on the same pairs prior to conditioning. Such an analysis was performed. It revealed that the strong preference for yellow prior to the four conditioning trials had indeed been reduced. Table 2 shows the results. Yellow water, although still consumed in considerable amounts following the four conditioning trials, was much less preferred in relation to the other colors than it had been prior to conditioning.

In summary, both species of quail showed unconditioned preferences among the five colors, with coturnix showing the stronger preferences. Following four conditioning trials in which drinking of the species-preferred color was followed ½ hr later by lithium chloride injection, both species significantly reduced their intake of the previously preferred water. Reduction in consumption of blue water by bobwhites was more pronounced than reduction in

Table 2

COTURNIX CHANGES IN PREFERENCE

Mean Amounts Consumed (ml)

Color Pair	Pre-Conditioning		Post-Conditioning	
	Yellow	Paired Color	Yellow	Paired Color
Yellow-Red★★	9.8	3.4	7.1	6.8
Yellow-Plain	9.4	4.6	7.4	7.1
Yellow-Blue★★	7.9	5.6	4.1	10.1
Yellow-Green★	8.3	5.6	4.6	8.9

★ p<.05 (for change between pre- and post-conditioning scores)
★★p<.01

drinking of yellow water by coturnix, probably because coturnix had a stronger pre-conditioning preference for yellow than the bobwhites had shown for blue water.

LONG-TERM RETENTION OF AVERSION TO SPECIFIC COLOR

Following completion of the study just described, we conducted a number of retention tests with the same bobwhites since they had conditioned so well, even though a formal investigation of retention had not been a part of the original plan. To our surprise, we learned that the aversion to blue water showed little if any attenuation in repetitions of the 4-day, 2-tube preference tests when given 1 week, 6 weeks, and 16 weeks after the original tests administered at the conclusion of the experiment. It seemed virtually certain that the presence of an alternative to blue water each day the tests were run (birds were on ad lib plain water between test series) had a great deal to do with the failure of the aversion to blue to extinguish. In our previous extinction tests, the 24-hr deprived birds had been offered only the color of water they had been conditioned to avoid. Under such circumstances, extinction of the aversion had appeared to be complete within a matter of a few days. Even so, it seemed remarkable that quail could "remember" to avoid one color from among four others for 4 months. We designed the following

436

study, therefore, to investigate this phenomenon deliberately, and in greater detail (Wilcoxon & Dwyer, 1973).

The main question we wanted to answer was whether the preference tests interspersed at intervals during the 4 months since conditioning were responsible, in whole or in part, for the birds' long retention. Perhaps the quail would not avoid a particular color which had been drunk prior to delayed illness if the first series of preference tests with that color versus the others occurred for the first time 4 months after the last illness. Maybe occasional "practice" of the aversion was required for relatively long-term retention.

Every effort was made to insure that the present experiment would be comparable to the one last described except for the deliberate manipulation of the number of preference tests intervening between the conditioning trials and the preference tests to be given after 4 months had passed.

Forty-eight naive adult male bobwhites that had been hatched and reared in our laboratory served as subjects. They were first put through a 20-day series of 2-tube preference tests with the five colors exactly as described in the previous study. Interestingly, these lab-reared birds did not show exactly the same order of preference for the five colors as had been shown by the bobwhites in the previous experiment which had been reared largely outdoors. Plain water turned out to be the water consumed in greatest overall average amounts by the new birds. Blue water, the favorite of the farm-reared birds, came in a close second, however, and none of the unconditioned preferences among the five colors was either large or statistically significant. We felt it best, all told, to use blue again as the color to be conditioned, especially since plain water was required for the long periods of ad lib water to be used between preference tests.

Following the 20 days of initial preference testing, all birds drank plain water from a pair of Richter tubes for 3 days (10 min daily drinking sessions) and on the succeeding 4 days drank green, red, yellow, and finally blue, which was followed on that day by a ½-hr-delayed injection of .15 molar lithium chloride solution (2% body weight). As in the previous experiment, all birds received four such conditioning trials on blue, with 2 recovery days between trials, and with water of a different color offered on successive recovery days.[1]

Subjects were assigned to four groups of 12 birds each, with each group scheduled to receive post-conditioning preference tests according to the plan shown in Table 3. Group I (IMR) received the 4-day series of preference tests (with blue versus first one and then

437

another of the four other colors on successive days) immediately after the series of conditioning trials, again 2 months later, and again 4 months after conditioning. Thus, this group closely paralleled the unplanned testing we had done after the previous experiment and may be regarded as our effort to confirm the earlier, serendipitous finding of surprisingly long retention. We had hoped that Group II (IR), tested the first 4 days after conditioning, and then 4 months later would show us whether preference tests immediately after conditioning would be sufficient to promote long retention. Group III (MR), tested at the middle and the end of the 4-month interval, and Group IV (R), which was tested only once, 4 months after conditioning, should provide direct evidence of how long bobwhite quail can remember to avoid a particular color in the absence of any opportunity to "practice" the aversion shortly after the conditioning trials.

Table 3

SCHEDULE FOR PREFERENCE TESTS

	Immediate (started day after conditioning)	Middle (2 mos later)	Remote (4 mos later)
Groups			
I (IMR)	Tested	Tested	Tested
II (IR)	Tested		Tested
III (MR)		Tested	Tested
IV (R)			Tested

Table 4 shows the mean amounts drunk by the four groups on the 5 days leading up to and including the first treatment, or conditioning trial, which was given on the last of these 5 days ½ hr after all birds had drunk blue water. The figures in the table simply show that all groups were drinking all of the five colors of water in essentially equal and normal amounts prior to conditioning.

Table 5 presents the mean drinking scores for all of the groups on each day throughout the course of the conditioning phase of the study. Water of the color indicated in the table was presented in a pair of tubes each day for 10 min. The reduction in drinking of blue water over trials was regular, substantial, and highly significant statistically.

438

Table 4

MEAN DRINKING SCORES (ml)
PRIOR TO TREATMENT

Color on Successive Days

	Plain	Green	Red	Yellow	Blue
Groups					
I (IMR)	13.4	10.7	11.3	12.6	12.0
II (IR)	10.7	10.6	10.2	10.7	12.1
III (MR)	11.7	10.8	12.1	11.7	12.9
IV (R)	10.6	9.3	11.1	10.6	12.0
Combined	11.5	10.3	11.2	11.4	12.2

In Table 6 are the data of primary interest. The numbers in the table are mean preference scores for blue versus the four other colors with which it was paired during the four days comprising each preference test. Preference scores were calculated for each bird by dividing the total amount of blue water the bird consumed during the four 2-tube tests by the total amount of blue plus the other four colored waters used in each test series. Thus, for example, the mean preference score of .057 for birds in Group I for the immediate test indicates that, of all the water consumed over the 4 days in which blue was paired each day with a different one of the other four colors, only 5.7% was blue water.

The first three columns in Table 6 show the principal results of the experiment. The main import of the preference scores shown in these columns is that it appears not to matter whether bobwhite quail "practice" their conditioned aversion in 2-tube preference tests given soon after the conditioning trials. They appear to remember to avoid the conditioned color very well when they encounter the preference tests for the first time at 2 months or even 4 months after the conditioning trials.

The mean preference scores shown in the last three columns of Table 6 come from preference tests identical to those already described, but which followed three extinction series in which only blue water was offered to the birds for 3 successive days. This is the condition in which we have always found that birds rapidly overcome their conditioned aversion to drinking water of a particular color if it is the only water offered to them in limited

Table 5

MEAN DRINKING SCORES (ml)
DURING CONDITIONING PHASE

Color on Successive Days

Groups	Blue*	Green	Red	Blue*	Yellow	Plain	Blue*	Green	Red	Blue*
I (IMR)	12.0	13.1	15.2	11.6	16.7	17.5	6.5	17.1	17.9	4.8
II (IR)	12.1	12.5	16.0	12.5	16.5	18.9	6.6	18.4	17.4	5.7
III (MR)	12.9	13.8	15.5	10.7	17.8	18.0	6.7	16.8	16.1	5.2
IV (R)	12.0	12.2	14.6	9.3	16.8	18.2	5.2	15.9	16.7	2.9
Combined	12.2	12.9	15.4	11.1	16.9	18.2	6.2	17.0	17.0	4.7

*Drinking of blue water was followed ½ hr later by 2 body weight IP injection of .15 molar lithium chloride.

440

Table 6

PREFERENCE SCORES AT DIFFERENT RETENTION
INTERVALS FOLLOWING CONDITIONING*

			Time of Preference Test			
	Immediate	Middle (2 mos)	Remote (4 mos)	After First Extinction	After Second Extinction	After Third Extinction
Groups						
I (IMR)	.057	.055	.053	.215	.242	.277
II (IR)	.059		.027	.183	.251	.318
III (MR)		.042	.110	.296	.379	.466
IV (R)			.056	.206	.408	.479

*Preference Score $= \dfrac{\text{Amount Blue}}{\text{Blue + Other Colors}}$ (Combined over the four days of each preference test)

441

daily drinking sessions under 24-hr water deprivation. The first "forced drinking" extinction of the aversion to blue water began the day after the remote (4 months post-conditioning) preference test was concluded. On the first day, drinking of blue (about 5 ml) was considerably below normal baseline levels, but on the second day it rose to around 10 ml, and on the third day was back up to baseline (means of 13 ml, 13 ml, 13 ml, and 12 ml for Groups I-IV respectively). Yet, as may be seen in Table 6, the aversion to blue water was still present to some extent in all groups as measured in the 2-tube preference tests after the first forced-drinking extinction series. The same was true after the second 3-day extinction except that, by that time, it began to look as if those birds which had had preference tests immediately after conditioning (Groups I and II) were maintaining their aversion to blue more strongly than those birds which had not had the immediate tests (Group III and IV). This trend was confirmed in the tests given after the third extinction series. In those final tests, the combined preference scores of Groups I and II were significantly different from the combined scores of Groups III and IV at well beyond the .01 level.[2]

THE DELAY GRADIENT

It is well known that the strength of taste aversions in rats is a decreasing function of time of delay between exposure to taste and onset of illness, even though very strong aversions are readily obtained with delays much longer than those typically found to be quite ineffective in the other kinds of avoidance learning. We investigated the effect of varying the delay between exposure to a distinctive visual cue and toxic injection with bobwhite quail (Wilcoxon & Fulmer, 1971, 1972) in the two studies next to be described.

Initial Experiment. Table 7 gives detailed results of an experiment first reported in preliminary form by Wilcoxon and Fulmer at the 1971 meeting of the Southeastern Psychological Association. The main variables were (a) duration of delay between drinking and the delivery of toxic injection, and (b) color of the water to be associated with illness. Fifty birds were randomly assigned to 10 groups of five each, the experimental conditions for which are outlined at the left of the table. Delay was varied at four levels, 5 min, 30 min, 60 min, and 120 min. For each delay condition, one group was given 9 days of baseline training in which they drank from two tubes (two tubes were used throughout the experiment) filled with distilled water made blue by adding 1.5 cc of food coloring; a comparable group received 9 days of similar training with plain distilled water. Sensitization control groups were included in the experimental design since the color that the birds would be drinking on conditioning trials, and tested on later, would not be the most familiar color in their recent drinking history, which made the possibility of heightened neophobia a factor to be considered. Clearly, however, such groups were not called for at all delay intervals. We ran them, therefore, only in the 120-min-delay condition, which seemed the most appropriate place to put them as a control for possible non-associative effects of illness per se.

The first column of numbers shown in the conditioning phase of the experiment (under B) gives the mean amounts drunk from both tubes on the last day of baseline training. The drinking is nicely uniform across groups despite their small size. The next column (TD_1) shows mean amounts drunk on the first treatment day. On this day and the 3 subsequent treatment days $(TD_2, TD_3,$ and $TD_4)$ all birds drank water of the color different from the one they had been exposed to in baseline training. They then received 2% body weight injections of .15 molar lithium chloride with delays between drinking and injection as called for by their group assignment. On each of the recovery days $(R_1$-$R_6)$ which intervened between treatment days, all birds drank water of their baseline training color.

By scanning the table across rows, one can see the gradual acquisition during the conditioning phase of an aversion to drinking water of the treatment-day color in all groups except (a) the 60-min-delay group whose treatment-day color was plain, (b) the two 120-min-delay groups, and (c) the two sensitization control groups whose drinking scores on the same color of water each day seem to have been elevated slightly, probably from the dehydrating effects of lithium injections given on treatment days. In general, the birds conditioned reasonably well to even plain water when the delay was either 5 min or 30 min $(p < .05)$, and very well to blue water at all the delay intervals $(p < .05$ or better in all cases) except the 120-min delay. The "delay gradient," however, is not regular unless one pools data from both groups at each delay interval—a procedure hardly justifiable given some of the substantial differences between groups conditioned to plain as opposed to blue water. Furthermore, there is the rather anomalous suggestion in the observed means that the 60-min-delay group may have developed a stronger aversion to blue than its 30-min-delay counterpart. There is no question, however, that the 120-min-delay conditioning group which was treated on plain water failed to show any evidence of

Table 7

MEAN AMOUNTS (ml) CONSUMED THROUGHOUT EXPERIMENT

	Groups			Conditioning Phase											Treatment Color	Recovery Color
Delay and Treatment (min)	Baseline Color	Treatment Color	Recovery Color	B	TD$_1$	R$_1$	R$_2$	TD$_2$	R$_3$	R$_4$	TD$_3$	R$_5$	R$_6$	TD$_4$		
5 LiCl	Blue	Plain	Blue	12.4	10.8	11.0	14.8	10.6	14.6	16.4	9.6	16.0	17.2	7.2	0.2	11.7
5 LiCl	Plain	Blue	Plain	12.6	11.6	12.8	16.4	5.4	18.8	20.2	1.6	19.2	16.0	0.0	0.0	13.3
30 LiCl	Blue	Plain	Blue	13.0	13.2	9.0	14.8	12.0	12.0	12.2	8.2	16.0	13.2	6.6	0.0	13.7
30 LiCl	Plain	Blue	Plain	12.8	11.0	11.2	14.4	8.8	16.2	16.2	5.2	18.4	16.0	6.6	0.0	13.9
60 LiCl	Blue	Plain	Blue	12.4	14.8	12.2	16.0	15.0	13.4	13.0	11.0	16.6	15.6	14.0	1.3	13.8
60 LiCl	Plain	Blue	Plain	12.6	11.6	12.4	16.4	3.6	18.4	18.2	3.6	22.0	19.8	3.4	0.4	16.7
120 LiCl	Blue	Plain	Blue	12.5	12.0	11.7	14.3	16.2	18.8	16.8	20.8	19.2	17.4	20.2	2.4	12.4
120 LiCl	Plain	Blue	Plain	13.0	10.2	13.8	17.8	12.0	13.6	14.6	10.8	16.0	15.2	10.2	2.4	14.0
120 LiCl*	Plain	Plain	Plain	12.5	11.7	14.2	14.7	15.7	20.4	22.8	20.0	21.0	17.6	18.6	7.0*	6.0*
120 LiCl*	Blue	Blue	Blue	12.0	13.2	10.2	16.0	16.5	14.5	15.5	14.0	13.5	13.0	12.8	8.0*	6.8*

*These two groups were sensitization control groups that received the same color throughout the experiment until the preference test. The mean amounts entered under "Recovery Color" in the preference test are the amounts they drank of blue (6.0), and of plain (6.8), i.e., the colors that were novel to them.

conditioning over the course of the four trials. Although there is a minor trend suggesting the development of a mild aversion to blue water in the other 120-min-delay group, it is not statistically significant. In short, the 2-hr delay did attenuate the strength of the aversion.

Two-tube preference tests given on the 6 successive days following conditioning showed virtually total avoidance of the water associated with illness, regardless of the delay interval used in conditioning, and regardless of whether the treatment-day water was plain or blue. These results are presented in the first two columns to the right of the conditioning phase data. The numbers are mean daily amounts (ml) drunk of each color over six daily sessions in which treatment color and recovery color were switched from left to right and right to left daily. Even the birds in the two 120-min-delay conditioning groups drank significantly less of the treatment-day color than of the recovery-day color (p < .01 with blue treatment color and p < .05 with plain treatment color). All of the other groups showed significant differences in the preference tests at levels ranging from p < .001 to p < .05. In contrast, the two sensitization control groups drank essentially equal amounts of the water they had been receiving each day from the beginning of baseline training (blue in one case, plain in the other) and water of the opposite color. The outcome of the preference tests in the two 120-min-delay conditioning groups cannot, therefore, be ascribed to sensitization.

There was, however, an interesting ambiguity in the preference test results, especially in the case of the two 120-min-delay conditioning groups. They clearly drank more water of the color that had been used on recovery days than they did of the water they had drunk on treatment days. But why? They had shown no significant decrease in consumption of the treatment-day color during the course of the four conditioning trials. Could it be that they had learned a preference for the recovery-day color, rather than an aversion to the treatment-day color? The follow-up experiment presented in Table 8 was designed to answer that question.

Follow-up Experiment. What seemed most needed was a neutral color to be used in post-conditioning preference tests, a color that had been associated with neither delayed illness nor recovery from illness. The use of such a color paired with treatment-day color could show us whether the treated birds had learned an aversion to the treatment-day color. The same neutral color paired with the color drunk on recovery days could show whether the birds had, instead, developed a liking for the recovery-day color. It was possi-

445

ble, of course, that the birds would learn both, i.e., an aversion to treatment color and a liking for recovery color.

TABLE 8

MEAN AMOUNTS (ml) CONSUMED
THROUGHOUT EXPERIMENT
(Abbrev. same as in Figure 7)

		120	120	120	120
Delay (min) and Treatment		LiCl	Sal	LiCl	Sal
Baseline Color		Red	Red	Red	Red
Treatment Color		Blue	Blue	Yellow	Yellow
Recovery Color		Yellow	Yellow	Blue	Blue
Successive	Days	B	15.5	15.8	14.6	15.7
		TD_1	17.2	15.8	13.2	16.3
		R_1	14.5	14.0	10.9	10.9
		R_2	16.9	15.2	14.1	13.1
		TD_2	15.0	16.0	10.9	15.9
		R_3	17.6	13.5	14.0	12.0
		R_4	18.2	15.0	15.8	13.7
		TD_3	10.6	13.8	11.88	12.4
		R_5	16.8	14.2	17.0	13.3
		R_6	17.2	14.0	15.0	12.1
		TD_4	9.5	13.0	10.9	14.1
Treatment Color			3.6	5.8	2.3	5.5
Recovery Color			13.9	7.6	11.1	5.9
Treatment Color			3.0	8.9	3.0	5.6
Baseline Color			12.8	5.6	10.7	7.0
Recovery Color			7.5	8.5	6.3	7.3
Baseline Color			8.9	5.4	6.8	5.9

Thirty-two bobwhite quail were randomly assigned to the four groups whose experimental conditions are outlined in Table 8. All groups received 7 days of baseline training in which they drank red distilled water from two tubes (1.5 cc food coloring per liter). Again, two tubes were used throughout the experiment. Saline con-

446

trol groups were included this time because, although red water would be made familiar to all of the birds during baseline training, it might be reacted to as novel and not truly neutral when seen for the first time again many days later during preference testing. Sensitization controls were not needed in light of the results from such groups run in the previous study. We selected blue and yellow for treatment and recovery colors with the expectation that discrimination between them would probably be easier than it had been between blue and plain in the previous study.

Examination of the rows of drinking scores during the conditioning phase of the follow-up experiment reveals that the birds treated on blue did show good discrimination between blue and yellow (the recovery-day color) over the course of the trials (p < .01), but the trend in the same direction for birds treated on yellow (with blue as recovery-day color) was not significant. Thus, the significant (in the case of blue) reduction in drinking of treatment-day color, despite a 2-hr delay between drinking and injection, supported the notion that the birds had come to see the treatment-day color as aversive. It remained to be seen whether the birds might also have learned to prefer recovery-day color over a neutral color. The answer to this question can be seen in the outcomes of the preference tests which were begun on the day after completion of the conditioning phase.

Preference tests between each pair of colors listed in the table were given on 2 successive days, with the spatial position of the colors reversed on the second day to control for possible position preferences. The figures in the table are the mean daily amounts drunk of each color averaged over the 2 days.

Our first priority was to replicate the previous finding that much more recovery-day water would be consumed than treatment-day water. As the values in the table show, this was the case for the two groups that received lithium injections, regardless of whether blue or yellow had been the color ingested 2 hr prior to the injections (p < .05). The two saline control groups, on the other hand, showed no such differences. Thus, the earlier finding held up on replication.

The critical preference tests, those at which the study really had been aimed, were conducted in a fairly complicated way. We needed to test the neutral baseline color against treatment-day color and against recovery-day color, but which test should come first? We did not want the order of testing to be a factor in the outcome of either test. Accordingly, we randomly divided each group into two subgroups, one of which received the treatment-color vs baseline-

447

color preference test first and the recovery-color vs baseline-color preference test next; the other subgroup received the tests in the reverse order. Each preference test spanned 2 days (color positions counterbalanced) and, as before, the figures in Table 8 are average amounts of the designated colors consumed over the 2 days of each test.

In the treatment-color vs. baseline-color test, it is clear that the treatment color was being avoided if the hypothesis that the baseline color was really neutral was tenable. Inspection of the scores of saline control groups shows that red was, indeed, essentially neutral with respect to treatment color; the small obtained differences are not statistically significant.

Finally, the recovery-color vs. baseline-color preference test shows that the recovery-day color had not come to be preferred over a neutral color by virtue of its having been drunk while the birds were recovering from illness. There were no significant differences obtained in that test.

It may be concluded, therefore, that bobwhite quail did learn to reduce their ingestion of colored water which had been followed on previous occasions by a 2-hr-delayed toxic injection. Also, the data provide no evidence that the birds learned to like the colored water which they drank on intervening recovery days.

GENERAL DISCUSSION AND CONCLUSIONS

I think the main significance of the findings reported above is that they demonstrate beyond reasonable doubt that long-delay learning of ingestive aversions in quail is a fact. Both mediation of the delay by any form of lingering peripheral stimulation, or reinstatement of such stimulation during illness, appear to have been effectively ruled out as explanations, as has sensitization. What we must look for now, in my view, is a central mechanism. I do not believe that we will find a ghost in the machine, but neither do I believe that the kinds of bridges we have traditionally used to span the temporal gap will bear the burden of these findings.

When we first became convinced that quail could in fact associate a purely visual cue with a long-delay illness, we suggested that the capacity to do so would likely turn out to be present in other highly visual species that rely heavily on vision in their normal foraging. Since then, several investigators have looked into this matter. Gorry and Ober (1970) have reported that squirrel monkeys can learn to avoid colored water on the basis of delayed illness, and Johnson, Beaton, and Hall (1974) have reported that

448

green monkeys can associate visual cues with delayed illness. Our own efforts (Wilcoxon & Etscorn, 1976) with rhesus monkeys, on the other hand, have been unsuccessful. While our monkeys readily learned taste aversions in the long-delay paradigm, they showed no evidence of associating a purely visual cue with delayed illness when sensitization and position preferences were adequately controlled.

Several rodent species that are less nocturnal than the rat, an animal well-known for its ineptitude for associating visual cues over long delays, have been studied. Braveman (this volume) has been able to show long-delay learning of aversions to visually distinctive ingestants in guinea pigs, even though the visual system of this animal is not very highly developed. In our own laboratory, we have been unsuccessful in establishing long-delay, illness-induced aversions to purely visual cues in gerbils (Abernathy, 1971) and spiny mice, *Acomys cahirinus* (Etscorn, 1977), although taste aversions were demonstrated in both species. It seems, therefore, that the question of how wide-spread the capacity is to associate visual cues with delayed illness is still very much an open one.

Garcia's pioneering work (e.g., Garcia, Ervin, & Koelling, 1966; Garcia & Koelling, 1966) in this fascinating research area indicated that only taste cues would turn out to be effective in long-delay aversion learning. This, and Brower's independent investigations (e.g., Brower et al., 1968) led us to speculate about birds and visual cues, and then to experiment with them. We are very happy that we did, and we are even more pleased that Garcia himself has taken up an interest in birds (Garcia & Hankins, this volume).

FOOTNOTES

[1]Neither sensitization control groups nor saline control groups were included in the above studies dealing with conditioned aversions to preferred colors and the long-term retention of aversions. Perhaps a few words need to be said about that. The rationale was that the colors to be used in the critical preference tests following conditioning would be, by that time, quite familiar to all subjects. Thus, if the birds showed a tendency to avoid only the color that had been ingested prior to illness, their avoidance could hardly be attributed to heightened neophobia resulting from sensitization by recent illnesses. In fact, the conditioned color would be the one most often and most recently seen. Similarly, there seemed no good reason to include saline control groups: we had never seen injection per se to have an effect when administered ½ hr following exposure to a color, and as for how unconditioned quail would respond to the various pairs of colors to be used in preference tests, such data had already been obtained in the 20-day series of preconditioning preference tests.

[2]The rapid extinction of aversions to colored water when water of the conditioned color is the only one available seems readily understandable. So does the rather prolonged retention of the aversion in the two-tube preference test situation wherein the birds, in choosing the alternative available to them, forego the opportunity to learn that ingestion of the color to which they are conditioned is no longer followed by a noxious consequence. The fact, however, that the aversion is still found to be present when measured by 2-tube preference tests after "forced drinking" extinction is somewhat puzzling. is testimony to the sensitivity of the 2-tube test, to be sure, but it also seems to suggest an almost cognitive element in the aversion (if I may be permitted to use loose language loosely) as opposed to a visceral one. In this connection, I should like to observe, finally, that the drinking behavior of our conditioned birds in the 2-tube tests lends no support to the interpretation that illness-induced aversions are based on "conditioned nausea." Birds so strongly conditioned to a particular color that they drink none of it whatever, nevertheless drink normal amounts of an alternate color in an adjacent tube, with both tubes in clear view. It is difficult to see how a bird nauseated at the sight of one color would drink another color in copious amounts from a tube placed about 1 cm to one side of the one that "looks nauseating."

450

ACKNOWLEDGEMENTS

Preparation of this chapter and the research reported in it were supported by NICHD Grant No. 00973. The author thanks the several reserach assistants and associates who have contributed to the research program, William B. Dragoin, James E. Dwyer, R. Stephen Fulmer, David E. Borrebach, James A. Czaplicki, and Frank T. Etscorn.

REFERENCES

Abernathy, W. B. The utilization of visual and gustatory cues by the gerbil in an illness-induced aversion. Unpublished master's thesis, George Peabody College for Teachers, Nashville, August 1971.

Bitterman, M. E. Flavor aversion studies. **Science**, 1976, **192**, 266-267.

Brower, L. P., Ryerson, W. N., Coppinger, L. L., & Glazier, S. C. Ecological chemistry and the palatability spectrum. **Science**, 1968, **161**, 1349-1351.

Etscorn, F. T. Illness-induced aversion learning in the spiny mouse to gustatory and visual cues. Unpublished doctoral dissertation, George Peabody College for Teachers, Nashville, 1977.

Fulmer, R. S. Colored water preferences in two quail species. Paper presented at the meeting of the Psychonomic Society, San Antonio, November 1970.

Garcia, John, Ervin, F. R., & Koelling, R. A. Learning with prolonged delay of reinforcement. **Psychonomic Science**, 1966, **5**(3), 121-122.

Garcia, John, & Koelling, R. A. Relation of cue to consequence in avoidance learning. **Psychonomic Science**, 1966, **4**, 123-124.

Gorry, T., & Ober, S. Stimulus characteristics of learning over long delays in monkeys. Paper presented at the meeting of the Psychonomic Society, San Antonio, 1970.

Johnson, C., Beaton, R., & Hall, K. Poison-based avoidance learning in nonhuman primates: Use of visual cues. **Physiology and Behavior**, 1975, **14**, 403-407.

Morgan, C. Lloyd. **Habit and instinct**. London: Edward Arnold, Publisher to the India Office, 1896.

Rothschild, M. Mimicry. **Natural History**, 1967, **76**, 44-50.

Smith, J. C., & Roll, D. L. Trace conditioning with x-rays as an aversive stimulus. **Psychonomic Science**, 1967, **9**, 11-12.

Smith, S. M. Innate recognition of coral snake pattern by a possible avian predator. **Science**, 1975, **187**, 759-760.

Wilcoxon, H. C. Change in colored water preference of two quail species through delayed-illness conditioning. Paper presented at meeting of the Psychonomic Society, San Antonio, November 1970.

Wilcoxon, H. C., Abernathy, W. B., Daly, W., Dragoin, W. B., Dwyer, J. E., & Kral, P. A. The comparative psychology of illness-induced aversions. A research program report presented at the meeting of the Southeastern Psychological Association, Louisville, April 1970.

Wilcoxon, H. C., Dragoin, W. B., & Kral, P. A. Illness-induced aversions in rat and quail: Relative salience of visual and gustatory cues. **Science**, 1971, **171**, 826-828.

Wilcoxon, H. C., & Dwyer, J. E. Long-term retention of conditioned aversion to colored water in bobwhite quail. Paper presented at the meeting of the Psychonomic Society, St. Louis, 1973.

Wilcoxon, H. C., & Etscorn, F. T. Failure to demonstrate illness-induced aversions to visual cues in rhesus monkeys. Paper presented at the meeting of the Southeastern Psychological Association, New Orleans, 1976.

Wilcoxon, H. C., & Fulmer, R. S. Conditioned aversions to distinctively-colored water in quail: The delay gradient. Paper presented at the meeting of the Southeastern Psychological Association, Miami Beach, 1971.

Wilcoxon, H. C., & Fulmer, R. S. Quail learn conditioned aversions to colored water with two-hour delay of aversive consequence. Paper presented at the meeting of the Southeastern Psychological Association, Atlanta, 1972.

XVIII

VISUALLY GUIDED AVOIDANCE OF POISONOUS FOODS IN MAMMALS

NORMAN S. BRAVEMAN
Memorial University of Newfoundland

One of the most provocative research areas in the investigation of learning mechanisms in food selection concerns the types of stimuli animals use to guide their acquired food aversions. This issue gained prominence primarily because of the outcome of what has come to be considered a classic experiment in this area (Garcia & Koelling, 1966). Rats were presented with water that had a distinctive sweet taste and which, when consumed, produced distinctive environmental changes in noise level and lighting. Consumption of the water was followed by contingent foot shock or by delayed toxicosis. When tested for aversions to the various components of the "bright-noisy-sweet" water, the subjects showed that pairings between either the gustatory component and multiple shock experiences or the audio-visual component and toxicosis were ineffective in conditioning aversions. In contrast, the shock was sufficiently aversive to produce aversions to the audio-visual component, and, similarly, the toxicosis conditioned aversions to the gustatory component.

The results of this and other similar experiments with laboratory rats (e.g., Domjan & Wilson, 1972; Garcia, McGowan, Ervin, & Koelling, 1968) have been used as the basis for what has become almost an axiom concerning the conditioning of food aversions in mammals. Simply stated, this relationship holds that mammals associate internal events (e.g., gustatory stimuli) with other internal events (e.g., gastrointestinal malaise) and external events (e.g., audio-visual cues) with other external events (e.g., foot shock). Associations between external and internal events are assumed to be, at best, more difficult, if not impossible, to establish.

There are at least two problems with the cue-consequence rule as it is generally stated. First, it generalizes from results obtained with laboratory rats to all mammals (Garcia, Hankins, & Rusiniak, 1974), even though the behavior of the laboratory rat may not be representative of other mammals (Lockhard, 1968). Second, it implies that there are no experimental conditions under which external events will become associated with internal consequences. However, the facility with which animals learn aversions to various ingested substances is, to a great extent, determined by a complex interaction among the various parameters of food-toxicosis experiences (Revusky & Garcia, 1970; Testa & Ternes, this volume). Thus, the failure to condition an aversion in any one experiment may reflect a problem with the parameters of that experiment.

Investigation of visually-guided food-aversion learning in various mammals serves to determine the species generality of the cue-consequence relationship as well as the parametric boundaries for this effect. In addition, such research is relevant to certain evolutionary hypotheses concerning the types of stimuli animals use to avoid poisonous food. Rozin and Kalat (1971), for example, state that "the tendency to associate tastes with aversive internal consequences—as opposed to associating either element with anything else—seems eminently sensible from an adaptive point of view. Gastrointestinal and related internal events are, in fact, very likely to be initiated or influenced by substances eaten, and taste receptors, by virtue of their location, provide information about these substances . . .an equal ability to associate lights and sounds with gastrointestinal consequences would be far less adaptive" (p. 471).

Such evolutionary arguments could also suggest, however, that associations between the visual aspects of food and aversive internal consequences are just as adaptive as associations between taste and internal consequences. Although information gained from taste receptors can sometimes "warn" the animal of an impending harmful post-ingestional experience, depending on the toxicity of the food, even a small taste may prove to be fatal. Therefore, it would be also advantageous for mammals to avoid the sight of food which in the past has led to poisoning.

Actually, I should modify this last statement somewhat in order to take into account certain environmental and evolutionary constraints. It is possible that some mammals have evolved so that only certain cues are available to them. The Israeli mole-rat, *Spalax ehrenbergi*, is an example of a muroid rodent which has completely adapted to a subterranean way of life (e.g., Nevo, 1961), has no eyes, and therefore is unable to select or avoid foods based on their visual characteristics. Other animals which may be able to taste, see, and smell food might live in environments where only some of these modalities can be used to reliably distinguish safe from toxic edibles. Such animals would presumably use cues to select food which differ from those employed by mammals that have evolved in environments where other modalities are important for survival. The specific cues which a particular group of mammals uses to select food depend on the selective pressures which have operated on the feeding behavior of that group, within the environment in which they have evolved. Since these pressures may vary from group to group, there is no a priori basis for concluding that members of all groups, no matter how biologically or physiologically similar, use the same cues in food selection. Thus, in addition to extending our knowledge of cues that different types of organisms use in the identification and selection of food, studies on visually-guided aversions in mammals other than the rat might provide insight into the evolutionary processes which underlie the conditioning of food aversions.

What is a Visually Guided Aversion? Until this point I have been using the phrase "visually-guided aversions" without having defined it. Simply stated, a visually-guided aversion is a specific type of conditioned food aversion in which animals use some aspect of the appearance of an ingested substance to avoid a food that, sometime in the past, has been ingested prior to the onset of non-fatal poisoning or toxicosis. Thus, I am excluding instances in which aversions to the appearance of the ingested substance are mediated by gustatory or olfactory cues.

The present chapter will consider two sources of visual cues which mammals use to avoid poisonous foods. The first, and the most natural source of visual information, involves the appearance of the food itself: its color, shape, or brightness. The second type of visual cue is provided by the visual characteristics of the food source, i.e., the shape, color, or brightness of the drinking tube or food hopper. Mammals can also avoid the visual aspects of environmental cues paired with toxicosis. However, since this phenomenon is discussed in detail elsewhere (Best, Best, & Henggeler, this volume), it will not be reviewed here.

Limited Scope of the Research. Perhaps the outstanding feature of research on mammalian visually-guided food aversions is that it has been very limited. Only four different kinds of mammals have been tested: rats, monkeys, cats, and guinea pigs. Since the research on cats (e.g., Masserman, 1964; Masserman & Pechtel, 1953) only incidentally involved feeding behavior and lacked controls for

457

obvious confounding factors such as olfactory cues (e.g., Masserman, Pechtel, & Schreiner, 1953), these studies will not be considered. The small range of the remaining species seriously restricts the conclusions that can be drawn from this research. However, hopefully the review will suggest areas of future investigation which may increase our systematic knowledge about visually-guided aversions in mammals.

CONDITIONED AVERSIONS TO THE APPEARANCE OF FOOD

Most of the studies on the conditioning of aversions to the appearance of the food by mammals involve the use of colored water as the "food." Typically, vegetable food dye, which is tasteless and odorless to humans, is added to tap water, and this mixture is presented to animals prior to the administration of an aversion-inducing treatment.

STUDIES WITH MONKEYS

One of the first studies reported using the colored-water technique was Stephen Ober's (1971) master's thesis. These experiments were also presented by Gorry and Ober (1971), but since there is no complete published account, I will describe them here in detail. Ober's strategy involved giving one group of squirrel monkeys (*Samiri sciurues*) 30 min access to a green-colored sucrose solution (.8 ml of food coloring per liter of 15% (W/V) sucrose solution) followed, 30 min later, by a 1% body weight intraperitoneal injection of .15M lithium chloride (Group G/Suc-Tox). Two additional groups either drank the green sucrose solution and were injected with physiological saline (Group G/Suc-NonTox) or drank tap water and received an injection of lithium (Group Wat-Tox). Animals were given two days to recover and then, on the third and fourth days after conditioning, were tested for aversions to the taste and/or appearance of the green sucrose solution. Sucrose preference was assessed by presenting animals with a choice between clear tap water and clear sucrose water; color aversions were assessed by allowing animals a choice between unflavored green water and tap water. Half of the animals in each of the three groups was given the taste test first and the color test second, while the reverse was true for the remaining animals. Finally, on the fifth day after training, all animals were given a preference test between unsweetened green tap water and uncolored sucrose-flavored tap water.

458

The results were presented in terms of preference scores computed by dividing the amount of the test solution that an animal consumed by the total amount ingested during a given test. Thus, scores less than .5 indicate that animals did not prefer the test substance, while scores greater than .5 show that they preferred the test solution to tap water. On the taste test, pooled over both days since there were no between-day differences, the average preference score for animals in Group G/Suc-Tox was approximately .18. In contrast, preference scores for animals in Groups G/Suc-NonTox and Wat-Tox were .66 and .75, respectively. The differences between the scores of animals in Group G/Suc-Tox and those in Groups G/Suc-NonTox or Wat-Tox were statistically significant. Thus, it is clear that animals in Group G/Suc-Tox formed strong aversions to the taste of the sucrose solution.

Results of the preference test between the green unflavored tap water and the uncolored tap water were, unfortunately, not quite so straightforward. The major problem stems from the fact that the animals in control Group G/Suc-NonTox drank relatively little green water. Overall, the preference score for these animals was approximately .33, while the scores for Groups G/Suc-Tox and Wat-Tox were .27 and .65, respectively. Statistical tests showed that Groups G/Suc-Tox and G/Suc-NonTox both had significantly lower preference scores than Group Wat-Tox. These results suggest that injections of physiological saline were as effective as injections of lithium in reducing preference for the green water.

Results of the third preference test, between the green tap water and the uncolored sucrose solution, clearly showed that the flavor cue was more salient than appearance. The average sucrose preference score for animals in Group G/Suc-Tox (.20) was significantly lower than the average preference score for animals in Group G/Suc-NonTox (.74) or in Group Wat-Tox (.80). Taken together, the outcome of this first experiment illustrates that monkeys can learn taste aversions. However, it remains to be demonstrated that they can also associate the visual features of edibles with subsequent poisoning per se rather than with the drug-administration procedure.

In the second of Ober's experiments, which began one week after the end of the first, half of the animals previously used in Group G/Suc-NonTox and half of Group Wat-Tox were given yellow water (4 cc of dye/5L) on the first day (Group Red-Tox); the remaining animals in these two groups were given red water of a similar concentration (Group Yellow-Tox). On day 2 animals in Group Red-Tox drank red water for 30 min while those in Group Yellow-Tox drank yellow water for 30 min. Thirty min after the end of the second drinking session all animals were injected with 1% body weight of .15 M lithium chloride. Three days later, animals in both of the newly formed groups were given a preference test between the yellow water and red water. Results showed that, overall, the average preference score was approximately .29 for Group Yellow-Tox and .56 for Group Red-Tox. During a second test session, average preference scores of approximately .59 and .62 were observed for Groups Yellow-Tox and Red-Tox, respectively.

Because animals in Group Yellow-Tox appeared to prefer the red tap water to the yellow water during the first test session, Ober and others (e.g., Gorry & Ober, 1971; Revusky, 1971) have concluded that the results of this experiment show that monkeys are able to associate the appearance of an ingested substance with delayed toxicosis. However, the low yellow-water consumption of Group Yellow-Tox may reflect an unconditioned aversion to that solution since animals in Group Red-Tox did not exhibit signs of aversions to the test substance. Moreover, Ober's unreferenced statement that squirrel monkeys cannot see colors at the long end of the spectrum does not appear to be supported by physiological or other behavioral evidence (e.g., Klüver, 1933; Walls, 1963).

STUDIES WITH GUINEA PIGS

Initial Demonstration of Visual Food Aversions. The first study with guinea pigs (*Cavia porcellus*) (Braveman, 1974) involved procedures similar to Ober's second experiment. The guinea pigs were allowed to consume tap water that had been colored red or blue (5 drops of dye/100 ml of tap water). One hour after the end of the 10-min drinking period, animals were injected with either lithium or physiological saline. Five one-bottle test sessions during which subjects were allowed to drink the red or blue water were then conducted at 3-day intervals. The amount consumed during each of these tests is summarized in Figure 1. There was a significant decline in consumption as a result of the lithium injections. In contrast, changes in colored water intake in the non-poisoned animals were not statistically significant. The results also show that for both types of colored water, the conditioned aversions extinguished relatively quickly. For example, on the second test session, animals in the red-sickness group consumed as much of the red water as they had on the training day. By the third test trial, animals in the blue-sickness group also drank as much of the blue water as they had on the training day.

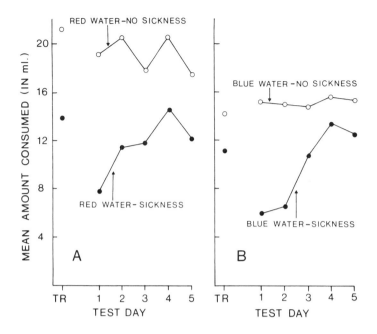

Figure 1

Mean amount of red tap water (Panel A) or blue tap water (Panel B) consumed on five test trials by guinea pigs that had been injected with lithium (Sickness) or physiological saline (No Sickness) 60 min after an initial exposure (TR) to the colored water. (From Braveman, 1974.)

It is possible that these results do not represent the effects of conditioning. Rather, the reduced consumption in poisoned animals may reflect sensitizing effects of the lithium injection. To evaluate this possibility, additional groups of animals were tested in a manner similar to that described above, except that injections of lithium or saline were administered 48 hr after consumption of red or blue water for the first time. Results of this experiment are summarized in Figure 2 and show that for both test solutions and for both types of injections there was an increase, rather than a decrease, in consumption between the first and second presentations of the test solution. Thus, our findings in the first experiment appear not to have been due to the sensitizing effects of lithium. These results indicate that the guinea pig, a mammal, can learn conditioned aversions to the appearance of an ingested solution, even when there is a 60-min delay between ingestion and toxicosis on a single training trial.

461

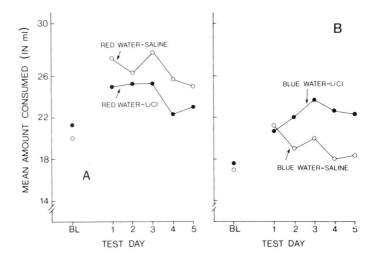

Figure 2
Mean amount of red water (Panel A) or blue water (Panel B)
consumed on five test trials by guinea pigs that had been injected with lithium or physiological saline 48 hr after an initial
exposure (BC) to the colored water. (From Braveman, 1974.)

These findings were unique in that, at the time they were reported, no other mammal had been shown to be unequivocally capable
of learning long-delayed, one-trial, visually-guided aversions to
edibles. The results were particularly unexpected since Wilcoxon,
Dragoin, and Kral (1971) had shown that, with a 30-min delay
between the ingestion of a similar blue solution and the injection of
lithium, albino rats were unable to learn an aversion to the blue
water. Our findings were also unexpected since histological (Walls,
1963) and behavioral (Messing, 1972) evidence indicated that vision in rats and guinea pigs is comparable. Thus, it was not possible to argue that guinea pigs learned visually-guided aversions
because they were visually more adept than rats. Nor was it possible to argue that they had learned aversions to the "color" of the
water since, like the rat, guinea pigs do not have the proper receptors for color vision.

Because of the uniqueness of our findings, we were particularly
interested in ruling out extraneous variables which may have been
confounded with the distinctive appearance of the test solutions.
The most obvious of these was that the guinea pigs were able to
taste the vegetable dye used to color the water. We evaluated this
possibility by presenting colored water to the animals on the train-

ing and test days in such a way that they could not see it. A bottle with blue water was mounted outside of the test chamber. The only contact that animals had with the solution was through the metal drinking spout which protruded through the solid wall of the chamber. To further guard against the possibility that animals would see the drops of blue water on the spout, all drinking was done in the dark. Repetition of our original experiment under these circumstances indicated that the flavor of colored water was not sufficient to guide ingestive aversions in guinea pigs.

Comparison of the Salience of Taste and Visual Cues. Our subsequent experiments were aimed at discovering which of the two cues, taste or appearance, was the more salient in guinea pig food-aversion learning. In the first of two experiments (Braveman, 1975), animals in different groups were presented with water that was both red and sweet. For six groups the test solution was colored by adding five drops of red vegetable dye to 100 ml of water that had been sweetened with various amounts of sodium saccharin. For two of these groups, the saccharin solution was .05% (W/V), for another two it was .15%, and for the remaining two it was .45%. In each two-group set, one was designated as an experimental group and received a lithium injection following consumption of the red sweet water; the other was designated as a control group and received an equivalent injection of physiological saline. Three days after training, all six groups were tested for aversions to the red element of the red sweet water by being presented with unsweetened red water.

A second set of six groups also consumed red sweet water on the training trial, but for all of these the concentration of the saccharin solution remained constant at .15%. For two of the groups only one drop of red food dye was added to 100 ml of the saccharin water, for another two groups 5 drops of dye were added, and for the third pair of groups 10 drops of dye were added. As before, one group of each pair was designated as experimental and the other as control. On the test trial, all subjects were tested for aversions to the sweet taste by being presented with a bottle of uncolored .15% saccharin.

The results of the test trial for the various groups are presented in Figures 3 and 4. Figure 3 shows the amount consumed by animals that were tested with the red solution. In none of the group pairs did the lithium-injected animals (E) drink significantly less than the saline-injected controls (C). In contrast, in each instance lithium-injected animals consumed less of the saccharin solution than their saline-injected controls (see Figure 4). These results show that when guinea pigs are presented with a solution that can

463

be characterized by both taste and appearance, they respond only to the gustatory feature. Taste cues appear to be relatively more salient in guinea pig food-aversion learning than visual stimuli.

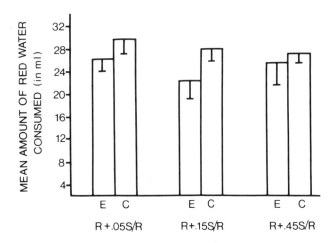

Figure 3
Mean amount of red tap water consumed on a test trial by guinea pigs that had received red-sweet water on the training day and then were injected with either lithium (E) or physiological saline (C). The solution presented on the training trial to animals in Group R+.05S/R was a .05% (W/V) saccharin solution which was colored with 5 drops of red food dye per 100 ml. Animals in Group R+.15S/R and R+.45S/r received water of a similar color but whose concentration of saccharin was .15% or .45%, respectively. (From Braveman, 1975.)

Modification of the Relative Salience of Taste and Visual Cues. Our next experiment was designed to determine whether the relative salience of taste and visual cues in guinea pig food-aversion learning is modifiable. Preliminary to this study we demonstrated, as expected on the basis of previous findings (e.g., Revusky & Bedarf, 1967), that aversion conditioning to the taste of saccharin is blocked if guinea pigs are given 10 daily drinking sessions with the saccharin solution prior to aversion training. Having shown that we could reduce the salience of a taste stimulus by pre-conditioning familiarization, we asked whether or not guinea pigs would learn aversions to the visual component of a solution which had a distinctive but familiar flavor (Braveman, 1975). Subjects were either preexposed (P) or not preexposed (N) to saccharin water and either injected with lithium (Li) or physiological saline (Na) on the train-

464

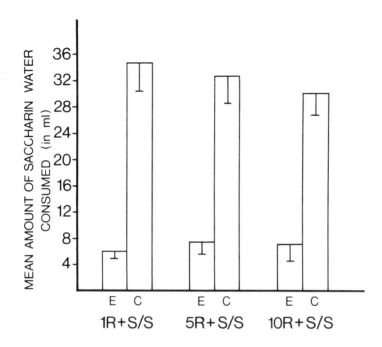

Figure 4

Mean amount of uncolored saccharin water consumed on a test trial by guinea pigs that had received red-sweet water on the training day and then were injected with lithium (E) or physiological saline (C). The solution presented on the training trial for animals in Group 1R+S/S was a .5% (W/V) saccharin solution which was colored with 1 drop of red food dye per 100 ml. Animals in Group 5R+S/S and 10R+S/S received a similarly flavored solution with 5 and 10 drops of red dye added per 100 ml, respectively. (From Braveman, 1975.)

ing day. Thus, Groups PNa and NNa were preexposed and not preexposed respectively and were injected with saline, while Groups PLi and NLi were preexposed and not preexposed respectively and injected with lithium. On the training day all subjects were presented with .15% saccharin colored with 5 drops of red dye per 100 ml. Three days later, each subject was tested with unsweetened red water.

Results of the test session are summarized in Figure 5 and show that only animals made familiar with the saccharin solution and injected with lithium learned aversions to the red water. Poisoned subjects for which the saccharin solution was novel during conditioning did not learn an aversion to the visual features of the solu-

465

tion. These findings indicate that reducing the salience of taste cues by pre-conditioning familiarization changed the relative salience of the visual and gustatory features of red sweet water and allowed guinea pigs to learn aversions to the visual component of this complex visual and gustatory stimulus.

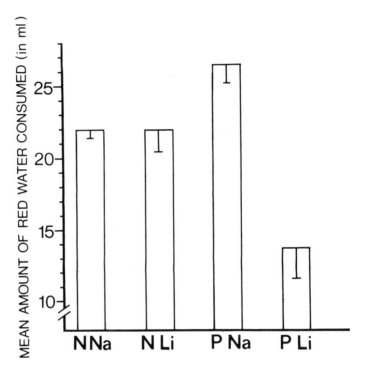

Figure 5
Mean amount of red water consumed by guinea pigs that were preexposed (P) or not preexposed (N) to saccharin and then injected with lithium (Li) or physiological saline (Na) on the training day after consumption of red water sweetened with saccharin. (Redrawn from Braveman, 1975).

STUDIES WITH RATS

Wilcoxon et al. (1971) demonstrated that albino rats do not learn long-delayed, one-trial aversions to blue water under conditions very similar to those we used in the studies on guinea pigs described above. However, the possibility remains that under other circumstances rats may be able to learn aversions to the visual aspects of food (see Nachman, Rauschenberger, & Ashe, this

466

volume). For example, shortening the delay between ingestion and toxicosis or using rats whose vision is somewhat more acute (e.g., Long-Evans) than that of the Sprague-Dawley strain might facilitate the learning of such visually-guided food aversions.

Results from a previously unpublished experiment from my laboratory suggest that either or both of these may be factors which determine whether rats learn aversions to the appearance of food. Two groups of hooded rats (n = 5) were adapted to a daily drinking schedule of 20 min in a special chamber designed to maximize attention to a graduated water bottle. On the training day, subjects were placed in the chamber with the water bottle absent after have been injected with either lithium (Group Tox) or physiological saline (Group NonTox). Approximately 10 min after the injection, the graduated drinking bottle containing blue water (5 drops of dye/100 ml water) was inserted into the chamber. All animals began drinking immediately, but those in Group Tox soon stopped and withdrew to the opposite side of the chamber where they spent the remaining portions of the 20-min session. Animals in Group NonTox drank more readily since they were not sick. However, each of these subjects was yoked to a corresponding animal in Group Tox and was allowed to drink only as much blue water as its yoked partner.

Three days later, all subjects were given a 20-min preference test between the blue water and tap water. Intakes during the test were converted into preference scores by dividing the amount of blue water consumed by the amount of tap water subjects drank. Group Tox had a significantly lower preference for blue water (mean = .31) than Group NonTox (mean = 1.16) (Mann-Whitney U, $p < .02$). This aversion in Group Tox was specific to the blue water and did not represent a generalized reduction of drinking in the test chamber. On the day before testing, Group Tox did not drink significantly less uncolored water in the experimental chamber than Group NonTox. Thus, by reducing the ingestion-toxicosis interval and by using hooded rats, it was possible to condition visually guided aversions to the appearance of blue water. Which, if either, of these variables is the more important is not known at this point.

CONDITIONED AVERSIONS TO THE FOOD CONTAINER

Animals can avoid poisonous foods by learning to avoid the container which regularly holds the food. Such avoidance may occur because of a direct association between container stimuli and toxicosis. Alternatively, the container avoidance may be mediated by learned aversions to the taste, olfactory, or other features of the food. Mediation of visually-guided aversions to food containers by food-aversion learning can be minimized by using highly familiar edibles, such as tap water or food pellets, which subjects do not readily learn to avoid.

STUDIES WITH MONKEYS

Johnson, Beaton, and Hall (1975) recently demonstrated conditioned aversions to the appearance of drinking bottles in green monkeys (*Cercopithecus sabeus*). The subjects were allowed to drink water from yellow and blue bottles on successive days. Following exposure to one bottle color, they were injected with lithium; after exposure to the other color, they were injected with physiological saline. Several days later, when given a choice of drinking water from the yellow and blue bottles, subjects avoided the color paired with lithium administration. This effect was obtained with both the yellow and blue stimulus bottles. Furthermore, the aversions persisted throughout five additional daily preference tests. These findings indicate that monkeys are able to learn visually-guided aversions to sources of ingestibles.

STUDIES WITH GUINEA PIGS

To demonstrate aversion learning to the visual features of drinking bottles in guinea pigs, I presented familiar-tasting tap water in bottles tinted either red or blue (Braveman, 1974). The colors were provided by sleeves of acetate (normally used as filters for theater lights) fitted to the inside of the drinking bottles and glass drinking spouts. Sixty minutes after the end of the drinking period, some animals exposed to each color were injected with lithium, while others were injected with physiological saline. Three days later, all subjects drank from the colored bottle presented on the training day. Four additional test trials were then administered at three-day intervals.

The results are presented in Figure 6 and show that there was a statistically significant reduction in consumption between training and testing for the lithium-injected animals. In contrast, saline-injected animals increased their intakes from the training to the test sessions, and this increase was significant for subjects tested with the blue bottle. With both the red and blue bottles, the conditioned aversions extinguished very rapidly. By the second test trial, lithium-injected animals consumed as much as they had on the training day. These results extend our earlier findings and show that guinea pigs are able to learn aversions to not only the appearance of water but also the appearance of the drinking bottle.

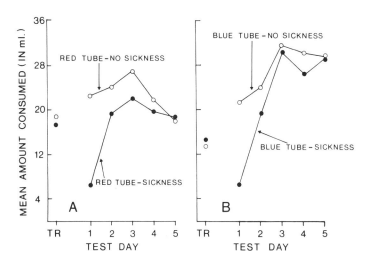

Figure 6
Mean amount of tap water consumed by guinea pigs from a red drinking bottle (Panel A) or from a blue drinking bottle (Panel B) on a training trial (TR) and on five test trials. Animals were injected with lithium (Sickness) or physiological saline (No Sickness) 60 min after consumption on the training trial. (From Braveman, 1974.)

STUDIES WITH RATS

Results of experiments with rats indicate that monkeys and guinea pigs are not the only mammals capable of learning to avoid a distinctive container. Rozin (1969), for example, showed that within two training trials, rats could learn to avoid a food container with distinctive visual and positional characteristics if there was no delay between ingestion and toxicosis. However, in this experiment rats drank a distinctively-flavored saccharin solution from familiar and novel containers. It is possible that the aversions were mediated by the taste of saccharin. In a less ambiguous demonstration, Revusky and Parker (1976) conditioned aversions to a distinctive drinking cup containing familiar tap water. Evidence of aversions to the drinking cup was apparent only after three training trials with a 30-min delay between ingestion and toxicosis. If the ingestion-toxicosis interval was increased to 1.5, 4.5, or 18 hr, conditioning did not occur even after 9 trials (see also Nachman, Rauschenberger, & Ashe, this volume).

SUMMARY AND CONCLUSION

As I noted at the outset, because of the sparsity of evidence, it is difficult to draw conclusions concerning visually-guided poison avoidance learning which might be valid for all mammals. However, it may be instructive to speculate about certain general principles and point out areas which require additional research.

First, the data discussed above clearly indicate that at least some mammals are capable of learning aversions to the appearance of food. Indeed, under certain conditions, this ability seems to be true even for rats. These findings are consistent with the suggestion that animals will associate toxicosis with whichever cues have the most predictive value in a particular setting (cf. Revusky & Parker, 1976; Testa & Ternes, this volume). If these cues happen to be gustatory, the animal will learn a conditioned taste aversion; if these cues happen to be visual, the animal will learn visually-guided aversions.

Although there seems little doubt that mammals can learn visually-guided food aversions, such aversions do not appear to be as robust as taste aversions. At this point, visually-guided food-aversion learning in mammals appears to require shorter ingestion-to-toxicosis intervals and more conditioning trials than taste-aversion learning. Visual conditioned aversions also appear to extinguish more quickly. However, no systematic attempts have been made to elucidate the relationship between the length of the delay interval, number of conditioning trials, and the strength or longevity of the visually-guided aversion. Moreover, in order to put this type of information into a useful perspective, additional research in which the intensity and relative novelty of visual and taste stimuli are equated and in which the training and test procedures are comparable to those in experiments on taste aversions would seem to be required.

Additional research on mammalian visual food-aversion learning may also provide clues to the evolutionary processes which underlie the learning of food aversions. Several investigators (e.g., Capretta, 1961; Rozin & Kalat, 1971) have suggested that the cues which guide animals in the avoidance of conditioned aversive foods are of the same class as the cues which they use in their normal feeding. Research directed toward elucidating the relationship between cues that animals use in normal feeding and

470

those which guide the learning of food aversions could further our understanding of the role that conditioned food aversions play in a naturally occurring and evolutionarily important process such as food selection.

ACKNOWLEDGEMENTS

Some of the research reported in the present chapter was supported by Grant A-8334 from the National Research Council of Canada and by a Supplementary Research Grant from the Dean of Science, Memorial University of Newfoundland, to the author. I would like to thank Emir Andrews, Carolyn Taylor and Gerard Martin who assisted with various aspects of the research.

REFERENCES

Braveman, N. S. Poison-based avoidance learning with flavored or colored water in guinea pigs. **Learning and Motivation**, 1974, **5**, 182-194.

Braveman, N. S. Relative salience of gustatory and visual cues in the formation of poison-based food aversions by guinea pigs (*Cavia porcellus*). **Behavioral Biology**, 1975, **14**, 189-199.

Capretta, P. J. An experimental modification of food preference in chickens. **Journal of Comparative and Physiological Psychology**, 1961, **54**, 238-242.

Domjan, M., & Wilson, N. E. Specificity of cue to consequence in aversion learning in the rat. **Psychonomic Science**, 1972, **26**, 143-145.

Garcia, J., & Koelling, R. A. Relation of cue to consequence in avoidance learning. **Psychonomic Science**, 1966, **4**, 123-124.

Garcia, J., Hankins, W. G., & Rusiniak, K. W. Behavioral regulation of the milieu interne in man and rat. **Science**, 1974, **185**, 823-831.

Garcia, J., McGowan, B. K., Ervin, F. R., & Koelling, R. A. Cues: Their relative effectiveness as a function of the reinforcer. **Science**, 1968, **160**, 794-795.

Gorry, T., & Ober, S. Stimulus characteristics of learning over long delays in monkeys. Paper delivered at the 10th annual meeting of the Psychonomic Society, San Antonio, November, 1971.

Johnson, D., Beaton, R., & Hall, K. Poison-based avoidance learning in non-human primates: Use of visual cues. **Physiology and Behavior**, 1975, **14**, 403-407.

Klüver, H. **Behavioral mechanisms in monkeys.** Chicago: The University of Chicago Press, 1933.

Lockhard, R. The albino rat: A defensible choice or a bad habit? **American Psychologist**, 1968, **23**, 734-742.

Masserman, J. H. **Behavior and neurosis: An experimental psychoanalytical approach to psychological principles.** New York: Hafner Publishing Company, 1964, 58-91.

Masserman, J. H., & Pechtel, C. Neurosis in monkeys: A preliminary report of experimental observations. **Annals of the New York Academy of Sciences**, 1953, **56**, 253-265.

Masserman, J. H., Pechtel, C., & Schreiner, L. The role of olfaction in normal and neurotic behavior in animals. **Psychosomatic Medicine**, 1953, **15**, 396-404.

Messing, R. The sensitivity of albino rats to lights of different wavelength: A behavioral assessment. **Vision Research**, 1972, **12**, 753-761.

Nevo, E. Observations on Israeli populations of the mole rat *Spalex E. ehrenybergi* Nehring 1898. **Mammalia**, 1961, **25**, 128-144.

Ober, S. Learned aversions to the taste and color of ingested substances due to delayed toxicosis in the squirrel monkey. Unpublished master's thesis. Northern Illinois University, 1971.

Revusky, S. H. The role of interference in association over a delay. In W. K. Honig & H. James (Eds.), **Animal memory**. New York: Academic Press, 1971.

Revusky, S. H., & Bedarf, E. W. Association of illness with prior ingestion of novel foods. **Science**, 1967, **155**, 219-220.

472

Revusky, S. H., & Garcia, J. Learned associations over long delays. In G. H. Bower & J. T. Spence (Eds.), **The psychology of learning and motivation: Advances in research and theory, IV.** New York: Academic Press, 1970, 1-84.

Revusky, S., & Parker, L. Aversions to drinking out of a container and to drinking unflavored water produced by delayed sickness. **Journal of Experimental Psychology: Animal Behavior Processes**, 1976, **2**, 342-353.

Rozin, P. Central or peripheral mediation of learning with long CS-UCS intervals in the feeding system. **Journal of Comparative and Physiological Psychology**, 1969, **67**, 421-429.

Rozin, P., & Kalat, J. W. Specific hungers and poison avoidance as adaptive specializations of learning. **Psychological Review**, 1971, **78**, 459-486.

Walls, G. L. **The vertebrate eye and its adaptive radiation**. New York: Hafner Publishing Company, 1963.

Wilcoxon, H. C., Dragoin, W. B., & Kral, P. A. Illness-induced aversions in rat and quail: Relative salience of visual and gustatory cues. **Science**, 1971, **171**, 826-828.

PHARMACOLOGICAL ASPECTS
OF
FOOD AVERSION
LEARNING

THE MULTIFACETED NATURE OF
TASTE-AVERSION-INDUCING AGENTS:
IS THERE A SINGLE COMMON FACTOR?

ELKAN GAMZU
Hoffman-La Roche Inc.

The earlier chapters of this book are ample testimony to the history of learned taste aversions. This chapter is devoted to summarizing recent studies that are directly or indirectly related to the question of the nature of the aversion-inducing agent and to asking the question of whether a single factor can be found that is common to all the effective aversion-inducing treatments.

CHARACTERIZING THE AVERSION-INDUCING TREATMENT

PRELIMINARY CONSIDERATIONS

The Nature of Reinforcement. Because of the limited scope of the present discussion, the conclusions are not intended to support or deny the capability of general principles of learning to explain the conditioned taste-aversion phenomenon. However, it seems reasonable to start by asking what contemporary animal learning theory has to say about the nature of reinforcers. The answer is—surprisingly little. With certain exceptions (e.g., Solomon & Corbit, 1974), this question is seldom addressed within a general framework. Indeed, a recent textbook in the area of animal learning specifically excludes questions concerning "the defining characteristics of reinforcers" (Mackintosh, 1974, preface). Certainly, incentive theorists have had much to say in this area (cf. Young, 1959) but the operational approach is apparently predominant today; i.e., reinforcers are most commonly defined by their general ability to change the rate of occurrence of a wide variety of behaviors. To avoid circularity, we add an independent measure such that appetitive reinforcers are events which the organism will seek out, try to maintain and not avoid; aversive reinforcers are those events which an organism will not seek, will make no effort to maintain, and will often try to terminate. [This is of course a paraphrase of Thorndike's (1911) definitions of satisfiers and annoyers.]

Whether or not the evidence of conditioned taste aversions fits neatly into these definitions, there is general agreement that the reinforcer or unconditioned stimulus (UCS) in this paradigm is aversive. It may be theorized that the organism avoids the flavored solution because it has associated the flavor with the UCS (Revusky, 1971), or because it has learned that the flavor is not safe (Rozin & Kalat, 1971), or because a hedonic shift has occurred (Garcia, Hankins, & Rusiniak, 1974). In any case, the change in behavior presupposes that the UCS is aversive.

Gastrointestinal Effects. Indeed, the nature of this aversive event has been further specified. In their classic paper, Garcia and Koelling (1966) talked about "agents which produce nausea and gastric upset." Rozin and Kalat (1971) similarly stressed the visceral consequences of UCS's used in taste-aversion studies, and although they recognized that other systems could also be affected, they focused on gastrointestinal distress or pain. Another term that has been used extensively to describe the UCS in taste aversion is toxicosis. The dictionary definition of toxicosis is a pathological condition caused by the action of a poison or toxin. Most of the original conditioned taste-aversion studies used X-radiation, apomorphine (cf. Garcia and Koelling, 1967) or lithium chloride (Nachman, 1970) as the UCS, and indeed these treatments produce severe gastrointestinal distress and emesis in man. Since the rat cannot exhibit emesis, we look for behavioral symptoms of malaise. By a combination of observation and anthropomorphizing, it seems reasonable that those treatments used to produce taste aversions in the early studies did indeed induce gastrointestinal distress.

Since these treatments also produce strong effects on other organ systems, one must ask why such emphasis has been placed on the gastrointestinal effects to the exclusion of other effects. The answer lies in the two most unique aspects of conditioning taste aversions: namely, its apparent specificity to food-related cues such as tastes in rats, and the prolonged delay of reinforcement which can still support conditioning. As has been pointed out very elegantly and convincingly by a number of authors (see especially Garcia et al., 1974, and Rozin & Kalat, 1971), it is adaptive for many organisms to associate tastes in particular with gastrointestinal (G-I) events

478

and for this associational system to work over appreciable delays since aversive G-I events often occur well after the taste stimulation has terminated.

The Range of Effective Drugs. Some recent findings, however, call into question the above characterizations of the UCS. Much of the interest and research in this domain has been stimulated by the fact that a wide variety of psychoactive compounds can be used to induce taste aversions. Among these are stimulants, such as amphetamine and some of its congeners; anticholinergic drugs, such as scopolamine; hallucinogens, such as mescaline, tetrahydrocannabinol and hashish; and compounds with various kinds of CNS depressant actions, including some barbiturates, ethanol, pyrazole, morphine, ether, chloral hydrate, some benzodiazepines (chlordiazepoxide, lorazepam, flurazepam), and imipramine. Indeed, even non-centrally active anticholinergics such as methyl scopolamine and methyl atropine have been used. This broad range of drugs is only a partial list of agents that can be used to produce taste aversions (see Appendix, this volume, for a comprehensive list), but is sufficient to indicate that inactive drugs are the exception to the rule. Cocaine (Cappell & LeBlanc, 1976; Coussens, 1975) and strychnine (Berger, 1972; Nachman & Hartley, 1975; Vogel, 1976) are the only compounds which have been so designated by more than one investigator and in both cases, the failures were only partial.[1]

It is unclear why such diverse compounds should all produce taste aversions. The ubiquity of compounds that can produce taste aversions would not be a problem if all the drugs were active only at toxic doses, since any active drug will have toxic effects at high enough doses. However, many studies have used doses that are standardly used in psychopharmacological tests (Berger, 1972), or doses that are capable of enhancing behavior in other situations (Cappell, LeBlanc, & Endrenyi, 1973), and in many cases these doses can be considered equivalent to therapeutic doses in man (Nachman & Ashe, 1973). Thus, although the question of toxicity may be one of definition, there is considerable agreement that many psychoactive compounds are capable of conditioning taste aversions in the absence of any signs of toxocity (see Cappell & LeBlanc, 1976; Vogel, 1976).

IS SICKNESS NECESSARY OR SUFFICIENT
FOR AVERSION CONDITIONING?

The foregoing raises the question of the effect these drugs have on the gastrointestinal (G-I) system. With such a broad spectrum of active drugs, it is not surprising to find that many have only minor G-I effects—at least at doses that are capable of producing taste aversions. The implication that sickness is not necessary for the production of taste aversions is compatible with Smith's (1971) observation that dose levels of X-radiation that produced conditioning did not always cause any noticeable symptoms of sickness (see Barker, Smith, & Suarez, this volume). In fact, apart from the evidence of a learned taste aversion it was impossible to distinguish a group of rats exposed to X-radiation from a sham-exposed group. In a similar vein, Nachman and Ashe (1973) reported no signs of sickness in response to a dose of lithium chloride (0.15 mEq/kg) that was sufficient to produce conditioning. Indeed, some of the anticholinergics that have been used to condition taste aversions are used therapeutically against certain types of G-I illness (Goodman & Gilman, 1970).

Although emesis cannot be studied directly in the rat, indirect evidence against emesis as a necessary condition comes from the work of Levy, Carroll, Smith, and Hofer (1974). They noticed a similarity in the magnitude of taste aversion and blood histamine levels as a function of the time since X-radiation, and hypothesized that radiation-induced histamine production was responsible for the "aversiveness of the irradiation." Pretreatment with an antihistamine blocked the formation of a taste aversion, but pretreatment with an anti-emetic had no effect. In a similar vein, Berger, Wise, and Stein (1973) investigated the effects of lesioning the area postrema on taste aversions. This site has been classified as an emetic chemoreceptor trigger zone and its ablation reduces drug-induced vomiting in cats (Borison & Wang, 1953). The lesions prevented the formation of a taste aversion based on methylscopolamine but *not* one based on amphetamine, indicating that the integrity of the area postrema is not necessary for taste aversion conditioning. Thus, there is a growing body of evidence and certainly considerable agreement (Berger, 1972; Cappell & LeBlanc, 1976; Gamzu, 1974; Vogel, 1976) that neither emesis, nausea, gastrointestinal disturbance, nor "sickness" in general are *necessary* consequences of treatments that are effective in producing taste aversions.

It is also the case that sickness in general may not even be a *sufficient* condition. Nachman and Hartley (1975) investigated this question by choosing drugs and doses that could be considered toxic. Indeed, rats treated with cyanide and strychnine exhibit pronounced signs of illness, and yet these drugs had no effect on intake of a sucrose solution with which they were paired once. In a second experiment, only a very mild taste aversion to sucrose was established when strychnine was repeatedly paired with the flavor, although the repeated strychnine injections resulted in death for half of the original group. Certainly, not even toxicosis is a sufficient condition for the establishment of taste aversions. Neither strychnine nor cyanide exert their action via the G-I system (Goodman & Gilman, 1970), so that the question of whether gastrointestinal distress alone is sufficient to produce a taste aversion is still open. Copper sulfate which reportedly causes emesis at a primarily peripheral level is very effective in producing conditioning at high doses (Nachman & Hartley, 1975). Therefore, it is still possible that gastrointestinal distress may be a sufficient condition.

MULTIFACETED NATURE OF AVERSION-INDUCING AGENTS

It is tempting at this point to revert to the operational definitions and simply describe the conditioning of taste aversions as reflecting the aversive or "punishing" aspects of drugs by virtue of the avoidance paradigm that is employed. Even this approach proves perplexing in at least two areas: (1) Certain positively reinforcing drugs can condition taste aversions, and (2) Chlordiazepoxide, which can be used to attenuate taste-aversion conditioning, is also effective in conditioning such aversions.

The Aversive Nature of Positively Reinforcing Agents. Some of the drugs that can induce conditioning have been considered "recreational" and are certainly abused by man (Jaffe, 1970). Furthermore, rats will readily intravenously self-administer drugs such as morphine (Weeks, 1962) and amphetamine (Pickens & Harris, 1968) at doses which can be used to establish taste aversions. Other drugs such as barbiturates (Davis, Lulenski, & Miller, 1968), alcohol (Meisch & Thompson, 1974), and even apomorphine (Baxter, Gluckman, Stein, & Scerni, 1974) have been demonstrated to support self-administration in the rat and all can be used as the UCS in taste-aversion conditioning. This paradox was first noted by Cappell and LeBlanc (1973) but has many parallels in other areas of research. A number of investigations (cf. McKearney, 1970) have shown that squirrel monkeys will make sequences of responses whose only consequence is the presentation of shock at levels that can also maintain avoidance behavior.

The paradoxical nature of these findings depends on a view of the drug-induced stimulus as a unifaceted event. That drugs have multiple actions is a fundamental pharmacological principle. For example, the drug diazepam is used therapeutically as a minor

481

tranquilizer, a muscle relaxant, an anticonvulsant, and as a pre-anesthetic. Thus it is not entirely inconceivable that a given drug should have different effects on different types of behavior. In fact the rate-dependency hypothesis (Kelleher & Morse, 1968) suggests that in a given animal a single dose of a drug can have opposite effects depending on the prevailing rate of responding. Indeed, even when rates of responding are equated, a single dose can have differential effects on the same behavior maintained by different schedules of reinforcement (Cook & Davidson, 1973; Cook & Sepinwall, 1975).

One way of resolving the "paradox" is to suggest that the hedonic effect of the drug depends on route of administration. Coussens, Crowder and Davis (1973) found that intravenous (i.v.) injection of amphetamine was less effective in taste-aversion conditioning than intraperitoneal (i.p.) injection of the same dose of amphetamine. In addition most taste-aversion conditioning paradigms use parenteral routes, whereas self-administration paradigms favor the i.v. route. However, both taste aversions and self-administration have been demonstrated orally, i.p., and i.v., and it seems unlikely that this particular difference in procedure can solve the "paradox."

Vogel (1976) has suggested that the important difference between the two procedures is the dimension of control. In self-administration studies, the rat controls the delivery of the drug, whereas this is not the case in taste-aversion studies. He argued that a similar effect is seen in the work of Steiner, Beer, and Shaffer (1969) who recorded individual patterns of reinforcement of rats responding for rewarding brain stimulation. In a subsequent session all the rats worked to terminate the same pattern of self-stimulation they had previously produced. It would be interesting to evaluate the preference for solutions that are paired with self-administration sessions but to the best of my knowledge this has not yet been attempted.[2]

Paradoxical Effects of Chlordiazepoxide (CDAP). Taste aversions can be readily established by pairing flavored solutions with i.p. injections of the drug chlordiazepoxide. For example, after appropriate adaptation to water (20 min each morning), Gamzu (1974) exposed independent groups of rats to 0.1% Na saccharin solution which was immediately followed by an i.p. injection of saline, 3.75, 7.5, 15, or 30 mg/kg of chlordiazepoxide. Two days later all rats were given a two-bottle choice test between a saccharin solution and water. The data shown in Figure 1 indicate clear evidence of conditioning, the magnitude of which varies directly with dose. However, chlordiazepoxide has also been used to attenuate condi-

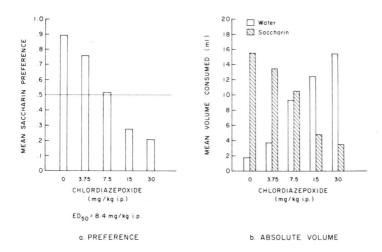

Figure 1
(a) Mean saccharin preference (saccharin consumption/saccharin consumption plus water consumption) and (b) mean volume consumed by 5 groups of rats. Each group had previously had an injection of either saline or chlordiazepoxide paired with saccharin. (From Gamzu, 1974.)

tioning. Cappell, LeBlanc, and Endrenyi (1972) first established aversion to a saccharin solution by pairing it with lithium chloride. Testing began 72 hr later and continued for 5 trials spaced at 72 hr. Thirty minutes before each test, groups were injected with either saline or CDAP (3, 4.5, or 6.75 mg/kg i.p.). They were then offered a single bottle of saccharin solution. Extinction over the five days was more rapid in each of the CDAP groups than in the control group. In a subsequent experiment Cappell and LeBlanc (1973) demonstrated reversal of amphetamine-induced taste-aversion conditioning by doses of 2.5 and 5 mg of CDAP. Vogel (1976), using latency to complete 100 licks of a flavored solution as the response measure, confirmed the action of CDAP (10 and 15 mg/kg) on amphetamine based conditioning and extended it to conditioning based on methyl atropine. Thus CDAP can be used to establish or attenuate taste-aversion conditioning. The latter finding is not in itself puzzling since it is widely established (Cook & Davidson, 1973; Cook & Sepinwall, 1975) that CDAP releases suppressed behavior. Thus, once again awareness of the multiple action of drugs to some extent resolves the discrepancy. Indeed, among other effects CDAP has a dipsogenic effect and actually increases consumption of flavored fluids (Poschel, 1971). Thus, increased consumption of flavored solutions in the studies of CDAP blocking may not reflect any effect on preference for the solution, but merely the dipsogenic effect of the drug since both sets of studies used single-bottle procedures. In an unpublished experiment Riley has re-examined this design using a two-bottle procedure and failed to find an effect of CDAP on preference, although the treatment elevated overall fluid intake.

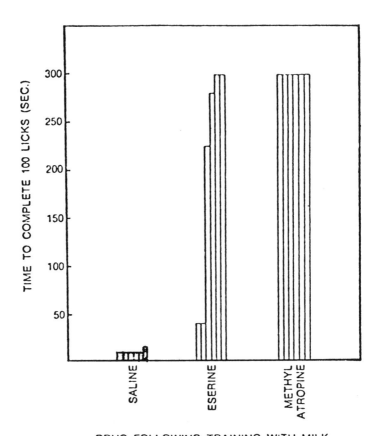

Figure 2
Individual times to complete 100 licks of sweetened condensed milk on the test session for groups previously injected with saline, eserine (0.5 mg/kg) or methyl atropine (1.0 mg/kg). (From Vogel & Clody, 1970.)

Even if an operational approach is taken, the question of why so many different drugs are all effective still remains. Basically, the procedures for producing and testing taste-aversion conditioning are very similar, despite differences in sensitivity (Grote & Brown, 1971). Is there a factor common to all UCSs?

Physiological and Biochemical Systems. The very diversity of the drugs that are effective in conditioning aversions rules out many simple notions. The notions of nausea and sickness as common factors have already been dismissed. A second possibility is that all the drugs affect some common physiological system. It is certainly not the CNS because some of the active drugs do not penetrate the blood-brain barrier (e.g., methyl scopolamine, methyl atropine, and copper sulfate) and this is confirmed by the Berger et al., (1973) area postrema study. Detailed examination of the action of a number of rodenticides has led Nachman and Hartley (1975) to conclude that there is no one common physiological system that can account for the establishment of conditioned taste aversions.

The possibility that a given biochemical substrate uniquely mediates conditioning is also unlikely.[3] Clody and Vogel (reported in Vogel, 1976) compared the conditioning of taste aversions with methyl atropine (1.0 mg/kg), an anti-cholinergic drug, and eserine (0.5 mg/kg), a drug which has effects on the cholinergic system opposite to anticholinergics. The results of this study are presented in Figure 2. Clearly both agonist and antagonist were effective in conditioning an aversion to milk. In a similar vein, both chlorpromazine and apomorphine, which have opposite effects on dopaminergic systems, are effective inducers of conditioned taste aversions. Treatments that increase histamine levels are effective (Levy et al., 1974), and so are drugs with some antihistaminic effects (e.g., chlorpromazine, Berger, 1972). Both morphine and the morphine antagonist naloxone can be used to establish conditioning (LeBlanc & Cappell, 1975).

Dose-Response Comparisons. The evidence for a common physiologically or biochemically based mechanism is not compelling. Beyond the lure of parsimony there are very few indices of a common mechanism. Recently in collecting dose-response data for cross-drug comparison, I was impressed by the parallel effects in the data which are plotted in Figure 3. In handling data from other laboratories I converted either latencies, single bottle volumes, or whatever was available into preference scores, using saline controls

485

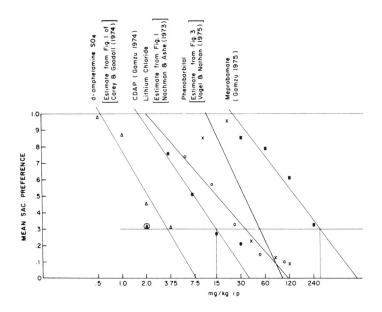

Figure 3
Dose-response regressions for five compounds that have been
used to induce learned taste aversions in naive rats.

where possible. Also, from the Nachman and Ashe (1973) data, I
excluded those points which were beyond what I considered
asymptote. Despite all these constraints, or maybe because of them,
the curves are remarkably similar in slope, although the drugs involved are quite different in chemistry and effect on other
behaviors. While this is no guarantee of a common mechanism, it is
often suggestive of one in pharmacological studies.

UCS PREEXPOSURE STUDIES:
EXPLICATING THE ROLE OF DRUG NOVELTY

The research reviewed so far suggests that the common aversion-
inducing mechanism, if one exists, has to be non-specific with
respect to psychoactive drugs. A similar conclusion is implied by
research on a phenomenon that is now known as the UCS preexposure effect. When the early work on psychoactive drugs was
blossoming, all of the taste-aversion studies used drug-naive rats
despite the fact that there are both behavioral and metabolic differences between naive and experienced rats, particularly in their
reactions to chlordiazepoxide (Cook & Sepinwall, 1975; Goldberg,

486

Manian, & Efron, 1967; Hoogland, Miya, & Bousquet, 1966; Sepinwall, 1973), flurazepam (Cannizzaro, Nigito, Provenzano, & Vitikova, 1972) and oxazepam (Margules & Stein, 1968). Was it

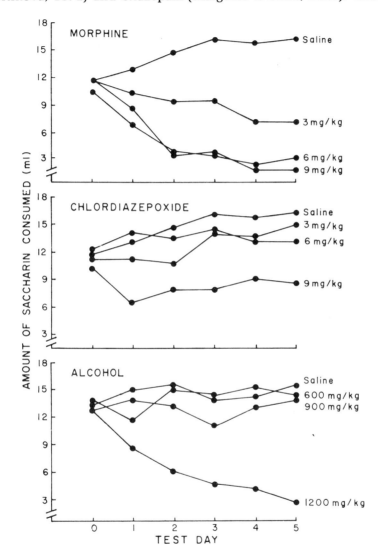

Figure 4
The effects of different doses of morphine, chlordiazepoxide and alcohol on saccharin consumption as a function of repeated saccharin-drug pairings on test days. (From Cappell et al., 1973.)

possible that a drug-experienced rat might not exhibit conditioning to a flavor paired with a familiar drug? If so, aversion conditioning to such drugs might be limited to drug-naive animals. Suggestive evidence of this was reported by Cappell et al., (1973). They exposed rats to repeated pairings of saccharin solution with different doses of morphine, CDAP, and alcohol. As can be seen in Figure 4, all three doses of morphine exerted a progressively greater effect with repeated conditioning trials (conducted once every 72 hr). When 3 mg/kg of CDAP was paired with saccharin there was initially reduced saccharin drinking compared to controls, which dissipated across trials. A similar though lesser recovery was also evident in the group exposed to 9 mg/kg of CDAP. This suggests that drug novelty might be important in establishing conditioning at least when CDAP is used, and that the effect may dissipate after experience with the compound.

EFFECTS OF PREEXPOSURE
TO CDAP AND APOMORPHINE

In order to investigate the possibility that drug novelty might be a common factor, I instituted a series of studies on the UCS preexposure effect. In one of these (Gamzu, 1974) groups of rats were first adapted to a limited access regimen of drinking. Food was available *ad libitum* throughout, but water was presented for only 20 min each morning. After a minimum of 5 days adaptation, all groups were given an i.p. injection of either saline or 15 mg/kg CDAP on each of 3 consecutive afternoons. One week later, a 0.1%

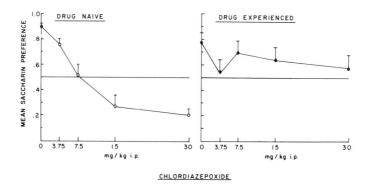

Figure 5
Comparison of the effects of pairing different doses of chlordiazepoxide with saccharin on mean saccharin preference in drug-naive and drug-experienced rats.

(w/v) Na saccharin solution was substituted for the water. Immediately on removal of the saccharin, the rats were injected i.p. with saline or 3.75, 7.5, 15 or 30 mg/kg CDAP. Two days later each rat was given a two-bottle choice between the 0.1% Na saccharin solution and water. The data are presented in Figure 5. Drug-experienced rats reacted very differently from drug-naive rats to the pairing of saccharin with CDAP. The left panel of Figure 5 indicates that all the naive rats showed evidence of conditioning and that the magnitude of the effect was directly related to dose. On the other hand, in drug-experienced rats there was little evidence of aversion conditioning and the outcome was not correlated with dose.

This experiment represents one of the more dramatic effects of preexposure because the formation of conditioning was completely blocked. Often a taste aversion is induced but of lesser magnitude than in drug-naive rats. This more typical effect can be seen in

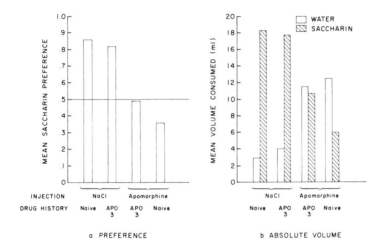

Figure 6
(a) Mean saccharin preference and (b) mean volume consumed by 4 groups of rats. Each group had previously received an injection of either saline or apomorphine paired with saccharin. Prior drug experience is also indicated. (From Gamzu, 1974.)

Figure 6. The drug used in this study was apomorphine HCL (10 mg/kg) and the procedure was identical to the one above with the exception that testing occurred three rather than two days after the saccharin-drug pairing, and two control groups were added. Drug-naive rats showed a clear taste aversion. Drug-experienced rats also

489

showed a taste aversion whether compared with either naive or experienced control groups, yet the drug-experienced group was significantly different from the drug-naive group in the magnitude of conditioning. In this case, prior exposure attenuated but did not eliminate conditioning.

CHARACTERISTICS OF THE PREEXPOSURE EFFECT

Demonstrations with Diverse Agents. This attenuation of conditioning by prior exposure to the UCS has been demonstrated for minor tranquilizers, barbiturates, amphetamine, fenfluramine, morphine, cyclophosphamide, ethanol, apomporphine, and lithium chloride (see Appendix for complete references). Only once has pretreatment with the UCS failed to affect a subsequent

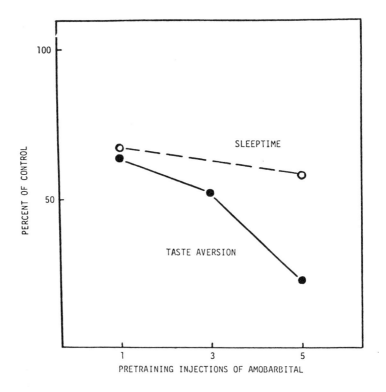

Figure 7
The effect of different degrees of preexposure to amobarbital on both learned taste aversions and sleeping time induced by amobarbital. Control values were obtained without preexposure. (From Vogel & Nathan, 1976.)

490

conditioned taste aversion. Elsmore (1972) gave repeated doses of Δ^9-THC prior to pairing with the saccharin and reported no effect. Whether this is a genuine difference between Δ^9-THC and all other drugs tested, a dose specific problem, or a procedural problem (cf. Cannon, Berman, Baker, & Atkinson, 1975) is not yet known, and deserves further investigation.

Effects of Number of Preexposures. Once again the generality of the UCS preexposure effect across so many drugs is surprising and suggests a non-specific mechanism. Before considering how these data might be explained, let us consider some parametric questions. One preexposure to the UCS is apparently sufficient to alleviate a subsequent conditioned taste aversion (Vogel, 1974b; Cannon et al., 1975), but the degree of attenuation increases with repeated preexposures, as is shown in Figure 7. In this study, Vogel (1974b) used 80 mg/kg amobarbital as both the pre-training and training drug and measured latency to 100 licks as the index of taste aversion. The solid circles clearly indicate that increasing the number of preexposures increases the attenuation of conditioning (see also Cannon et al., 1975; Cappell & LeBlanc, 1975).

Retention of Preexposures. There is also agreement that the magnitude of the preexposure effect is greatest when preexposure and pairing are close in time, and that the greater the delay between preexposure and flavor-UCS pairing the weaker the effect. Cannon et al. (1975) suggested 4 days as a maximum delay using lithium chloride, but Cappell and LeBlanc (1976) have reported preexposure effects at a delay of 14 days with amphetamine and at a delay of 28 days for morphine. These differences are probably drug and dose specific.

Magnitude and Persistence of the Preexposure Effect. The questions of the degree of attenuation and its persistence have less clear answers. Many of the experiments on preexposure have examined the effects of that variable on a single-trial or in extinction. When repeated pairings are used the preexposure effect sometimes dissipates after 5 or more pairings (Riley, Jacobs, & LoLordo, 1975), although this is not uniformly the case (cf. Brookshire & Brackbill, 1971; Berman & Cannon, 1974). This discrepancy might be very important, but at the present time it is impossible to assess whether the durability of the preexposure effect depends on the specific drug. Similarly, the magnitude of the effect varies. In my studies, preexposure to minor tranquilizers completely blocks the development of conditioning (i.e., preexposed groups simply do not learn taste aversions). On the other hand, most other investigators do not find a complete block of conditioning. Since complete blockade

491

has only been consistently reported for the minor tranquilizers chlordiazepoxide, diazepam, and meprobamate (Gamzu, 1974, 1975), it is possible that the complete elimination of conditioning by preexposure is quite specific. Although my experiments have always employed a single conditioning trial, Pat Gay (personal communication) has shown a maintained preexposure effect with chlordiazepoxide over repeated pairings.

Part of the problem of making general statements in this area is not only the differences in procedure but also the lack of any consistent way of choosing comparable doses of different compounds. It was exactly this reasoning that led me to compute the drug-dose relationships shown in Figure 3. Using this as a guide, I have compared equivalently effective doses of chlordiazepoxide, meprobamate and amphetamine. The latter differed from the two minor tranquilizers in that preexposure did not completely eliminate the conditioning although it did significantly attenuate it. Whether these differences in magnitude and duration of the preexposure effect are quantitative or qualitative is not at present answerable.

Specificity of Preexposure. Another fascinating feature of the preexposure paradigm is the investigation of the effects of prior exposure to one drug on the establishment of a conditioned taste

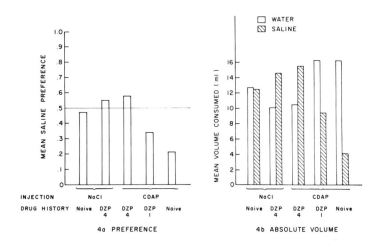

Figure 8
(a) Mean saline preference and (b) mean volume consumed by 5 groups of rats. Each group had previously received an injection of either saline or chlordiazepoxide (CDAP) paired with saline. Prior drug experience is also indicated. See text for further explanation. (From Gamzu, 1974.)

492

aversion based on a second drug. One example of a positive effect is seen in Figure 8. These data are from the second stage of a preexposure study. Animals in the DZP-1 group had previously been administered a single injection of diazepam (DZP) 7.5 mg/kg i.p. paired with a saccharin solution. The rats in the DZP-4 groups had 4 prior experiences with 7.5 mg/kg DZP. These data are from a twobottle choice test 10 days after the last DZP injection and 4 days after a normal saline solution had been paired with an i.p. injection of either saline or 15 mg/kg CDAP. As is readily seen, prior exposure to diazepam either attenuated or eliminated the CDAP based taste aversion. In some sense this is not surprising because the drugs belong to the same chemical class (benzodiazepines) and have some common therapeutic uses.

Encouraged by this success, I attempted to assess the effect of preexposure to CDAP on aversion conditioning with amphetamine. Groups of ten rats each were exposed to three i.p. injections of saline, amphetamine (2 mg/kg) or CDAP (15 mg/kg). A week later a saccharin solution was paired with an i.p. injection of either saline or amphetamine (2 mg/kg). The results of the test data are shown in Figure 9. Preexposure to amphetamine attenuated the conditioning

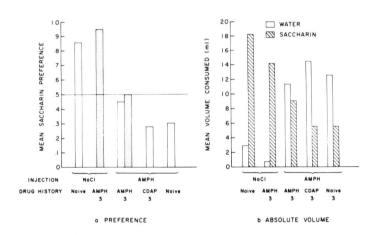

Figure 9
(a) Mean saccharin preference and (b) mean volume consumed by 5 groups of rats. Each group had previously received an injection of either saline or d-amphetamine sulfate paired with saccharin. Prior drug experience is also indicated. The stippled bar represents the mean saccharin preference for an additional group of 10 rats run in an independent replication. (From Gamzu, 1974.)

493

and indeed this effect was replicated some time later (this is shown in the stippled bar). However, pretreatment with a dose of CDAP that was sufficient to eliminate a CDAP based taste aversion had no effect when amphetamine was the UCS. A similar lack of effect of CDAP preexposure on morphine and amphetamine based conditioning has recently been reported by Cappell, LeBlanc, and Herling (1975). The possibility that the pretreatment effect with CDAP would extend to non-benzodiazepine minor tranquilizers was negated when pretreatment with CDAP failed to affect an aversion based on meprobamate (at an equivalently effective dose) as is seen in Figure 10.

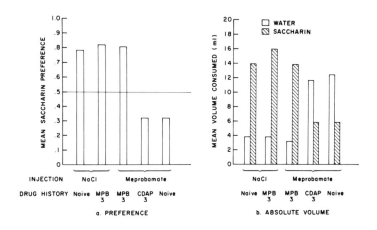

Figure 10
(a) Mean saccharin preference and (b) mean volume consumed by 5 groups of rats. Each group had previously had an injection of either saline or meprobamate paired with saccharin. Prior drug experience is also indicated. (From Gamzu, 1975.)

Cross-over effects have now been shown between many different treatments—the most interesting of which is Braveman's (1975b) demonstration that preexposure to amphetamine, lithium chloride or methyl scopolamine can eliminate conditioning based on rotation (see Braveman, this volume, for more details).

EXPLANATIONS OF THE PREEXPOSURE EFFECT

1. Drug Tolerance. A variety of possible explanations for the pretreatment effect require examination. The possibility that physiological tolerance or dependence was being established was suggested by Parker, Failor, and Weidman (1973). Since they had used 25 consecutive days of exposure to high doses of morphine, physiological tolerance and dependence probably did affect their result. However, these concepts are clearly not relevant to studies using lithium chloride or rotation. Moreover, Vogel (1974b) studied both conditioned taste aversions and sleeping time (see Figure 7) and found that preexposure had a much lesser effect on sleeping time than it did on aversion conditioning. Gamzu (1975) similarly reported sedation in 80% of rats 3 hr after they had been exposed to meprobamate—even though two days later the drug-naive rats clearly showed aversion conditioning while drug-experienced rats did not. Another possibility, that repeated exposure has resulted in increased drug blood levels, has been directly examined for LiCl and rejected (Suarez & Barker, 1976). Indeed, some studies have been specifically designed with long delays between the preexposure and the conditioning stages to eliminate such possibilities (cf. Cannon et al., 1975; Gamzu, 1975).

Cappell and LeBlanc have gathered a great deal of information to support their contention that the preexposure effect can be explained by the concept of drug tolerance (see Cappell & LeBlanc, 1976, for an excellent summary). Drug tolerance is defined behaviorally as being evident when (a) an increased dose is required to maintain an effect of constant magnitude, and (b) a constant dose elicits effects of diminishing magnitude. Both Gamzu (1975) and Goudie and Thornton (1975) have pointed out that this position is little more than descriptive, and without further specification is not really explanatory. Indeed it is difficult to conceive how a notion of tolerance can adequately deal with Braveman's data indicating what would have to be called "cross-tolerance" between rotation and a variety of drug treatments.

2. UCS Habituation. Cappell and LeBlanc's definition does point out the similarity of the preexposure effect to the concept of habituation. In classical conditioning experiments on eyelid conditioning, prior exposure to the UCS does in fact attenuate the conditioned response (Kimble & Dufort, 1956; Mis & Moore, 1973). The possibility that the preexposure effect is simply a reflection of UCS habituation has been raised, but there are no strong supporters. The two most common objections are that preexposure sometimes completely eliminates taste-aversion conditioning and that preexposure to one drug attenuates conditioning based on a second drug. Neither of these effects has been demonstrated in more conventional classical conditioning paradigms (Gamzu, 1975; Braveman, 1975a). Obviously, these facts and omissions are far from being un-

495

equivocal and this issue requires more attention before being discarded.

3. Associative. Another set of explanations for the preexposure effect can be classified as associative. These would suggest that at the time of preexposure some unspecified (possibly background) stimulus was associated with the UCS and that this association either interfered with (Revusky, 1971) or blocked (Kamin, 1968) the formatio of conditioned aversion. Cannon et al. (1975) designed an elegant test of this type of explanation. Two groups of rats had preexposure to either LiCl or saline followed by saccharin paired with LiCl. All treatments took place in the home cage. Another two groups had their preexposure injections in distinctively different cages in which they remained for 24 hr. Later, the taste-drug pairing occurred in the home cage. Regardless of the preexposure environment, animals preexposed to LiCl did not exhibit a taste aversion on the first day of testing, whereas those rats preexposed only to saline did. If an association between the preconditioning UCS and the home cage were responsible for the preexposure effect in earlier studies, pretreatment with LiCl in a distinct environment followed by training and testing in the home cage should have had no effect. In a similarly motivated study, Braveman (1975a) demonstrated that the preexposure effect cannot be attributed to interference based on association between the preexposure drug injection and level of deprivation (cf. Suarez & Barker, 1976). Finally, both Cannon et al. (1975) and Riley et al. (1975) have reported that after a prior pairing of a taste CS with the UCS, there will be an attenuation of the taste aversion formed by pairing a new taste CS with that UCS (but see Revusky, Parker, Coombes, & Coombes, 1976). Consequently it is unlikely that the preexposure effect is due to association of the prior drug injections with some other (nontaste) stimulus.

4. "Learned Helplessness." Yet another possibility is that the preexposure effect is an example of "learned helplessness" (Seligman & Maier, 1967), in which the rats have learned that aversive events occur independently of their behavior. Although appealing, the concept is not specific enough to handle the fact that a given pretreatment (e.g., chlordiazepoxide) can eliminate conditioning in some instances (e.g., when chlordiazepoxide or diazepam is the UCS) but not in others (e.g., when amphetamine or meprobamate is the UCS).

5. Other Mechanisms. Two non-specific mechanisms which have been proposed to explain the preexposure effect are of interest because it may be possible to extrapolate from them to other aspects of taste-aversion conditioning. One of these is based on a concept of stress and will be described by Braveman (see Braveman, this volume). The second mechanism is based on a notion of drug novelty, and has been proposed in varying forms by Gamzu (1974, 1975) and Vogel and Nathan (1975a, b). The remainder of this chapter will be devoted to this concept.

THE DRUG-NOVELTY HYPOTHESIS

In attempting to explain apparently paradoxical effects of drugs on extinction of a conditioned avoidance response, Amit and Baum (1970) proposed that all novel drug states are aversive. The concepts suggested here are clearly related although there is no claim that novel drug states are aversive *per se*. What is suggested is that novel drug treatments have the common feature of disrupting the "milieu interne." As a result of a variety of very sensitive homeostatic mechanisms, most physiological systems operate within fairly narrow limits. Drug treatments clearly cause changes in some of these systems resulting in a variety of internal stimuli, all of which are uniquely novel in an untreated rat. Some of these may not be inherently aversive, but it is suggested that these states may be difficult for the organism to assess. To the extent that internal functioning is disrupted by novel states, these states may be classified as potentially harmful in the absence of any additional information, just as Kalat and Rozin (1973) have assumed that animals initially classify foods as potentially dangerous. This argument allows one to understand why humans do not always react adversely to initial exposure to medication—they are often informed of what might happen and that it will not be harmful. (As we shall see below in the absence of information human reactions to drugs are quite different.) After repeated exposure an organism might learn that some components (possibly all) of the novel drug-induced stimuli are not necessarily dangerous to its continued functioning. The biological adaptiveness of such a system is as appropriate to internal stimuli as it is for taste stimuli.

Supporting Human Evidence. Human clinical evidence is quite supportive of this view of novel drug states. In a double-blind study, Lasagna, vonFelsinger, and Beecher (1955) reported considerable variability in the subjective reactions of normal patients to a variety of drugs including amphetamine, morphine and heroin. Even the stimulant/depressant qualities of amphetamine were equivocally evaluated by the subjects. A more "ex-

497

perienced" group also described the drug-effects predominantly as unpleasant. These reactions can be attributed to the subjects' lack of knowledge of what drug they were receiving. Jaffe (1970) claims that "many confirmed users of narcotics relate that their first experiences with opioids were not at all pleasurable." Similarly, initial experiences with marijuana are often completely neutral, although subsequently similar doses cause a subjective "high" (Snyder, 1971). Finally, in a more controlled experimental environment, Schachter and Singer (1962) gave college students injections of epinephrine. The behavior and reported mood of the subjects was primarily dependent on the actions of a confederate. When the confederate was euphoric, so were the subjects; when the confederate was irritable, so were the subjects. Moreover, this tendency was stronger in subjects who had not been given information of the pharmacological effects of epinephrine, e.g., tachycardia. Thus, it seems quite plausible that the pharmacologically non-specific effects of certain psychoactive compounds might indeed be difficult to classify on initial exposure. In lower organisms, it is difficult to see how prior information can be arranged other than through experience with the drug.

Acceptance of this view of drug induced stimuli implies that the only necessary feature of a treatment that will enable it to condition a taste aversion in *naive* rats is that the treatment-induced state has to be discriminable from the standard state of eunoia. This is independent of the fact that many drug-induced stimuli may well be aversive.

RESEARCH IMPLICATIONS

The drug novelty hypothesis is not offered as an explanation of all instances of taste-aversion conditioning, but rather as an additional organizing concept that may resolve some of the "paradoxical" findings. The hypothesis has several implications: (1) All drugs that produce discriminable internal changes should be effective UCSs in taste-aversion conditioning drug-naive animals. (2) Pretreatment with such drugs prior to training should invariably attenuate the magnitude of subsequently conditioned aversions, and this attenuation effect should increase with additional experience with the drug state. (3) Some drugs may not cause any inherently aversive internal stimuli (the benzodiazepines for example) and yet be effective UCSs in naive rats. Experience with these latter drugs should eliminate their effectiveness in this paradigm. Conversely, some drug treatments may produce aversive stimulation, in which

498

case preexposure would only attenuate but never completely eliminate their ability to condition taste aversions. (4) To the extent that two treatments result in discriminably similar internal states, pretreatment with one drug ought to attenuate the magnitude of conditioning based on the second drug. Moreover, to the extent that two treatments result in discriminably different internal states, pretreatment with one of them may have absolutely no effect when the second one is paired with a novel taste.

The flexibility of the novelty hypothesis is both a blessing and a curse because in its present form it is not sufficiently specific to allow for refutation. One possible way to increase precision in the predictions would be to independently measure the discriminability of different drugs both from control injections and among each other. The state dependence technique of Overton (1971) might prove useful in this regard. Indeed, those drugs that have been studied extensively in both state-dependent and conditioning paradigms are classified by Overton as exerting either moderate or strong discriminative control of behavior. Unfortunately, the procedure is arduous and there is little data on the interesting question of between-drug discriminability.[4]

DIFFICULTIES

Asymmetrical Cross-over Effects. There are three sets of data that are not readily encompassed by the drug novelty approach. The first is what might be called asymmetrical cross-over effects in which pretreatment with drug A affects conditioning using drug B but not vice versa. Vogel (1974b) reported a study in which the treatments included were injections of vehicle, amobarbital (120 mg/kg) and amphetamine (2 mg/kg). All three possible pretreatments were combined with all three possible training treatments in a 3 x 3 factorial design. Pretreatment with amobarbital attenuated conditioning based on either amobarbital or amphetamine. However, pretreatment with amphetamine had little effect on conditioning with amobarbital or amphetamine.

Such findings are clearly an anathema to the theory outlined above. One aspect of these results is surprising in light of the data in Figure 9 showing a preexposure effect with 2 mg/kg amphetamine. This is not simply an artifact of the difference between Vogel's latency to lick and my two-bottle choice procedure since others have also reported a preexposure effect with amphetamine (cf. LeBlanc & Cappell, 1974; Cappell & LeBlanc, 1975; Goudie, Thornton, & Wheatley, 1975) using single-bottle tests and similar

499

doses. Thus Vogel's data are probably not representative and do not constitute a refutation of the novelty concept. In another example of asymmetrical drug effects, Braveman (1975b) presented data showing a quantitative difference between the effects of amphetamine pretreatment on a methylscopolamine based conditioned taste aversion as compared to the effects of methylscopolamine pretreatment on an amphetamine based conditioning. This evidence is less difficult to deal with because the difference is not qualitative. Indeed, if one examines the control group data, the amphetamine dose (2 mg/kg) was less effective in producing conditioning than the methylscopolamine dose (1 mg/kg). Clearly one would expect pretraining with a more potent treatment to exert a greater effect on a milder training treatment than vice versa. A similar argument can be applied to Goudie et al's. (1975) study of the pretreatment effect using fenfluramine and amphetamine. Here preexposure to either drug attenuated an amphetamine based taste aversion, but only pretreatment with fenfluramine attenuated conditioning based on fenfluramine. Interpretation of these data is confounded by the fact that in the saline pretreated control groups, fenfluramine (6 mg/kg) produced a significantly greater aversion than did amphetamine (2 mg/kg).

Transfer Across Different UCSs. A second area of research findings that may turn out to be difficult to encompass within the present admittedly tentative version of the drug novelty hypothesis is that prior exposure to some treatments affect taste aversions based on seemingly different UCSs (e.g. Braveman's work with rotation cited above). Without further modification, I would have to ascribe some common internal stimulation to all of these treatments. It is possible that use of additional principles might overcome this difficulty, but without any supportive evidence the problem remains unsolved.

Strychnine and Cocaine: Anomalies? The third set of data that is not easily encompassed by the drug novelty approach involves the partial failures of strychnine and cocaine to reliably produce taste aversions. It is ironic that the question that generated a great deal of this research—namely, why do all drugs produce conditioned taste aversions—is now inverted to how to explain the rare exceptions. Certainly we would expect both of these drugs to produce discriminable internal states. In the case of cocaine, the very fact that it is readily self-administered indicates that rats can discriminate the internal stimuli it produces. Indeed, these two negative instances provide an obstacle for theoretical approaches that are designed to find a single common factor for all aversion-

500

inducing agents. Both Coussens (1975) and Cappell and LeBlanc (1976) have suggested that cocaine does not induce taste-aversion conditioning because of its very short half-life, resulting in a UCS which is too brief to be effective. However, there seems to be little direct evidence to support this contention, and Nachman and Hartley (1975) reported no discernible relationship between duration of sickness symptoms and ability to induce a conditioned taste aversion. Moreover, Nachman et al. (1970) indicated only a small difference between conditioning effected by intraperitoneal and intracardiac administration of ethanol, although both onset and duration should be greatly affected by this difference of route of administration. Another possible reason for the failure of strychnine and cocaine (and possibly cyanide) to produce taste-aversion conditioning may reside in their ability to produce convulsions, which could cause amnesia for the CS, the UCS, or both. In this regard, it is interesting that Berger (1972) failed to establish taste-aversion conditioning using ECS, and that ECS can interfere with the establishment of taste aversions (Kral & Beggerly, 1973) or temporarily disrupt an established taste aversion (Vogel, 1974a). This hypothesis is similarly difficult to evaluate in view of the lack of relevant data and the weakness of the aforementioned ECS effects.

The absence of satisfactory resolution of why cocaine and strychnine do not induce taste aversions seems to be the most compelling argument against any common factor being involved in the induction of taste aversions—whether the emphasis is on novelty, stress, or any other organizing concept. Resolution of this issue would clearly enhance our understanding of the nature of the UCS in taste-aversion conditioning.

SUMMARY AND CONCLUSIONS

The phenomenon of learned taste aversions has generated considerable interest and research because it appears to be relatively stimulus-specific and occurs over delays that are longer than those used in standard animal learning tasks. In explaining its uniqueness, most theories have stressed the visceral—and in particular—the gastrointestinal effects of the UCS and have related these features to the ethological and/or evolutionary value of very specific mechanisms of associating taste with sickness. This characterization of the UCS as a sickness-inducing stimulus is undermined by a number of findings, including the fact that the list of effective drugs is lengthy and the exceptions few. Other data confirm that the effectiveness of the UCS does not depend on its ability to affect the gastrointestinal system, nor on its ability to produce symptoms of sickness.

This multifaceted nature of the UCS makes it unlikely that a single common factor is responsible for the effectiveness of diverse UCSs. It also introduces several anomalies such as the fact some drugs can be employed both in conditioning taste aversions and self-administration paradigms—which supposedly reflect opposite mechanisms of reinforcement. This "paradox," and others, are not unique to the taste-aversion conditioning phenomenon and are partially explicated by stressing the multiple functions of stimuli in general, and drugs in particular.

It is suggested that consideration of drug-induced UCSs in a manner similar to the way we consider the taste stimuli in conditioned aversions might provide a common factor. Regardless of the hedonic features of a given drug-induced state the organism is expected to be neophobic to a novel drug state. This explains the ubiquity of the conditioning phenomenon, and why prior experience always attenuates the effect. It also explains why some drugs that probably do not cause aversive states can be used to induce taste aversions in drug-naive rats. Drug novelty is not a comprehensive explanation of the conditioning phenomenon but is suggested as an additional principle that explains some features of taste-aversion conditioning. Many drugs appear to produce unpleasant states *per se* as indicated by their continued efficacy in the preexposure effect. As yet there does not appear to be a mechanism of action that is common to all these latter treatments.

FOOTNOTES

[1]Other failures to produce conditioned taste aversions have been reported, but are understandable either in terms of the extreme delay between injection and onset of activity (e.g., 72 hr for Warfarin; see Nachman & Hartley, 1975) or have only been studied at one dose. Another candidate for a drug that might fail to establish conditioning is cyanide (Nachman & Hartley, 1975) but it seems reasonable to await replication before accepting this negative finding.

[2]Since preparation of this chapter, Wise, Yokel, and DeWit (1976) have reported an attempt to evaluate the effect of pairing a novel flavor with self-administered apomorphine. Rats were first trained to self-administer amphetamine. Once this behavior was established, the self-administered substance was changed to apomorphine. Just prior to the first session with apomorphine, the rats were exposed to a novel saccharin solution. Consumption of saccharin was measured the following day. The data are difficult to evaluate both in terms of degree of positive reinforcement demonstrated (as opposed to extinction) and the equivalence of dose and delay between the saccharin exposure and the apomorphine infusions. Wise et al., (1976) concluded that conditioning had occurred, but the technical difficulties inherent in this type of study are extreme and the conclusions are equivalently limited.

[3]Investigation of biochemical substances is hampered by the fact that some of the depleting agents such as α-methyl-paratyrosine (Carey & Goodall, 1974a) and para-chlorphenylalanine (Nachman et al., 1970) are themselves capable of producing taste aversions.

[4]The taste aversion paradigm has an interesting feature that depends only on the assumption that the UCS produces a state that is discriminably different from normal. Most studies of the discriminative properties of drugs (cf. Thompson & Pickens, 1971) are quite prolonged and require that the organism's behavior be studied while it is under the direct pharmacological action of the drug. Taste-aversion conditioning offers a relatively rapid technique—and one in which the animal is no longer under the direct effects of the drug.

ACKNOWLEDGEMENTS

I would like to acknowledge the helpful comments of Drs. Cook, Davidson and Sepinwall. I am especially indebted to Linda Volpe for her valuable efforts in the preparation of the manuscript. Thanks are also due to Drs. Cappell and Vogel who have granted permission to use their data.

REFERENCES

Amit, Z., & Baum, M. Comment on the increased resistance-extinction of an avoidance response induced by certain drugs. **Psychological Reports,** 1970, **27,** 310.

Austin, T. M. Taste aversion learning: Convergent and divergent evolution. Paper presented at the 45th Annual Meeting of the Eastern Psychological Association, Philadelphia, 1974.

Baxter, B. L., Gluckman, M. I., Stein, L., & Scerni, R. A. Self-injection of apomorphine in the rat: Positive reinforcement by a dopamine receptor stimulant. **Pharmacology, Biochemistry and Behavior,** 1974, **2,** 387-391.

Berger, B. D. Conditioning of food aversion by injections of psychoactive drugs. **Journal of Comparative and Physiological Psychology,** 1972, **81,** 21-26.

Berger, B., Wise, C. D., & Stein, L. Area postrema damage and bait shyness. **Journal of Comparative and Physiological Psychology,** 1973, **82,** 475-479.

Berman, R. F., & Cannon, D. S. The effect of prior ethanol experience on ethanol-induced saccharin aversions. **Physiology and Behavior,** 1974, **12,** 1041-1044.

Borison, H. L., & Wang, S. C. Physiology and pharmacology of vomiting. **Pharmacological Review,** 1953, **5,** 193-230.

Braveman, N. S. Absence of taste aversion following prior exposure to sickness. Paper presented at a symposium entitled "Psychopharmacology and learned taste aversions," American Psychological Association, Chicago, 1975. (a)

Braveman, N. S. Formation of taste aversions in rats following prior exposure to sickness. **Learning and Motivation,** 1975, **6,** 512-534. (b)

Brookshire, K. H., & Brackbill, R. M. Habituation to illness: Effects on acquisition and retention of a conditioned taste-aversion. Paper presented at the Annual Meeting of the Psychonomic Society, St. Louis, 1971.

Cannizzaro, G., Nigito, S., Provenzano, P. M., & Vitikova, T. Modification of depressant and disinhibitory action of flurazepam during short term treatment in the rat. **Psychopharmacologia,** 1972, **26,** 173-184.

Cannon, D., Berman, R. F., Baker, T. B., & Atkinson, C. A. Effect of preconditioning unconditioned stimulus experience on learned taste aversions. **Journal of Experimental Psychology: Animal Behavior Processes,** 1975, **104,** 270-284.

Cappell, H., &LeBlanc, A. E. Punishment of saccharin drinking by amphetamine in rats and its reversal by chlordiazepoxide. **Journal of Comparative and Physiological Psychology,** 1973, **85,** 97-104.

Cappell, H., & LeBlanc, A. E. Conditioned aversion by amphetamine: Rates of acquisition and loss of the attenuating effects of prior exposure. **Psychopharmacologia,** 1975, **43,** 157-162.

Cappell, H., & LeBlanc, A. E. Gustatory avoidance conditioning by drugs of abuse: Relationships to general issues in research on drug dependence. In N. W. Milgram, L. Krames, & T. M. Alloway, (Eds.), **Food aversion learning.** Plenum Press, 1976, in press.

Cappell, H., LeBlanc, A. E., & Endrenyi, L. Effects of chlordiazepoxide and ethanol on the extinction of a conditioned taste aversion. **Physiology and Behavior,** 1972, **9,** 167-169.

Cappell, H., LeBlanc, A. E., & Endrenyi, L. Aversive conditioning by psychoactive drugs: Effects of morphine, alcohol and chlordiazepoxide. **Psychopharmacologia,** 1973, **29,** 239-246.

Cappell, H., LeBlanc, A. E., & Herling, S. Modification of the punishing effects of psychoactive drugs in rats by previous drug experience. **Journal of Comparative and Physiological Psychology,** 1975, **89,** 347-356.

Carey, R. J., & Goodall, E. B. Amphetamine-induced taste aversion: A comparison of d- versus l-amphetamine. **Pharmacology, Biochemistry and Behavior,** 1974, **2,** 325-330.

Catania, A. C. Discriminative stimulus functions of drugs: Interpretations I. In T. Thompson & R. Pickens (Eds.), **Stimulus properties of drugs.** New York: Appleton-Century-Crofts, 1971.

Cook, L., & Davidson, A. B. Effects of behaviorally active drugs in a conflict-punishment procedure in rats. In S. Garattini, E. Mussini, & L. O. Randall, (Eds.), **The benzodiazepines.** New York: Raven Press, 1973.

Cook, L., & Sepinwall, J. Parameters of emotion: Psychopharmacological parameters and methods. In L. Levi (Ed.), **Emotions—The parameters and measurement.** New York: Raven Press, 1975.

Coussens, W. R. Route of administration and conditioned taste aversion. Paper presented at a symposium entitled "Psychopharmacology and learned taste aversions," American Psychological Association, Chicago, 1975.

Coussens, W. R., Crowder, W. F., & Davis, W. M. Morphine induced saccharin aversion in α-methyl-tyrosine pretreated rats. **Psychopharmacologia,** 1973, **29,** 151-157.

Davis, J. D., Lulenski, G. C., & Miller, N. E. Comparative studies of barbiturate self-administration. **International Journal of the Addictions,** 1968, **3,** 207-214.

Dragoin, W., McCleary, G. E., & McCleary, P. A comparison of two methods of measuring conditioned taste aversion. **Behavior Research Methods and Instrumentation,** 1971, **3,** 309-310.

Elsmore, T. F. Saccharin aversion induced by $\triangle^9$-tetrahydrocannabinol: Effects of repeated doses prior to pairing with saccharin. **Proceedings of the 80th Annual Convention of the American Psychological Association,** 1972, **7,** 817-818.

Gamzu, E. Preexposure to unconditioned stimulus alone may eliminate taste aversions. Paper presented at the 15th Annnual Meeting of the Psychonomic Society, Boston, 1974.

Gamzu, E. Elimination of taste aversions by pretreatment: Cross-drug comparisons. Paper presented at a symposium entitled "Psychopharmacology and learned taste aversions," American Psychological Association, Chicago, 1975.

Garcia, J., & Ervin, F. R. Gustatory-visceral and telereceptor-cutaneous conditioning—Adaptation in internal and external milieus. **Communications in Behavioral Biology,** 1968, **1,** 389-415.

Garcia, J., Hankins, W. G., & Rusiniak, K. W. Behavioral regulation of the milieu interne in man and rat. **Science,** 1974, **185,** 824-831.

Garcia, J., & Koelling, R. A. Relation of cue to consequence in avoidance learning. **Psychonomic Science,** 1966, **4,** 123-124.

Garcia, J., & Koelling, R. A. A comparison of aversion induced by X-rays, toxins, and drugs in the rat. **Radiation Research,** 1967, **7** (Suppl.), 439-450.

Garcia, J., McGowan, B. K., & Green, K. F. Biological constraints on conditioning. In A. Black & W. F. Prokasy (Eds.), **Classical conditioning II: Current theory and research.** New York: Appleton-Century-Crofts, 1972.

Goldberg, M. E., Manian, A. A., & Efron, D. H. A comparative study of certain pharmacologic responses following acute and chronic administration of chlordiazepoxide. **Life Sciences,** 1967, **6,** 481-491.

Goodman, L. S., & Gilman, A. (Eds.), **The pharmacological basis of therapeutics.** New York: MacMillan, 1970.

Goudie, A. J., & Thornton, E. W. Effects of drug experience on drug induced conditioned taste aversions: Studies with amphetamine and fenfluramine. **Psychopharmacologia,** 1975, **44,** 77-82.

Goudie, A. J., Thornton, E. W., & Wheatley, J. Attenuation by alphamethyltyrosine of amphetamine induced conditioned taste aversion. **Psychopharmacologia,** 1975, **45,** 119-123.

Grote, F. W., & Brown, R. T. Conditioned taste aversions: Two-stimulus tests are more sensitive than one-stimulus tests. **Behavior Research Methods and Instrumentation,** 1971, **3,** 311-312.

Hoogland, D. R., Miya, T. S., & Bousquet, W. F. Metabolism and tolerance studies with chlordiazepoxide-2-^{14}C in the rat. **Toxicology and Applied Pharmacology,** 1966, **9,** 116-123.

Jaffe, J. H. Drug addiction and drug abuse. In Goodman & Gilman (Eds.), **The pharmacological basis of therapeutics.** New York: The MacMillan Company, 1970.

Kalat, J. W., & Rozin, P. "Learned safety" as a mechanism in long-delay taste-aversion learning in rats. **Journal of Comparative and Physiological Psychology,** 1973, **83,** 198-207.

Kamin, L. J. Attention-like processes in classical conditioning. In M. R. Jones, (Ed.), **Miami symposium on the prediction of behavior: Aversive stimulation.** Miami, Florida: University of Miami Press, 1968.

Kelleher, R. T., & Morse, W. H. Determinants of the specificity of behavioral effects of drugs. **Ergeb. Physiol. Biol. Chem. Exp. Pharmakol.,** 1968, **60,** 1.

Kimble, G. A.,'& Dufort, R. H. The associative factor in eyelid conditioning. **Journal of Experimental Psychology,** 1956, **52,** 386-391.

Koechlin, B. A., & D'Arconte, L. Determination of chlordiazepoxide (Librium) and of a metabolite of lactam character in plasma of humans, dogs and rats by a specific spectrofluorometric micromethod. **Analytical Biochemistry,** 1963, **5,** 195.

Kral, P. A., & Beggerly, H. D. Electroconvulsive shock impedes association formation: Conditioned taste aversion paradigm. **Physiology and Behavior,** 1973, **10,** 145-147.

Lasagna, L., vonFelsinger, J. M., & Beecher, H. K. Drug-induced mood changes in man. **Journal of the American Medical Association,** 1955, **157,** 1006-1020.

LeBlanc, A. E., & Cappell, H. Attenuation of punishing effects of morphine and amphetamine by chronic prior treatment. **Journal of Comparative and Physiological Psychology,** 1974, **87,** 691-698.

LeBlanc, A. E., & Cappell, H. Antagonism of morphine-induced aversive conditioning by naloxone. **Pharmacology, Biochemistry and Behavior,** 1975, **3,** 185-188.

Levy, C. J., Carroll, M. E., Smith, J. C., & Hofer, K. G. Antihistamines block radiation-induced taste aversions. **Science,** 1974, **186,** 1044-1046.

Mackintosh, N. J. **The Psychology of animal learning.** New York: Academic Press, 1974.

Margules, D. L., & Stein, L. Increase of "antianxiety" activity and tolerance of behavioral depression during chronic administration of oxazepam. **Psychopharmacologia,** 1968, **13,** 74-80.

McKearney, J. W. Responding under fixed-ratio and multiple fixed-interval fixed-ratio schedules of electric shock presentation. **Journal of the Experimental Analysis of Behavior,** 1970, **14,** 1-6.

Meisch, R. A., & Thompson, T. Rapid establishment of ethanol as a reinforcer for rats. **Psychopharmacologia,** 1974, **37,** 311-321.

Mis, F. W., & Moore, J. W. Effect of preacquisition UCS exposure on classical conditioning of the rabbit's nictitating membrane response. **Learning and Motivation,** 1973, **4,** 108-114.

Nachman, M. Learned taste and temperature aversions due to lithium chloride sickness after temporal delays. **Journal of Comparative and Physiological Psychology,** 1970, **73,** 22-30.

Nachman, M., & Ashe, J. H. Learned taste aversions in rats as a function of dosage, concentration and route of administration of LiCl. **Physiology and Behavior,** 1973, **10,** 73-78.

Nachman, M., & Hartley, P. L. Role of illness in producing learned taste aversions in rats: A comparison of several rodenticides. **Journal of Comparative and Physiological Psychology,** 1975, **89,** 1010-1018.

Nachman, M., Lester, D., & LeMagnen, J. Alcohol aversion in the rat: Behavioral assessment of noxious drug effects. **Science,** 1970, **168,** 1244-1246.

Overton, D. Discriminative control of behavior by drug states. In T. Thompson & R. Pickens (Eds.), **Stimulus properties of drugs.** New York: Appleton-Century-Crofts, 1971.

Parker, L., Failor, A., & Weidman, K. Conditioned preferences in the rat with an unnatural need state: Morphine withdrawal. **Journal of Comparative and Physiological Psychology,** 1973, **82,** 294-300.

Peck, J. H., & Ader, R. Illness-induced taste aversion under states of deprivation and satiation. **Animal Learning and Behavior,** 1974, **2,** 6-8.

Pickens, R., & Harris, W. C. Self-administration of d-amphetamine by rats. **Psychopharmacologia,** 1968, **12,** 158-163.

Poschel, B. P. H. A simple and specific screen for benzodiazepine-like drugs. **Psychopharmacologia,** 1971, **19,** 193-198.

Rachlin, H. **Introduction to modern behaviorism.** San Francisco: W. H. Freeman, 1970.

Revusky, S. The role of interference in association over a delay. In W. Honig & H. James (Eds.), **Animal memory.** New York: Academic Press, 1971.

Revusky, S., Parker, L., Coombes, J., & Coombes, S. Flavor aversion learning: Extinction of the aversion to an interfering flavor after conditioning does not affect the aversion to the reference flavor. **Behavioral Biology,** 1976, in press.

Riley, A. L., Jacobs, W. J., & LoLordo, V. M. The effect of drug exposure on the acquisition and retention of a conditioned taste aversion. Paper presented at a symposium entitled "Psychopharmacology and learned taste aversions," American Psychological Association, Chicago, 1975.

Rozin, P., & Kalat, J. W. Specific hungers and poison avoidance as adaptive specializations of learning. **Psychological Review,** 1971, **78,** 459-486.

Schachter, S., & Singer, J. E. Cognitive, social and physiological determinants of emotional state. **Psychological Review,** 1962, **69,** 379-399.

Seligman, M. E. P., & Maier, S. F. Failure to escape traumatic shock. **Journal of Experimental Psychology,** 1967, **74,** 1-9.

Sepinwall, J. Some pharmacological aspects of benzodiazepines. **Folha Médica,** 1973, **67,** 727-735.

Smith, J. C. Radiation: Its detection and its effects on taste preferences. In E. Stellar & J. M. Sprague (Eds.), **Progress in physiological psychology,** (Vol. 4). New York: Academic Press, 1971.

Snyder, S. H. **Uses of marijuana.** New York: Oxford University Press, 1971.

Solomon, R. L., & Corbit, J. D. An opponent-process theory of motivation: I. Temporal dynamics of affect. **Psychological Review,** 1974, **81,** 119-145.

Steiner, S., Beer, B., & Shaffer, M. M. Escape from self-produced rates of brain stimulation. **Science,** 1969, **163,** 90-91.

Suarez, E. M., & Barker, L. M. Effects of water deprivation and prior LiCl exposure in conditioning taste aversions. **Physiology and Behavior,** 1976, **17,** 555-559.

Thompson, T., & Pickens, R. (Eds.), **Stimulus properties of drugs.** New York: Appleton-Century-Crofts, 1971.

Thorndike, E. L. **Animal intelligence: Experimental studies.** New York: MacMillan Press, 1911.

Vogel, J. R. Antagonism of a learned taste aversion following repeated administrations of electroconvulsive shock. **Physiological Psychology,** 1974, **2,** 493-496. (a)

Vogel, J. R. Prior exposure to a drug (US) attenuates learned taste aversions. Paper presented at the meeting of the Psychonomic Society, Boston, November, 1974. (b)

Vogel, J. R. Conditioning of taste aversions by drugs of abuse. In H. Lal & J. Singh (Eds.), **Neurobiology of drug dependence (Vol. 1). Behavioral analysis of drug dependence.** New York: Futura, 1976.

Vogel, J. R., & Clody, D. E. Some determinants of conditioned aversion. Paper presented at the Behavior Pharmacology Society Meeting, Princeton, 1970.

Vogel, J. R., & Nathan, B. A. Learned taste aversions induced by hypnotic drugs. **Pharmacology, Biochemistry and Behavior,** 1975, **3,** 189-194.

Vogel, J. R., & Nathan, B. A. Reduction of learned taste aversions by preexposure to drugs. **Psychopharmacologia,** 1976, in press.

Vogel, J. R., & Nathan, B. A. Paper presented at a symposium entitled "Psychopharmacology and learned taste aversions," American Psychological Association, Chicago, 1975.

Weeks, J. R. Experimental morphine addiction: Method for automatic intravenous injections in unrestrained rats. **Science,** 1962, **138,** 143-144.

Wise, R. A., Yokel, R. A., & DeWit, H. Both positive reinforcement and conditioned aversion from amphetamine and from apomorphine in rats. **Science,** 1976, **191,** 1273-1275.

Young, P. T. The role of the affective processes in learning and motivation. **Psychological Review,** 1959, **66,** 104-125.

XX

WHAT STUDIES ON PREEXPOSURE TO PHARMACOLOGICAL AGENTS TELL US ABOUT THE NATURE OF THE AVERSION-INDUCING AGENT

NORMAN S. BRAVEMAN
Memorial University of Newfoundland

The purpose of the present chapter is to discuss the nature of the postingestional consequence (i.e., the aversive event) that is responsible for the conditioning of aversions to ingested substances. As has been noted elsewhere (see Gamzu, this volume), a wide variety of pharmacological interventions have been found effective in conditioning taste aversions. Data from studies in which animals are exposed to the aversion-inducing treatment prior to conditioning, however, suggest that there may be a single aversive element which is common to all of the many different treatments that have been employed to produce conditioned aversions. In the present chapter I will present evidence which I feel supports this position.

THE PREEXPOSURE PARADIGM: THE EFFECT AND THE ISSUES

The effect of preexposing animals to aversion-inducing treatments on the subsequent formation of conditioned food aversions is relatively easy to demonstrate. Animals are exposed to an aversion-inducing treatment prior to pairing the ingestion of a distinctive food or solution with the same (e.g., Austin, 1974; Berman & Cannon, 1974; Braveman, 1975a; Brookshire & Brackbill, 1976; Cappell & LeBlanc, 1976; Elkins, 1974) or with a different (e.g., Braveman, 1975a; Gamzu, 1975; Vogel & Nathan, 1975) aversion-inducing treatment. It is typically found that, after a sufficient number of preexposures, subsequent conditioning is either weakened or completely prevented. That is to say, animals that have been exposed to an aversion-inducing treatment, prior to the time when that, or a different, treatment is used to condition an aversion to a distinctively flavored solution, generally do not learn aversions as readily to the distinctively flavored solution as animals that have not been so preexposed.

Interestingly, there is little disagreement among researchers that the effect occurs. It is known, for example, that conditioning can be disrupted (a) with as few as one preexposure (e.g., Austin, 1974; Braveman, 1975a), (b) when there are as many as 10 days between the last preexposure and training (e.g., Braveman, 1975a; Cappell & LeBlanc, 1975; Gamzu, 1974; Vogel & Nathan, 1975), and (c) if any one of a number of aversion-inducing treatments, training and testing procedures are employed. In the present chapter I will concentrate on one particular experimental strategy that has provided insight into the nature of the postingestional consequence.

CROSSOVER EXPERIMENTS

Transfer Between Methylscopolamine and Amphetamine. "Crossover" experiments involve preexposing animals to one aversion-inducing treatment and then training them to avoid a novel-tasting solution by administering another treatment. In most instances (e.g., Cappell & LeBlanc, 1975; Gamzu, 1974), pharmacologically dissimilar agents are used during preexposure and training phases of the experiment. For example, in one experiment (Braveman, 1975a, 1975b) animals were preexposed to intraperitoneal (i.p.) injections of 1 mg/kg of methylscopolamine (MS) on 0, 3, 5 or 7 occasions and then trained to avoid a .15% (w/v) solution of saccharin by injecting them, i.p., with 2 mg/kg of d-amphetamine sulfate (AM). As in most of our studies, preexposures were administered once every fifth day when animals were 20 hr deprived of food and water, and the last preexposure occurred 10 days prior to the single training trial. Finally, animals that received 0 preexposures and those in an additional group (referred to as Control Level in the following figures) received equivolume injections of physiological saline during preexposure. Animals in the Control Level condition also received physiological saline injections on the training trial.

Training consisted of providing animals with access to saccharin for 15 min and then injecting them either with the AM or physiological saline. Three days later, on a test trial, animals were presented with the saccharin solution for a second 15 min drinking period but were not injected. The amount of saccharin animals drank during this test session is summarized in Figure 1. Analysis of these results showed that animals that had been preexposed to MS on five occasions formed weaker aversions than animals that had been preexposed to MS on 0 or 3 occasions. Animals that had been preexposed on 7 occasions did not form aversions to the sacharin solution; consumption by these animals was not reliably

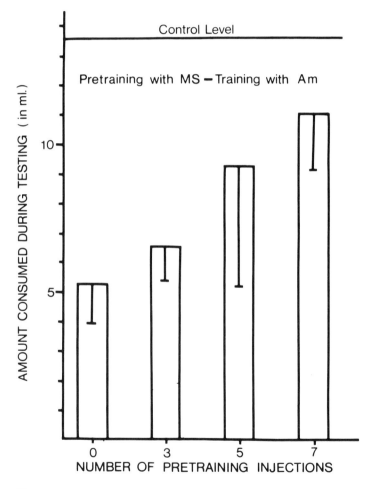

Figure 1
Test trial consumption of saccharin by animals that had been preexposed to methylscopolamine (MS) on 0, 3, 5 or 7 occasions and then trained with d-amphetamine sulfate (AM). (From Braveman, 1975a).

different from consumption by animals tested in the Control Level condition. In other words, seven preexposures blocked the conditioning of saccharin aversions while five preexposures merely attenuated them.

This result has been replicated in experiments in my own laboratory and in those of other investigators using different drugs, including one experiment in which animals were preexposed with AM and trained with MS. Crossover effects with amphetamine and methylscopolamine are of particular interest because these agents appear to produce conditioned food aversions by different mechanisms. Berger, Weiss, and Stein (1973) have noted that methylscopolamine produces aversions via a peripheral mechanism which acts through the area postrema, while d-amphetamine produces aversions by direct action on the central nervous system. This relationship suggested to us that there may be a single, nonpharmacologically based, mechanism which mediates the crossover effect we observed between MS and AM in the previous experiment. However, before developing my reasoning along these lines, I want to present additional evidence on the crossover effect.

Transfer Between Lithium and Methylscopolamine. One experiment indicated, once again, that the specific pharmacological nature of the aversion-inducing treatments appeared not to be important in producing the crossover effect. In this experiment, animals were preexposed on five different occasions with a 0.5% body weight injection of a 0.3M solution of lithium chloride (LiCl) and then trained with either a 1% body weight injection of 0.3M solution of LiCl or 1 mg/kg of methylscopolamine. Control subjects received physiological saline injections during preexposure. The procedure differed slightly from what was used in the previous experiment in that preexposure treatments were administered 1 hr after animals had received 1.5 hr access to their daily food and tap water. This allowed us to assess whether or not the crossover effect was procedure-specific.

Three days after the training trial animals were tested for aversions to the saccharin solution in a 15 min test trial. The amount of the saccharin that animals in the various groups drank on the conditioning day prior to the injection (i.e., Pretraining) and on the test trial (i.e., Test) are summarized in Figure 2. These results show that animals that had been preexposed and trained with LiCl (PT-L) drank as much saccharin on the test trial as they had during pretraining. In contrast, animals that had not been preexposed and then were trained with LiCl (C-L) showed a reliable reduction in consumption between the training and the test sessions. Similar results were obtained for animals that had been preexposed to LiCl and trained with methylscopolamine (PT-M) and for those that had not been preexposed and then trained with methylscopolamine (C-M). Thus it appears that the crossover effect also occurs with drugs other than MS and AM, and that the schedule of administering the preexposure does not influence the outcome of the experiment.

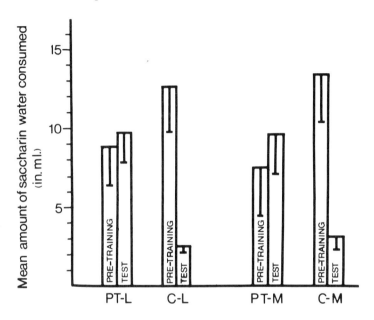

Figure 2
Mean amount of saccharin water consumed prior to a single training trial (pretraining) and on a one-bottle test Trial (Test) in animals that had been preexposed to LiCl (PT) or to physiological saline (C) and then trained with LiCl (L) or methylscopolamine (M). Preexposures in this experiment were administered one hr after animals had received their daily ration of food and water. (From Braveman, 1975a).

CROSSOVER EFFECTS BETWEEN DRUG
AND NON-DRUG TREATMENTS

There are a number of reasons for wanting to discover if the crossover effect occurs between drug and non-drug treatments. One of these involves discovering whether or not the crossover effect occurs primarily for pharmacological reasons, such as the

515

establishment of tolerances between different drugs. Since we had already demonstrated that crossover effects occurred between pairs of drugs which are as dissimilar as AM and MS and LiCl, and since others have reported crossover effects with other drugs (e.g., Gamzu, 1975; Vogel & Nathan, 1975), we had reason to believe that the effect had a non-pharmacological basis. The following two experiments provide additional support for a non-pharmacological interpretation of crossover effects.

Interference With Rotation-Induced Preexposure. The first of these experiments involves the use of rotation which, in independent experiments (Braun & McIntosh, 1973; Green & Rachlin, 1973), had been shown to be an effective aversion-inducing treatment. In this experiment, animals in different groups were preexposed on five separate occasions to one of five different treatments including intraperitoneal injections of physiological saline, 2 mg/kg of d-amphetamine sulfate, 1 mg/kg of methylscopolamine, or a 1% body weight injection of a .3M solution of LiCl. A fifth group of animals was rotated on each of these occasions at 60 rpm for 15 min. It is important to remember that each of these treatments, except the saline injection, is capable of producing aversions if they are administered for the first time following consumption of a distinctive solution. All other unspecified procedural details of this experiment were similar to the one involving AM and MS.

Ten days after the last preexposure treatment, animals in all groups were presented with a .15% (w/v) solution of sodium saccharin during their normal 15 min drinking period; 90-180 sec later, they were placed in a special transparent chamber and rotated for 15 min at 60 rpm. At the end of this rotation session, animals were replaced in their home cages and, 3 hr later, given access to food and tap water for 30 min. On the next day, they received tap water during their normal 15 min drinking period and were not rotated. Alternation of saccharin-rotation days with water-no rotation days continued until animals received three two-day cycles. This procedure provided the opportunity to use the amount consumed prior to rotation on a conditioning trial as an evaluation of the effects of prior conditioning experiences. On Test Trial 3 animals were given saccharin to drink but this was not followed by rotation.

Figure 3 shows the amount of saccharin that animals consumed during the 15-min drinking sessions prior to each rotation session and on Test Trial 3. Analysis of these results showed that prior to the first rotation, (PT), there were no reliable differences among the five groups, nor were the changes in consumption between PT and

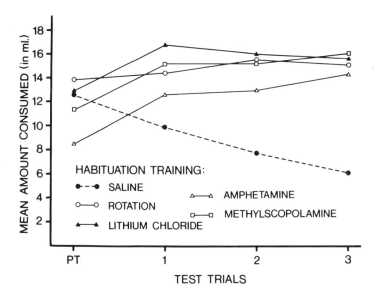

Figure 3
Consumption of saccharin water prior to each of three training
sessions (i.e., PT, Test Trials 1 and 2) and prior to no training
(i.e., Test Trial 3) by animals that had been preexposed to
either lithium chloride, methylscopolamine, d-amphetamine
sulfate, rotation, or physiological saline. All animals were
rotated on each of the training trials. (From Braveman, 1975a).

Test Trial 1 (i.e., following one training trial) reliable. However, on
Test Trial 2, after animals had received two pairings of saccharin
water and rotation, and from then on, those that had been preexposed to saline injections consumed reliably less than they had on
PT and reliably less than animals in any of the other groups. In
contrast, animals that had been preexposed to any of the aversion-
inducing treatments revealed what appeared to be a reduction of
neophobia in that, in spite of the intervening training trials, they
increased their consumption between PT and the test trials. These
results suggest that five preexposures to any one of a variety of
pharmacological aversion-inducing agents can completely block
the conditioning of rotation-induced food aversions.

The fact that animals that were rotated both during preexposure
and training exhibited the preexposure effect extends findings from
other studies and shows that the preexposure effect can be produced when non-pharmacological treatments are employed. The
fact that preexposure to any one of several drugs also reduced the
effectiveness of a non-drug treatment also suggests that the

crossover effect is not tied to the pharmacological nature of the drug treatments.

Transfer Between Shock and Lithium. Subsequent research (Braveman, 1975b) involving LiCl and electric footshock appears to confirm and extend the above conclusion. This research, which was conducted by Karen Jacobson, a graduate student at the University of Haifa (Israel), and myself replicated the results of the previous experiment. Since we are not concerned here with the question of whether or not the animals associate eating-related cues with exteroceptive pain, I will only briefly describe the procedure that we used to produce conditioned food aversions with the electric shock.

Animals in this experiment were implanted with subcutaneous electrodes which terminated in their forepaws. Following recovery from the operation and adaptation to a 15 min per day drinking schedule on which they received tap water from two drinking tubes that were presented simultaneously in their home cages, animals drank either 2% (w/v) saccharin or 50% (v/v) sweetened condensed milk which was presented to them from a single tube in their home cages. Thirty minutes later, one-half of the animals that drank the saccharin water was placed in a special chamber and received, through the electrodes, 4 ma of pulsed, constant electric shock which was delivered on a variable interval (VI) 1-min schedule for 1 hr. The VI schedule ranged from 15 to 105 sec in gradations of 15 sec, and each shock presentation lasted for 4 sec. The remaining animals that had consumed the saccharin received similar shock treatment 24 hr after they drank the sweetened water. For animals that drank the sweetened condensed milk, the drinking-shock intervals were 4 and 24 hr, respectively.

Three days later animals were presented with the solution that they had consumed prior to the shock session and an equivalent amount of tap water. This 15 min two-bottle test session was carried out in the home cages. Figure 4 shows the relative preference that animals had for the test solution on the test trial. Scores of .5 indicate that animals had no preference for the test solution over the tap water, scores greater than .5 indicate a preference for the test solution, while scores less than .5 indicate a preference for the tap water or an aversion to the test solution. These results show that animals that had been shocked 30 min or 4 hr after drinking saccharin or milk, respectively, preferred the tap water. Those that had been shocked 24 hr after drinking preferred the test substance to the tap water. Moreover, differences in mean preference scores between the 30 min delay group and its respective 24 hr control

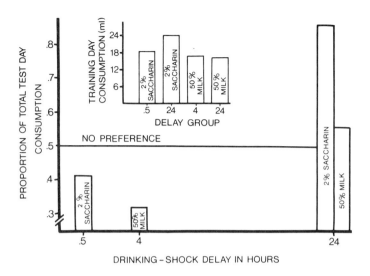

Figure 4

Preference scores from a two-bottle test trial for animals that had been trained to avoid saccharin or sweetened condensed milk. Preference scores were calculated by dividing the amount of the test solution, saccharin or milk, consumed by the total consumption.

and between the 4 hr delay group and its 24 hr control were statistically reliable.

This finding, in and of itself, is important since it appears to extend results reported by Krane and Wagner (1975). However, for the present purposes I want to consider what happens to aversion formation following preexposure to either unavoidable shock or LiCl. Based on our previous findings, the specific treatment to which animals are preexposed should not be an important factor in determining whether or not subsequent aversions are attenuated. In the present experiment, animals were preexposed to injections of LiCl or to unavoidable and uncontrollable shock on five different occasions. Each session was scheduled to occur every fourth day. A single training trial occurred seven days after the last preexposure session. On this trial animals drank a 50% solution of sweetened condensed milk. One-half of the animals that had previously received shock were then injected with LiCl and one-half of the previously LiCl-injected animals received the uncontrollable and unavoidable shock. The remaining animals in each of these groups were trained with the treatment that was used during preexposure.

519

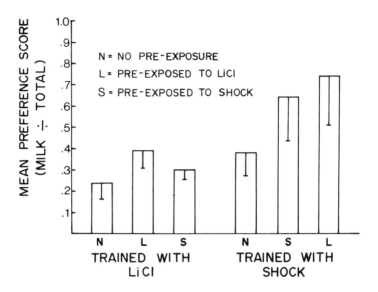

Figure 5
Preference scores from a two-bottle test trial for animals that had been either not preexposed (N) or preexposed to shock (S) or LiCl (L) and then trained with either LiCl or shock.

A single, two-bottle preference test between the sweetened condensed milk solution and tap water was administered two days after the training session. The preference that animals exhibited for the milk solution on this test trial is presented in Figure 5. All animals that were trained with LiCl formed aversions of varying strength to the milk since all of their preference scores were less than .5. However, those that were preexposed to LiCl (Group L) or shock (Group S) showed a tendency to form weaker aversions than animals that had not been preexposed (Group N). In contrast, for animals that were trained with shock, only those that had not been preexposed to either shock (Group S) or to LiCl (Group L) appeared to prefer the milk to water. In other words, preexposure to either LiCl or shock attenuated LiCl-induced aversions whereas preexposure to the same treatments completely blocked the formation of shock-induced aversions.

MANY AVERSIVE TREATMENTS: A SINGLE CAUSE?

What, then, do the results of these experiments indicate about the nature of the postingestional consequence in the conditioning of aversions? I feel that they, and other experiments like them (e.g.,

Gamzu, 1975; Vogel & Nathan, 1975), show that the many different types of treatments share a common property that is responsible for producing the aversion. Thus, preexposure to one treatment reduces, in an unspecified way at this point, the aversiveness of that and other treatments. This conclusion, however, is open to possible criticism on two grounds.

EVIDENCE AGAINST A SINGLE CAUSE

First, not all experiments show that preexposure to one treatment is effective in reducing the aversiveness of all other treatments. In fact, in some experiments preexposure to treatment A will reduce the effectiveness of treatment B, but when B is used during preexposure the effectiveness of A is unaffected (e.g., Cappell & LeBlanc, 1975). Such findings would suggest that there is not a factor which is common to all of the treatments. Rather, they indicate that there may be a specific, pharmacologically based, relationship among some treatments. In order to reconcile these asymmetrical results with those which indicate that the relationship among treatments is symmetrical, and hence indifferent to the types of treatments that are employed, I would like to suggest that instances of asymmetries have resulted from parametric problems which are related to the facility with which various treatments produce aversion. For example, we know from independent experiments that the doses of LiCl used in the experiment by Jacobson and myself produce stronger aversions under less favorable conditions than electric footshock does under relatively more favorable conditions. The same appears to be true of other types of aversion-inducing treatments (e.g., Berger, 1972; Nachman & Ashe, 1973). If an animal is preexposed to one of the "weaker" treatments the effect on a "stronger" treatment will be less (unless the number of preexposures is extended) than if preexposure is to one of the "stronger" treatments. I have tested the limits of this proposal in my own laboratory by preexposing animals to doses of LiCl or of strychnine sulfate that are known not to produce conditioned food aversions and then training them with doses of LiCl that are known to produce aversions (e.g., Braveman, 1975b). In these instances the preexposure effect does not occur. Thus, it appears that, if preexposure involves treatments that are so weak that they do not produce aversions, the preexposure effect, both with the same and different drugs, does not occur. This result lends support to the argument that the asymmetries which have been reported may have resulted from parametric problems. It follows that if treatments that produce equivalent aversions are used, the asymmetrical results should disappear.

A second criticism of the proposal that there is an aversive property which is common to all treatments stems from the fact that, to date, no one has been able to specify conclusively the nature of this property. Gamzu (this volume) has suggested that drug novelty may be the common factor, yet it is known that nonpharmacological treatments are capable of producing very strong aversions. Others have argued that sickness is the common property, yet it is known that not all of the treatments that are used to produce aversions, in the doses that are employed, make animals sick. Still others (e.g., Wise, Yokel, & DeWit, 1976; Vogel & Nathan, 1975) have argued that lack of control over the onset or duration of the drug effects is the aversive factor which produces aversions.

THE STRESS HYPOTHESIS

Each of the above positions claims a certain degree of empirical support, yet none accounts for all of the data. It is obvious to anyone who has used LiCl, for example, that a rat that has been injected with 1% body weight of .3M solution of LiCl becomes very sick shortly after the injection. At the same time, the same behavioral indices of sickness are not present when animals are injected with drugs such as amphetamine or methylscopolamine. Yet we know that all of these drugs produce aversions. This suggests to me that the aversive property which is common to all treatments is something which is more general than either sickness, novelty or lack of control. I would like to propose that this general aversive property is the stress that results from the application of aversion-inducing treatments. More specifically, I want to argue that certain stress-related physiological changes which are common to and produced by the application of the various aversion-inducing treatments are responsible for what appears to be a commonality among different treatments. In fact, results of recent research appear to be consistent with this position and point to changes in corticosterone or its precursor, ACTH, as the single underlying factor which makes aversion-inducing treatments aversive.

Evidence for Stress Mediation. In one series of experiments, Riley (personal communication) has shown that following the injection of various aversion-inducing drugs, there are characteristic changes in blood corticosterone levels. The procedure employed by Riley involved adapting rats to a schedule on which they received water for 20 min daily for the first twelve days of the experiment.

During this phase they were also injected with physiological saline to adapt them to the injection procedure. On the training day all animals were given access to saccharin for 20 min, followed immediately by i.p. injections of either a .15M solution of LiCl (1.8 mEq/kg) or an equivalent volume of physiological saline. Animals were then decapitated at 10, 30, 60 or 240 min after the injection and blood samples were taken and analyzed by fluorometric methods.

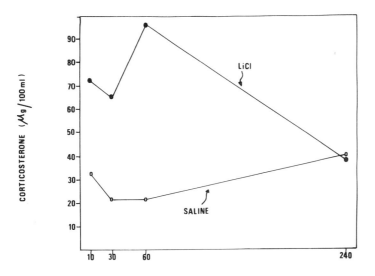

MINUTES SINCE INJECTION

Figure 6
Mean number of micrograms of corticosterone per 100 ml of blood plasma in animals that were trained with LiCl or physiological saline. (From Riley, personal communication.)

The results of this experiment are summarized in Figure 6. It is apparent from this figure that there were large differences in blood corticosterone levels between LiCl- and saline-injected animals beginning at 10 min and peaking at 60 min following injection. The corticosterone levels returned to baseline level by 240 min after injection.

In a second experiment, Riley employed a similar procedure except this time he injected 50 mg/kg of morphine sulfate or an equivalent dose of physiological saline on the training day. Figure 7 shows that the corticosterone response for this drug was different

523

from that for LiCl. The peak response occurred 10 min after the injection, after which plasma concentrations began to return to baseline levels.

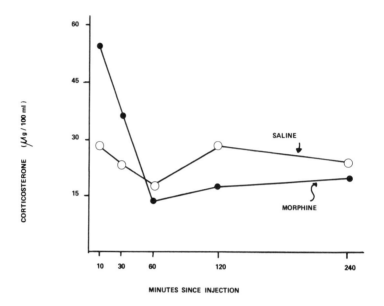

Figure 7
Mean number of micrograms of corticosterone per 100 ml of blood plasma in animals that were trained with morphine or with physiological saline. (From Riley, personal communication.)

An interesting aspect of the data from these two experiments is that they correspond to the facility with which these two drugs condition food aversions. It is generally thought that LiCl is one of the most effective drugs in producing aversions (Nachman & Hartley, 1975), while morphine is much more equivocal in its effectiveness as an aversion-inducing agent (Berger, 1972; Jaquet, 1973). Based on correlational evidence such as this, Riley (personal communication) has argued that the effectiveness of a treatment in conditioning food aversions may be determined by the rate at which the level of corticosterone or ACTH reaches or is maintained at a specified level. Furthermore, he suggested that the effective association in the food-aversion paradigm may be between the eating-related cue (e.g., taste) and this change in the level of corticosterone or ACTH.

524

Recent data from the laboratory of Dr. Robert Ader (1976) would appear to confirm Riley's notion. In a series of experiments, Ader has attempted to measure the level of corticosterone at various times during the conditioning of food aversions. In one experiment a "conditioned" (C) group of rats was injected with 50 mg/kg of cyclophosphamide (CY) 30 min after they had consumed a .1% solution of sodium saccharin for 15 min. A "non-conditioned" group (NC) received an equivalent injection of distilled water. Two or five days later, equal numbers of animals in the C and NC groups were either given access to saccharin or tap water, or were merely deprived of water for 23¾ hr. Behavioral tests showed that only animals that had been injected with CY on the training trial learned a conditioned aversion. Corticosterone determinations showed that, as in the Riley experiments, it was possible to elevate the level of corticosterone over the level that was measured in non-deprived animals by injecting them with CY as well as by water depriving them for 23¾ hr or by allowing animals to drink saccharin water. The rise in corticosterone, however, was reliably greater to CY than to any of the other experimental manipulations.

Postconditioning determinations of the corticosterone response in animals that had been conditioned to avoid saccharin showed that the corticosterone levels on both test days approximated the level reached during the preconditioning phase of the experiment in response to CY alone. In other words, following one conditioning trial, the taste of saccharin was sufficient to produce a corticosterone response which was equivalent to that produced by CY. A similar finding was presented in a second experiment in which LiCl was used to produce conditioned aversions and in an independent study by Smotherman, Hennessy, and Levine (1976). The increase in corticosterone level in response to saccharin in animals that had learned to avoid the saccharin solution was not only too indistinguishable from that produced by the CY alone, but it was also reliably higher than that attained by animals in several control groups that had been included to insure the rise was "conditioned" and not the effect of an artifact.

Further research has been aimed at delineating causal relationships between both corticosterone and ACTH and food-aversion learning. For example, both Riley and Ader have suggested that corticosterone is necessary for the acquisition of conditioned aversion—perhaps because a process which activates the memory of the initial conditioning experience is not present on the test trial. If this hypothesis is correct, it follows that the formation of conditioned aversion should be blocked if the rise of corticosterone is blocked. Indeed, Hennessy, Smotherman, and Levine (1976) have shown that pretreatment with dexamethasone, a drug which suppresses adrenal-pituitary activity, attenuated LiCl-induced aversions to milk. In addition, extinction of conditioned aversions should be paralleled by a concomitant reduction in the adrenal-pituitary response. If, on the other hand, ACTH levels are maintained at conditioning levels, extinction of the aversions should be retarded. In fact, Rigter and Popping (1976) have shown that injections of certain ACTH analogues, as well as other drugs which are known to stimulate ACTH production, prolong already conditioned aversions.

The foregoing studies show rather conclusively that corticosterone and/or ACTH are crucial in the formation of conditioned taste aversions. Clearly, this conclusion is consistent with findings from research involving other types of avoidance learning and points, once again (see Revusky, this volume), to the general nature of the processes which govern the various types of learning. However, at some point it will be important to discover exactly what aspect of the change in corticosterone or ACTH is responsible for making treatments aversive. Such information will, for example, allow one to predict whether or not a given treatment will produce a conditioned aversion. Finally, it appears that histamine—a chemical involved in the stress syndrome—also plays an important role in the formation of aversions (Levy, 1975; Levy, Carroll, Smith, & Hofer, 1974). It would, therefore, appear to be profitable for further research to investigate the relationship between histamine and corticosterone in the formation of conditioned aversions. In other words, there is still much to be discovered about the single mechanism which seems to underlie the formation of conditioned aversions.

SUMMARY

The results of experiments involving the crossover preexposure effect point to two very interesting aspects of this phenomenon. The first is the relative indifference of the effect to the type and/or kind of treatments that are employed during preexposure and training. The second aspect of these experiments points to the fact that the effect does not appear to be dependent upon the use of pharmacological agents as treatments. Thus, it is possible to weaken the effectiveness of rotation or shock to produce aversions by preexposing animals to treatments, such as LiCl, that are basically pharmacological in nature. It is these two aspects of the preexposure effect which have led me to postulate that there is a single aversive property which is common to the various treatments that have been used to condition aversions.

Elsewhere (e.g., Braveman, 1975b) I have argued that the mechanism which is responsible for the preexposure effect is basically associative in nature. However, this position begs the questions regarding the nature of the aversive property which is shared by the many different treatments in that it is based on the supposition that preexposure to an unspecified aversive stimulus makes associations between the taste of an ingested solution and that aversion-inducing stimulus more difficult. However, a growing body of literature now points to the role of stress-related neurohumoral changes which appear to be common to several different aversion-inducing treatments. It is not known, at this point, exactly how these neurohumoral changes operate to provide an aversive substrate for the various treatments and additional research is dictated. Such research appears, to me, to be very promising for a number of reasons. First of all, it is known that there are similar changes which underlie other, more traditional forms of avoidance conditioning (e.g., Anisman, 1975; Levine & Brush, 1967; Weiss, Stone, & Harrell, 1970). Thus, research which is aimed at understanding the relationship between these neurohumoral changes and the conditioning of food aversions is one means of relating food avoidance learning to other forms of avoidance learning.

Secondly, by gaining an understanding of the nature of the postingestional consequence, we will be in a much better position to understand the heretofore unexplained and elusive preexposure effect. A relatively straightforward account of the preexposure effect follows when the aversive consequence is viewed as being a product of an underlying neurohumoral change. Specifically, it is possible to argue that repeated exposures to an aversion-inducing treatment, as typically occurs in studies on preexposure, dampens or otherwise interferes with a neurochemical process which is necessary for the formation of conditioned aversions. Thus, when the same or a different treatment is administered following preexposure, the necessary cause of aversions is not produced or, if it is, it is produced at a level which only allows for the formation of weakened or attenuated aversions. Obviously, these assertions require direct empirical validation. However, it appears that research along these lines will provide promising and interesting information about mechanisms which underlie the conditioning of food aversions.

ACKNOWLEDGEMENTS

Some of the research on preexposure was supported by a Research Grant from the Dean of Science, Memorial University of Newfoundland, and by Grant A-8334 from the National Research Council of Canada to the author. Emir Andrews, Gerard Martin, Richard Noseworthy and Joan Crane assisted with various aspects of this research, and their help is greatly appreciated. The studies on preexposure were conducted while the author was a Visiting Research Professor at the University of Haifa (Israel). I am deeply indebted to Karen Jacobson and Ron Backner for their help and to Dr. Barry Berger for providing equipment and space. Finally, I want to thank Dr. A. Riley for granting permission to include his unpublished data, and Dr. Earle Thomas, whose critical and perceptive comments of earlier ideas helped in the formulation of some of the ideas presented in the present chapter.

Ader, R. Conditioned adrenocortical steroid elevations in the rat. **Journal of Comparative and Physiological Psychology,** 1976, **90,** 1156-1163.

Anisman, H. Time-dependent variations in aversely motivated behaviors: Nonassociative effects of cholinergic and catecholaminergic activity. **Psychological Review,** 1975, **82,** 359-385.

Austin, T. M. Control of conditioned taste aversions by previous learning. Paper presented at the Forty-fifth Annual Meeting of the Eastern Psychological Association, Philadelphia, 1974.

Berger, B. D. Conditioning of food aversions by injections of psychoactive drugs. **Journal of Comparative and Physiological Psychology,** 1972, **81,** 21-26.

Berger, B., Wise, C., & Stein, L. Area postrema and bait shyness. **Journal of Comparative and Physiological Psychology,** 1973, **82,** 475-479.

Berman, R. F., & Cannon, D. S. The effect of prior ethanol experience on ethanol-induced saccharin aversions. **Physiology and Behavior,** 1974, **12,** 1041-1044.

Braun, J. J., & McIntosh, H. Learned taste aversions induced by rotational stimuli. **Physiological Psychology,** 1973, **1,** 301-304.

Braveman, N. S. Formation of taste aversions in rats following prior exposure to sickness. **Learning and Motivation,** 1975, **6,** 512-534. (a)

Braveman, N. S. Absence of taste aversions following prior exposure to sickness. Paper presented at the Eighty-third Annual Meeting of the American Psychological Association, 1975 (b).

Brookshire, K., & Brackbill, R. Formation and retention of conditioned taste aversions and UCS habituation. **Bulletin of the Psychonomic Society,** 1976, **7,** 125-128.

Cappell, H., & LeBlanc, A. Tolerance explanation of effects of prior drug exposure on gustatory aversions. Paper presented at the Eighty-third Annual Meeting of the American Psychological Association, 1975.

Elkins, R. Bait-shyness acquisition and resistance to extinction as functions of US exposure prior to conditioning. **Physiological Psychology,** 1974, **2,** 341-343.

Gamzu, E. Preexposure to an unconditioned stimulus alone may eliminate taste aversions. Paper presented at the Fifteenth Annual Meeting of the Psychonomic Society, 1974.

Gamzu, E. Elimination of taste aversions by pretreatment: Cross-drug comparisons. Paper presented at the Eighty-third Annual Meeting of the American Psychological Association, 1975.

Green, L., & Rachlin, H. The effect of rotation on the learning of taste aversions. **Bulletin of the Psychonomic Society,** 1973, **1,** 137-138.

Hennessy, J. W., Smotherman, W. P., & Levine, S. Conditioned taste aversion and the pituitary-adrenal system. **Behavioral Biology,** 1976, **16,** 413-424.

Jaquet, Y., F. Conditioned aversion during morphine maintenance in mice and rats. **Physiology and Behavior,** 1973, **11,** 527-541.

Krane, R., & Wagner, A. Taste aversion learning with delayed-shock US: Implications for the "generality of the laws of learning." **Journal of Comparative and Physiological Psychology,** 1975, **88,** 882-889.

Levine, S., & Brush, F. R. Adrenocortical activity and avoidance learning as a function of time after avoidance training. **Physiology and Behavior,** 1967, **2,** 385-388.

Levy, C. J. Histamine in taste aversions. Paper presented at the Eighty-third Annual Meeting of the American Psychological Association, 1975.

Levy, C. J., Carroll, M. E., Smith, J. C., & Hofer, K. G. Antihistamines block radiation-induced taste aversions. **Science,** 1974, **186,** 1044-1046.

Nachman, M., & Ashe, J. H. Learned taste aversions in rats as a function of dosage, concentration and route of administration of LiCl. **Physiology and Behavior,** 1973, **10,** 73-78.

Nachman, M., & Hartley, P. The role of illness in producing learned taste aversions in rats: A comparison of several rodenticides. **Journal of Comparative and Physiological Psychology,** 1975, **89,** 1010-1018.

Rigter, H., & Popping, A. Hormonal influences on the extinction of conditioned taste aversions. **Psychopharmacologia** (Berl.), 1976, **46,** 255-261.

Riley, A. Changes in blood-corticosterone levels following the administration of lithium chloride and morphine. Personal communication.

Smotherman, W. P., Hennessy, J. W., & Levine, S. Plasma corticosterone levels during recovery from LiCl produced taste aversions. **Behavioral Biology,** 1976, **16,** 401-412.

Vogel, J., & Nathan, B. Antagonism of a taste aversion by preexposure to a dissimilar drug. Paper presented at the Eighty-third Annual Meeting of the American Psychological Association, 1975.

Weiss, J. M., Stone, E. A., & Harrell, N. Coping behavior and brain norepinephrine level in rats. **Journal of Comparative and Physiological Psychology**, 1970, **72,** 153-160.

Wise, R. A., Yokel, R. A., & DeWit, H. Both positive reinforcement and conditioned aversion from amphetamine and from apomorphine in rats. **Science**, 1976, **191,** 1273-1275.

_____ XXI _____

"SICKNESS" AND THE BACKWARD CONDITIONING
OF TASTE AVERSIONS

LEWIS M. BARKER
Baylor University

JAMES C. SMITH
Florida State University

E. MARTIN SUAREZ
Miami VAH

The necessary and sufficient conditions for an event to act as an unconditioned stimulus (UCS) in taste-aversion conditioning remain an enigma despite the considerable amount of research that has been directed to this question (see Gamzu; Braveman, this volume). The experiments to be reported here were developed within the research program of James C. Smith and his students who, in the 1960's, accompanied John Garcia and colleagues in their search for the unconditioned stimulus properties of ionizing radiation (see Garcia, Kimeldorf, & Hunt, 1961). Much of this work has been described in detail elsewhere (Smith, 1971), and only the more recent research concerned with the delineation of radiation and drug or toxin-induced sickness will be treated here. Specifically, in this chapter we will examine (1) the relationship of overt signs of induced-sickness to the efficacy of taste-aversion conditioning, and (2) evidence for taste-aversion conditioning resulting from a procedure in which the sickness-inducing event precedes the taste experience (i.e., postexposure, or "backward" conditioning). Various hypotheses concerning this latter phenomenon will then be examined.

RELATIONSHIP OF SIGNS OF SICKNESS
TO EFFICACY OF CONDITIONING

SICKNESS AS THE UNCONDITIONED RESPONSE (UCR)
IN TASTE-AVERSION CONDITIONING

Smith (1971) has described a series of studies which were modeled after the radiation-induced taste-aversion conditioning experiments first reported by Garcia, Kimeldorf, and Koelling (1955), and by Garcia and Kimeldorf (1957). Smith used variations on a "standard experiment" in which rats ingested an initially palatable saccharin solution in temporal conjunction with exposure to ionizing radiation. In comparison with various control groups, the rats subsequently showed an aversion to the saccharin solution. Following the theoretical interpretation of Garcia et al. (1955) and of Garcia and Kimeldorf (1957), these taste preference changes were viewed as conditioned responses (CRs) resulting from a Pavlovian-like conditioning procedure in which the saccharin taste was a conditioned stimulus (CS) and exposure to ionizing radiation was an unconditioned stimulus (UCS). Both of the above stimuli could be easily manipulated and, along with the CR, were readily measured. Radiation-induced malaise (or sickness, or illness) was inferred to be the analogue of a Pavlovian unconditioned response (UCR). Unlike Pavlovian defense conditioning, however, in which the UCR to an aversive UCS is observable (e.g., paw flexion to electric shock), the UCR to ionizing radiation is not readily measurable. This inability to specify the UCR to radiation continues to present difficulties for a Pavlovian interpretation of taste-aversion conditioning. The irradiated rat does not appear sick and yet the subsequent taste-aversion behavior has traditionally been interpreted in terms of a sickness model (see Garcia & Ervin, 1968; Garcia, McGowan, & Green, 1972).

COMPARISON OF RADIATION- AND
LITHIUM CHLORIDE-INDUCED CONDITIONING

In the late 1960's rat poisoning experiments (Richter, 1950; cf. "bait-shyness" experiments of Rzoska, 1953, 1954) were integrated into the radiation-induced taste-aversion literature by Garcia, Ervin, and Koelling (1966, 1967). The problems of a sickness model of conditioning were exacerbated by equating poisoning experiments in which agents administered to rats produced obvious signs of sickness with irradiation experiments that did not involve any change in the appearance of the rat when the UCS was administered. An example of one such comparison can be seen in Figure 1, in which taste-aversion conditioning induced by radiation is compared to conditioning produced by a dosage of lithium chloride (LiCl) which Nachman (1970) previously reported to readi-

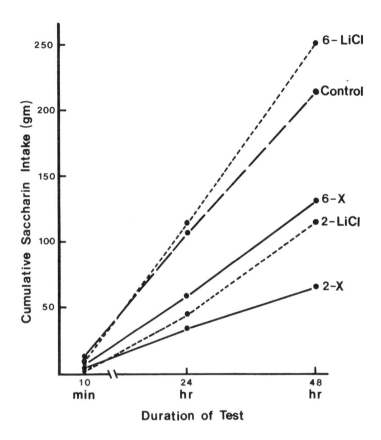

Figure 1
The cumulative 0.1% saccharin consumption of four treatment groups (n = 8) and a pooled control group (n = 36) during a 48-hr two-bottle preference test with water. During the first 10 min, only the saccharin bottle was available. Treatment consisted of 20 min access to 0.1% saccharin solution, followed by 100R gamma radiation or 20 ml/kg, 0.15M lithium chloride. CS-UCS delays were 2 hr (2-X, 2-LiCl) or 6 hr (6-X, 6-LiCl) duration. Pooled controls consisted of saccharin CS/sham UCS and Sham (water) CS/LiCl or Radiation UCS groups—none of which differed statistically from each other during the 48-hr preference test. (Replotted from Barker & Smith, 1974).

ly cause signs of sickness and be highly effective in long-delay conditioning of taste aversions. Differential conditioning of these two UCSs can be seen by comparing the 10-min, 24-hr, and 48-hr cumulative saccharin intakes which followed aversion conditioning to saccharin three days earlier. Groups 2-LiCl and 6-LiCl were conditioned by being allowed access for 20 min to 0.1% saccharin solution, followed 2 hr and 6 hr later by 20 ml/kg, 0.15M LiCl, administered i.p. Groups 2-X and 6-X were treated in a similar manner except that they were exposed to 100 roentgens (R) gamma radiation in place of LiCl, 2 hr and 6 hr after access to the saccharin solution. The LiCl-treated animals invariably looked abnormal 5-10 min post-injection as evidenced by marked inactivity and diarrhea—two signs commonly used to designate "sickness" in the rat. In contrast to this, the irradiated animals did not exhibit abnormal signs that could be interpreted as sickness. On the basis of a sickness model of conditioning, one would expect the LiCl-treated rats to exhibit the greatest amount of conditioning. Figure 1 clearly shows that this is not the case. With 2-hr delays between saccharin ingestion and the aversive LiCl or radiation treatment, taste aversions were clearly conditioned in both groups in comparison to levels of saccharin consumed by control groups. With 6-hr delays, however, there is no evidence of conditioning in the LiCl-treated group after 24 hr of testing. The 6 hr-delay radiation group by contrast exhibited aversion conditioning at the 24-hr and 48-hr intervals which was comparable to the 2-hr LiCl group (Barker & Smith, 1974).

QUANTIFICATION OF SICKNESS IN RATS

We have recently completed a more systematic investigation into the relationship of signs of induced-sickness to efficacy of taste-aversion conditioning. Groups of rats were conditioned to avoid 0.25% saccharin by allowing 10 min access to this solution followed by one of two dose levels of radiation, LiCl, or cyclophosphamide (Schmitt & Barker, 1976). Three experienced rat observers rated each rat in this study on a scale of 1 (no overt signs of sickness) to 7 (extremely sick, near death) approximately 15 min following administration of the radiation, drug, or toxin in an attempt to quantify the sickness-inducing properties of these UCSs. The overall inter-rater reliability (r) equalled 0.63. The mean values of the three raters were used as data points in an analysis of variance, and the significant differences that were found are summarized in Table 1. Only the high dosage cyclophosphamide group and both LiCl groups were rated discriminably sicker than controls.

Not surprisingly, the high dose levels of LiCl made these rats appear significantly sicker than the low dose levels. The same trend was seen in the cyclophosphamide-treated animals, but the difference was not significant.

TABLE 1

GROUPS AND MEANS	100R x-ray	50R x-ray	Control	33mg/kg cyclo.	66mg/kg cyclo.	1.5 mEq LiCl	3.0 mEq LiCl
100R $X=1.33$	-	.17	.43	1.11	1.67**	1.97**	3.17**
50R $X=1.50$		-	.26	.94	1.50**	1.81**	3.00**
Control $X=1.76$			-	.68	1.24**	1.55**	2.74**
33 mg/kg cyclo. $X=2.44$				-	.56	.86	2.06**
66 mg/kg cyclo. $X=3.00$					-	.31	1.50**
1.5 mEq LiCl $X=3.31$						-	1.19*
3.0 mEq LiCl $X=4.50$							-

* $p < .05$ ** $p < .01$

Table 1
Summary table of Tukey's HSD tests and the absolute differences between means for the rating data. Each number represents the mean of three individual raters' mean rating for each group of 5 rats, where on a scale of 1-7, 1 = "normal" and 7 = "near death."

The sickness ratings of these groups can be compared to the degree of aversion conditioning to saccharin in Figure 2. The 100R x-ray group appeared normal yet was readily conditioned to a level indistinguishable from the high dosage LiCl and cyclophosphamide groups during three 10-min extinction tests. In fact, the x-ray and LiCl groups showing comparable conditioned aversions were rated as appearing the *most normal* and the *most sick*, respectively. While the post-conditioning time of observation (~15 min) was arbitrary, these data are in substantial agreement with our previous, less systematic observations over longer durations.

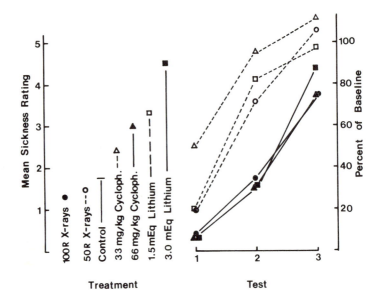

Figure 2

The mean sickness ratings made approximately 15 min following radiation, lithium chloride, or cyclophosphamide treatment
are plotted in the left portion of the figure. Starting three days
later the conditioned aversion to 0.1% saccahrin for these
groups was assessed in three 10 min, one-bottle tests at 48-hr
intervals. These intakes are expressed as percentages of
pseudoconditioning control groups. Note the lack of correspondence between overt signs of sickness and subsequent conditioning. (From Schmitt & Barker, unpublished manuscript).

FURTHER EVIDENCE AGAINST A
SICKNESS MODEL OF CONDITIONING

Perhaps it should not be too surprising that how "sick" a rat appears does not predict the effectiveness of the aversive treatment in
conditioning taste aversions. A number of examples exist which
argue against a simple sickness model of conditioning. Dosages of
ethanol, for instance, sufficient to make an animal comatose, produce little conditioning of taste aversions (Lester, Nachman, &
LeMagnen, 1971), even following repeated saccharin-ethanol pairings (Cannon, Berman, Baker, & Atkinson, 1975; Barker & Johns,
1976). Dosages of apomorphine which make rats look exceedingly
sick typically require multiple pairings with a distinctive taste
before aversion conditioning occurs (Garcia, Ervin, & Koelling,

538

1966). Furthermore, marked individual differences in the oc-curence of overt signs of disorder have been reported for high (75mg/kg) dosages of cyclophosphamide, including the absence of any symptomology for 30-40% of the treated rats; no relationship between the presence or absence of sickness signs and the degree of conditioned aversion was found (Barker, Suarez, & Gray, 1974).

Indeed, it can be argued that the rat need not even consciously experience the UCR to a radiation UCS for conditioning to occur. Roll and Smith (1972) allowed rats access to a saccharin solution, then anesthetized the rats, and x-irradiated them 1 hr later. Anesthetization was continued for 8 hr post-radiation. They found that relative to similarly anesthetized but sham-radiated controls, rats not allowed to experience the presumed noxious stimulus properties of radiation still formed profound conditioned aversions. The demonstration of conditioning in unconscious rats exposed to agents other than radiation has not been reported.

POSTEXPOSURE OR "BACKWARD" CONDITIONING OF TASTE AVERSIONS

IDENTIFICATION OF CR AND UCR COMPONENTS IN RADIATION-INDUCED CONDITIONING

The problem that unconditioned stimuli in taste-aversion condi-tioning procedures present for a traditional Pavlovian analysis is exemplified by the ionizing radiation UCS. As noted above, ap-plication of sublethal amounts of radiation typically used in aversion conditioning elicit no visible response from the organism, precluding measurement of a UCR. However, because decrements in the consumption of flavored fluids subsequent to a conditioning procedure are interpreted as the conditioned response, it is not un-reasonable to look for an *unconditioned* response in the form of decrements in the consumption of flavored fluid in the immediate post-irradiation exposure period. With this in mind, some of the first experiments on "postexposure conditioning" (where a radia-tion UCS precedes an ingested saccharin CS) were confounded due to a failure to identify and separate the CS aspects of saccharin in-gestion from the UCR and CR interpretations of the reduced sac-charin ingestion following radiation exposure (see below). Finally, identification of the onset and time course of the UCR to radiation as measured by differential saccharin ingestion in the post-radiation exposure period paralleled the above interest in condi-tioning parameters.

Initial observations that conditioned taste aversions could result from stimulus sequences in which the radiation (UCS) preceded the ingestion of saccharin (CS) were reported by Morris and Smith (1964) and by Scarborough, Whaley, and Rogers (1964).[1] The work of Smith and his students on this problem during the 1960's has recently been presented in detail (Smith, 1971) and, therefore, will only be briefly summarized here to provide perspective for subsequent sections.

A series of studies demonstrated that long-term saccharin aversion could be conditioned in rats that had ingested saccharin in close temporal relationship with exposure to ionizing radiation; it was not necessary for the rat to ingest saccharin prior to being irradiated (Smith, Taylor, Morris, & Hendricks, 1965; Smith & Schaeffer, 1967), but saccharin ingestion did have to occur within 6 hr following radiation exposure (Morris & Smith, 1964).

Methodological Considerations. Postexposure radiation experiments by Scarborough and his students (Scarborough & McLaurin, 1964; McLaurin & Scarborough, 1963; Scarborough et al., 1964; McLaurin, Farley, Scarborough, & Rawlins, 1964) differed from those by Smith in that they typically did not specify a conditioned stimulus. For example, McLaurin et al. (1964) allowed rats access to water, a saccharin solution, or nothing, and then exposed the rats to radiation. Immediately thereafter water and a saccharin solution was made accessible in each animal's home cage. Over the ensuing days all groups avoided the saccharin solution relative to sham-irradiated groups, leading Scarborough and colleagues to question the necessity of a CS in radiation conditioning. Scarborough et al. (1964) hypothesized that saccharin consumed in the home cage in the immediate post-irradiation period might have CS properties that were associated with a "lingering physiological disturbance" instigated by the radiation exposure. Smith and Schaeffer (1967) showed conclusively that Scarborough's hypothesis was correct by using electronic drinkometer circuits to measure which fluid was consumed at what time in the home cage following radiation. They found that, indeed, it was necessary for saccharin solution to be consumed either before or during a several hour post-radiation exposure period (i.e., the CS) for the subsequent conditioned aversion to saccharin (i.e., the CR) to occur.

Extending the Parameters of Postexposure Conditioning. Demonstrations of postexposure conditioning remain remarkable and inexplicable to the present. In more recent experiments we have attempted to measure the intensity and duration of the UCR to radiation by systematically manipulating the UCS-CS interval in a taste aversion conditioning paradigm. Significant conditioning was found for radiation-to-saccharin intervals up to and including 6 hr using two different procedures to assess the aversion (Carroll & Smith, 1974; Barker & Smith, 1974). A 12 hr UCS-CS interval has been demonstrated to yield significant conditioning using yet a third procedure (Scarborough et al., 1964). The optimal pairing of radiation with saccharin (i.e., the sequencing which yields maximum saccharin aversion conditioning) occurs with a UCS-CS interval of 0.5 - 1.5 hr (Carroll & Smith, 1974; Barker & Smith, 1974), and this has been uniformly interpreted as a reflection of the peak of the physiological disturbance initiated by sublethal radiation exposure.[2]

Further support for the above interpretation of the UCR to radiation was provided by Smith and his colleagues who looked for physiological changes following radiation exposure which coincided with the 30-90 min optimum of postexposure conditioning. Noting that systemic histamine levels peak 60-120 min post-irradiation (Weber & Steggerda, 1949), they successfully demonstrated that preadministration of antihistamines could block the formation of radiation-induced taste aversions (Levy, Carroll, Smith, & Hofer, 1974). This and a subsequent series of experiments demonstrated that histamine production was the probable basis for the "aversiveness of radiation," but was not the common aversive element of all agents which can be used to condition taste aversions. Lithium chloride-induced taste aversions, for example, were shown to be unaffected by preadministration of antihistamines, and neither was antihistamine pretreatment totally effective in blocking the taste aversions induced by cyclophosphamide, a radiomimetic (Levy et al., 1974; Levy, 1975).

BACKWARD CONDITIONING USING OTHER UCSs

The post-radiation exposure conditioning phenomenon has now been extended to agents that induce signs of sickness, and which apparently do not effect conditioning via histamine release. Figure 3 compares the "backward" conditioning of LiCl, alloxan, and cyclophosphamide with that of radiation at dose levels which produce substantially equivalent conditioned taste aversions in a forward conditioning paradigm (cf. Figure 2). The alloxan dosage used was found to be effective in 6-hr "forward" delays as well as a

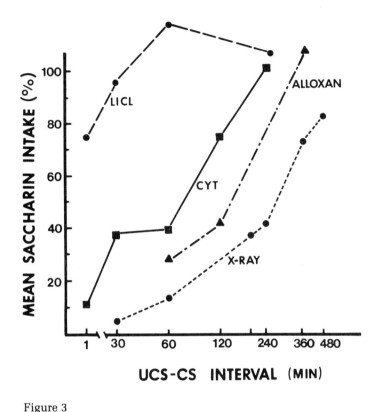

Figure 3

A comparison of postexposure conditioning for LiCl, radiation, cyclophosphamide, and alloxan UCSs. The LiCl and radiation data are replotted from Barker and Smith (1974). The cyclophosphamide function has been replotted from Barker, Suarez, and Gray (1974), and the alloxan data from Brookshire (1974, Figure 1). Each point on the radiation and LiCl functions was computed by dividing the amount of saccharin consumed in a 48-hr, 2-bottle test by control group saccharin consumption for the same period. The pseudoconditioning controls had water CSs and radiation or LiCl UCSs. The cyclophosphamide scores were computed in a similar manner but as assessed in a single 10-min test initiated 72 hr post-conditioning. The alloxan function was generated by dividing the saccharin preference of each alloxan-saccharin group by an alloxan-water (pseudoconditioning) control group's saccharin preference during a 2-hr test initiated 7 days post-conditioning. The UCS parameters for the LiCl and radiation are as reported for the respective high dose groups in Table 1. The cyclophosphamide dosage was 75 mg/kg while the alloxan monohydrate dosage was 120 mg/kg. The CS was 0.1% saccharin for all experiments

542

except 0.25% saccharin paired with cyclophosphamide. Compare comparable conditioning in forward paradigm (Figure 2) yet grossly different effectiveness of UCSs in postexposure procedure. Maximum postexposure conditioning intervals reported are 1.0 hr for LiCl (Domjan & Gregg, 1976), and for cyclophosphamide (Barker, Suarez, & Gray, 1974), 2 hr for alloxan (Brookshire, 1974), and 12 hr for radiation (Scarborough et al., 1964).

2-hr "backward" interval (Brookshire, 1974). In contrast to the relatively poor conditioning exhibited by the LiCl-treated groups in Figure 3, significant backward conditioning at a 1.0 hr UCS-CS interval has recently been found for lithium chloride (Domjan & Gregg, 1977).

Unlike the radiation UCS, lithium chloride, cyclophosphamide, alloxan, and presumably most other commonly used UCSs in taste-aversion studies produce optimal conditioning in CS-UCS sequences in which the rat begins experiencing the UCR either during or shortly following ingestion of the distinctively flavored fluid CS. The majority of taste-aversion conditioning studies employing backward sequences (for listing, see Appendix) typically inject the rat with a drug or toxin (UCS) and then allow access to a taste CS. It has been argued elsewhere (Nachman, 1970; Barker & Smith, 1974) that such "backward" procedures are effectively "forward" due to the delay of onset of drug effect. Significant conditioning at UCS-CS intervals greater than 30 min, however, has been demonstrated for both lithium chloride and cyclophosphamide; in both instances the rats appear visibly sick *prior to ingestion of the taste CS*. To the extent that signs of sickness represent the effective UCR, such conditioning is construed to be backward.

THEORETICAL CONSIDERATIONS:
POSTEXPOSURE OR "BACKWARD" CONDITIONING?

Smith (1971) has preferred to use the descriptive term "postexposure conditioning" rather than "backward conditioning" because the latter typically does not yield the stable, long-lasting behavioral changes attributed to associative conditioning, and as seen, for example, in Figure 3.[3] In fact, our lack of theoretical understanding of backward conditioning affords little insight into why, for the radiation groups in Figure 3, for example, profound saccharin aversion was found at the 0.5 hr UCS-CS interval, with decreasing aversion as the interval was extended beyond 6 hr. Several alternative hypotheses are presented below. While formulated to account for the UCR to 100R radiation, these hypotheses are presumably applicable to other agents successfully used in backward conditioning.

(1) UCR Time-Course Hypothesis.[4] The level of conditioned aversion for the 0.5 - 8.0 hr UCS-CS groups may reflect pairings of saccharin ingestion overlapping with (i.e., contiguous with) a radiation-induced physiological disturbance. The maximum physiological effect occurs 60-120 min post-radiation exposure (see Figure 4) and saccharin drinking during this time period results in maximal subsequent aversion (cf. Figure 3). As the physiological disturbance declines (for example at 3-4 hr postexposure), a saccharin drinking period (CS) would be paired with a UCR of a reduced magnitude, resulting in less conditioned aversion. To the extent that this hypothesis is valid, the aversion conditioning function in Figure 3 plots the time course of the UCR to a 100R radiation exposure. As previously noted, support for this hypothesis comes from the observation that histamine levels peak 60-120 min post-radiation. The CS event can be construed as being "embedded" within the UCR (i.e., the UCR both precedes and follows the CS; cf. Heth & Rescorla, 1973); this analysis, therefore, preserves CS-UCR contiguity theory.[5]

(2) "Queasy Stomach" Hypothesis. An interesting variation on the above hypothesis preserves CS-UCR contiguity in another way. The ingestion of saccharin in recently-radiated rats might *initiate* a noxious UCR ("unfamiliar food on a queasy stomach"). Radiation exposure may "sensitize" the rat by disrupting the internal milieu in a manner perceptible but not necessarily aversive, *until* saccharin is ingested. The "queasy stomach" hypothesis, unfortunately, cannot account for long-delay saccharin-radiation forward conditioning (i.e., CS-UCS delays of more than a couple of hours) in which rats with empty stomachs readily learn taste aversions. Secondly, this hypothesis merely changes the nature of the already unspecified UCR to radiation, without changing the necessity that this "new" UCR (i.e., "queasiness") have a time course similar to that depicted in Figure 4. Finally, conditioning results even when the abrupt onset of signs of sickness following treatment with LiCl and cyclophosphamide occur *prior* to, and independent of, saccharin ingestion.

(3) UCR Habituation Hypothesis. A second variation of the *UCR Time-Course Hypothesis* also preserves CS-UCR contiguity but ac-

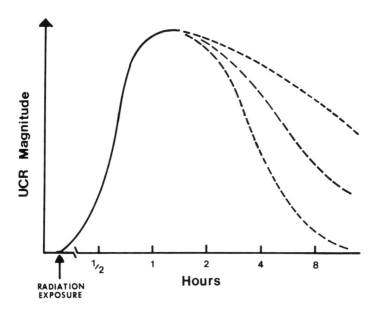

Figure 4
Hypothetical time-course of the UCR following exposure to 100 R radiation, as inferred from taste aversion conditioning function. The dashed lines indicate that the offset of the UCR cannot be predicted from the conditioning data.

counts for the backward delay gradient by postulating that the radiation UCR peaks shortly following radiation exposure, following which the rat becomes progressively habituated to the UCR. The loss of associability at longer UCS-CS delays may occur because the UCR is no longer novel when the saccharin is ingested (cf. the UCS preexposure effect, Gamzu, Braveman, this volume).

While this hypothesis is difficult to disprove, it can be argued equally well that long-delay UCS-CS conditioning is due to the *failure* of the UCR to habituate; this lack of UCR habituation allows for associability of saccharin ingestion with a radiation UCR several hours after the UCR onset. Following this reasoning, it may be that the greater effectiveness of radiation in UCS-CS paradigms compared to cyclophosphamide and LiCl can be attributed to the more complete habituation of these latter stimuli. This in turn may be accounted for by the rapidity of onset and perceptible aversiveness of these agents which allows them to habituate more quickly compared to the radiation stimulus. Since the magnitude and number of drug or radiation preexposures has been demonstrated to be inversely related to their effectiveness in conditioning taste aversions (for a review, see Gamzu, this volume), it can be further argued that higher dose levels of drugs or radiation which presumably produce more habituation would yield *less* conditioning over long UCS-CS delays. This counter-intuitive notion is currently being tested.[6]

(4) Backward Conditioning Hypothesis. The formation of backward associations (i.e., backward conditioning) has been reported in several recent animal conditioning studies (Heth & Rescorla, 1973; Kieth-Lucas & Guttman, 1975; Wagner & Terry, 1975; Tait, 1975, reported in Gormezano & Tait, 1976). While only modest evidence for conditioning was reported by Wagner and Terry (1975) and Gormezano and Tait (1976), the other two investigations yielded relatively stable and long-lasting CRs that varied systematically with manipulations of the UCS-CS interval.[7] Of these studies, 10 sec was the longest UCS-CS interval for which successful conditioning was reported (Kieth-Lucas & Guttman, 1975); the relevance of these studies for explication of the backward conditioning of taste aversions over several hours, therefore, is questionable.

According to a backward conditioning hypothesis, the delay gradient of conditioning in Figure 3 results from the reduced association between two events (i.e., the peak UCR and saccharin ingestion) that occur further apart in time. (This backward delay gradient using radiation is strikingly similar—almost a mirror image—of the forward, CS-UCS, delay gradient. See Barker & Smith, 1974). The time-course of the radiation UCR is of little importance for this hypothesis, other than postulating a maximum response shortly following exposure to radiation.

(5) Two-way conditioning. Elsewhere in this volume Solomon has contended that learning about the consequences of ingesting tasty foods is categorically different from learning about exteroceptive stimulus events. Palatable tastes are UCSs, not CSs, he argues, and UCS_1-UCS_2 pairings typically yield durable, single-trial conditioning (see Solomon, this volume, for examples). According to Razran (1971), moreover, such UCS_1-UCS_2 sequences are likely to produce *reverse* associations as well as the usual forward associations. While an expanded theoretical treatment of two-way, or "bidirectional" conditioning is beyond the scope of this paper, this theory predicts that potent biological events, such as the ingestion of a novel, tasty solution, and an aversive, post-ingestive episode, would become readily associated regardless of the precise temporal sequencing.[8]

546

DISCUSSION

Demonstrations of postexposure conditioning of taste aversions has raised a number of questions about taste-aversion conditioning in general, and about the nature of the unconditioned stimuli and responses in particular. Outstanding among these questions is that of the lack of correspondence between the overt and covert aspects of drug and radiation treatments. If there exist aversive aspects common to these various treatments, the rats do not reflect this in their overt behavioral response—indeed, they need not even be conscious for the conditioning to occur.

A second issue raised by these experiments concerns our difficulty of incorporating into a satisfactory theoretical framework the existence of postexposure conditioning of taste aversions. The five hypotheses listed above are neither mutually exclusive nor exhaustive, and, moreover, are not readily testable. It is difficult to formally discuss the "contiguity" of stimulus and response events that have such poorly specifiable durations. For example, in many of our investigations the CS is defined as " . . . 20 min access to 0.1% saccharin solution." The exact CS duration is difficult to define because rats seldom drink for the entire 20-min period, yet it is possible that the rat experiences the aftertaste of 0.1% saccharin in excess of 20 min. Furthermore, there is visceral afferent activity associated with stomach distention for some time following ingestion which presumably is a part of the CS complex (cf. Testa & Ternes, this volume). With respect to the UCS, as discussed above, the as yet unspecified responses to radiation, drugs, and toxins that are involved in conditioning taste aversions have onsets, magnitudes, and durations that have not been independently measured. The duration of these UCRs are more than likely measured in hours. It may be unreasonable, then, to compare UCS-CS taste-aversion conditioning with UCS-CS procedures employing levels of electric shock (Heth & Rescorla, 1974; Kieth-Lucas & Guttman, 1975) or of corneal air puffs (Gormezano & Tait, 1976) that produce UCRs of a few seconds to a few minutes at most.

The attempts to account for associative conditioning within a more traditional Pavlovian time frame (i.e., the CS-UCS contiguity hypotheses, Hypotheses 1-3, above) are questionable on the same grounds; even when the radiation-saccharin sequences are analyzed as embedded or overlapping contiguous stimulus and response events, the temporal parameters are measured in hours.

An additional problem these data encounter are their relationship to the so-called "medicinal" effect first reported by Green and Garcia (1971) (see also Zahorik, this volume). Using a similar UCS-followed-by-CS design, these investigators reported *increases* in the rat's preference for the CS after repeated trials (i.e., on successive days rats drank a distinctive-tasting CS during post-injection periods, UCS = apomorphine). We have consistently found *decrements* in saccharin preference using four different UCSs (see Figure 3). It is possible that the UCR following administration of apomorphine has onset and time-course characteristics that preclude backward conditioning. This hypothesis is currently being tested by systematically varying the amount of injected apomorphine, thereby producing UCRs which vary in onset and intensity, and relating these effects to the magnitude of subsequent taste-aversion conditioning in a backward design (see Footnote 6).

In conclusion, it is suggested that our understanding of backward conditioning of taste aversions is hampered by two overriding considerations. The first is methodological and concerns our inability to independently measure the time-course of physiological responses to complex stimuli such as tastes and drugs. Inferences about the UCR can be made from backward conditioning functions such as those shown in Figure 3, but a number of alternative explanations (Hypotheses 2-5, above) rule out a simple "mapping" of the UCR time-course by this method.

The second consideration is theoretical and is concerned (as are other chapters in this book) with the integration of findings of taste-aversion conditioning experiments with more general conceptualizations of learning. There is a certain irony in the fact that long-delay UCS-CS conditioning in the taste-aversion paradigm is as difficult to reconcile with backward conditioning experiments employing tones, shocks, and air puffs as is long-delay forward conditioning in the respective paradigms.

548

FOOTNOTES

[1]It is somewhat ironic that an early failure to produce conditioned taste aversion when radiation exposure preceded saccharin ingestion (Garcia & Kimeldorf, 1957) was used as evidence to support the argument that taste-aversion formation was, in fact, due to classical conditioning. See Smith (1971, p. 71) for an analysis of this failure to find backward conditioning.

[2]Carroll and Smith (1974) and Barker and Smith (1974) used 100R gamma radiation exposures delivered in 10 min; Scarborough, et al. (1964) used 68 R in a 10 min exposure to x-rays. Neither the rate of irradiation or type of radiation exposure (i.e., gamma rays, x-rays, or fast neutrons) have been found to affect the magnitude of conditioned taste aversions—which varies directly with total dose (see Smith, 1971, for a review). Systematic dosage comparisons in postexposure taste-aversion designs have not been made, however, and it is not known if higher or lower radiation dosages or rates of exposure would shift the peak UCR from the 0.5-1.5 hr reported for 100R.

[3]While some learning theorists accord an important status to backward conditioning (e.g., Razran, 1971), most treat UCS-CS sequences as non-associative control procedures for associative conditioning—probably because as Razran (1971, p. 88) has observed, the existence of backward conditioning " . . . plainly contravenes the contingency concept."

[4]Marilyn Carroll-Santi provided valuable criticism and insight in formulating this hypothesis for radiation postexposure conditioning and the function displayed in Figure 4.

[5]In a similar manner Brookshire (1974, p. 1072) interpreted the 2 hr backward conditioning he found using alloxan to the " . . . association of the (saccharin) CS with the initial hyperglycemia, with associated destruction of the beta cells (of the pancreas), or with temporary renal damage—all of which are in evidence within a few hours after alloxan injection."

[6]Ongoing dissertation entitled "A comparison of the taste aversions induced by x-rays, lithium chloride, apomorphine, and ethanol in US-CS paradigms," George F. Schmitt, Baylor University.

[7]Cautela (1965) has noted that the only reports of backward conditioning that cannot be discounted due to lack of comparison with sensitization and/or pseudoconditioned control groups involve "noxious stimulation." The demonstration of a CR gradient resulting from systematic UCS-CS interval manipulations, he further argues, may be taken as evidence of associative conditioning, in that pseudoconditioning procedures generally yield "flat" CR functions.

[8]Gormezano and Tait (1976) provide an excellent summary of the theoretical development of "bidirectional" conditioning as well as a critical evaluation of the empirical data for the theory. In brief, all stimulus pairings produce both forward, and to a lesser degree, backward associations. CS_1-CS_2 pairings (cf. sensory preconditioning) yield the most unstable bidirectional conditioning; UCS-CS procedures yield in-

549

termediate, but for the most part unstable backward conditioning. UCS_1-UCS_2 conditioning is the most rapidly developed and most durable, producing UCR_1's to UCS_2 as readily as UCR_2's to UCS_1. See also Razran (1971, Pp. 99-106).

ACKNOWLEDGEMENT

Some of the research reported here, as well as the writing of this chapter, was supported by an "Encouragement of Scholarship" award by Baylor University to the first author.

REFERENCES

Barker, L. M., & Johns, T. Assessment of tolerance to ethanol in the rat by taste aversion conditioning: Effects of ethanol preexposure and water scheduling. Unpublished ms., 1976.

Barker, L. M., & Smith, J. C. A comparison of taste aversions induced by radiation and LiCl in CS-US and US-CS paradigms. **Journal of Comparative and Physiological Psychology,** 1974, **87,** 644-654.

Barker, L. M., Suarez, E. M., & Gray, D. Backward conditioning of taste aversions in rats using cyclophosphamide as the US. **Physiological Psychology,** 1974, **2,** 117-119.

Boland, F. Saccharin aversions induced by lithium chloride toxicosis in a backward conditioning paradigm. **Animal Learning & Behavior,** 1973, **1,** 3-4.

Brookshire, K. H. Function of the "onset of illness" in the preference changes of alloxan-diabetic rats. **Journal of Comparative and Physiological Psychology,** 1974, **87,** 1069-1072.

Cannon, D. S., Berman, R. F., Baker, T. B., & Atkinson, C. A. Effect of preconditioning unconditioned stimulus experience on learned taste aversions. **Journal of Experimental Psychology: Animal Behavior Processes,** 1975, **104,** 270-284.

Carroll, M. E., & Smith, J. C. Time course of radiation-induced taste-aversion conditioning. **Physiology and Behavior,** 1974, **13,** 809-812.

Cautela, J. R. The problem of backward conditioning. **Journal of Psychology,** 1965, **60,** 135-144.

Domjan, M., & Gregg, B. Backward taste-aversion conditioning with lithium: Effects of CS duration and CS concentration. **Physiology and Behavior,** in press.

Garcia, J., & Ervin, F. R. Gustatory-visceral and telereceptor-cutaneous conditioning—adaptation in internal and external milieus. **Communications in Behavioral Biology,** 1968, **1,** 389-415.

Garcia, J., Ervin, F. R., & Koelling, R. A. Learning with prolonged delay of reinforcement. **Psychonomic Science,** 1966, **5,** 121-122.

Garcia, J., Ervin, F. R., & Koelling, R. A. Bait-shyness: A test for toxicity with n =2. **Psychonomic Science,** 1967, **7,** 245-246.

Garcia, J., & Kimeldorf, D. J. Temporal relationship within the conditioning of saccharin aversion through radiation exposure. **Journal of Comparative and Physiological Psychology,** 1957, **50,** 180-183.

Garcia, J., Kimeldorf, D. J., & Hunt, E. L. The use of ionizing radiation as a motivating stimulus. **Psychological Review,** 1961, **68,** 383-395.

Garcia, J., Kimeldorf, D. J., & Koelling, R. A. Conditioned aversion to saccharin resulting from exposure to gamma radiation. **Science,** 1955, **122,** 157-158.

Garcia, J., McGowan, B., & Green, K. F. Biological constraints on conditioning. In A. Black & W. F. Prokasy (Eds.), **Classical conditioning II: Current research and theory.** New York: Appleton-Century-Crofts, 1972.

551

Gormezano, I., & Tait, R. W. The Pavlovian analysis of instrumental conditioning. **The Pavlovian Journal of Biological Science,** 1976, **11,** 37-55.

Green, K. F., & Garcia, J. Recuperation from illness: Flavor enhancement for rats. **Science,** 1971, **173,** 749-751.

Heth, C. D., & Rescorla, R. A. Simultaneous and backward fear conditioning in the rat. **Journal of Comparative and Physiological Psychology,** 1973, **82,** 434-443.

Kieth-Lucas, T., & Guttman, N. Robust single-trial delayed backward conditioning. **Journal of Comparative and Physiological Psychology,** 1975, **88,** 468-476.

Lester, D., Nachman, M., & LeMagnen, J. Aversive conditioning by ethanol in the rat. **Quarterly Journal of Studies on Alcohol,** 1970, **31,** 578-586.

Levy, D. Histamine in taste aversions. Paper presented at the 83rd Annual Convention of the American Psychological Assoc. Chicago, Illinois, 1975.

Levy, C., Carroll, M., Smith, J. C., & Hofer, K. G. Antihistamines block radiation-induced taste aversions. **Science,** 1974, **186,** 1044-1046.

McLaurin, W. A., Farley, J. A., Scarborough, B. B., & Rawlings, T. D. Postirradiation saccharin avoidance with non-coincident stimuli. **Psychological Reports,** 1964, **14,** 507-512.

McLaurin, W. A., & Scarborough, B. B. Extension of the interstimulus interval in saccharin avoidance conditioning. **Radiation Research,** 1963, **20,** 317-324.

Morris, D., & Smith, J. C. X-ray conditioned saccharin aversion induced during the immediate postexposure period. **Radiation Research,** 1964, **21,** 513-519.

Nachman, M. Learned taste and temperature aversions due to lithium chloride sickness after temporal delays. **Journal of Comparative and Physiological Psychology,** 1970, **73,** 22-30.

Razran, G. **Mind in evolution.** New York: Houghton Mifflin, 1971.

Richter, C. P. Taste and solubility of toxic compounds in poisoning rats and man. **Journal of Comparative and Physiological Psychology,** 1950, **43,** 358-374.

Roll, D. L., & Smith, J. C. Conditioned taste aversion in anesthetized rats. In M. E. P. Seligman & J. L. Hager (Eds.), **Biological boundaries of learning.** New York: Appleton-Century-Crofts, 1972.

Rzoska, J. Bait shyness, a study in rat behavior. **British Journal of Animal Behavior,** 1953, **1,** 128-135.

Rzoska, J. The behavior of white rats towards poison baits. In D. Chitty (Ed.) **Control of rats and mice. Vol. 2, Rats.** Oxford: Clarendon Press, 1954.

Scarborough, B. B., & McLaurin, W. A. Saccharin avoidance conditioning instigated immediately after the exposure period. **Radiation Research,** 1964, **21,** 299-307.

Scarborough, B. B., Whaley, D., & Rogers, J. G. Saccharin avoidance behavior instigated by x-irradiation in backward conditioning paradigms. **Psychological Reports,** 1964, **14,** 475-481.

552

Schmitt, G. F., & Barker, L. M. A comparison of taste aversions and neophobia induced by radiation, LiCl, cyclophosphamide, and apomorphine. Unpublished manuscript, 1976.

Smith, J. C. Radiation: Its detection and its effects on taste preferences. In E. Stellar & J. M. Sprague (Eds.), **Progress in physiological psychology, Vol. 4.** New York: Academic Press, 1971.

Smith, J. C., & Schaeffer, R. W. Development of water and saccharin preferences after simultaneous exposures to saccharin and gamma rays. **Journal of Comparative and Physiological Psychology,** 1967, **63,** 434-438.

Smith, J. C., Taylor, H. L., Morris, D., & Hendricks, J. Further studies of x-ray conditioned saccharin aversion during the postexposure period. **Radiation Research,** 1965, **24,** 423-431.

Tait, R. W. Assessment of the bidirectional conditioning hypothesis through the UCS_1-UCS_2 conditioning paradigm. Unpublished doctoral dissertation, University of Iowa. (Cited in Gormezano & Tait, 1976)

Wagner, A. R., & Terry, W. S. Backward conditioning to a CS following an expected vs. a surprising UCS. **Animal Learning and Behavior,** 1975, **3,** 370-374.

Weber, R. P., & Steggerda, F. R. Histamine in rat plasma; correlation with blood pressure changes following x-irradiation. **Proceedings of the Society for Experimental Biology and Medicine,** 1949, **70,** 261.

CONCLUSION

XXII

THE SIGNIFICANCE OF LEARNING MECHANISMS IN FOOD SELECTION: SOME BIOLOGY, PSYCHOLOGY AND SOCIOLOGY OF SCIENCE

PAUL ROZIN
University of Pennsylvania

The field represented by the papers in this volume began, as an organized research endeavor, ten years ago, with the publication of two brief papers by John Garcia and his colleagues (Garcia & Koelling, 1966; Garcia, Ervin, & Koelling, 1966). It seems appropriate, on this tenth birthday, to take stock of where the field has gone and where it is going. In this paper, I shall discuss those aspects of the research that I feel have been of most significance and that have directed my own thinking and research. First is the significance of learning mechanisms and the novel-familiar distinction for understanding food selection in omnivores. Second is the application of these principles to the understanding of human food selection, including the nature and function of cuisines, and the problem of addiction. Third is the way in which the progress of this area has exposed some interesting issues in the sociology of science, in terms of the reaction to and assimilation of "anomalous" results. Fourth, and intimately tied to the sociology, is the significance and impact of the elaboration of learning mechanisms in food selection on the psychology of learning: the re-introduction of adaptive-evolutionary thinking into the field. Fifth, I will describe some of my own broad theoretical views, relating to the concept of accessibility, that have grown out of the work in this field.

UNDERSTANDING FOOD SELECTION IN OMNIVORES

Food and food-related activities are surely the most time-consuming waking behavior of most animals. In keeping with the central role of food in survival, adaptations leading to improvements in the discovery, procurement, and selection of foods have been a major factor in species success, and hence a major force in evolution. A number of the major orders of mammals, such as the Carnivora or Insectivora, take their names from feeding habits. Virtually all mammalian orders owe their origins to invasion of a new food niche (Mayr, 1974). Most anthropologists believe that the most critical steps in the evolution of man relate to the shift to a more carnivorous diet consequent upon a gradual invasion of the savannah environment.

Food Selection Strategies. The problem of food selection has been solved through two diametrically opposed strategies. The first opts for a rather narrow, well-defined class of foods, and preprograms sensory recognition of these, along with a central process that signals the need for these foods. Such systems are probably at work in animals that eat foods that are easy to categorize in a sensory system (e.g., the insect food of many frogs, or a related group of plants with common chemical properties). Dethier's analysis of feeding in the blowfly provides a classic example of such an innate or "closed" system (Dethier, 1969). Richter (1942-1943) argued that much of food selection in omnivores could be also accounted for with such a specific model. His own work on sodium hunger is strong support for a specific, prewired system. However, it appears that sodium hunger and "water hunger" represent the only clearcut specific systems in the omnivorous mammals studied (see Rozin, 1976a, for a more extensive discussion).

A more general system would seem to be necessary to understand the wide-ranging adaptive food selection of omnivores in the real world, and in particular, the specific hungers and "cafeteria" self-selection demonstrated in laboratory rats. A prewired system designed to deal with possible deficiences in over 30 nutrients would have to involve separate sensory recognition systems for each of these, and internal detection systems to recognize deficiency in each. Even if it were possible to construct such a system within the biological constraints of a developing organism with limited brain size, it would be in large part an exercise in futility, since most of the deficiences programmed would never be actually experienced by any particular animal.

The Omnivore's Paradox. The primary advantage of omnivory is that it provides greater assurance of a food supply. While the omnivore is not the best exploiter of any particular food source, knowledge of the varieties of available nutrient sources in the environment allows it to smoothly negotiate seasonal changes, blights, and especially high competition for any particular food source. Anything of nutritional value is of interest to the omnivore. There is no simple way to define this very loose category in sensory terms. To be sure, certain biases, such as sugar and salt receptors, may be provided, and a few specific systems such as sodium or water hungers. But, basically the omnivore has to gather its own information. The problems and challenges are many: the animal is faced with a wide variety of potential foods, some nutritious, most of no food value, and some harmful. The omnivore's problem, or "paradox," is that it must try and explore the full nutritional potential of its environment, while at the same time minimizing ingestion of poisonous substances. Hence, a conflict exists between neophobia and neophilia (or what, in more Freudian terms, one might call the "edible complex"). It is this central importance of experience in omnivore food selection that makes food selection of great importance in the evolution of complex and plastic functions in animals. In contrast to communication and other systems, the food selection system of omnivores cannot be heavily determined by genetic programming: it is what Mayr (1974) calls an "open system," and hence of particular interest to psychologists. Given the importance and complexity of the problem of defining what is food for an omnivore, it is surprising how little research has been devoted specifically to this problem. Hogan's studies (1973; this volume) on the development of food selection in chicks, and Reisbick's (1973) studies on guinea pigs are excellent beginnings in this area.

FOOD SELECTION IN THE RAT

Work on specific hungers and poison avoidance over the last 15 years is a natural extension of the classic work on food selection by Curt Richter (1942-1943), P. T. Young (1948) and others, and on poison avoidance by Richter (1953), Rzoska (1953) and others (see Barnett, 1963; Chitty & Southern, 1954). On the basis of this research, it is now possible to describe in some detail, how one omnivore, the common rat (*Rattus norvegicus*) solves some of the problems of food selection.[1] The basic mechanisms have been reviewed in other publications (Rozin & Kalat, 1971; Rozin, 1976a), and are described in some detail in some of the papers in this volume. Three categories of adaptations can be outlined.

Novelty vs. Familiarity. First is the subdivision of the world of potential foods into two major subcategories: the novel and the familiar. Novel "foods" are approached with hesitation and in a conflicted manner, especially by wild rats. Familiar foods are reacted to with much more certainty, and in a manner reflecting the nature of the past experience with them. They can probably be subdivided into three subcategories: dangerous, neutral and positive (Rozin & Kalat, 1971; Rozin, 1976a; Zahorik, this volume).[2]

The existence of these categories assumes an ability to evaluate the consequences of foods (see below). Remarkably, a food may pass from the "novel" category to the categories of familiar-aversive, familiar-safe, or possibly familiar-preferred after only a single exposure of a few minutes (Kalat & Rozin, 1973). At this time there is no reason to believe that there is anything unique about the novel-familiar dimension with respect to foods: animals in general probably tend to associate new consequences with new precursors, and also tend to be suspicious of new, non-food objects or events. However, it does appear that this dimension is particularly salient in food selection, and is easily studied there.

Belongingness and Long-Delay Learning. The second group of adaptations constitute what might be called the "Message from Garcia": belongingness and long-delay learning (Garcia & Koelling, 1966; Garcia, Ervin, & Koelling, 1966; Garcia & Ervin, 1968). These two features of learning about foods provide a neat adaptive fit to the special problems of food selection: the reliable relation between oral stimulation and subsequent entry into the body, and the inherent delay between ingestion and its metabolic consequences. Appropriately, the "field" of stimuli easily associated with metabolic consequences changes with the sensory basis of food selection: thus, visually dominant feeders, such as birds, may selectively associate sights with visceral events (Wilcoxon, Dragoin, & Kral, 1971; Wilcoxon, this volume). In general, animals seem to have a predisposition to associate food-relevant cues with the consequences of ingested foods (Rozin & Kalat, 1971). Given the predicament of rats, with the frequent threat of poisoning, it is not surprising that this system seems to be biased toward learning more rapidly about the negative consequences of food (Rozin & Kalat, 1971; Seward & Greathouse, 1973). In general this type of learning occurs reliably and rapidly, and is retained for long periods of time.

Natural Feeding Patterns. A third group of adaptations concerns certain apparently natural feeding and food related patterns that facilitate operation of the learning mechanisms. These include a tendency of wild rats to cautiously sample a new food, and then withdraw for a while to "evaluate the consequences" (Rzoska, 1953), and the tendency of rats faced with multiple new foods to try them one at a time (Rozin, 1969). [Some additional adaptations are described by Rozin (1967a), Richter et al. (1938) and Richter and Rice (1945).]

Remaining Problems. These three groups of adaptations satisfactorily explain how rats avoid dangerous foods and come to prefer foods that alleviate their deficiencies (along with the prewired mechanisms for sodium and water). Presumably, with respect to recognition of general foods (caloric sources), it is reasonable to consider "hunger" as a "deficiency," and repletion as a rewarding visceral event. But there are still problems. Most vexing, perhaps, are the cafeteria data, which suggest that at least under some circumstances healthy rats can self-select a balanced diet (Richter, 1942-1943). All of the mechanisms discussed here presume a state of *imbalance* prior to or after ingestion. There are three possible, noncomplementary resolutions to this problem: (1) There are incipient deficiencies and recoveries maintaining the cafeteria performance; (2) There are some new principles yet to be discovered; (3) The cafeteria performance may not be as precise as it appears to be. Some rats do not perform well on such a regime (Pilgrim & Patton, 1947; Lat, 1967). Furthermore, there is a rather wide range of choices among the constituents that could lead to normal growth. All the choices had some basic nutritional value [the same may be said for the Davis (1928) study on young children]. Yet, the stability of Richter's results and the sensitivity of the pattern of choice to mild nutritional stresses forbid dismissal of the impressive cafeteria results.

UNDERSTANDING FOOD SELECTION IN HUMANS

Since humans are omnivores, one might expect them to possess some of the same adaptations to food selection as rats and other omnivores. One can argue for some innate biases, such as sweet preference and bitter avoidance (Steiner, 1973; Rozin, 1976a,b), and a rat-like ability to learn about the consequences of foods. Of course, with the advent of human culture, a substantial part of the decision making about foods has been shifted away from the individual, but I shall argue here that even at the level of culture, some of the individual mechanisms discussed, especially the neophobia factors, can be seen to operate.

Belongingness and Long-Delay Learning. The manifestation of the long-delay learning and belongingness principles in humans is evidenced primarily by an almost endless series of anecdotes about learned avoidances of particular foods following food-poisoning or other negative gastrointestinal events. Seligman's (1970) "sauce bearnaise" phenomenon is probably the most widely cited anecdote. The proof of the pudding (as it were) that this type of learning is not reasoned or cognitive comes from instances where the source of illness is identified post hoc as having nothing to do with food. For example, the gastrointestinal upset may be referrable to the "flu," or other diners eating the same food may not have become sick. Food related aversions still persist under these circumstances, according to the anecdotes. This type of observation has led some investigators to suggest that taste-aversion learning in humans and other animals is rather primitive, and unmodifiable by "cognitions" (Seligman, 1970; Rozin & Kalat, 1971; Seligman & Hager, 1972). Hard evidence supporting the delay and belongingness principles in humans is scarce. The only systematic study is by Garb and Stunkard (1974), who obtained information on food aversions and their origins from a diverse population. Eighty-eight percent of the food aversions reported were referred to a gastrointestinal upset, and 83% of the respondents reporting such upsets perceived food as the active agent. These types of aversions imply both belongingness and long-delay learning.[3]

Novelty vs. Familiarity. Data from humans on the issue of familiarity and neophobia are much richer. There is much evidence in favor of suspicion of new foods. Reluctance to eat new foods has been reported in nonhuman primates, both in the laboratory (Weiskrantz & Cowey, 1963) and in the field (Itani, 1958), and has been anecdotally reported many times for humans. It is clearly evident in many young American children in the two to four year old age range (Kram & Owen, 1972; Benjamin, 1942), and also in the reluctance of traveling adults to eat strange foods. This (anecdotally) seems especially true for travelers from temperate zone, developed countries, when visiting underdeveloped tropical countries, where the perceived risk of food-borne disease is high. The accentuated desire of humans for familiar foods when ill (Mitchell et al., 1968) is probably another manifestation of this same neophobia (cf. Domjan, this volume).

There is an extensive literature in human social and experimental psychology on the relation between familiarity and preference. It is masterfully and charmingly reviewed in a paper by Zajonc (1968), in which he marshalls much evidence in favor of the notion that mere exposure will enhance preference. One could say, to twist an old phrase, *familiarity breeds content*. The basic experimental support for this comes from a variety of studies showing that repeated exposure of human subjects to stimuli as diverse as unfamiliar music, Turkish words or cookies leads to enhanced preference rating (or choice) of these particular items (Zajonc, 1968; Maslow, 1937). There is usually a gradual increase in preference with repeated exposures. This contrasts with the rapid "categorization" of food as familiar after a single exposure in rats (Kalat & Rozin, 1973). Of course, the measure usually used in rat studies has been resistance to subsequent association with poison, rather than "preference." However, the major source of discrepancy may be in the reliance on non-food stimuli in the human literature. A few studies dealing explicitly with new foods indicate that much of the battle in attempting to develop acceptance of a food is won if the "subject" can be induced to *try* the food (Hollinger & Roberts, 1929; Torrance, 1958). Here we seem to have a substantial one-trial effect.

There is another side to this relationship that has only been minimally explored in rats (e.g., Holman, 1973). That is reduced preference on repeated exposure. Negative hedonic or monotony factors have been reported in human food preferences (Siegel & Pilgrim, 1958) and in rated palatability of tastes in experimental situations (Stang, 1975). This *familiarity breeds contempt* (or to continue the Freudian analogs, *repetition revulsion*) obviously represents the other side of the omnivore's paradox, the urge to explore new food sources. Altogether, the familiarity data on humans serve as a demonstration of both sides of the omnivore's paradox.[4]

ROLE OF CUISINES IN HUMAN FOOD SELECTION

In the face of real world human food selection, this discussion seems rather abstract. Human (and animal) food choices in the real world are highly constrained by the psychologically uninteresting variable of availability. Rats in spaghetti factories eat spaghetti; Eskimos do not eat mangoes. But the real world situation for humans is further removed from the individual mechanisms described, because most foods eaten by most humans are determined culturally, by their cuisines. Availability of particular foods is in part determined by whether they are considered to be edible by the body of food practices called cuisine. Almost all foods never eaten by a particular person were not tried and rejected, but simply never experienced, because they fell outside of that person's cuisine. Although the limits and biases in food selection established by cuisine are particularly weak in upper socioeconomic classes and in mixed cultures such as the United States, the vast majority of people in the world are strongly associated with well-defined peasant cuisines. I will try to show that the same adaptive learning mechanisms that operate in individual humans and rats to facilitate food selection, can also be seen at the cultural level, in cuisines. In particular, I believe that the novelty-familiarity dimension has great importance in understanding the nature of cuisine and its adaptive value. Parallels between cultural and individual choice should not be surprising, since cuisines represent the accumulated efforts and knowledge of individual humans.

The Nature of Cuisines. Cuisines can be described as culturally transmitted food practices that determine (E. Rozin, 1973): (1) the *basic foods* (staple and secondary foods) which provide the principal sources of calories and other nutrients, (2) the methods of *preparation* of these foods, (3) the *flavorings* added to the basic foods, and (4) a variety of *limitations* on mixing of certain types of foods, taboos, and rules concerning eating.

Thus, for example, Southern Chinese (Cantonese) cuisine has a rice staple and a large variety of secondary foods (including pork, chicken, fish, shellfish, bean curd, bean sprouts, and many other vegetables) which are characteristically prepared by stir-frying (brief heating in an oil-coated pan) and typically flavored with soy sauce and gingerroot. The characteristic flavorings of a cuisine, which are used with most of the foods, have been called *flavor principles* (E. Rozin, 1973). These are usually quite simple and include, for example, chili and tomato for much of Mexican cuisine, and olive oil, tomato, and oregano for Southern Italian cuisine. More than any other particular aspect of a cuisine, the flavor principles seem to convey its identity (E. Rozin, 1973). Unlike the basic foods, which can be easily justified in nutritional terms, the flavorings may serve some "psychological" function. Indeed, the persistent use of characteristic flavorings raises the question of the function of cuisine.

Nutritional Functions of Cuisines. Surely there are many functions of cuisine, some best defined in symbolic or social terms, such as group identity, and not related to the issues raised in this paper or volume (see Rozin, 1976b; Simoons, 1976). However, cuisines do appear to have functions relevant to basic individual food selection mechanisms. They form a means for transmission across generations of the experience with foods of individuals in previous generations. Although suggestions of such transmission appear in infrahumans (Galef, 1976, and this volume; Itani, 1958; Kawai, 1965), it occurs on a massive scale in humans. The notion of cuisine as institutionalized nutritional wisdom can be illustrated in many ways. For example, the crushing and rinsing treatment of bitter manioc, a staple food widely used in South America and Africa, serves to wash away potentially toxic levels of cyanide (Jones, 1959). The adoption of bitter manioc by many Old World cultures after its introduction from South America seemed to go hand-in-hand with the detoxification mechanism. Similarly, both the Chinese tradition of sucking on sweet and sour spare-ribs by lactating mothers (the acid vinegar makes some of the bone calcium utilizable) (Winfield, 1948) and the regular addition of the mineral lime to tortillas in Mexico (Cravioto et al., 1945) serve as important sources of calcium in diets basically low in calcium. There are abundant examples of this sort, which must surely be accounted for as discoveries of individuals, often through the mechanisms discussed here. There are, of course, also harmful culinary practices.

Cuisine as a Cultural Form of Neophobia. A second and psychologically more interesting potential function for cuisine, relates to neophobia and familiarity. The conception of cuisine as a cultural form of neophobia is strongly suggested by what Elisabeth Rozin has called the conservatism of cuisine (E. Rozin, 1975; P. Rozin, 1976a,b). Many of the world's major modern peasant cuisines, including those of India (Prakash, 1961), Mexico (May & McLellan, 1972), and Iran (Flannery, 1969) have existed, more or less unchanged, over thousands of years, in spite of extensive contact with other cuisines over at least the last few hundred years. In this regard, it is notable that the food habits of immigrant groups are more resistant to change than any of the other outward manifestations of culture, such as language or dress. Food habits are often the last outward signs of ethnic identity in second or third generation immigrant groups, and are a matter for significant attention in the adjustment of immigrant groups (Freedman, 1973) and marketing of foods to ethnic groups (Alexander, 1958). The flavor principles, which seem even more resistant to change than the basic food items, are probably the most conservative aspect of cuisine (Bavly, 1966; Rozin, 1976a,b).

I suggest that one function of flavorings is to label foods as familiar, and thus safe. Given the real possibilities of harm produced by ingested foods, and the psychological commitment made by putting strange things into the mouth, the act of eating can be permeated by conflict and anxiety. A distinctive, repeated flavor can serve to reduce this anxiety, and allow the pleasures of eating to predominate. This interpretation is supported by the apparently higher reliance placed by stressed people on characteristic items of their cuisine (Burgess & Dean, 1962; Mitchell et al., 1968). Again, the importance of familiarity in acceptance is suggested by the experience of investigators who have attempted to change food habits by inducing acceptance of a new food into a cuisine. Reduction of the novelty of the proposed new food is commonly suggested (Mead, 1943; Seaton & Gardner, 1959). Similarly, and in accordance with common sense, introduction of new foods to children is often done by mixing them with a preferred food (Leibowitz & Holcer, 1974).

Flavor Marking and the Introduction of New Foods. Neophobia notwithstanding, the history of cuisines is replete with the adoption of new foods. This was most marked after the discovery of the New World, and its rich variety of indigenous plants, including potatoes, tomatoes, corn, manioc, tobacco, chocolate and chili peppers. Here, of course, is the other side of the omnivore's paradox, at the cultural level. Since the adoption of new *basic* foods (corn, potatoes, etc.) is most significant nutritionally, and since the basic foods contribute less distinctively to food taste than the flavors and preparation techniques, it makes some sense to surmise that the conservative flavor principles could be used as a vehicle to make new staple foods more familiar, and hence acceptable into a cuisine. Thus, within the notion of flavor principle, we see the novel-familiar principle and the omnivore's paradox.

The importance of making food taste familiar is illustrated by some observations made by my wife and me at a Vietnamese refugee camp in Pennsylvania. We found that most of the camp residents were doing their best to flavor the basic fare in such a way as to make it taste Vietnamese. The Vietnamese "flavor principle" is a salty, fermented fish sauce (Nuc Mam), supplemented with hot chili pepper, sugar, and vinegar or lemon. This was unavailable at the camp. However, the residents were mixing soy sauce and hot chili sauce into an approximation of their flavor principle, and putting it on their food. In response to this, the Army had placed bottles of soy sauce and hot chili sauce on each table in the dining room.

OTHER UNIQUE ASPECTS OF HUMAN FOOD SELECTION

In addition to cuisines, two other human reactions to food are either unique or almost unique in the animal kingdom. One of these is the strong attachment or preference that develops for particular foods (e.g., milk) or flavors (flavor principles), which usually lasts through a lifetime. The other is the inclusion among strongly desired foods of substances which are initially rejected, because of their taste qualities.

Persistence of Food Preferences. It is not clear whether the strong attachment to foods in humans results from variations of the basic learning mechanisms described here, some additional special mechanisms (e.g., imprinting) in humans, or possibly some aspect of the overwhelming importance of culture and social influence in humans. What is clear is that laboratory rats raised on Purina chow are quite ready to abandon it, after a short transitional period, for some other food, while a Mexican child raised on Mexican cuisine is likely to stick with it, even when tempted by other foods. Relatively few serious attempts have been made to establish lasting preferences in omnivorous animals. A recent encouraging study by Capretta and Rawls (1974) demonstrated, however, a garlic preference in rats based on garlic exposure pre and/or immediately post weaning (see also Capretta, this volume). The preference was demonstrated a month after garlic exposure had been terminated.

Preference for Initially Rejected Substances. The preference in humans for initially rejected substances may have direct relevance to some of the principles discussed here. The most obvious examples in the world are alcohol, tobacco, coffee, and chili pepper. Given the almost invariable initial rejection of these substances by young children and uninitiated adults (but see Richter, 1941), it is hard to imagine how these substances ever became part of the human diet. However, once they were accepted in a group of individuals or culture, it is reasonable to assume that social pressure, the desire to seem adult, etc. (Albrecht, 1973) guaranteed exposure and experimentation with them by youngsters. For the case of chili, mere exposure, social "reinforcement," and general association with the home, family and eating might be sufficient to maintain ingestion and induce a strong preference. The adaptive value of this preference, which must be clearly distinguished from the way in which the preference is established in individuals, might relate to chili's high vitamin A content, hypothermic effects, or bacteriocidal action (Rozin, 1976b).

Unlike chili, coffee, alcohol, and tobacco are all potentially addictive substances. Thus their maintained use and strong preference may be accounted for by the termination of the noxious state of withdrawal or the avoidance of that state (Solomon, 1976). Now, here is where some learning principles may come into play. In order to establish an addiction, the potential addict must discover the relation between withdrawal symptoms and the ingestion of the addictive substance (Solomon, 1976). This could be discovered by incidental sampling of the substance during withdrawal symptoms. If this occurred, the withdrawal symptoms would disappear or decrease after a modest period of time—a situation calling for long-delay learning. The "CSs" in this case would be typical for taste-aversion learning, but the "US," relief of withdrawal symptoms, might be quite different, since these symptoms are not primarily gastrointestinal, and include cramps, headaches, irritability, etc.

The question then remains, are the stimuli which accompany the relief of withdrawal symptoms preferentially associable with tastes? Not only may the withdrawal-termination association be outside the realm of belongingness, but at a cognitive level, where learning could also take place, it is counterintuitive. Why should symptoms following some hours after ingestion of a substance be relieved by that same substance? I suspect that it is for this reason that the great majority of addicts probably learn of the withdrawal termination properties of alcohol or heroin by hearsay, such as the advice of other addicts. It has been rather difficult to establish orally based addictions in animals. This, in spite of the fact that through appropriate reinforcement procedures, or forced ingestion, steady high intakes, tolerance and subsequent withdrawal symptoms for alcohol can be produced (Mello, 1973). Apparently the weak link in animals is in learning about the termination of withdrawal, a long-delay learning problem. There is no one who can "tell" them about it, and the US may fall outside the realm of their specialized food learning system. After all, the general withdrawal symptomatology probably does not, in the real world, strongly correlate with something that was eaten. In the case of "mainlined" heroin or morphine, the consequences of administration are much more rapid, and may support learning of a more traditional type. In any event, it should be clear that there are real problems related to food selection mechanisms, in the area of addiction in both animals and humans.

THE SOCIOLOGY OF SCIENCE AND THE "MESSAGE FROM GARCIA"

The field of taste-aversion learning, as we now know it, can be said to have originated ten years ago, in the now classic pair of papers by Garcia and his colleagues (Garcia & Koelling, 1966; Garcia, Ervin, & Koelling, 1966). It is instructive to examine, for a moment, why it is so easy to mark the origin of the field. After all, phenomena of taste-aversion learning, both evidence for belongingness and food aversions with long delays, were briefly described by Pavlov (1927). The two 1966 papers were preceded by a great deal of work on radiation-based aversion, from the laboratories of Garcia and J. C. Smith (reviewed in Smith, 1971), among others. Further back in time, clear demonstrations of poison avoidance, which must have been learned, were reported by Richter (1953), Rzoska (1953) and others, and described in some detail in Barnett's excellent book on the rat (1963). Similarly, Nachman's (1963) work on sodium hunger and lithium aversion, and the work of my colleagues and myself on specific hungers (Rozin, Wells, & Mayer, 1964; Rozin, 1967a) extending the early work, pointed strongly towards a unique type of learning. Prior to 1966, in the printed record, at least, psychologists basically ignored this work. At least some biologists (e.g., Harris et al., 1933) were quite willing to grant to the rat special learning abilities that were contrary to the prevailing theories of learning. For learning psychologists, the work on specific hungers and poisoning could best be left to rest quietly in the motivation sections of introductory or second level textbooks. Although the fact that rats can self-select foods and avoid poisons seemed to indicate some type of learning, it had never been proven, and more importantly, no one had ever really shown that a special kind of learning was involved. After all, who was to say that ingested poisons did not produce at least some rapid, unpleasant effects, which could form the basis for learning with temporal contiguity?[5]

Importance of the Clarity of Garcia's Message. What was special about the two Garcia et al. experiments was that they focused on those aspects of poison avoidance that seemed to directly challenge learning theory. While in prior studies learning *seemed* to occur with CS-US intervals of many minutes or hours, in the Garcia, Ervin, and Koelling (1966) study, this conclusion was inescapable. In this study, the US was administered some 30 min or more *after* the CS, so that it would be impossible to resort to subtle rapid aversive effects of the US to provide temporal contiguity.

It was the clarity of the two Garcia et al. experiments—the forceful way in which they addressed the contradictions to existing doctrine—that accounts both for the present reverence in which they are held, and the great difficulties that were encountered in publishing them. Prior and contemporaneous studies by Garcia and his colleagues, J. C. Smith and his colleagues, myself and my colleagues, and others, which flirted with these same ideas did not experience such resistance *because* they were flirtations rather than outright statements or demonstrations.

I can illustrate this best from my own experience. In 1965, before discovering the "Message from Garcia," I was doing a set of experiments and observations on the development of an aversion to thiamine deficient diet by thiamine deficient rats. Having discovered the existence of an aversion to deficient diet, I set out to analyze the source of the aversion. In particular, was it the diet itself, or its container or location? I did an experiment on the response of deficient rats to the deficient diet in a new container, or a new diet in the old container and location. The results were clear: the rat's behavior indicated aversion to the diet (taste-smell cues) and not to the container or location (exteroceptive cues). This, of course, is a less elegant demonstration of "belongingness." I had no trouble getting this "specific aversion" paper published (Rozin, 1967b), because it was primarily designed to show that specific hungers were better described as specific aversions to deficient diets. I didn't know what I had found and didn't strongly play up the belongingness sub-experiment. When I read the "Message from Garcia," my paper was already in press. I immediately saw the significance of the message when I got it from Garcia (not surprising, since my own work pointed to it over and over again), but I was too blind or conventional to do the clean, direct study. On the other hand, I would like to think that I was the first person (other than Garcia, Ervin, and Koelling) to appreciate the significance of their findings.

Widespread Acceptance of the "Message from Garcia." So it was Garcia who first clearly stated, in experimental form, the fundamental challenge to general process learning theory. He received, initially, the brunt of the organized opposition of the powers that be, and subsequently (possibly through some opponent process) the status of hero and paradigm breaker. For by now, the phenomena of taste-aversion learning are widely accepted, and the debate has shifted from their validity to their significance. This can be best illustrated by the appearance of taste-aversion learning in the ultimate standard of acceptance in the field: introductory psychology textbooks. As an introductory psychology teacher, I am the lucky recipient of many of the texts published each year. I have fortunately saved them (about 12 running feet of bookshelf at this time). I examined some 50 of them, to see if they reported on taste-aversion learning in poison avoidance or specific hungers as special types of learning, and/or as an argument for biological-adaptive approaches to learning. Of 15 books published between 1968 and 1970, only one mentions this type of learning process in food selection, and none deal with the general issue of learning as an adaptation. Over the period of 1971-1973, which spans the publication of biologically oriented reviews by Garcia, McGowan, and Green (1972), Seligman (1970), Rozin and Kalat (1971,1972), and Shettleworth (1972), five of 12 books mention the learning in food selection issue, and 3 explicitly deal with the relation to general theories of learning. Over the last 3 years (1974-1976), of the 22 books I surveyed, 15 discuss learning in food selection and 11 deal explicitly with adaptive approaches to learning that arise from taste-aversion learning. This discussion is most frequently in the form of a presentation of Seligman's (1970; Seligman & Hager, 1972) concept of preparedness. I think it is fair to say that the "Message from Garcia" has arrived. There are now enough people working in this field so that taste-aversion papers or grants are likely to be reviewed by other workers in the field, with improving prospects for support. As indicated by the rich variety of papers in this volume, the task is now the detailed study of these learning mechanisms, and the determination of the extent to which they can be assimilated into traditional theory, or the extent to which they require significant modification of that theory.

PARADIGMS, ANOMALIES, AND GENERAL IMPLICATIONS FOR A PSYCHOLOGY OF LEARNING

Clash Between General Process and Adaptive-Evolutionary Paradigms. The relevance of belongingness and long-delay learning to food selection has never been in question. These principles were welcome additions to the already acknowledged mechanisms of food selection in animals and humans. The new findings were controversial within a wider framework of general views held by most experimental psychologists, and it is from this source that resistance was offered. From the point of view of the psychology of learning, as of 10 years ago, the belongingness and long-delay "phenomena" were anomalous. I use the term here in the sense employed by Thomas Kuhn (1968), meaning inconsistent with the prevailing paradigm or general framework of the field. The paradigm in question can be described as general process learning theory, which claims that essentially all of learned behavior (which, for many adherents of this view, means essentially all behavior) can be accounted for in terms of two types of conditioning, classical and instrumental. These have certain properties, such as the requirement for temporal contiguity, extinction, and generalization. These processes were seen to be essentially the same across situations and across wide phylogenetic gaps. While most learning studies from the laboratory seemed to support this framework, the work on poison avoidance challenged both the notions of equipotentiality and close temporal contiguity. Hence, the anomaly.

However, this is an unusual instance of an anomaly, because there is a co-existing "paradigm" which forms the framework of thought for many biologists, within which the special learning mechanisms for food selection are the expected result. This paradigm is, of course, the Darwinian adaptive-evolutionary viewpoint. With its emphasis on adaptation and selection for phenotypes that deal most effectively with environmental problems, the unique fit between environmental demands and the characteristics of taste-aversion learning would be expected. Views with this type of adaptive flavor were widely expressed within experimental psychology in earlier times, and are even salient in the earlier writings of Clark Hull (1929), one of the major figures in general process theory. Over the years, largely under the influence of Skinner and his followers, these adaptive-evolutionary considerations, with their often teleological flavor, have given way to the search for mechanisms, and universal mechanisms, at that. Evolutionary-adaptive thought has remained on the periphery of psychology, primarily in the writings of the ethologists. Tinbergen (1951) and Lorenz (1965) have both written eloquently about learning as an adaptation to particular situations. Studies from within psychology itself, such as the work of Bolles (1970) on species-specific avoidance responses, or Breland and Breland (1961) on instinctive drift, surely suggested some of the same flavor. But again, it was the starkness of the 1966 Garcia et al. papers which seemed to focus the issue for psychologists.

Reconciliation of General Process and Adaptive-Evolutionary Paradigms. There is, indeed, a paradigm clash between the general process learning view and the Darwinian adaptive-evolutionary view. I feel, however, that the adaptive-evolutionary view has been caricatured a bit, and is not as inconsistent with a general process view as might appear on first glance. It would seem unnecessary to comment on the great similarities among living species, or subgroups such as genera or families. These similarities come about as homologies or analogies. Animal organisms all share certain problems in life, and would be expected to show common solutions. When new and exceptionally good solutions arise, be they rudimentary kidneys, elementary nerve nets or homeostatic feedback systems, they are likely to spread. A given solution, once established, will tend to remain in force, even with the possibility of a superior solution along different lines, simply because the establishment of new solutions that would involve extensive up-heavals in physiological organization are likely to involve some maladaptive intermediate forms. Thus, there is every reason for an adaptive-evolutionary view to be comfortable with general pro-cesses, and such widespread adaptations as neurons and kidneys are clear instances. The critical issue is that the adaptive-evolutionary view sees common mechanisms as the working material with which to shape solutions to a given problem. Given the basic general properties of neurons and nerve nets, how does one solve *this* problem? Changes in some mechanisms or new com-binations of elements may be necessary. Yes, all vertebrates have kidneys, with certain common mechanisms, but there are impor-tant variations when one compares the kidneys of salt or fresh water fish, or either of these with different types of mammals. In short, both the theme (common mechanism) and the variations (divergence) are critical to the adaptive-evolutionary view. The general process paradigm has neglected the divergent features.

In my opinion, as a consequence of premature crystallization of views about processes and relevant phenomena in the under-standable rush to a science of behavior, the general process theory supporters have left behind possibly most of the actual learning that goes on in the real world: habituation, navigation, insight, memory, and in general, storage of important information about the environment. In the attempt to simplify, and provide elegant mechanisms, the field was defined in terms of two basic learning processes, instead of being defined in terms of the effect of ex-perience on behavior. Of course, this had important virtues, since it allowed a concentration of effort in elucidating the characteristics of what do appear to be some fundamental features of plastic mechanisms in animals.

I believe that the proper view is that animals must profit from ex-perience in order to get around better in the world, and that, through natural selection, they have come to be creatures that can take advantage of experience in many ways. Recent work in animal learning has itself emphasized this view, through concentration on contingency or informativeness of stimuli, rather than contiguity (Rescorla & Wagner, 1972). In the context, "what are the problems in learning about foods?" a central issue for survival in omnivores, the recent food selection work makes sense. It is only an anomaly if one accepts the biologically rather unsound position that because two basic learning processes have been uncovered in a number of species, and intensively investigated there, they must be the "whole story" in learning. Why should learning ability differ from all other characteristics in being immune to "shaping" by specific problems?

As I see it, then, the issue is not "convergence" versus "divergence," but striking a balanced view between general processes and specific adaptations. Probably the most important consequence of the "Message from Garcia" has been its role in calling attention to the adaptive-evolutionary factors, and creating renewed interest among psychologists in the writings of the ethologists, evolutionary theory, and the wide range of plastic phenomena in animals. The re-entry of such types of thinking into experimental psychology has been most effectively stimulated by Seligman's writings on "preparedness" (Seligman, 1970; Seligman & Hager, 1972). Although a number of other general views representing the adaptive-evolutionary view have emerged in the last 5-6 years (e.g., Shettleworth, 1972; Rozin & Kalat, 1971,1972; Garcia, McGowan, & Green, 1972; Rozin, 1976c), Seligman's has had the most impact. I believe the reasons are: (1) that his work was published in a central psychology journal, the *Psychological Review*; (2) that more than any of the critics of the general process view, Seligman is himself associated with that view, and emphasized materials from the learning laboratory in establishing his position; (3) that the notion of preparedness is easy to understand and applies to the total range of learned behaviors, whereas many of the other reviews (e.g., Bolles, 1970; Rozin & Kalat, 1971) focused on examples from one sub-area; and (4) that his theoretical synthesis pretty much leaves general process theory intact, by saying that the addition of the preparedness principle is all that is needed. The intrusion of adaptive-evolutionary thinking into the analysis of learning, in Seligman's hands, is significant, but still minimal. This shall be discussed in more detail below.

RESPONSES TO THE "MESSAGE FROM GARCIA"

In order to clarify the implications of special types of learning mechanisms in food selection for a psychology of learning, I would like to describe what I take to be the varied responses that psychologists have made to these new findings.

Ignoring the Phenomena. At one extreme, as might be expected for "anomalous" results, the response is to ignore them. This is illustrated by the failure to mention either food-selection learning mechanisms or evolutionary-adaptive aspects of learning in many current and recent introductory textbooks, and the "business as usual" approach of many practitioners in the field. This is, in part, an adaptive response, since most anomalous findings probably turn out to be either unreplicable or become assimilated into existing doctrine. One cannot be distracted by all the anomalies: normal science must proceed apace.

Denying the Phenomena. A second response is denial. That is, the findings are recognized, but claimed to be unreplicable, a statistical fluke, etc. I expect that this was a common view early in the game, but it is virtually absent now. There have been too many replications in too many research laboratories and undergraduate psychology laboratories. A modification of this view accepts the findings as reported, but claims that the experiments are methodologically poor. If done properly, the results might well turn out to be congruent with traditional general process theory (Bitterman, 1975). I must confess that I fail to see how anyone conversant with the full literature on taste-aversion learning could hold this view. An impressive number of studies have, for example, validated long-delay learning as a *central* phenomenon, not mediated by temporal contiguity produced via aftertaste or "stomach taste" (see Revusky & Garcia, 1970, or Rozin & Kalat, 1971, for a tabulation of this evidence). It is testimony to the strength of the general process view that some need resort to a series of unlikely and different minor methodological flaws for each of the many experiments in this area in order to come up with the *possibility* that there is no long delay effect (Bitterman, 1976). I cannot be persuaded that the burden of proof should lie so heavily on the side of this issue that has biological common sense behind it. Taste-aversion learning is not like ESP: on the contrary, the phenomena of taste-aversion learning are in harmony with a basic paradigm that has more scientific merit behind it, at this time, than does current learning theory.

Explaining the Phenomena in Conventional Terms. A third approach has been acceptance of the basic taste-aversion findings, but not their adaptive-evolutionary implications. This involves the constructive activity of attempting to explain the apparently anomalous findings with often ingenious applications of general principles within the field. I expect that this enterprise will be partially successful; the extent of the success remains to be seen. The chapter by Testa and Ternes in this volume is an interesting venture along these lines.

Treating the Phenomena as Isolated Exceptions. A fourth response, and I suspect the most common one at this time among learning psychologists, is to accept taste-aversion learning as a genuine anomaly, but assume that it has little to do with the rest of the field. This is the treatment provided in many texts. It is, in general, the way imprinting has been treated within the field of learning; it is dutifully described, and followed or preceded by a full exposition of general process theory.

Modifying Existing Theory to Explain the Phenomena. A fifth approach is to preserve the general framework of general process theory, but to recognize that the new, "anomalous" findings require some modifications of the theory. This approach has been clearly articulated in two different forms: one by Revusky (Revusky, 1971; Revusky & Garcia, 1970) and the other by Seligman (1970). Revusky deals specifically with taste-aversion learning. He proposes addition of the belongingness principle to present theory, and then uses belongingness, with other learning principles, to derive the long-delay learning effect. The basic idea is that CS-US (or other delay) intervals are limited by retroactive interference. With the belongingness principle, relevant interference is limited to tastes, with respect to certain types of visceral USs. Taste experience, and hence taste interference, is severely limited, allowing for much longer delay intervals. Revusky and his colleagues (Revusky, 1971, and this volume) have performed a number of experiments supporting this view of taste-aversion learning, and, in general, the centrality of interference in determination of the maximum delays consistent with learning. There seems little doubt that interference factors contribute at least a component to the long-delay phenomenon, though it is not at all clear that they are sufficient to explain it (Kalat & Rozin, 1971; Kalat, this volume). Ironically, in a recent paper, Krane and Wagner (1975) have proposed a resolution of taste-aversion learning and general process theory which is somewhat the inverse of Revusky's interference theory. They suggest accepting something like a long-delay principle (extended length of central representations of taste) and try to derive belongingness from this and other learning principles.

Seligman (1970; Seligman & Hager, 1972) has created a formulation basically consistent with general process theory, which extends well beyond the domain of taste-aversion learning. He postulates a dimension, preparedness, which encompasses at its extremes the most readily learned "connections" or associations (prepared) and those least readily learned (contraprepared). He postulates a set of characteristics which vary together and distinguish prepared (biologically adapted and at least partly preprogrammed learning) from contraprepared learning. Thus, for example, prepared systems are acquired more rapidly and extinguish more slowly. Although this scheme has considerable merit and has most effectively raised the issue of biological-adaptive approaches to learning, it seems to me to be in part guilty of the same shortcomings that it criticizes. That is, it adds another *general* principle. While recognizing that some types of learning are of special importance in real life, and thus somewhat overdetermined, it draws a sharp line at the amount of divergence it will permit. What are the grounds (other than a general process orientation) for assuming that one package of adaptations will serve all important areas of function equally well? Surely animals face different *types* of problems in different situations. Thus, in the area of imprinting, relatively rapid acquisition and strong resistance to extinction (the "preparedness package") seem appropriate. However, consider the bee's problem in learning about the location of food sources. It must quickly exploit a particular clump of flowers when it comes into bloom and abandon it quickly once it goes out of bloom. Here, rapid learning and rapid extinction would be most desirable. Preparedness does not allow a tight fit between the organism's abilities and the problem at hand, but this is just what nature strives for.

Integration of the Adaptive-Evolutionary Approach Into the Study of Learning. A final (sixth) approach more strongly challenges general process theory, by emphasizing the fit between the characteristics of learning and the demands of the situation. This approach also integrates the learning under study into the total solution of the problem at hand. That is, it relates the learning to the other behaviors involved in the same functional sequences. This is basically the view of evolutionary biology, originally represented in this area by the writings of Tinbergen (1951) and Lorenz (1965). In more recent incarnations, it has been described as adaptive specialization of learning mechanisms (Rozin & Kalat, 1971,1972; Rozin, 1976c) or constraints on learning (Shettleworth, 1972; Hinde & Stevenson-Hinde, 1973; see also Lockard, 1971, for a more extreme view). The basic thrust of these views is that learning should be treated just as any other phenotype: a system specifically evolved in response to environmental pressures. The demands of the natural situation (as is so clearly the case in taste-aversion learning) provide at least a framework for searching for types of learning mechanisms. This view is quite comfortable with the existence of some general processes, but it assumes there will also be some special adaptations, since the situations in which learning is useful are quite varied. It holds (Rozin & Kalat, 1971, 1972) that much of real-world learning has some of this specialized flavor, including many of the most impressive plastic feats of animals, such as the navigation abilities of bees (see Schwartz, 1977, for an excellent integration of this viewpoint with more traditional approaches to learning.)

THE DIMENSION OF ACCESSIBILITY

The "adaptive specialization" view has led me to a more general view of learning and intelligence, which I shall briefly describe here (see Rozin, 1976c, for more details). In this view, adaptive specializations of learning, the "packages" of often impressive abilities integrated in the service of a particular problem, form the building blocks of yet more versatile adjustments. Specifically, the adaptive specialization to food selection described for rats is seen, not as a special and anomalous situation, but rather as a more typical state of affairs (Rozin & Kalat, 1972; Rozin, 1976c). Other adaptive specializations of learning would include imprinting, specialized navigations systems such as in salmon and bees, both the syntax and phonology acquisition systems in humans, and the complex system of visual inference (Helmholtz's unconscious inference) responsible for constancies, some illusions and other complex visual phenomena. Each of these systems is impressive in its accomplishments, but sharply limited in its applicability to a specific set of situations. I use the term *inaccessible* to describe this state of affairs. Insofar as such a sophisticated system incorporated features that would be of value in other situations, it would be adaptive if it could be extended, through natural selection, to such situations. This process can be described as increasing accessibility (see Rozin, 1976c, for a discussion of possible mechanisms for accomplishing this). The claim is that the evolution of intelligence and learning involves not only the appearance of new abilities, but new applications of already existing "programs," and a movement from specifically limited or inaccessible "programs" to generally available or accessible "programs." The basic classical conditioning package, for example, probably arose initially in response to anticipation of some important environmental event. At this time in evolutionary history, the process may have been limited to one or a few stimulus-stimulus or stimulus-response combinations. This, presumably, is why it has been difficult to find classical conditioning in some invertebrates: the appearance of the phenomenon is highly dependent on the specific situation and stimuli. This useful adaptation, which reflects the basic causal structure of the world, may have been extended in evolution over wider and wider domains. How much easier to reapply an old invention than to reinvent it each time it is needed. The end result, of course, as illustrated by many mammals, is a system in which classical conditioning processes are highly accessible, and appear in recognizable forms over a wide range of stimuli, behaviors, and situations.

Accessibility in Development and Pathology. I find the dimension of accessibility useful, as well, in the understanding of development. Here, within the Piagetian scheme (Flavell, 1963), one sees a specific "logical" ability, such as conservation, manifested originally in only a narrow range of situations (e.g., number conservation), and gradually extended over years to other domains (volume, area, etc.) until it becomes completely accessible, and thus statable as a general principle. This phenomenon of décalage can be restated as increasing accessibility, and seems to be representative of many aspects of development. Conversely, much of neuropathology (Geschwind, 1965), including the decline of function in senility, can be conveniently described as loss of access. Most often, the pathology consists of a reduced domain of application of particular cognitive functions. These functions appear in special narrowly defined situations, but are not as generally available as they were before. As a result, clinicians or investigators frequently disagree as to whether a function is lost or not: often it is just hard to find. It is as if certain processing centers were disconnected from some of their inputs and outputs, a concrete form of inaccessibility (Geschwind, 1965; Rozin, 1976c).

Increasing Access as a Type of Learning. Finally, I find this same dimension of accessibility useful in the understanding of learning and education. Although some types of access may be accomplished through natural selection, some seem to occur through experience within the lifetime. It is at least strange that we must be taught to "understand" the rules of syntax that we are already successfully applying in our day-to-day speech; to learn the segmentation of speech into phonemes in order to understand the alphabet, when we have already been doing this for years in the normal decoding and encoding of speech; to learn the laws of perspective in art class, when our visual system has already been using them for most of our life; or to learn mnemonic devices, such as organization, which we regularly use without any specific acquisition in normal memory function. All these and many other underlying cognitive capacities apparently are relatively limited in accessibility and, most critically, are not accessible to awareness. For this reason, call this mass of abilities the cognitive unconscious. We must either learn them as entirely new processes or somehow gain access to existing representations in the head.

This line of thought suggests that it may be useful to carve out a subcategory of learning that consists of learning what is already known, in the form of inaccessible systems in the head. Is the process of learning the same for arbitrary and new events as for increasing access of something already known? What is actually going on when a child finally realizes, in the course of alphabetic instruction, that the word "hat" has three sounds (Gleitman & Rozin, 1976; Rozin & Gleitman, 1976)? Is this ultimately highly intuitive realization not, in some sense, a tapping into those mental processes in the cognitive unconscious that perform this segmentation in the course of normal speech processing? These are, at the moment, areas of extensive speculation and little information. I propose that we should at least consider increasing access as a new type of learning.

SUMMARY

In my view, the analysis of learning mechanisms in feeding has paid double dividends. It has widely extended our understanding of one of the most important behavior systems of animals. This is especially true for the omnivores, who happen to include most species of special interest to psychologists, notably humans and rats. Since successful omnivory seems closely tied to sensory and motor capacity, motivation and intelligence, we have in fact made contact with much of psychology.

Most significantly and controversially, the field has by example had a substantial and growing impact on the general views of learning held within psychology. The emphasis in the discussion above has been on the findings that appear "anomalous" and that strain the credibility of a rigorously interpreted general process theory. But it is appropriate to remember that in many respects these same taste-aversion learning phenomena follow the text-book laws (see Testa & Ternes, this volume), and, in fact, without too much strain, traditional terminology can be used to describe most of the effects. The lesson is surely that there is virtue in the general processes we have all grown up with, but something to be learned from the new phenomena of taste-aversion learning. One can continue to search for general mechanisms, but with awareness of and sensitivity to the importance of adaptive modification of these to fit particular situations. Surely it seems a bit bizarre that in the service of endowing animals with great plasticity and flexibility, we grant to them a set of absolutely inflexible processes for the acquisition of information. It makes little sense a priori, and seems not to be the case. Nonetheless, the major thrust of the psychology of learning over the last 30 years or so, with its general process orientation, has resulted in some striking general laws and commonalities: similarities in the behavior of rats and pigeons in Skinner boxes cannot and should not be ignored. The question is not whether such research should be done, but whether it should be *the* field of learning, or whether it is sensible to continue to ignore a set of potent plastic factors that lie outside the realm of the field as traditionally defined. I believe that the elaboration of the field of learning mechanisms in food selection has provided the critical push necessary to reopen the eyes of learning psychologists to the world of Darwin, and his descendents in our field, the ethologists. Surely, workers in both traditions have much to gain from this reunion.

FOOTNOTES

[1]The extension of the rat analysis to other species with different types of food niches is only in its infancy. Excellent work has been done on avian species by Hogan (1973, this volume) and Wilcoxon (this volume), and on a variety of mammals (Gustavson, this volume).

[2]This general framework was recognized prior to the recent spurt of research activities. The issue of novelty and neophobia figured prominently in the work of Barnett (1956) and Richter (1953) in the 1950s and was directly implicated in research on specific hungers (Rodgers & Rozin, 1966). But until novelty and neophobia was related to "belongingness" and long-delay learning (Revusky & Bedarf, 1967; Rozin, 1968), it managed to escape the notice of almost all psychologists.

[3]The existence and occasional success of chemical aversion therapy using emetic agents is some testimony in favor of these mechanisms, although the delay is minimized in these procedures. A weak test of the applicability of "belongingness" (which has made little dent into the practice of aversion therapy) would be to compare the relative effectiveness of chemical and electric aversion therapy for the treatment of ingestive versus other types of disorders. The data are cloudy, but in a recent review of aversion therapy for alcoholism, Nathan (1976) suggested that there is a "slight edge" for chemical aversion treatment. This very weak support is further diluted by the report of approximately equivalent effectiveness of chemical and electric aversion therapy in the treatment of homosexuality (Marks, 1976). At present, one must be content with extensive anecdotal evidence and common sense as support for the two basic learning adaptations in humans.

[4]The relation between familiarity and preference in humans has been explored extensively enough for there to be the expected conflicts and inconsistencies in the literature. It appears likely that preference enhancement, as opposed to reduction, on repeated exposure, will be facilitated if the stimuli are initially novel and relatively complex (Berlyne, 1970). Most critically, while it makes sense that reduction of perceived risk is a natural partial explanation of the rapid increase in preference for unfamiliar foods, it seems less likely for unfamiliar music, where gradual appreciation of structure and development of fulfilled expectations would seem a more appropriate mechanism.

[5]Actually, McLaurin (1964) performed an experiment in 1964 which demonstrates long-delay learning, using saccharin preference and X-irradiation. Although effects were shown for delays ranging from 3 to 180 min, the centrality of these findings for the study of classical conditioning was not emphasized. In fact, in the abstract, the author concludes that saccharin avoidance conditioning does not fall within the classical conditioning paradigm. This paper, although it appeared in a psychology journal, did not appear to attract the attention of psychologists. As it turns out, the results are somewhat confounded,

582

since McLaurin began testing his rats before the full effects of the radiation US had appeared, so that there was an opportunity to learn to avoid saccharin during the test period (see Smith & Schaeffer, 1967). However, McLaurin's data show a clear avoidance of saccharin with a CS-US delay of 180 min, even taking backward effects into account, through comparison with a control group that he ran.

ACKNOWLEDGEMENTS

I thank the National Science Foundation for support of some of the research described in this chapter.

REFERENCES

Albrecht, G. L. The alcoholism process: A social learning view. In P. G. Bourne & R. Fox (Eds.), **Alcoholism: Progress in research and treatment.** New York: Academic Press, 1973. Pp. 11-42.

Alexander, M. The significance of ethnic groups in marketing new-type packaged foods in greater New York. **Proceedings of the American Marketing Association,** 1958, 557-561.

Barnett, S. A. Behaviour components in the feeding of wild and laboratory rats. **Behaviour,** 1956, **9,** 24-43.

Barnett, S. A. **The rat: A study in behaviour.** London: Methuen, 1963.

Bavly, S. Changes in food habits in Israel. **Journal of the American Dietetic Association,** 1966, **48,** 488-495.

Benjamin, E. The period of resistance in early childhood: Its significance for the development of the problem child. **American Journal of Diseases of Children,** 1942, **63,** 1019-1079.

Berlyne, D. E. Novelty, complexity, and hedonic value. **Perception and Psychophysics,** 1970, **8,** 279-286.

Bitterman, M. E. The comparative analysis of learning: Are the laws of learning the same in all animals? **Science,** 1975, **188,** 699-709.

Bitterman, M. E. Technical comment on flavor aversion studies. **Science,** 1976, **192,** 266-267.

Bolles, R. C. Species-specific defense reaction and avoidance learning. **Psychological Review,** 1970, **77,** 32-48.

Breland, K., & Breland, M. The misbehavior of organisms. **American Psychologist,** 1961, **16,** 681-684.

Burgess, A., & Dean, R. F. A. **Malnutrition and food habits.** New York: Macmillan, 1962.

Capretta, P. J., & Rawls, L. H., III. Establishment of a flavor preference in rats: Importance of nursing and weaning experience. **Journal of Comparative and Physiological Psychology,** 1974, **86,** 670-673.

Chitty, D., & Southern, H. N. **Control of rats and mice.** London: Oxford University Press, 1954.

Cravioto, R. O., Anderson, R. K., Lockhart, E. E., Miranda, F. deP., & Harris, R. S. Nutritive value of the Mexican tortilla. **Science,** 1945, **102,** 91-93.

Davis, C. M. Self-selection of diets by newly weaned infants: An experimental study. **American Journal of Diseases of Children,** 1928, **36,** 651-679.

Dethier, V. G. Feeding behavior of the blowfly. In D. S. Lehrman, R. A. Hinde, & E. Shaw (Eds.), **Advances in the study of behavior** (Vol. 2). New York: Academic Press, 1969. Pp. 112-266.

Flannery, K. V. Origins and ecological effects of early domestication in Iran and the Near East. In P. J. Ucko & G. W. Dimbleby (Eds.), **The domestication and exploitation of plants and animals.** London: Gerald Duckworth, 1969. Pp. 73-100.

Flavell, J. H. **The developmental psychology of Jean Piaget.** Princeton, New Jersey: Van Nostrand-Reinhold, 1963.

Freedman, R. L. Nutrition problems and adaptation of migrants in a new cultural milieu. **International Migrations,** 1973, **11,** 15-31.

584

Galef, B. G., Jr. Social transmission of acquired behavior: A discussion of tradition and social learning in vertebrates. In J. Rosenblatt, R. A. Hinde, C. Beer, & E. Shaw (Eds.), **Advances in the study of behavior** (Vol. 6). New York: Academic Press, 1976. Pp. 77-100.

Garb, J., & Stunkard, A. Taste aversions in man. **American Journal of Psychiatry**, 1974, **131**, 1204-1207.

Garcia, J., & Ervin, F. R. Gustatory-visceral and telereceptor-cutaneous conditioning—adaptation to internal and external milieus. **Communications in Behavioral Biology**, 1968, 1 (Part A), 389-415.

Garcia, J., Ervin, F. R., & Koelling, R. A. Learning with prolonged delay of reinforcement. **Psychonomic Science**, 1966, **5**, 121-122.

Garcia, J., & Koelling, R. A. Relation of cue to consequence in avoidance learning. **Psychonomic Science**, 1966, **4**, 123-124.

Garcia, J., McGowan, B. K., & Green, K. F. Biological constraints on conditioning. In A. H. Black & W. F. Prokasy (Eds.), **Classical conditioning II: Current theory and research**. New York: Appleton-Century-Crofts, 1972. Pp. 3-27.

Geschwind, N. Disconnexion syndromes in animals and man. Part I. **Brain**, 1965, **8**, 237-294.

Gleitman, L. R., & Rozin, P. The structure and acquisition of reading. I. Relations between orthographies and the structure of language. In A. S. Reber & D. Scarborough (Eds.), **Markers to meanings**. Potomac, Maryland: Erlbaum, in press.

Harris, L. J., Clay, J., Hargreaves, F., & Ward, A. Appetite and choice of diet: The ability of the vitamin B deficient rat to discriminate between diets containing and lacking the vitamin. **Proceedings of the Royal Society**, 1933, **113** (Part B), 161-190.

Hinde, R. A., & Stevenson-Hinde, J. (Eds.). **Constraints on learning**. London: Academic Press, 1973.

Hogan, J. A. How young chicks learn to recognize food. In R. A. Hinde & J. Stevenson-Hinde (Eds.), **Constraints on learning**. London: Academic Press, 1973. Pp. 119-139.

Hollinger, M., & Roberts, J. L. Overcoming food dislikes: A study with evaporated milk. **Journal of Home Economics**, 1929, **21**, 923-932.

Holman, E. W. Temporal properties of gustatory spontaneous alternation in rats. **Journal of Comparative and Physiological Psychology**, 1973, **85**, 536-539.

Hull, C. L. A functional interpretation of the conditioned reflex. **Psychological Review**, 1929, **36**, 498-511.

Itani, J. On the acquisition and propagation of a new food habit in the natural group of Japanese monkeys at Takasaki Yama. **Journal of Primatology**, 1958, **1**, 84-98.

Jones, W. O. **Manioc in Arica**. Stanford, California: Stanford University Press, 1959.

Kalat, J. W., & Rozin, P. The role of interference in taste-aversion learning. **Journal of Comparative and Physiological Psychology**, 1971, **77**, 53-58.

Kalat, J., & Rozin, P. "Learned safety" as a mechanism in long-delay taste-aversion learning in rats. **Journal of Comparative and Physiological Psychology**, 1973, **83**, 198-207.

Kawai, M. Newly acquired precultural behavior of the natural troop of Japanese monkeys on Koshima islet. **Primates**, 1965, **6**, 1-30.

585

Kram, K. M., & Owen, G. M. Nutritional studies on United States preschool children: Dietary intakes and practices of food procurement, preparation and consumption. In S. J. Fomon & T. A. Anderson (Eds.), **Practices of low-income families in feeding infants and small children, with particular attention to cultural subgroups**. Washington, D.C.: U.S. Government Printing Office (Dept. H.E.W. Publication No. 72-5605), 1972. Pp. 3-18.

Krane, R. V., & Wagner, A. R. Taste aversion learning with a delayed shock US: Implications for the "generality of the laws of learning." **Journal of Comparative and Physiological Psychology**, 1975, **88**, 882-889.

Kuhn, T. **The structure of scientific revolutions**. Chicago: University of Chicago Press, 1968.

Lat, J. Self-selection of dietary components. In C. F. Code & W. Heidel (Eds.), **Handbook of physiology**. Washington, D.C.: American Physiological Society, 1967. Pp. 367-386.

Leibowitz, J. M., & Holcer, P. Building and maintaining self-feeding skills in a retarded child. **American Journal of Occupational Therapy**, 1974, **28**, 545-548.

Lockard, R. B. Reflections on the fall of comparative psychology: Is there a message for us all? **American Psychologist**, 1971, **26**, 168-179.

Lorenz, K. **Evolution and the modification of behavior**. Chicago: University of Chicago Press, 1965.

Marks, I. M. Management of sexual disorders. In H. Leitenberg (Ed.), **Handbook of behavior modification and behavior therapy**. Englewood Cliffs, N.J.: Prentice-Hall, 1976. Pp. 255-300.

Maslow, A. The influence of familiarization on preference. **Journal of Experimental Psychology**, 1937, **21**, 162-180.

May, J. M., & McLellan, D. L. **The ecology of malnutrition in Mexico and Central America**. New York: Hafner, 1972.

Mayr, E. Behavior programs and evolutionary strategies. **American Scientist**, 1974, **62**, 650-659.

McLaurin, W. A. Postirradiation saccharin avoidance in rats as a function of the interval between ingestion and exposure. **Journal of Comparative and Physiological Psychology**, 1964, **57**, 316-317.

Mead, M. The problem of changing food habits. **Bulletin of the National Research Council**, 1943, **108**, 20-31.

Mello, N. K. A review of methods to induce alcohol addiction in animals. **Pharmacology, Biochemistry and Behavior**, 1973, **1**, 89-101.

Mitchell, H. S., Rynbergen, H. J., Anderson, L., & Dibble, M. V. **Cooper's nutrition in health and disease** (15th Edition). Philadelphia: Lippincott, 1968. Chapter 11.

Nachman, M. Learned aversion to the taste of lithium chloride and generalization to other salts. **Journal of Comparative and Physiological Psychology**, 1963, **56**, 343-349.

Nathan, P. E. Alcoholism. In H. Leitenberg (Ed.), **Handbook of behavior modification and behavior therapy**. Englewood Cliffs, N.J.: Prentice-Hall, 1976. Pp. 3-44.

Pavlov, I. P. **Conditioned reflexes**. (G. V. Anrep, Ed. & Trans.) New York: Dover, 1960. (Reprinted)

586

Pilgrim, F. J., & Patton, R. A. Patterns of self-selection of purified dietary components by the rat. **Journal of Comparative and Physiological Psychology**, 1947, **40**, 343-348.

Prakash, O. **Food and drink in ancient India**. Delhi: Munshi Ram Manohar Lal, 1961.

Reisbick, S. H. Development of food preferences in newborn guinea pigs. **Journal of Comparative and Physiological Psychology**, 1973, **85**, 427-442.

Rescorla, R. A., & Wagner, A. R. A theory of Pavlovian conditioning: Variations in the effectiveness of reinforcement and nonreinforcement. In A. H. Black & W. F. Prokasy (Eds.), **Classical conditioning II: Current research and theory**. New York: Appleton-Century-Crofts, 1972. Pp. 64-99.

Revusky, S. H. The role of interference in association over a delay. In W. Honig & H. James (Eds.), **Animal memory**. New York: Academic Press, 1971. Pp. 155-213.

Revusky, S. H., & Bedarf, E. W. Association of illness with prior ingestion of novel foods. **Science**, 1967, **155**, 219-220.

Revusky, S. H., & Garcia, J. Learned associations over long delays. In G. H. Bower & J. T. Spence (Eds.), **The Psychology of learning and motivation** (Vol. 4). New York: Academic Press, 1970. Pp. 1-84.

Richter, C. P. Alcohol as food. **Quarterly Journal of Studies on Alcohol**, 1941, **1**, 650-662.

Richter, C. P. Total self regulatory functions in animals and human beings. **Harvey Lecture Series**, 1942-43, **38**, 63-103.

Richter, C. P. Experimentally produced reactions to food poisoning in wild and domesticated rats. **Annals of the New York Academy of Science**, 1953, **56**, 225-239.

Richter, C. P. Salt appetite of mammals: Its dependence on instinct and metabolism. In Fondation Singer Polignac (Ed.), **L'Instinct dans le comportement des animaux et de l'homme**. Paris: Masson, 1956. Pp. 577-629.

Richter, C. P., Holt, L. E., Barelare, B., Jr., & Hawkes, C. D. Changes in fat, carbohydrate, and protein appetite in vitamin B deficiency. **American Journal of Physiology**, 1938, **124**, 596-602.

Richter, C. P., & Rice, K. K. Self-selection studies on coprophagy as a source of vitamin B complex. **American Journal of Physiology**, 1945, **143**, 344-354.

Rodgers, W. L., & Rozin, P. Novel food preferences in thiamine-deficient rats. **Journal of Comparative and Physiological Psychology**, 1966, **61**, 1-4.

Rozin, E. **The flavor principle cookbook**. New York: Hawthorn, 1973.

Rozin, E. A lunch in Brooklyn: The conservatism of cuisine. Unpublished manuscript, 1975.

Rozin, P. Thiamine specific hunger. In C. F. Code & W. Heidel (Eds.), **Handbook of physiology 6: Alimentary canal** (Vol. 1). Washington, D.C.: American Physiological Society, 1967a. Pp. 411-431.

Rozin, P. Specific aversions as a component of specific hungers. **Journal of Comparative and Physiological Psychology**, 1967b, **64**, 237-242.

Rozin, P. Specific aversions and neophobia as a consequence of vitamin deficiency and/or poisoning in half-wild and domestic rats. **Journal of Comparative and Physiological Psychology**, 1968, **66**, 82-88.

Rozin, P. Adaptive food sampling patterns in vitamin deficient rats. **Journal of Comparative and Physiological Psychology**, 1969, **69**, 126-132.

Rozin, P. The selection of foods by rats, humans, and other animals. In J. Rosenblatt, R. A. Hinde, C. Beer, & E. Shaw (Eds.), **Advances in the study of behavior** (Vol. 6). New York: Academic Press, 1976a. Pp. 21-76.

Rozin, P. Psychobiological and cultural determinants of food choice. In T. Silverstone (Ed.), **Appetite and food intake**. Berlin: Dahlem Konferenzen, 1976b. Pp. 285-312.

Rozin, P. The evolution of intelligence and access to the cognitive unconscious. In J. A. Sprague & A. N. Epstein (Eds.), **Progress in psychobiology and physiological psychology** (Vol. 6). New York: Academic Press, 1976c. Pp. 245-280.

Rozin, P., & Gleitman, L. R. The structure and acquisition of reading. II. The reading process and the acquisition of the alphabetic principle. In A. S. Reber & D. Scarborough (Eds.), **Markers to meanings**. Potomac, Maryland: Erlbaum, 1976.

Rozin, P., & Kalat, J. Specific hungers and poison avoidance as adaptive specializations of learning. **Psychological Review**, 1971, **78**, 459-486.

Rozin, P., & Kalat, J. Learning as a situation-specific adaptation. In M. E. P. Seligman & J. Hager (Eds.), **The biological boundaries of learning**. New York: Appleton-Century-Crofts, 1972. Pp. 66-97.

Rozin, P., Wells, C., & Mayer, J. Thiamine specific hunger: Vitamin in water versus vitamin in food. **Journal of Comparative and Physiological Psychology**, 1964, **57**, 78-84.

Rzoska, J. Bait shyness, a study in rat behavior. **British Journal of Animal Behavior**, 1953, **1**, 128-135.

Seaton, R. W., & Gardner, B. W. Acceptance measurements of unusual foods. **Food Research**, 1959, **24**, 271-278.

Schwartz, B. **Learning and behavior theory**. New York: W. W. Norton, 1977.

Seligman, M. E. P. On the generality of the laws of learning. **Psychological Review**, 1970, **77**, 406-418.

Seligman, M. E. P., & Hager, J. (Eds.). **The biological boundaries of learning**. New York: Appleton-Century-Crofts, 1972.

Seward, J. P., & Greathouse, S. R. Appetitive and aversive conditioning in thiamine-deficient rats. **Journal of Comparative and Physiological Psychology**, 1973, **83**, 157-167.

Shettleworth, S. Constraints on learning. In D. S. Lehrman, R. A. Hinde, & E. Shaw (Eds.), **Advances in the study of behavior** (Vol. 4). New York: Academic Press, 1972. Pp. 1-68.

Siegel, P. S., & Pilgrim, F. J. The effect of monotony on the acceptance of food. **American Journal of Psychology**, 1958, **71**, 756-759.

Simoons, F. J. Food habits as influenced by human culture: Approaches in anthropology and geography. In T. Silverstone (Ed.), **Appetite and food intake**. Berlin: Dahlem Konferenzen, 1976. Pp. 313-329.

Smith, J. C. Radiation: Its detection and its effects on taste preferences. In E. Stellar & J. M. Sprague (Eds.), **Progress in physiological psychology**. New York: Academic Press, 1971.

Smith, J. C., & Schaeffer, R. W. Development of water and saccharin preferences after simultaneous exposures to saccharin solution and gamma rays. **Journal of Comparative and Physiological Psychology**, 1967, **63**, 434-438.

Solomon, R. L. An opponent-process theory of motivation. IV. The affective dynamics of drug addiction. In J. Mazer & M. E. P. Seligman (Eds.), **Psychopathology: Laboratory models**. San Francisco: Freeman, 1976.

Stang, D. J. When familiarity breeds contempt, absence makes the heart grow fonder: Effects of exposure and delay on taste pleasantness ratings. **Bulletin of the Psychonomic Society**, 1975, **6**, 273-275.

Steiner, J. The human gustofacial response. In J. F. Bosma (Ed.), **Fourth symposium on oral sensation and perception: Development in the fetus and infant**. Washington, D.C.: U.S. Government Printing Office, 1974.

Tinbergen, N. **The study of instinct**. London: Oxford University Press, 1951.

Torrance, E. P. Sensitization versus adaptation in preparation for emergencies: Prior experience with an emergency ration and its acceptability in a simulated survival situation. **Journal of Applied Psychology**, 1958, **42**, 63-67.

Weiskrantz, L., & Cowey, A. The aetiology of food reward. **Animal Behaviour**, 1963, **11**, 225-234.

Wilcoxon, H. C., Dragoin, W. B., & Kral, P. A. Illness-induced aversions in rat and quail: Relative salience of visual and gustatory cues. **Science**, 1971, **171**, 826-828.

Winfield, G. W. **China: The land of the people**. New York: William Sloan, 1948.

Young, P. T. Appetite, palatability and feeding habit: A critical review. **Psychological Bulletin**, 1948, **45**, 289-320.

Zajonc, R. B. Attitudinal effects of mere exposure. **Journal of Personality and Social Psychology**, 1968, **9**, 1-27.

APPENDIX

APPENDIX

CONDITIONED TASTE AVERSIONS: A BIBLIOGRAPHY

Anthony L. Riley and Constance M. Clarke
Department of Psychology
The American University

The following is a bibliographic list of 632 articles dealing specifically with conditioned taste aversions from 1950-1976. The references are classified according to six major categories in a topical index. The major categories are Conditioning Variables, Extinction and Retention Variables, Methodological Variables, Physiological Manipulations, Comparative/Field Aspects, and General Information. References were obtained from individual journals in psychology, physiology, pharmacology, and animal behavior and were supplemented and extended by *Psychological Abstracts* and *Pharmacological Abstracts*. A final source of references was provided by individual researchers who contributed preprints and reprints. In using the reference list it should be noted that for a given investigation, single-author papers precede all two-author papers, which in turn precede three-author papers.

1. Abel, E. L. Cannabis: Effects on hunger and thirst. **Journal of Behavioral Biology,** 1975, **15,** 255-281.

2. Ader, R. "Strain" differences in illness-induced taste aversion, **Bulletin of the Psychonomic Society,** 1973, **1,** 253-254.

3. Ader, R. Effects of early experiences on shock- and illness-induced passive avoidance behaviors. **Developmental Psychobiology,** 1973, **6,** 547-555.

4. Ader, R. Letter to the editor. **Psychosomatic Medicine,** 1974, **36,** 183-184.

5. Ader, R. Behaviorally conditioned immunosuppression. **Psychosomatic Medicine,** 1975, **37,** 333-340.

6. Ader, R. Conditioned adrenocortical steroid elevations in the rat. **Journal of Comparative and Physiological Psychology,** 1976, **90,** 1156-1163.

7. Ahlers, R. H., & Best, P. J. Novelty vs. temporal contiguity in learned taste aversions. **Psychonomic Science,** 1971, **25,** 34-36.

8. Ahlers, R. H., & Best, P. J. Retrograde amnesia for discriminated taste aversions: A memory deficit. **Journal of Comparative and Physiological Psychology,** 1972, **79,** 371-376.

9. Alcock, J. Punishment levels and the response of black-capped chickadees *(Parus atricapillus)* to three kinds of artificial seeds. **Animal Behavior,** 1970, **18,** 592-599.

10. Alcock, J. Punishment levels and the response of white-throated sparrows *(Zonotrichia albicollis)* to three kinds of artificial models and mimics. **Animal Behavior,** 1970, **18,** 733-739.

11. Alcock, J. **Animal Behavior.** New York: Sinauer Press, 1975.

12. Aleksanyan, Z. A., Buresova, O., & Bures, J. Modification of unit responses to gustatory stimuli by conditioned taste aversions in rats. **Physiology and Behavior,** 1976, **17,** 173-179.

13. Aleksanyan, Z. A., Buresova, O., Dolbakyan, E., & Bures, J. Unit activity changes induced by taste

aversion conditioning in rats. **Physiologia Bohemoslovaca**, 1974, **23**, 341.

14. Amit, Z., Levitan, D. E., Brown, Z. W., & Rogan, F. Possible involvement of central factors in the mediation of conditioned taste aversion. **Neuropharmacology**, in press.

15. Andrews, E. A., & Braveman, N. S. The combined effects of dosage level and interstimulus interval on the formation of one-trial poison-based aversions in rats. **Animal Learning and Behavior**, 1975, **3**, 287-289.

16. Arthur, J. B. Taste aversion learning is impaired by interpolated amygdaloid stimulation but not by posttraining amygdaloid stimulation. **Behavioral Biology**, 1975, **13**, 369-376.

17. Balagura, S., & Smith, D. F. Role of LiCl and environmental stimuli on generalized learned aversion to NaCl in the rat. **American Journal of Physiology**, 1970, **219**, 1231-1234.

18. Balagura, S., Brophy, J., & Devenport, L. D. Modification of learned aversion to LiCl and NaCl by multiple experiences with LiCl. **Journal of Comparative and Physiological Psychology**, 1972, **81**, 212-219.

19. Balagura, S., Ralph, T. L., & Gold, R. Effect of electrical brain stimulation of diencephalic and mesencephalic structures on the generalized NaCl aversion after LiCl poisoning. **Physiologist**, 1972, **15**, 77.

20. Barker, L. M. CS duration, amount, and concentration effects in conditioning taste aversions. **Learning and Motivation**, 1976, **7**, 265-273.

21. Barker, L. M., & Smith, J. C. A comparison of taste aversions induced by radiation and lithium chloride in CS-US and US-CS paradigms. **Journal of Comparative and Physiological Psychology**, 1974, **87**, 644-654.

22. Barker, L. M., Best, M. R., & Domjan, M. (Eds.). **Learning Mechanisms in Food Selection**. Waco, Texas: Baylor University Press, 1977.

23. Barker, L. M., Smith, J. C., & Suarez, E. M. "Sickness" and the backward conditioning of taste aversions. In L. M. Barker, M. R. Best, & M. Domjan (Eds.), **Learning Mechanisms in Food Selection**. Waco, Texas: Baylor University Press, 1977.

24. Barker, L. M., Suarez, E. M., & Gray, D. Backward conditioning of taste aversions in rats using cyclophosphamide as the US. **Physiological Psychology**, 1974, **2**, 117-119.

25. Barnett, S. A. **The rat: A study in behavior**. Chicago: Aldine Press, 1963.

26. Barnett, S. A. **The rat: A study in behavior**. Chicago: Aldine Press, 1975.

27. Barnett, S. A., Cowan, P. E., Radford, G. G., & Prakash, I. Peripheral anosmia and the discrimination of poisoned food by *Rattus rattus* L. **Behavioral Biology**, 1975, **13**, 183-190.

28. Bauer, E. R., & Reynolds, E. V., III. D-Amphetamine and palatability of a saccharin solution. **Psychonomic Science**, 1971, **23**, 3-4.

29. Bauermeister, J. J., & Schaeffer, R. W. Relations between preconditioned rate of solution ingestion and rate of post-irradiation intake. **Physiology and Behavior**, 1969, **4**, 1019-1021.

30. Baum, M., Foidart, D. S., & Lapointe, A. Rapid extinction of a conditioned taste aversion following unreinforced intraperitoneal injection of the fluid CS. **Physiology and Behavior**, 1974, **12**, 871-873.

31. Beckoff, M., Gustavson, C. R., Kelly, D. J., & Garcia, J. Technical comment: Predation and aversive conditioning in coyotes. **Science**, 1975, **187**, 1096.

32. Berg, D., & Baenninger, R. Predation: Separation of aggressive and hunger motivation by condi-

tioned aversion. **Journal of Comparative and Physiological Psychology**, 1974, **86**, 601-606.

33. Berger, B. D. Conditioning of food aversions by injections of psychoactive drugs. **Journal of Comparative and Physiological Psychology**, 1972, **81**, 21-26.

34. Berger, B. D. Properties of the unconditioned stimulus. In N. W. Milgram, L. Krames, & T. Alloway (Eds.), **Food Aversion Learning**. New York: Plenum Press, in press.

35. Berger, B. D., Wise, C. D., & Stein, L. Area postrema damage and bait shyness. **Journal of Comparative and Physiological Psychology**, 1973, **82**, 475-479.

36. Berman, R. F., & Cannon, D. S. The effect of prior ethanol experience on ethanol-induced saccharin aversions. **Physiology and Behavior**, 1974, **12**, 1041-1044.

37. Best, M. R. Conditioned and latent inhibition in taste-aversion learning: Clarifying the role of learned safety. **Journal of Experimental Psychology: Animal Behavior Processes**, 1975, **1**, 97-113.

38. Best, M. R., & Barker, L. M. The nature of "learned safety" and its role in the acquisition gradient. In L. M. Barker, M. R. Best, & M. Domjan (Eds.), **Learning Mechanisms in Food Selection**. Waco, Texas: Baylor University Press, 1977.

39. Best, P. J., & Orr, J., Jr. Effects of hippocampal lesions on passive avoidance and taste aversion conditioning. **Physiology and Behavior**, 1973, **10**, 193-196.

40. Best, P. J., & Zuckerman, K. Subcortical mediation of learned taste aversion. **Physiology and Behavior**, 1971, **7**, 317-320.

41. Best, P. J., Best, M. R., & Ahlers, R. H. Transfer of discriminated taste aversion to a leverpressing task. **Psychonomic Science**, 1971, **25**, 281-282.

42. Best, P. J., Best, M. R., & Henggeler, S. The contribution of environmental non-ingestive cues in conditioning with aversive internal consequences. In L. M. Barker, M. R. Best, & M. Domjan (Eds.), **Learning Mechanisms in Food Selection**. Waco, Texas: Baylor University Press, 1977.

43. Best, P. J., Best, M. R., & Lindsey, G. P. The role of cue additivity in salience in taste aversion conditioning. **Learning and Motivation**, 1976, **7**, 254-264.

44. Best, P. J., Best, M. R., & Mickley, G. A. Conditioned aversion to distinct environmental stimuli resulting from gastrointestinal distress. **Journal of Comparative and Physiological Psychology**, 1973, **85**, 250-257.

45. Biederman, G. B. The search for the chemistry of memory: Recent trends and the logic of investigation in the role of cholinergic and adrenergic transmitters. In G. A. Kerkut & J. W. Phillis (Eds.), **Progress in Neurobiology (Vol. 2)**. Oxford: Pergamon Press, 1974, 289-307.

46. Biederman, G. B., Milgram, N. W., Heighington, G. A., Stockman, S. M., & O'Neill, W. Memory of conditioned food aversion follows a U-shape function in rats. **Quarterly Journal of Experimental Psychology**, 1974, **26**, 610-615.

47. Bitterman, M. E. The comparative analysis of learning: Are the laws of learning the same in all animals. **Science**, 1975, **188**, 699-709.

48. Bitterman, M. E. Reply to Garcia, Hankins, and Rusiniak. **Science**, 1976, **192**, 266-267.

49. Boland, F. J. Saccharin aversions induced by lithium chloride toxicosis in a backward conditioning paradigm. **Animal Learning and Behavior**, 1973, **1**, 3-4.

50. Bolles, R. C. The comparative psychology of learning: The selective association principle: Some problems with "general" laws of learning. In G. Ber-

mant (Ed.), **Perspectives on Animal Behavior.** Glenview: Scott, Foresman, 1973, 280-306.

51. Bolles, R. C. **Learning Theory.** New York: Holt, Rinehart, and Winston, 1975.

52. Bolles, R. C., Riley, A. L., & Laskowski, B. A further demonstration of the learned safety effect in food-aversion learning. **Bulletin of the Psychonomic Society,** 1973, **1,** 190-192.

53. Bond, N. W., & DiGiusto, E. L. Amount of solution drunk is a factor in the establishment of taste aversion. **Animal Learning and Behavior,** 1975, **3,** 81-84.

54. Bond, N. W., & DiGiusto, E. L. One trial higher-order conditioning of a taste aversion. **Australian Journal of Psychology,** 1976, **28,** 53-55.

55. Bond, N. W., & Harland, W. Higher order conditioning of a taste aversion. **Animal Learning and Behavior,** 1975, **3,** 295-296.

56. Bond, N. W., & Harland, W. Effect of amount of solution drunk on taste-aversion learning. **Bulletin of the Psychonomic Society,** 1975, **5,** 219-220.

57. Booth, D. A. Taste reactivity in satiated, ready to eat, and starved rats. **Physiology and Behavior,** 1972, **8,** 901-908.

58. Booth, D. A. Some characteristics of feeding during streptozotocin-induced diabetes in the rat. **Journal of Comparative and Physiological Psychology,** 1972, **80,** 238-249.

59. Booth, D. A. Conditioned satiety in the rat. **Journal of Comparative and Physiological Psychology,** 1972, **81,** 457-471.

60. Booth, D. A. Food intake compensation for increase or decrease in the protein content of the diet. **Behavioral Biology,** 1974, **12,** 31-40.

61. Booth, D. A., & Davis, J. D. Gastrointestinal factors in the acquisition of oral sensory control of satiation. **Physiology and Behavior,** 1973, **11,** 23-29.

62. Booth, D. A., & Jarman, S. P. Ontogeny and insulin-dependence of the satiation which follows carbohydrate absorption in the rat. **Behavioral Biology,** 1975, **15,** 159-172.

63. Booth, D. A., & Pilcher, C.W.T. Behavioral effects of protein synthesis inhibitors: Consolidation blockade or negative reinforcement? In G. B. Ansell & P. B. Bradley (Eds.), **Macromolecules and Behavior.** Birmingham, England: MacMillan, 1973, 105-112.

64. Booth, D. A., & Simson, P. C. Food preferences by association with variations in amino acid nutrition. **Quarterly Journal of Experimental Psychology,** 1971, **23,** 135-145.

65. Booth, D. A., & Simson, P. C. Aversion to a cue acquired by its association with effects of an antibiotic in rats. **Journal of Comparative and Physiological Psychology,** 1973, **84,** 319-323.

66. Booth, D. A., & Simson, P. C. Taste aversion induced by an histidine-free amino acid load. **Physiological Psychology,** 1974, **2,** 349-351.

67. Booth, D. A., Lee, M., & McAleavey, C. Acquired sensory control of satiation in man. **British Journal of Psychology,** in press.

68. Booth, D. A., Lovett, D., & McSherry, G. M. Postingestive modulation of the sweetness preference gradient in the rat. **Journal of Comparative and Physiological Psychology,** 1972, **78,** 485-512.

69. Booth, D. A., Toates, F. M., & Platt, S. V. Control system for hunger and its implications in animals and man. In D. Norvin, W. Wyrwicka, & G. Bray (Eds.), **Hunger: Basic Mechanisms and Clinical Implications.** New York: Raven Press, 1976, 127-143.

70. Brackbill, R. M., & Brookshire, K. H. Conditioned taste aversions as a function of the number of CS-US pairs. **Psychonomic Science,** 1971, **22,** 25-26.

71. Brackbill, R. M., Rosenbush, S. N., & Brookshire, K. H. Acquisition and retention of conditioned taste aversions as a function of the taste quality of the CS. **Learning and Motivation,** 1971, **2,** 341-350.

72. Bradley, R. M., & Mistretta, C. M. Intravascular taste in rats as demonstrated by conditioned aversion to sodium saccharin. **Journal of Comparative and Physiological Psychology,** 1971, **75,** 186-189.

73. Braun, J. J., & McIntosh, H., Jr. Learned taste aversions induced by rotational stimulation. **Physiological Psychology,** 1973, **1,** 301-304.

74. Braun, J. J., & Rosenthal, B. Relative salience of saccharin and quinine in long-delay taste aversion learning. **Behavioral Biology,** 1976, **16,** 341-352.

75. Braun, J. J., & Snyder, D. R. Taste aversions and acute methyl mercury poisoning in rats. **Bulletin of the Psychonomic Society,** 1973, **1,** 419-420.

76. Braun, J. J., Slick, T. B., & Lorden, J. F. Involvement of gustatory neo-cortex in the learning of taste aversions. **Physiology and Behavior,** 1972, **9,** 637-641.

77. Braveman, N. S. Poison-based avoidance learning with flavored or colored water in guinea pigs. **Learning and Motivation,** 1974, **5,** 182-194.

78. Braveman, N. S. Formation of taste aversions in rats following prior exposure to sickness. **Learning and Motivation,** 1975, **6,** 512-534.

79. Braveman, N. S. Relative salience of gustatory and visual cues in the formation of poison-based food aversions by guinea pigs (*Cavia porcellus*). **Behavioral Biology,** 1975, **14,** 189-109.

80. Braveman, N. S. Visually guided avoidance of poisonous foods in mammals. In L. M. Barker, M. R. Best, & M. Domjan (Eds.), **Learning Mechanisms in Food Selection.** Waco, Texas: Baylor University Press, 1977.

81. Braveman, N. S. What studies on pre-exposure to pharmacological agents tell us about the nature of the aversion-inducing agent. In L. M. Barker, M. R. Best, & M. Domjan (Eds.), **Learning Mechanisms in Food Selection.** Waco, Texas: Baylor University Press, 1977.

82. Brett, L. P., Hankins, W. G., & Garcia, J. Prey-lithium aversions III: Buteo hawks. **Behavioral Biology,** 1976, **17,** 87-98.

83. Bronstein, P. M., & Crockett, D. P. Maternal rations affect the food preferences of weanling rats: II. **Bulletin of the Psychonomic Society,** 1976, **8,** 227-229.

84. Brookshire, K. H. Changes in the rat's preference for saccharin and sodium chloride solutions following injection of alloxan monohydrate. **Journal of Comparative and Physiological Psychology,** 1974, **87,** 1061-1068.

85. Brookshire, K. H. Function of the "onset of illness" in the preference changes of alloxan-diabetic rats. **Journal of Comparative and Physiological Psychology,** 1974, **87,** 1069-1072.

86. Brookshire, K. H., & Brackbill, R. M. Formation and retention of conditioned taste aversions and UCS habituation. **Bulletin of the Psychonomic Society,** 1976, **7,** 125-128.

87. Brookshire, K. H., Stewart, C. N., & Bhagavan, H. N. Saccharin aversion in alloxan-diabetic rats. **Journal of Comparative and Physiological Psychology,** 1972, **79,** 385-393.

88. Browder, J. A., Upchurch, W. M., & Kirby, R. H. Preference for drinking deionized water over D_2O in the rat. **Physiological Psychology,** 1974, **2,** 461-463.

89. Brower, L. P. Ecological chemistry. **Scientific American,** 1969, **220,** 22-29.

90. Brown, R. T. Taste aversion learning in dead rats: A procedural note. **The Worm Runner's Digest,** 1974, **16,** 105.

595

91. Brown, R. T., Stewart, R. I., & Hall, T. L. Extinction of a taste aversion in the absence of the consummatory response. **Animal Learning and Behavior,** 1976, **4,** 213-216.

92. Brozek, G., Buresova, O., & Bures, J. Effect of bilateral cortical spreading depression on the hippocampal theta activity induced by oral infusion of aversive gustatory stimulus. **Experimental Neurology,** 1974, **42,** 661-668.

93. Buchwald, N. A., Garcia, J., Feder, B. H., & Bach-y-Rita, G. Ionizing radiation as a perceptual and aversive stimulus. In T. J. Haley & R. S. Snider (Eds.), **Response of the Nervous System to Ionizing Radiation.** New York: Litte, Brown, 1964, 687-699.

94. Bures, J., & Buresova, O. Behavioral and electrophysiological analysis of the conditioned taste aversion in rats. **Modern Trends in Neurophysiology,** in press.

95. Bures, J., & Buresova, O. Gustatory recognition times in rats with conditioned taste aversion. **Physiologia Bohemoslovaca,** in press.

96. Bures, J., & Buresova, O. Physiological mechanisms of conditioned food aversion. In N. W. Milgram, L. Krames, & T. Alloway (Eds.), **Food Aversion Learning.** New York: Plenum Press, in press.

97. Buresova, O. Differential role of the cerebral cortex and subcortical centres in the acquisition and extinction of conditioned taste aversion. **Activitas Nervosa Superior** (Prague), 1976, **18,** 1-2.

98. Buresova, O., & Bures, J. Cortical and subcortical components of the conditioned saccharin aversion. **Physiology and Behavior,** 1973, 11, 435-439.

99. Buresova, O., & Bures, J. Cortical and subcortical components of conditioned saccharin aversion in rats. **Acta Neurologia Experimentalis,** 1973, **33,** 689-698.

100. Buresova, O., & Bures, J. The mechanism of conditioned saccharin aversion. In H. Matthies (Ed.), **Neurobiological Basis of Memory Formation.** Berlin: Veb Verlag Volk und Gesundheit, 1974, 298-313.

101. Buresova, O., & Bures, J. Functional decortication in the CS-US interval decrease efficiency of taste aversive learning. **Behavioral Biology,** 1974, **12,** 357-364.

102. Buresova, O., & Bures, J. The antagonistic influence of anesthesia and functional decortication on conditioned taste aversion. **Activitas Nervosa Superior** (Prague), 1975, **17,** 58.

103. Buresova, O., & Bures, J. Functional decortication by cortical spreading depression does not prevent forced extinction of conditioned saccharin aversion in rats. **Journal of Comparative and Physiological Psychology,** 1975, **88,** 47-52.

104. Buresova, O., & Bures, J. The effect of anesthesia on acquisition and extinction of conditioned taste aversion. **Behavioral Biology,** in press.

105. Burghardt, G. M. Chemical prey preference polymorphism in newborn garter snakes (*Thamnophis sirtalis*). **Behaviour,** 1975, **52,** 202-225.

106. Burghardt, G. M., Wilcoxon, H. C., & Czaplicki, J. A. Conditioning in garter snakes: Aversion to palatable prey induced by delayed illness. **Animal Learning and Behavior,** 1973, **1,** 317-320.

107. Cannon, D. S., Berman, R. F., Baker, T. B., & Atkinson, C. A. Effect of preconditioning unconditioned stimulus experience on learned taste aversions. **Journal of Experimental Psychology: Animal Behavior Processes,** 1975, **104,** 270-284.

108. Cappell, H. D., & LeBlanc, A. E. Conditioned aversion to saccharin by single administrations of mescaline and d-amphetamine. **Psychopharmacologia,** 1971, **22,** 352-356.

109. Cappell, H. D., & LeBlanc, A. E. Aversive conditioning by d-amphetamine. In J. M. Singh, L. Miller, & H. Lal (Eds.), **Drug Addiction: Experimental Pharmacology.** New York; Futura, 1972, 99-105.

110. Cappell, H. D., & LeBlanc, A. E. Punishment of saccharin drinking by amphetamine in rats and its reversal by chlordiazepoxide. **Journal of Comparative and Physiological Psychology,** 1973, **85,** 97-104.

111. Cappell, H. D., & LeBlanc, A. E. Conditioned aversion by psychoactive drugs: Does it have significance for an understanding of drug dependence? **Addictive Behaviors,** 1975, **1,** 55-64.

112. Cappell, H. D., & LeBlanc, A. E. Conditioned aversion by amphetamine: Rates of acquisition and loss of the attenuating effects of prior exposure. **Psychopharmacologia,** 1975, **43,** 157-162.

113. Cappell, H. D., & LeBlanc, A. E. Gustatory avoidance conditioning by drugs of abuse: Relationships to general issues in research on drug dependence. In N. W. Milgram, L. Krames, & T. M. Alloway (Eds.), **Food Aversion Learning.** New York: Plenum Press, in press.

114. Cappell, H. D., LeBlanc, A. E., & Endrenyi, L. Effects of chlordiazepoxide and ethanol on the extinction of a conditioned taste aversion. **Physiology and Behavior,** 1972, **9,** 167-169.

115. Cappell, H. D., LeBlanc, A. E., & Endrenyi, L. Aversive conditioning by psychoactive drugs: Effects of morphine, alcohol, and chlordiazepoxide. **Psychopharmacologia,** 1973, **29,** 239-246.

116. Cappell, H. D., LeBlanc, A. E., & Herling, S. Modification punishing effects of psychoactive drugs in rats by previous drug experience. **Journal of Comparative and Physiological Psychology,** 1975, **89,** 347-356.

117. Capretta, P. J. An experimental modification of food preferences in chicks. **Journal of Comparative and Physiological Psychology,** 1961, **54,** 238-242.

118. Capretta, P. J. Establishment of food preferences by exposure to ingestive stimuli early in life. In L. M. Barker, M. R. Best, and M. Domjan (Eds.), **Learning Mechanisms in Food Selection.** Waco, Texas: Baylor University Press, 1977.

119. Capretta, P. J., & Moore, M. J. Appropriateness of reinforcement to cue in the conditioning of food aversions in chickens (*Gallus gallus*). **Journal of Comparative and Physiological Psychology,** 1970, **72,** 85-89.

120. Capretta, P. J., & Rawls, L. H., III. Establishment of a flavor preference in rats: Importance of nursing and weaning experience. **Journal of Comparative and Physiological Psychology,** 1974, **86,** 670-673.

121. Capretta, P. J., Moore, M. J., & Rossiter, T. R. Establishment and modification of food and taste preferences: Effects of experience. **The Journal of General Psychology,** 1973, **89,** 27-46.

122. Capretta, P. J., Petersik, J. T., & Stewart, D. J. Acceptance of novel flavours is increased after early experience of diverse tastes. **Nature,** 1975, **254,** 689-691.

123. Carey, R. J. Acquired aversion to amphetamine solutions. **Pharmacology, Biochemistry, and Behavior,** 1973, **1,** 227-229.

124. Carey, R. J. Long-term aversion to a saccharin solution induced by repeated amphetamine injections. **Pharmacology, Biochemistry, and Behavior,** 1973, **1,** 265-270.

125. Carey, R. J., & Goodall, E. B. Amphetamine-induced taste aversion: A comparison of d-versus l-

amphetamine. **Pharmacology, Biochemistry, and Behavior**, 1974, **2**, 325-330.

126. Carey, R. J., & Goodall, E. B. A conditioned taste aversion induced by α-methyl-p-tyrosine. **Neuropharmacology**, 1974, **13**, 595-600.

127. Carroll, M. E., & Smith, J. C. Time course of radiation-induced taste aversion conditioning. **Physiology and Behavior**, 1974, **13**, 809-812.

128. Carroll, M. E., Dinc, H. I., Levy, C. J., & Smith, J. C. Demonstrations of neophobia and enhanced neophobia in the albino rat. **Journal of Comparative and Physiological Psychology**, 1975, **89**, 457-467.

129. Chambers, K. C. Hormonal influences in sexual dimorphism in rate of extinction of a conditioned taste aversion in rats. **Journal of Comparative and Physiological Psychology**, 1976, **90**, 851-856.

130. Chambers, K. C., & Sengstake, C. B. Sexually dimorphic extinction of a conditioned taste aversion in rats. **Animal Learning and Behavior**, 1976, **4**, 181-185.

131. Chitty, D. (Ed.). **Control of Rats and Mice (Vol. 1)**. Oxford: Clarendon Press, 1954.

132. Chitty, D. (Ed.). **Control of Rats and Mice (Vol. 2)**. Oxford Clarendon Press, 1954.

133. Chitty, D. The study of the brown rat and its control by poison. In D. Chitty (Ed.), **Control of Rats and Mice (Vol. 1)**. Oxford: Clarendon Press, 1954, 160-305.

134. Clark, M. M., & Galef, B. G., Jr. The effects of forced nest-site feeding on the food preferences of wild rat pups at weaning. **Psychonomic Science**, 1972, **28**, 173-175.

135. Clody, D. E., & Vogel, J. R. Drug-induced conditioned aversion to mouse-killing in rats. **Pharmacology, Biochemistry, and Behavior**, 1973, **1**, 477-481.

136. Clody, D. E., Vogel, J. R., & Taub, P. Chlordiazepoxide antagonism of the acquisition and performance of a conditioned food aversion in rats. **Pharmacology, Biochemistry, and Behavior**, in press.

137. Colavita, F. B. Saccharine preference in rats as a function of age and early experience. **Psychonomic Science**, 1968, **12**, 311-312.

138. Colby, J. J., & Smith, N. F. The effect of three elimination procedures on the unlearning of a conditioned taste aversion in the rat. **Learning and Motivation**, in press.

139. Cooper, A., & Capretta, P. J. Olfactory bulb removal and taste aversion learning in mice. **Bulletin of the Psychonomic Society**, 1976, **7**, 235-236.

140. Corcoran, M. E. Role of drug novelty and metabolism in the aversive effects of hashish injections in rats. **Life Sciences**, 1973, **12**, 63-72.

141. Corcoran, M. E., Bolotow, I., Amit, Z., & McCaughran, J. A., Jr. Conditioned taste aversions produced by active and inactive cannabinoids. **Pharmacology, Biochemistry, and Behavior**, 1974, **2**, 725-728.

142. Cott, H. B. **Adaptive Coloration in Animals.** London: Metheun, 1940.

143. Coussens, W. R. Conditioned taste aversion: Route of drug administration. In J. M. Singh & H. Lal (Eds.), **Drug Addiction: Neurobiology and Influences on Behavior (Vol. 3)**. Miami: Symposium Specialists, 1974.

144. Coussens, W. R., Crowder, W. F., & Davis, W. M. Morphine-induced saccharin aversion in α-methyltyrosine pretreated rats. **Psychopharmacologia**, 1973, **29**, 151-157.

145. Cullen, J. W. Modification of salt-seeking behavior in the adrenalectomized rat via gamma-ray irradiation. **Journal of Comparative and Physiological Psychology**, 1969, **68**, 524-529.

146. Cullen, J. W. Modification of NaCl appetite in the adrenalectomized rat consequent to extensive LiCl poisoning. **Journal of Comparative and Physiological Psychology**, 1970, **72**, 79-84.

147. Czaplicki, J. A., Borrebach, D. E., & Wilcoxon, H. C. Stimulus generalization of an illness-induced aversion to different intensities of colored water in Japanese quail. **Animal Learning and Behavior**, 1976, **4**, 45-48.

148. Czaplicki, J. A., Porter, R. H., & Wilcoxon, H. C. Olfactory mimicry involving garter snakes and artificial models and mimics. **Behaviour**, 1975, **54**, 60-72.

149. D'Amato, M. R. Derived motives. **Annual Review of Psychology**, 1974, **25**, 83-106.

150. Danguir, J., & Nicolaidis, S. Impairment of learned aversion acquisition following paradoxical sleep deprivation in the rat. **Physiology and Behavior**, 1976, **17**, 489-492.

151. Davidson, W. S., III. Studies of aversive conditioning for alcoholics: A critical review of theory and research methodology. **Psychological Bulletin**, 1974, **81**, 571-581.

152. Davis, J. L. Saccharin aversion acquired during unilateral spreading depression. **Physiological Psychology**, 1975, **3**, 253-254.

153. Davis, J. L., & Bures, J. Disruption of saccharin-aversion learning in rats by cortical spreading depression in the CS-US interval. **Journal of Comparative and Physiological Psychology**, 1972, **80**, 398-402.

154. Davison, C. S., & House, W. J. Alcohol as the aversive stimulus in conditioned taste aversion. **Bulletin of the Psychonomic Society**, 1975, **6**, 49-50.

155. Davison, C. S., Corwin, G., & McGowan, T. Alcohol induced taste aversion in the golden hamster. **Journal of Studies on Alcohol**, 1976, **37**, 606-610.

156. Decastro, J. M., & Balagura, S. Fornicotomy: Effect on the primary and secondary punishment of mouse killing by LiCl poisoning. **Behavioral Biology**, 1975, **13**, 483-489..

157. Der-Karabetian, A., & Gorry, T. Amount of different flavors consumed during the CS-US interval in taste-aversion learning and interference. **Physiological Psychology**, 1974, **2**, 457-460.

158. Deutsch, J. A., Molina, F., & Puerto, A. Conditioned taste aversion caused by palatable nontoxic nutrients. **Behavioral Biology**, 1976, **16**, 161-174.

159. Deutsch, R. Conditioned hypoglycemia: A mechanism for saccharin-induced sensitivity to insulin in the rat. **Journal of Comparative and Physiological Psychology**, 1974, **86**, 350-358.

160. Devenport, L. D. Aversion to a palatable saline solution in rats: Interactions of physiology and experience. **Journal of Comparative and Physiological Psychology**, 1973, **83**, 98-105.

161. Dinc, H. I., & Smith, J. C. Role of the olfactory bulbs in the detection of ionizing radiation by the rat. **Physiology and Behavior**, 1966, **1**, 139-144.

162. Divac, I., Gade, A., & Wikmark, R. E. G. Taste aversion in rats with lesions in the frontal lobes: No evidence for interceptive agnosia. **Physiological Psychology**, 1975, **3**, 43-46.

163. Domjan, M. CS preexposure in taste-aversion learning: Effects of deprivation and preexposure duration. **Learning and Motivation**, 1972, **3**, 389-402.

164. Domjan, M. Role of ingestion in odor-toxicosis learning in the rat. **Journal of Comparative and Physiological Psychology**, 1973, **84**, 507-521.

165. Domjan, M. Poison-induced neophobia in rats: Role of stimulus generalization of conditioned taste aversions. **Animal Learning and Behavior**, 1975, **3**, 205-211.

166. Domjan, M. The nature of the thirst stimulus: A factor in conditioned taste-aversion behavior. **Physiology and Behavior**, 1975, **14**, 809-813.

167. Domjan, M. Determinants of the enhancement of flavored-water intake by prior exposure. **Journal of Experimental Psychology: Animal Behavior Processes**, 1976, **2**, 17-27.

168. Domjan, M. Selective suppression of drinking during a limited period following aversive drug treatment in rats. **Journal of Experimental Psychology: Animal Behavior Processes**, in press.

169. Domjan, M. Attenuation and enhancement of neophobia for edible substances. In L. M. Barker, M. R. Best, & M. Domjan (Eds.), **Learning Mechanisms in Food Selection**. Waco, Texas: Baylor University Press, 1977.

170. Domjan, M., & Bowman, T. G. Learned safety and the CS-US delay gradient in taste-aversion learning. **Learning and Motivation**, 1974, **5**, 409-423.

171. Domjan, M., & Gillan, D. Role of novelty in the aversion for increasingly concentrated saccharin solutions. **Physiology and Behavior**, 1976, **16**, 537-542.

172. Domjan, M., & Gregg, B. Long-delay backward taste-aversion conditioning with lithium. **Physiology and Behavior**, in press.

173. Domjan, M., & Levy, C. J. Taste aversions conditioned by the aversiveness of insulin and formalin: Role of CS specificity. **Journal of Experimental Psychology: Animal Behavior Processes**, in press.

174. Domjan, M., & Wilson, N. E. Specificity of cue to consequence in aversion learning in the rat. **Psychonomic Science**, 1972, **26**, 143-145.

175. Domjan, M., & Wilson, N. E. Contribution of ingestive behaviors to taste-aversion learning in the rat. **Journal of Comparative and Physiological Psychology**, 1972, **80**, 403-412.

176. Domjan, M., Schorr, R., & Best, M. R. Early environmental influences on conditioned and unconditioned ingestional and locomotor behaviors. **Developmental Psychobiology**, in press.

177. Dragoin, W. Conditioning and extinction of taste aversions with variations in intensity of the CS and UCS in two strains of rats. **Psychonomic Science**, 1971, **22**, 303-305.

178. Dragoin, W., McCleary, G. E., & McCleary, P. A comparison of two methods of measuring conditioned taste aversions. **Behavior Research Methods and Instrumentation**, 1971, **3**, 309-310.

179. Dragoin, W., Hughes, G., Devine, M., & Bently, J. Long-term retention of conditioned taste aversions: Effects of gustatory interference. **Psychological Reports**, 1973, **33**, 511-514.

180. Eckardt, M. J. Conditioned taste aversion produced by the oral ingestion of ethanol in the rat. **Physiological Psychology**, 1975, **3**, 317-321.

181. Eckardt, M. J. The role of orosensory stimuli from ethanol and blood-alcohol levels in producing conditioned taste aversion in the rat. **Psychopharmacologia**, 1975, **44**, 267-271.

182. Eckardt, M. J. Alcohol-induced conditioned taste aversion in rats: Effect of concentration and prior exposure to alcohol. **Journal of Studies on Alcohol**, 1976, **37**, 334-346.

183. Eckardt, M. J., Skurdal, A. J., & Brown, J. S. Conditioned taste aversion produced by low doses of alcohol. **Physiological Psychology**, 1974, **2**, 89-92.

184. Elkins, R. L. Attenuation of drug-induced bait-shyness to a palatable solution as an increasing function of its availability prior to conditioning. **Behavioral Biology**, 1973, **9**, 221-226.

185. Elkins, R. L. Individual differences in bait shyness: Effects of drug dose and measurement technique. **The Psychological Record**, 1973, **23**, 349-358.

186. Elkins, R. L. Bait-shyness acquisition and resistance to extinction as functions of US exposure prior to conditioning. **Physiological Psychology**, 1974, **2**, 341-343.

187. Elkins, R. L. Conditioned flavor aversions to familiar tap water in rats: An adjustment with implications for aversion therapy treatment of alcoholism and obesity. **Journal of Abnormal Psychology**, 1974, **83**, 411-417.

188. Elkins, R. L. Aversion therapy for alcoholism: Chemical, electrical, or verbal imaginary? **The International Journal of the Addictions**, 1975, **10**, 157-209.

189. Elkins, R. L. A note on aversion therapy for alcoholism. **Behavior Research and Therapy**, 1976, **14**, 159-161.

190. Elsmore, T. F., & Fletcher, G. V. Δ⁹-tetrahydrocannabinol: Aversive effects in rats at high doses. **Science**, 1972, **175**, 911-912.

191. Elton, C. Research on rodent control by the bureau of animal population, September 1939 to July 1947. In D. Chitty (Ed.), **Control of Rats and Mice (Vol. 1)**. Oxford: Clarendon Press, 1954, 1-24.

192. Emmerick, J. J., & Snowdon, C. T. Failure to show modification of male golden hamster mating behavior through taste/odor aversion learning. **Journal of Comparative and Physiological Psychology**, 1976, **90**, 857-869.

193. Erspamer, R., & Crow, L. T. A depression of ethanol consumption in rats as a result of intraperitoneal injections of pyrazole. **Psychonomic Science**, 1972, **26**, 29-30.

194. Etscorn, F. Effects of a preferred vs. a nonpreferred CS in the establishment of a taste aversion. **Physiological Psychology**, 1973, **1**, 5-6.

195. Etscorn, F., & Miller, R. L. Variations in the strength of conditioned taste-aversion in rats as a function of time of inducement. **Physiological Psychology**, 1975, **3**, 270-272.

196. Etscorn, F., & Stephens, R. Establishment of conditioned taste aversions with a 24-hour CS-US interval. **Physiological Psychology**, 1973, **1**, 251-253.

197. Farber, P. D., Gorman, J. E., & Reid, L. D. Morphine injections in the taste aversion paradigm. **Physiological Psychology**, 1976, **4**, 365-368.

198. Farley, J. A., McLaurin, W. A., Scarborough, B. B., & Rawlings, T. D. Pre-irradiation saccharin habituation: A factor in avoidance behavior. **Psychological Reports**, 1964, **14**, 491-496.

199. Feinberg, A. Effect of treatment-test interval and proferrin on X-irradiation-induced saccharin aversion. **JSAS Catalog of Selected Documents in Psychology**, 1973, **3**, 119-141.

200. Fenwick, S., Mikulka, P. J., & Klein, S. B. The effect of different levels of pre-exposure to sucrose on the acquisition and extinction of a conditioned aversion. **Behavioral Biology**, 1975, **14**, 231-235.

201. Fernandez, B., & Ternes, J. W. Conditioned aversion to morphine with lithium chloride in morphine-dependent rats. **Bulletin of the Psychonomic Society**, 1975, **5**, 331-332.

202. Fjerdingstad, E. J. Chemical transfer of radiation induced avoidance: A replication. **Scandinavian Journal of Psychology**, 1972, **13**, 145-151.

203. Fregly, M. J. Specificity of the sodium chloride appetite of adrenalectomized rats: Substitution of lithium chloride for sodium chloride. **American Journal of Physiology**, 1958, **195**, 645-653.

204. Frey, A. H., & Feld, S. R. Avoidance by rats of illumination with low power non-ionizing electromagnetic energy. **Journal of Comparative and Physiological Psychology**, 1975, **89**, 183-188.

598

205. Frumkin, K. Interaction of LiCl aversion and sodium-specific hunger in the adrenalectomized rat. **Journal of Comparative and Physiological Psychology**, 1971, **75**, 32-40.

206. Frumkin, K. Effects of deprivation schedule on the maintenance of a preoperative salt aversion by adrenalectomized rats. **Physiological Psychology**, 1975, **3**, 101-106.

207. Frumkin, K. Failure of sodium- and calcium-deficient rats to acquire conditioned taste aversions to the object of their specific hunger. **Journal of Comparative and Physiological Psychology**, 1975, **89**, 329-339.

208. Frumkin, K. Differential potency of taste and audiovisual stimuli in the conditioning of morphine withdrawal in rats. **Psychopharmacologia**, 1976, **46**, 245-248.

209. Gadusek, F. J., & Kalat, J. W. Effects of scopolamine on retention of taste-aversion learning in rats. **Physiological Psychology**, 1975, **3**, 130-132.

210. Gaines, T. B., & Hayes, W. J., Jr. Bait shyness to antu in wild Norway rats. **Public Health Report**, 1952, **63**, 306-311.

211. Galef, B. G., Jr. Social effects in the weaning of domestic rat pups. **Journal of Comparative and Physiological Psychology**, 1971, **75**, 358-362.

212. Galef, B. G., Jr. The social transmission of acquired behavior. **Biological Psychiatry**, 1975, **10**, 155-160.

213. Galef, B. G., Jr. Social transmission of acquired behavior: A discussion of tradition and social learning in vertebrates. In J. S. Rosenblatt, R. A. Hinde, E. Shaw, & C. Beer (Eds.), **Advances in the Study of Behavior (Vol. 6)**. New York: Academic Press, 1976, 77-100.

214. Galef, B. G., Jr. Mechanisms for the social transmission of acquired food preferences from adult to weanling rats. In L. M. Barker, M. R. Best, & M. Domjan (Eds.), **Learning Mechanisms in Food Selection**. Waco, Texas: Baylor University Press, 1977.

215. Galef, B. G., Jr., & Clark, M. M. Parent-offspring interactions determine time and place of first ingestion of solid food by wild rat pups. **Psychonomic Science**, 1971, **25**, 15-16.

216. Galef, B. G., Jr., & Clark, M. M. Social factors in the poison avoidance and feeding behavior of wild and domesticated rat pups. **Journal of Comparative and Physiological Psychology**, 1971, **75**, 341-357.

217. Galef, B. G., Jr., & Clark, M. M. Mother's milk and adult presence: Two factors determining initial dietary selection by weanling rats. **Journal of Comparative and Physiological Psychology**, 1972, **78**, 220-225.

218. Galef, B. G., Jr., & Heiber, L. The role of residual olfactory cues in the determination of the feeding site selection and exploration patterns of domestic rats. **Journal of Comparative and Physiological Psychology**, in press.

219. Galef, B. G., Jr., & Henderson, P. W. Mother's milk: A determinant of the feeding preferences of weanling rat pups. **Journal of Comparative and Physiological Psychology**, 1972, **78**, 213-219.

220. Galef, B. G., Jr., & Sherry, D. F. Mother's milk: A medium for the transmission of cues reflecting the flavor of mother's diet. **Journal of Comparative and Physiological Psychology**, 1973, **83**, 374-378.

221. Gamzu, E. The multifaceted nature of taste-aversion learning agents: Is there a single common factor? In L. M. Barker, M. R. Best, & M. Domjan (Eds.), **Learning Mechanisms in Food Selection**. Waco, Texas: Baylor University Press, 1977.

222. Garb, J. L., & Stunkard, A. J. Taste aversions in man. **American Journal of Psychiatry**, 1974, **131**, 1204-1207.

223. Garcia, J. The faddy rat and us. **New Scientist and Science Journal**, 1974, **49**, 254-256.

224. Garcia, J., & Ervin, F. R. Appetites, aversions, and addictions: A model for visceral memory. In J. Wortis (Ed.), **Recent Advances in Biological Psychiatry (Vol. 10)**. New York: Plenum Press, 1968, 284-293.

225. Garcia, J., & Ervin, F. R. Gustatory-visceral and telereceptor-cutaneous conditioning: Adaptation in internal and external milieus. **Communications in Behavioral Biology**, 1968, **1**, 389-415.

226. Garcia, J., & Hankins, W. G. The evolution of bitter and the acquisition of toxiphobia. In D. A. Denton & J. P. Coghlan (Eds.), **Olfaction and Taste (Vol. 5)**. New York: Academic Press, 1975, 39-47.

227. Garcia, J., & Hankins, W. G. On the origin of food aversion paradigms. In L. M. Barker, M. R. Best, & M. Domjan (Eds.), **Learning Mechanisms in Food Selection**. Waco, Texas: Baylor University Press, 1977.

228. Garcia, J., & Kimeldorf, D. J. Temporal relationship within the conditioning of a saccharin aversion through radiation exposure. **Journal of Comparative and Physiological Psychology**, 1957, **50**, 180-183.

229. Garcia, J., & Kimeldorf, D. J. The effect of ophthalectomy upon responses of the rat to radiation and taste stimuli. **Journal of Comparative and Physiological Psychology**, 1958, **51**, 288-291.

230. Garcia, J., & Kimeldorf, D. J. Some factors which influence radiation-conditioned behavior of rats. **Radiation Research**, 1960, **12**, 719-727.

231. Garcia, J., & Kimeldorf, D. J. Conditioned avoidance behaviour induced by low-dose neutron exposure. **Nature**, 1960, **185**, 261-262.

232. Garcia, J., & Koelling, R. A. Relation of cue to consequence in avoidance learning. **Psychonomic Science**, 1966, **4**, 123-124.

233. Garcia, J., & Koelling, R. A. A comparison of aversions induced by X-rays, toxins, and drugs in the rat. **Radiation Research Supplement 7**, 1967, 439-450.

234. Garcia, J., & Koelling, R. A. The use of ionizing rays as a mammalian olfactory stimulus. In L. M. Beidler (Ed.), **Handbook of Sensory Physiology (Vol. IV), Chemical Senses: Olfaction (Part 1)**. New York: Springer-Verlag, 1971, 449-464.

235. Garcia, J., Clark, J. C., & Hankins, W. G. Natural responses to scheduled rewards. In P. P. G. Bateson & P. H. Klopfer (Eds.), **Perspectives in Ethology**. New York: Plenum Press, 1973, 1-41.

236. Garcia, J., Ervin, F. R., & Koelling, R. A. Learning with prolonged delay of reinforcement. **Psychonomic Science**, 1966, **5**, 121-122.

237. Garcia, J., Ervin, F. R., & Koelling, R. A. Bait-shyness: A test for toxicity with N = 2. **Psychonomic Science**, 1967, **7**, 245-246.

238. Garcia, J., Ervin, F. R., & Koelling, R. A. Toxicity of serum from irradiated donors. **Nature**, 1967, **213**, 682-683.

239. Garcia, J., Green, K. F., & McGowan, B. K. X-ray as an olfactory stimulus. In C. Pfaffman (Ed.), **Olfaction and Taste**. New York: Rockefeller University Press, 1969, 299-309.

240. Garcia, J., Hankins, W. G., & Coil, J. D. Koalas, men, and other conditioned gastronomes. In N. W. Milgram, L. Krames, & T. Alloway (Eds.), **Food Aversion Learning**. New York: Plenum Press, in press.

241. Garcia, J., Hankins, W. G., & Rusiniak, K. W. Behavioral regulation of the milieu interne in man and rat. **Science**, 1974, **185**, 823-831.

242. Garcia, J., Hankins, W. G., & Rusiniak, K. W. Flavor aversion studies. **Science**, 1976, **192**, 265-266.

599

243. Garcia, J., Kimeldorf, D. J., & Hunt, E. L. Conditioned responses to manipulative procedures resulting from exposure to gamma radiation. **Radiation Research**, 1956, **5**, 79-87.

244. Garcia, J., Kimeldorf, D. J., & Hunt, E. L. Spatial avoidance behavior in the rat as a result of exposure to ionizing radiation. **British Journal of Radiology**, 1957, **30**, 318-320.

245. Garcia, J., Kimeldorf, D. J., & Hunt, E. L. The use of ionizing radiation as a motivating stimulus. **Psychological Review**, 1961, **68**, 383-395.

246. Garcia, J., Kimeldorf, D. J., & Koelling, R. A. Conditioned aversion to saccharin resulting from exposure to gamma radiation. **Science**, 1955, **122**, 157-158.

247. Garcia, J., Kovner, R., & Green, K. F. Cue properties vs palatability of flavors in avoidance learning. **Psychonomic Science**, 1970, **20**, 313-314.

248. Garcia, J., McGowan, B. K., & Green, K. F. Biological constraints on conditioning. In A. H. Black & W. F. Prokasy (Eds.), **Classical Conditioning II: Current Research and Theory**. New York: Appleton-Century-Crofts, 1972, 3-27.

249. Garcia, J., McGowan, B. K., & Green, K. F. Biological constraints on conditioning. In M. E. P. Seligman & J. L. Hager (Eds.), **Biological Boundaries of Learning**. New York: Appleton-Century-Crofts, 1972, 21-43.

250. Garcia, J., Rusiniak, K. W., & Brett, L. P. Conditioning food-illness aversions in wild animals: Caveat canonici. In H. David & H. M. B. Hurwitz (Eds.), **Operant-Pavlovian Interactions**. New Jersey: Lawrence Erlbaum Associates, in press.

251. Garcia, J., Hankins, W. G., Robinson, J. H., & Vogt, J. L. Bait shyness: Tests of CS-US mediation. **Physiology and Behavior**, 1972, **8**, 807-810.

252. Garcia, J., McGowan, B. K., Ervin, F. R., & Koelling, R. A. Cues: Their relative effectiveness as a function of the reinforcer. **Science**, 1968, **160**, 794-795.

253. Garcia, J., Buchwald, N. A., Feder, B. H., Koelling, R. A., & Tedrow, L. F. Ionizing radiation as a perceptual and aversive stimulus. In T. J. Haley & R. S. Snider (Eds.), **Response of the Nervous System to Ionizing Radiation**. New York: Little, Brown, 1964, 673-686.

254. Gay, P. E., Leaf, R. C., & Arble, F. B. Inhibitory effects of pre- and post-test drugs on mouse-killing by rats. **Pharmacology, Biochemistry, and Behavior**, 1975, **3**, 33-45.

255. Gelperin, A. Rapid food-aversion learning by a terrestrial mollusc. **Science**, 1975, **189**, 567-570.

256. Gibbs, J., Young, R. C., & Smith, G. P. Cholecystokinin decreases food intake in rats. **Journal of Comparative and Physiological Psychology**, 1973, **84**, 488-495.

257. Gleitman, H. Getting Animals to understand the experimenter's instructions. **Animal Learning and Behavior**, 1974, **2**, 1-5.

258. Gold, R. M., & Proulx, D. M. Bait-shyness acquisition is impaired by VMH lesions that produce obesity. **Journal of Comparative and Physiological Psychology**, 1972, **79**, 201-209.

259. Goudie, A. J., & Thornton, E. W. Effects of drug experience on drug induced conditioned taste aversions: Studies with amphetamine and fenfluramine. **Psychopharmacologia**, 1975, **44**, 77-82.

260. Goudie, A. J., Taylor, M., & Atherton, H. Effects of prior drug experience on the establishment of taste aversions in rats. **Pharmacology, Biochemistry, and Behavior**, 1975, **3**, 947-952.

261. Goudie, A. J., Thornton, E. W., & Wheatley, J. Effects of p-chloro-phenylalanine on drinking suppressed by punishment. **IRCS Medical Science: Neurobiology and Neurophysiology; Pharmacology; Psychology**, 1975, **3**, 265.

262. Goudie, A. J., Thornton, E. W., & Wheatley, J. Attenuation by alpha-methyltyrosine of amphetamine induced conditioned taste aversion in rats. **Psychopharmacologia**, 1975, **45**, 119-123.

263. Goudie, A. J., Thornton, E. W., & Wheeler, T. J. Drug pretreatment effects in drug induced taste aversions: Effects of dose and duration of pretreatment. **Pharmacology, Biochemistry, and Behavior**, 1976, **4**, 629-633.

264. Green, K. F. Aversions to grape juice induced by apomorphine. **Psychonomic Science**, 1969, **17**, 168-169.

265. Green, K. F., & Churchill, P. A. An effect of flavors on strength of conditioned aversions. **Psychonomic Science**, 1970, **21**, 19-20.

266. Green, K. F., & Garcia, J. Recuperation from illness: Flavor enhancement for rats. **Science**, 1971, **173**, 749-751.

267. Green, K. F., & Parker, L. A. Gustatory memory: Incubation and interference. **Behavioral Biology**, 1975, **13**, 359-367.

268. Green, K. F., Holmstrom, L. S., & Wollman, M. A. Relation of cue to consequence in rats: Effect of recuperation from illness. **Behavioral Biology**, 1974, **10**, 491-503.

269. Green, L., & Rachlin, H. The effect of rotation on the learning of taste aversions. **Bulletin of the Psychonomic Society**, 1973, **1**, 137-138.

270. Green, L., & Rachlin, H. Learned taste aversions in rats as a function of delay, speed, and duration of rotation. **Learning and Motivation**, 1976, **7**, 283-289.

271. Green, L., Bouzas, A., & Rachlin, H. Test of an electric-shock analog to illness-induced aversion. **Behavioral Biology**, 1972, **7**, 513-518.

272. Gross, N. B., Fisher, A. H., & Cohn, V. H., Jr. The effect of rachitogenic diet on the hoarding behavior of rats. **Journal of Comparative and Physiological Psychology**, 1955, **48**, 451-455.

273. Grote, F. W., & Brown, R. T. Conditioned taste aversions: Two-stimulus tests are more sensitive than one-stimulus tests. **Behavior Research Methods and Instrumentation**, 1971, **3**, 311-312.

274. Grote, F. W., Jr., & Brown, R. T. Rapid learning of passive avoidance by weanling rats: Conditioned taste aversion. **Psychonomic Science**, 1971, **25**, 163-164.

275. Grote, F. W., Jr., & Brown, R. T. Deprivation level affects extinction of a conditioned taste aversion. **Learning and Motivation**, 1973, **4**, 314-319.

276. Grupp, L. A., Linesman, M. A., & Cappell, H. Effects of amygdala lesions on taste aversions produced by amphetamine and LiCl. **Pharmacology, Biochemistry, and Behavior**, 1976, **4**, 541-544.

277. Gustavson, C. R. Taste aversion conditioning of predators. **The Chronicle of the Horse**, 1975, **38**, 12-13.

278. Gustavson, C. R. Breakthrough on the Honn Ranch. **Defenders of Wildlife International**, in press.

279. Gustavson, C. R. Comparative and field aspects of learned food aversions. In L. M. Barker, M. R. Best, & M. Domjan (Eds.), **Learning Mechanisms in Food Selection**. Waco, Texas: Baylor University Press, 1977.

280. Gustavson, C. R. & Garcia, J. Aversive conditioning: Pulling a gag on the wily coyote. **Psychology Today**, 1974, **8**, 68-72.

281. Gustavson, C. R. & Gustavson, J. C. Spiked lamb dulls coyote appetite. **Defenders of Wildlife International**, 1974, **49**, 293-294.

600

282. Gustavson, C. R. Brett, L. P., Garcia, J., & Kelly, D. J. A working model and experimental solutions to the control of predatory behavior. In H. Markowitz & V. Stevens (Eds.), **Studies of Captive Wild Animals**. Chicago: Nelson Hall, in press.

283. Gustavson, C. R. Kelly, D. J., Sweeney, M., & Garcia, J. Prey-lithium aversions I: Coyotes and wolves. **Behavioral Biology**, 1976, **17**, 61-72.

284. Gustavson, C. R., Garcia, J., Hankins, W. G., & Rusiniak, K. W. Coyote predation control by aversive conditioning. **Science**, 1974, **184**, 581-583.

285. Halpern, B. P., & Marowitz, L. A. Taste responses to lick-duration stimuli. **Brain Research**, 1973, **57**, 473-478.

286. Halpern, B. P., & Tapper, D. N. Taste stimuli: Quality coding time. **Science**, 1971, **171**, 1256-1258.

287. Hamilton, L. W., & Capobianco, S. Consumption of sodium chloride and lithium chloride in normal rats and in rats with septal lesions. **Physiological Psychology**, 1973, **1**, 213-218.

288. Hankins, W. G., Garcia, J., & Rusiniak, K. W. Dissociation of odor and taste in baitshyness. **Behavioral Biology**, 1973, **8**, 407-419.

289. Hankins, W. G., Garcia, J., & Rusiniak, K. W. Cortical lesions: Flavor illness and noise-shock conditioning. **Behavioral Biology**, 1974, **10**, 173-181.

290. Hargrave, G. E., & Bolles, R. C. Rat's aversion to flavors following induced illness. **Psychonomic Science**, 1971, **23**, 91-92.

291. Harlow, H. F. Effects of radiation on the central nervous system and on behavior: General survey. In T. J. Haley & R. S. Snider (Eds.), **Response of the Nervous System to Ionizing Radiation**. New York: Academic Press, 1962, 627-644.

292. Haroutunian, V., & Riccio, D. C. Acquisition of rotation-induced taste aversion as a function of drinking-treatment delay. **Physiological Psychology**, 1975, **3**, 273-277.

293. Harriman, A. E., & Kare, M. R. Preference for sodium chloride over lithium chloride by adrenalectomized rats. **American Journal of Physiology**, 1964, **207**, 941-943.

294. Harriman, A. E., Nance, D. M., & Milner, J. S. Discrimination between equimolar NaCl and LiCl solutions by anosmic, adrenalectomized rats. **Physiology and Behavior**, 1968, **3**, 887-889.

295. Hawkins, R., III. Learning to initiate and terminate meals: Theoretical, clinical, and developmental aspects. In L. M. Barker, M. R. Best, & M. Domjan (Eds.), **Learning Mechanisms in Food Selection**. Waco: Baylor University Press, 1977.

296. Hennessy, J. W., Smotherman, W. P., & Levine, S. Conditioned taste aversion and the pituitary-adrenal system. **Behavioral Biology**, 1976, **16**, 413-424.

297. Hinde, R., & Stevenson-Hinde, J. (Eds.). **Constraints on Learning**. London: Academic Press, 1973.

298. Hobbs, S. H., & Elkins, R. L. Baitshyness retention in rats with olfactory-bulb ablations. **Physiological Psychology**, 1976, **4**, 391-394.

299. Hobbs, S. H., Clingerman, H., & Elkins, R. L. Illness-induced taste aversions in normal and bulbectomized hamsters. **Physiology and Behavior**, 1976, **17**, 235-238.

300. Hobbs, S. H., Elkins, R. L., & Peacock, L. J. Taste-aversion conditioning in rats with septal lesions. **Behavioral Biology**, 1974, **11**, 239-245.

301. Hogan, J. A. How young chicks learn to recognize food. In R. A. Hinde & J. Stevenson-Hinde (Eds.), **Constraints on Learning**. London: Academic Press, 1973, 119-139.

302. Hogan, J. A. Development of food recognition in young chicks: I. Maturation and nutrition. **Journal of Comparative and Physiological Psychology**, 1973, **83**, 355-366.

303. Hogan, J. A. Development of food recognition in young chicks: II. Learned associations over long delays. **Journal of Comparative and Physiological Psychology**, 1973, **83**, 367-373.

304. Hogan, J. A. Development of food recognition in young chicks: III. Discrimination. **Journal of Comparative and Physiological Psychology**, 1975, **89**, 95-104.

305. Hogan, J. A. The ontogeny of food preferences in chicks and other animals. In L. M. Barker, M. R. Best, & M. Domjan (Eds.), **Learning Mechanisms in Food Selection**. Waco, Texas: Baylor University Press, 1977.

306. Holland, P. C., & Rescorla, R. A. The effect of two ways of devaluing the unconditioned stimulus first- and second-order appetitive conditioning. **Journal of Experimental Psychology: Animal Behavior Processes**, 1975, **1**, 355-363.

307. Holman, E. W. Temporal properties of gustatory spontaneous alternation in rats. **Journal of Comparative and Physiological Psychology**, 1973, **85**, 536-539.

308. Holman, E. W. Immediate and delayed reinforcers for flavor preferences in rats. **Learning and Motivation**, 1975, **6**, 91-100.

309. Holman, E. W. Some conditions for the dissociation of consummatory and instrumental behavior in rats. **Learning and Motivation**, 1975, **6**, 358-366.

310. Holman, E. W. The effect of drug habituation before and after taste aversion learning in rats. **Animal Learning and Behavior**, 1976, **4**, 329-332.

311. Holman, R. B., Hoyland, V., & Shillito, E. E. The failure of p-chloro-phenylalanine to affect voluntary alcohol consumption in rats. **British Journal of Pharmacology**, 1975, **53**, 299-304.

312. Holt, J., Antin, J., Gibbs, J., Young, R. C., & Smith, G. P. Cholecystokinin does not produce bait shyness in rats. **Physiology and Behavior**, 1974, **12**, 497-498.

313. Horowitz, G. P., & Whitney, G. Alcohol-induced conditional aversion: Genotypic specificity in mice (*Mus musculus*). **Journal of Comparative and Physiological Psychology**, 1975, **89**, 340-346.

314. Howard, W. E., & Marsh, R. E. Mestranol as a reproductive inhibitor in rats and moles. **The Journal of Wildlife Management**, 1969, **33**, 403-408.

315. Howard, W. E., Palmateer, S. D., & Nachman, M. Aversion to strychnine sulfate by Norway rats, roof rats, and pocket gophers. **Toxicology and Applied Pharmacology**, 1968, **12**, 229-241.

316. Hulse, E. V., & Dempsey, B. C. Radiation conditioning: A specific aversion to feeding after a single exposure to 50R. **International Journal of Radiation Biology**, 1964, **8**, 97-99.

317. Hunt, E. L., & Kimeldorf, D. J. The humoral factor in radiation-induced motivation. **Radiation Research**, 1967, **30**, 404-419.

318. Hunt, E. L., Carroll, H. W., & Kimeldorf, D. J. Humoral mediation of radiation-induced motivation in parabiont rats. **Science**, 1965, **150**, 1747-1748.

319. Hutchison, S. L., Jr. Taste aversion in albino rats using centrifugal spin as an unconditioned stimulus. **Psychological Reports**, 1973, **33**, 467-470.

320. Ionescu, E., & Bures, J. Ontogenetic development of the conditioned food aversion in chickens. **Behavioral Processes**, in press.

321. Ionescu, E., Buresova, O., & Bures, J. The significance of gustatory and visual cues for conditioned food aversion in rats and chickens. **Physiologia Bohemoslovaca**, 1975, **24**, 58.

322. Jacquet, Y. F. Conditioned aversion during morphine maintenance in mice and rats. **Physiology and Behavior**, 1973, **11**, 527-541.

323. Johnson, C., Beaton, R., & Hall, K. Poison-based avoidance learning in nonhuman primates: Use of visual cues. **Physiology and Behavior**, 1975, **14**, 403-407.

324. Johnston, R. E., & Zahorik, D. M. Taste aversions to sexual attractants. **Science**, 1975, **189**, 893-894.

325. Kakolewski, J. W., & Valenstein, E. S. Glucose and saccharin preference in alloxan diabetic rats. **Journal of Comparative and Physiological Psychology**, 1969, **68**, 31-37.

326. Kalat, J. W. Taste-aversion learning in dead rats. **The Worm Runner's Digest**, 1973, **15**, 59-60.

327. Kalat, J. W. Taste salience depends on novelty, not concentration, in taste-aversion learning in the rat. **Journal of Comparative and Physiological Psychology**, 1974, **86**, 47-50.

328. Kalat, J. W. Taste-aversion learning in infant guinea pigs. **Developmental Psychobiology**, 1975, **8**, 383-387.

329. Kalat, J. W. Should taste-aversion learning experiments control duration or volume of drinking on the training day? **Animal Learning and Behavior**, 1976, **4**, 96-98.

330. Kalat, J. W. Food aversion learning: Biological significance. In N. W. Milgram, L. Krames, & T. Alloway (Eds.), **Food Aversion Learning**. New York: Plenum Press, in press.

331. Kalat, J. W. Status of "learned safety" or "learned non-correlation" as a mechanism in taste aversion learning. In L. M. Barker, M. R. Best, & M. Domjan (Eds.), **Learning Mechanisms in Food Selection**. Waco, Texas: Baylor University Press, 1977.

332. Kalat, J. W., & Rozin, P. "Salience": A factor which can override temporal contiguity in taste-aversion learning. **Journal of Comparative and Physiological Psychology**, 1970, **71**, 192-197.

333. Kalat, J. W., & Rozin, P. Role of interference in taste-aversion learning. **Journal of Comparative and Physiological Psychology**, 1971, **77**, 53-58.

334. Kalat, J. W., & Rozin, P. You can lead a rat to poison but you can't make him think. In M. E. P. Seligman & J. L. Hager (Eds.), **Biological Boundaries of Learning**. New York: Appleton-Century-Crofts, 1972, 115-122.

335. Kalat, J. W., & Rozin, P. "Learned safety" as a mechanism in long-delay taste-aversion learning in rats. **Journal of Comparative and Physiological Psychology**, 1973, **83**, 198-207.

336. Kanarek, R. B., Adams, K. S., & Mayer, J. Conditioned taste aversion in the Mongolian gerbil (*Meriones unguiculatus*). **Bulletin of the Psychonomic Society**, 1975, **6**, 303-305.

337. Kay, E. J. Aversive effects of repeated injections of THC in rats. **Psychological Reports**, 1975, **37**, 1051-1054.

338. Kemble, E. D., & Nagel, J. A. Failure to form a learned taste aversion in rats with amygdaloid lesions. **Bulletin of the Psychonomic Society**, 1973, **2**, 155-156.

339. Kendler, K., Hennessy, J. W., Smotherman, W. P., & Levine, S. An ACTH effect on recovery from conditioned taste aversion. **Behavioral Biology**, 1976, **17**, 225-229.

340. Kesner, R. P., Berman, R. F., Burton, B., & Hankins, W. G. Effects of electrical stimulation of amygdala upon neophobia and taste aversion. **Behavioral Biology**, 1975, **13**, 349-358.

341. Kimeldorf, D. J. Radiation-conditioned behavior. In T. J. Haley & R. S. Snider (Eds.), **Response of the Nervous System to Ionizing Radiation**. New York: Academic Press, 1962, 683-690.

342. Kimeldorf, D. J., & Hunt, E. L. Conditioned behavior and the radiation stimulus. In T. J. Haley & R. S. Snider (Eds.), **Response of the Nervous System to Ionizing Radiation**. Boston: Little, Brown, 1964, 652-661.

343. Kimeldorf, D. J., & Hunt, E. L. **Ionizing Radiation: Neural Function and Behavior**. New York: Academic Press, 1965.

344. Kimeldorf, D. J., Garcia, J., & Rudadeau, D. O. Radiation-induced conditioned avoidance behavior in rats, mice, and cats. **Radiation Research**, 1960, **12**, 710-718.

345. Klein, S. B., Mikulka, P. J., & Hamel, K. Influence of sucrose preexposure on acquisition of a conditioned aversion. **Behavioral Biology**, 1976, **16**, 99-104.

346. Klein, S. B., Barter, M. J., Murphy, A. L., & Richardson, J. H. Aversion to low doses of mercuric chloride in rats. **Physiological Psychology**, 1974, **2**, 397-400.

347. Klein, S. B., Mikulka, P. J., Domato, G. C., & Hallstead, C. Retention of internal experience in juvenile and adult rats. **Physiological Psychology**, in press.

348. Klein, S. B., Domato, G. C., Hallstead, C., Stephens, I., & Mikulka, P. J. Acquisition of a conditioned aversion as a function of age and measurement technique. **Physiological Psychology**, 1975, **3**, 379-384.

349. Kral, P. A. Interpolation of electroconvulsive shock during CS-US interval as an impediment to the conditioning of taste aversion. **Psychonomic Science**, 1970, **19**, 36-37.

350. Kral, P. A. Electroconvulsive shock during the taste-illness interval: Evidence for induced dissociation. **Physiology and Behavior**, 1971, **7**, 667-670.

351. Kral, P. A. ECS between tasting and illness: Effects of current parameters on a taste aversion. **Physiology and Behavior**, 1971, **7**, 779-782.

352. Kral, P. A. Effects of scopolamine injection during CS-US interval on conditioning. **Psychological Reports**, 1971, **28**, 690.

353. Kral, P. A. A localized ECS impedes taste aversion learning. **Behavioral Biology**, 1972, **7**, 761-765.

354. Kral, P. A., & Beggerly, H. D. Electroconvulsive shock impedes association formation: Conditioned taste aversion paradigm. **Physiology and Behavior**, 1973, **10**, 145-147.

355. Kral, P. A., & St. Omer, V. V. Beta-adrenergic receptor involvement in the mediation of learned taste aversions. **Psychopharmacologia**, 1972, **26**, 79-83.

356. Krames, L., Milgram, N. W., & Christie, D. P. Predatory aggression: Differential suppression of killing and feeding. **Behavioral Biology**, 1973, **9**, 641-647.

357. Krane, R. V., & Wagner, A. R. Taste aversion learning with a delayed shock US: Implications for the "generality of the laws of learning." **Journal of Comparative and Physiological Psychology**, 1975, **88**, 882-889.

358. Krane, R. V., Sinnamon, H. M., & Thomas, G. J. Conditioned taste aversions and neophobia in rats with hippocampal lesions. **Journal of Comparative and Physiological Psychology**, 1976, **90**, 680-693.

359. Kulkosky, P. J., Riley, A. L., Woods, S. C., & Krinsky, R. Interaction of brain stimulation and conditioned taste aversion: Osmotically induced drinking. **Physiological Psychology**, 1975, **3**, 297-299.

360. Kverno, N. B., & Hood, G. A. Evaluation procedures and standards chemical screening and development for forest wildlife damage. U.S. Fish and

Wildlife Service, Wildlife Research Center, Denver, 1963, 1-59.

361. Lavin, M. J. The establishment of flavor-flavor associations using a sensory preconditioning training procedure. **Learning and Motivation**, 1976, **7**, 173-183.

362. Leary, R. W. Food-preference changes of monkeys subjected to low-level irradiation. **Journal of Comparative and Physiological Psychology**, 1955, **48**, 343-346.

363. LeBlanc, A. E., & Cappell, H. Attenuation of punishing effects of morphine and amphetamine by chronic prior treatment. **Journal of Comparative and Physiological Psychology**, 1974, **87**, 691-698.

364. LeBlanc, A. E., & Cappell, H. Antagonism of morphine-induced aversive conditioning by naloxone. **Pharmacology, Biochemistry, and Behavior**, 1975, **3**, 185-188.

365. Lehr, P. P., & Nachman, M. Lateralization of learned taste aversion by cortical spreading depression. **Physiology and Behavior**, 1973, **10**, 79-83.

366. Le Magnen, J. La Facilitation differentielle des reflexes d'ingestion par l'odour alimentaire. **Compte Rendus des Seances de la Societe de Biologie et de ses Filiales** (Paris), 1963, **157**, 1165-1170.

367. Le Magnen, J. Habits and food intake. In C. F. Code (Ed.), **Handbook of Physiology (Section 6): Alimentary Canal (Vol. 1): Control of Food and Water Intake**. Washington, D.C.: American Physiological Society, 1967, 11-20.

368. Le Magnen, J. Olfaction and nutrition. In L. M. Beidler (Ed.), **Handbook of Sensory Physiology (Vol. VI): Chemical Senses (Part 1): Olfaction**. New York: Springer-Verlag, 1971, 465-482.

369. Lester, D. M., Nachman, M., & Le Magnen, J. Aversive conditioning by ethanol in the rat. **Quarterly Journal of Studies on Alcohol**, 1970, **31**, 578-586.

370. Lett, B. T. Delayed reward learning: Disproof of the traditional theory. **Learning and Motivation**, 1973, **4**, 237-246.

371. Lett, B. T. Visual discrimination learning with a 1-min delay of reward. **Learning and Motivation**, 1974, **5**, 174-181.

372. Lett, B. T. Long delay learning in the t-maze. **Learning and Motivation**, 1975, **6**, 80-90.

373. Lett, B. T. Long delay learning: Implications for learning and memory theory. In N. S. Sutherland (Ed.), **Tutorial Essays in Experimental Psychology (Vol. 2)**, in press.

374. Lett, B. T., & Harley, C. W. Stimulation of lateral hypothalamus during sickness attenuates learned food aversions. **Physiology and Behavior**, 1974, **12**, 79-83.

375. Le Van, H., & Moos, W. S. An effect of DMSO on post-irradiation saccharin avoidance in mice. **Experientia**, 1967, **23**, 276-277.

376. Le Van, H., & Moos, W. S. Possible effects of radiation produced hydrogen peroxide on post-irradiation aversion in mice. **Experientia**, 1967, **23**, 749-751.

377. Le Van, H., Moos, W. S., & Hebron, D. L. Direct and indirect effect of X-irradiation on conditioned avoidance behavior. **Medicina Experimentalis**, 1968, **18**, 161-168.

378. Le Van, H., Moos, W. S., & Mason, H. C. Attenuation of transferability of radiation-induced behavior by dimethyl sulfoxide in mice. **Journal of Biological Psychology**, 1970, **12**, 41-44.

379. Levine, M. J., & Brownstein, P. M. Replication report: I. Maternal rations affect the food preferences of weanling rats. **Bulletin of the Psychonomic Society**, 1976, **8**, 230.

380. Levy, C. J., Ervin, F. R., & Garcia, J. Effect of serum from irradiated rats on gastrointestinal function. **Nature**, 1970, **225**, 463-464.

381. Levy, C. J., Carroll, M. E., Smith, J. C., & Hofer, K. G. Antihistamines block radiation-induced taste aversions. **Science**, 1974, **186**, 1044-1046.

382. Levy, C. J., Carroll, M. E., Smith, J. C., & Hofer, K. G. Reply to Sessions. **Science**, 1975, **190**, 403.

383. Liebling, D. S., Eisner, J. D., Gibbs, J., & Smith, G. P. Intestinal satiety in rats. **Journal of Comparative and Physiological Psychology**, 1975, **89**, 955-965.

384. Lindsey, G. P., & Best, P. J. Overshadowing of the less salient of two novel fluids in a taste-aversion paradigm. **Physiological Psychology**, 1973, **1**, 13-15.

385. Lorden, J. F. Effects of lesions of the gustatory neocortex on taste aversion learning in the rat. **Journal of Comparative and Physiological Psychology**, 1976, **90**, 665-679.

386. Lorden, J. F., Kenfield, M., & Braun, J. J. Response suppression to odors paired with toxicosis. **Learning and Motivation**, 1970, **1**, 391-400.

387. Lovett, D., & Booth, D. A. Four effects of exogenous insulin on food intake. **Quarterly Journal of Experimental Psychology**, 1970, **22**, 406-419.

388. Lovett, D., Goodchild, P., & Booth, D. A. Depression of intake of nutrient by association of its odor with effects of insulin. **Psychonomic Science**, 1968, **11**, 27-28.

389. Lowe, W. C., & O'Boyle, M. Suppression of cricket killing and eating in laboratory mice following lithium chloride injections. **Physiology and Behavior**, 1976, **17**, 427-430.

390. Luongo, A. F. Stimulus selection in discriminative taste-aversion learning in the rat. **Animal Learning and Behavior**, 1976, **4**, 225-230.

391. MacKay, B. Conditioned food aversion produced by toxicosis in Atlantic cod. **Behavioral Biology**, 1974, **12**, 347-355.

392. Mackintosh, N. J. **The Psychology of Animal Learning**. London: Academic Press, 1974.

393. Maier, S. F., Zahorik, D. M., & Albin, R. W. Relative novelty of solid and liquid diet during thiamine deficiency determines development of thiamine-specific hunger. **Journal of Comparative and Physiological Psychology**, 1971, **74**, 254-262.

394. Malone, P. E., & Cox, V. C. Development of taste aversions to individual components of a compound gustatory stimulus. **Communications in Behavioral Biology**, 1971, **6**, 341-344.

395. Manning, F. J., & Jackson, M. C., Jr. Enduring effects of morphine pellets revealed by conditioned taste aversion. **Psychopharmacologia**, in press.

396. Margules, D. L. Alpha-adrenergic receptors in the hypothalamus for the suppression of feeding behavior by satiety. **Journal of Comparative and Physiological Psychology**, 1970, **73**, 1-12.

397. Margules, D. L. Beta-adrenergic receptors in the hypothalamus for learned and unlearned taste aversions. **Journal of Comparative and Physiological Psychology**, 1970, **73**, 13-21.

398. Marsh, R. E. Recent and future developments in rodenticides. **Bulletin of the Society of Vector Ecologists**, 1975, **2**, 1-7.

399. Marsh, R. E., & Howard, W. E. Evaluation of mestranol as a reproductive inhibitor of Norway rats in garbage dumps. **The Journal of Wildlife Management**, 1969, **33**, 133-138.

400. Marsh, R. E., & Howard, W. E. New perspectives in rodent and mammal control. In J. M. Sharpley & A. M. Kaplan (Eds.), **Proceedings of the Third International Biodegradation Symposium**. London: Applied Science Publishers, Ltd., 1975, 317-329.

603

401. Marsh, R. E., Passof, P. C., & Howard, W. E. Anticoagulants and alpha-naphthylthiourea to protect conifer seeds. In H. C. Black (Ed.), **Wildlife and Forest Management in the Pacific Northwest**. Oregon State University School of Forestry, 1974, 75-83.

402. Martin, G. M., & Storlien, L. H. Anorexia and conditioned taste aversions in the rat. **Learning and Motivation**, 1976, 7, 274-282.

403. Martin, G. M., Bellingham, W. P., & Storlien, L. H. The effects of varied color experience on chickens formation of color and texture aversions. **Physiology and Behavior**, in press.

404. Martin, J. C. Spatial avoidance in a paradigm in which ionizing irradiation precedes spatial confinement. **Radiation Research**, 1966, 27, 284-289.

405. Martin, J. C. Saccharin preference and aversion as a function of irradiation and supplier in the albino rat. **Psychonomic Science**, 1968, 13, 251-252.

406. Martin, J. C., & Ellinwood, E. H., Jr. Conditioned aversion to a preferred solution following methamphetamine injections. **Psychopharmacologia**, 1973, 29, 253-261.

407. Martin, J. C., & Ellinwood, E. H., Jr. Conditioned aversion in spatial paradigms following methamphetamine injection. **Psychopharmacologia**, 1974, 36, 323-335.

408. McFarland, D. J. Stimulus relevance and homeostasis. In R. Hinde & J. Stevenson-Hinde (Eds.), **Constraints on Learning**. London: Academic Press, 1973, 141-155.

409. McGowan, B. K., Hankins, W. G., & Garcia, J. Limbic lesions and control of the internal and external environment. **Behavioral Biology**, 1972, 7, 841-852.

410. McGowan, B. K., Garcia, J., Ervin, F. R., & Schwartz, J. Effects of septal lesions on bait-shyness in the rat. **Physiology and Behavior**, 1969, 4, 907-909.

411. McKeever, S. Compound 1080 and forest regeneration: Characteristics of the poison in relation to bait shyness, poison shyness, toxicity to rodents, and phytotoxicity to conifer seeds. State of California, Resources Agency, Department of Conservation, Division of Forestry, 1974.

412. McLaurin, W. A. Postirradiation saccharin avoidance in rats as a function of the interval between ingestion and exposure. **Journal of Comparative and Physiological Psychology**, 1964, 57, 316-317.

413. McLaurin, W. A., & Scarborough, B. B. Extension of the interstimulus interval in saccharin avoidance conditioning. **Radiation Research**, 1963, 20, 317-324.

414. McLaurin, W. A., Farley, J. A., & Scarborough, B. B. Inhibitory effect of preirradiation saccharin habituation on conditioned avoidance behavior. **Radiation Research**, 1963, 18, 473-478.

415. McLaurin, W. A., Scarborough, B. B., & Farley, J. A. Delay of postirradiation test fluids: A factor in saccharin avoidance behavior. **Radiation Research**, 1964, 22, 45-52.

416. McLaurin, W. A., Farley, J. A., Scarborough, B. B., & Rawlings, T. D. Post-irradiation saccharin avoidance with non-coincident stimuli. **Psychological Reports**, 1964, 14, 507-512.

417. Middleton, A. D. Rural rat control. In D. Chitty (Ed.), **Control of Rats and Mice (Vol. 2)**. Oxford: Clarendon Press, 1954, 414-418.

418. Mikulka, P. J., Leard, B., & Klein, S. B. Illness alone (US) exposure as a source of interference with the acquisition and retention of a taste aversion. **Journal of Experimental Psychology: Animal Behavior Processes**, in press.

419. Mikulka, P. J., Krone, P. D., Rapisardi, P. L., & Kirby, R. H. Discrimination between deionized water and D_2O in a runway using olfaction in the rat. **Physiological Psychology**, 1975, 3, 92-94.

420. Milgram, N. W., Krames, L., & Alloway, T. (Eds.). **Food Aversion Learning**. New York: Plenum Press, in press.

421. Milgram, N. W., Krames, L., & Caudarella, M. Control of interspecific aggression by toxicosis. In N. W. Milgram, L. Krames, & T. Alloway (Eds.), **Food Aversion Learning**. New York: Plenum Press, in press.

422. Miller, C. R., Elkins, R. L., & Peacock, L. J. Disruption of a radiation-induced preference shift by hippocampal lesions. **Physiology and Behavior**, 1971, 6, 283-285.

423. Miller, C. R., Elkins, R. L., Fraser, J., Peacock, L. J., & Hobbs, S. H. Taste aversion and passive avoidance in rats with hippocampal lesions. **Physiological Psychology**, 1975, 3, 123-126.

424. Miller, L. L., & Drew, W. G. Cannabis: Review of behavioral effects in animals. **Psychological Bulletin**, 1974, 81, 401-417.

425. Millner, J. R., & Palfai, T. Metrazol impairs conditioned aversion produced by LiCl: A time dependent effect. **Pharmacology, Biochemistry, and Behavior**, 1975, 3, 201-204.

426. Mineka, S., Seligman, M. E. P., Hetrick, M., & Zuelzer, K. Poisoning and conditioned drinking. **Journal of Comparative and Physiological Psychology**, 1972, 79, 377-384.

427. Mitchell, D. Experiments on neophobia in wild and laboratory rats: A reevaluation. **Journal of Comparative and Physiological Psychology**, 1976, 90, 190-197.

428. Mitchell, D., Fairbanks, M., & Laycock, J. D. Suppression of neophobia by chlorpromazine in wild rats. **Behavioral Biology**, in press.

429. Mitchell, D., Kirschbaum, E. H., & Perry, R. L. Effects of neophobia and habituation on the poison-induced avoidance of exteroceptive stimuli in the rat. **Journal of Experimental Psychology: Animal Behavior Processes**, 1975, 104, 47-55.

430. Mitchell, D., Parker, L. F., & Johnson, R. Absence of a generalization decrement in the poison-induced avoidance of interoceptive stimuli in the rat. **Physiological Psychology**, 1976, 4, 121-123.

431. Mitchell, D., Parker, L. F., & Woods, S. C. Cyclophosphamide-induced sodium appetite and hyponatremia in the rat. **Pharmacology, Biochemistry, and Behavior**, 1974, 2, 627-630.

432. Moore, M. J., & Capretta, P. J. Changes in colored or flavored food preferences in chickens as a function of shock. **Psychonomic Science**, 1968, 12, 195-196.

433. Morris, D. D., & Smith, J. C. X-ray-conditioned saccharin aversion induced during the immediate postexposure period. **Radiation Research**, 1964, 21, 513-519.

434. Morrison, G. R., & Collyer, R. Taste-mediated conditioned aversion to an exteroceptive stimulus following LiCl poisoning. **Journal of Comparative and Physiological Psychology**, 1974, 86, 51-55.

435. Morrison, J. H., Olton, D. S., Goldberg, A. M., & Silbergeld, E. K. Alterations in consummatory behavior of mice produced by dietary exposure to inorganic lead. **Developmental Psychology**, 1975, 8, 389-396.

436. Mountjoy, P. T., & Roberts, A. E. Radiation produced avoidance to morphine. **Psychonomic Science**, 1967, 9, 427-428.

604

437. Murphy, L. R., & Brown, T. S. Hippocampal lesions and learned taste aversion. **Physiological Psychology**, 1974, **2**, 60-64.

438. Nachman, M. Learned aversion to the taste of lithium chloride and generalization to other salts. **Journal of Comparative and Physiological Psychology**, 1963, **56**, 343-349.

439. Nachman, M. Taste preferences for lithium chloride by adrenalectomized rats. **American Journal of Physiology**, 1963, **205**, 219-221.

440. Nachman, M. Learned taste and temperature aversions due to lithium chloride sickness after temporal delays. **Journal of Comparative and Physiological Psychology**, 1970, **73**, 22-30.

441. Nachman, M. Limited effects of electroconvulsive shock on memory of taste stimulation. **Journal of Comparative and Physiological Psychology**, 1970, **73**, 31-37.

442. Nachman, M. Stimulus properties. In N. W. Milgram, L. Krames, & T. Alloway (Eds.), **Food Aversion Learning**. New York: Plenum Press, in press.

443. Nachman, M., & Ashe, J. H. Learned taste aversions in rats as a function of dosage, concentration, and route of administration of LiCl. **Physiology and Behavior**, 1973, **10**, 73-78.

444. Nachman, M., & Ashe, J. H. Effects of basolateral amygdala lesions on neophobia, learned taste aversions, and sodium appetite in rats. **Journal of Comparative and Physiological Psychology**, 1974, **87**, 622-643.

445. Nachman, M., & Cole, L. P. Role of taste in specific hungers. In L. M. Beidler (Ed.), **Handbook of Sensory Physiology (Vol. IV): Chemical Senses (Part 2): Taste**. New York: Springer-Verlag, 1971, 337-362.

446. Nachman, M., & Hartley, P. L. Role of illness in producing learned taste aversions in rats: A comparison of several rodenticides. **Journal of Comparative and Physiological Psychology**, 1975, **89**, 1010-1018.

447. Nachman, M., & Jones, D. R. Learned taste aversions over long delays in rats: The role of learned safety. **Journal of Comparative and Physiological Psychology**, 1974, **86**, 949-956.

448. Nachman, M., Lester, D., & Le Magnen, J. Alcohol aversion in the rat: Behavioral assessment of noxious drug effects. **Science**, 1970, **168**, 1244-1246.

449. Nachman, M., Rauschenberger, J., & Ashe, J. H. Studies of learned aversions using non-gustatory stimuli. In L. M. Barker, M. R. Best, & M. Domjan (Eds.), **Learning Mechanisms in Food Selection**. Waco, Texas: Baylor University Press, 1977.

450. Nakajima, S. Conditioned aversion of water produced by cycloheximide injection. **Physiological Psychology**, 1974, **2**, 484-486.

451. Nathan, B. A., & Vogel, J. R. Taste aversions induced by d-amphetamine: Dose-response relationship. **Bulletin of the Psychonomic Society**, 1975, **6**, 287-288.

452. Nowlis, G. H. Conditioned stimulus intensity and acquired alimentary aversions in the rat. **Journal of Comparative and Physiological Psychology**, 1974, **86**, 1173-1184.

453. O'Boyle, M., Looney, T. A., & Cohen, P. S. Suppression and recovery of mouse killing in rats following immediate lithium-chloride injections. **Bulletin of the Psychonomic Society**, 1973, **1**, 250-252.

454. Omura, K., Takagi, S. F., & Harada, O. On the mechanism of the repellant action of naramycin to rats. **Gunma Journal of Medical Sciences**, 1961, **10**, 217-227.

455. Opitz, K. Effect of fenfluramine on alcohol and saccharin consumption in the rat. **South African Medical Journal**, 1972, **46**, 742-744.

456. Overall, J. E., Brown, W. L., & Logie, L. C. Instrumental behaviour of albino rats in response to incident X-radiation. **British Journal of Radiology**, 1959, **32**, 411-414.

457. Overmann, S. R. Dietary self-selection by animals. **Psychological Bulletin**, 1976, **83**, 218-235.

458. Pain, J. F., & Booth, D. A. Toxiphobia for odors. **Psychonomic Science**, 1968, **10**, 363-364.

459. Parker, L. A., & Revusky, S. Failure of Sprague-Dawley rats to transfer taste-aversions or preferences by odor-marking the spout. **Behavioral Biology**, 1975, **15**, 383-387.

460. Parker, L. F. "Neophobia": The effects of initial duration of exposure on subsequent saccharin intake in rats. **Bulletin of the Psychonomic Society**, 1976, **8**, 298-300.

461. Parker, L. F., & Radow, B. L. Morphine-like physical dependence: A pharmacologic method for drug assessment using the rat. **Pharmacology, Biochemistry, and Behavior**, 1974, **2**, 613-618.

462. Parker, L. F., & Radow, B. L. Effects of parachlorophenylalanine on ethanol self-selection in the rat. **Pharmacology, Biochemistry, and Behavior**, 1976, **4**, 535-540.

463. Parker, L. F., Failor, A., & Weidman, K. Conditioned preferences in the rat with an unnatural need state: Morphine withdrawal. **Journal of Comparative and Physiological Psychology**, 1973, **82**, 294-300.

464. Passof, P. C., Marsh, R. E., & Howard, W. E. Alpha-naphthylthiourea as a conditioning repellant for protecting conifer seed. In W. V. Johnson (Ed.), **Proceedings: Sixth Vertebrate Pest Conference**. Anaheim, California, 1974.

465. Peacock, L. J., & Watson, J. A. Radiation-induced aversion to alcohol. **Science**, 1964, **143**, 1462-1463.

466. Peck, J. H., & Ader, R. Illness-induced taste aversion under states of deprivation and satiation. **Animal Learning and Behavior**, 1974, **2**, 6-8.

467. Perry, N. W., Jr. Avoidance conditioning of NaCl with X-irradiation of the rat. **Radiation Research**, 1963, **20**, 471-476.

468. Peters, R. H., & Reich, M. J. Effects of ventromedial hypothalamic lesions on conditioned sucrose aversions in rats. **Journal of Comparative and Physiological Psychology**, 1973, **84**, 502-506.

469. Pilcher, C. W., & Stolerman, I. P. Conditioned food aversions for assessing precipitated morphine abstinence in rats. **Pharmacology, Biochemistry, and Behavior**, 1976, **4**, 159-163.

470. Prakash, I., & Jain, A. P. Bait shyness of two gerbils, *Tatera indica* Hardwicke and *Meriones hurrianae* Jerdon. **Annals of Applied Biology**, 1971, **69**, 169-172.

471. Prakash, I., Rena, B. D., & Jain, A. P. Bait shyness in three species of *Rattus*. **Zeitschrift fur Angewandte Zoologie**, in press.

472. Puerto, A., Deutsch, J. A., Molina, F., & Roll, P. L. Rapid rewarding effects of intragastric injections. **Behavioral Biology**, 1976, **18**, 123-134.

473. Puerto, A., Deutsch, J. A., Molina, F., & Roll, P. L. Rapid discrimination of rewarding nutrient by the upper gastrointestinal tract. **Science**, 1976, **192**, 485-487.

474. Ralph, T. L., & Balagura, S. Effect of intracranial electrical stimulation on the primary learned aversion to LiCl and the generalized aversion to NaCl. **Journal of Comparative and Physiological Psychology**, 1974, **86**, 664-669.

475. Revusky, S. Aversion to sucrose produced by contingent X-irradiation: Temporal and dosage parameters. **Journal of Comparative and Physiological Psychology**, 1968, **65**, 17-22.

476. Revusky, S. The role of intereference in association over a delay. In V. Honig (Ed.), **Animal Memory.** New York: Academic Press, 1971. 155-213.

477. Revusky, S. Some laboratory paradigms for chemical aversion treatment of alcoholism. **Journal of Behavior Therapy and Experimental Psychiatry,** 1973, **4,** 15-17.

478. Revusky, S. Long-delay learning in rats: A black-white discrimination. **Bulletin of the Psychonomic Society,** 1974, **4,** 526-528.

479. Revusky, S. Learning as a general process with an emphasis on data from feeding experiments. In N. W. Milgram, L. Krames, & T. M. Alloway (Eds.), **Food Aversion Learning.** New York: Plenum Press, in press.

480. Revusky, S. The concurrent interference approach to delay learning. In L. M. Barker, M. R. Best, & M. Domjan (Eds.), **Learning Mechanisms in Food Selection.** Waco, Texas: Baylor University Press, 1977.

481. Revusky, S., & Bedarf, E. W. Association of illness with ingestion of novel foods. **Science,** 1967, **155,** 219-220.

482. Revusky, S., & De Venuto, F. Attempt to transfer aversion to saccharin solution by injection of RNA from trained to naive rats. **Journal of Biological Psychology,** 1967, **9,** 18-22.

483. Revusky, S., & Garcia, J. Learned associations over long delays. In G. H. Bower & J. T. Spence (Eds.), **Psychology of Learning and Motivation: Advances in Research and Theory (Vol. IV).** New York: Academic Press, 1970, 1-84.

484. Revusky, S., & Gorry, T. Flavor aversions produced by contingent drug injections: Relative effectiveness of apomorphine, emetine, and lithium. **Behavior Research and Therapy,** 1973, **11,** 403-409.

485. Revusky, S., & Parker, L. A. Aversions to unflavored water and cup drinking produced by delayed sickness. **Journal of Experimental Psychology: Animal Behavior Processes,** 1976, **2,** 342-353.

486. Revusky, S., & Taukulis, H. Effects of alcohol and lithium habituation on the development of alcohol aversions through contingent lithium injection. **Behavior Research and Therapy,** 1975, **13,** 1-4.

487. Revusky, S., Taukulis, H. K., & Peddle, C. Learned associations between pentobarbital sedation and later lithium sickness in rats. **Pharmacology, Biochemistry, and Behavior,** in press.

488. Revusky, S., Parker, L. A., Coombes, J., & Coombes, S. Flavor aversion learning: Extinction of the aversion to an interfering flavor after conditioning does not affect the aversion to the reference flavor. **Behavioral Biology,** in press.

489. Revusky, S., Parker, L. A., Coombes, J., & Coombes, S. Rat data which suggest alcoholic beverages should be swallowed during chemical aversion therapy, not just tasted. **Behavior Research and Therapy,** 1976, **14,** 189-194.

490. Richter, C. P. Taste and solubility of toxic compounds in poisoning rats and man. **Journal of Comparative and Physiological Psychology,** 1950, **43,** 358-374.

491. Richter, C. P. Experimentally produced behavior reactions to food poisoning in wild and domesticated rats. **Annals of the New York Academy of Sciences,** 1953, **56,** 225-239.

492. Riege, W. H. Possible olfactory transduction of radiation-induced aversion. **Psychonomic Science,** 1968, **12,** 303-304.

493. Riege, W. H. Disruption of radiation-induced aversion to saccharin by electroconvulsive shock. **Physiology and Behavior,** 1969, **4,** 157-161.

494. Rigter, H., & Popping, A. Hormonal influences on the extinction of conditioned taste aversion. **Psychopharmacologia,** 1976, **46,** 255-261.

495. Riley, A. L., & Baril, L. L. Conditioned taste aversions: A bibliography. **Animal Learning and Behavior,** 1976, **4,** 1S-13S.

496. Riley, A. L., & Clarke, C. M. Conditioned taste aversions: A bibliography. In L. M. Barker, M. R. Best, & M. Domjan (Eds.), **Learning Mechanisms in Food Selection.** Waco, Texas: Baylor University Press, 1977.

497. Riley, A. L., & Waxman, G. I. The social relevance of psychological research on animals: Conditioned taste aversion in the giant mutant rat. **The Worm Runner's Digest,** 1975, **17,** 121-122.

498. Riley, A. L., Jacobs, W. J., & LoLordo, V. M. Drug exposure and the acquisition and retention of a conditioned taste aversion. **Journal of Comparative and Physiological Psychology,** 1976, **90,** 799-807.

499. Rodgers, W., & Rozin, P. Novel food preferences in thiamine-deficient rats. **Journal of Comparative and Physiological Psychology,** 1966, **61,** 1-4.

500. Rohles, F. H., Overall, J. E., & Brown, W. L. Attempts to produce spatial avoidance as a result of exposure to X-radiation. **British Journal of Radiology,** 1959, **32,** 244-246.

501. Roll, D. L., & Smith, J. C. Conditioned taste aversion in anesthetized rats. In M. E. P. Seligman & J. L. Hager (Eds.), **Biological Boundaries of Learning.** New York: Appleton-Century-Crofts, 1972, 98-102.

502. Roll, D., Schaeffer, R. W., & Smith, J. C. Effects of a conditioned taste aversion on schedule-induced polydipsia. **Psychonomic Science,** 1969, **16,** 39-41.

503. Rolls, B. J., & Rolls, E. T. Effects of lesions in the basolateral amygdala on fluid intake in the rat. **Journal of Comparative and Physiological Psychology,** 1973, **83,** 240-247.

504. Rolls, E. T., & Rolls, B. J. Altered food preferences after lesions in the basolateral region of the amygdala in the rat. **Journal of Comparative and Physiological Psychology,** 1973, **83,** 248-259.

505. Rondeau, D. B., Jolicoeur, F. B., Kachanoff, R., Scherzer, P., & Wayner, M. J. Effects of phenobarbitol on ethanol intake in fluid deprived rats. **Pharmacology, Biochemistry, and Behavior,** 1975, **3,** 493-497.

506. Rossi, N. A., & Reid, L. D. Affective states associated with morphine injections. **Physiological Psychology,** 1976, **4,** 269-274.

507. Roth, S. R., Schwartz, M., Teitelbaum, P. Failure of recovered lateral hypothalamic rats to learn specific food aversions. **Journal of Comparative and Physiological Psychology,** 1973, **83,** 184-197.

508. Rozin, P. Thiamine specific hunger. In C. F. Code (Ed.), **Handbook of Physiology (Section 6): Alimentary Canal (Vol. 1): Control of Food and Water Intake.** Washington, D.C.: American Physiological Society, 1967, 411-431.

509. Rozin, P. Specific aversions as a component of specific hungers. **Journal of Comparative and Physiological Psychology,** 1967, **64,** 237-242.

510. Rozin, P. Specific aversions and neophobia resulting from vitamin deficiency or poisoning in half-wild and domestic rats. **Journal of Comparative and Physiological Psychology,** 1968, **66,** 82-88.

511. Rozin, P. Central or peripheral mediation of learning with long CS-US intervals in the feeding system. **Journal of Comparative and Physiological Psychology,** 1969, **67,** 421-429.

512. Rozin, P. Adaptive food sampling patterns in vitamin deficient rats. **Journal of Comparative and Physiological Psychology,** 1969, **69,** 126-132.

513. Rozin, P. Psychobiological and cultural determinants of food choice. In T. Silverstone (Ed.),

Appetite and Food Intake. Berlin: Dalham Konferenzen, 1976, 285-312.

514. Rozin, P. The selection of foods by rats, humans, and other animals. In J. Rosenblatt, R. A. Hinde, C. Beer, & E. Shaw (Eds.), **Advances in the Study of Behavior (Vol. VI)**. New York: Academic Press, 1976, 21-76.

515. Rozin, P. The significance of learning mechanisms in food selection: Some biology, psychology, and sociology of science. In L. M. Barker, M. R. Best, and M. Domjan (Eds.), **Learning Mechanisms in Food Selection**. Waco, Texas: Baylor University Press, 1977.

516. Rozin, P., & Kalat, J. W. Specific hungers and poison avoidance as adaptive specializations of learning. **Psychological Review**, 1971, **78**, 459-486.

517. Rozin, P., & Kalat, J. W. Learning as a situation-specific adaptation. In M. E. P. Seligman & J. L. Hager (Eds.), **Biological Boundaries of Learning**. New York: Appleton-Century-Crofts, 1972, 66-96.

518. Rozin, P., & Ree, P. Long extension of effective CS-US interval by anesthesia between CS and US. **Journal of Comparative and Physiological Psychology**, 1972, **80**, 43-48.

519. Rozin, P., & Rodgers, W. Novel-diet preferences in vitamin-deficient rats and rats recovered from vitamin deficiency. **Journal of Comparative and Physiological Psychology**, 1967, **63**, 421-428.

520. Rudy, J. W., Iwens, J., & Best, P. J. Pairing novel exteroceptive cues and illness reduce illness-induced taste aversions. **Journal of Experimental Psychology: Animal Behavior Processes**, in press.

521. Rusak, B., & Zucker, I. Fluid intake of rats in constant light and during feeding restricted to the light or dark portion of the illumination cycle. **Physiology and Behavior**, 1974, **13**, 91-100.

522. Rusiniak, K. W., Garcia, J., & Hankins, W. G. Bait shyness: Avoidance of the taste without escape from the illness in rats. **Journal of Comparative and Physiological Psychology**, 1976, **90**, 460-467.

523. Rusiniak, K. W., Gustavson, C. R., Hankins, W. G., & Garcia, J. Prey-lithium aversions II: Laboratory rats and ferrets. **Behavioral Biology**, 1976, **17**, 73-85.

524. Rzoska, J. Bait shyness: A study in rat behaviour. **The British Journal of Animal Behaviour**, 1953, **1**, 128-135.

525. Rzoska, J. The behavior of white rats towards poison baits. In D. Chitty (Ed.), **Control of Rats and Mice (Vol. 2)**. Oxford: Clarendon Press, 1954, 374-394.

526. Sanders, B. Reduction of alcohol selection by pargyline in mice. **Psychopharmacologia**, 1976, **46**, 159-162.

527. Sanders, B., Collins, A. C., & Wesley, V. H. Reduction of alcohol selection by pargyline in mice. **Psychopharmacologia**, 1976, **46**, 159-162.

528. Scarborough, B. B., & McLaurin, W. A. The effect of intraperitoneal injection on aversive behavior conditioning with X-irradiation. **Radiation Research**, 1961, **15**, 829-835.

529. Scarborough, B. B., & McLaurin, W. A. Saccharin avoidance conditioning instigated immediately after the exposure period. **Radiation Research**, 1964, **21**, 299-307.

530. Scarborough, B. B., Whaley, D. L., & Rogers, J. G. Saccharin avoidance behavior instigated by X-irradiation in backward conditioning paradigms. **Psychological Reports**, 1964, **14**, 475-481.

531. Schaeffer, A. A. Habit formation in frogs. **Journal of Animal Behavior**, 1911, **1**, 309-335.

532. Schaeffer, R. W., & Smith, J. C. Lick rates in rats exposed to gamma-irradiation. **Psychonomic Science**, 1966, **6**, 201-202.

533. Schaeffer, R. W., Hunt, E. L., & Kimeldorf, D. J. Application of Premack's theory to a classically conditioned sucrose aversion induced by X-ray exposure. **The Psychological Record**, 1967, **17**, 359-367.

534. Schwartz, B. On going back to nature: A review of Seligman and Hager's **Biological Boundaries of Learning**. **Journal of the Experimental Analysis of Behavior**, 1974, **21**, 183-198.

535. Schwartz, B. **Learning and Behavior Theory**. New York: W. W. Norton, 1977.

536. Schwartz, M., & Teitelbaum, P. Dissocation between learning and remembering in rats with lesions in the lateral hypothalamus. **Journal of Comparative and Physiological Psychology**, 1974, **87**, 384-398.

537. Seligman, M. E. P. On the generality of the laws of learning. **Psychological Review**, 1970, **77**, 406-418.

538. Seligman, M. E. P. Phobias and preparedness. **Behavior Therapy**, 1971, **2**, 307-320.

539. Seligman, M. E. P., & Hager, J. L. **Biological Boundaries of Learning**. New York: Appleton-Century-Crofts, 1972.

540. Seligman, M. E. P., & Hager, J. L. Biological boundaries of learning: The sauce-bearnaise syndrome. **Psychology Today**, 1972, **6**, 59-61.

541. Sessions, G. R. Histamine and radiation-induced taste aversion conditioning. **Science**, 1975, **190**, 402-403.

542. Seward, J. P., & Greathouse, S. R. Appetitive and aversive conditioning in thiamine-deficient rats. **Journal of Comparative and Physiological Psychology**, 1973, **83**, 157-167.

543. Shettleworth, S. J. Constraints on learning. In D. S. Lehrman, R. S. Hinde, & E. Shaw (Eds.), **Advances in the Study of Behavior (Vol. IV)**. New York: Academic Press, 1972, 1-68.

544. Shettleworth, S. J. The role of novelty in learned avoidance of unpalatable "prey" by domestic chicks (*Gallus gallus*). **Animal Behavior**, 1972, **20**, 29-35.

545. Shettleworth, S. J. Stimulus relevance in the control of drinking and conditioned fear responses in domestic chicks (*Gallus gallus*). **Journal of Comparative and Physiological Psychology**, 1972, **80**, 175-198.

546. Shorten, M. The reaction of the brown rat towards changes in its environment. In D. Chitty (Ed.), **Control of Rats and Mice (Vol. 2)**. Oxford: Clarendon Press, 1954, 307-334.

547. Siegel, S. Flavor preexposure and "learned safety." **Journal of Comparative and Physiological Psychology**, 1974, **87**, 1073-1082.

548. Simson, P. C., & Booth, D. A. Effect of CS-US interval on the conditioning of odour preferences by amino acid loads. **Physiology and Behavior**, 1973, **11**, 801-808.

549. Simson, P. C., & Booth, D. A. Olfactory conditioning by association with histidine-free or balanced amino acid loads in rats. **Quarterly Journal of Experimental Psychology**, 1973, **25**, 354-359.

550. Simson, P. C., & Booth, D. A. Dietary aversion established by a deficient load: Specificity to the amino acid omitted from a balanced mixture. **Pharmacology, Biochemistry, and Behavior**, 1974, **2**, 481-485.

551. Simson, P. C., & Booth, D. A. The rejection of a diet which has been associated with a single administration of an histidine-free amino acid mixture. **British Journal of Nutrition**, 1974, **31**, 285-296.

552. Sinclair, J. D. Morphine suppresses alcohol drinking regardless of prior alcohol access duration.

Pharmacology, Biochemistry, and Behavior, 1974, 2, 409-412.

553. Sinclair, J. D., Adkins, J., & Walker, S. Morphine-induced suppression of voluntary alcohol drinking in rats. Nature, 1973, 246, 425-427.

554. Smith, C. U. M. Discrimination between heavy water and water by the mouse. Nature, 1968, 217, 760.

555. Smith, D. F., & Balagura, S. Role of oropharyngeal factors in LiCl aversion. Journal of Comparative and Physiological Psychology, 1969, 69, 308-310.

556. Smith, D. F., Balagura, S., & Lubran, M. Some effects of adrenalectomy on LiCl intake and excretion in the rat. American Journal of Physiology, 1970, 218, 751-754.

557. Smith, J. C. Radiation as an aversive stimulus. American Zoologist, 1967, 7, 402.

558. Smith, J. C. Radiation: Its detection and its effects on taste preferences. In E. Stellar & J. M. Sprague (Eds.), Progress in Physiological Psychology, IV. New York: Academic Press, 1971, 53-118.

559. Smith, J. C., & Birkle, R. A. Conditioned aversion to sucrose in rats using X-rays as the unconditioned stimulus. Psychonomic Science, 1966, 5, 271-272.

560. Smith, J. C., & Morris, D. D. Effects of atropine sulfate on the conditioned aversion to saccharin fluid with X-rays as the unconditioned stimulus. Radiation Research, 1963, 18, 186-190.

561. Smith, J. C., & Morris, D. D. The use of X-rays as the unconditioned stimulus in five-hundred-day-old rats. Journal of Comparative and Physiological Psychology, 1963, 56, 746-747.

562. Smith, J. C., & Morris, D. D. The effects of atrophine sulfate and physostigmine on the conditioned aversion to saccharin with X-rays as the unconditioned stimulus. In T. J. Haley & R. S. Snider (Eds.), Response of the Nervous System to Ionizing Radiation. New York: Little, Brown, 1964, 662-672.

563. Smith, J. C., & Roll, D. L. Trace conditioning with X-rays as an aversive stimulus. Psychonomic Science, 1967, 9, 11-12.

564. Smith, J. C., & Schaeffer, R. W. Development of water and saccharin preferences after simultaneous exposures to saccharin solution and gamma rays. Journal of Comparative and Physiological Psychology, 1967, 63, 434-438.

565. Smith, J. C., Morris, D. D., & Hendricks, J. Conditioned aversion to saccharin solution with high dose rates of X-rays as the unconditioned stimulus. Radiation Research, 1964, 22, 507-510.

566. Smith, J. C., Taylor, H. L., Morris, D. D., & Hendricks, J. Further studies of X-ray conditioned saccharin aversion during the postexposure period. Radiation Research, 1965, 24, 423-431.

567. Smith, R. G. The role of alimentary chemoreceptors in the development of taste aversions. Communications in Behavioral Biology, 1970, 5, 199-204.

568. Smith, R. G. Intake differentiation by rats of equimolar sodium chloride and lithium chloride solutions. Psychonomic Science, 1971, 23, 11-12.

569. Smotherman, W. P., Hennessy, J. W., & Levine, S. Plasma corticosterone levels during recovery from LiCl produced taste aversions. Behavioral Biology, 1976, 16, 401-412.

570. Sofia, R. D., & Knobloch, L. C. Comparative effects of various naturally occurring cannabinoids on food, sucrose, and water consumption by rats. Pharmacology, Biochemistry, and Behavior, 1976, 4, 591-599.

571. Solomon, R. L. An opponent-process theory of motivation: V. Affective dynamics of eating. In L. M. Barker, M. R. Best, & M. Domjan (Eds.), Learning Mechanisms in Food Selection. Waco, Texas: Baylor University Press, 1977.

572. Southern, H. N. Control of Rats and Mice (Vol. 3). Oxford: Clarendon Press, 1954.

573. St. Omer, V. V., & Kral, P. A. Electroconvulsive shock impedes the learning of taste aversions: Absence of blood-brain-barrier involvement. Psychonomic Science, 1971, 24, 251-252.

574. Stricker, E. M., & Zigmond, M. J. Effects on homeostasis of intraventricular injections of 6-hydroxydopamine in rats. Journal of Comparative and Physiological Psychology, 1974, 86, 973-994.

575. Strom, C., Lingenfelter, A., & Brody, J. F. Discrimination of lithium and sodium chloride solutions by rats. Psychonomic Science, 1970, 18, 290-291.

576. Strouthes, A. Saccharin drinking and mortality in rats. Pharmacology, Biochemistry, and Behavior, 1973, 10, 781-791.

577. Stunkard, A. Presidential address-1974: From explanation to action in psychosomatic medicine: The case of obesity. Psychosomatic Medicine, 1975, 37, 195-236.

578. Stunkard, A. Satiety is a conditioned reflex. Psychosomatic Medicine, 1975, 37, 383-387.

579. Suarez, E. M., & Barker, L. M. Effects of water deprivation and prior LiCl exposure in conditioning taste aversions. Physiology and Behavior, 1976, 17, 555-559.

580. Supak, T. D., Macrides, F., & Chorover, S. L. The bait-shyness effect extended to olfactory discrimination. Communications in Behavioral Biology, 1971, 5, 321-324.

581. Sutker, L. W. The effect of initial taste preference on subsequent radiation-induced aversive conditioning to saccharin solution. Psychonomic Science, 1971, 25, 1-2.

582. Tapper, D. N., & Halpern, B. P. Taste stimuli: A behavioral categorization. Science, 1968, 161, 708-710.

583. Taukulis, H. K. Odor aversions produced over long CS-US delays. Behavioral Biology, 1974, 10, 505-510.

584. Taukulis, H. K., & Revusky, S. H. Odor as a conditioned inhibitor: Applicability of the Rescorla-Wagner model to feeding behavior. Learning and Motivation, 1975, 6, 11-27.

585. Ternes, J. W. Circadian cyclic sensitivity to gamma radiation as an unconditioned stimulus in taste aversion conditioning. In L. E. Scheving, F. Halberg, & J. E. Pauly (Eds.), Chronobiology. Tokyo: Igaku Shoin, 1974, 544-547.

586. Ternes, J. W. Conditioned aversion to morphine with naloxone. Bulletin of the Psychonomic Society, 1975, 5, 292-294.

587. Ternes, J. W. Naloxone-induced aversion to sucrose in morphine-dependent rats. Bulletin of the Psychonomic Society, 1975, 5, 311-312.

588. Ternes, J. W. Resistance to extinction of a learned taste aversion varies with time of conditioning. Animal Learning and Behavior, 1976, 4, 317-321.

589. Testa, T. J. Causal relationships and the acquisition of avoidance responses. Psychological Review, 1974, 81, 491-505.

590. Testa, T. J. Effects of similarity of location and temporal intensity pattern of conditioned and unconditioned stimuli on the acquisition of conditioned suppression in rats. Journal of Experimental Psychology: Animal Behavior Processes, 1975, 104, 114-121.

608

591. Testa, T. J., & Ternes, J. W. Specificity of conditioning mechanisms in the modification of food preferences. In L. M. Barker, M. R. Best, & M. Domjan (Eds.), **Learning Mechanisms in Food Selection**. Waco, Texas: Baylor University Press, 1977.

592. Thomas, J. B., & Smith, D. A. V. M. H. Lesions facilitate bait-shyness in the rat. **Pharmacology, Biochemistry, and Behavior**, 1975, **15**, 7-11.

593. Thomka, M. L., & Brown, T. S. The effect of hippocampal lesions on the development and extinction of a learned taste aversion for a novel food. **Physiological Psychology**, 1975, **3**, 281-284.

594. Thompson, H. V. The consumption of plain and poisoned cereal baits by the brown rat. In D. Chitty (Ed.), **Control of Rats and Mice (Vol. 2)**. Oxford: Clarendon Press, 1954, 352-373.

595. Tucker, A., & Gibbs, M. Cycloheximide-induced amnesia for taste aversion memory in rats. **Pharmacology, Biochemistry, and Behavior**, 1976, **4**, 181-184.

596. Vitiello, M. V., & Woods, S. C. Caffeine: Preferential consumption by rats. **Pharmacology, Biochemistry, and Behavior**, 1975, **3**, 147-149.

597. Vogel, J. R. Antagonism of a learned taste aversion following repeated administrations of electroconvulsive shock. **Physiological Psychology**, 1974, **2**, 493-496.

598. Vogel, J. R. Conditioning of taste aversion by drugs of abuse. In H. Lal & J. Singh (Eds.), **Neurobiology of Drug Dependence (Vol. 1): Behavioral Analysis of Drug Dependence**. New York: Futura, in press.

599. Vogel, J. R., & Clody, D. E. Habituation and conditioned food aversion. **Psychonomic Science**, 1972, **28**, 275-276.

600. Vogel, J. R., & Nathan, B. A. Learned taste aversions induced by hypnotic drugs. **Pharmacology, Biochemistry, and Behavior**, 1975, **3**, 189-194.

601. Vogel, J. R., & Nathan, B. A. Learned taste aversions induced by high doses of monosodium L-glutamate. **Pharmacology, Biochemistry, and Behavior**, 1975, **3**, 935-937.

602. Vogel, J. R., & Nathan, B. A. Reduction of learned taste aversions by pre-exposure to drugs. **Psychopharmacology**, 1976, **49**, 167-172.

603. Volo, A., & Strouthes, A. Saccharin ingestion, weight loss, and mortality in rats. **Physiological Psychology**, 1974, **2**, 323-325.

604. Wallace, P. Animal behavior: The puzzle of flavor aversion. **Science**, 1976, **193**, 989-991.

605. Watson, J. S. Control of the ship rat (*Rattus rattus*) in London. In D. Chitty (Ed.), **Control of Rats and Mice (Vol. 2)**. Oxford: Clarendon Press, 1954, 490-499.

606. Watson, J. S., & Perry, J. S. Experiments on rat control in Palestine and the Sudan. In D. Chitty (Ed.), **Control of Rats and Mice (Vol. 2)**. Oxford: Clarendon Press, 1954, 500-521.

607. Wayner, M. J., Jolicoeur, F. B., Rondeau, D. B., & Merkel, A. D. The effect of sodium phenobarbital on forced and voluntary alcohol consumption in the rat. In J. D. Sinclair & K. Kiianmaa (Eds.), **The Effects of Centrally Acting Drugs on Voluntary Alcohol Consumption**. Helsinki: The Finnish Foundation for Alcohol Studies, 1975, 35-48.

608. Wayner, M. J., Rondeau, D. B., Jolicoeur, F. B., & Wayner, E. A. Effects of phenobarbital on saccharin and citric acid intake in fluid deprived rats. **Pharmacology, Biochemistry, and Behavior**, 1976, **4**, 335-337.

609. Weijnen, J. A. W. M. Current licking: Lick-contingent electrical stimulation of the tongue. In J. A. W. M. Weijnen & J. Mendelson (Eds.), **Drinking**

Behavior, Oral Stimulation, Reinforcement, and Preference. New York: Plenum Press, 1977.

610. Weisinger, R. S., Parker, L. F., & Skorupski, J. D. Conditioned taste aversions and specific need states in the rat. **Journal of Comparative and Physiological Psychology**, 1974, **87**, 655-660.

611. Weisman, R. N., Hamilton, L. W., & Carlton, P. L. Increased conditioned gustatory aversion following VMH lesions in rats. **Physiology and Behavior**, 1972, **9**, 801-804.

612. Whaley, D. L., Scarborough, B. B., & Reichard, S. M. Traumatic shock, X-irradiation, and avoidance behavior. **Physiology and Behavior**, 1966, **1**, 93-95.

613. Wickler, W. **Mimicry in Plants and Animals**. New York: McGraw-Hill, 1968.

614. Wilcoxon, H. C. Learning of ingestive aversions in avian species. In L. M. Barker, M. R. Best, & M. Domjan (Eds.), **Learning Mechanisms in Food Selection**. Waco, Texas: Baylor University Press, 1977.

615. Wilcoxon, H. C., Dragoin, W. B., & Kral, P. A. Illness-induced aversions in rat and quail: Relative salience of visual and gustatory cues. **Science**, 1971, **171**, 826-828.

616. Wing, J. F., & Birch, L. A. Relative cue properties of novel-tasting substances in avoidance conditioning. **Animal Learning and Behavior**, 1974, **2**, 63-65.

617. Winn, F. J., Jr., Kent, M. A., & Libkumin, T. M. Learned taste aversion induced by cortical spreading depression. **Physiology and Behavior**, 1975, **15**, 21-24.

618. Wise, R. A., & Albin, J. Stimulation-induced eating disrupted by a conditioned taste aversion. **Behavioral Biology**, 1973, **9**, 289-297.

619. Wise, R. A., Yokel, R. A., & DeWit, H. Both positive reinforcement and conditioned aversion from amphetamine and from apomorphine in rats. **Science**, 1976, **191**, 1273-1274.

620. Wittlin, W. A., & Brookshire, K. H. Apomorphine-induced conditioned aversion to a novel food. **Psychonomic Science**, 1968, **12**, 217-218.

621. Woods, S. C., Weisinger, R. S., & Wald, B. A. Conditioned aversions produced by subcutaneous injections of formalin in rats. **Journal of Comparative and Physiological Psychology**, 1971, **77**, 410-415.

622. Woods, S. C., Lawson, R., Haddad, R. K., Rabe, A., & Lawson, W. E. Reversal of conditioned aversions in normal and micrencephalic rats. **Journal of Comparative and Physiological Psychology**, 1974, **86**, 531-534.

623. Wright, W. E., Foshee, D. P., & McCleary, G. E. Comparison of taste aversion with various delays and cyclophosphamide dose levels. **Psychonomic Science**, 1971, **22**, 55-56.

624. Zahler, C. L., & Harper, A. E. Effects of dietary amino acid pattern on food preference behavior of rats. **Journal of Comparative and Physiological Psychology**, 1972, **81**, 155-162.

625. Zahorik, D. M. Conditioned physiological changes associated with learned aversions to tastes paired with thiamine deficiency in the rat. **Journal of Comparative and Physiological Psychology**, 1972, **79**, 189-200.

626. Zahorik, D. M. The role of dietary history in the effects of novelty on taste aversions. **Bulletin of the Psychonomic Society**, 1976, **8**, 285-288.

627. Zahorik, D. M. Associative and non-associative factors in learned food preferences. In L. M. Barker, M. R. Best, & M. Domjan (Eds.), **Learning Mechanisms in Food Selection**. Waco, Texas: Baylor University Press, 1977.

628. Zahorik, D. M., & Bean, C. A. Resistance of "recovery" flavors to later association with illness. **Bulletin of the Psychonomic Society**, 1975, **6**, 309-312.

629. Zahorik, D. M., & Houpt, K. A. The concept of nutritional wisdom: Applicability of laboratory learning models to large herbivores. In L. M. Barker, M. R. Best, & M. Domjan (Eds.), **Learning Mechanisms in Food Selection**. Waco, Texas: Baylor University Press, 1977.

630. Zahorik, D. M., & Johnston, R. E. Taste aversions to food flavors and vaginal secretion in golden hamsters. **Journal of Comparative and Physiological Psychology**, 1976, **90**, 57-66.

631. Zahorik, D. M., & Maier, S. F. Appetitive conditioning with recovery from thiamine deficiency as the unconditioned stimulus. **Psychonomic Science**, 1969, **17**, 309-310.

632. Zahorik, D. M., Maier, S. F., & Pies, R. W. Preferences for tastes paired with recovery from thiamine deficiency in rats. **Journal of Comparative and Physiological Psychology**, 1974, **87**, 1083-1091.

TOPICAL INDEX

610

611

613

ACKNOWLEDGEMENT

This article is an extension and update of Riley and Baril (1976). The authors would like to thank the many colleagues who generously contributed information for this bibliography—especially V. M. LoLordo for his time and helpful suggestions throughout this project. We also thank C. T. Barrett and D. A. Zellner for their invaluable editorial help.

616

NAME INDEX [1]

---

[1] The name index excludes those names appearing in the Appendix, pages 593-610.

618

619

Gleitman, L. R. 580
Gluckman, M. S. 481
Goldberg, M. E. 486
Goodall, E. B. 503
Goodman, L. S. 480, 481
Gormezano, I. 546, 547, 549
Gorry, T. H. 25, 49, 448, 458, 460
Goudie, A. J. 495, 499
Gower, E. C. 275
Gray, D. 171, 174, 539, 542, 543
Greathouse, S. R. 183, 184, 560
Green, K. F. 151, 160, 171, 186, 234, 280, 303, 333, 337, 534, 547, 571, 574
Green, L. S. 11, 215, 248, 516
Greenwood, M. R. C. 215
Gregg, B. 153, 175, 543
Grice, G. R. 320
Grinker, J. A. 215
Grossman, M. I. 205
Grote, F. W. 154, 230, 485
Gudnason, G. V. 108
Gurwitz, S. B. 215
Gustavson, C. R. 13, 23, 24, 25, 26, 30, 31, 32, 34, 36, 49, 50, 582
Guttman, N. 286, 546, 547
Hager, J. L. 15, 562, 571, 574, 576
Halgren, C. R. 297
Hall, D. 11
Hall, K. 27, 448, 468
Hall, W. G. 85, 202
Hammond, L. J. 296
Hankins, W. G. 3, 9, 11, 13, 14, 16, 23, 24, 25, 26, 30, 32, 35, 49, 50, 204, 242, 243, 247, 374, 390, 449, 456, 478
Haralson, J. 25
Haralson, S. 25
Hargreaves, F. J. 7, 47, 181, 569
Harland, W. 285
Harlow, H. F. 27
Harner, J. P. 56
Harrell, N. 527
Harris, L. J. 7, 47, 181, 569
Harris, R. S. 565, 584
Harris, W. C. 481
Hawkins, R. C. 201, 285
Hartley, P. L. 245, 246, 479, 480, 481, 485, 501, 503, 524
Hebb, D. O. 90, 162
Heiber, L. 132, 133
Hein, A. 275

Held, R. 275
Hellwald, H. 75
Helmholtz, H. 578
Henderson, P. W. 107, 138, 139, 146
Hendricks, J. 9, 540
Henggeler, S. 10, 234, 371, 381, 399, 457
Hennessy, J. W. 525, 526
Herling, S. 494
Hess, E. H. 88, 91, 99, 101, 104, 152
Heth, C. D. 544, 546, 547
Hewitt, M. I. 211
Hill, S. W. 211
Hinde, R. A. 88, 93, 124, 577
Hirsch, J. 214, 215
Hofer, K. G. 9, 249, 480, 526
Hoffman, A. C. 155
Hoffman, H. S. 259
Hogan, J. A. 71, 74, 75, 76, 77, 78, 79, 80, 81, 82, 83, 88, 89, 90, 91, 93, 95, 104, 143, 152, 173, 192, 559, 582
Hogan-Warburg, A. J. 83, 84, 92
Hogan-Warburg, L. 95
Hollinger, M. 152, 563
Holman, E. W. 163, 243, 563
Holstron, L. S. 186
Holcer, P. 566
Holt, J. 205
Homer, A. L. 27, 29
Hoogland, D. R. 487
Houpt, K. A. 33, 45, 49
Howard, W. E. 62
Huenemann, R. L. 209
Hull, C. L. 92, 99, 572
Hunt, E. L. 9, 10, 375, 378, 533
Itani, J. 562, 564
Ivens, J. D. 54, 61
Iwens, J. 386
Jackson, M. 95
Jacobs, W. J. 387, 491
Jacobson, K. 518, 521, 528
Jaffe, J. H. 481, 498
Jahnke, J. 119
Jain, A. P. 27
Janzen, D. H. 60
Jarka, R. G. 204
Jaquet, Y. F. 524
Jenkins, H. M. 386
Jensen, D. D. 375
Johns, T. 538

620

622

624

SUBJECT INDEX [1]

---

[1] The subject index excludes those names appearing in the Appendix, pages 593-610.

627

631